PUBLIC FINANCES: NEEDS, SOURCES, AND UTILIZATION

NATIONAL BUREAU OF ECONOMIC RESEARCH

Special Conference Series

Public Finances: Needs, Sources, and Utilization

A CONFERENCE OF THE
UNIVERSITIES-NATIONAL BUREAU
COMMITTEE FOR ECONOMIC RESEARCH

A REPORT OF THE
NATIONAL BUREAU OF ECONOMIC RESEARCH, NEW YORK

PUBLISHED BY
PRINCETON UNIVERSITY PRESS, PRINCETON
1961

Printed in the United States of America

RELATION OF NATIONAL BUREAU DIRECTORS TO
PUBLICATIONS REPORTING CONFERENCE PROCEEDINGS

Since the present volume is a record of conference proceedings, it has been exempted from the rules governing submission of manuscripts to, and critical review by, the Board of Directors of the National Bureau. It has, however, been reviewed and accepted for publication by the Director of Research.

(Resolution adopted July 6, 1948 *and revised November* 21, 1949)

Contents

CONTENTS

Introduction

CONSENSUS among scholars has never been attained concerning the appropriate definition of the subject matter of Public Finance. International as well as intranational differences of opinion on the proper limits of the field have existed for many years. Scholarship on the European continent has, by and large, approached the discipline in terms of the institution under scrutiny, the fiscal system. In the English-speaking world, Public Finance has been more limited in that it has been confined within the methods and procedures of traditional economic analysis. As a result of this orientation, English and American works have, until quite recently, tended to concentrate attention on the impact of the fiscal system on the private market economy. Decisions made by governments have been assumed to be exogenous to the private economic calculus of individuals and firms.

This is not to suggest that English-language scholars have been uninterested in the choice of that set of legislative enactments constituting what may be called "the fiscal system" of a political entity. The study of the effects of alternative tax schemes on private behavior assumes a purpose only in the potential assistance to individuals confronted with some freedom of choice among the alternatives considered. But implicit in this traditional approach has been the assumption that criteria for judging alternative systems, or portions thereof, are to be located independently of the fiscal decision itself.

There is a rather subtle difference between this approach, which has, broadly speaking, characterized English-language work, and that which looks on the fiscal system as the means through which individuals make decisions concerning the appropriate amount of resources to be devoted to public rather than to private uses. The difference is sufficient to explain, at least in part, the relative neglect of the expenditure side and, perhaps more importantly, the failure of scholars in this country to devote much attention to the fiscal decision-making process as such.

Recent developments represent a belated recognition of this doctrinal gap. Inspired by a wider knowledge of the European tradition in the field and marrying this tradition to an extension of modern welfare economics, scholars are now paying increasing attention to the collective decision-making process. Because of these recent developments, Public Finance seems to be on the threshold of becoming one of the most stimulating fields of inquiry in all of the social sciences. At such a stage of ferment, any conference set of papers that genuinely represents work in the whole disciplinary field should include widely heterogeneous individual contributions in terms of method, scope, and level of abstraction. The papers included in this volume seem to qualify fully under this norm.

Few of the papers in this volume discuss what might be called "orthodox" topics in Public Finance. At least three of the papers introduce material that might appear to some readers to be more appropriate in modern political science. Two others deal almost exclusively with budgetary and administrative problems. Yet another seems to be welfare economics in disguise. And, finally, one paper seems to introduce elements of location economics into Public Finance. The point to be emphasized is that all of the papers are devoted to separate aspects of the larger problem of collective decision-making. It is, I think, worth observing that not a single paper is either explicitly or primarily devoted to an examination of individual behavior in response to government fiscal action. Instead, the focus is, in almost all cases, on individual behavior in making decisions which constitute fiscal action.

This is, in my opinion, an important sign of progress. For the first time, the empirical-analytical skills of the American economist are being brought to bear on an increasingly important form of human behavior. And, in so doing, the economist is recognizing that he must disregard to a large extent the traditional boundaries among the separate disciplines. There is much to be gained from a continuation, even an acceleration, of such efforts. And, if the conference at which these papers were discussed has served its purpose, work of this general description will become increasingly stimulating to the research scholar.

The fiscal expert, the practical man who is called on to design improvements in legislation, who must provide advice and counsel to the legislator seeking guidance as to modifications in the existing fiscal structure, may quite properly object to the abstract nature of much of the modern work. For rarely has there existed a wider gap between theory and practice than that between the normative theory of the optimal budget and the way in which budgets are actually made. The practitioner, who is constantly under pressure, is appropriately impatient at the seemingly irrelevant attempts of the welfare economists to develop the models of an ideally neutral fiscal system. Such impatience may be tempered somewhat when it is recognized that the optimality theorists are working over rather new ground. An extension of the conventional welfare analysis to its limits in respect to the public sector of the economy can only be viewed as a healthy development. Only when the analysis is pushed so far can its inherent shortcomings as well as its possible usefulness be revealed.

The broad and uncharted area between the day-to-day problems facing the legislative adviser and the rarified problems discussed by the optimality theorist seems to offer the greatest opportunity for genuine contributions in Public Finance. We need to know much more than we do know about the way in which individuals of a political system organize and finally make collective decisions. The extension of conventional rationality norms to governmental decisions may or may not lead to "improvements." It is in moving in the direction of problems such as these that several of the papers in this volume deserve special mention. These papers embody the recognition that the institutions of collective decision-making are the appropriate variables to be examined in any attempt to "improve" the decision-making process itself. Substantial agreement on criteria for "improvements" in the process represents a plausible objective. Agreement on criteria for objectively measurable "improvements" in the *results* of political action, apart from the process by which decisions are made, seems not only to be impossible but undesirable.

The Program and Planning Committee for the conference at which the papers in this volume were discussed included the following members:

> L. L. Ecker-Racz
> Walter Heller
> Charles E. Lindblom
> Roland N. McKean
> Richard A. Musgrave
> Lawrence Seltzer
> James M. Buchanan, Chairman
> C. Harry Kahn, Secretary

The views and interests of this committee were perhaps as heterogeneous as are the papers included in this volume. It seems a real measure of success to be able to report that genuine consensus was reached on all issues involved in the planning of the conference and the publication of these papers. Especial thanks of the committee must go to Harry Kahn for his patient work as Secretary of the Committee. Mr. Kahn's generous allotment of time to the many tasks of reviewing and assembling this volume has made it possible to bring out the conference report in considerably less months than has hitherto been possible for this series.

JAMES M. BUCHANAN

Charlottesville, Virginia

PUBLIC FINANCES: NEEDS, SOURCES, AND UTILIZATION

Financial Needs and Resources Over the Next Decade: At All Levels of Government

GERHARD COLM and MANUEL HELZNER

NATIONAL PLANNING ASSOCIATION

1. *Projections and Forecasts*

MAKING economic projections is fraught with great occupational hazards. Therefore, self-preservation of the practitioners in this field makes it necessary to emphasize that projections are hypothetical estimates and to state with all possible clarity the hypotheses on which they are based. This applies with particular force to projections in the public sector.

In this introductory section of our paper we will state the assumptions made in estimating government expenditures for the next decade. These assumptions are not meant to be arbitrary or merely for the sake of experiments in economic arithmetic. They are meant to be "life hypotheses" and therefore must be related to the present and foreseeable historical situation.

By insisting that our projections are only hypothetical and will not become reality unless our assumptions happen to become reality, we are protecting ourselves. On the other hand, by selecting those assumptions—the "life hypotheses"—which are believed relevant for this particular period, the projectors of necessity stick their neck out. They cannot entirely avoid the hazards inherent in any effort which tries to provide some light, dim as it may be, for groping our way through an uncertain future.

As an analytical device we have prepared alternative projections based on different assumptions. However, we are also presenting a "judgment" model which is based on what we regard as the most plausible assumption, or more precisely as the assumptions most suitable for the use for which the projections are designed.

The assumption that no major war or major economic depression will occur during the next decade does not imply any statement about the improbability of such events. A major war would have such drastic consequences that entirely different kinds of emergency programs would have to be considered than those discussed in this paper. The topic of this session—a reappraisal of the financial needs

3

of the various levels of government—seems to imply the assumption that a major international crisis can be avoided. However, this assumption is entirely compatible with assuming that international tension and the struggle of "competitive coexistence" will be continued or even aggravated.

In our judgment model we have assumed not only that war will be avoided but also that the national security programs will develop approximately in line with present plans. This assumption has been made not because it is believed to be most probable or militarily adequate. Rather, it appeared that, in the absence of convincing evidence to the contrary, the most prudent operating assumption was that defense programs would proceed as currently planned, fully recognizing the uncertainty implied in this assumption. To assume as a working hypothesis a drastic increase or a substantial reduction in defense would be to anticipate major changes in other government programs and private plans. The high and low defense models have been added in order to demonstrate the problems which would be involved in major changes in defense—up or down.

We also assume the absence of a major economic depression but not the absence of economic fluctuations. In our program discussion no specific antidepression programs are included. Programs are discussed solely on the ground of their own merits. However, it may well be considered that the speed with which these programs are carried out may be changed in line with an anticyclical government policy. We assume that such changes in pace would not affect the average rate of expenditures over a number of years.

Projections and Economic Growth

We assume that the present concern with *economic growth* is not merely a passing fad, but a challenge which will influence government decisions during the next decade. By assuming a continuing concern with economic growth, we do not necessarily assume that the United States will engage in a GNP race with the Soviet bloc. We only mean that the people will be aware of the many public and private needs and will seek to provide for these needs by expanding productive capacity and by operating at levels of economic activity approximating the growth potential of the economy. The fact that our way of life is challenged by a communistic rival system will heighten the determination to succeed in this endeavor and to overcome obstacles.

Projections of the public sector are conceived as part of general projections which reflect a 4 to 5 per cent annual growth rate for the American economy as a whole.[1] The anticipated increases in the labor force of close to 1.75 per cent per year would raise our production potential while still allowing for some continued reduction in the standard work week.

In addition, the continued high research effort, particularly for national defense, is likely to yield a continuing stream of technological advances for peacetime application.

There is an interrelationship between economic growth and activity in the public sector. On the one hand, government programs will be needed to support economic growth; on the other, economic growth will make it possible to finance additional programs without sacrificing other wants. The need for government programs in support of economic growth will influence the selection of programs and the priority which determines the sequence in which they are undertaken.

An example may illustrate what we mean when speaking of growth consciousness. Recent advances in air transportation have outgrown the available ground facilities. In such a situation two possible courses of action may be followed. One course of action would put the brakes on or delay further advances in air transportation until in the course of time more adequate ground facilities are provided. In support of such a course some may argue that with more use of railroads and road and water transportation we could get along without jets for many years just as we have in the past. In contrast, a growth-conscious policy will make an effort to speed up the modernization of ground facilities in order to remove an obstacle which is in the way of a particular development. Unlike most other times and cultures, the public attitude in our present culture strongly favors the second course of action.

Method of Projections

The projections of government expenditures are based primarily on direct estimates for major government programs. Only for a few minor programs has it been assumed that they will expand in proportion to the GNP. In a few cases—e.g., in the field of metropolitan renewal programs, health (including mental health) and water development programs—it was assumed that by 1970 the pressing

[1] The projections used in this paper are based on the NPA long-range projections for 1965 and 1970, prepared with the assistance of a Ford Foundation grant and continued on a self-supporting subscription basis.

need will result in essentially new and large programs for which only relatively small expenditures are being made at the present time. In a few cases (e.g., agriculture) it was assumed that policy solutions will be found which make a substantial reduction in expenditures possible.

While recognizing the high social priority of public programs in support of economic growth, we have assumed that these programs will rise gradually. A prolonged period of international tension and "competitive coexistence" requires not only continuously large and possibly rising military programs, but also large nonmilitary programs, both for implementing the government's foreign economic policy and for promoting domestic economic growth and welfare. We have assumed that a wasteful policy of alternatingly blowing hot and cold can be avoided and that heavy fluctuations in the relationship between the private and public sector will be absent. This means that changes in the tax *rates*—upwards or downwards—would be of limited size and that rising government expenditures would be largely financed by the additional yield resulting from an expanding tax base rather than from rising tax rates. We assume, therefore, that in the case of the need for substantially higher defense expenditures, other government programs will rise somewhat more slowly. However, should a drastic reduction in defense expenditures become possible, a somewhat enhanced rise in nondefense programs plus a substantial reduction in tax rates is assumed.

Scope of Projections

The projections of needs for public programs presented in this paper define public programs in a very broad way. They include programs irrespective of whether they would be financed or administered by the federal government, state and local government, or by any kind of public authorities or other public agencies set up for specific purposes. Only after needs and resources in the aggregate have been projected is it possible to examine whether the needs can be met if the traditional division of functions and resources among the various levels of government are continued or whether some modification in these relationships is needed.

Another question of definition arises in cases in which the borderline between the private and public sector of the economy is blurred. Our projections of government goods and services purchases use the consolidated national income and product accounts as a frame of reference. Therefore social security, veterans' benefit payments, and other transfer, interest, and subsidy payments are accounted for as receipts of individuals and businesses and the use of these receipts appear in the account as spending or saving of individuals and business. In this paper we show both government purchases of goods and services and transfer payments of the government.

Another such "borderline" case is the following: Does a FHA or VA housing program belong to the public or private sector of the economy if the houses are financed by private funds protected by government guarantee or insurance? We have in these projections excluded privately financed but publicly guaranteed or insured programs and have regarded them as part of the private sector of the economy. The proper method would probably be to allocate these programs in part to the private, in part to the public sector. NPA has a special study of these programs under way and it is hoped that the result of that study may provide some meaningful guide line for distinguishing between private and public aspects of these programs. For the present, we recognize that the exclusion of these programs from the public sector results in some underestimate of the relative significance of the public sector. Also, industries supervised and regulated by the government are regarded as purely private for purposes of our projection. Therefore, the ratio between the size of the public and private sector in our projections does not give a full picture of the actual significance of government for the economy as a whole.

COMPARATIVE PROJECTIONS—A SUPPLEMENT[2]

In Table 1 an attempt has been made to compare our own estimates with those of Dick Netzer[3] and Otto Eckstein.[4] The possibility of a comparison is limited by the fact that Netzer has dealt only with state-local expenditures while Eckstein has selected a different target period for his projection. Netzer uses the Census Bureau concept of government expenditures; Eckstein combines the budget concept for federal programs with a national income and product concept for state-local programs. Both sets of estimates are on a fiscal year

[2] This section incorporates supplementary material not included in the original manuscript but presented at the conference session.

[3] Dick Netzer, "Financial Needs and Resources Over the Next Decade: State and Local Governments," in this volume. (Data have been converted to 1958 dollars.)

[4] Otto Eckstein, *Trends in Public Expenditures in the Next Decade*, Committee for Economic Development, April 1959.

TABLE 1

Projections of Government Activity—A Comparison
(billions of 1958 dollars)

| | ECKSTEIN PROJECTIONS MEDIUM MODEL (FISCAL YEAR-BUDGET CONCEPT) | | NETZER PROJECTIONS (FISCAL YEAR-CENSUS BUREAU CONCEPT) | | COLM-HELZNER PROJECTIONS JUDGMENT MODEL (CALENDAR YEAR GNP CONCEPT) | |
| | | | *1970, Moderate* | *1970, Substantial* | | |
	1964	*1968*	(constant costs)		*1964*	*1970*[a]
GNP	554	624	(736–784)		602	790
Total govt. expend.[b]	153.6	171.4	–	–	159.9	204.7
Federal	106.2	117.7	–	–	101.9	124.2
State-local	47.4	53.7	65.8	78.4	64.6	90.0
Federal						
National security	50.7	56.0	–	–	50.9	54.6
Other	55.5	61.7	–	–	51.0	69.6
State-local						
Education	22.4	25.9	23.9	30.3	24.0	30.7
Highways	8.0	9.1	11.9	14.1	11.4	13.1
Health and Hosp.	2.9	3.0	5.0	5.7	7.1	9.8
Housing and Community redevelopment	.7	.8	.8	1.1	2.7	7.9
Other	13.4	14.9	24.2	27.2	19.4	28.5
Federal grants-in-aid	–	–	8.2	10.7	6.6	9.5
Govt. expenditures as a % of GNP						
Total	27.7	27.5			26.6	25.9
Federal	19.2	18.9			16.9	15.7
State-local	8.5	8.6	(8.4-8.9)	(10.0-10.6)	9.7	10.2

[a] Projections for 1970 incorporate revisions made since preparation of original manuscript.
[b] Federal grants-in-aid are excluded from total government expenditures to avoid duplication. Eckstein has excluded federal grants-in-aid from state-local government expenditures, as well.

basis. Our projections follow the GNP concept on a calendar year basis. Nevertheless the comparison, limited as it is, may be useful.

In substance, the main difference between our projection and that of Eckstein is that in our judgment model we anticipate a higher rate of economic growth. Our estimates of state-local expenditures are very similar to those of Netzer, except for the extraordinary increase we have allowed for new programs in the field of metropolitan renewal, health (including mental health) and water development. The same is the case also in the comparison of our state-local estimates with those of Eckstein.

Various studies show that there already is a great need in these program areas and that the need will increase with further development. It seems to us only reasonable to assume that over the next decade more nearly adequate programs in these fields will be initiated. All economic projections, whether they show a 3 or 4 or 5 per cent rate of GNP growth imply that technological advances which are now only in the drafting board stage will be adopted in the private sector of the economy. It would be wholly inconsistent if we assumed that in the field of government only *present* programs would grow but no new programs adopted for which an urgent demonstrable need can be shown. We believe that our estimates may be regarded as conservative because they do not assume adoption of programs which are not yet in the discussion stage. On the other hand, our estimates for agricultural support programs imply substantially lower expenditures than those given by Eckstein. We have assumed that over the coming decade an agricultural policy will be formulated which gives effective support but with reduced expenditures.

2. *Projected Public Needs and Resources*
Government Programs and Economic Resources

Economic growth in the coming decade will create a multiplicity of economic and social needs requiring private and government action. The role of government programs in meeting these needs will in large part be influenced by the requirements for defense, both military and civilian. But regardless of defense requirements economic growth will be accompanied by rising nondefense needs. Expanded programs will be required to meet the increased demands for public services traditionally performed by government (e.g., education, highways and skyways, public health and hospital care). In addition, economic progress would be stifled unless substantial improvement is made in such areas as urban renewal, research and development (particularly basic research), and conservation and utilization of our natural resources (including air and water resources).

Since it cannot be assumed that all of the needs for government services can or will be met simultaneously, a projection of government programs should be viewed in the context of trends and developments in other sectors of the economy and in the perspective of the growth potential for the economy as a whole. Economic projections provide a frame of reference for appraising the role of government programs over the next ten years.

TABLE 2
Projected Patterns of Economic Growth—1970
(billions of 1958 dollars)

	Disposable Receipts	Percentage of GNP	Purchases of Goods and Services	Percentage of GNP
1970 JUDGMENT MODEL				
Consumers	566.0	71.6	514.5	65.1
Domestic investment	77.0	9.8	115.1	14.6
Net international	1.1	.1	5.7	.7
Total government	195.9	24.8	204.7	25.9
Less: transfers, interest, subsidies	49.9	6.3	49.9	6.3
Government	146.0	18.5	154.8	19.6
GNP	790.1	100.0	790.1	100.0
1970 LOW GROWTH, LOW GOVERNMENT MODEL				
Consumers	550.9	74.7	523.3	71.0
Domestic investment	75.7	10.3	92.4	12.5
Net international	1.1	.1	5.7	.8
Total government	149.1	20.2	155.4	21.0
Less: transfers, interest, subsidies	39.4	5.3	39.4	5.3
Government	109.7	14.9	116.0	15.7
GNP	737.4	100.0	737.4	100.0
1970 HIGH GROWTH, HIGH GOVERNMENT MODEL				
Consumers	581.4	71.8	524.9	64.8
Domestic investment	75.6	9.3	102.4	12.7
Net international	1.1	.2	5.7	.7
Total government	205.1	25.3	230.2	28.4
Less: transfers, interest, subsidies,	53.8	6.6	53.8	6.6
Government	151.3	18.7	176.4	21.8
GNP	809.4	100.0	809.4	100.0
1970 HIGH DEFENSE MODEL				
Consumers	572.0	70.1	517.8	63.4
Domestic investment	77.3	9.5	112.4	13.8
Net international	1.1	.1	5.7	.7
Total government	206.6	25.3	221.2	27.1
Less: transfers, interest, subsidies	40.6	5.0	40.6	5.0
Government	166.1	20.3	180.6	22.1
GNP	816.5	100.0	816.5	100.0
1970 LOW DEFENSE MODEL				
Consumers	573.2	72.9	529.8	67.4
Domestic investment	77.1	9.8	113.6	14.5
Net international	1.1	.2	5.7	.7
Total government	188.5	24.0	190.9	24.3
Less: transfers, interest, subsidies	54.2	6.9	54.2	6.9
Government	134.5	17.1	136.8	17.4
GNP	785.9	100.0	785.9	100.0

(continued)

TABLE 2 (concluded.)

1958 ACTUAL

Consumers	311.6	71.2	290.6	66.4
Domestic investment	45.0	10.3	54.4	12.4
Net international	1.3	.3	1.4	.3
Total government	114.4	26.1	124.6	28.5
Less: transfers,				
interest, subsidies	33.3	7.6	33.3	7.6
Government	81.1	18.5	91.2	20.9
Statistical discrepancy	−1.2	−.3		
GNP	437.7	100.0	437.7	100.0

Note: Details may not add to total due to rounding.
Source: Department of Commerce and National Planning Association, Economic Projections Series (1959).

In this section attention will be given to the growth prospects in a number of specific program areas. In deriving these projections it was recognized that alternative patterns of economic growth would be possible under full employment conditions. These would have different implications for the size and character of government activities. Thus, projections of government activity should take into account possible differences in the rate of economic growth and possible alternative patterns of resource distribution among the various economic sectors.

For these reasons, Table 2 presents five economic model projections for 1970, all in 1958 dollars. The first two alternative models postulate conditions of low and high rates of economic growth and low and high levels of nondefense government programs. National defense expenditures are assumed in these models to remain close to current levels. The high defense model considers the possibility that expenditures for military purposes will increase and will represent a slightly higher per cent of GNP than currently. A fourth model explores the implications of a significant easing of international tensions that would permit a substantial reduction in defense outlays. Finally, a fifth model represents what in our "judgment" is the most likely pattern for economic growth in the coming decade assuming no substantial change in the international situation. These models are presented together with the most recent data for 1958.[5]

Although the focus of this paper is on government needs and resources, a few brief general observations would be in order before examining specific government programs. First, compared to 1958,

[5] Program expenditures for 1958 represent a breakdown of government purchases of goods and services using Census Bureau function categories.

11

the 1970 Judgment Model implies a growth rate for the economy of 5 per cent per year. However, since economic conditions in 1958 fell considerably below full employment levels, the long-term growth trend implied by our judgment model is 4.2 per cent per year. Second, total government revenues and expenditures in the judgment model account for a smaller percentage of GNP than in 1958. Although 1958 may not be a suitable base period for comparison purposes, nevertheless, the relationship of projected government activity to GNP in the judgment model does not represent a significant change from recent levels. Government purchases of goods and services relative to GNP would account for only a slightly higher proportion than in the 1955–57 period. Third, the projected excess of government expenditures in 1970 in the judgment model does not necessarily imply government operating deficits throughout the period. The "deficit" allows for the financing of authorities which might be set up for dealing with large scale urban renewal and other capital outlay programs. Government revenues are projected assuming a moderate reduction in the over-all tax burden.

Government Programs

A. NATIONAL DEFENSE. (Table 3.) The outlook for defense expenditures by 1970 is largely conditioned by one's outlook regarding the state of world tension and turmoil. Nevertheless, certain conclusions

TABLE 3

Projected National Defense Expenditures—1970

(billions of 1958 dollars)

1970	
Judgment model	54.6
Low growth—low government	49.3
High growth—high government	49.3
High defense	87.6
Low defense	27.3
1958 actual	44.0

and implications for government programs would follow from adopting one or another assumption. Except in the cases of the low and high defense models, continuation of the present state of international tension and of approximately current levels of defense preparedness are assumed. Defense expenditure projections in all models include $1.1 billion of foreign military cash grants (which under present national income and product accounting practices

12

appear as "Transfer Payments"). These cash grants are excluded in deriving government "Goods and Services Purchases."

In the two alternative models defense expenditures rise moderately. In our judgment model, we assume that recent structural changes in the defense establishment will continue. Modern weapons and military equipment (e.g., jet planes, missiles, atomic submarines, etc.) require heavier capital investment per military person than do conventional armaments. Thus, our projection of current levels of defense preparedness would not be inconsistent with a projection of somewhat smaller armed forces (estimated at 2.3 million) but higher total expenditures. In the event that a substantial reduction in expenditures for military preparedness becomes possible, additional resources would be available for expanding research and development activities and for overcoming some of the serious deficiencies in other nondefense areas.

B. EDUCATION. (Table 4.) A well-educated and properly trained

TABLE 4

Projected Education Expenditures—1970

(billions of 1958 dollars)

1970	
Judgment model	30.7
Low growth—low government	24.0
High growth—high government	36.8
High defense	29.6
Low defense	33.4
1958 actual	15.6

labor force has become a virtual *sine qua non* for continued economic growth and technological progress. Expenditures for education by government have experienced a significant spurt during the post-World War II period. Outlays for education in real terms have more than doubled; expenditures per school-age child (five to seventeen years) have been rising by 4.5 per cent per year. In part this increase represents an effort to overcome some of the deficiencies which accumulated during the prewar and wartime periods.

However, in spite of increased outlays, a substantial backlog of deficiencies in education still remains and needed improvements in our educational system are still delayed. In the years ahead the expected rise in student population and in the proportion enrolled in school (especially in institutions of higher learning) will create further inadequacies in our educational system unless adequate facilities and sufficient qualified teachers are provided. Moreover, many workers whose skills will be made obsolete by the advance of technology will require reeducation and retraining. Thus, there is good reason to believe that government educational programs will have to expand appreciably over the coming decade. In our judgment model, the increase in per student educational outlays over the next ten years would proceed at approximately the same rate as during the past decade.

C. HIGHWAYS AND SKYWAYS. (Table 5.) Public road and highway expenditure programs will be greatly influenced by the provisions of the Federal Aid Highway Act of 1956. Outlays for interstate highway construction under this program are estimated to rise by roughly

TABLE 5

Projected Expenditures for Highways—1970

(billions of 1958 dollars)

1970	
Judgment model	13.1
Low growth—low government	9.8
High growth—high government	16.9
High defense	12.6
Low defense	14.2
1958 actual	8.4

50 per cent between 1958 and 1970. In addition, increased expenditures can be expected for improving the nation's primary and secondary road systems. Substantial outlays will also be required in areas not now covered under these programs. For example, improvements in our interstate and major road systems will create a need for adequate access and rural roads.

In the skyways, no less than on the highways, advances in transportation would be hindered by inadequate public programs. By 1970 the volume of air travel is expected to double. However, the age of the jet will find its growth prospects severely limited without adequate airport and ground facilities. In addition, more effective air traffic control systems will be needed if our skyways are to meet the increased demand for high speed air travel. Substantial investment in terminals, runways, control systems, etc. will be required over the coming decade if the anticipated growth in air transportation is to take place.[6]

[6] An allowance for an increase in this program has been included under "other nondefense programs."

D. HEALTH AND HOSPITALS. (Table 6.) Expenditures for health and hospitals particularly at the state and local level have been rising steadily during the postwar period. Substantial increases in expendi-

TABLE 6

Projected Health and Hospital Expenditures—1970

(billions of 1958 dollars)

1970	
Judgment model	9.8
Low growth—low government	4.7
High growth—high government	14.1
High defense	9.3
Low defense	11.0
1958 actual	3.3

tures, however, will be required to overcome present deficiencies in hospital facilities and to provide adequate medical and hospital care for the growing number of aged in our population. In addition, the rise in living standards which economic growth would bring will heighten the demand for improvements in health and hospital services generally. Our judgment model suggests that if considerable progress in this area is to be achieved, a significant increase in government assistance will be required.

E. HOUSING, COMMUNITY REDEVELOPMENT, AND URBAN RENEWAL. (Table 7.) Government programs for housing and community development currently constitute minor expenditure items although the government does exert a significant influence on private housing

TABLE 7

Government Expenditures for Housing, Community Redevelopment and Urban Renewal—1970

(billions of 1958 dollars)

1970	
Judgment model	7.9
Low growth—low government	3.3
High growth—high government	11.0
High defense	6.6
Low defense	8.2
1958 actual	.6

through its insurance and guarantee programs. Past or current expenditure levels in this area, however, have little relevancy to the magnitude of the problem which communities face in the coming decade. The cost of modernizing our urban communities and of

15

preventing deterioration in our metropolitan areas is staggering.[7] And yet, substantial economic growth cannot take place in communities incapable of providing the necessary health, transportation, water, recreation, and other essential facilities. Urban redevelopment includes not only slum clearance. The further development of metropolitan areas will also depend on providing a transportation system which can cope with the changing patterns of urbanization. In a growing number of areas, the ever-expanding problems of the metropolis have become the problem of the emerging megalopolis.

In an economy of rapid growth and technological change there will always be some areas which will lag behind and which in severe and persistent cases of localized depression will require government support. Programs for developing community facilities which would attract new industries are likely to become of growing importance in a dynamic economy. Such programs may be supported both by private and public resources.

F. OTHER NONDEFENSE PROGRAMS. (Table 8.) Recent advances in technology have contributed substantially to rising productivity and economic growth during the past decade. These technological innova-

TABLE 8

Projected Programs for General Administration and
Other Nondefense Programs—1970

(billions of 1958 dollars)

1970	
Judgment model	39.8
Low growth—low government	26.0
High growth—high government	49.4
High defense	36.0
Low defense	43.4
1958 actual	19.3

tions, however, are themselves largely the result of expanded public and private programs for research and development. In the coming decade the promise of economic growth will likewise depend heavily upon advances in our store of knowledge. Continued progress, however, will require increased private and public outlays. Government expenditures for research and development currently finance more than half of the nation's research and development effort.

[7] The cost to the government of undertaking needed urban renewal programs over the coming decade has been estimated at roughly $20 billion annually. This does not include an estimated $130 billion of capital expenditures by private enterprises which would be required annually as a result of the redevelopment program. See: Reginald Isaacs, "The Real Cost of Urban Renewal," *Problems of United States Economic Development*, Vol. 1, Committee for Economic Development, 1958.

Moreover, our tax system encourages private enterprise to undertake research and development activities by regarding such functions as essential business expenses and hence deductable from business income. In agriculture, health, and resource development, the government has traditionally supported research activities, while in the field of national security and atomic energy most research and development programs are financed entirely by the government. Beyond these fields, applied research is regarded largely as the responsibility of business and private research organizations. However, there is an urgent need for increased expenditures particularly for basic research without which applied research and continued technological advancement would be stifled. Increased expenditures by the government for research and development activities would thus provide essential support for continued economic growth.

Economic growth will also require an expansion in various other functions of government. These include such housekeeping activities as police and fire protection, postal service, public welfare institutions, and the general administration and regulating functions of government. In addition, rising population, community development, and industrial expansion could lead to serious problems of resource utilization and conservation. The prospect of a serious water shortage, for example, would become more critical and more widespread in the face of an expected 50 per cent increase in the demands upon our water resources for irrigation, industrialization, and consumption. Government programs are required not only to combat waste and contamination but also to provide additional water sources, such as through the conversion of saline or brackish water. Capital expenditures alone for public water supply facilities are expected at least to double by 1970.

G. TRANSFERS, INTEREST, AND SUBSIDIES. (Table 9.) Government transfer expenditures consist primarily of benefit payments under the social security program (OASI and unemployment compensation), government pension and insurance benefits (including veterans benefits), and payments under public assistance programs. Recent amendments to the Social Security Act have provided for significant increases both in coverage and in benefit payments. Under existing legislation, projected benefit payments would just about double by 1970. Expenditures for veterans benefits are expected to rise only slightly under present laws. However, the experience of the past indicates that recipients under the various social security and government benefit programs have shared in the real productivity increases which have taken place in the economy. For this reason, our judgment-model projections of government social insurance and pension programs provide for an increase in the level of benefits in line with the increase in real income.

TABLE 9

Projected Expenditures for Transfers, Interest, and
Subsidies less Current Surplus
(billions of 1958 dollars)

	Transfers	Interest	Subsidies less Current Surplus	Total
1970				
Judgment model	44.3	8.6	−3.0	49.9
Low growth—low government	35.0	6.6	−2.2	39.4
High growth—high government	47.1	10.0	−3.3	53.8
High defense	33.3	10.4	−3.1	40.6
Low defense	48.5	8.8	−3.2	54.2
1958 Actual	25.5	6.3	1.5	33.3

TABLE 10

Government Expenditures 1958–70
(dollars in 1958 prices)

	1958 ACTUAL			1970 JUDGMENT MODEL		
	Billions	Per Capita	Percentage of GNP	Billions	Per Capita	Percentage of GNP
Goods and services:						
National defense	$44.0	$253	10.1%	53.5	$250	6.8%
Education	15.6	90	3.6	30.7	144	3.9
Highways	8.4	48	1.9	13.1	61	1.7
Health and hospitals	3.3	19	.8	9.8	46	1.2
Housing and urban renewal	.6	3	.1	7.9	37	1.0
Other nondefense programs	19.3	111	4.4	39.8	186	5.0
Total goods and services	$91.2	$524	20.9%	$154.8	$724	19.6%
Transfers, int., etc.	33.3	191	7.6	49.9	233	6.3
Total gov't expenditures	$124.5	$715	28.5%	$204.7	$957	25.9%

Projected net interest paid in the high government model assumes an increase in government debt at about the same rate as in the postwar years including the Korean war period. In the low expenditure model, total interest payments change little from current levels.

Finally, with regard to subsidies (less current surplus of government enterprises), the projections assume that by 1970 government subsidy programs (particularly for agriculture) can be substantially reduced and that government enterprises will be managed so as to yield a smaller deficit (or a larger surplus).

H. JUDGMENT MODEL SUMMARY. The foregoing discussion suggests a number of reasonable alternative patterns of government activity within the framework of a full employment economy. In our judgment neither of the alternative patterns represents the most likely combination of programs which might be expected to prevail by 1970. In arriving at our own judgment-model estimates, therefore, it was necessary to consider the most likely course of government action regarding needs and priorities. In summary Table 10 above, our judgment-model estimates for 1970 are compared with actual expenditures for 1958 both on a per capita basis and as a percent of GNP.

3. *Government Financial Resources and Intergovernmental Relationships*

A. FINANCIAL NEEDS AND RESOURCES. (Table 11.) Rising personal income and increased business activity provide a higher revenue base for financing government programs. At the same time, however, economic growth and rising incomes are influenced by government

TABLE 11

Projected Government Revenues—1970

(billions of 1958 dollars)

	Personal Taxes	Corporate Taxes	Indirect Business Taxes	Contributions to Social Insurance	Total Receipts
Judgment model	63.0	35.1	70.3	27.4	195.9
Low growth— low government	35.1	25.0	65.5	23.3	149.1
High growth— high government	64.6	40.3	71.1	29.1	205.1
High defense	70.8	35.6	71.3	29.0	206.6
Low defense	56.7	34.6	69.6	27.5	188.5
1958 Actual	42.8	18.6	38.6	14.4	114.4

tax and revenue policies. Thus, in deriving the alternative and judgment models the revenue programs of the government, like its expenditure programs, were related to the growth prospects for the economy as a whole.

Because of the nature of our tax structure, some parts of government revenues tend to increase faster than the growth in GNP, while other revenue sources tend to lag behind the increase in economic activity. Projected changes in tax rates also had to take into account differences in the pattern of economic growth. For example, if economic growth is achieved with high levels of consumption or investment, the tax rate on personal and corporate income is assumed to be lower than if a substantial portion of our resources is devoted to higher defense or nondefense government programs. In our judgment model the increase in government programs is accompanied by a moderate reduction in taxes. In the aggregate, taxes on individual incomes, profits, and business activity would represent approximately the same percentage of GNP in 1970 as in 1958.

B. INTERGOVERNMENTAL RELATIONSHIPS. In our judgment model, which assumes a small increase in national security expenditures, we estimate that aggregate annual government expenditures (defense and nondefense; federal, state, and local) would rise by 66 per cent from 1958 to 1970; GNP (all measured in 1958 prices) would rise by 80 per cent.[8] This means that the increase in the *ratio* of nondefense expenditures to GNP would not quite offset the decline in the ratio of defense expenditures to GNP. If we were to look only at the aggregates, financing would seem to present no problem because public programs would account for approximately the same percentage of GNP. However, as soon as we look at the federal, state, and local functions separately, a very serious problem becomes apparent.

Under the traditional distribution of functions between federal programs on the one hand, and state and local on the other, this projection would indicate a much smaller rise in federal expenditures than in those at the state-local level. However, under the traditional distribution of the tax sources, federal revenues would rise much more in response to expanding incomes and production than state and local revenues. This discrepancy in the prospective development of expenditures and revenues creates a problem requiring more drastic measures than those contemplated in the past. There are a number of alternatives through which the problem could be attacked: These are:

1. Reduce or abolish certain federal taxes and increase certain state—local tax rates
2. A change in the division of functions between federal and state and local government
3. A change in the division of tax sources

[8] Compared to 1957, government expenditures and GNP by 1970 would both rise by about 80 per cent.

4. Adoption of some system by which state and local governments would share in the yield of federal income and estate taxes
5. Additional use of grants-in-aid
6. Additional use of the federal tax credit device
7. Federal support of state or local borrowing
8. The use of intergovernmental semi-independent agencies for some functions (e.g., urban renewal) with federal support of financing (including borrowing).

This problem of the discrepancy between federal and state-local expenditures and revenues becomes even more critical if a reduction in national security expenditures should become feasible. Only in case of a substantial increase in national security expenditures beyond what has here been contemplated, might there develop a situation in which some increase in tax rates at all levels of government may be needed. For the purpose of this Conference we deal primarily with the situation in which only a moderate increase in defense expenditures (i.e., a decline in the ratio of defense expenditures to GNP) would be needed. Both of the other cases would require more drastic measures for channeling a higher portion of purchasing power from the public into private hands, in the one case, and from private into public hands in the other. The basic problem of Federal, state-local relations can best be studied if one assumes that the ratio of public to private functions in the *aggregate* remains approximately constant.

In this paper we do not intend to deal with the respective merits or demerits of the various possible solutions as set forth, either individually or in combination. We only want to suggest that our projections strongly indicate some change is imperative in the present relationship between the federal and state-local governments. Thereby, we have posed the problem with which subsequent papers in this session of the Conference will deal directly.

Financial Needs and Resources over the Next Decade: State and Local Governments

DICK NETZER

THIS paper constitutes a considerably revised version of a preliminary exploration of the same subject which was presented at the December 1957 meetings of the American Economic Association in Philadelphia.[1] The basic approach remains the same: in both papers I have eschewed global methods of making projections related to assumed trends in GNP, population, and the like. Rather, each expenditure and receipt category in the Census classification of state-local government finance has been examined separately and individual projections developed on the basis of uniform economic and population assumptions.

Thus, the aggregates suffer from the familiar defect of partial analysis, in that they neglect dynamic interrelationships. More concretely, in this case, the revenue projections probably do not adequately reflect the impact on the economy of society's choice among alternative scales of state-local expenditure. The various hypothetical scales of aggregate state-local expenditure probably do not adequately reflect the impact of the aggregate on the parts, although the direction of the impact here is far from clear. For example, I am not at all sure whether a social choice for high patterns of expenditure in some major functional areas would lead to greater pressure for complementary outlays in other areas or whether it would lead to retrenchment due to pressures on the revenue. I rather suspect that the interrelations in state-local finance are modest and often offsetting in their effects on the final outcome, hence my choice of approach.

These partial projections in both papers at the outset have been based on "as-is" assumptions—that is, on the impact of the economy's assumed behavior on state and local finance assuming the continuance of existing programs. For the receipts side, this means combining existing revenue laws and administration with the expected economic growth. For the expenditure side, this means combining existing standards of public service with the expected increase in underlying workload. Expenditures by function, in the next stage, were examined

[1] *American Economic Association Papers and Proceedings*, May 1958, pp. 317–27.

on the basis of two alternative subjective appraisals of potential improvements in standards—one labeled, in the present paper, "moderate" improvements in standards, and one labeled "substantial" improvements in standards.

1. *Background for the Projections*

The objective background for the projections shown in the tables and discussed in the remainder of this paper consists of the population and economic assumptions I have employed. Population growth and movement is the principal dynamic factor making for rising expenditure requirements: here Series II of the Census Bureau's November 1958 projections of the population is the fundamental assumption.[2] This projection indicates that the total population will rise by about 25 per cent, to nearly 214 million, from 1957 to 1970, with increases of 32 per cent for the population sixty-five and older, 29 per cent for elementary-school age children, 56 per cent for high-school age children, and 63 per cent for the college-age group. I assume that about 80 per cent of the growth in the total population will be within the confines of standard metropolitan areas and that the growth will continue to be particularly rapid outside the core cities of the large metropolitan areas. Furthermore, continued above-national-average rates of growth in the West and Southwest are expected.

In the earlier paper, the twentieth century average rate of growth in GNP, 3.5 per cent annually, was employed. In this paper, in an effort to rest upon a foundation having some features in common with Dr. Colm's paper, two alternative growth rates are utilized— 3.7 per cent, the Colm-Helzner low rate, and 4.2 per cent, the rate in their "judgment" model. All magnitudes are stated in 1957 dollars, and at least initially I assume away inflation: that is, the *over-all* price level will remain stable, however one chooses to measure this. I also assume that the period will be a generally prosperous one, and in particular that 1970, the year for which the projected data are presented, will be one of substantially full employment.

An awareness of the subjective background to what follows is also essential for the reader. There are two basic, though interrelated, elements here. First, I view state and local governments as passive, reacting to the changing environment which they confront, rather than as bold innovators. This means that they do not anticipate

[2] U.S. Bureau of the Census, *Illustrative Projections of the Population of the United States, by Age and Sex, 1960 to 1980*, Current Population Reports, Series P–25 No. 187, November 10, 1958.

demand for their services, but rather respond to changes in workload as they arise. In my models, new programs and the expansion of old ones are based only on needs which exist at the time of action or which will develop so shortly and so certainly that they cannot be overlooked, even by traditionally short-sighted public agencies.

Second, I do not anticipate that the federal government will have very large surpluses which will be seeking outlets as aids in financing expanded state and local government programs. That is, I assume that increased outlays on expenditure programs which do not involve state-local participation at present will absorb most of the increased Federal revenues available from a growing GNP. This is principally because I quite seriously do not believe that any discussion of 1970, contingent on the preservation of democratic institutions (not to mention a population of 214 million and a stock of physical assets two-thirds or more larger than at present), is at all relevant, if one does not contemplate a defense effort far larger than the present one. In addition, numerous proposed large-scale expansions of Federal efforts in other areas—natural resources, health research, health insurance, etc.—do not necessarily involve new programs on the state-local level. Finally, if we are successful in making the decade of the 1960's a generally prosperous one, we will be fighting inflation most of the time and appropriate federal fiscal policies would produce large surpluses.

A few qualifications are in order at this point. First, the projections here assume a smooth and gradual increase in expenditures as well as receipts from 1957 to 1970. With steady economic growth, the gradual expansion of tax bases over a decade and more is impressively large in dollar terms, and permits very large increases in expenditures. But the influences making for increases in outlays are not likely to be smooth or gradual. First of all, the underlying workload is likely to increase rather unevenly—for example, take the very rapid increase in high-school enrollments which is now upon us. Secondly, congestion and deficiencies in facilities and services, as measured by prevailing public attitudes, exist here and now, and we may reasonably expect efforts to overcome them in the immediate future rather than evenly over the entire thirteen-year period. Thus, even if any one set of my expenditure projections is assumed to be providing an "adequate" level of services in 1970, however one defines adequacy in this connotation, it will probably not be providing adequate services in 1960.

Another qualification: I have ignored geographic differences and differences among levels of government within the total state-local government sector of the economy. Geographic differences present no problem if, in the parts of the country in which population (and hence needs for public services) is growing at a more than average rate, gross product and income are growing at a rate equally in excess of the national average and if tax bases in the fast growing areas are at least as sensitive to economic growth as those elsewhere. However, there is some evidence that this is in fact not the case: that the western states, for example, have been experiencing a rate of increase in population which is a good deal more above the national average than is their rate of increase in income. From 1950 to 1957, California, for instance, had a rate of increase in population more than double the national rate but a rate of increase in personal income less than one and one-half as great as the national rate. Therefore, the techniques used here probably conceal some real problems.

The projections below follow the Governments Division, Bureau of the Census, classifications and definitions of state-local financial transactions, with a few exceptions. The Census scheme of financial reporting essentially presents *gross* cash receipts from and payments to the public, with internal transactions within the unit of government (or for the aggregates, among the units within the aggregate) washed out. The activities of state-local government are comprehended within three major revenue and expenditure categories—general, utility (including liquor store systems), and insurance trust. In this paper, insurance trust transactions are ignored entirely. The category is dominated by unemployment insurance, which can more easily be handled as a Federal program. It may be that my failure to include employee retirement system finances is a not inconsequential omission, for many such systems appear to be seriously under-financed and may therefore in coming years occasion sizeable drains on general revenues. Nonetheless, I have not found it possible to cover any more than general and utility revenue and expenditure. One exception to the Census scheme within these categories: I have chosen not to treat liquor monopoly systems as utility operations but rather strictly as revenue devices, and have included only their excess of revenue over expenditures in my accounts. This shows up on the revenue side as an addition to receipts from selective sales taxes on alcoholic beverages. (See Table 1.)

TABLE 1

Revenue and Expenditure, 1957: Reconciliation of Bureau of
Census Figures with This Paper's
(millions of dollars)

REVENUE	
Census Bureau	
General revenue	38,162
Utility revenue	2,935
Liquor store revenue	1,185
Insurance trust revenue	3,639
Total	45,922
Less:	
Insurance trust revenue	3,639
Liquor store expenditure	936
Equals: Revenue total used in this paper	41,347
EXPENDITURE	
Census Bureau	
General expenditure	40,420
Utility expenditure	3,518
Liquor store expenditure	936
Insurance trust expenditure	2,752
Total	47,626
Less:	
Insurance trust expenditure	2,752
Liquor store expenditure	936
Equals: Expenditure total used in this paper	43,938

SOURCE: U.S. Bureau of the Census, *State and Local
Government Finances in 1957*, 1957 Census of Governments Advance Release No. 8, February 1959, Table 1,
p. 13.

2. *Revenue*

In this effort, revenues have been projected on two wholly different
bases. Revenues which are associated with the scale and nature of
expenditure programs have been projected as corollaries of the
independently developed expenditure estimates, while general tax
revenues have been separately estimated, on the basis of an expansion
of the base for each major source of tax revenue which appears to be
consistent with the assumed over-all economic environment.

Program-associated revenues here include Federal aid, highway-
user taxes, receipts from utility operations, charges for services, and
miscellaneous general revenue. This distinction is to some extent an
arbitrary one, for some general tax revenues are partly dependent on
the scale of spending programs—e.g., general levies which tax some
aspects of motor vehicle ownership and use—and some of the other
group of revenue producers are relatively insensitive to program

27

scale. This is particularly true of some elements of the miscellaneous general revenue category; they are grouped here because it seems just marginally more reasonable to relate them to state-local programs than to the growth in the economy at large. The following tabulation indicates the major items (for 1957, in billions of dollars) in the breakdown used:

General tax revenue		24.7
Property taxes	12.9	
Other taxes	11.9	
Program-associated revenue		16.6
Federal aid	3.8	
Highway-user taxes	4.3	
Utility revenue	2.9	
Other charges for services	3.8	
Miscellaneous general revenue	1.7	

The general tax revenue projections here are estimates of collections at constant (1957) rates, in 1957 dollars, assuming alternatively that real GNP will grow from 1957 to 1970 at rates of 3.7 and 4.2 per cent per year. By tax rates, I mean effective rates against the economic rather than the legal base; all changes in law and administrative practice—in nominal tax rates, in exemptions, deductions and coverage, in assessment ratios, in use of particular taxes by units of government—are treated as changes in effective rates. Thus, for the property tax, constant rates mean that assessments will rise as rapidly as the market value of taxable property or nominal property tax rates will rise to offset any lags in assessments.

Under these assumptions, then, the fundamental task has been to estimate the increase in the economic bases of each major tax, which is likely to accompany the assumed rise in GNP. Such estimates have been based on a reconstruction, using rather heroic procedures, of the postwar (1946–57) real expansion in tax bases, adjusted for apparent anomalies in the postwar period not apt to recur, in my judgment.

Tables 2–5 indicate the procedures and results. Table 2 shows the results of the reconstruction of underlying tax bases, in the form of percentage increases in the tax bases for the entire period and for the first six years and second five years of the period since 1946. I should note at this point that the income and death and gift tax bases include the estimated effect of the characteristic progressive

28

rate structures, and perhaps might better be labeled as the change in tax collections at constant rates. Because this was a period with a fair amount of inflation, it is not surprising that ad valorem tax bases rose very much more rapidly than the bases for specific taxes, notably those on liquor and tobacco and in the "all other" group. Likewise, it is not surprising that the increases were generally much more marked in the first half of the period, when price levels advanced steeply, than in the second half. The large rise in the estimated property tax base is perhaps the only eyebrow-raiser in the Table.

TABLE 2

Estimated Growth in State-Local Tax Bases
(Excluding Highway-User Taxes), Fiscal 1946–57

| | PERCENTAGE CHANGE IN TAX BASE | | |
TAX	1946–57	1946–52	1952–57
Property	151	90	32
Income	153	103	28
Individual	167	83	46
Corporation	140	89	16
Sales and gross receipts[a, b]	83	45	26
General	100	58	26
Alcoholic beverage[a]	9	−5	14
Tobacco products	27	22	4
Other[b]	158	84	40
Death and gift	217	90	67
All other, including licenses and permits[c]	48	28	16
Total	127	75	30
Total, excluding property taxes	97	57	24

[a] Includes excess of revenue over expenditure of liquor monopoly systems.
[b] Excludes motor fuel taxes.
[c] Excludes motor vehicle and operators' licenses.

I repeat that this is a measure of the rise in the current market value of taxable property, not a measure of assessed values.

Table 3 is the complement to Table 2, showing estimated changes in effective tax rates, broadly defined, for major classes of taxes. I estimate that effective property tax rates declined by nearly a tenth from 1946 to 1952, but rose fairly sharply thereafter, to yield a rather small rise for the entire period. The stiff rise in consumption tax rates was due to the widespread adoption of sales and gross receipts levies by additional states and local units, as well as to increases in rates of existing taxes.

Table 4 compares the tax base change results (shown in Table 2)

TABLE 3

Estimated Changes in Effective Rates of Major Classes of
State-Local Taxes (Excluding Highway-User Taxes)
Fiscal 1946–57

	PERCENTAGE CHANGE IN EFFECTIVE TAX RATES		
TAX	1946–57	1946–52	1952–57
Property	+5	−9	+15
Income	+25	+5	+16
Sales and gross receipts[a]	+67	+44	+18
All other[b]	+60	+34	+24
Total	+24	+7	+16
Total, excluding property taxes	+54	+31	+18

[a] Includes excess of revenue over expenditure of liquor monopoly systems; excludes motor fuel taxes.

[b] Including death and gift taxes and licenses and permits; excludes motor vehicle and operators' licenses.

TABLE 4

GNP Elasticity of State-Local Tax Bases
(Excluding Highway-User Taxes)
Estimated Fiscal 1946–57 and Assumed Fiscal 1957–70

	PERCENTAGE CHANGE IN TAX BASES ASSOCIATED WITH 1.00 PER CENT RISE IN GNP	
TAX	*Estimated 1946–57*	*Assumed 1957–70*
Property	1.00[a]	1.00
Income	1.40	1.50
Individual	1.53	1.70
Corporation	1.28	1.10
Sales and gross receipts[b,c]	*	1.00
General	.92	1.00
Alcoholic beverage[b]	.19[d]	.50
Tobacco products	.62[d]	.80
Other[c]	1.45	1.40
Death and gift	1.98	1.80
All other, including licenses and permits[e]	1.09[d]	1.10
Total	*	1.10
Total, excluding property taxes	*	1.20

Note: Subtotals and totals in column 2 are computed from the results shown in Table 5.

* Not computed because computation would involve combining current and constant dollar GNP relationships. Data not footnoted in column 1 are current dollar GNP elasticities.

[a] Change in deflated base compared with change in GNP in constant dollars.

[b] Includes excess of revenue over expenditure of liquor monopoly systems.

[c] Excludes motor fuel taxes.

[d] Change in base compared with change in GNP in constant dollars; these are largely specific rather than ad valorem taxes.

[e] Excludes motor vehicle and operators' licenses.

TABLE 5

State-Local Government Tax Revenue (Excluding Highway-User Taxes)
by Source, Fiscal 1946, 1957, and 1970 (Projected)
(millions of dollars)

TAX	ACTUAL 1946[a]		1957	PROJECTED, 1970 3.7% Growth Rate	4.2% Growth Rate
Property		4,986	12,851	20,600	21,900
Income		869	2,751	5,250	5,650
Individual	422	1,767		3,600	3,900
Corporation	447	984		1,650	1,750
Sales and gross receipts[b,c]		2,241	6,859	11,100	11,700
General	962	4,027		6,450	6,850
Alcoholic beverages[b]	559	840		1,100	1,150
Tobacco products	213	604		900	950
Other[c]	507	1,388		2,650	2,750
Death and gift		141	346	700	800
All other, including licenses and permits[d]		654	1,932	3,200	3,450
Total		8,891	24,739	40,850	43,500
Total, excluding property taxes		3,905	11,888	20,250	21,600

SOURCE: 1946—U.S. Bureau of the Census, *Historical Statistics on State and Local Government Finances, 1902–1953* (1955) 1957—U.S. Bureau of the Census, *State and Local Government Finances in 1957*, 1957 Census of Governments Advance Release No. 8, February 1959, and *Summary of Governmental Finances in 1957*, August 24, 1958. Property taxes as shown in former release; other detail as shown in latter, except that eight million dollar difference in total nonproperty taxes between two releases is all allocated to "all other" category.
[a] Some detail for local governments partly estimated.
[b] Includes excess of revenue over expenditure of liquor monopoly systems.
[c] Excludes motor fuel taxes.
[d] Excludes motor vehicle and operators' licenses.

with GNP changes. In this comparison, changes in the bases for ad valorem taxes generally are compared with changes in GNP in current dollars, while for specific taxes the comparison is with constant dollar GNP. The exception to this rule is the property tax; since the purpose of these computations has been to secure data on which to construct a no-inflation model, deflators have been applied to the current dollar estimates of property values and the deflated result compared with constant dollar GNP. The second column of the Table shows the elasticity figures chosen for use in the projections. Where significant differences exist between the figures calculated for 1946–57 and those used for 1957–70, they are explained below in the sections dealing with the major taxes in detail.

Finally, Table 5 indicates my tax revenue projections assuming (a) that real GNP grows at a rate of 3.7 per cent per year and (b) that real GNP grows at a rate of 4.2 per cent per year. The over-all

31

rise in revenue from 1957 to 1970 is about two-thirds under the first GNP assumption and about three-fourths under the latter. This compares with a rise of about 125 per cent from 1946 to 1957, adjusted for changes in effective tax rates. In the 1946–57 period, property taxes accounted for just about one-half of the total increase of nearly 16 billion dollars; if effective rates of all taxes had remained at 1946 levels property taxes would have produced about two-thirds of an 11 billion dollar rise in total tax revenue. In contrast, in my projections, property taxes will account for somewhat less than half of increases in the totals projected at 16–19 billion dollars.

My December 1957 paper suggested that perhaps the major difference in my prophecies and those frequently voiced elsewhere, relates to the very large difference between the GNP elasticity of state-local tax revenues in my model and the elasticities computed by other investigators.[3] The latter data suggest over-all elasticity figures ranging from no less than half to no more than 75 per cent of unity, with estimates of property tax elasticity, which is really the crucial factor, of as little as 0.22.

From 1946 to 1957, actual tax revenues (as defined here) including the impact of effective rate changes rose 1.63 per cent for each 1 per cent rise in current dollar GNP. Excluding property taxes, the elasticity figure was 1.87. Estimated tax revenues, had effective rates remained constant at 1946 levels, rose 1.17 per cent for each 1 per cent rise in current dollar GNP; the nonproperty tax figure was 0.89. Measuring changes in deflated ad valorem tax bases and actual specific tax bases against constant dollar GNP changes produces an elasticity figure of 1.04 for both the total and the nonproperty group.

In the projections the over-all elasticity figure used is 1.1 for total taxes and 1.2 for nonproperty sources. This is somewhat above the deflated 1946–57 results, but below the undeflated results (at constant effective rates) for all tax sources combined. I continue to be persuaded that the difference between my computations and those of others are more apparent than real, since I have been concerned less with actual changes in receipts which include the impact of effective tax rate changes (as I define them here) than with estimated changes in the underlying economic phenomena which state and local agencies tax. To repeat the conclusions of the earlier paper, in an environment free from inflation or major declines in

[3] *A.E.A. Papers and Proceedings*, May 1958, pp. 323–4.

activity, it is rather difficult to find many state and local tax bases which are likely to grow appreciably less rapidly than GNP. The transactions which are the measure of most consumption and business taxes tend to comprise an expanding rather than a contracting share of total activity. And taxes with progressive rate structures, principally the individual income tax, will automatically produce disproportionately large increases in revenues at constant rates, along with rising activity.[4]

Property Taxes

Probably no feature of the December 1957 paper received more abuse than the assumption of unit elasticity in projecting property tax revenues. The criticisms took two forms. First, it was asserted that whatever my estimates of the elasticity of the underlying base— the market value of taxable property—history has demonstrated that changes in assessments lag changes in value to a major extent and that therefore in an environment of growing output, income and wealth, state and local agencies will find themselves relying on a revenue source which inadequately reflects growth. It was the use of assessments, not market values, that produced the 0.22 elasticity figure for the periods between 1929 and 1950 alluded to above.[5]

I reject this contention, for several reasons. First, there is no real evidence to indicate that assessments are in fact insensitive to secular changes in GNP, however sticky they are in the short run in the face of cyclical changes. The evidence that does exist is meager, but it suggests the contrary conclusion. It must be repeated that the present projections assume away cyclical movements which are large or prolonged.

Second, this criticism implies that with growth but no inflation, the ratio of assessed to market values of existing properties will continuously decline and/or new improvements and additions will be ignored on a wholesale scale by tax assessors. This seems wholly unreasonable. To be sure, reassessments are periodic rather than continual and increases in real value which are a consequence of growth in the economy rather than changes in the physical character

[4] An exception to these generalizations might occur in the event that a large proportion of the rise in GNP took the form of massive increases in defense outlays, financed by broad-based federal taxes which pre-empt the additional income *before* it affects state-local tax bases. This is not entirely inconceivable.

[5] See Harold M. Groves and C. Harry Kahn, "The Stability of State and Local Tax Yields," *American Economic Review*, March 1952, pp. 87–102.

of the property (e.g., the rising value of potential homesites now in farm use on the fringes of growing metropolitan areas) are apt to be inadequately reflected by assessors. However, for the economy as a whole in the environment postulated, it is inconceivable that such lags would lower the elasticity figure by more than, say, 0.15. And, as will be seen shortly, there is good reason to believe that the conservative elasticity figure used—1.00—is actually a good deal more than 0.15 below the true post-war experience. Moreover, there are offsets to these deficiencies in assessment practices. Assessment practices *are* improving, albeit more slowly than reasonable men can abide, in part through the adoption of just passably good practices by the more primitive jurisdictions and in part through continual improvements in all sorts of procedures, techniques, and assessment aids and equipment of a mundane sort, on the part of more advanced assessment offices and officers. In addition, if there is to be no more inflation, the lags occasioned by the recent inflation will be caught up with, as assessors begin to regard current market values as more "normal."

Third, even if there are moderate lags in assessments, the goal here is to appraise fiscal resources available to state-local governments, not, at least in the first instance, to gauge how heavily they will tap these resources. In the assumed economic environment, market values, not assessments (or putting it otherwise, a measure which holds effective, not nominal rates constant) seem very much the appropriate measure of available resources.

The second major criticism, less frequently voiced, is much more to the point. This, simply, questions my estimates of changes in the underlying base, market values. Walter Heller, the formal discussant of the earlier paper, queried whether offsetting influences had been at work among the components of the property tax base in the post-war period and whether it is reasonable to assume their continuance.[6] The projections here are based on a new set of estimates of changes in the property tax base, not a repetition of the earlier computations, although the resulting elasticity figures are identical.

The method used was to prepare separate estimates of changes in current market values (or depreciated replacement cost) for the major classes of property ordinarily subject to levy, and to combine these series into an index, weighting the components on the basis of

---

[6] *A.E.A. Papers and Proceedings*, May 1958, p. 332.

their share of total assessed value in 1956, as reported in the 1957 Census of Governments.[7] The separate series were also expressed in 1946 dollars, and combined on the basis of these weights, into a 1946 dollar index. The four series used were: residential nonfarm real estate, which accounted for about 42 per cent of 1956 assessments; other nonfarm real estate, including here all state-assessed rail and public utility property, about 30 per cent of the 1956 tax base; farm real estate, about 10 per cent of the tax base; and tangible personal property-inventories, producer durables, and motor vehicles, about 17 per cent of the tax base. Intangibles, which amount to only about one-half of the 1 per cent of total assessed values, most of this concentrated in a single state, were ignored. The basic approach was to bring forward to the present, somewhat crudely, on the basis of available evidence various components of the national wealth estimates presented by Raymond Goldsmith in *A Study of Savings.*[8] For residential nonfarm real estate, this method produces results for 1956 very close to the equalized value total based on the Census Bureau's assessment-ratio survey for six months in 1956.[9] For nonresidential real estate, the results, while not as close to the Census data, are not unacceptably far off that benchmark. Department of Agriculture data were used for farm real estate, rather than the Goldsmith-based approach.

Table 6 indicates the results of these methods. The current value-current GNP elasticities are relatively low for farm real estate and relatively very high for inventories and durables, and in general the elasticity figures are higher for the first half of the period than for the second half, which is understandable in view of the rapid rises in the price level in the 1945–51 period. On a deflated basis, the elasticity figures for the earlier years are far lower than for the more recent years, especially for the nonfarm real estate categories which together comprised nearly three-fourths of the 1956 tax base.

There are two reasons why I suggested above that the use of unit elasticity in the projections is conservative. First, the deflators used are probably much too large. Essentially, they are based on the rise in the costs of producing new properties (improvements to real estate and tangible personalty), and they imply an immediate and

[7] U.S. Bureau of the Census, *Property Tax Assessments in the United States,* 1957 Census of Governments Advance Release No. 5, December 1957.

[8] See Volume III, Table W–1.

[9] U.S. Bureau of the Census, *Assessed Values and Sales Prices of Transferred Real Property,* 1957 Census of Governments Advance Release No. 7, May 1958.

TABLE 6

Estimated Changes in Values of Taxable Classes of Property for Taxes Payable
in Fiscal 1946–57[a]

	Residential Nonfarm Real Estate	Other Nonfarm Real Estate	Farm Real Estate	Inventories and Durables	Weighted Total[b]
Percentage increase in tax base, current market values:					
1945–56	149	135	105	238	151
1945–51	87	71	73	139	90
1951–56	33	37	19	41	32
GNP elasticities of revenues at: constant effective rates— current dollar GNP *vs.* current market values:					
1946–57	1.37	1.24	0.97	2.18	1.38
1946–52	1.34	1.09	1.12	2.14	1.38
1952–57	1.22	1.37	0.70	1.52	1.19
constant dollar GNP *vs.* deflated values:					
1946–57	1.02	0.68	0.30	2.18	1.00
1946–52	0.60	0.20	0.24	1.92	0.64
1952–57	1.67	1.54	0.47	2.20	1.54

[a] Tax base computations apply to values in calendar year preceding fiscal year in which taxes are payable; to give effect to lags in collections, GNP changes between tax payment years are used in computing elasticities.

[b] Weighted by proportion which each class is of total assessed value in 1956.

proportionate revaluation of existing properties. This is no doubt a considerable exaggeration of actual price effects. Second, I suspect that the 1952–57 period may be a better indicator for the future than the earlier period, because of the relative magnitudes of inflation in the two periods, as well as the relative volumes of investment activity. To give some weight to lags in the assessment process, a rather conservative elasticity figure has been employed in the projections. However, ignoring these lags, and throwing caution to the winds, an elasticity figure of 1.4–1.5 would seem to be indicated.

Income Taxes

In the December 1957 paper, employing the glib (and erroneous) assumption that state *individual income tax* structures were only mildly progressive over the range of incomes which is really significant, little allowance for progressivity was made, either in the separation of postwar period base and effective rate changes (as defined here), or in projections for the future. That a fair degree of progressivity actually does obtain was pointed out by Heller.[10]

[10] *A.E.A. Papers and Proceedings*, May 1958, p. 332.

Consequently new computations have been made for the 1946–57 period using a procedure designed to include the impact of progressivity. First, an effort was made to develop a pattern of rates and exemptions which is average, when weighted by income or individual income tax collections, for the governments using the tax in the base year.

These tax provisions were applied to income distribution data in various postwar years to gauge the rise in tax liability which accompanies a given rise in taxable types of personal income. I conclude that under this characteristic income tax structure, tax liability rises by about 1.7 per cent for each 1.0 per cent increase in income which is ordinarily taxable. Ordinarily taxable income here means the Commerce personal income series, for the governments with individual income taxes, excluding estimated amounts of imputed and other nonmoney income and various types of nontaxable money income. The following is the result of these efforts:

Increase in:	*1946–57*	*1946–52*	*1952–57*
taxable types of personal income	92%	49%	29%
tax base including effect of progressivity	167%	83%	46%

Increase in:	*1946–56*	*1946–52*	*1952–56*
tax rates, this paper	58%	29%	22%
tax rates, December 1957 paper	112%	63%	30%

In other words, ignoring progressivity one would conclude that the GNP elasticity of the individual income tax base in the postwar years has been a good deal less than unity, while considering the actual prevailing rate structures, I conclude now that the elasticity has been more than 1.5, and that the increase in effective tax rates has been only about half as great as was asserted in the earlier paper.

Table 4 indicates that for the projections a higher elasticity figure has been used than is estimated to have been the experience in the 1946–57 period. This is so because in the immediate postwar years the growth in personal income appreciably lagged the rise in GNP. For the states with personal income taxes, personal income rose only about three-fourths as rapidly as GNP from 1946 to 1952, and the elasticity figure for the tax base is around 1.3. From 1952 to 1957, personal income rose about as fast as GNP, and the elasticity figure is 1.7, that which is used in the projections. This implies that personal income of taxable types in states using the tax will rise *pari passu* with GNP; application of a 1.7 progressivity factor to this assumption produces the elasticity figure employed here.

For *corporate income taxes*, an elasticity figure somewhat *below* the postwar experience has been used. The postwar period includes one particularly abnormal period for corporate profits—the 60 per cent rise in the two years between 1949 and 1951, largely under the impact of the Korean War. Since then corporate profits have risen only about one-third as rapidly as GNP. Over the next decade or so, it seems likely that corporate profits before taxes may rise somewhat faster relative to GNP than recently, perhaps approaching unit elasticity. The figure of 1.1 results from giving effect to the modest degree of progression in existing state-local corporate tax structures.

Sales and Gross Receipts Taxes

Consumption taxes as a group appear in the postwar period to have had a constant dollar GNP elasticity of somewhat less than unity. The ad valorem taxes had a current dollar GNP elasticity of just around unity. The *general sales component* figure was .92; in the projections this is raised slightly, to unity, to take account of the generally more comprehensive retail sales tax base now than was characteristic in 1946. This reflects more widespread inclusion of services and less widespread exemption of food.

The two specific tax sources covered here, sales of *alcoholic beverages* and *tobacco products*, exhibited rather low elasticities in the postwar period. In the early postwar years, consumption of alcoholic beverages declined significantly from the wartime peaks; since 1952 the constant dollar GNP elasticity has been only slightly below unity. Considering consumption trends for alcoholic beverages more generally over a longer period and also the changing age distribution of the population, I would guess that the future GNP elasticity will be substantially above the abnormal postwar period (which includes the decline in consumption), but far below unity. On the other hand, consumption of tobacco products rose only slightly less rapidly than GNP in the early postwar years, but has risen hardly at all since 1952 in the wake of the disclosure of the links between smoking and cancer. My elasticity figure of 0.8 is based on the assumption that the health issue will continue to act as a drag on consumption, but will not be nearly as decisive an influence as in the last few years.

Other Taxes

Reconstruction of the bases of *death and gift taxes* in the post-war period has proven to be at least as unsatisfying a job as working with the property tax base. Relevant data is scarce and not readily amenable to the manipulations required. The basic raw material here has been federal estate and gift tax data, which are available for some but not all years of the 1946–57 period. I have attempted to adjust the series, partially interpolated, on gross estates for the typical progressive rate structure.

One big problem in working with this data relates to the only major changes in effective rates in the period on both the federal and state levels, the estate-splitting marital deduction changes around 1948. Because of the effects of these changes on progressivity, I have somewhat fewer qualms about the results for the 1950–57 period, after the changes had become effective, than about the results for the entire eleven-year span. The following are the calculations for the two periods:

	1946–57	1950–57
Percentage increase in base, not adjusted for progressivity	140	67
GNP elasticity	1.28	1.21
Percentage increase in base, adjusted for progressivity	217	96
GNP elasticity	1.98	1.73
Progressivity factor	1.55	1.43

For the projections, I have assumed that bequests and gifts subject to tax will have a GNP elasticity of 1.2 and the progressivity factor will be 1.5, producing an assumed GNP elasticity of death and gift tax collections at constant rates of 1.8. The 1.2 figure corresponds to the 1950–57 experience; it seems reasonable to expect that, as incomes and wealth rise and poverty decreases, the volume of bequests and gifts subject to tax will rise somewhat faster than GNP.

The major components of the *all other* taxes group are severance taxes and license and similar taxes on corporations in general and

39

on a wide variety of occupations and businesses. These miscellaneous business taxes are largely specific rather than ad valorem and there seems no reason to anticipate anything other than unit elasticity. The use of a 1.1 figure is based on the assumption that oil and gas output, the main source of severance tax receipts, will continue to rise more rapidly than real GNP.

3. *Expenditures*

The projections discussed in this section cover the Census categories of general and utility expenditures, excluding liquor store outlays, and aside from interest payments. Debt service requirements are treated in another section; they have been computed essentially as residuals, based on the implications for changes in indebtedness resulting from various alternative combinations of receipts and expenditures.

Three basic sets of expenditure projections have been developed, function by function. The differences among the three sets of projections relate to the degree of improvement in standards of state-local services and facilities allowed for. The term "standards" of public services in this paper refers, in concept, to objective physical standards. For example, constant standards of highway services would permit vehicles to move at the same rate of speed with no greater exposure to accident, regardless of increases in the number of vehicles travelling between similar points at the same time. However, the expression of such standards in dollar terms presents great difficulties. In some cases, this is based on what are presumably expert judgments of other investigators. More often, good or adequate standards are equated with the recent expenditure experience of public agencies reputed to be performing a particular service moderately or substantially above average in both dollar and real terms. This recent expenditure experience has been reduced to unit costs—per capita, per vehicle, per student enrolled, etc. In applying these dollar standards, shifts in the population and the resulting workload interregionally and to and within urban areas have been considered.

The first set of projections allows only for matching increases in workload due to population growth and movement and the like. It assumes constant (fiscal 1957) standards of services and facilities, insofar as this can be quantified, and, of course, is highly unreal. No one can anticipate that expenditures, in an environment of buoyant revenues, would increase this little; the exercise, however, does provide a floor for each function.

The other two sets of projections allow, respectively, for "moderate" and "substantial" improvements in standards. In general, "moderate" improvement means raising the 1957 level of performance for the country as a whole to that achieved by "good" performers at present, whether groups of cities, individual cities, or state-wide averages. "Substantial" improvement generally means raising the 1957 level of performance for the entire spectrum of state-local governments to an average equal to that of the very best performers in 1957. The choice of "good" and "superlative" performers is of course an entirely subjective affair. In neither set of projections is there any effort to make allowances for the strength of competitive claims on the revenue. Rather, the functions are treated in isolation from each other, and from revenues.

Despite my assumption of stable price levels over-all, it is worthwhile considering expenditure totals in an environment of adverse relative prices for the goods and services state and local agencies buy. Throughout the postwar period, as Mr. Heller pointed out in his comment,[11] the prices paid by state and local governments appear to have risen substantially more rapidly than the general price level. I say "appear" because, as Heller also points out, the implicit GNP deflator for the state-local sector quite clearly makes no allowance for increases in productivity. Any increase in state-local wage rates is treated as a price increase, without regard for the fact that this more highly paid labor may be steadily producing more and better final output—public services. One cannot really maintain that state-local productivity is stagnant; as a matter of fact, there have been striking improvements in productivity in "housekeeping" and staff services almost everywhere, as these activities have become more capital-intensive and less labor-intensive.

Nonetheless, state and local governments remain on the whole far more labor-intensive than the economy as a whole, and they are also heavy purchasers of the output of the construction industry. Both these factors suggest that productivity increases may well continue to lag those in the economy as a whole, and thus, in effect, relative prices may rise for state and local agencies in an atmosphere of price stability for the economy. To illustrate the impact of a modest lag in productivity, I have computed the effect of a 0.5 per cent

[11] *A.E.A. Papers and Proceedings*, May 1958, p. 331.

TABLE 7

State-Local Government Expenditures, by Functional Groups
Fiscal 1946, 1957, and 1970 (Projected)[a]
(millions of dollars)

FUNCTIONAL GROUPS	ACTUAL 1946[b]	ACTUAL 1957	PROJECTED, 1970, WITH INDICATED CHANGES IN STANDARDS No Change	Moderate Improvement	Substantial Improvement
Education	3,356	14,134	19,300	23,350	29,600
Highways	1,672	7,798	10,300	11,600	13,800
Health and welfare, total	2,227	6,598	7,750	8,500	9,350
Public assistance	1,230	2,800*	2,800	2,800	2,800
Public hospitals	567	2,487*	3,300	3,900	4,600
Other community facilities and services, total[c]	2,346	8,618*	11,200	13,550	16,100
Water and sanitation	726	2,948*	3,850	4,650	5,450
Police and fire	773	2,302	3,100	3,350	3,950
Miscellaneous[d]	1,866	5,410*	6,800	7,250	7,700
Total	11,485	42,559	55,350	64,250	76,550
Exhibit: capital outlays	1,305	12,710	14,350	18,650	22,775

SOURCE: 1946—U.S. Bureau of the Census, *Historical Statistics on State and Local Government Finances, 1902–1953* (1955).
1957—U.S. Bureau of the Census, *State and Local Government Finances in 1957*, 1957 Census of Governments Advance Release No. 8, February 1959, and *Summary of Governmental Finances in 1957*, August 24, 1958. Totals and most subtotals from former release; starred (*) detail and subtotals from latter release, or in part estimated where information presented in Advance Release No. 8 suggests significant revision in this detail.

[a] Excludes all debt service payments, insurance trust expenditures, and liquor store expenditures.
[b] Some underlying detail in part estimated.
[c] Includes, in addition to functions shown, local parks and recreation, nonhighway transportation, housing and community redevelopment, and electric, gas, and transit utilities.
[d] Includes general control, natural resources, and other and unallocable general expenditures.

per year rise in over-all cost levels (per unit of stable quality), applied to the totals in the projections previously developed. This price rise is applied across the board; I have made no attempt to gauge which functions are likely to do best in productivity. To the extent that the 0.5 per cent figure is reasonable, applying it to the totals overstates the case, since they include close to three billion dollars in assistance and subsidy payments (mostly public assistance) which are not subject to the same price-productivity considerations.

Table 7 summarizes the three sets of projections, by major functional groups, without allowance for increases in relative prices or lags in productivity, however one chooses to put it. From a level of 42.6 billion dollars in fiscal 1957 general and utility expenditures, excluding interest, are projected to rise 12.8 billion, 21.7 billion, and 34.0 billion in the three respective patterns, depending on the changes in standards assumed. In contrast to the changes in 1946–57 period, a considerably larger proportion of the over-all increase is accounted for by education—40–46 per cent versus about 35 per cent in the postwar period—and a considerably smaller proportion by health and welfare activities—8–9 per cent versus 14 per cent in the earlier period—due to the assumed stability of public assistance outlays which is only partially offset by the assumed steep rise in hospital expenditures. Highways and the "other community facilities and services" category each accounted for about one-fifth of the rise in the 1946–57 period. In the projections allowing for improvements in standards highways will account for a slightly smaller part of the rise and the "other community facilities" category for a slightly larger part. This is largely because I judge levels of performance at present to be a good deal less "adequate" for water supply and sewerage than for roads, and hence expect a steeper rise for the former, despite the vastly expanded Federal aid program enacted in 1956.

At present, education absorbs about one-third of state-local expenditures included in Table 7. By 1970, I would expect the proportion to be closer to 40 per cent. I anticipate declines in the relative importance of both health and welfare and the miscellaneous group, which is composed mostly of fairly slowly growing activities. Highway spending should maintain its relative role—about 18 per cent of the total—and the "other community facilities" group should increase slightly in importance, to about 21 per cent of the total.

Applying an increase in costs to the totals produces the following results, as compared with the totals in Table 7 (in millions of dollars):

Total Expenditures	Constant Costs	Cost Rising at 0.5 Per Cent per Year
Constant standards	55,350	58,950
Moderate improvement	64,250	68,400
Substantial improvement	76,550	81,450
Increase in Expenditures, 1957–70		
Constant standards	12,791	16,391
Moderate improvement	21,691	25,841
Substantial improvement	33,991	38,891

TABLE 8
Projected State-Local Expenditures in Fiscal 1970
as a Per Cent of GNP

| | CHANGES IN STANDARDS ASSUMED | | |
	No Change	*Moderate Improvement*	*Substantial Improvement*
At constant costs:			
General and utility expenditures, excluding interest			
with GNP rising at 3.7% per year	7.7	8.9	10.6
with GNP rising at 4.2% per year	7.3	8.4	10.0
Estimated purchases of goods and services			
with GNP rising at 3.7% per year	6.6	7.8	9.4
with GNP rising at 4.2% per year	6.2	7.3	8.8
With costs rising 0.5% per year:			
General and utility expenditures, excluding interest			
with GNP rising at 3.7% per year	8.2	9.5	11.3
with GNP rising at 4.2% per year	7.7	8.9	10.7
Estimated purchases of goods and services			
with GNP rising at 3.7% per year	7.1	8.3	10.0
with GNP rising at 4.2% per year	6.7	7.8	9.4

On a per capita basis, total expenditures (per Table 7) amounted to around 250 dollars in 1957. Under my constant standards assumption they would rise to close to 260 dollars (or 275 with rising relative costs) in 1970; the rise is due to the disproportionate increases in school and college enrollments and the shifting of population, which make constant standards more costly per capita on a nationwide basis. The moderate improvement projections suggest per capita outlays of around 300 dollars (or 320 with rising costs), while the substantial improvement projections indicate per capita spending of around 355 dollars (or 380 with rising costs).

In 1957 general and utility expenditures, excluding interest, amounted to slightly less than 10 per cent of GNP, while state-local purchases of goods and services were somewhat over 8 per cent of GNP. Table 8 indicates the GNP relationships of the various sets of projections. The 1957 proportions of GNP absorbed by state-local government activities are substantially above the constant standards projection figures, and moderately above the moderate improvement projection, assuming no adverse shift in the terms of trade, as it were. Assuming that GNP rises at 3.7 per cent annually, and that

44

state-local costs are constant, the proportion of the much larger GNP absorbed by the state-local sector would be a good deal larger than at present under the substantial improvement model. This is especially so when the measure is purchases of goods and services, which excludes assistance and subsidies (largely public assistance), the current operating expenses (but not the capital outlays) of public enterprises, and all capital spending for land and existing structures. With adverse relative costs—at the hypothetical rate of 0.5 per cent per year—the results under the moderate improvement model approximate the current proportions, while those under the substantial improvement model are quite a bit above the current relationships.

Is this reasonable, in view of the very large postwar increase in the share of gross output used by the state-local sector? It is, if one views state and local bodies as passive reactors rather than active initiators, and if one does not assume revolutionary changes, the bare outlines of which are not even hazily perceptible on the distant horizon at present. I confess, however, that these GNP comparisons lead me to believe that my substantial improvement model may be of a higher order of likelihood than my moderate improvement model, not necessarily for all functions, but for the major ones. The basis for the projections for individual activities is discussed in the following paragraphs.

Education

Education expenditures have been projected separately for current and capital outlays for each of the major components of this function. The results are shown in Table 9. In 1957, school districts, other local governments, and a few state governments spent a total of 9.1 billion dollars for current operating expenses of *local school systems*. By 1970, the school-age population is expected to rise about 39 per cent—31 per cent for the elementary-school age group and 63 per cent for the high-school age group. Because of these markedly differential rates of growth, and because high school per pupil costs are a good deal higher than elementary-school costs—probably two-thirds higher on the average—expenditures have been projected separately for high schools and elementary schools. In the constant standards model, current expenditures rise only with the rise in enrollment, and because of the high-school growth and cost differential, are slightly higher on a per pupil basis over-all.

TABLE 9

State-Local Expenditures for Education, Fiscal 1957 and 1970 (Projected)

(millions of dollars)

FUNCTION	ACTUAL 1957	No Change	PROJECTED, 1970, WITH INDICATED CHANGES IN STANDARDS	
			Moderate Improvement	*Substantial Improvement*
Local school systems, total	11,852	15,400	18,600	23,500
capital outlays	2,753	2,500	3,050	3,250
other expenditures	9,099	12,900	15,550	20,250
State institutions of higher education, total	1,958	3,400	4,150	5,400
capital outlays	484	450	650	900
other expenditures	1,474	2,950	3,500	4,500
Other education	324	500	600	700
Total	14,134	19,300	23,350	29,600
Exhibit: total capital outlays[a]	3,237	2,950	3,700	4,200
total current expenditures[a]	10,897	16,350	19,650	25,400

SOURCE for 1957 data: U.S. Bureau of the Census, *State and Local Government Finances in 1957*, 1957 Census of Governments Advance Release No. 8, February 1959, and *U.S. Census of Governments: 1957, Vol. III, No. 1, Finances of School Districts*, November 1958. Capital outlays for local school systems operated by local governments other than school districts are estimated on the basis of the data in *Summary of Governmental Finances in 1957*, August 24, 1958. School district data exclude interest and insurance trust outlays.

[a] Includes amounts not shown by character in detail above.

In the moderate improvement model, I assume a rise in per pupil costs over-all of about 20 per cent. This is in effect assuming that by 1970, nation-wide, average costs will be equal to the state-wide average for the states apparently doing the best job today. Of the 32 states operating their schools largely through independent school districts, and thus adequately covered in 1957 Census of Governments material already published, California and Oregon rank highest on a per pupil expenditure basis; their per pupil outlays are about one-fifth above the national average.

For the substantial improvement model, per pupil outlays of individual school districts reputed to be doing an outstanding job were examined. These, in the main, are school districts operating in upper-income suburbs of the major cities. As a standard of excellence, I chose two nationally renowned suburban Chicago districts, one the Glencoe elementary-school district, and the other the high-school district of which Glencoe forms a part. These districts spend half to two-thirds again as much per pupil as the national average, and applying their expenditure levels to the anticipated enrollment increases produces an over-all per pupil average almost 60 per cent greater than the current level. The increase in total expenditures over 1957 is 120 per cent in this model, as compared with about 70 per cent in the moderate improvement model and 40 per cent in the constant standards model.

Capital outlay needs for local school systems also have been projected separately for high schools and elementary schools. All capital expenditures are expressed in classroom-equivalents and estimates of current average-per-classroom costs are applied. The constant standards model provides for meeting the needs of increasing enrollments at current standards of occupancy, plus provision for depreciation of older existing facilities, fire losses and the like, and the underutilization of some facilities due to reorganization of school districts and population shifts. The result is a construction program averaging over the 13-year period, only about 56,000 classrooms a year, compared to the 68,000–70,000 rate of recent years, but costing, due to the high-school spurt, less than one-tenth less than was spent in 1957. The moderate improvement model includes these increased needs, plus provision for replacement of classrooms deemed unsatisfactory and additional needs alleged on account of overcrowding as of the fall of 1957. This yields a building program averaging slightly over 68,000 rooms per year over the period, about the 1957 rate, but about 20 per cent more costly. To this, the substantial improvement projection adds allowance for about 10 per cent more space (or its equivalent in other facilities or equipment) per pupil in newly built facilities. In all models, the really significant rise is not in bricks and mortar, but in current (largely instructional) spending.

The basic statistic for projections for *state institutions of higher education* is the anticipated increase in college enrollments nation-wide—somewhere between 90 and 95 per cent. This is based on a two-thirds increase in the college-age group, plus an increase in the proportion attending college which is conservative relative to historical trends. Since public institutions are almost certain to experience a disproportionate share of the enrollment increase, a doubling of their enrollments is (conservatively) assumed. The improved standards models combine the approach used for current expenditures of local school systems with information in the 1957 report of the President's committee.[12] The latter suggests, to me,

[12] The President's Committee on Education Beyond the High School, *Second Report to the President*, July 1957.

estimates compounded of varying assumptions as to the rise in faculty salaries and the possible or probable economies of scale, including changes in the faculty-student ratio. In the moderate improvement model, I have assumed that per student costs in 1970 on the average will equal those borne by those states currently supporting relatively high quality state universities, in which costs are about one-third above the current national average. The resulting figure has been reduced by some allowance for economies of scale. In the substantial improvement model, I have distinguished between commercial auxiliaries and noncommercial activities at state institutions, because of the very large differences among the very best performing states occasioned by the auxiliary activities. I assume that noncommercial per student outlays will rise 80 per cent, this being the Michigan relationship to the national average in 1957; per student outlays for the commercial auxiliaries are expected to rise only slightly. Here, too, some allowance has been made for scale economies. In effect, the substantial improvement projection of 4.5 billion dollars, three times 1957 outlays of 1.5 billion, would permit faculty salaries to more than double by 1970.

Recent experience suggests that it will cost about 5.6 billion dollars (in 1957 dollars) to accommodate the anticipated rise in enrollment with additional plant and equipment at current standards. This averages about 450 million dollars a year over the 1957–70 period, less than the 1957 outlays. The improved standards projections relate to the appraisals of annual capital outlay needs through 1970 in the President's Committee's 1957 *Report*, with the substantial improvement model fully providing for these needs and the moderate improvement model falling somewhat below.

Highways

Shortly after the enactment of the new federal program in 1956, I prepared an appraisal of the financial impact of the federal action, including its likely effect on expenditures by state and local agencies on road work not eligible for federal aid.[13] Since then, highway expenditure prospects have been changed by greatly increased estimates of the cost of the interstate program, as well as by the 1958 amendments to the basic highway act. The projections here are based on the calculations for the earlier appraisal adjusted for

---

[13] "Financial Policy for Highways: Impact of the 1956 Federal Legislation," *National Tax Journal*, June 1957, pp. 114–25.

changes in the outlook since early 1957. The following table indicates the composition of the projected figures, compared with fiscal 1957 amounts (in billions of dollars):

| | CAPITAL OUTLAYS | | CURRENT |
	Federal Aid Work	Other	EXPENDITURES
Fiscal 1957	1.8	3.5	2.5
Fiscal 1970:			
Constant standards	4.0	2.5	3.8
Moderate improvement	5.0	3.6	3.0
Substantial improvement	6.2	4.5	3.1

The constant standards model provides for increases in total capital outlays to match the rise in traffic. Nonfederal aid work is expected to stay at current levels, excluding toll road capital outlays which amounted to over one billion dollars in 1957 and are expected to virtually vanish very shortly. Federal aid work will provide all of the increase, but not as much of an increase as now seems required to provide the quality improvements anticipated when the 1956 act was passed. The moderate improvement model essentially corresponds, in quality of highway services produced, to what had been expected from the 1956 legislation, but will involve at least one billion dollars more per year in Federal funds than was forecast two years ago. The substantial improvement model provides for capital outlays about 25 per cent greater than this, in effect providing a good deal more in the way of quality improvements within urban areas than the original interstate program anticipated.

Maintenance costs are expected to rise proportionately with traffic under the constant standards assumption. However, under the other two assumptions, the considerably greater mileage of new high-quality roads is expected to retard the rise in maintenance costs on the more heavily traveled roads.

Health and Welfare

The declining relative importance of health and welfare outlays is a function of the assumption that *public assistance* costs, in all three models, will remain at current levels in the face of inflation-free prosperity. Assistance to the needy aged, which absorbs about 60 per cent of public assistance funds currently, should decline or at least not increase as the expanding scope of social insurance relieves the pressure of a rising over-sixty-five population. In an economy with full employment and substantially higher per capita incomes, it is hard to see why the other public assistance programs should not be less, rather than more, costly in 1957 dollars.

Hospital expenditures, on the other hand, can be expected to rise sharply indeed. In the 1946–57 period, the increase was large even when reduced to real per capita terms. For the constant standards model I have assumed that current per capita costs will continue, but that the increase in the underlying workload will be greater than the one-fourth rise in the population would suggest; rather, it is set at about one-third, which is close to the proportion by which the population over sixty-five is expected to increase. Various sources suggest that by some objective standards the country "needs" to add 50,000 public (nonfederal) hospital beds (including the bed-equivalents of other facilities) annually over the next decade, compared to the recent construction rate of around 20,000 beds. This appraisal has been used for the substantial improvement model, together with the increase in operating expenses the resulting 70 per cent increase in capacity implies. In addition, for this model, I have assumed a 20 per cent rise in the cost per patient at state mental hospitals, reflecting the very poor quality of patient care prevalent at present. In the moderate improvement model, similar assumptions apply but the construction rate, and the resulting increase in capacity and operating expenses, is set lower, at 35,000 beds (and bed-equivalents).

I suspect that these estimates are rather on the low side, in view of the steeply rising per patient costs, in constant dollars, for both plant and equipment and current expenses, consequent on technological advances. However, in part at least, these must be counted as quality improvements and would affect only the two improvement models. Moreover, there well could be an explosion of public revulsion at the state of the mental hospitals, resulting in vastly improved standards of patient care, costing as much as one billion dollars more than the 4.6 billion figure for total hospital expenditures shown in Table 10 for the substantial improvement model.

Other health and *other public welfare* programs have exhibited only modest increases in real per capita terms in recent years. Their growth is likely to continue to be sluggish, for some components—institutional care in welfare institutions, for example—may change hardly at all. On the other hand, the likelihood of large new

TABLE 10

State-Local Expenditures for Health and Welfare, Fiscal 1957 and 1970 (Projected)

(millions of dollars)

| FUNCTION | ACTUAL 1957 | PROJECTED, 1970, WITH INDICATED CHANGES IN STANDARDS | | |
		No Change	Moderate Improvement	Substantial Improvement
Public hospitals, total	2,487	3,300	3,900	4,600
capital outlays	350	450	500	750
other expenditures	2,137	2,850	3,400	3,850
Other health	715	900	950	1,000
Total health and hospitals	3,202	4,200	4,850	5,600
Public assistance	2,800	2,800	2,800	2,800
Other welfare	596	750	850	950
Total public welfare	3,396	3,550	3,650	3,750
Total	6,598	7,750	8,500	9,350
Exhibit: total capital outlays[a]	400	500	600	875
total current expenditures[a]	6,198	7,250	7,900	8,475

SOURCE for 1957 data: Totals for health and hospitals and public welfare categories from U.S. Bureau of the Census, *State and Local Government Finances in 1957*, 1957 Census of Governments Advance Release No. 8, February 1959; "other health" and public assistance as in *Summary of Governmental Finances in 1957*, August 24, 1958, thereby attributing the entire 65 million dollar increase in the total for health and hospitals in Advance Release No. 8 to public hospitals, and the entire 15 million dollar decrease in the total for public welfare to "other welfare." The breakdown between current and capital outlays is estimated on the basis of all published Census Bureau material relating to 1957 finances, including the State and City *Compendiums*.

[a] Includes amounts not shown by character in detail above.

programs, such as health insurance on the state level, or social work programs for adolescents in urban areas which cost really large amounts of money, seems small.

Other Community Facilities and Services

This functional category groups together activities, other than those previously discussed, which by and large bear a direct relation to urbanization. That is, under these programs, facilities and services are provided which in sparsely settled communities or rural areas are usually provided privately by the consumer of the service himself—such as water supply and sanitation services—or are not consumed at all—such as police services in general, local parks, airports, public housing, and transit.

In 1957, water and sanitation expenditures accounted for more than one-third of all outlays in this category. Water supply and sewerage have been, aside from schools, unquestionably the greatest public problem in the rapidly expanding peripheries of metropolitan

TABLE 11

State-Local Expenditures for Other Community Facilities and
Services, Fiscal 1957 and 1970 (Projected)

(millions of dollars)

FUNCTION	ACTUAL 1957	PROJECTED, 1970, WITH INDICATED CHANGES IN STANDARDS No Change	Moderate Improvement	Substantial Improvement
Water supply utilities, total[a]	1,464	1,900	2,250	2,550
capital outlays	694	850	1,000	1,200
other expenditures[a]	770	1,050	1,250	1,350
Sanitation, total	1,484	1,950	2,400	2,900
capital outlays	700	900	1,150	1,350
other expenditures	784	1,050	1,250	1,550
Police and fire protection	2,302	3,100	3,350	3,950
Local parks and recreation	585	750	1,000	1,150
Housing and community redevelopment, total	460	400	800	1,050
capital outlays	252	100	500	700
other expenditures	208	300	300	350
Nonhighway transportation, total	541	600	750	900
capital outlays	368	300	450	550
other expenditures	173	300	300	350
Transit utilities[a]	600	600	800	1,000
Electric power and gas supply utilities, total[a]	1,182	1,900	2,200	2,600
capital outlays	391	625	800	875
other expenditures[a]	791	1,275	1,400	1,725
Total	8,618	11,200	13,550	16,100
Exhibit: total capital outlays[b]	2,795	3,250	4,500	5,450
total current expenditures[b]	5,823	7,950	9,050	10,650

SOURCE for 1957 data: U.S. Bureau of the Census, *State and Local Government Finances in 1957*, 1957 Census of Governments Advance Release No. 8, February 1959, for totals for sanitation, police and fire protection, water supply utilities (less interest), and other utilities (with difference of 3 million dollars, net of interest, from earlier estimates allocated to current operations of electric power and gas supply utilities).

Summary of Governmental Finances in 1957, August 24, 1958, for other functions, both totals and character breakdowns.

Character breakdown for water, sanitation, police and fire, and other utilities based on or estimated from published 1957 Census Bureau data, including the 1957 *Summary* and the State and City *Compendiums*.

[a] Excluding interest on utility debt.

[b] Includes amounts not shown by character in detail above.

areas. For *water supply* expenditures, I assume that the lags at present are so great that large capital outlays will be required continuously to maintain the same standards. The constant standards model therefore applies current per capita costs with adjustment for increasing urbanization and for a continuing shift in the population to the more arid parts of the country with substantially higher per capita costs for water—probably nearly 50 per cent above the national average. In this model, per capita costs—with no change in quality—are thus about 5 per cent higher than at present.

The moderate improvement model allows, in addition, for a considerable increase in water use per capita, by customers, domestic and industrial, of public water supply systems—an increase of about one-sixth. The substantial improvement model further assumes that state-local systems will be providing a fair amount of water for purposes not now ordinarily associated with local water supply activities, largely irrigation. The result is per capita consumption 35 to 40 per cent greater than in 1957, and a very sizable increase in the capital facilities needed to do this job.

Sanitation expenditures are projected separately for sewers and sewage disposal, the major component, and other sanitation, largely refuse disposal, but also including street cleaning in larger cities. The constant standards model applies current per capita outlays to the increased population, with a significant adjustment for the disproportionate increase in the urban populations requiring high levels of expenditure. The moderate improvement model allows for very considerable increases in sewerage outlays, in view of the large current deficiencies, assuming that the entire country will be served at average per capita costs comparable to those in a relatively good performing state (Illinois) today, costs more than one-third above the national average in 1957. The substantial improvement model provides for average per capita outlays about 55 per cent above the 1957 level, comparable to outlays in a few of the most urbanized, high performing states currently (such as New Jersey).

For other sanitation outlays, similar methods are applied, but the moderate improvement model allows for a much smaller implied improvement in quality—about 15 per cent; the substantial improvement model essentially assumes that all metropolitan areas will be receiving these services at levels of quality equivalent to those in the large city which is probably doing the best job today—Washington, D.C.

Police and fire protection expenditures are markedly influenced by increased urbanization. In addition, increased motor vehicle use has a strong influence on police costs, especially state highway police. Because of urbanization, in the constant standards model, per capita police costs are expected to average about 5 per cent more than in 1957 and per capita fire protection costs about 4 per cent more. The improvement models apply to various levels of government and urban size groupings the 1957 per capita costs of various good and outstanding performing states and cities. Differences among states and cities performing at what seem to be different standards are a good deal more marked in per capita expenditure terms for police than for fire protection services, and thus increased police costs account for the bulk of the increase in the improvement models.

Local government expenditures for *parks and recreation* amounted to only a little over 1 per cent of total state-local expenditures in 1957. Here, too, urbanization has a marked impact. In view of the characteristic low levels of performance of this service in the suburban and fringe areas, which are the most rapidly growing parts of the country, the improvement models allow for increases in outlays which are very large in relative terms, even compared with the post-war experience (in real per capita terms).

The estimates for *housing and community redevelopment* are linked to various hypothetical federal program scales, since federal programs provide both the impetus and the funds for the over-whelming bulk of local activities here. The constant standards model assumes that the federal public housing program will end after the early 1960's, and that the federal urban renewal program will not be any larger than at present, involving capital outlays of no more than 100 million dollars a year by 1970. The moderate improvement model assumes the indefinite continuation of the recent 35,000 unit public housing program (per year) plus a renewal program which is moderately larger. The substantial improvement model allows for an increase in the current public housing program, plus a 200 million dollar capital outlay urban renewal program. More probable is a somewhat smaller public housing program, perhaps even below that of recent years—say, no more than 200 million dollars in capital outlays—but much larger urban renewal efforts, perhaps as much as 500 million dollars a year in capital outlays by 1970. In any case, capital expenditures nearly three times the 1957 level seem by no means farfetched.

For *nonhighway transportation*, mainly airports and port facilities, the constant standards model here again assumes a tapering of capital outlays after the mid-1960's, as airports and Great Lakes port facilities become adequate to handle the increased traffic. The moderate improvement model assumes a continued gradual rise in capital outlays, providing new facilities improved in quality over those merely sufficient to handle rising traffic volumes in the air and on the waterways. The substantial improvement model allows some room for new dimensions of airport needs, for new types of aircraft and the like, as well as for increased outlays on publicly owned terminal facilities for highway traffic, including parking.

The estimates for expenditures on publicly owned *transit systems* depend on varying guesses as to the likelihood, of future extensions of rapid transit plant. The lowest figure assumes a continued secular fall in the proportion of urban traffic carried by transit, offset by planned extensions now in the works and by growth in the urban population, to produce expenditures equal to those of recent years. The improvement models allow, in the moderate case, for extensions to enable transit volume to rise along with the population growth, and in the substantial case, for large capital outlays for new systems and extensions, as well as further public ownership, operation, and/or subsidy of suburban mass transportation. Much larger increases in outlays could conceivably occur if the most grandiose of the views reflected in the latter model prevail in many communities. After paying a good deal of attention to the transit problem, in other connections, I am inclined to be rather skeptical about the possibilities for, the economic case to support, and the likelihood of vast expansion of transit undertakings, and this skepticism is reflected in my projections.

Projections for expenditures on local *electric power* and *gas supply* utilities depend upon whether recent rates of growth in electric and gas consumption and output will continue and whether publicly owned local utilities will maintain their relative importance. In general, I incline to the view that consumption and output nationally will continue to grow at rather rapid rates, but that local public utilities will continue to shrink in relative importance, as they have in recent years. It must be remembered that the largest metropolitan areas in which a large proportion of the growth in population and gross product will occur, are in the main served by private utility companies. My own bias is reflected most adequately in the moderate improvement projections, which assume expenditures will not quite double by 1970: this seems to me to be the most likely result, not the substantial improvement projection.

Other Functions

This miscellaneous group includes some functions for which expenditures historically have shown marked secular improvement

TABLE 12

State-Local Expenditures for All Other Functions[a]
Fiscal 1957 and 1970 (Projected)
(millions of dollars)

| | | PROJECTED, 1970, WITH INDICATED CHANGES IN STANDARDS | | |
FUNCTION	ACTUAL 1957	No Change	Moderate Improvement	Substantial Improvement
General control	1,722	2,150	2,300	2,450
Natural resources	1,030	1,250	1,400	1,550
Other and unallocable general expenditures	2,658	3,400	3,550	3,700
Total	5,410	6,800	7,250	7,700
Exhibit: total capital outlays	1,014	1,150	1,250	1,500
total current expenditures	4,396	5,650	6,000	6,200

SOURCE for 1957 data: U.S. Bureau of the Census, *State and Local Governments Finances in 1957*, 1957 Census of Governments Advance Release No. 8, February 1959, for totals for general control and natural resources. The "all other" category equals the total amount shown for "all other" in Advance Release No. 8, less the amounts shown in *Summary of Governmental Finances in 1957*, August 24, 1958, for local parks and recreation, housing and community redevelopment, and nonhighway transportation (see Table 10), thus allocating the entire 102 million dollar difference indicated in the Advance Release to the catch-all category. The capital outlay figure is based on the total capital outlay figure shown in the Advance Release, less all the estimates presented in Tables 9, 10, and 11 for capital outlays and less highway capital outlays.

[a] Excluding interest, insurance trust, and liquor store expenditures.

and others which have evidenced little per capita real change. Expenditures for *general control* are assumed to be largely responsive to population increases, with modest (and rather arbitrary) allowances for quality changes. Here there appears to be substantial room for scale economies as well as for productivity—increasing applications of capital equipment, and these figures may well be a good deal too high.

NATURAL RESOURCES. There is apt to be some population pressure, including the effect of urbanization, on conservation activities, especially drainage, but little effect on agriculture or fish and wildlife outlays. The only areas where changes in standards are likely to be noticeable are state parks and power programs. Thus, this function overall shows only modest changes in all three projections.

Program-Associated Revenue

Tied to each of the expenditure projections presented heretofore, there is a set of projections, by function, of receipts associated with program scale and nature (Tables 13, 14, and 15). As indicated earlier,

TABLE 13

Sources of Funds for Projected State-Local Expenditures in Fiscal 1970:
Constant Standards Assumption
(millions of dollars)

| | | SOURCE OF FUNDS | | |
FUNCTION	EXPENDITURES[a]	Federal Aid	User Taxes and Charges and Miscellaneous General Revenue[b]	Residual: General Taxes and Borrowing[c]
Education	19,300	800	2,500	16,000
Highways	10,300	2,800	7,000	500
Health and welfare, total	7,750	1,750	800	5,200
Public hospitals	3,300	50	800	2,450
Public assistance	2,800	1,600	–	1,200
Other	1,650	100	–	1,550
Other community facilities and services, total	11,200	250	5,550	5,400
Water supply utilities	1,900	–	1,700	200
Sanitation	1,950	50	650	1,250
Police and fire protection	3,100	–	–	3,100
Local parks and recreation	750	–	150	600
Housing and community redevelopment	400	150	350	–100
Nonhighway transportation	600	50	350	200
Transit utilities	600	–	550	50
Electric and gas utilities	1,900	–	1,800	100
Miscellaneous, total	6,800	600	1,900	4,300
General control	2,150	–	–	2,150
Natural resources	1,250	150	200	900
All other	3,400	450	1,700	1,250
Total	55,350	6,200	17,750	31,400
Exhibit: 1957 totals	42,559	3,843	12,764	25,948

[a] Excludes all debt service payments, insurance trust expenditures, and liquor store expenditures.

[b] Includes highway user taxes, utility revenues, and all charges and miscellaneous (nontax) general revenue. Charges for services are allocated to the appropriate function, although the receipts frequently are covered into general funds and not available for that particular function. Similarly, miscellaneous (nontax) general revenues have been crudely allocated to functions, although frequently not earmarked. Special assessments are divided evenly between highways and sanitation. All interest earnings (this excludes insurance trust interest earnings) are allocated to education, although it is recognized that substantial portions represent earnings on sinking funds and unexpended construction funds, particularly for utilities and highways. Revenues from sale of property and miscellaneous sources are allocated to "other and unallocable general expenditures," except for a portion assumed to be oil and gas royalties earmarked for schools. Thus the functional breakdown is not very useful by itself; its purpose was to aid in arriving at a total for nongeneral tax revenues which is likely to be more realistic than a projection of these revenues as a lump sum.

[c] Requirements for general taxes and borrowing are larger than the amounts shown here by the amount of debt requirements. Where small or negative figures appear, it is usually because substantial debt service requirements on debt issued for these functions are covered in whole or in part from user charges (and federal aid, in the case of housing). For example, total utility debt service requirements would, no doubt, be in the range of 1.0 to 1.5 billion dollars under the three expenditure projections presented here, which implies residual requirements after user charge receipts anywhere from two to four times as large as those shown in the last column of this series of tables. Implicitly, the presumption is that federal aid and user charges are utilized first for direct current operating and capital expenditures and the remainder, if any, for debt service needs. Thus, the functional figures here, again, are misleading, although the totals for all functions plus debt service may be realistic.

TABLE 14

Sources of Funds for Projected State-Local Expenditures in Fiscal 1970:
Moderate İmprovement in Standards Assumption
(millions of dollars)

FUNCTION	EXPENDITURES[a]	Federal Aid	User Taxes and Charges and Miscellaneous General Revenue[b]	Residual: General Taxes and Borrowing[c]
		SOURCE OF FUNDS		
Education	23,350	1,200	3,000	19,150
Highways	11,600	3,800	7,200	600
Health and welfare, total	8,500	1,800	1,000	5,700
Public hospitals	3,900	100	1,000	2,800
Public assistance	2,800	1,600	–	1,200
Other	1,800	100	–	1,700
Other community facilities and services, total	13,550	600	6,250	6,700
Water supply utilities	2,250	–	1,950	300
Sanitation	2,400	100	750	1,550
Police and fire protection	3,350	–	–	3,350
Local parks and recreation	1,000	–	200	800
Housing and community redevelopment	800	400	350	50
Nonhighway transportation	750	100	400	250
Transit utilities	800	–	600	200
Electric and gas utilities	2,200	–	2,000	200
Miscellaneous, total	7,250	650	1,950	4,650
General control	2,300	–	–	2,300
Natural resources	1,400	150	250	1,000
All other	3,550	500	1,700	1,350
Total	64,250	8,050	19,400	36,800
Exhibit: 1957 totals	42,559	3,843	12,764	25,948

See Table 13 for notes.

these receipts include all nongeneral tax revenues—federal aid, highway-user taxes, utility revenue, charges for services, and miscellaneous general revenue.

Where I have assumed no fundamental change in the nature of programs, federal aid is generally estimated at the amounts existing legislation may be expected to provide. By this I do not mean the dollar authorization provisions of existing laws, but the apparent legislative intent to finance a program of a particular level of "adequacy." Where fairly radical expansion of program is assumed, for example, in education in the highest set of projections, new legislation is expected to provide significantly more federal money, though by no means all the funds required for the large expansion of service.

TABLE 15

Sources of Funds for Projected State-Local Expenditures in Fiscal 1970:
Substantial Improvement in Standards Assumption
(millions of dollars)

FUNCTION	EXPENDITURES[a]	SOURCE OF FUNDS		
		Federal Aid	User Taxes and Charges and Miscellaneous General Revenue[b]	Residual: General Taxes and Borrowing[c]
Education	29,600	2,000	3,500	24,100
Highways	13,800	5,000	8,000	800
Health and welfare, total	9,350	1,900	1,250	6,200
Public hospitals	4,600	200	1,250	3,150
Public assistance	2,800	1,600	–	1,200
Other	1,950	100	–	1,850
Other community facilities and services, total	16,100	800	7,200	8,100
Water supply utilities	2,550	–	2,100	450
Sanitation	2,900	150	900	1,850
Police and fire protection	3,950	–	–	3,950
Local parks and recreation	1,150	–	250	900
Housing and community redevelopment	1,050	500	450	100
Nonhighway transportation	900	150	450	300
Transit utilities	1,000	–	700	300
Electric and gas utilities	2,600	–	2,350	250
Miscellaneous, total	7,700	750	2,050	4,900
General control	2,450	–	–	2,450
Natural resources	1,550	200	300	1,050
All other	3,700	550	1,750	1,400
Total	76,550	10,450	22,000	44,100
Exhibit: 1957 totals	42,559	3,843	12,764	25,948

See Table 13 for notes.

Increasing reliance on user charges is generally anticipated, with larger increases for those functions for which user charges are most suited and for which expenditures show the largest relative increases. Recent experience has weighed heavily in quantifying this. In a sense, these increases in user charges are "rate increases" which I have excluded in dealing with general taxes. However, I feel it is more realistic to view them as increased prices (where the prices are in fact increased, not where the dollar increase comes from a larger volume of services consumed) which match quality changes or which are necessary to elicit additional units of output of a quasi-commercial service produced under conditions of increasing costs. In this sense, the "constant rates" feature of the income side of the statement is retained.

TABLE 16

State-Local Expenditures, Revenues, and Debt, Fiscal 1957 (Actual) and 1970 (Projected):
Expenditures Projected Assuming No Rise in Relative Costs of State-Local Purchases
(billions of dollars)

	Expenditures Excluding Debt Service[a]	Debt Service[b]	Tax Revenues[c]	Federal Aid and User Charges	Deficit or Surplus (—)	Exhibit: Debt at Year-End
Actual, 1957	42.6	4.1	24.7	16.6	5.4	53.2
Projected, 1970:						
Assuming no change in standards and—						
GNP rising at 3.7%	55.4	2.5	40.9	24.0	−7.0	22.2
GNP rising at 4.2%	55.4	1.3	43.5	24.0	−10.8	4.5
Assuming moderate improvement in standards and—						
GNP rising at 3.7%	64.3	5.1	40.9	27.5	1.0	62.1
GNP rising at 4.2%	64.3	4.0	43.5	27.5	−2.7	44.2
Assuming substantial improvement in standards and—						
GNP rising at 3.7%	76.6	8.5	40.9	32.5	11.7	113.0
GNP rising at 4.2%	76.6	7.3	43.5	32.5	7.9	95.0
Borrowing (deficit) limited to 7.5 billion dollars per year	76.6	7.8	44.4[d]	32.5	7.5	100.3

[a] Excludes insurance trust and liquor store expenditures.

[b] Excludes debt retirement by refunding. The projected figures for debt service are the cumulative results of assuming an even rate of change in expenditures and revenues from 1957 to 1970 and assuming that each year's deficit or surplus will be reflected immediately in equivalent debt operations.

[c] Including net revenues of liquor stores.

[d] Residual needs assuming borrowing of 7.5 billion dollars in each year of period.

4. Combined Income Statements

In all, in Tables 16 and 17, I present fourteen combinations of receipts and expenditures. There are six alternative expenditures projections—the three assumptions as to standards with and without an assumed rise in the relative prices confronting state and local agencies—each with its own projection of program-associated revenue. Each of these six projections is compared with the two alternative tax revenue estimates, one assuming a 3.7 per cent rate of growth in GNP and the other assuming a 4.2 per cent growth rate. Finally, the highest expenditure pattern, under both relative costs assumptions, is compared with tax revenues computed as a residual with borrowing fixed at 7.5 billion dollars a year.

TABLE 17

State-Local Expenditures, Revenues, and Debt, Fiscal 1957 (Actual) and 1970 (Projected):
Expenditures Projected Assuming Rise in Relative Costs of State-Local Purchases*
(billions of dollars)

	Expenditures Excluding Debt Service[a]	Debt Service[b]	Tax Revenues[c]	Federal Aid and User Charges	Deficit or Surplus (−)	Exhibit: Debt at Year-End
Actual, 1957	42.6	4.1	24.7	16.6	5.4	53.2
Projected, 1970						
Assuming no change in standards and—						
GNP rising at 3.7%	59.0	3.5	40.9	25.5	−3.8	37.7
GNP rising at 4.2%	59.0	2.3	43.5	25.5	−7.7	19.8
Assuming moderate improvement in standards and—						
GNP rising at 3.7%	68.4	6.3	40.9	29.2	4.7	79.1
GNP rising at 4.2%	68.4	5.1	43.5	29.2	.8	61.1
Assuming substantial improvement in standards and—						
GNP rising at 3.7%	81.5	9.8	40.9	34.5	16.0	131.8
GNP rising at 4.2%	81.5	8.6	43.5	34.5	12.1	113.9
Borrowing (deficit) limited to 7.5 billion dollars per year	81.5	7.8	47.3[d]	34.5	7.5	100.3

See Table 16 for other notes.
* Over-all costs rising at 0.5 per cent annually in an environment of general price-level stability.

These tables, for the first time in this paper, include debt service costs and thus compare total needs and total resources. Debt service requirements, and the figures for outstanding indebtedness, have been computed under the assumption that both receipts and expenditures will rise smoothly from 1957 to the 1970 totals indicated. As I suggested earlier in this paper, this is hardly a realistic prospect, and I would anticipate more rapid rises in expenditures in the early years with greater indebtedness and therefore a higher level of debt service requirements for the entire 13-year period. It is further assumed that there will be no time lags between borrowing and spending and no change in cash holdings. This means that any deficiency of revenues below the indicated requirements, in any of the interim years, will immediately be borrowed and utilized. The "deficit" thus will equal new borrowing, here restricted to long-term borrowing on the assumption that short-term indebtedness is rolled over without increasing.

The net outcomes shown in Tables 16 and 17 are hardly surprising, for it has been noted elsewhere (see Table 8) that the over-all GNP elasticities of four of the six expenditure projections are less than unity, while the tax revenue projections are based on an elasticity of 1.1. Thus for all the comparisons except those involving the substantial improvement expenditure projections, the deficit (as defined in these tables) is smaller than it was in fiscal 1957. The moderate improvement comparisons range, in their net results, from a moderate surplus and indebtedness 9 billion dollars lower than in 1957, to a deficit about the size of that experienced recently and indebtedness 50 per cent higher than at the end of 1957.

What then of prospects if substantial improvements in the quality of public services are in fact achieved? If prices do not move adversely against state and local governments, and if GNP grows at a 4.2 per cent annual rate, the resulting deficiency in fiscal resources will rise gradually from 5.4 billion dollars in fiscal 1957 to 7.9 billion in 1970. With expanding output and income, borrowing of that magnitude—only slightly above the calendar 1958 peak levels of state-local borrowing—could be easily assimilated by the economy and total state-local debt of 95 billion dollars would not be particularly burdensome. This is the most favorable combination.

At the other extreme, if relative prices confronting state-local agencies do actually rise (at the rate illustrated here), and GNP grows no more than 3.7 per cent annually, the deficiency would soar to 16 billion dollars and outstanding debt to 132 billion dollars. Even in the much larger economy expected in 1970, these seem burdensome and not easily assimilated levels. No doubt with sufficient institutional changes—such as scrapping of debt and interest rate limits and surrender of the Federal tax exemption to appeal to new classes of investors—a much larger volume of state-local debt instruments could be marketed, providing other claims on the supply of long-term funds were not equally avid. But the general economic climate I have assumed would in fact generate very large demands from other sources for long-term funds.

To illustrate the impact of limited ability to market debt, the results shown in the last lines of Tables 16 and 17 have been computed. In these computations, expenditures and program-associated revenues are taken as given, from the substantial improvement projections, and gross borrowing limited to 7.5 billion dollars a year, about the recent peak. The general tax revenues needed are thus residuals. These residuals are larger than the tax revenues projected independently by relatively modest amounts. The following indicates the percentage increases in tax rates suggested by the 7.5 billion borrowing limit models:

	GNP GROWTH RATE	
	3.7%	4.2%
No change in relative costs	+8	+2
Rising relative costs	+15	+9

If pressed to choose among the fourteen alternative combinations on the score of likelihood, I would opt for the most unfavorable (in terms of financial results) combination with borrowing limited to 7.5 billion dollars a year—that is, a 3.7 per cent growth rate with rising relative costs. The tax revenues needed to support such levels would be about 15 per cent greater than those produced by a GNP growing at a rate of 3.7 per cent.

A 15 per cent rise in effective tax rates, across the board, over a 13-year period is hardly staggering. Within the five-year period from 1952 to 1957, I estimate that both property and nonproperty tax effective rates rose in the 15 to 18 per cent range (see Table 3). This was a period with a fair amount of real growth and relatively modest inflation. If all states in 1970 employed a full array of general sales and income taxes at rates comparable to the average in 1957, it is likely that total tax receipts would be about 7.5 billion dollars higher than they would be with no new adoptions, at a 3.7 per cent growth rate. This would be more than enough to cover the revenue deficiency in my most "probable" combination.

No doubt, however, the problem could not be solved nearly so neatly. While only three of the dozen largest states now use the full array of retail sales, individual income, and corporate profits taxes, there are a few large states and a number of smaller but rapidly growing ones which already tap all three sources. California, which no doubt will be the largest state in 1970, has the full array, while New York, with state income taxes and widespread local sales taxes, in effect does so. Even so, the tax rate increases required in particular areas, above and beyond the adoption of universal state retail sales and income taxation, are not very large ones.

In short, I conclude that if the economy grows at a real rate comparable to that of recent years, without inflation in general, the most likely consequence is a scale of state-local finance about double that of 1957 by 1970—disbursements including debt service requirements of nearly 90 billion dollars (purchases of goods and services of about 72 billion) and receipts from taxes and program revenues of about 82 billion dollars, with debt of around 100 billion dollars at the end of the period. In effect what I am saying is that the kind of economy I envisage can support, with relatively modest increases in the rates of state-local taxes, a very large degree of improvement in the *quality* of public services.

An Inflation Model

If in fact the decade of the 1960's is a generally inflationary one, the outlook for state-local finance is not nearly so sanguine. Under such conditions, it would appear justifiable to postulate lagging property tax assessments, and thus less than unit elasticity of revenues projected at constant nominal rather than effective rates. Also, the bases of the taxes whose rates are specific rather than ad valorem would lag rather badly.

Suppose for example, that the price level over-all advances by an average of 2.5 per cent annually from 1957 to 1970, with a resulting price level 38 per cent higher at the end of the period. If effective rates of nonproperty taxes remain constant, and if property tax nominal rates remain constant, I would anticipate an increase in tax revenues of less than 15 per cent over those shown in Table 5. On the other hand, expenditures would be 38 per cent higher than those shown in Table 7, or 47 per cent higher if state-local costs advance at an annual average rate of 3 per cent, rather than 2.5 per cent. I assume that program-associated revenues would rise proportionately with expenditures.

In this example, fiscal requirements, including debt service, if standards are to be substantially improved, would be in the 120–130 billion dollar range, while total revenues would be in 90–100 billion dollar range, depending on the growth rate and relative price change assumed. That is, the over-all deficit would be at the least in excess of 20 billion dollars, and at the most, close to 40 billion. In this environment, very large tax rate increases—in part rises in nominal property tax rates—would be needed to support substantially improved public services. In the worst, and most likely, combination of circumstances—that is, with a 3.7 per cent real growth rate and faster increases in state-local costs than in the over-all price level— the tax rate increases needed would be 80 per cent or greater across the board. This is very large indeed even by the exceptional standards of the postwar period.

Moreover, in this kind of inflationary environment, long-term borrowing by state-local agencies on a massive scale would not be easily accommodated. In fact, the atmosphere for all long-term borrowers would be hostile indeed. All this suggests that, if the 1960's are like the 1950's, the quality of public services in 1970 may be only marginally better than at present, and that the frequently forecast "crisis" in state-local finances will really be upon us, at long last.

COMMENTS

ALLEN D. MANVEL, Bureau of the Census

Probably most of you, like myself, have been interested in trying to compare and relate these two papers to each other. Such an effort is given a tantalizing quality by differences of approach—not merely because Mr. Netzer is focusing on state-local amounts, while Messrs. Colm and Helzner are looking at all-government data, but also because the latter use concepts found in the national income amounts while Mr. Netzer's data follow fairly closely the classification used for Census Bureau reporting on governmental finances, and are considerably more detailed.

It is possible, nonetheless, to discern important areas of resemblance between the projections—for example, each of them anticipates an approximate doubling of public spending for the two most costly nondefense functions, education and highways. On the other hand, the judgment model of Colm and Helzner seems to anticipate a considerably stronger rise than is indicated by Netzer's projection in other areas of nondefense spending—health and hospitals, housing and urban renewal, and the rest.

Most public expenditure for these purposes now is made by state and local governments, and with relatively little federal financing. The question arises: What portion of the sharp rise that Colm and Helzner project in these fields is likely to be contingent upon a drastic increase in their financing from resources of the central government—either directly by federal assumption of new responsibilities, or indirectly through new or greatly increased grants for functions that now benefit little or none from federal aid?

But the sharpest difference between the two papers has to do with national defense. Although this function is outside the direct framework of reference for most of Mr. Netzer's presentation, he very properly recognizes that assumptions about it must strongly influence any set of projections for state-local finances. So, in support of his view that only a moderate rise may reasonably be anticipated for federal grants to state and local governments, Mr. Netzer expresses a belief that most of the increase in federal revenue that results from a growing GNP will be absorbed by direct federal spending—in particular, by defense, which he considers likely to require an effort "far larger than the present one." This is in striking contrast to the judgment projection of Messrs. Colm and Helzner, in which defense spending would represent in 1970 less than 7 per cent of GNP as compared with the present 10 per cent.

It is probably too much to hope that the Conference can provide any approach to a consensus favoring one or the other of these defense projections, or some alternative to either, but it will be helpful if the summary treatment which the formal papers accord to this crucial issue can be thoughtfully supplemented in the discussion at this and subsequent sessions.

In any effort to ask useful questions about the Colm-Helzner projections, I face the particular hazard of disclosing my own remoteness from the complexities of national income accounting. Nevertheless, let me take that risk in raising the following points:

1. Is it reasonable to anticipate a 20-fold multiplication in public spending for housing and urban renewal by 1970? All of us will concede the existence of tremendous needs in this field, but surely a condition for drastic growth in public spending to deal with these needs is the gestation of new governmental attitudes and mechanisms of which there is little present evidence. As a matter of fact, gross governmental spending for housing and community redevelopment, as shown in annual Census Bureau reports, has lagged behind the trends evidenced for practically every other function during the past decade, and is now at about the same dollar level as in 1950.

2. Also on grounds of reasonableness rather than desirability, I have serious reservations about the amount anticipated for "subsidies less current surplus of government enterprises." For all

governments combined, this component in 1957 involved expenditure on a national accounting basis of $1.3 billion, representing the net effect of federal subsidy amounts (mainly for farm support and the postal deficit) that totaled $3.1 billion and were thus only partly offset by a current surplus of $1.8 billion for enterprises of state and local governments. Achievement of the projected shift to an over-all net surplus figure of $3 billion in 1970 would appear to involve the use of approaches about which, I strongly suspect, at least the Secretary of Agriculture and the Postmaster General would like to have further information.

3. Has a generous enough allowance been made for the future rise in transfer payments? The text discussion says that "the judgment model incorporates a moderate increase in the level of benefits," but it would appear from the aggregate that any such allowance must be relatively small. If one accepts other features of the judgment model—in particular, a lesser increase in national defense spending than in gross national product, and some reduction in federal taxes—should not one also postulate a climate that would produce a more generous broadening of various benefit programs than appears to be indicated?

Turning to Mr. Netzer's paper, I shall resist the temptation to attempt comments upon particular items in the very impressive array of data he has developed. However, I have one major quantitative question. It concerns the effect of two simplifying limitations that Mr. Netzer used in developing his figures—namely, the omission of any allowance for financing of employee-retirement costs from general government revenues, and of any allowance for growth in the fund holdings of state and local governments.

As to the former, Mr. Netzer says "It may be that my failure to include employee-retirement system finances is a not inconsequential omission, for many such systems appear to be seriously under-financed and may therefore in coming years occasion sizable drains on general revenues." As a matter of fact, state and local government contributions to retirement systems for their employees already involve a considerable sum, which has moved up from less than three-quarters of a billion dollars in 1953 to about $1\frac{1}{4}$ billion dollars in 1957. It seems not unreasonable to project contributions of this kind aggregating $15 to $25 billion for the interval 1958 to 1970.

Recent experience also suggests an understandable tendency for state and local governments to expand their fund balances as the scale of their financial transactions is increased. Leaving out of account their holdings for insurance trust funds, the financial assets of state and local governments have recently averaged about one-half of the total volume of their annual revenue and expenditure. While this fraction could be reduced by drastic simplification in the fund structure of these governments, such a desirable development is hardly to be expected. Thus, in the light of recent trends, Mr. Netzer's projected rise of $30 to $40 billion in annual rate of state-local expenditure might reasonably create pressure for a growth of $15 to $20 billion in their aggregate holdings of cash and securities.

If these two simplifying assumptions are eliminated, therefore, additional financing of something between $30 and $50 billion would appear to be indicated for the 13-year interval as a whole, either from revenue or from borrowing.

I am more interested, however, in exploring another aspect of Mr. Netzer's paper. As you know, he develops three alternative sets of expenditure projections, one assuming no improvement in the standards of state and local government services and facilities, one involving "moderate" improvement, and one providing for "substantial" improvement. He then calculates the additional costs that would arise if prices paid by state and local governments were to gain over the general price level by approximately 0.5 per cent annually. Comparing the results of these calculations with the assumed trend in gross national product, Netzer states his opinion that the substantial improvement model, with rising relative costs, seems more reasonable than any of the less costly projections.

Especially since I am inclined to share his opinion, the question arises: Why should the results found at an extreme end of the spectrum of alternatives appear to be the most likely? For whatever it may be worth—and perhaps they should be expressed as questions rather than assertions—let me offer three observations.

1. I have the impression that an element of conservatism has entered into projections for various individual functions. It seems possible that in this kind of process the estimator is subject to the psychology which is often observed in revenue estimates for governmental budgeting, where an error in one direction may have serious consequences, while a mistake on the other side of the ledger would still leave what is imprecisely known as a "balanced" budget. Is it possible that Mr. Netzer, in trying to avoid projecting what he would

like to see happen in some functional areas, may have leaned too far in the other direction?

2. I wonder whether working in terms of summary national aggregates may not cause underaccounting for tendencies at work toward improved standards of state and local government services. Mr. Netzer himself seems to recognize this in commenting that his projection for no over-all improvement is highly unreal. I wonder, though, whether the amount of upgrading allowed for in his other models takes enough initial account of the pressures toward a higher over-all average level which are inherent in the existence of widely diverse standards as among various functions and various geographic areas. Perhaps this comes down to questioning the propriety of regarding state and local governments as passive reactors to their environment. In any event, it seems reasonable to expect, at least with the kind of economic climate anticipated, that pressures toward upgrading of public services will considerably outweigh resistance to such upgrading, and that gains which are made, especially in underdeveloped geographic and functional areas, will not be offset by losses elsewhere.

3. Is it not proper to assume, from the very outset, the kind of relative price trend which Mr. Netzer introduces as a final hypothetical adjustment? (As an aside, I should be interested in knowing whether his use of an annual change rate of 0.5 per cent in relative governmental prices is based upon some historical evidence, or whether some other rate might reasonably be postulated.) Mr. Netzer's references to this adjustment put it in an unfavorable light. He terms it an allowance for "adverse relative costs," which is introduced to measure the effects if "prices move adversely against state and local governments." Technically, of course, this is all a proper description. However, if we consider the phenomenon in the light of general economic doctrine, it need not sound so bad.

In a price economy, resources are presumed to move from one kind of use to another, in response to competitive rates of payment in the form of profits, rent, or wages. We are well aware of the historical shift of major emphasis of economic activity from agricultural production toward industrial production and more recently toward distributional and service activities. If this trend is to continue, with a high-level economy and an increasingly urban society, it seems reasonable to expect also a further relative growth in the scale of state and local government activities, which so predominantly involve the provision of services and of urban facilities. The attraction of additional resources into public uses, then, may reasonably be expected to involve what Mr. Netzer terms adverse relative costs but which might instead be viewed as a stronger competitive position for state and local governments, in their employment of personnel and their purchase of other services and goods.

In offering these observations, I hope that I have managed to achieve at least one purpose—namely, keeping well within the time allotted to me—so that other participants in the Conference may not be limited in their full opportunity to discuss these very challenging papers.

I. M. LABOVITZ, Library of Congress

Because I share Mr. Manvel's impression that the expenditure projections for various functions are influenced by an element of caution in the direction of understatement, I want to ask whether population trends have been given enough weight in either the Colm-Helzner or the Netzer estimates.

In the one area where the Census Bureau offers projections, it has called attention to several striking and pertinent facts. Its estimates (in *Current Population Reports*, series P-25, no. 187, November 10, 1958; esp. pp. 3–4) indicate:

1. For the next 10 to 15 years, the population twenty-five to forty-four years old will remain virtually unchanged—about 48 million in 1970, compared with 47 million in 1957.

2. The forty-five to sixty-four year group will grow only moderately after 1957, from 35 million in 1957, to 42 million in 1970.

3. The college-age group, eighteen to twenty-four, will grow relatively fast, increasing by about 10 million over the 1957 figure to about 25 million in 1970.

4. Persons of high-school age, fourteen to seventeen, will number nearly 16 million in 1970, compared with 10 million in 1957—another rapid increase.

5. The population of age sixty-five and over will continue to grow substantially. Not until well after 1980 will the birth declines of the 1920's and 1930's affect this age group. By 1970 we shall have

more than 19.5 million people of age sixty-five or older, compared with fewer than 15 million in 1957. Moreover, there will be a continuing decline in the ratio of males to females in the sixty-five-and-older group. This ratio already has dropped sharply. In 1940 we had 95 males for every 100 females of age sixty-five and over. In 1957, the ratio was 85 to 100. It will decline further. The projected ratio for 1970 is 75 males for 100 females—and for 1980 it is 72 to 100 in this age group.

These population projections have substantial implications for our public expenditure projections. In a period in which the number of very old people and of young people increases rapidly, while the age group that contributes by far the bulk of the labor force remains practically stable, the impact on public programs may be quite direct and quite substantial. The growth, in short, will be in the very segments of the population whose current contributions to production are comparatively slight and whose use of publicly provided goods and services and reliance on public transfer payments are especially large.

Thus, quite apart from any other forces that might tend to increase the relative importance of governmental programs, the population estimates suggest strongly that by 1970 the public sector will account for an even bigger proportion of all goods and services than it does today.

C. HARRY KAHN, Rutgers University

Dr. Netzer's study presents us with a detailed and far-reaching examination of the state-local sector of the economy. Although there is no doubt that this is an important and excellent contribution, I want to comment critically on three points.

1. Perhaps the most striking conclusion reached by Netzer, mainly because it contradicts widely held current opinion, is that state-local financial resources are equal to, and probably even greater than, financial needs. If correct it would obviate much of the concern expressed by Colm and Helzner in the preceding paper, that the "discrepancy in the prospective development of expenditures and revenues [between the federal sector, on the one hand, and the state and local sector on the other] creates a problem requiring more drastic measures than those contemplated in the past." One does not have to search much for the more important reasons for Netzer's

sanguine outlook. He has been careful and candid in stating his assumptions and methods.

By far the most important revenue source in the combined state-local picture is the property tax, and Netzer's conclusion that it has unit long-run elasticity accounts largely for the difference between him and others. This conclusion is based on two considerations. First, it is based on the finding that effective property tax rates (ratios of tax yields to market value of property), as well as the ratio of property values to GNP, rose over the period 1946–57, suggesting a GNP elasticity of at least unity. During those years the decline in assessment ratios was offset by a steady rise in nominal rates. Second, Netzer points out that in a no-inflation model, one may assume stable assessment ratios so that assessments will rise in proportion to market values.

Both of Netzer's points seem well-taken, and yet they do not quite meet the immediate problem. Indeed by setting up a no-inflation model for the 1957–70 period, Netzer avoids the difficulty which has been posed by postwar developments in the property tax. Though lagging assessments can always be offset by rising nominal rates, the fact that the property tax does not automatically respond to changing market values as do other ad valorem taxes poses a problem in periods of inflation.[1] Compensating for the lag in assessments by raising nominal rates is only possible as long as legal rate ceilings and voter-resistance (however misguided) do not become acute. Yet these factors may well be the major reason for the so-called crisis in local finance. Definitions which obscure these differences between the property tax and taxes which directly, or indirectly, reflect market transactions are therefore not very appropriate to a comparison of long-term elasticities.

If the property tax has the high secular elasticity which Netzer attributes to it, this should be apparent from figures for a period longer than the post-World War II years. But when we compare property tax collections with GNP (the measure adopted by Netzer) we find that the property tax yield had in 1957 not yet returned to the position it occupied prior to World War II:

[1] The difference between these taxes becomes very explicit on p. 30 of Netzer's paper: "In this comparison, changes in the bases for ad valorem taxes generally are compared with changes in GNP in current dollars, while for specific taxes the comparison is with constant dollar GNP. The exception to this rule is the property tax; since the purpose of these computations has been to secure data on which to construct a no-inflation model, deflators have been applied to the current dollar estimates of property values and the deflated result compared with constant dollar GNP."

	Property Taxes	GNP	Property Taxes as Percentage of GNP
		(billions of dollars)	
1929	4.7	104.4	4.5
1932	4.5	85.5	8.3
1936	4.1	82.7	6.0
1940	4.4	100.6	4.4
1946	5.0	210.7	2.4
1952	6.1	347.0	2.5
1955	10.7	397.5	2.7
1957	13.1	442.5	3.0

SOURCES: Col. 1: Census Bureau, *Governmental Finances in the United States, 1902 to 1957;* figure for 1929 from Commerce Department, *National Income* (A Supplement to the Survey of Current Business), 1954.

Col. 2: Commerce Department, *U.S. Income and Output* (A Supplement to the Survey of Current Business), 1959 and *Survey of Current Business,* July 1959.

Though GNP has risen manyfold since the 1930's, property tax collections have not increased commensurately. For the most part this is explained by the lag in assessments behind market values.[2] If one were to apply Netzer's measure to state income taxes one would, as expected, find that they have risen more than GNP since 1929 or, if preferred, since 1938.

2. While over-all price-stability is assumed for the period 1957–70, the effect of increases in the cost of state and local government output on future expenditure needs is considered. Netzer reasons that productivity increases in the state-local government sector "may well continue to lag those in the economy as a whole" because "state and local governments remain on the whole far more labor-intensive . . . and they are also heavy purchasers of the output of the construction industry" (p. 41). Movements in relative prices for the goods and services state and local agencies buy may in fact have been adverse, and may so continue. Netzer considers this the

[2] All this has been noted previously by Mabel Newcomer, "The Decline of the General Property Tax," *National Tax Journal,* March 1953.

most likely development (pp. 43–46). But the reason cited—greater labor intensity in the state-local sector—does not seem to me sufficient to expect it. As far as I am aware there is little evidence on the question of relative labor intensities. Solomon Fabricant found 15 per cent of total capital assets (excluding military assets, roads, streets and land) owned by governments (1946), but only 12 per cent of the labor force employed by governments (1949).[3] The share of state and local governments in capital assets held by governments was considerably greater than their share in government-employment.[4] These figures thus would suggest greater capital, rather than greater labor, intensity.

But even if we were to grant Netzer's premise of greater labor intensity, this by itself does not imply smaller productivity increases for state-local governments. It may merely signify a lower *level* of output per unit of labor input, whereas relative increases in productivity may nevertheless be the same, or even greater, in the state local sector.

3. The possibility is briefly discussed that state-local agencies might have to borrow at a rate of $16 billion in 1970—that is, if relative prices confronting them rise 0.5 per cent and GNP by no more than 3.7 per cent annually and if the quality of public services is substantially improved (Table 17). Netzer thinks that, among other institutional changes, "surrender of the Federal tax exemption to appeal to new classes of investors" would permit a larger volume of state-local debt to be marketed (p. 62). It is difficult to see how this can be so. The exemption of interest from federal income tax may not help states and localities very much, and most of the gain may go to high-tax bracket individuals, but there is no reason why the exemption should ever make such debt *less* saleable in the aggregate.

SELMA J. MUSHKIN, Department of Health, Education, and Welfare

Mr. Netzer has forged an important tool for evaluation of state and local governmental finances in the decade ahead. However, by his combination of two political assumptions—a national government engrossed in defense, and state and local governments reacting passively to public services—he has postulated a vacuum in government. Political processes insure positive action in meeting emerging

---

[3] *Trend of Government Activity Since 1900*, National Bureau of Economic Research, 1952, Tables 1 and 3.
[4] *Ibid.*, Tables 8 and 9.

social and technical problems, e.g., to provide controls against radiation hazards from peacetime uses of nuclear materials, to use television as a teaching aid, or psychotherapy for mental patients who become accessible for treatment through new drugs.

Although the models presented reflect the program impacts of metropolitan concentrations of population, account is not taken of changes in program levels resulting from migration out of the poorer states with relatively low levels of public services to the higher income, higher program level states. Some preliminary computations of the effects on educational outlays resulting from these interstate population flows suggest that these shifts (isolated from population growth and other changes) account for increases of 15–20 per cent in school operating expenditures over the nation.

The central issue of Mr. Netzer's paper is his assumption of a gross product elasticity of the property tax base of 1.0. Earlier studies on the gross product (or income) elasticity of the property tax base suggest a substantially lower elasticity ratio.[1] To gain some perspective on the assumed ratio, the relative movements of full values of real property and personal income were computed for five states for which at least partial but reasonably comparable trend data were readily available.[2]

These five states are among approximately twenty-four states that have initiated market sales ratios or appraisal studies for porperty tax equalization purposes. The findings for these states summarized in Table 1 support the assumed elasticity ratio as a conservative projection of recent experience, but at current, not constant dollars.

The income elasticity of full property values in the period 1948 to 1955 exceeded a ratio of 1.0. The computed ratios for these three years ranged from 1.7 to 2.0. While data for this period are not available for New Jersey and California, the information for the six-year interval between 1951 and 1957 for these two states indicate an elasticity ratio of 1.3 and 1.7 respectively.

A number of underlying factors help to explain the relative movements of real property and personal income since World War II. Farm property values (Census of Agriculture) approximately

---

[1] Harold M. Groves and C. H. Kahn, "The Stability of State and Local Tax Yields," *American Economic Review*, March 1952, pp. 87–102.

David M. Blank, "The Role of Real Property Tax in Municipal Finances." *National Tax Journal*, December 1954, pp. 319–26.

[2] From a study in process, jointly with Eugene P. McLoone.

TABLE 1

Income Elasticity of Full Market Values of Real Property,
Selected States and Years

		PERCENTAGE CHANGE OVER PERIOD		
STATE	PERIOD	*Full Market Value* (assessed real property)	*State Personal Income*	ELASTICITY RATIOS
Illinois	1928–55	116	188	.6
Wisconsin	1929–55	130	231	.6
California	1937–55	482	489	1.0
Illinois	1938–55	302	310	1.0
Kentucky	1938–55	318	362	.9
Illinois	1941–55	270	193	1.4
Kentucky	1941–55	242	238	1.0
Wisconsin	1941–55	203	212	1.0
Illinois	1948–55	62	36	1.7
Kentucky	1948–55	78	39	2.0
Wisconsin	1948–55	81	42	1.9
California	1951–57	96	55	1.7
New Jersey	1951–57	52	41	1.3

doubled; the farm component of gross product changed very little. Construction prices have increased faster than consumer prices. Even at constant prices private construction increased faster between 1948 and 1955 than gross product.

More intensive use of relatively scarce land in metropolitan core areas, coupled with upgrading of land uses in fringe areas, has caused a rise in real estate disproportionate to income.

The income elasticity of property values has varied widely in different periods. Over the period 1928–29 to 1955 the elasticity ratio was about 0.6 in Illinois and Wisconsin; for the years 1937–38 to 1955, near 1.0 in three states. (It may be of some interest to note that from 1928–29 to 1955 little change occurred in the effective property tax rate in either Illinois or Wisconsin.) In constant dollars, the private real property component of national estimates of wealth, compiled by Raymond Goldsmith, declined over the period 1929–48 despite the rise in constant dollar gross product.[3] In current dollars for this time period, private real estate increased 59 per cent and gross product rose 146 per cent, yielding an elasticity ratio of 0.4. The

---

[3] Raymond W. Goldsmith, *A Study of Saving in the United States*, Princeton University Press, 1955. Tables W-3 and W-4.

earlier study of property base elasticity by Groves and Kahn and David Blank underscore these marked differences. It should be emphasized, however, that the Groves-Kahn conclusion of stability (or low-income elasticity) of property taxes compared with other levies over a cyclical period is not essentially inconsistent with the Netzer assumtion of 1.0. The Groves-Kahn findings on the cyclical insensitivity of the property tax, especially the projected stability of yields in the face of declining business activity, reflect property assessment practices, base-period evaluation norms, lags in re-assessment, and the drop-off in new construction.

An Economic Theory of Fiscal Decentralization

CHARLES M. TIEBOUT
UNIVERSITY OF CALIFORNIA, LOS ANGELES

FISCAL federalism involves the relations of multilevel governments. A normative approach may take the political structure as given and then see what economic consequences result. Conversely, one may neutralize political variables and arrange governments solely on the basis of economic efficiency.

This paper is concerned with fiscal federalism—fiscal decentralization—purely from the point of view of economic efficiency. Alternatively stated, the problem is defined such that—as nearly as possible—political federalism is neutral. This framework can be varied as alternative forms of political federalism come under consideration as discussed by Richard Musgrave in this volume.

1. Introduction

To begin with, assume there are no states, counties, metropolitan authorities and so on. Private goods are produced by activities organized along the lines of a Lösch spatial patterning.[1] The task—to organize for the provision of public goods.

A. Assumptions

The following is assumed:

1. The set of goods which are to be publicly provided has been decided.

2. The average cost of producing each of the public goods is "U" shaped; i.e., there are economies of scale.

3. The central government may establish agencies for the provision of each public good. In turn, each agency can establish "branch governments" where efficiency requires more than one site of production.

Note. This study was carried out with the aid of a grant from the Institute of Public Administration. Richard Musgrave offered many useful comments and suggestions as did my colleagues, H. L. Miller, W. L. Hansen, and D. B. Houston. Errors are the unique property of the author.

[1] August Lösch, *The Economics of Location*, trans. by William Wolgom with the assistance of Wolfgang Stolper, Yale University Press, 1954.

4. All taxes are on a pure benefits basis, therefore redistribution in the form of taxes and transfers between individuals or regions is not allowed.

These assumptions will be spelled out in the discussion which follows. Later some will be relaxed to see what implications can be drawn.

B. Public Goods

The public goods which are to be provided satisfy social wants and cannot be provided on a fee basis.[2] Assume, in other words, the polar case of public goods.[3] (In some cases we use examples of public goods where fees might be charged. Indeed, most public goods are a blend of pure private and pure public goods; i.e., benefits show externalities between 0 and 100 per cent. *Interest here is only in the externalities!*)

C. Spatial Setting

Space is of considerable importance to our problem. The reason is not transport costs, as in the private market. The reason is that public goods have a spatial extent on the benefits side. Moreover, benefits from public services may not accrue equally to all residents of a region. More specifically:

1. *Benefits from some services accrue in the same amount to all persons within a region.* By way of examples: The soldier who protects the resident of California provides the same protection for the resident of Maine. Police patrol cars provide, more or less, uniform protection for all residents throughout the precinct covered. Trucks which spray against mosquitoes are likely to spray uniformly throughout the municipality.

2. *Benefits from some services taper off from the site of production.* By way of examples: An air raid siren at the corner of Hollywood and Vine in Los Angeles provides more protection to a person who lives one block away than a person living forty blocks away. The siren provides no protection to a resident of Bangor, Maine. Emergency hospitals provide more protection to people living nearby, as do fire houses.

[2] The nature of public goods has been discussed by Musgrave and Samuelson. See especially, Richard Musgrave, *The Theory of Public Finance*, McGraw-Hill, 1959; Paul A. Samuelson, "The Pure Theory of Public Expenditures," *Review of Economics and Statistics*, November 1954, pp. 87–9.

[3] A polar or pure public good implies A's consumption leaves B no worse off.

3. *Benefits from some services have a spillover effect.* Suppose community X provides a set of public services; e.g., mosquito spraying, air raid sirens, fire protection, and so forth. Its neighbor, community Y, provides none of these services. Residents of Y will still benefit from X's provision of some of these services: fewer mosquito bites; some residents near X can hear the air raid siren; and some fire protection can be given—assuming the X fire department is willing to cross community boundaries. This "spillover" occurs whether or not the service is provided uniformly throughout X, mosquito spraying; or with diminishing benefits within X, air sirens.

4. *Benefits from some services reinforce each other while others do not.* As a result of mosquito spraying, residents of X receive benefits. Now suppose community Y sprays. Residents of X are provided with even more benefits. In other words, the spillover effect is associated with benefits which reinforce each other.[4]

Benefits would not reinforce each other in the following spillover case. Suppose Mr. Jones lives on the edge of community X, ten miles from the hospital. His benefits from the good "emergency hospital service" are less than those of residents with more central locations. Now community Y builds a hospital, also ten miles from Mr. Jones. Mr. Jones, however, is no better off, nor is anybody else in X.[5]

These four characteristics of public goods together with the benefit principle and economies of scale pose one of the problems of spatial arrangement to be discussed below.

D. Uniformities in Tastes and Incomes

The spatial patterning of public goods will differ depending on differences in tastes and incomes of various spatial groupings of people; i.e., taste and income heterogeneity within the nation. A community of Quakers, for example, might wish no provision of Nike sites. Two communities with the same tastes might want different amounts of fire protection if one community has a higher

[4] Public goods may well reinforce each other with varying degrees of intensity. For mosquitoes it may be slight. On the other hand, protection against a two alarm fire might be more than twice as effective when two communities are considered as opposed to one. We are not interested in the degree of reinforcement.

[5] Clearly, one can think of many reasons why Mr. Jones will be better off because of the new hospital in community Y; e.g., extra bed space, more specialized treatment, etc. Again, we are concerned only from the point of view of the pure public good, "emergency hospital treatment."

income level. In turn, with more output this may call for a somewhat larger geographic fire district for the wealthier community. These issues will be taken up below.

2. Basic Patterning with Uniform Tastes and Incomes

Let us assume first that tastes and incomes are uniform throughout the nation. Each agency of the central government needs to determine how many "branch governments"—separate sites of production—are required for its particular public good given the spatial extent of benefits and the technological aspects of supply. Consider the case of uniform benefit services and then diminishing benefit services.

A. Uniform Benefits Throughout the District Served

The following is illustrative of the case of uniform benefits throughout the districts served.

Assume a city of 100 square miles in which the population is evenly distributed, there are no differences in income within the population, and further, a uniform demand for police protection. Assume the demand is known. Further, suppose that police protection is a pure public good within a patrolled precinct. That is to say, the patrol car which protects your house also protects mine. Thus, total output $X_p = x_1 = x_2 \ldots = x_n$, where n is the number of consumers who all consume in common. A unit of output is some number indicating a certain amount of protection spread evenly throughout a police precinct. Thus, to say a five-square-mile precinct has 600 units of output implies that each resident receives 600 units of protection.[6] (We grant that it is difficult to define units of output—units of production—in operational terms. If a patrol car passes everybody's house three times a day instead of twice, *cet. par.* output has gone up by some amount.)

The problem is to set up an optimum number of precincts within the city and provide uniform police protection. (Whether these units are independent police forces or precincts is not an issue. The

---

[6] Even with a uniform population spread, some problems of district size appear. Clearly, square miles and miles along a radial line are not the same thing. It is easier, however, to treat the police problem as if population were spread along a line. Thus, although we incorrectly say "square" miles where "line" miles should be used, it does not affect the analysis and is useful for exposition.

same type of analysis applies to both cases. It is analogous to firm and plant economies.)

It is necessary to be clear on the meaning of costs. Total cost is the usual cost of supplying the output. In the case of police protection, total cost will increase for one of two reasons: (1) Given a district to be protected, say five square miles, the total cost will rise with the level of protection offered; i.e., with increasing output. (2) Total cost will also increase, given the level of output per person, as the area served increases. The key in understanding this is in the meaning of "output."

Suppose a precinct covered three square miles and received 300 units of protection. Total output, therefore, is 300 units and, for a pure public good, each resident receives 300 units of output. The total cost of providing this protection is, say $75,000 a year. Now the precinct is enlarged to seven square miles. Unless the precinct budget is increased, the protection is spread thinner and thinner and, in turn, the units of protection received per resident go down. On the other hand, with economies of scale, increasing the budget to $150,000 a year may allow the same 300 units of protection to be provided for all residents within seven square miles. In an obvious sense, total output has risen even though output per resident has remained constant. Supposedly, with pure public goods, output per resident equals total output. Evidently, total output needs to be defined for a specified region. Thus, while the relationship—total output equals each individual's share—holds for public goods such as national defense, for nonnational goods it needs to be defined with respect to the region served.

For present purposes, the relevant cost is the cost per resident. This, given our assumptions, indicates the tax bill each resident must pay for police protection. The tax bill will depend on the amount of service offered and the number of people who benefit. Each resident, with uniform demand, will pay in taxes the total cost divided by the population. Note that greater population lowers the cost per resident, but not the amount of the pure public service received. Thus, a new family building on a vacant lot next door requires no more effort from the patrol car which passes anyway, but its presence does lower the cost per resident.[7]

---

[7] This is, clearly, an extreme assumption. Police protection costs are a function of the number of people protected, given the geographic bounds of the district. We are, however, sticking with the polar case of a public good.

Figure 1 shows the variables which are assumed to affect the cost per resident. Consider cost per resident, holding the number of square miles—and, by assumption, population—constant (*CLD*). As output per resident increases the cost per resident increases. Why? Simply because to produce more output per resident in a given

FIGURE I

Police Protection: Assumed Relationship of Cost/Resident to Output/Resident and Miles or Population

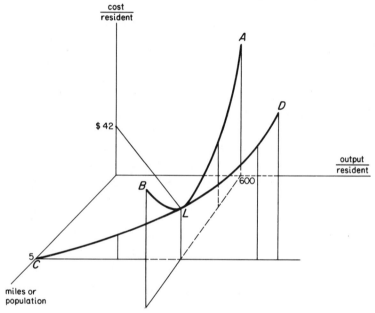

area costs more in total cost for extra policemen, patrol cars, and so forth. With population constant, cost per resident must rise.

Turning to Figure 2 for a moment, here the *Z* axis measures unit-cost/resident. Again holding the number of square miles serviced (and population) constant, consider the cost to each resident per unit of protection (*C′L′D′*). The "U" shape with a low point at 600 units reflects the economies of scale in the ordinary sense of the term; e.g., better utilization of equipment.

Turning back to Figure 1, holding output per resident constant, consider an increase in the geographic size of the precinct; i.e., in square miles (and population)—(*ALB*). Here a second set of economies are assumed to enter. If 600 units of protection are provided for a very small precinct, the cost per resident will be quite high. As the level of output increases because of a larger precinct, certain economies of scale enter. Some are the same forces which provide economies of scale in Figure 2 with respect to increased output per resident, given the precinct size. Thus, costs per resident

FIGURE 2

Police Protection: Assumed Relationship of Unit Cost per Resident to Output per Resident and Miles or Population

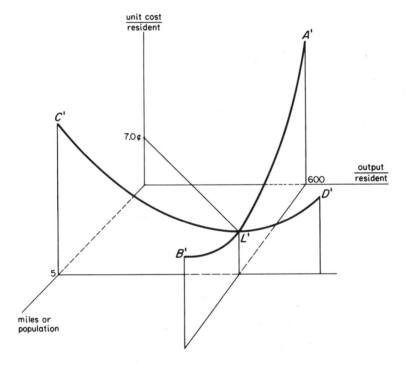

fall for awhile. Eventually, costs per resident rise as diseconomies, especially transport costs, enter. In Figure 2, the curve at 600 units of output per resident $(A'L'B')$ is of the same shape as Figure 1, except that it is 1/600 as high in terms of costs.

Table 1 presents a set of per person costs as a function of square miles and total output. Holding square miles constant, reading up the columns, cost increases per resident as the level of output increases. Holding output per resident constant, reading across the rows, cost per resident declines and then rises as more square miles

TABLE 1
Cost Per Resident: Output Per Resident And Square Miles Covered
(cost in dollars)

Output Per Resident	1	2	3	4	5	6	7	8	9
900	104	96	84	81	79	73	**72**	120	260
800	92	87	67	61	59	**55**	68	119	151
700	78	68	53	49	48	**46**	63	103	130
600	60	57	51	47	**42**	45	57	101	127
500	48	44	41	38	**36**	43	53	85	99
400	36	35	32	**29**	34	39	46	71	82
300	28	27	24	**22**	25	37	41	58	69
200	18	16	**15**	17	23	28	34	39	61
100	12	10	**8**	9	13	17	22	31	34
0	0	0	0	0	0	0	0	0	0

Square Miles

and larger populations are covered. For each level of output per resident there is one precinct size where cost per person is lowest. These values are in bold face. Note that at an output of 600 units per resident a five-mile precinct is optimal and the cost per resident is 42 dollars. This corresponds to Figure 1.

Another implication of Table 1 is given by the following: Suppose a precinct were three square miles and provided 700 units of protection per resident. Operating as efficiently as possible it will cost each taxpayer 53 dollars. If taxpayers are willing to join with their neighbors and increase the precinct to six square miles, cost to each taxpayer will be reduced to forty-six dollars. If for some reason, say political, they object to enlarging their precinct, they will not be at an efficiency point in terms of the economics of federalism. This does not deny that such an operation might not be efficient under some form of political federalism. Under the present rules, however, the precinct would be six square miles.

The northeast drift of the lowest cost per resident point in Table 1 reflects the economies of scale discussed above. Dividing each **circled** value in Table 1 by the corresponding units of output gives the unit cost of supplying each, and every, resident. The intersection of the demand and supply curve is the same for one and all. Moreover, it determines the level of output and given the size of the city, the number of precincts is determined.[8] Assuming average cost pricing, each person will pay the same tax. The net residuum, benefits

[8] The issue of possible inequalities in precinct size and city size is disregarded. For example, what if five square miles is optimal but the city contains twenty-seven square miles? This problem is encountered and discussed in monopolistic competition theory.

minus taxes, will be zero for each resident.[9] The benefits principle is satisfied.

B. *Diminishing Benefits*

The technological problems in providing public goods take on additional complexities when the benefits accruing diminish as a function of distance from the site of production. Fire protection, air raid sirens, emergency hospital treatment, parks, and so forth, provide examples of benefits diminishing with distance. Some of the problems involved may be illustrated by the following exercise—which is merely suggestive and not presented as a tight technical solution.

Suppose a city of 10,000 population has to set up fire precincts. Again, we are not concerned with the optimal number of precincts to a fire district. As noted, protection falls as distance from the fire house increases. For a given fire house, people in the first-mile ring all receive some amount of protection. Those in the second ring, because of the time involved in getting to the fire, receive less protection. And so it goes. Beyond some point, benefits (protection) will be zero.

We assume various kinds of fire houses can be built. For example, a fire house with two pumpers and one hook and ladder, or four pumpers and two hook and ladders. Suppose some level of output at the fire house can be defined, say 110 units of protection. Whatever combination of equipment that provides this level for the least cost is most efficient. For other levels of output some other combination may be optimal. There is one level which provides the lowest cost per unit of fire protection. Thus, the cost curve is "U" shaped. (For purposes of a solution a less general ordering is satisfactory. All we imagine is that there is a list of possible types and sizes of fire houses.)

In order to focus on externalities, we again assume that fire protection is a *pure public good*. This implies that there is no loss of service to people in the first-mile zone when the second-mile zone is brought under protection. To be sure, the people in the first-mile zone will be better off to the extent that their tax bill is lowered. Further, by assumption, no extra dollar costs are incurred by including the second mile zone. Of course, both will be better off if the third mile zone is included.

[9] See James Buchanan, "Federalism and Fiscal Equity," *American Economic Review,* September 1950, pp. 583–99.

TABLE 2

Values and Cost: i^{th} Type of Fire House

(population = 10,000)

Miles from Fire House (1)	Value to Resident (2)	Total Value to the City (3)	Average Value Per Resident (4)	Total Cost to City (5)	Cost Per Resident (6)	Surplus Per Resident (7)[a]	Tax on Each Resident (8)	Surplus to Each Resident After Tax (9)[b]
1	$100	$1,000,000	$100	$2,000,000	$200.0	$−100.0	$44.4	$55.6
2	90	950,000	95	1,000,000	100.0	−5.0	40.0	50.0
3	80	900,000	90	666,000	66.7	+23.3	35.6	44.4
4	70	850,000	85	500,000	50.0	+35.0	31.1	38.9
5	60	800,000	80	400,000	40.0	+40.0	26.7	33.3
6	50	750,000	75	300,000	33.3	+41.7	22.2	27.8
7	40	700,000	70	285,000	28.5	+41.5	22.2	27.8
8	30	650,000	65	248,000	24.8	+40.2	26.7	33.3

[a] (7) is (4) less (6).
[b] (9) is (2) less (8).

The demand for protection, as before, is the same for all individuals. The problem is to find the optimum sized fire precinct. This problem contains elements of two problems discussed in the literature: (1) the average cost-marginal cost pricing problem for decreasing cost industries; and (2) the boundary problem under spatial duopoly—in essence, what determines the boundary where one producer's market area stops and another's begins. The latter problem has been discussed by Hotelling and Smithies—among others.[10]

One possible approach is given by the following procedure.[11] A city planner interviews various residents, asking them how much they are willing to pay for a fire house—type one—within one mile of their home or none at all. "How much are you willing to pay to have it within two miles of your home or none at all?"—and so on. "How about for fire house—type two—(perhaps larger)? How about for type three?"—and so on. The residents are assumed to reveal their true preferences.

Table 2 presents a hypothetical set of data for the city for the ith type of fire house. Columns 1 and 2 present the values placed on fire protection as a function of distance from the fire house. Column

[10] Harold Hotelling, "Stability in Competition," *The Economic Journal*, February 1929, pp. 41–57; Arthur Smithies, "Optimum Location in Spatial Competition," *Journal of Political Economy*, October 1941, pp. 423–39. Both articles are reprinted in *Readings in Price Theory*, George Stigler and Kenneth Boulding (eds.), Irwin, 1952.

[11] H. L. Miller was extremely helpful in pointing out this type of approach.

3 shows the value to all residents of the city. For example, with a fire house every four miles, half of the population will live within one mile and the other half within two miles.[12] Thus, the total value to the city of 10,000 population is 950,000 dollars; i.e.,

$$\$100 \times 5,000 + \$90 \times 5,000.$$

Column 4 presents the average value per resident. Column 5 shows the total cost to the city if a fire house is located every two miles, four miles, six miles, and so forth. The cost per resident is given in Column 6. This is not necessarily the tax each resident pays. Column 7 shows the "surplus" per resident, where surplus is defined as total value less total cost. Columns 8 and 9 will be discussed below.

The planner notes that for the ith type of fire station, this surplus is a maximum and equal to 41.7 per person with a six-mile precinct; i.e., with fire stations every twelve miles. For the $i + 1$ type of fire station some other maximum surplus exists and corresponds, perhaps, to some other precinct size. The same holds for all other types of fire stations.

In choosing the optimum fire station and its corresponding precinct size, the planner could simply pick that one with the largest surplus. Let us assume, however, that the rule is to pick the combination which yields the largest surplus in proportion to the cost per resident. That is, if the kth fire house offers a surplus of 100 dollars per resident and a cost of 100 dollars per resident, it is preferable to the jth station type where the surplus is 150 dollars, but the cost per resident is 200 dollars. Other rules governing choice can be devised.

We assume that the ith type of station, given in Table 2, yields the largest surplus in proportion to costs.

The planner indicates that the city should build fire stations of type i every twelve miles. In order to just cover costs, 33.3 dollars per resident will need to be raised in taxes. The problem is now turned over to the tax bureau.

The tax bureau proceeds to raise the needed funds. The benefits principle requires that each taxpayer have a zero net residuum. The average tax per resident will be 33.3 dollars. At least two schemes appear as possibilities.

---

[12] Again there are problems of square miles versus line miles. (Footnote 6.) Once more assume the city is spread along a line, even though the term "square" miles is used in the discussion and calculations.

One scheme would tax each taxpayer *in proportion to his share of the total benefits.* Assuming one resident per mile for a radial of six miles, the benefits to the six people are 450 dollars; i.e., from Column 2, 100 + 90 + etc. These peoples' share of the total tax is 200 dollars; i.e., 33.3 dollars times the six people. Mr. Jones who lives in the first-mile zone receives 100/450 of the benefits. His tax is 100/450 × 200 dollars, or 44.4 dollars as shown in Column 8 of Table 2. Mr. Smith who lives in the sixth-mile zone pays 50/450 × 200 dollars, or 22.2 dollars. Other residents' taxes are calculated in the same manner. The people living seven and eight miles away will be the sixth- and fifth-mile residents of an adjoining precinct.

Under this proportion to benefits scheme, the "surplus" received by each individual will not be equal, but proportional, to the tax paid. Mr. Jones pays 44.4 dollars in taxes and receives 100 in the value of benefits to him. His surplus is 55.6 dollars given in Column 9 of Table 2 which is 125 per cent of his tax bill. Mr. Smith of the sixth-mile zone receives a surplus of only 27.8 dollars, which is also 125 per cent of his taxes.

An alternative scheme would be to tax so that *each person's surplus is equal.* Since the average surplus per resident is 41.7 dollars, each person's tax is the value to him of the benefits less 41.7 dollars. Here Mr. Jones of the first mile would pay 58.3 dollars in taxes and Mr. Smith of the sixth mile would pay only 8.3 dollars in taxes. Both, and all others as well, would have a "surplus" of 41.7 dollars.

The first tax scheme corresponds to the method by which the optimum station was chosen, namely to seek to make the proportion of surplus over cost as large as possible. This tax scheme will give a "surplus" of about 1.25 dollars for every dollar of cost for all taxpayers.

C. Cost Problems

The discussion of fire and police protection assumed benefits were independent of the population size. This may be the case for national defense and air raid sirens, but it does not hold for police and fire protection. As more people are added to a given size fire or police precinct, the total cost of providing the same per capita amount of protection will go up. An important question is, will it cost more per resident or less? A priori information offers no conclusive hints on this question. It is true that most studies indicate that increasing population is associated with increased per capita expenditures.[13] It may be that the level of, say police protection, has increased. Yet, in larger urban areas the same amount of protection may not result in less net crime. Insofar as larger cities are a well-spring of crime—somehow defined—greater units of protection may not be enough to offset the relatively greater crime potential in urban areas as opposed to small communities.

Economies of scale are extremely difficult to measure. Studies in the private sector, for the most part, have been limited to those industries where the product is readily identifiable—such as the petroleum industry. Even here, economies of scale are extremely difficult to measure. In the case of public goods one immediately runs into the problem of holding product constant. Nevertheless, many governmental reorganization studies seem to imply that empirical studies of economies of scale will provide a major basis for reorganization.[14] A possible pitfall in this approach is that it leads to undue attention to the supply aspects in providing public goods to the detriment of the demand aspects.

D. *Final Patterning*

The discussion of the technological aspects of supply given, the problem of providing public goods is conceptually simple. With uniform demand each public good agency will establish as many branch agencies as economies of scale indicate. The national defense agency will be a one branch agency. The national agency in charge of fire protection will have n branches.

When all agencies and branch governments are operating, the spatial patterning will be similar to that for the private sector. All public goods will be produced at the capital. Some will be national for single branch agencies. Others will serve the immediate needs of the capital region; e.g., the fire department. Other communities will produce within their borders only a subset of the total number of different public goods; e.g., they will provide fire protection, but not a Supreme Court. The public sector, in other words, will develop along a Lösch pattern.[15]

It should be noted that the problem of spillover discussed above

---

[13] See Harvey Brazer, "The Role of Major Metropolitan Centers in State and Local Finance," *American Economic Review, Proceedings*, May 1958, pp. 305–16.

[14] For example, Metropolitan St. Louis Survey, *Path of Progress for Metropolitan St. Louis*, August 1957, p. 51.

[15] Lösch, *op.cit.*

is of no concern in this simplified model. With uniform demand, population, income, and, in turn, uniform services, each community will receive back as much in spillover as it contributes to its neighbors. Each sprays uniformly against mosquitoes and the per capita benefits exchanged are equal.

3. Complications with Demands and Income Variable

Certain complications which arise because of differences in taste and incomes and the resulting unequal spillover of benefits are now introduced.

A. Differences in Taste

Keeping incomes equal for the moment, how is it possible to allow for differing demands? Suppose that within a geographic area tastes differ. People being where they are, what principles should the central government (still assuming that it has full powers over the branch governments) adopt in laying out public service boundaries for each branch?

A general rule, similar to that used in the fire protection example, might be to make the "surplus" in proportion to taxes as large as possible. Operationally, this is not of much use. Conceptually, the costs of providing various amounts of public goods in various locations should be compared with the benefits received by residents. That combination which yields the largest surplus should be chosen. Clearly, this is a trial and error method and, even if demands were known, one could not be certain that the combination is a maximum maximorium without trying all possible combinations. A similar problem arises in determining the location of firms in the private sector.[16]

Fortunately, an alternative approach exists. Instead of taking the people as given and trying to fit the nonnational public goods pattern to them, offer a varied pattern of public goods and make it possible for the people to move to suit their tastes. People who want good schools will then be able to move to communities where good schools are provided. To the extent that communities offer a varied pattern of public goods, each resident can, conceptually, choose the pattern

[16] See Charles M. Tiebout, "Location Theory, Empirical Evidence, and Economic Evolution," *Regional Science Association, Papers and Proceedings*, III, 1957, pp. 74–86.

which best satisfies his preferences. (The details of this type of approximate solution have been given elsewhere.[17]) That people with similar tastes move together is a first principle of fiscal federalism.

B. Differences in Income

If the assumption that incomes are equal is relaxed, a new variable enters. People in choosing communities with differing expenditure patterns will consider their share of the cost. One of the major variables determining their share will be the incomes of the other residents. Given the tax structures and incomes of various communities offering about the same pattern of public services, a person will choose the community where his tax bill is least. In fact, he may well choose a community where the pattern of services offered is not as nearly to his liking as another community, but his tax bill is sufficiently lower to make this a more favorable location.

As a result of unequal incomes, the resulting pattern of public goods will be less optimal, in a sense, than in the case where incomes are equal. However, two modifications appear which somewhat offset any distortions introduced by unequal incomes.

At a conceptual level, with many communities from which to choose, a person will consider both the cost and pattern of services. How will differential costs modify his choice of patterns? Suppose a set of k equally wealthy suburbs surround a city. From the cost (tax) point of view alone, a person will pick one of these k suburbs as opposed to some other community. Of these k communities, one will have a pattern of services which best suits his preferences.

In effect, the presence of wealthy communities has lowered the cost to the prospective resident. It is true that at a lower cost he will pick a different pattern of public goods than at a higher cost. Thus, he may move to a community which spends 12 per cent of its budget on parks when his cost is low. At a higher cost, he may prefer a community which spends only 8 per cent on parks. Other residents, with higher incomes, are also content with 12 per cent spent on parks. If the cost to these people was lowered so that they paid the same as the low income family, they might desire 18 per cent spent on parks. Thus, the fiscal rule that people with similar tastes should

[17] See Charles M. Tiebout, "A Pure Theory of Local Expenditures," *Journal of Political Economy*, October 1956, pp. 416–24.

move together needs qualification. People with the same fiscal tastes, given the costs to each of them, should move together.

At the real world level, the existence of unequal incomes has lead to the "tax colony." That is, people with high incomes band together in communities which keep low income residents out of the community. Zoning laws, building restrictions, and so forth, are some of the means of control. Moreover, it does appear that communities with high levels of public service tend to have high rental and housing prices. When you seek good schools for your children, you often find the rents and housing prices are high. This is not to suggest any single direct causality, for other factors do influence the level of rents and housing prices. It is simply a suggestion as to how it is the rich avoid paying taxes for the poor.

So far the analysis has assumed that the pattern of public goods is given and that people adapt to the pattern which suits their preferences. Public service patterns, however, can be changed: (1) as a condition for entering a community; and (2) once a person is a resident of a community. Firms are much more likely to obtain a change in fiscal arrangements as a condition of moving than are individuals. Community efforts to entice industry into their bounds frequently involve fiscal bargains. The granting of a tax free status for a period of years seems to be a favorite ploy. The fiscal logic of such a move, evidently, is that in the long run the firm will more than pay its share of costs. Even if the pattern of public goods is initially changed, the residents will eventually be better off in terms of a lower tax benefit ratio.

Other people may pick a community with an eye towards changing the pattern of goods provided once residence is established. Other things equal, the smaller the community, the more likely one is to have influence. Further, small group theory suggests that the smaller the community, the more likely the people are to agree on the issues at hand and clearly identify the problem. Thus, tastes are apt to be more uniform.

C. Spillover

One major problem still confronts us under fiscal federalism with varied tastes and incomes. Most public goods have a spillover effect. A simple example will illustrate the problem.

Suppose a whole ring of communities surrounding a town decide to spray against mosquitoes. Community A does not spray. Clearly,

A residents are better off, and without paying any extra taxes. As noted earlier, the same sort of spillover analysis holds for other public goods.[18] The question is, should A residents be forced to pay something?

In terms of benefits taxation, residents of community A should be taxed and a transfer doled out to the spraying communities. Yet, if it is decided that community A should pay something, how should its share be assessed? Under a nonunitary system, this involves a decision by a higher level of government, and one of the major functions of a higher level government, under fiscal federalism, is to arbitrate such spillovers.

In practice it appears that this arbitration is carried out by a provision of minimum standards.[19] Usually minimum standards of service are set up for certain public goods; such as, all children shall have so much education, and a community must provide so many dollars per student. The normative justification for minimum standards may be simply in the notion of the welfare state—knowing what is best for people. It seems feasible to suggest that a second reason for minimum standards is the question of spillover. If community A is forced to spray against mosquitoes, neighboring communities will receive greater benefits from their own spraying. If they wish to spray even more than the minimum, that is their privilege, but they cannot expect community A to share the cost. Thus, minimum standards are seen not so much in the welfare sense, but as a substitute for intercommunity transfers.

Summary

This paper has set forth an efficiency framework for an evaluation of fiscal federalism. On the supply side, benefits may be uniform throughout the district served or may diminish as a function of distance from the site of production. The existence of benefit spillovers indicates that one community's well being, in part, depends on the public goods provided by its neighbors. As a result, higher level governments may be called upon to arbitrate differential spillovers.

On the demand side, the problem of determining taxpayer preferences still exists. The demand for national public goods such as defense

---

[18] Other aspects of spillover are discussed by James Buchanan, "Federal Expenditure and State Functions," in *Federal Expenditure Policy for Economic Growth and Stability*, Joint Economic Committee, Washington, D.C., November 1957, pp. 174–9.

[19] Insofar as communities offering similar patterns of public goods cluster together—such as wealthy areas—spillovers tend to be equal.

and, as a matter of degree, nonnational goods such as schools is determined through the political process. To the extent that demands differ, a partial solution at the nonnational level is offered through the mobility of people to communities where the pattern of services provided suits their tastes.

Approaches to A Fiscal Theory of Political Federalism

RICHARD A. MUSGRAVE

UNIVERSITY OF MICHIGAN

THE preceding paper deals with the fiscal structure of a community as determined by considerations of economic efficiency.[1] These considerations demanded central provision for services the benefits of which accrue equally throughout the federation, while leaving the supply of other services to various regional units of government. This study is concerned with a quite different approach, where the role of the central fisc is not limited to considerations of efficiency, but set by the very objectives of political federalism. When independent states join in a federation, they may do so to develop a common foreign defense, or establish a customs union, or they may wish to pursue certain objectives which require central government interference in the finances of the member states.[2] It is this interference which is the subject of this paper.

Central interference in state finances may be based on various objectives. One set of objectives relates the central fisc to the *groups of individuals* comprising the various states. Here the central fisc respects the determination of fiscal policies at the state level, and leaves the individual citizen of the federation at the fiscal mercy of the political process in which he partakes as a citizen of his particular state. However, the central fisc may influence the terms at which public services are provided at the state level. Thus, it may choose to equalize the fiscal operations of the various states, where equalization may be defined in a number of ways. Or, the objective might be to provide incentives to states to raise their service levels. Finally, central policy may wish to assure a minimum level of state services, independent of self-finance by the states.

Another set of objectives relates the central fisc to the *individual citizens* of the federation, whatever the particular state to which they

Note. I am indebted to H. E. Brazer and M. Krzyzaniak for helpful comments.

[1] See C. M. Tiebout's "An Economic Theory of Fiscal Decentralization," in this volume.

[2] The terms "central" and "state" are used here in a generic sense of reflecting higher and lower levels of government.

belong. Here the central fisc may try to equalize differentials in the position of federal citizens which arise from their respective citizenships in particular states. Thereby the central fisc attempts to isolate federal citizens from the fiscal consequences of their respective state citizenships. As such, this approach is less federalist and more centralist in spirit than the preceding view, wherein the central fisc deals with the states as political entities.

The final choice among these approaches, and among various forms of each, is a matter of political philosophy rather than economics. However, the various plans differ in their economic consequences. My purpose is to explore these differences, especially as they apply to various interpretations of the first approach. The second approach will be considered but briefly.

1. Plans Relating Central Fisc to Member States of Federation

Plans involving relationships between the central fisc and the political units of the various states will be considered first. Here it is the purpose of the central fisc to influence the fiscal performance of the various states. The objective may be to bring about various forms of equalization, be it in actual performance, in fiscal capacity, or in fiscal potential; or the objective may be to induce the states as a group to raise their service levels.

The various plans will be examined as to their distributional results and their incentive or disincentive effects on state services. To make this a meaningful investigation, each case must allow for such central taxes or transfers as may be needed to finance the plan and to clear the central budget. This budget equation appears to have been overlooked in most discussions of such plans and is the crux of our analysis. The following symbols will be used:

n = number of states
T_i = taxes collected by the ith state, in dollars
S_i = subsidy (+ or −) received by the ith state, in dollars
A_i = total dollar outlay by the ith state
P_i = level of performance in the ith state
N_i = index of need in the ith state
t_i = tax rate in the ith state ·
t_c = tax (+) or subsidy (−) rate of central government, required to clear the central budget
t_s = standard rate
B_i = tax base of ith state
m = minimum outlay per unit of need
k = rate of matching grant
K = lump sum grant, in dollars
   Use of bars indicates averages.

To simplify matters, these rather heroic assumptions are made:

1. There is only one type of state service.
2. Taxes collected by any one state are in fact borne by the citizens of that state. This rules out the possibility of exporting tax burden, or shifting taxes to the citizens of other states.
3. Benefits from expenditures in any one state are limited to citizens of that state. This rules out spillover of benefits.
4. All state expenditures are tax financed. This rules out borrowing.
5. A full-employment income prevails. This rules out problems which arise from cyclical fluctuations.
6. Changes in policy of any one state will not lead to retaliatory measures by other states. This rules out strategy.

These assumptions will be reconsidered briefly later on.

PURE EQUALIZATION PLANS:

A. Equalization of Actual Outlay or Performance

PLAN 1. A first and rather primitive approach to equalization is one where the central government equalizes actual per capita dollar outlays on state services in all states. In other words, it taxes away the above-average revenue from high-revenue states, and pays transfers to meet the deficiency in low-revenue states.

The definitional equation is:

$$(1\text{-}1) \qquad A_i = T_i + S_i \qquad i = 1, 2, \ldots, n,$$

one such equation being given for each of the n states. Since it is the object of central government policy to equalize the outlay A_i in all the states, it must meet the condition:

$$(1\text{-}2) \qquad A_i = \frac{\Sigma_i A_i}{n} \text{ arises.}$$

Finally the central budget must be balanced, so that

$$(1\text{-}3) \qquad \Sigma_i S_i = 0.$$

This leaves $n + (n - 1) + 1 = 2n$ equations. Given the T_i's, all A_i's and all S_i's can be determined.

The S_i's represent a subsidy from the central government if they are positive, and a charge if they are negative.

Obviously, $\quad S_i > 0 \quad$ if $\quad T_i < \dfrac{\Sigma_i T_i}{n} = \bar{T}$; also

$$S_i = 0 \quad \text{if} \quad T_i = \bar{T}; \text{ and}$$
$$S_i < 0 \quad \text{if} \quad T_i > \bar{T}.$$

The plan results in a redistribution from states whose tax yield exceeds the national average to states whose tax yield falls short of the average.

Summing the n equations under (1-1), solving the system for S_i and taking a partial derivative with respect to an autonomous change in taxation by the state i,[3] gives the following:

$$(1\text{-}4) \qquad \frac{\partial S_i}{\partial T_i} = \frac{1}{n} - 1.$$

The partial derivative is negative, so that an increase in the tax yield of any state getting a subsidy reduces that subsidy, part of the yield being drained off to other states.

Effects of changes in the state's tax yield on its total outlays are obtained by solving for A_i and taking the partial derivative with regard to T_i. The result is:

$$(1\text{-}5) \qquad \frac{\partial A_i}{\partial T_i} = \frac{1}{n}.$$

Since n represents the number of states, $1/n$ is always a fraction. The partial derivative falls short of one so that the substitution effect imposes a disincentive to state taxation. State i only retains a fraction of its own yield and the own-cost of state services is increased. If the number of states is large, $1/n$ becomes very small and the benefit to any one state from increased taxation approaches zero. Thus, this system has an extreme disincentive effect on state taxation. All states will reduce their own revenue, and the system may tend towards a zero level of taxation.[4]

PLAN 2. Quite apart from its extreme disincentive effects, Plan 1 is unsatisfactory because there is no allowance for differences in the needs of various states. Equal dollar outlays may result in great differences in performance levels; and if public policy is to aim at equalization of actual levels of some sort, it will be more meaningful to equalize performance levels. This is done in Plan 2.

Two sets of definitional equations apply:

$$(2\text{-}1) \qquad A_i = T_i + S_i, \qquad\qquad i = 1, 2, \dots, n;$$

$$(2\text{-}2) \qquad P_i = \frac{T_i + S_i}{N_i}$$

---

[3] Summing (1-1) gives $\Sigma_i A_i = \Sigma_i T_i + \Sigma_i S_i$, and substituting from (1-3) gives $\Sigma_i A_i = \Sigma_i T_i$, or $n\bar{A} = \Sigma_i T_i$, or $\bar{A} = \frac{\Sigma_i T_i}{n}$. Since by (1-2) it is known that $A_i = \bar{A}$, this can be substituted in (1-1) to obtain $S_i = \frac{\Sigma_i T_i}{n} - T_i$, from which (1-4) follows.

[4] In addition to this substitution effect, gaining states may increase their taxation due to income effect, while losing states may reduce theirs, but these effects will tend to wash out on balance.

where A_i, T_i, and S_i are defined as before. P_i is the performance level of the state i and equals the ratio of outlays in state i to the index of need for state i.[5] The index N_i may be standardized so that

$$\bar{N} = \frac{\Sigma_i N_i}{n} = 1$$

Thus, a state with an index $N_i = 1$ has needs equal to the average for all states in the country. If $N_i > 1$, the state is needier than the average, and if $N_i < 1$, the state is less needy.

As before, it is assumed that the central government pursues a policy such that its proceeds from and disbursements to the states are balanced, or

(2-3) $\Sigma_i S_i = 0.$

The purpose of these central subsidies and taxes is to equalize performance levels in all states, so that

(2-4) $P_i = \frac{\Sigma_i P_i}{n}.$

Considering T_i's and N_i's as given, there are $n + n + 1 + (n - 1) = 3n$ equations. Thus, all A_i's, S_i's, and P_i's can be determined.

As may be seen from equation (2-2)

$$S_i \gtreqless 0 \quad \text{if} \quad P_i \cdot N_i - T_i \gtreqless 0.$$

The redistribution now is from low need-high tax yield to high need-low tax yield states. A state which is average in both respects remains unaffected, as are states which combine proper degrees of excess or deficiency on both counts.

As before, the (2-1) equations can be summed, the system solved for S_i, and a partial derivative with regard to T_i taken.[6] The result is:

(2-5) $\frac{\partial S_i}{\partial T_i} = \frac{N_i - n}{n}.$

Since $\frac{\Sigma_i N_i}{n} = 1$, the derivative is negative. An increase in the tax

---

[5] If public services are in the form of education, N may be an index of school-age children. In the case of highways it may be an index of traffic needs, e.g., dispersion of population and so forth. Construction of appropriate indices for all services creates difficult though not insurmountable problems.

[6] From equation (2-2) comes $P_i N_i = T_i + S_i$. Summing and substituting from (2-3) gives $\Sigma_i P_i N_i = \Sigma_i T_i$, or $P_i = \frac{\Sigma_i T_i}{n}$. Substituting into (2-2), we get $S_i = \frac{\Sigma_i T_i N_i}{n} - T_i$, from which (2-5) follows.

yield of any one state always reduces its subsidy, the loss being smaller the larger is the state's need.

In order to determine the effects of changes in a state's tax yield on its total outlays, the system is solved for A_i and a partial derivative with regard to T_i taken to obtain:

$$(2\text{-}6) \qquad \frac{\partial A_i}{\partial T_i} = \frac{N_i}{n}.$$

Since the partial derivative is a fraction, the substitution effect always imposes a disincentive to state taxation. For the average state, where $N_i = 1$, the disincentive is the same as under Plan 1. It is smaller for more needy states and greater for less needy states. As before, the system tends toward a zero level of taxation.[7]

PURE EQUALIZATION PLANS:

B. Equalization of Differentials in Need and Capacity

Next, the central fisc may wish to equalize differentials in fiscal capacity, rather than in actual outlays or performance.

PLAN 3. The yield or performance level which the states themselves choose to provide is now disregarded and attention focused on their ability to provide for a centrally set level of performance. The two definitional equations are:

$$(3\text{-}1) \qquad A_i = T_i + S_i \qquad i = 1, 2, \ldots, n,$$
$$(3\text{-}2) \qquad S_i = m(N_i - \bar{N}) + t_s(\bar{B} - B_i).$$

Equation (3-2) defines the subsidy to any one state in two parts. The first is the deficiency in yield, obtained by applying a standard rate in state i, as compared to what is obtained by applying it in the average state; and the second part is the excess of expenditure required to give a set performance level m, as compared to the amount required in the average state. Each part of the subsidy will equal zero for the group as a whole, so that the central budget will balance. Such is the case at whatever levels t_s and m are set, but it is reasonable to assume that

$$(3\text{-}3) \qquad t_s\bar{B} = m\bar{N}$$

so that the standard rate provides the required revenue for a state of average base and need. Given m and the values of T_i, N_i, B_i, as well as $\bar{N}$ and $\bar{B}$, the system can be solved for the values of A_i, S_i, and t_s.

[7] With regard to income effects, the same observations apply as to Plan 1.

Setting $\bar{N} = 1$ as before, and substituting, the result is

(3-4) $$S_i = t_s(\bar{B}N_i - B_i).$$

Redistribution is from low need-high base, to high need-low base states.

This approach may also be looked upon as providing for a block grant, adjusted to need so as to assure an equal level of performance, and financed by a proportional central tax t_c. Thus, in place of (3-2)

(3-2a) $$S_i = mN_i - t_c B_i \quad \text{and}$$

(3-3a) $$m\bar{N} = t_c \bar{B} \quad \text{can be written,}$$

from which an expression similar to (3-4) may be obtained.

Written in either form, the essential feature of this plan is that t_i, the state's own tax rate, does not appear. Therefore, the plan has no substitution effect. This is a great advantage as compared to Plans 1 or 2, where the disincentive effect was of prohibitive magnitude. However, Plan 3 still retains the disadvantage that no allowance is made for the state's own tax effort. Thus, state X may be forced to contribute to public services in state Y, even though the residents of Y fail to make even a modest effort to meet their own problems. This, the residents of state X will rightly object to.

PURE EQUALIZATION PLANS:

C. Equalization of Potentials for State Finance

This disadvantage can now be removed and a more sophisticated approach considered, where the function of the central fisc is not to equalize actual levels or capacities in the various states, but to equalize fiscal potentials. Underlying this approach is a philosophy of fiscal federalism which says that the societies of each state should be permitted to determine their own levels of fiscal activity, but that the central government should equalize the fiscal opportunities of the various states, or the potential levels which they might achieve with their own action.

PLAN 4. A first variant of this approach is equalization of fiscal capacities, in the sense of equalizing the tax revenue which various states might obtain by imposing any given rate of tax. To simplify, this rate is here defined as the ratio of state revenue to the tax base of the state. The tax base, in turn, may be defined as private income in the state.[8] Differences in need are disregarded for the time being.

[8] The question whether property as well as income should be allowed for in measuring the tax base is not here entered into. For the present purposes, the simple definition of the tax base in terms of income will do.

Under this plan each state will obtain a subsidy or pay a tax equal to the difference between the revenue which would be obtained if its tax rate was applied to the average tax base, and the revenue which *is* obtained by applying its tax to its own base. If the claims of small-base states exceed the contributions of large-base states, a further central tax is needed to clear the budget, and a further central transfer is required if contributions exceed claims. It is assumed that this central tax or transfer is assessed proportional to state income.[9]

Proceeding as before, two sets of definitional equations arise:

$$(4\text{-}1) \qquad A_i = B_i t_i + S_i, \qquad i = 1, 2, \ldots, n,$$

$$(4\text{-}2) \qquad S_i = (\bar{B} - B_i)t_i - B_i t_c, \quad \text{where} \quad \bar{B} = \frac{\Sigma_i B_i}{n},$$

and the condition

$$(4\text{-}3) \qquad \Sigma_i S_i = 0.$$

Equation (4-1) is similar to that in previous plans. The subsidy as defined by equation (4-2) now consists of two parts. The first part equals the state's own tax rate times the excess of the average tax base over its own tax base; and the second part equals the product of central tax (or transfer) rate times the state's tax base. Either part, and hence the total, may be positive or negative. There are now $2n + 1$ equations, and, given the values of B_i and t_i as parameters, they can be solved for all A_i's and S_i's, and for t_c.

Solving for t_c[10]

$$(4\text{-}4) \qquad t_c = \frac{\Sigma_i(\bar{B} - B_i)t_i}{n\bar{B}} \quad \text{is obtained.}$$

Thus, $t_c \gtrless 0$, depending on whether $\Sigma_i B_i t_i \lessgtr \bar{B}\Sigma_i t_i$. If tax rates in small-base states are high relative to tax rates in large-base states, t_c is positive and vice versa.

From equation (4-2) the pattern of redistribution can be determined, as shown in Table 1, where $+$ indicates gain, $-$ indicates loss, and 0 indicates no change.

Whatever t_c is, there will be a redistribution from states with larger bases to states with smaller bases. If tax rates in small-base states are high relative to those in large-base states ($t_c > 0$), the gaining

---

[9] If allocation is on a progressive basis, the redistribution effects of the plan between small and large base states is accentuated.

[10] Equation (4-2) is summed, set equal to zero according to (4-3), and solved for t_c.

group will include states with less than average bases only. If tax rates in large-base states are high relative to those in small-base states ($t_c < 0$), the gainers may include some states with above-average bases.

TABLE 1
Redistribution Between States

B_i	t_c		
	> 0	0	< 0
$< \bar{B}$	$+$ or $-$	$+$	$+$
$= \bar{B}$	$-$	0	$+$
$> \bar{B}$	$-$	$-$	$+$ or $-$

Moreover, it follows from equation (4-2) that, for any given value of t_c, states with a base below the average base will be better off (gain more or lose less) if their own tax rate is high; and that states with a base above the average will be better off if their tax rate is low. Thus redistribution is primarily among high-rate states.

However, equation (4-2) does not tell what happens to a state if it changes its own tax rate, since resulting effects on the central rate must be allowed for. Solving the system for S_i and taking a partial derivative with regard to t_i,[11] the following is obtained:

$$(4\text{-}5) \qquad \frac{\partial S_i}{\partial t_i} = (\bar{B} - B_i)\left(1 - \frac{B_i}{n\bar{B}}\right).$$

Since $n\bar{B} = \Sigma_i B_i$, the expression $\left(1 - \dfrac{B_i}{n\bar{B}}\right)$ is always a positive fraction, and the partial derivative is positive, zero, or negative, depending on whether $B_i \lessgtr \bar{B}$. Thus, the state with a less than average base always increases its gains or reduces its losses from the central tax-transfer process by raising its own tax rate; and the opposite holds for a state with a more than average base.

Most important will be the effect of the plan on the total outlays of any state, including finance out of its own revenues and by subsidy. The system is now solved for A_i and a partial derivative with regard to t_i taken. The answer is:

$$(4\text{-}6) \qquad \frac{\partial A_i}{\partial t_i} = B_i + (\bar{B} - B_i)\left(1 - \frac{B_i}{n\bar{B}}\right).$$

[11] The value of t_c as given in (4-4) is substituted into (4-2) from which (4-5) is obtained.

The substitution effect is such as to give an incentive to (reduce the cost of) state services if the second term on the right is positive, and to pose a disincentive to (raise the cost of) state services if it is negative.[12] Since the second term equals $\dfrac{\partial S_i}{\partial t_i}$ the conclusions are the same as in the preceding paragraph. States with a less than average base are subject to an incentive effect, and states with a more than average base suffer a disincentive effect.

Assuming the income elasticity of demand for public services to be unity in all states, and price elasticity to be equal for all states and to exceed zero, tax rates will be higher in small-base states. As shown by equation (4-4) this means $t_c > 0$. This being the case, equation (4-2) reveals that only states with a base below the average will gain. The losers will include states with an average base, and may include states with less than average base.[13] This suggests that there may be a disincentive effect for the group as a whole, although no definite conclusions can be drawn without introducing behavior assumptions and assigning weights to various states.[14]

PLAN 5. In the preceding Plan, the equalization objective was stated in terms of revenue capacity. This Plan considers equalization in terms of need. The purpose under this Plan is to enable all states to obtain the same performance levels per dollar of their own tax revenue collected. Differences in base are completely disregarded. Again a federal tax or subsidy may be needed to clear the budget.

Proceeding as before, the definitional equations are:

(5-1) $\quad A_i = B_i t_i + S_i, \qquad i = 1, 2, \ldots, n;$

(5-2) $\quad S_i = (N_i - \bar{N})t_i B_i - B_i t_c;$ and the usual condition

(5-3) $\quad \Sigma_i S_i = 0.$

Given the n values of B_i, $\bar{B}$, and the parameters t_i, the $2n + 1$ equation permits the determination of n values of A_i and S_i, as well as t_c. Equations (5-1) and (5-3) are the same as before. According to (5-2) the subsidy again consists of two parts. The first part adjusts

[12] The fraction by which cost is increased (if $-$) or reduced (if $+$) is given by $(\bar{B} - B_i)\dfrac{(n\bar{B} - B_i)}{n\bar{B}B_i}$.

[13] This result is reinforced if income elasticity is less than unity, but need not apply if income elasticity exceeds unity, or if price elasticities differ by states.

[14] Also, allowance must again be made for income effects, which go to increase public services where $S_i > 0$, and decrease public services where $S_i < 0$.

the state's own tax yield so as to provide average performance per dollar of self-financed outlay; and the second again reflects the state's participation in the central tax or transfer such as may be needed to clear the central budget.

Solving for t_c,[15] the following equation is obtained:

$$(5\text{-}4) \qquad t_c = \frac{\Sigma_i(N_i - \bar{N})t_iB_i}{n\bar{B}}.$$

Thus, $t_c \gtrless 0$, depending on whether $\Sigma_i(N_i - \bar{N})t_iB_i \gtrless 0$. The central rate, t_c, will be positive if the yield of state taxes or t_iB_i is large (be it due to high rates and/or large bases) in high-need states relative to the yield in low-need states, and t_c will be negative if the opposite holds.

From equation (5-2) the pattern of redistribution may again be determined, as shown in Table 2.

TABLE 2
Redistribution Between States

N_i	t_c		
	> 0	0	< 0
$< \bar{N}$	—	—	+ or −
$= \bar{N}$	—	0	+
$> \bar{N}$	+ or −	+	+

Whatever t_c, there will be a redistribution to more needy from less needy states. If state tax yields are relatively high in high-need states $(t_c > 0)$, the gaining group will include states with more than average need only. If yields are relatively high in low-need states $(t_c < 0)$, the gaining group will include some states with less than average need.

Also, it follows from equation (5-2) that, for any given value of t_c, states that one subjects to a more than average need will be better off if their tax rate is high, while states with less than average need will be better off if their tax rates are low. Redistribution will be again primarily among high rate states.

In order to determine the effects on a state's position which result from changes in its tax rate, resulting changes in t_c must be allowed

[15] As before, equation (5-2) is summed and, substituting from (5-3), we obtain (5-4).

for. Solving the system for S_i and taking a partial derivative with regard to t_i[16] gives this equation:

$$(5\text{-}5) \qquad \frac{\partial S_i}{\partial t_i} = (N_i - \bar{N})\left(1 - \frac{B_i}{n\bar{B}}\right)B_i.$$

Since $\frac{B_i}{n\bar{B}}$ is always a fraction, the derivative will be positive, zero, or negative depending on whether $N_i \gtrless \bar{N}$. The state with a more than average need always increases its gain (or reduces its loss) by raising its own tax rate, whereas the state with less than average need reduces its loss or raises its gain by reducing its tax rate.

Turning again to the effects of changes in a state's tax rate on its total outlays, the system is solved for A_i and a partial derivative taken with regard to t_i. The result is:

$$(5\text{-}6) \qquad \frac{\partial A_i}{\partial t_i} = B_i + (N_i - \bar{N})\left(1 - \frac{B_i}{n\bar{B}}\right)B_i.$$

The substitution effect is such as to give an incentive to (or reduce the cost of) state services if the second term on the right side is positive, and to result in disincentive if the term is negative. Since the second term equals $\frac{\partial S_i}{\partial t_i}$, the conclusions are again similar to those of the preceding paragraph. States with more than average need are subject to an incentive effect, while those with less than average need are subject to a disincentive effect.

In the absence of incentive or disincentive effects, there is reason to expect that tax yields in high-need states will be high relative to those of low-need states.[17] This finding is reinforced by the incentive and disincentive effects of the Plan. Therefore, equation (5-4) tells that t_c will tend to be positive, and equation (5-2) permits the conclusion that only states with more than average need will gain. The losers will include states with less than average and states with average need, and may also include some states with more than average need. Again it appears that there may be a disincentive effect for all states as a whole, but it must again be noted that no definite conclusions can be drawn without introducing behavioral assumptions and assigning weights to various states.[18]

[16] The value of t_c, as determined in (5-4) is substituted into (5-2) from which (5-5) is obtained.
[17] It should be recalled that need as here defined is independent of fiscal capacity.
[18] As noted in Plan 4, the result will depend further on the operation of the income effect.

PLAN 6. While Plan 4 neglected differences in need, Plan 5 neglected differences in fiscal capacity. Plan 6 is a more nearly perfect equalization scheme where both sets of differences are allowed for. In this plan, performance per effort unit, as measured by the state's own tax rate is equalized. The definitional equations are:

$$(6\text{-}1) \qquad A_i = B_i t_i + S_i, \qquad i = 1, 2, \ldots, n;$$

$$(6\text{-}2) \qquad S_i = (\bar{B} - B_i)t_i + (N_i - \bar{N})\bar{B}t_i - B_i t_c.$$

It will be noted that equation (6-2) is similar to (4-2) in the treatment of differences in tax base, but differs from (5-2) in the treatment of differences in need. In the present case, the correction for need is applied to the yield from the equalized base, whereas in Plan 4 (with capacity differences disregarded) it was applied to actual yield. The more refined treatment of (6-2) is in keeping with Plan 6 which is designed to make full allowance for both capacity and need differentials.

As before, the condition of clearance in the central budget is:

$$(6\text{-}3) \qquad\qquad \Sigma_i S_i = 0.$$

Given the n values of B_i, N_i, and the n parameters t_i, the n values of A_i and S_i, as well as t_c, may be determined.

Solving for t_c, the following equation results:

$$(6\text{-}4) \qquad t_c = \frac{\Sigma_i(\bar{B} - B_i)t_i + \bar{B}\Sigma_i(N_i - \bar{N})t_i}{n\bar{B}}.$$

Thus, t_c tends to be positive if tax rates are high in small-base and high-need states relative to those in large-base and low-need states; and t_c tends to be negative if the opposite holds. However, it will be noted from (6-4) that need differentials are now weighted, reflecting application of the need correction to the average tax base in (6-2).

Turning now to the pattern of redistribution, equation (6-2) is considered. The results which may be derived from inspection of that equation are summarized in Table 3.

The tendency is for a redistribution from low need-large base states to high need-small base states. For any given level of t_c, a high rate of state tax will increase gains for winning states and losses for losing states, provided that low bases are paired with large needs and vice versa. If these characteristics are crossed, the opposite result may prevail. The earlier conclusion, that redistribution is primarily among high-rate states, need not apply here.

TABLE 3

Redistribution Between States

N_i	$t_c > 0$			$t_c = 0$			$t_c < 0$		
	B_i			B_i			B_i		
	$< \bar{B}$	$= \bar{B}$	$> \bar{B}$	$< \bar{B}$	$= \bar{B}$	$> \bar{B}$	$< \bar{B}$	$= B$	$> \bar{B}$
$< \bar{N}$	+ or −	−	−	+ or −	−	−	+ or −	+ or −	+ or −
$= \bar{N}$	+ or −	−	−	+	0	−	+	+	+ or −
$> \bar{N}$	+ or −	+ or −	+ or −	+	+	+ or −	+	+	+ or −

Proceeding as before, the system may be solved for S_i and a partial derivative taken with regard to t_i. The result:

$$(6\text{-}5) \qquad \frac{\partial S_i}{\partial t_i} = \left(1 - \frac{B_i}{n\bar{B}}\right)[(\bar{B} - B_i) + (N_i - \bar{N})\bar{B}].$$

Since $\dfrac{B_i}{n\bar{B}}$ is a fraction, the sign of the partial derivative now depends on B_i and N_i, as given in Table 4. An increase in the state's tax rate

TABLE 4

Relation Between State Tax Rate and Subsidy

$$\left(\text{sign of } \frac{\partial S_i}{\partial t_i}\right)$$

N_i	B_i		
	$> \bar{B}$	$= \bar{B}$	$< \bar{B}$
$< \bar{N}$	−	−	+ or −
$= \bar{N}$	−	0	+
$> \bar{N}$	+ or −	+	+

tends to increase the gain or reduce the loss for the high need-small base states, and to reduce the gain for low need-large base states.

The gain in state outlays to be obtained by raising the state tax is now given by

$$(6\text{-}6) \qquad \frac{\partial A_i}{\partial t_i} = B_i + \left(1 - \frac{B_i}{n\bar{B}}\right)[(\bar{B} - B_i) + (N_i - \bar{N})\bar{B}].$$

The second term on the right equals $\dfrac{\partial S_i}{\partial t_i}$, so that the results of Table 4 will again apply. The substitution effect is such as to provide an incentive to state taxation for small-base, high-need states; and a disincentive for large-base, low-need states. If state tax rates can be expected to be higher in the former group, the central tax rate [as shown by equation (6-4)] will be positive and the redistribution pattern will be as shown in the left quadrant of Table 3. No definite statement can be made regarding the net effect of the plan on aggregate yield of state taxes in all states, but the earlier comments in connection with Plans 4 and 5 suggest that the over-all level of service may well be reduced.

Plan 6 is superior to Plan 3 in that the degree of benefit received by low-capacity, high-need states is made to depend on their own tax effort. This removes the serious defect inherent in Plan 3 that receiving states may enjoy a free ride while the contributing states are held responsible for their lack of tax effort. At the same time, is not Plan 6 inferior to Plan 3 in that it reintroduces substitution effects? I do not think so. Since it is the very objective of Plan 6 to equalize the tax effort (rate level) required to obtain any given level of performance, the resulting incentive or disincentive effects are not to be looked upon as undesirable side-effects of the plan, such as is the case with Plan 2. Rather, the resulting changes in the relative cost of public services reflect the central objective of the Plan, which is to equalize the relationship between tax effort and performance.

PURE INCENTIVE PLANS

The preceding plans were concerned primarily with matters of equalization. While these plans may raise or lower the total level of state outlays in the process, these changes in over-all level were incidental byproducts of the main objective of equalization. Here is a different set of plans where the objective is to give an incentive, by way of matching grants, to all states to *raise* their tax and service levels. Such plans may have redistributional results (with regard to fiscal capacity and/or need) but these now become incidental.

PLAN 7. A pure incentive plan is illustrated by a system of matching grants, where the central fisc matches all state revenues or outlays at a uniform rate. The system is given by the definitional equations:

(7-1) $\qquad A_i = B_i t_i + S_i, \qquad i = 1, 2, \ldots, n;$

(7-2) $\qquad S_i = kt_i B_i - t_e B_i;$ and the usual condition

(7-3) $\qquad \Sigma_i S_i = 0.$

Given k and n values of B_i, as well as the n parameters t_i, there

111

are $2n + 1$ equations with which to determine n values of A_i and S_i, and the value of t_c.

The central tax now equals

(7-4) $$t_c = \frac{k\Sigma_i t_i B_i}{n\bar{B}}$$

which is always positive. As may be seen from equation (7-2),

$$S_i \gtreqless 0, \text{ depending on whether } t_i \gtreqless \frac{t_c}{k}.$$

There will be a redistribution from states with low tax rates to states with high tax rates. A large base means a higher gain to the winner and a higher loss to the loser, redistribution now being centered among the large-base states.

Solving the system for S_i and differentiating with respect to t_i, the following is obtained:

(7-5) $$\frac{\partial S_i}{\partial t_i} = kB_i\left(1 - \frac{B_i}{n\bar{B}}\right).$$

A state may always increase its subsidy by raising its tax rate. The resulting gain will be the greater the larger is the state's tax base, and the smaller is its share in the aggregate base for all states.

Solving for A_i and differentiating with respect to t_i, the result is:

(7-6) $$\frac{\partial A_i}{\partial t_i} = B_i + kB_i\left(1 - \frac{B_i}{n\bar{B}}\right).$$

Since the second term on the right, equal to $\dfrac{\partial S_i}{\partial t_i}$, is positive, the substitution effect offers an incentive to all states to increase their tax rates. The cost of state services is reduced for all states, but especially for states with a large base. The plan is likely to raise the aggregate level of state services, but again we cannot be quite sure of the over-all result.[19]

[19] Suppose there is only one citizen, who consumes units of X and Y. Now let the central government impose a lump sum tax on him, and use the proceeds to subsidize X. It may be shown that this will result in increased consumption of X and reduced consumption of Y. However, our case is more complex, as a number of states are involved, and each may react differently. Any one state finds the cost of state services reduced, and this is an inducement for higher taxes and outlays on such services. However, due to the action of other states, the residents of any one state also find their income reduced since the central tax t_c must be paid. This will lead them to reduce outlays on state services. In states where the demand for state services is highly elastic with respect to income but inelastic with respect to price, the level of state services may decline, and this may outweigh the resulting increase in other states. However, this does not seem a likely outcome.

EVALUATION

Additional forms might be developed, combining the character- istics of the various plans. Block grants of the Plan 3 type may be made subject to a minimum-effort requirement. The equalization of fiscal potential, of the Plan 4 to 6 type, may be combined with incentive factors of the matching grant type. And the incentive or matching grant approach of Plan 7 may be tempered by allowing for equalization features.[20] In all cases where a central tax is needed, this tax may be rendered progressive in terms of B_i, and so forth. There is no end to possible combinations, but the above sets will suffice to show the nature of the problem.

Final choice among these plans is a matter of political philosophy as well as economics. However, some plans are more sensible in objective than others, and some have less disturbing secondary results. Thus, Plan 2 is more sensible than Plan 1, if equalization of actual budgets is to be achieved. Both Plans 1 and 2 are untenable, however, as they have violent disincentive effects and tend to a zero level of state services. If there is to be equalization of actual per- formance, central finance has to be substituted for state finance. A high degree of absolute equalization is not compatible with a work- able system of fiscal federalism.

Equalization of capacity to meet a centrally set level of perform- ance, as described in Plan 3, renders any one state's position in the scheme (its own gains or losses) independent of its own tax rate. The disincentive effect on state taxation disappears, but there remains the disadvantage that some states are called upon to contribute to the services of others which, while needy, refuse to make an adequate effort of their own. This remains a serious detriment to the establish- ment of an orderly system of fiscal federalism.

Equalization of potentials, as provided by Plans 4 to 6, does not give rise to this objection. A state now receives support only to the extent that it qualifies by its own tax effort; and other states will

---

[20] For instance, the subsidy under Plan 7 may be redefined as

$$S_i = kt_i\bar{B} + (N_i - \bar{N})kt_i\bar{B} - t_cB_i.$$

Since $\bar{N} = 1$, we have

$$S_i = kt_i\bar{B}N_i - t_cB_i$$

and

$$\frac{\partial A_i}{\partial t_i} = B_i + kN_i\left(\bar{B} - \frac{B_i}{n}\right).$$

113

contribute more, if they themselves value public services more highly. Incentive or disincentive effects again result. They differ for various types of states, and the over-all level of state services may now be affected in either direction. Substitution effects are less severe than under Plan 2, and they differ in nature. Substitution effects are now an essential part of the approach, designed to equalize the tax effort required to reach various levels of performance. Equalization of potentials may thus be accomplished within an orderly system of fiscal federalism, and among the various plans here described, Plan 6 is my favorite. It offers the most comprehensive approach to equalization. By leaving the level of state services to their own determination, it also appears to be most compatible with the spirit of fiscal federalism.

Incentive schemes such as Plan 7, are designed to raise the over-all level of state services. The distributional results of the plan are incidental and tend to contradict equalization objectives as usually conceived. However, these results may be neutralized by rendering the central tax progressive, or, as noted before, equalization and incentive objectives may be combined.

REVIEW OF ASSUMPTIONS

It remains to review the assumptions listed at the beginning of this discussion.

1. Allowance for various categories of state services complicates matters but does not change the principle involved. A state may now have different indexes of need for various services. Equalization plans may be applied to taxes for (or outlays on) particular services only, or a generalized equalization plan may be based on a composite index of need. Incentive plans may now involve different matching rates for different types of services, so that the losses or gains for any one state come to depend on its budget pattern.

2. If taxes collected by any state may be shifted to residents of other states, the simplicity of the argument breaks down. However the case may be salvaged, provided that the fraction of a state's taxes the burden of which actually falls within the state can be determined.[21] Only this fraction can be taken as an index of tax effort within the state. In the absence of a matching spillover of

---

[21] For a discussion of the difficulties involved see R. A. Musgrave and D. Daicoff, "Who Pays the Michigan Taxes," in *Staff Papers, Michigan Tax Study Committee.*

benefits, state taxes which are exported constitute an anarchic element in a system of fiscal federalism.[22]

3. If spillover effects are allowed for, an efficient fiscal system permits the state to tax outside its jurisdiction, be it directly, or by appropriate shifting of tax burdens to outside residents. Where this cannot be handled on the state level, a central tax-transfer system may serve to neutralize spillovers. However, such a system does not provide for redistribution or equalization. On the contrary, it serves to prevent regional redistribution, and bears no relation to the problems here considered. This function of the central fisc belongs to the efficiency problems considered in the preceding paper.

4. Introduction of loan finance breaks the equality between tax yield and amount spent, but this does not matter. In the long run at least, there is no reason why the revenue effort might not be measured in terms of "own" finance, be it in taxes or loans.

5. By assuming full employment and price level stability the problem of stabilization policy has been eliminated. Substitution of B_i^f and $\bar{B}^f$ (where superscript f stands for full employment) for B_i and $\bar{B}$, permits insertion of a stabilization feature into the discussion; and it may be desirable also, in this context, to substitute a term t_s (statutory tax rate) for our term t_i. Lest there remain a mere regional equalization of cyclical differentials, a spreading of income losses and gains over the cycle, it will be necessary in this case to drop the requirement that the central budget should be cleared and to introduce deficit and surplus finance.

6. Finally, it has been assumed that changes in the tax rate by any one state will not affect tax rates imposed by other states. In reality this may not be the case, and considerations of strategy may become important in the tax policy of large states. This must be allowed for when the stability of the various plans is considered.

EMPIRICAL APPLICATION

These various equalization plans, or variants thereof, might be applied to available fiscal data in order to determine the resulting

[22] Taxation of income by state X, even though such income is received by residents of state Y, should be considered as falling within state X, provided that such income is earned in state X, and the tax is in line with benefits which accrue to such income from expenditures by state X. The same holds for benefit taxation of commuters. On the other hand, it is not part of the tax effort of state X, as defined for purposes of this argument, if X taxes residents of state Y (through use of taxes which are exported or shifted to the outside) who do not benefit from expenditures in state X.

values of t_c and patterns of redistribution between the fifty states in the United States. This may be done either with regard to total state finances, or various segments thereof such as education finance. Time did not permit the undertaking of such applications, but they are quite possible. While the definition of appropriate indexes of fiscal capacity and need is troublesome, it can be handled.[23] Also, the various plans here outlined may be compared with recommendations of the Royal Commission on Dominion-Provincial Relations[24] and with actual practices in such countries as Australia, Germany, and Switzerland, where fairly refined methods of fiscal equalization are used.

As far as such applications are concerned, the preceding models of central interference in state finance are quite operational. However, the discussion left open the question of just how various states would react to changes in their fiscal resources and to changes in the own-cost of public services, and what would happen to the total level of state services as a result. In order to permit conclusions in this respect, the models must be supplemented by behavioral assumptions, but unhappily little empirical data is available on which such assumptions may be based.

2. Plans Relating Central Fisc to Individual Citizens of Federation

The philosophy of fiscal federalism underlying the preceding plans was that all states of the federation should be placed in a more or less equal fiscal position, be it in the sense of service levels, capacities or potentials, and that all states should be induced to raise their services. Beyond this, there was no attempt to equalize the gains which *individual* citizens of the federation may derive from state fiscal activities. Rather, the individual is left to the mercy of the political decisions arrived at in their particular states. By its very nature, this approach required transactions between the central and the state fiscs.

There is a second and quite different philosophy of fiscal federalism. Here, the idea is that the central fisc should neutralize the individual citizen of the federation against the fiscal operations of

[23] See Selma Mushkin and Beatrice Crowther, *Federal Taxes and the Measurement of State Capacity*, Washington, Public Health Service, U.S. Department of Health, Education, and Welfare, May 1954.

[24] See *Report of the Royal Commission on Dominion-Provincial Relations*, Book II, *Recommendations*, Ottawa, 1940.

the particular state in which he resides. This requires direct trans-actions between the central fisc and the individual citizens of the federation. For this reason it seems more centralist in spirit, but this need not render it necessarily inferior or superior. The choice, as noted before, remains one of political philosophy and social preference.

No attempt will be made to explore this second approach in detail, but a brief discussion is needed, if only to place the first approach in its proper perspective. It is necessary to distinguish between (1) objectives relating to problems of "horizontal equity" or the principle that equals should be treated equally, (2) objectives relating to "vertical equity" or the requirement of differential treatment of unequals, and (3) efficiency objectives.

EQUITY OBJECTIVES:

A. Horizontal Equity

It is assumed that the fiscs for each state meet the requirement of horizontal equity among their own citizens, and that the same holds for the operations of the central fisc in providing federation-wide services. As a result, horizontal equity is assured for citizens of state X insofar as the combined state X and central fiscs are concerned, and the same holds for citizens of state Y and other states. However, the same need not hold as between citizens of states X and Y. While their positions are the same under the central fisc, the position of equals may differ with regard to their respective state fiscs. Hence their positions may differ with regard to the total (combined state and central) fisc.

J. M. Buchanan, in his pioneering paper, has suggested that it should be the function of the central fisc to eliminate such differences, so that all citizens of the Federation who are otherwise equal will be treated equally under the total fisc, no matter what state they live in.[25] Buchanan argues that this objective has a certain claim for priority because: (1) it is more sensible to consider relationships of the central fisc to individuals, rather than to the states "as such"; (2) as a matter of equity, the requirement of horizontal equity is more meaningful than is that of vertical equity; and (3) the scheme tends to neutralize distorting effects on resource allocation which

[25] See J. M. Buchanan, "Federalism and Fiscal Equity," *American Economic Review*, September 1950, pp. 583–600, reprinted in *Readings in the Economics of Taxation*, R. A. Musgrave and C. Shoup, eds. Also, see the subsequent discussion by H. P. Jenkins and J. M. Buchanan, in *Journal of Political Economy*, August 1951, pp. 353–9.

result from differences in the fiscal activities of states. Leaving (3) for later consideration, I should note that to me neither (1) nor (2) are convincing.[26] However this may be, the matter of priority need not be debated here. For present purposes, it is quite sufficient to recognize Buchanan's interesting case as one among possible objectives.

Suppose first that the requirement of horizontal equity is applied with regard to taxation only. Assuming tax structures in all states to be proportional, an opposite of Plan 1 could be applied, except that the subsidy now would go to each individual citizen rather than to his state. Redistribution is from low-rate to high-rate states, and severe incentive effects result with regard to the level of state taxes. If the tax structures of states are progressive by varying degrees, a more complex pattern of interstate redistribution results. However this may be, there is still a strong disincentive effect.

This difficulty is avoided by Buchanan's proposal to reinterpret the requirement of horizontal equity in terms of equality of fiscal residue, defined as expenditure benefits minus tax payments. Given the crucial assumption that benefits from state expenditures are equal for all citizens of the state, Buchanan can easily compute the fiscal residue for taxpayers at various points in the income scale. In a state which relies only on poll-tax finance, the fiscal residue equals zero for all residents, regardless of income. For any tax structure less regressive than a poll tax, the residue falls from a positive to a negative level when moving up the income scale. As states do not use poll tax finance and the tax structures and service levels of various states differ, individuals with equal incomes but living in different states are left with different fiscal residues. A central tax-transfer plan is devised to equalize them.

A comparison may be drawn between State X with a high, and State Y with a low, per capita income. We assume that both pay a proportionate tax. If the rate is the same in both states, an individual with a given income would have a higher fiscal residue if living in X

[26] With regard to (1), I would not interpret the preceding plans as relating the central fisc to the states "as such." Rather, the central fisc takes as given the political process of social preference determination as arrived at by various groups of citizens of various states. This indeed would seem the essence of political federalism.

With regard to (2), how can it be held that "equal treatment of equals" as a matter of *equity*, is more important than is the proper differentiating between unequals? If the latter does not matter (because it cannot be determined or otherwise), how can any meaning be imputed to the former, other than that of establishing a rule which avoids malicious differentiation? If so, tax distribution by lottery would do as well.

than if living in Y. This follows because he pays the same tax in both cases but receives more benefits if residing in X. Similarly, the residents of X will be better off than their counterparts in Y if the same total revenue is collected in both states, since now a person with a given income pays less tax if living in X while receiving the same benefits. In both these cases in which the residents in X are better off, the central equalization scheme will favor the residents of Y. The same conclusion applies to the in-between cases, where the tax rate in X is lower than in Y while total revenue in X is still higher. No simple rule can be set down, however, for situations where total revenue in X is less than in Y, or where the tax rate in X exceeds that in Y. In these cases the outcome depends on the relative levels of tax rate as well as per capita incomes.

It should be noted that these particular results, as well as Buchanan's illustrations, are based on the assumption that ex-penditure benefits may be distributed on a per capita basis. If we assume instead that benefits are proportional to income, the result changes. In a state with a proportional tax structure the fiscal residue is now zero at all income levels, and the principle of equal treatment of equals now holds as between the residents of all states which have proportional tax structures, whatever their service levels. While this does not change the formal nature of Buchanan's argument, it indicates that the specific results will depend entirely on one's assumptions regarding the distribution of benefits. While the redefinition of horizontal equity in terms of fiscal residue is an interesting and sensible idea, its implementation is exceedingly difficult.

This leads me to a more basic point. If state taxes, imposed to finance public services, are allocated on a benefit basis, all citizens of the federation will be taxed on a benefit basis by their respective states. In this case, no central equalization is needed since the require-ment of horizontal equity is met by the very condition of universal taxation according to benefits received.[27] Differences in treatment can arise only out of tax transfer schemes, imposed by states to

---

[27] The concepts of horizontal and vertical equity do not fit into a normative system, where public services are supplied on a benefit basis and a tax-transfer mechanism is used to redistribute income. The principle of equality then becomes that everybody is subjected to benefit taxation, and everybody is made subject to the same scheme of redistribution. On this division of functions see Chs. 1 and 2 of my *The Theory of Public Finance*, McGraw-Hill, 1959.

This leaves open the question whether benefit taxation (and hence the principle of equality) should be defined in terms of equal *marginal* benefits or equal *total* benefits. In the first case, everyone is taxed so that the marginal benefits which *he* derives from

implement their particular notions as to what constitutes the socially desirable state of distribution.

B. Vertical Equity

The problem, in this case, becomes one of desired central interference into income-redistribution policies of the states. Let us suppose that both central and state fiscs have distributional objectives. If the state adjustment is made first (where state taxes and transfers apply to income before central tax) and the central adjustment comes second (where central taxes and transfers apply to income after state taxes), the state adjustments will not affect the end-result, but only determine the particular pattern of federal taxes and transfers. If the central adjustment comes first, the state pattern is the one which finally prevails in each state. If both levels insist on their pattern as the final goal, an unstable situation results.

Since one level must be given priority, there is much to be said for making this adjustment at the central level. Looking at the matter in a normative way, it is clear that state taxes will then be based properly on income minus those central taxes or plus those central transfers which reflect distributional adjustments by the central fisc. Central taxes raised to provide for central services will not be allowed in deducting for purposes of state taxation, as they may be considered use of income. Central taxes in turn would be assessed on total income, without allowance for state taxes to provide state services.

EFFICIENCY OBJECTIVES

In the preceding discussion, the Buchanan plan was looked upon as a formula for horizontal equity. Alternatively, it may be considered a design to neutralize distorting effects on location which result from differentials between the fiscal operations of various states.

Let it be assumed that, in the absence of differentials among state

---

his outlays on public services equals the marginal benefit which *he* derives from his private outlay. In the second case, there is an equating of the total benefits which various people derive from their transactions with the fisc. This includes the consumer surplus which Mr. X derives because his co-citizens like public services so that the unit cost to him is low, as compared to that derived by Mr. Y who lives in a state where his co-citizens do not wish to pay for public services. This difference corresponds to gains which the consumer derives in his private purchases if his preferences are dissimilar from those of rival consumers. Since the latter gains are usually taken as given when defining a "proper" distribution of income, it seems preferable to apply the same reasoning to the tax case, and to define benefit taxation in marginal terms.

fiscs, market forces lead to an optimal location of economic activity in the private sector. Now fiscal differentials are introduced between the states, and the pattern of location changes. Buchanan suggests that such changes could be avoided if fiscal residues were neutralized. Following the preceding argument, it is again concluded that such differences would not arise, and that locational distortions would be avoided, if all state taxes were imposed on a benefit basis, even though at different levels.[28] Differences in net residue would remain only if various states pursued different distribution policies, in which case the appropriate adjustment would be to let the central plan for distribution dominate.

All this is a much too simplified view of the problem. For one thing, there is again the question of just how the benefits are distributed among individual residents. For another, there are a host of difficulties which arise from interstate commerce and the structure of the corporation. Even if it is assumed that all tax revenue is obtained from personal income tax, benefit taxation or equalization of net residue at the personal level neutralizes the location of firms only if management is identified completely with the owner, which is surely an unrealistic assumption. Moreover, certain benefits accrue to business firms rather than to individuals, and many state and local taxes are (and for benefit purposes must be) levied on the firm rather than the owner. This poses difficult problems of interregional shifting of benefits and burdens, all of which complicate benefit taxation by regional units, as well as interregional equalization of net residues. As shown in the preceding paper, certain gains in efficiency may be derived by appropriate regional dispersion of the fiscal system. At the same time, the mechanism of decentralization is apt to be imperfect. It will tend to introduce unneutralities and, by narrowing the "common market," add new inefficiencies. Not only may location of industry be interfered with by differential fiscal policies, but also the threat of capital flight to low-tax (or, rather, high net-residue) states may prevent a proper allocation of resources between the satisfaction of public and of private wants.

Apart from all this, there remains the question of how efficiency in location is affected by various plans for equalization between states, such as were discussed in the first section of this paper.[29]

[28] On this point, see comments by Buchanan and my rejoinder.

[29] See James M. Buchanan, "Federal Grants and Resource Allocation," *Journal of Political Economy*, June 1952, pp. 208–17; also see the literature there referred to and the discussion with A. D. Scott in the December 1952 issue of the same journal.

By increasing the economic capacity of poor regions, the outflow of resources is checked, and this may interfere with speedy transition to more efficient location. At the same time, mobility may be limited to begin with, and appropriate plans for regional equalization may aid rather than hinder efficiency for the country as a whole.

COMMENTS

JAMES M. BUCHANAN, University of Virginia

An ancient proverb suggests that being the "big frog in the little pond" is sometimes a desirable state of affairs. My comment is designed to demonstrate that this state of affairs is achieved only at a cost, and that the fully rational frog (whose utility function is independent of those of his fellows except as to be developed herein) must *always* choose the big pond precisely because there are likely to be bigger and better frogs present.

This proverbial analogy gets us directly to one of the central economic problems of federalism. At the expense of neglecting the many other provocative aspects of the two papers, I shall confine my formal discussion to this central issue. I do so partially to exploit this occasion to modify and to correct certain portions of my own analysis that appeared in the work to which both Musgrave and Tiebout refer. This seems warranted since Musgrave seems to accept, at least by inference, certain implications of my earlier argument which I now believe to be in need of substantial correction. Tiebout specifically discusses the issue I want to raise when he introduces income differences into his analysis, but he does not examine the implications fully.

I begin with a brief examination of the word "redistribution" as this is used in the discussion of a fiscal system. I have previously characterized a fiscal system as being "redistributive" if the higher income individuals bear a "net tax" and the lower income receivers receive a "net benefit." The fiscal residuum, that is to say, the net tax or net benefit, is computed by estimating for the individual his share of total taxes and total benefits from governmental services, *in cost values*. If the residuum resulting from this subtraction of benefits from taxes is positive, the individual pays a "net tax," if negative, he receives a "net benefit." If the residuum is zero, a *quid pro quo* exists between the individual and the fisc, and, in so far as this particular individual is concerned, the system is defined to be distributionally neutral.

On the basis of this means of calculating the over-all fiscal residua of individuals in the separate subordinate units of a federation (states), and adopting the normative rule of "equal treatment for equals," or as Musgrave calls it, the rule of horizontal equity, I proposed a conceptual scheme for computing a set of interarea transfers of revenue.

The inference of this analysis is that, if the separate subordinate units attempt to accomplish some redistribution, in the sense here defined, some interarea or interstate fiscal adjustment is suggested by equity as well as efficiency considerations. But, as Musgrave has properly shown, the negative inference from my model is perhaps more important than the positive. The inference is clear that, if the subordinate units do not attempt to undertake redistribution through their fiscal systems, redistribution in the sense defined above, each individual is confronted with a zero fiscal residuum, and, consequently, the argument for interarea fiscal transfers vanishes.

Up to this point there is no error in my earlier analysis or in Musgrave's interpretation of it. The modification or correction that now seems required is to make quite clear that the presence of the *quid pro quo* relationship between the individual and the government does not necessarily guarantee that the individual is subjected to equal over-all fiscal "treatment" with his "equals" in other subordinate units. This fiscal equivalent of the diamond-water paradox rises to confuse us here. Economists have failed to distinguish carefully between benefit taxation defined in *total* and *marginal* terms. Musgrave points to this distinction in a footnote, and Tiebout also recognizes the distinction in his analysis, but, somewhat surprisingly, neither of them follows up the implications for the problems of federalism.

Interpreted in terms of some equality between total contributions made and total benefits received, the benefit principle is, of course, nonsensical. As Jevons and Einaudi have both emphasized, governments could, on such a principle, exact from the individual almost everything above the bare subsistence minimum. The only relevant benefit principle must be that of equalizing marginal benefits received from government services with the marginal taxes paid. This makes the benefit principle analogous to market pricing in respect to the *quid pro quo* relationship that is established between the buyer and seller of government services. The individual gives up the maximum amount that he is willing to give up to secure the *specified* amount of public services available. He does not give up the maximum amount that he would be willing to give up were he to be faced with an all-or-none choice. He receives a genuine "taxpayer's surplus," and it is worth noting that this "taxpayer's surplus" may still be positive in situations where the individual is subjected to a "net tax." In other words, the individual may be forced to pay more for government than he would pay, were government services available to him at uniform market prices, and still enjoy some "taxpayer's surplus."

The presence of the *quid pro quo* relationship suggests only that the individual is confronted with a marginal tax rate equal to the marginal benefits he receives from public services. The total fiscal situation in which the individual finds himself is determined on the other hand by the total tax pressure exerted on him by the fisc in comparison with the total benefits he receives from having public services available to him. The *quid pro quo* is, therefore, only a necessary, not a sufficient, condition to insure that all individuals are subjected to equal fiscal treatment. Viewed in this way, it is clear that, even if all the states in a federation adopted the pure benefit principle in organizing fiscal systems, there would still remain major fiscal advantages to locating in a community with a relatively larger number of high-income receivers, as Tiebout recognizes. The taxpayer's surplus for any given individual, otherwise indifferent as to location as among communities, will normally be higher in the community with the largest proportion of high-income receivers. This conclusion is obvious, and it stems from the spillover or external effects arising out of the consumption of public goods, effects that the Lindahl-Musgrave-Bowen-Samuelson models have made clear.

It is quite easy to illustrate the main point in very simple terms. Take two suburban areas, one rich, the other poor. Neither unit possesses taxing power so that all local collective action must be genuinely voluntary. Each of the two areas needs to add some playground equipment in its centrally located park. It is evident that the amount of equipment per capita will be larger in the richer community than in the poorer. Other things equal, the individual, faced with a choice, will locate in the richer community.

Even if no collective action takes place, a situation where an extreme form of "benefit" taxation applies, the effects discussed here will be present. Examples are close at hand. If an individual has decided to spend $30,000 on the purchase of a house, and his utility function is not influenced by relative standing in his local community, he will, other things equal, find it more advantageous to buy a home in an area dominated by $60,000 houses as compared with another in which $15,000 units abound. Why is this true? For the reason that, in moving to the "rich" community, the individual is able to secure some of the spillover effects of private actions taken by other homeowners in preserving and beautifying the landscape; e.g., the care of lawns, flower gardens, etc. Note here that there need be no interdependence among private decisions resulting in *collective action* of any sort. The individual who considers purchasing the $30,000 house may be quite unwilling to pay more than a *zero* marginal price or tax to insure that his richer neighbors *expand* their flower gardens. Interference with the private market process is justified only if the interdependence among individuals' decisions involves the marginal decisions of individuals considered. Modern welfare economists have not always steered clear of this modern version of the diamond-water paradox.

But I must return to the main point. The application of the benefit principle of taxation, in the only meaningful sense that this principle can be applied, does not, indeed cannot, eliminate the differential fiscal advantages conferred on the average resident of the relatively richer communities in a federation. This true fiscal differential is present solely by fact of the community's relative richness. These differentials will be present in all cases where there is interdependence among individual decisions, either marginal or inframarginal.

The differentials are real, and any consideration of over-all efficiency in resource usage must take them into account. If we continue to assume that states in a federation do, in fact, finance all public services on the basis of marginal benefit, we must try to describe the resulting equilibrium. In small communities, such as the residential suburbs of metropolitan regions, the fiscal advantages and disadvantages may, at least for a considerable time period, be almost fully capitalized. The original developers and early settlers of the community will reap the differential gains, and the prospective residents entering the community after its pattern has more or less been determined will find the community's expected future net fiscal advantages capitalized into the original price of land. The cost of land will be higher than that of similar land in the poorer community.

If we look at the larger units, say, the states in this country, the description of full resource equilibrium is more difficult. Land values will still, to some extent, reflect the net fiscal advantages and disadvantages of location. But land, broadly considered, is as producible as any other capital good. Investors in the production of "land" will not find it profitable to develop areas expected to be dominated by clusters of low-income residents. Such areas will tend to be "underdeveloped" relative to those geographic areas more favorably situated in terms of expected occupational cluster. If this differential developmental pattern materializes, the prospective purchaser of land in the two areas may find developed land prices substantially equivalent. If this is true, the net fiscal advantage or disadvantage must take the form of an equalizing difference in the returns to labor. The individual must be rewarded for moving into the low-income area by the expectation of a slightly higher salary or wage in relation to living costs. On balance, both of these effects seem likely to occur. Land values would tend to be higher, and wage and salary levels for comparable skills slightly lower in the states with proportionately larger numbers of higher income receivers. Such differentials will characterize full resource adjustment only if all other forms of equalizing differences are assumed away. In the real world, other equalizing differentials may, of course, more than offset the ones considered here. But it should be noted that in a period when public or collective activity, especially at the local level, is increasing rapidly the differentials discussed here assume increasing importance over time.

Before we proceed further, we must examine somewhat more carefully the characteristics of a fiscal system that is organized on the basis of pure economic considerations, that is, a system embodying taxation in accordance with the principle of marginal benefit. In order for resources to be efficiently allocated as between the private goods and the public goods sector, this principle must be followed, as Musgrave and Samuelson have shown. In any position where the necessary conditions for Pareto optimality are satisfied, the rate at which each individual is willing to substitute public goods for private goods must be equal to the rate at which he is forced to give up public goods for private goods. To this point, the analogy with the welfare conditions for the purely private goods world is complete. But here it stops. The marginal rates of substitution between public goods and private goods are not necessarily equal as among the separate individuals. If the externality features of public goods were not present, individuals would find it advantageous to "trade" public goods among themselves until a uniform price were established. But such trading is impossible by definition. In a federation, however, "trading" can take place indirectly. Individuals can, in effect, "trade" public goods by shifting from one locality to the other. In this way, the total taxpayers' surplus is increased.

All of the preceding discussion has been based on the assumption that states do, in fact, organize their internal fiscal systems on the basis of efficiency considerations. Of course they do not. State systems, although less "redistributive" than the federal system, are "redistributive" in the sense defined. There remains the question: Does the criterion of equalizing fiscal residua for equals in the separate states, the criterion I proposed several years ago, retain any validity from the efficiency point of view?

If no interarea transfers of revenue are undertaken by the central government, and states do attempt some net "redistribution," there will clearly be some excessive shifting of resources to the states characterized by concentrations of high-income receivers. Not only will the "true" fiscal differential discussed above be present, but also the effects of the attempted redistribution policies will provide still a further fiscal incentive for individuals to migrate toward the richer states. The net fiscal advantages and disadvantages will tend to be equalized by a system of interarea transfers based on the equity criterion. In effect, the implementation of a set of transfers based on this rule would introduce uniform pricing for government as among "equals" in the separate locations. The individual would be insured that he could "purchase" the same amount of government for the same price regardless of geographic location. This policy would act directly on the geographically discriminatory pricing of government services that is implicit in the principle of state taxation in accordance with marginal benefit, and which is even more pronounced in the more realistic fiscal systems actually existing. This policy would act directly to remove the fiscal differentials instead of forcing the burden of adjustment on resource movement to equalize the net advantages and disadvantages.

There is an analogue to this in price theory. Under what conditions should price discrimination be prohibited legally? If the consumer is assumed to have available to him sufficient alternatives, no attempt is normally made to prohibit sellers from discriminating in price if they so desire. The full adjustment is placed on the workings of the market. On the other hand, if the buyer is assumed not to have open sufficient alternatives, price discrimination by sellers may be subjected to direct prohibition. The case with fiscal federalism is quite similar. On economic grounds, no case can be made for interarea revenue transfers if the geographic mobility of resources and the multiplicity of state and local fiscal systems are considered sufficient to constitute acceptable alternatives to the buyer of government services. From this position, the inherent geographical discrimination in the pricing of governmental services in a federation need not be cause for concern or for specific public action in the form of transfers among the state units. On the other hand, a second position would suggest that the geographic mobility of resources and the existence of the several states do not constitute effective alternatives to the individual, and that, on both equity and efficiency grounds, the fiscal differentials should be attacked directly by a system of revenue transfers.

As Tiebout has shown, if the "early settlers" of the "richer" communities take action, by means of zoning restriction or otherwise, to prevent the "trading through migration" from taking place, the second position becomes stronger. One way or the other the "rich" should be willing, not to "pay taxes for the poor" (Tiebout's words are ill-chosen here for there are no strictly distributional issues involved), but rather to share the benefits of their own collectively provided services. Insofar as the goods in question are purely "public" in the Samuelson-Musgrave polar sense, the "rich" can share these goods without cost to themselves. In fact, per capita costs can be actually reduced as Tiebout shows in his model. Hence, for the "early settlers" to refuse to share "public goods" with new migrants would seem to represent a genuine dog-in-the-manger attitude. But, of course, complications arise as soon as it is recognized that the extreme polar case does not describe reality. As Tiebout suggests, all collectively provided goods and services are partially "public" and partially "private." This being the case, the immigration of new citizens into the "richer" communities will always reduce, to some extent, the taxpayers' surplus of the early settlers. Prohibitions on entry become economically rational, provincially considered. As Margolis suggests in his paper, land owners will forego capital gains in order to prevent entry of "undesirables" into the community. But this sacrifice of capital gains on possible land holdings may be more than offset by the retention of a greater share of taxpayers' surplus. In a very real sense, zoning restrictions and other like devices can be considered as means through which "early settlers" attempt to create a structure of property rights in "taxpayers' surplus."

As we now compute GNP, the policy of providing some interarea revenue transfers to offset fiscal differentials would tend to increase national measures of product. Despite this fact, and despite Samuelson's interesting recent note on the economics of marriage, I must somewhat reluctantly conclude that my position in support of substantial interarea transfers has been modified under the influence of the Musgrave-Samuelson clarification of the nature of public goods and the interesting local government models of Stigler and Tiebout. These influences, coupled with the fact that serving as a discussant on this program has forced me to rethink some of my earlier analysis, lead me to put much less emphasis than previously on the efficiency basis of intergovernmental revenue transfers.

This leads to my final point. Unless intergovernmental fiscal transfers of revenue can be justified on equity or efficiency grounds, there remains only the interarea fiscal interdependence producing the spillover effects mentioned by Tiebout. Here the whole question boils down to determining the extent of importance of these effects, and, at least at the currently important margins of decision, I do not think these effects are significant.

C. LOWELL HARRISS, Columbia University

Most of us probably join with Professor Musgrave in endorsing the principle that the power of government can be wisely used to reduce economic inequality.[1] Presumably the general public welfare will be served. In at least one respect, however, substantial *inequality* may serve the *general public interest* constructively—the public of the entire economy or the entire free world. I speak of education, the largest nonnational expenditure and perhaps the single type assumed by Professor Musgrave. (Of course, it has spillover effects, but I can think of no significant state expenditure having no spillover.)

The world needs people with superior education. Everyone has

---

[1] I now feel that the reduction of poverty rather than the reduction of inequality ought to receive the major emphasis. This, however, is a different issue from the one I want to discuss here.

an interest—one he may not always appreciate adequately—in the existence and the efficient use of people with the highest of training. Excellence—in diplomacy, statesmanship, art, science, medicine, architecture, entertainment, religion, judicial decision, national defense, or economics—requires great skill. It calls for extensive and expensive training. Not many school districts can afford top quality elementary or secondary schooling, at least not until we are a much wealthier nation than today. But some communities are able and willing to provide much more than others. In doing so, these communities serve the *general* public. Inequality makes possible a kind of accomplishment for the whole society which would not be attainable under conditions of equality.

The transfer of resources from high- to low-income areas (or people) will permit some to improve the quality of education they offer (or obtain). Such improvement is in the general public interest. Not improbably, there will be an increase in the average level. Yet financing the transfer may reduce significantly the ability of the few to provide excellence. If so, the general public will suffer. Raising an average does not meet the need for superior human achievement. I wish that we had the income and the willingness to make every school system better than the best today. Unfortunately, we do not. If I am right, therefore, if there is a national interest in excellence in education, this fact has a place in models for the transfer of income. A program of equalization will reduce the ability, and perhaps the willingness, of a relatively few school districts to provide high quality education. What the country loses as a result may be different in kind from the gains it enjoys from bettering the quality a little in many times as many schools.[2]

To repeat: The whole public benefits from excellence. The communities which offer superior education thereby help meet a need of the nation as a whole. Equalization programs may increase the total of educational opportunity and serve the entire society. Yet these programs may also reduce the supply of a type of education which is an essentially different product from that which is added.

[2] Our present system, heavens knows, is not an efficient arrangement for developing excellence. In this respect we suffer from an aspect of the problem noted by Professor Tiebout—space. If children are to live with their parents, much human potential cannot in our generation be offered top quality opportunity in elementary and secondary schools. Moreover, good schools will be wasted on many people of mediocre capacity. One advantage of cities is that educational facilities of varying quality can be made accessible to many children.

Equality cannot permit us to serve all our needs—and the "our" is the general public, society as a whole—including those for superior training, until the economy has much higher income than it does today.

BURTON A. WEISBROD, Washington University of St. Louis

External, or spillover effects are at the heart of many problems of fiscal federalism. Professor Tiebout argues that under certain circumstances these effects may be disregarded with impunity by the analyst —a most important conclusion, if correct. Thus, he states:

"With uniform demand, population, income, and, in turn, uniform services, each community will receive back as much in spillover as it contributes to its neighbors . . . and the per capita benefits exchanged are equal. . . . [Thus], the problem of spillover . . . is of no concern."

If by "no concern" is meant that in the case outlined there would be no need for an ethical arbiter to make transfer payments because of inequalities in exchange of spillovers, then Tiebout is quite right. But, equity aside, there remains the question of the efficiency of the aggregate output of public goods—where the "efficient" rate of output is that at which marginal social benefit (defined according to some social welfare function) equals marginal social cost; and in this regard, there is no cancelling out of the spillover effects; there is reason for concern. The output of the good (e.g., Tiebout's example of mosquito spraying) by each community, and, hence, both communities, will be, in general, too low.

In presenting the case, I assume that each community takes as "given" the anticipated level of spillover benefits it is to receive from the other community, and then makes its expenditures decisions. Of course, the efficiency of the resulting levels of expenditure depends on whether each community (1) errs in assuming a *higher* level of output by the other than actually occurs, or (2) errs in assuming a *lower* level, or (3) correctly anticipates the other community's output.

The point to be recognized here is that, even if each community *correctly* estimates the other's production, aggregate output of both communities will be nonoptimal in the sense defined above—i.e., will be too small. The argument is simple: Each community produces

Note: I have benefited from discussion of this subject with my colleague, Ronald G. Ridker.

the level of output at which, given the spillover benefits from the other community's output, *its* marginal *community* benefits equal its marginal community cost; but, since marginal community benefits (i.e., within one community) are less than marginal *social* benefits (to both communities), by virtue of the external (spillover) benefits, each community stops short of the social optimal level of production, presumably being unconcerned about benefits from its actions which fall outside its boundaries. *Each* community produces too little; there is no "canceling out" of inefficiencies, although, as Tiebout correctly points out, "the per capita benefits exchanged [by the communities] are equal." Note that this result occurs even though we assume complete knowledge—that each community realizes that it is both a provider and a recipient of spillover benefits, and moreover, knows the amounts of spillover in both directions; the result is just another example of the generalization that output may be expected to be suboptimal whenever there exist external economies in production or consumption. Hence, the achievement of social optimality necessitates some intercommunity cooperation, or a higher level government to see to it that the formerly external benefits are given proper consideration when output decisions are made. Contrary to Tiebout, there *is* reason for concern.

Finally, it is interesting to note that, dropping the assumption that each community correctly predicts its spillover receipts, each community's attempt to achieve its (community) optimum level of output *could* lead to the social optimum, *if* it *under*estimated by the appropriate amount the spillovers it actually received. We saw above that the deviation of social from community marginal benefit led the community which *correctly* knew what spillovers it was to receive to *under*produce; ignorance (underestimation) of spillover receipts would, *ceteris paribus*, lead it to overproduce. The counteracting effects of these two factors could lead to the social optimum level of output, though we can hardly count on such a result.

REPLY by Mr. Musgrave

If I understand Professor Buchanan's comments correctly, he now proposes a double standard. As far as *equity considerations* are concerned, he agrees with me that adherence to benefit taxation by states equalizes net residues, thus rendering central interference unnecessary. This assumes the usual interpretation of benefit taxation as equating the marginal utility of tax and private outlays for any one taxpayer. However, Professor Buchanan suggests that such a policy would not do the job of neutralizing the *allocation effects* of state fiscs. In order to accomplish this, so he argues, there would have to be equalization of total net benefits (including consumer surplus) as between taxpayers. Thus, equity and efficiency considerations require different standards and are, in fact, incompatible.

Suppose that citizen x obtains a greater total net gain from his transactions with the fisc in X land than does y in Y land, both x and y having equal tastes and incomes. This will be the case where the cost share for x in public services will be smaller if he resides in X land than if he resides in Y land because (1) the tastes of other residents place a higher preference on public services in X land than in Y land or (2) average income is higher in X land than in Y land. Depending on the importance of these factors relative to the weight of other locational considerations, fiscal factors may have a significant effect on x's choice of location. Such will be the case even though the tax structure in both X and Y adheres to benefit taxation in the marginal sense.

However, I am not at all certain that such influences on the location of X should be classified as "distorting" the regional allocation of resources. Rather it appears that they constitute a given datum for location, just as does the geographical distribution of natural resource deposits. The fact that the benefit incidence of public services is spacially limited, and that this has a bearing on how people wish to group themselves, is part of the economic map which determines resource allocation. Efficiency is not served by erasing this feature of the map. Indeed, a central policy aimed at nullifying resulting differentials (such as remain with universal benefit taxation) in state finance will interfere with efficiency in the regional structuring of public finances.

Practical Solutions to Financial Problems Created by the Multilevel Political Structure

I. M. LABOVITZ
LIBRARY OF CONGRESS

L. L. ECKER-RACZ
U.S. TREASURY

1. Introduction

THIS paper examines ways and means of increasing the financial capabilities of state governments through adjustments in federal-state-local fiscal relations. Federalism, to be sure, creates problems at the federal level as well, but these do not relate primarily to fiscal capability. In a sense our primary concern is for the financial capabilities of local governments, since much of the initial impact of rising civilian governmental costs is on them. However, cities, counties, towns and school districts are the wards of the states and their problems the states' problems.

During the last five years for which official data are available, 1953–57, state and local "general government" absorbed nearly $200 billion for direct general expenditures, capital outlay for local utilities, debt redemption, employee-retirement systems and increases in fund balances (Table 1).

To finance these expenditures, state and local governments raised $149 billion from their own revenue sources—from taxes, fines, fees and licenses, interest earnings and the operation of utility and other business enterprises. This left a gap of about $49 billion, bridged by financial aid from the federal government (about $16 billion) and and by borrowing (about $33 billion).

This gap—about $10 billion per annum—is one quantitative approximation of the fiscal problem of state and local governments with which we are here concerned and for which solutions are sought. It is, however, little more than an approximation of that problem.

The magnitudes cited measure state and local performance—the amounts spent—and not the amounts that would have been spent if adequate resources had been available to finance a level of governmental service consistent with need. No measure is available of the

Note. This paper does not necessarily reflect the views of the above agencies.

TABLE 1

State and Local "General Government" Operations, 1953–57

Use of funds:	In millions
Direct general expenditure	$169,484
Capital outlay for local government utilities	5,146
Debt redemption	12,037
Contribution to employee retirement systems	5,116[a]
Increase in cash and security holdings (exclusive of insurance trust funds)	7,095
Total (net of duplication)	$198,003[b]
Source of funds:	
General revenue from own sources	$144,229
Net current surplus of utilities and liquor stores	4,407[c]
Intergovernmental revenue from Federal Government	16,140
Borrowing	33,057
Total	$197,833

SOURCE: Bureau of the Census, Governments Division.

[a] Derived by subtracting from the total increase ($6,427 million) in retirement fund assets, the excess ($1,311 million) of their receipts from employee contributions and investment earnings over their payments of benefits and withdrawals.

[b] Less than the sum of detail by $875 million, representing employer contributions by local governments to state administered employee retirement systems, included above in both "Direct general expenditure" and "Contributions to employee retirement systems."

[c] The excess of aggregate utility revenues over expenditures for utility operations and utility interest.

degree to which state and local performance fell short of need, apart from such fragmentary information as classroom shortages, deficient instruction programs, substandard health and recreation facilities, etc.

Moreover, the magnitudes cited pertain to the past. They have been increasing and will continue to increase. During these five years alone, the size of the annual gap as here defined, i.e., the amounts borrowed and obtained as federal aid, increased from $6.4 billion to over $10 billion. The projections presented to this conference and other forecasts suggest continuing increases in future years.

The magnitudes shown in Table 1 understate the problem also because they are global for the country as a whole, and conceal substantial deviations from the average in individual jurisdictions. Despite the upgrading of the less productive sections of the country, economic inequality continues to characterize the states and the political subdivisions within individual states. As subsequent discussion indicates, this uneven geographic distribution of resources is the genesis of many problems in federal-state fiscal relations.

In posing the problem in terms of state-local financial requirements, there is no intention to suggest that it exclusively or primarily concerns only state and local governments. Problems at the state level quickly become matters for national and federal concern. Current preoccupation with the inadequacy of the states' public education systems provides a timely illustration, but one no more dramatic than national concern in earlier years with the inability of state governments to cope adequately with unemployment or the inadequacy of their resources for the payment of unemployment benefits during the 1957-58 recession. Neither is it our intention to suggest that the problem of federalism is primarily one of dollars and cents. The philosophical values involved are indeed important and their implications for the functioning of the political institutions —for democratic government itself—recognized.[1] It is, however, in financial terms that the problem of intergovernmental relations is generally presented. It is in financial terms that it will be relieved.

One or two additional stipulations. Intergovernmental problems in a federalism do not admit of absolute solutions. A system of government wherein the several states with unequal economic resources undertake to conduct many of their affairs as one nation while retaining an important measure of sovereignty with respect to large sectors of governmental activity, can never be free of problems. If some of these do not lend themselves to neat solutions, they do lend themselves to accommodation.[2] Such accommodation, moreover, is likely to involve the established tools of intergovernmental relationships, rather than new arrangements still uninvented. The tools are familiar; the debate concerns largely the use to be made of them, how and when and under what circumstances? This paper answers very few of these questions. It aims to be constructive, not by providing new answers—but rather, by examining old ones and by disposing of some misconceptions. This accounts for the uneven allotment of space among the subjects treated, frequently at variance with their relative revenue importance. The purpose here is not to treat federal-state-local relations comprehensively and systematically. We limit ourselves to problems which we can illuminate with the quantitative data we have been able to assemble.[3]

[1] For a constructive formulation of the philosophy of contemporary American federalism see the *Report* of the Commission on Intergovernmental Relations, GPO, June 1955, and William Anderson, *The Nation and the States, Rivals or Partners?*, University of Minnesota Press, 1955.

[2] Committee on Intergovernmental Fiscal Relations, *Federal, State, and Local Government Fiscal Relations*, Senate Doc. 69, 78th Cong., 1st sess., GPO, 1943.

[3] The presentation is unbalanced even in this restricted sense, because our examination has proceeded further on some phases of the subject than on others.

The sections which follow examine a variety of suggestions for augmenting the financial resources of state and local governments through intergovernmental action. The areas of taxation, debt financing, and federal financial aid are discussed in this order.

2. *Revenues of State and Local Governments from their Own Sources*

In fiscal year 1957, taxes produced $29 billion for state and local governments and financed approximately 70 per cent of their general government expenditures. Borrowing, federal aid and miscellaneous charges and receipts, including utility and liquor store profits, provided the balance. Our concern in this section is with tax revenues; how adjustments in federal-state relations would affect them. The revenue import of the several components of the state and local tax structure is summarized in Table 2.

TABLE 2

State and Local Tax Revenues, 1953 and 1957

(amounts in millions)

Item	1953	1957[a]	Percentage Increase	1957 Distribution
Taxes, total	$20,908	$29,042	38.9	100.0%
Property	9,375	13,097	39.7	45.1
Individual income	1,065	1,767	65.9	6.1
Corporation income	817	984	20.4	3.4
Sales and gross receipts	6,927	9,461	36.6	32.6
General sales and gross receipts	2,860	4,027	40.8	13.9
Motor fuel	2,019	2,851	41.2	9.8
Alcoholic beverage	465	591	27.1	2.0
Tobacco products	469	604	28.8	2.1
Other selective taxes	1,114	1,388	24.6	4.8
Death and gift	226	346	53.1	1.2
Other, including licenses and permits	2,497	3,387	35.6	11.6
Motor vehicle and operator licenses	1,012	1,462	44.5	5.0
All other taxes	1,485	1,924	29.6	6.6

SOURCE: Bureau of the Census, *Summary of Governmental Finances.*

[a] *The 1957 Census of Governments* reports total state and local taxes of $28,817 million. The property tax accounts for most of the $225 million reduction.

A. PROPERTY TAX

The number one revenue producer is still the long-maligned property tax. It supplies 45 per cent of the tax revenues of state and local governments and since it has become principally a local as distinguished from a state tax, its contribution to local revenues is relatively much larger, 87 per cent.[4]

Despite its well-publicized limitations, including alleged unresponsiveness to changing levels of employment and economic activity, the property tax is holding its own. Between 1953 and 1957, when total state and local tax collections increased 38.9 per cent, the property tax yield increased 39.7 per cent. By virtue of its dominant role in state-local tax systems, the property tax influences appreciably the behavior of total tax collections. Several factors are contributing to the rising revenue yield of property taxes. The large volume of new construction and the steady upward trend in the level of tax rates are the principal ones. Lesser, but nonetheless significant contributors are improved assessment techniques and reduced tax delinquencies. State legislatures are taking an increased interest in up-dating tax assessments to relieve the pressure for state financial aid to local jurisdictions, and where distribution of state aid is partially based on local need, to curb the tendency to reduce local assessments in order to demonstrate greater local need.

Since the federal government levies no property taxes, problems of overlapping do not arise. Note should be taken, however, of deductibility of property taxes for federal income tax purposes, since it reduces the net burden of local property taxes for federal income taxpayers who itemize deductions. Deductibility of property taxes is especially important for the larger corporations, since it effectively shifts approximately half of their tax to the federal government.

A problem of major importance for a limited number of local jurisdictions is the immunity of federal property from local taxation, and for a substantially larger number of communities, the tax exemption of properties owned by the state and by religious, educational, charitable and similar nonprofit organizations. Federal-state relations are involved in only the first of these.[5]

Under the doctrine of reciprocal tax immunity first enunciated by

---

[4] As used in this document, the term "states" excludes Alaska and Hawaii.

[5] In view of the dominant role of the property tax in the fiscal capabilities of local governments and the impairment of these capabilities by deficient tax administration, an examination of possibilities for enhancing local fiscal capacity through federal action should properly explore opportunities available at the national level for influencing the quality of property tax administration. The data on assessment practices (ratios) assembled in connection with the *1957 Census of Governments*, underscore the urgency of this problem and could serve as the basis of a nation-wide effort to improve assessment practices through the dissemination of information and technical assistance, or possibly through matching grants to finance state-wide assessment procedure studies.

Chief Justice Marshall in 1817 and still generally maintained, property owned by the federal government or its instrumentalities is not subject to state or local taxation without explicit congressional consent. Congress has consented in only a few instances, notably with respect to the real property of the now-liquidated Reconstruction Finance Corporation and certain other lending agencies. More often but still infrequently, Congress has authorized payments designated as "in lieu of taxes," and in a few situations, federal grants in recognition of the tax immunity of federal properties. For the fiscal year 1955, aggregate payments associated with the nontaxability of federal property were estimated at $276 million and consisted of:

	In millions
Property taxes	$2.9
Payments in lieu of taxes	13.8
Revenue-sharing	52.4
Other related payments:	
Federally affected	
school districts,	
for construction	121.1
for operation and	
maintenance	81.9
Indian education and	
welfare (off-reservation	
tuition)	3.5
Total	$275.6[6]

The vast bulk of federal property, whether measured by acreage, number of parcels, or value, is at present immune from payments directly or indirectly associated with the prevailing property tax system for financing local government. While its current value is not known, it clearly is substantial. The accumulated historical cost of real property owned by the federal government within the continental United States was estimated in 1958 at approximately $55 billion for land and improvements. The accumulated cost of federally owned tangible personal property was probably over $150 billion. The bulk

[6] Senate Committee on Government Operations, 84th Cong., 2d sess., *Payments of Taxes, or in Lieu of Taxes, to State or Local Taxing Units*, Hearings on S. 826 . . . (and other bills), part 2, pp. 337–41, April 19 and 20, 1956.

of the land acreage is in the public domain and never was in taxable ownership; moreover, it includes vast areas with little present market value.[7]

Many of the government's most valuable properties—and those most nearly resembling in physical characteristics and use typical privately owned taxable properties—were acquired or built during and after World War II. Federal properties sold to private users and turned to otherwise taxable business use have been held off the tax rolls until title passed from the federal government or payments under purchase contracts were completed. Moreover, some federal agencies, such as the military services and the AEC, have taken title and thus have extended the federal tax immunity to much personal property acquired and used or held by private contractors under their direction.

Questions concerning payments to state and local governments on account of federal government properties have been the subject of long controversy, numerous studies, voluminous documentation, dozens of legislative proposals, and a few limited statutory enactments over the last two decades.

Investigators generally agree that the central question is one of equity—equity between the taxpayers of the federal and of the several local governments. As in most questions of equity, the disagreement arises over what constitutes a fair arrangement for action. The broad practical question is essentially this: How can the national government carry on its operations and hold property without imposing special burdens upon the taxpayers of communities where the operations or properties are disproportionately large?[8] There are, however, subsidiary practical questions. One relates, for example, to the like treatment of similarly used properties where the use of the federally owned property is in competition with taxable private property. This and other collateral issues complicate any effort to draft a concrete program or policy.

Canada has tried a solution involving payments, in a limited category of cases, for disproportionate amounts of national government property. A somewhat similar proposal, but with a "hardship

---

[7] House Committee on Government Operations, 85th Cong., 2d sess., *Federal Real and Personal Property Inventory Report as of June 30, 1958*, pp. 11, 139. The real property total includes $9 billion public domain realty estimated at approximate current value.

[8] Council of State Governments, *Federal-State Relations*, Senate Doc. 81, 81st Cong., 1st sess., pp. 114–20.

test" attached, was received by the Congress without enthusiasm or action.[9]

Court decisions have highlighted some issues. One group of three interrelated Supreme Court decisions, rendered in 1958, is of particular current interest. The Court ruled that:

1. Leased realty exempt to the United States as owner may, nevertheless, under a Michigan statute relating to tax-exempt property, be taxable to a private corporate lessee (the Borg-Warner Corporation) using the property in a business conducted for profit. Two justices dissented. (*U.S. et al., v. City of Detroit*, March 3, 1958, 355 U.S. 466.)

2. Real property exempt to the United States as owner but used by a private corporation (the Continental Corporation) under a use-permit, without rental payment, in performing supply contracts for the government may, under the same Michigan statute, be taxable to the private user. In this case, also, the decision was 7 to 2. (*U.S. v. Township of Muskegon, et al.*, March 3, 1958, 355 U.S. 484.)

3. Personal property owned by the United States and used by a subcontractor under a prime contract between two other private companies and the United States may be taxable under the Michigan personal property tax law to the party in possession. In this decision, in which the Court was divided 5 to 4 [but a rehearing was later denied], the tax was considered by the majority to be a tax "for the privilege of using or possessing" the personal property, rather than a tax on the government's interest in the property. (*City of Detroit, et al., v. Murray Corporation of America, et al.*, March 3, 1958, 355 U.S. 489.)

Mr. Justice Black's majority opinion in the Continental case included this comment:

"The case might well be different if the government had reserved such control over the activities and financial gain of Continental that it could properly be called a 'servant' of the United States in agency terms. But here Continental was not so assimilated by the government as to become one of its constituent parts." (355 U.S. 486.)

Mr. Justice Black observed for the majority in the Borg-Warner decision:

"Today the United States does business with a vast number of private parties. In this Court the trend has been to reject immunizing these private parties from non-discriminatory state taxes as a matter of constitutional law. Cf. *Penn-Dairies v. Milk Control System*, 318 U.S. 261, 270. Of course, this is not to say that Congress, acting within the proper scope of its power, cannot confer immunity by statute where it does not exist constitutionally. Wise and flexible adjustment of intergovernmental tax immunity calls for political and economic considerations of the greatest difficulty and delicacy. Such complex problems are ones which Congress is best qualified to resolve." (355 U.S. 474.)

In his prevailing opinion in the Murray case, Mr. Justice Black added:

"We find nothing in the Constitution which compels us to strike down these state taxes. There was no discrimination against the federal government, its property or those with whom it does business. There was no crippling obstruction of any of the government's function, no sinister effort to hamstring its power, not even the slightest

[9] Senate Committee on Government Operations, 84th Cong., 2d sess., Hearings on S. 826 . . . , part 2, pp. 327–33.

142

interference with its property. Cf. *McCulloch v. Maryland*, 4 Wheat, 316. In such circumstances, the Congress is the proper agency, as we pointed out in *U.S. v. City of Detroit*, to make the difficult policy decisions necessarily involved in determining whether and to what extent private parties who do business with the Government should be given immunity from state taxes." (355 U.S. 495.)

If inferences are warranted from the 1958 decisions and recent congressional consideration of the subject, they may perhaps be summarized in this way:

1. In certain circumstances, even in the absence of explicit congressional consent to taxation, the Supreme Court is disposed to uphold the authority of the states to levy nondiscriminatory taxes upon private industrial users of government-owned property, real or personal, and to permit the amount of the tax to be measured by the value of the property. There is a greater division over personal property than over real property.

2. Congressional action will be required if there is to be any marked shift of policy from the present prevalent pattern of immunity of federal property from both actual taxes and the payment of amounts "in lieu of property taxes."

3. The interest generated by World War II and the Korean property acquisitions brought forth many proposals but no comprehensive congressional action. At present there is nothing to suggest that Congress will soon be disposed to lay down a general policy providing comprehensively for payments either of property taxes or in lieu of property taxes on account of federally owned properties. Doubtless there will continue to be piecemeal enactments dealing with selected problems, much as the court decisions will continue to resolve particular cases or to focus attention upon the complexities of the problem.

As controversy continues, both the local governments and the property-owning federal agencies publicize estimates of tremendous amounts of property tax revenue that are supposed to be involved in the issue of federal immunity. Often, however, these estimates make little or no allowance for prevailing practices of underassessment and nonassessment and for other institutional characteristics of the property tax system which would—or, at least, should—be invoked to assure equitable treatment of the federal government. As a result, the relative fiscal importance of even the broadest proposals is often exaggerated. Currently active legislative proposals are of relatively limited proportions—to relieve communities genuinely damaged.[10]

[10] S. 910, 86th Cong., 1st sess.

143

Substantially broader programs appear unlikely at this time in view of the widespread, almost emotional attachment to the concept of constitutional immunity and the unyielding attitude of state and local governments to the income tax immunity of their own securities.

In summary, then, a significant modification of the tax immunity now generally applicable to property of the federal government does not appear to be among the reasonable expectations for near-term practicable solutions to the revenue needs of local governments. Indeed, there is no visible prospect for an accommodation or innovation that would still the continuing controversy in this area of inter-level fiscal relations.

B. INDIVIDUAL INCOME TAX

The classic example of tax overlapping is the individual income tax, now employed at all three governmental levels, federal, state, and local.

Individual income taxation was introduced at approximately the same time by the federal government and some states. Most of the states, however, entered the field a decade or more after adoption of the federal income tax in 1913. City and county levies are largely a World War II phenomenon.

Thirty-one states (and the District of Columbia) now tax individual incomes.[11] All but two of these use broaldy based taxes applying generally to all income. The two exceptions, New Hampshire and Tennessee, limit their taxes to interest and dividends. Local governments in five states levy income taxes. In only two (Ohio and Pennsylvania), however, are local taxes widespread and neither of these has a state-wide tax. Of the other three in which the local tax overlaps the state tax, in Alabama and Missouri the local tax occurs only once each; in Kentucky five times. Local taxes are uniformly imposed at low flat rates and typically apply only to salaries, wages and net profits of unincorporated businesses and professions. Some local tax bases include rental income; none is believed to include investment income.

In 1957 individual income taxes produced about 6 per cent of state and local tax revenues. This represented some increase since 1953, when they accounted for about 5 per cent, and presumably is attributable to the rise in the level of personal income and to tax rate

[11] The descriptions of state tax systems throughout this chapter are as of January 1, 1959, as reported by Commerce Clearing House, *State Tax Reporter*. Significant changes can be anticipated in 1959 since revenue problems confront many of the 46 States in which the legislatures meet in regular sessions this year.

increases. More effective enforcement, notably the introduction of withholding at the source by eleven states, has also been a factor. Significantly, not a single new state individual income tax has been enacted in twenty years and more than one-third (36.3 per cent) of the United States population is still free of income taxation in its home state. Significantly, also, these people are concentrated in the older industrial states; Connecticut, Illinois, Michigan, New Jersey, Ohio, and Pennsylvania.

On a national scale and measured in terms of tax dollars collected, federal-state tax overlapping in individual income taxation is relatively small. All individual income taxes collected by state governments in 1958 aggregated $1.6 billion, equivalent to 4.5 per cent of federal tax collections from this source. In other words, the aggregate impact of all state imposed taxes is of the general magnitude of a 1 1/4 percentage point change in the first bracket rate of the federal tax. In the 31 states with income taxes, 1958 state collections averaged about 8 per cent of federal collections. However, as will be noted by reference to Table 3, the weight of state income tax collections, as measured by the amount of federal tax collections, has been increasing steadily, if slowly, during the past few years (reflecting in part federal tax reductions and in part the sharper graduation of state rate schedules).

The relative weight of state income taxes varies widely. In seven states the ratio of state to federal collections in 1958 was less than 5 per cent and in another twelve less than 10 per cent. In twelve states, this percentage exceeded 10 percent and in five of these, 15 per cent (Table 4).

These percentages, it should be emphasized, serve only as approximations of the relative weight of state taxes. Federal tax collections are tabulated on the basis of states in which they were paid, which in some cases does not conform to liability for state taxes. Moreover, since federal tax collection statistics combine the individual income tax with the OASI employment taxes, the amount of federal income tax collections had to be estimated. This was done by applying the national ratio of income tax collections to combined income and payroll tax collections for the particular year to the combined collections reported for each state. As a result, federal collections in the less industrialized states are probably somewhat understated.[12]

---

[12] However, a state-by-state comparison of state tax collections with federal tax liabilities reported on unaudited income tax returns (as reported in *Statistics of Income*) does not provide too much support for this generalization.

TABLE 3

Individual Income Tax: State Collections as Percentage of
Federal Collections, 1953–58

STATE	FISCAL YEARS ENDING IN						1953–1958
	1953	1954	1955	1956	1957	1958	
Alabama[a]	5.2%	4.9	5.6	7.7[c]	8.0	7.8	6.7
Arizona[a]	6.6	7.6	7.9	10.1	9.0	6.5	7.9
Arkansas	4.0	4.1	4.7	4.8	4.7	6.3	4.8
California	3.3	3.4	4.0	4.1	4.1	4.3	3.9
Colorado	3.6	3.8	4.7[c]	4.6	4.9	4.9	4.5
Delaware	1.5	5.3[c]	6.1	6.7	6.2	9.0	5.8
Georgia	4.2	4.0	4.9	6.3	6.6	6.7	5.5
Idaho	9.3	7.8	8.5	12.9[c]	12.1	13.8	10.9
Iowa	6.0	6.7	7.2	7.9	8.5	8.3	7.5
Kansas	4.4	4.6	5.4	5.0	4.9	5.4	4.9
Kentucky	8.4	8.6	14.8[c]	11.8	16.3	17.1	13.0
Louisiana[a]	4.6	4.2	4.8	5.6	5.9	5.8	5.2
Maryland[b]	2.8	3.3	3.8	7.1[c]	7.3	7.8	5.3
Massachusetts	7.9	7.5	8.5	10.7	10.2	10.0	9.2
Minnesota	10.0	10.5	11.8	11.9	11.5	12.7	11.4
Mississippi	6.2	6.0	4.6	4.6	5.6	5.9	5.5
Missouri[a]	1.9	2.0	2.3	2.7	2.8	3.1	2.5
Montana	6.3	6.6	7.2	9.7[c]	8.9	11.0	8.4
New Hampshire[d]	1.8	1.8	2.0	1.9	1.8	1.8	1.8
New Mexico[a]	3.6	3.9	4.3	4.8	4.8	4.9	4.4
New York	6.8	6.9	7.4	6.1	8.1	8.7	7.7
North Carolina	11.1	11.6	12.5	12.9	13.2	13.8	12.6
North Dakota	6.9	5.8	6.2	6.0	6.1	6.1	6.2
Oklahoma	3.2	3.4	3.8	4.2	4.0	4.2	3.8
Oregon	15.3	15.5	16.5	23.5[e]	29.4	28.7[e]	21.7
South Carolina	9.0	9.4	9.7	10.9	10.8	11.2	10.2
Tennessee[d]	1.2	1.2	1.3	1.3	1.3	1.4	1.3
Utah	6.4	6.9	8.0	9.1	9.7	11.1	8.7
Vermont	15.0	14.1	15.3	20.9	20.6	21.6	18.1
Virginia	9.3	10.8	12.1	11.4	24.3[f]	14.0	14.0
Wisconsin	11.4	12.5	13.8	16.0	16.7	17.4	14.8
Total (31 states)	5.7	6.0	6.6	7.6	8.0	8.1	7.1
Total (U.S.)	3.2	3.3	3.7	4.2	4.3	4.5	3.9

Caution: These data are subject to important limitations and the reader is urged to consider the qualifications noted in the accompanying text in interpreting them.

SOURCE: Federal collections from Annual *Report*(s) *of the Commissioner of Internal Revenue.* State collections from Bureau of the Census, *State Tax Collections.*

[a] Since reported state income tax collections include both the individual and corporate tax, the computation is based on state and federal collections from both taxes.

[b] Includes District of Columbia.

[c] Includes more than one year's liabilities incident to the introduction of withholding.

[d] The state tax is limited to interest and dividends.

[e] Reflects increases in the rate of withholding.

[f] Includes more than one year's liabilities resulting from advancement of tax due dates.

146

TABLE 4

Individual Income Tax: State Collections as a Percentage of
Federal Collections, 1953 and 1958

		FREQUENCY DISTRIBUTION					
Under 5 Per Cent		5 Per Cent to 10 Per Cent		10 Per Cent to 15 Per Cent		15 Per Cent and Over	
			1953				
Arkansas	4.0	Alabama[a]	5.2	Minnesota	10.0	Oregon	15.3
California	3.3	Arizona[a]	6.6	North Carolina	11.1	Vermont	15.0
Colorado	3.6	Idaho	9.3	Wisconsin	11.4		
Delaware	1.5	Iowa	6.0				
Georgia	4.2	Kentucky	8.4				
Kansas	4.4	Massachusetts	7.9				
Louisiana[a]	4.6	Mississippi	6.2				
Maryland[b]	3.7	Montana	6.3				
Missouri[a]	1.9	New York	6.8				
New Hampshire	1.8	North Dakota	6.9				
New Mexico[a]	3.6	South Carolina	9.0				
Oklahoma	3.2	Utah	6.4				
Tennessee	1.2	Virginia	9.3				
13		13		3		2	
			1958				
California	4.3	Alabama[a]	7.8	Idaho	13.8	Kentucky	17.1
Colorado	4.9	Arizona[a]	6.5	Massachusetts	10.0	Oregon	28.7
Missouri[a]	3.1	Arkansas	6.3	Minnesota	12.7	Vermont	21.6
New Hampshire	1.8	Delaware	9.0	Montana	11.0	Virginia	14.0
New Mexico[a]	4.9	Georgia	6.7	North Carolina	13.8	Wisconsin	17.4
Oklahoma	4.2	Iowa	8.3	South Carolina	11.2		
Tennessee	1.4	Kansas	5.4	Utah	11.1		
		Louisiana[a]	5.8				
		Maryland[b]	7.8				
		Mississippi	5.9				
		New York	8.7				
		North Dakota	6.1				
7		12		7		5	

Caution: These data are subject to important limitations and the reader is urged to consider the qualifications noted in the accompanying text in interpreting them.

SOURCE: Federal collections from Annual *Report*(s) *of the Commissioner of Internal Revenue.* State collections from Bureau of the Census, *State Tax Collections.*

[a] Since state income tax collections include both the individual and corporate tax, the computation is based on state and federal collections from both taxes.

[b] Includes District of Columbia.

Despite these limitations, the computed percentage relationships between state and federal income tax collections demonstrate a striking variation in the relative weight of state income taxes, explained largely by differences in tax rates and personal exemptions. Two-thirds of the states with relatively low state collections allow the federal tax as a deduction for state income tax purposes. This, however, is only a partial explanation of the variation in the

147

productivity of state income taxes since about the same proportion of relatively high-yield state taxes also allow this deduction.

These statistics illuminate the divergence in state attitudes toward the personal income tax as a source of state revenue. Seventeen states choose not to use the income tax and have held to this view even in the last twenty years, when the pressure for revenue was great; two choose to tax only income from intangibles; the remaining 29 states employ broadly based taxes but employ them with varying degrees of intensity, ranging from about 3 per cent of federal tax liabilities in Missouri to over 25 per cent in Oregon. (The yield of the New Hampshire and Tennessee taxes restricted to income from intangibles is less than 2 per cent of federal collections.)

This divergence in state attitudes toward income taxation, quite apart from the States' desire to preserve freedom of action with respect to the structure of their respective income taxes, makes impracticable some frequently proposed devices for federal-state income tax coordination.

It has been suggested, for example, that the federal government share a part of its individual income tax revenue with the states in return for the states discontinuing their own income taxes. Such an arrangement would necessarily have to be voluntary on the part of all the 31 states since, in the absence of a constitutional amendment, it could not be forced upon states and would probably be workable only if elected by all the states. It follows that the sharing would have to be on a scale adequate to reimburse the state which currently is making the most intensive use of this tax. Oregon, for example, with individual income tax collections approximating one-quarter of federal collections could not be expected voluntarily to surrender its own tax for substantially less than a corresponding proportion of federal income tax collections reported from that state. Since practical political considerations would probably prescribe uniform sharing with all the states,[13] it would require (at current federal collection levels) an additional federal tax levy of the general magnitude of $10 billion to finance this coordination device. In other words, the federal government would have to distribute to the states, on the average, about $6 for every $1 of their own tax they abandoned. This is the general magnitude of the federal cost of a sharing basis adequate to

[13] Uniform treatment of all the states is assumed to be one of the essential differences between a shared tax and a grant-in-aid. In an exchange of state income taxes for a federal grant, it would, of course, be possible to relate the amount of the grants to the income tax revenues abandoned by the individual states.

compensate fully every state for giving up its own individual income tax. Inevitably most states would receive windfalls, relatively the largest accruing to those which now impose no income taxes or employ them at relatively very low effective tax rates. The largest windfalls would accrue to the older industrial states without individual income taxes.

Another coordination device occasionally suggested for possible use in the individual income tax area is the tax supplement. It involves the states imposing their taxes on the federal income tax base and the federal government collecting them at the time it collects its own tax. Each state would be free to determine its own tax rate, expressed preferably as a percentage of the federal tax liability. The tax supplement technique has had some acceptance in the joint collection of state and local sales taxes, pioneered by Mississippi in 1950 and now in widespread use in California and Illinois, and to a lesser degree, in New Mexico. The supplement differs from the use of an identical tax base by two independent taxing jurisdictions discussed below only in that the tax supplement involves one jurisdiction collecting the taxes of both.

The applicability of the tax supplement to income taxation presents difficulties quite apart from the reluctance of the states to surrender the privilege of administering their own taxes. The federal taxpayer can file his tax return and pay his taxes either at his place of residence or his place of business. Whatever place he chooses, his tax return must cover all his income wherever derived—in the state of filing, in any of the other 48 states or in a foreign country. States generally follow a similar rule; their residents are taxable on all their income, from whatever geographic source. In the case of nonresidents, however, states limit their jurisdiction to income originating within their own borders. Use of the tax supplement for collecting state income taxes from nonresidents would pose problems, because federal administrative agencies would be reluctant to undertake the determinations necessary to differentiate between income derived within and without a state on the basis of varying state rules. For this reason the tax supplement device would probably be practicable only if the states abandoned the taxation of nonresidents.[14]

The tax supplement is closely akin to the utilization of similar tax bases and methods of tax computation by two or more independent

[14] Assuming univeral state income taxation, this would leave the total income subject to state taxation unchanged, but would alter its distribution among the states.

taxing jurisdictions. An advanced form of this coordination has been proposed in New York. It contemplates the state utilizing the federal provisions governing the definition of taxable income, subject only to such adjustments as the state legislature prescribes. New York's corporation franchise tax has long been geared to the federal tax base.[15]

Use of the federal tax base for state tax purposes can take several forms depending upon the degree of coordination and simplification desired. In its most complete form, the state tax is simply expressed as a percentage of the federal liability. The outstanding example is the territorial income tax of Alaska imposed at 14 per cent of federal tax liability. In this way Federal Revenue Code revisions affecting tax liability were automatically applicable for purposes of the Alaskan tax. Questions of constitutionality may be involved since it can be interpreted as a delegation of state legislative powers to the Congress. New Mexico avoided the constitutional question by making the use of this device optional. Between 1953 and 1955 it gave its taxpayers (with adjusted gross incomes under $10,000) a choice between 4 per cent of Federal tax liability and liability computed under New Mexico's own tax law.

A second possibility is for the state to utilize the federal definition of taxable net income under current law, to which its own independently determined tax rates apply. Alternatively, the state may employ the federal definition of taxable income as of a certain date, disregarding subsequent changes in the Federal Code.

State use of federal definitions of taxable income is not untried. Between 1953 and 1955 Utah's taxpayers with adjusted gross income under $5,000 were permitted to compute their taxes either on the basis of the Utah statute or on the basis of federal taxable income reduced by the amount of federal income tax paid. Currently, Vermont taxpayers have the option to employ definitions under the Federal Revenue Code in effect on April 26, 1957. Kentucky permits its taxpayers to compute their tax on the basis of the Federal Code in effect on January 1, 1956. Iowa bases its tax on the 1954 Code as enacted (disregarding subsequent amendments). Specifically it defines net income for Iowa state purposes as adjusted gross income under the 1954 Code (plus interest from municipal bonds and Iowa income taxes deducted on the federal tax return, and minus interest and dividends from federal securities).

[15] Peter Miller, "Proposal for a Federally Based New York Personal Income Tax," *Tax Law Review*, January 1958, pp. 183–209.

Adoption of federal definitions of the tax base for purposes of the states' taxes would simplify the preparation of tax returns and state enforcement of the tax laws. Presumably it would involve some loss of revenue to the states since their own statutes do not generally provide as many exceptions to the general rule (for the benefit of selected groups of taxpayers) as does the Federal Code. This revenue loss could possibly be more than offset, however, by the increased revenue the states could derive by capitalizing on the results of the more effective federal tax enforcement.

In the interest of completeness, mention should be made of the widespread and growing practice of state legislatures to adopt Federal Code provisions pertaining to one or more details in the computation of tax liability for purposes of their own taxes. Capital gains and losses and loss carryover provisions are examples.

In terms of national aggregates and in relation to federal tax magnitudes, state income taxes would appear to have substantial potential for expansion. The deductibility of state taxes for federal income tax purposes contributes to this potential, since it shifts a part of the increased state tax burdens from the taxpayer to the federal government. In effect, the federal treasury absorbs a share of the burden of any increase in the state tax (of a taxpayer who itemizes deductions) corresponding to the marginal federal tax rate applicable to the taxpayer in the absence of the increased deduction. An extreme example of this approach was rejected by the California electorate in November 1958.[16] The threat of driving residents and their activities to other low income tax states effectively inhibits movement in this direction, although experience appears to lend little credence to the argument that variations in tax rates significantly influence decisions concerning the location of industries.

C. CORPORATION INCOME TAX

The corporate income tax generally occupies a prominent place in the list of overlapping taxes but has not figured prominently among coordination proposals. It has on occasions been singled out for such proposed arrangements as revenue sharing but few appear to regard it a pressing problem.

Corporate net income is now taxed in 34 states and the District of

---

[16] Proposed constitutional amendment (Proposition 17) which would have reduced the sales tax and the lower range income tax rates and substantially increased tax rates in the higher income ranges.

TABLE 5
State Corporation Income Tax Rates

1. FLAT RATE TAXES

Under 2 Per Cent	2 Per Cent	3 Per Cent	4 Per Cent	5 Per Cent	6 Per Cent	Other
New Jersey, 1.75%	Iowa	Alabama	California	Colorado	North Carolina	Idaho, 8%
	Missouri	Kansas, 3.75%	Georgia	Delaware	Oregon	Minnesota, 7.3%
	New Mexico	Connecticut, 3.75%	Louisiana	District of	Pennsylvania	
		Tennessee, 3.75%	Oklahoma	Columbia	Massachusetts,	
			Utah	Maryland	6.765%	
				Montana		
				South Carolina		
				Vermont		
				Virginia		
				New York, 5.5%		
				Rhode Island, 5.5%		

2. GRADUATED RATES

State	Rates	Number of Brackets	Maximum Rate Applies Over
Arizona	1%–5%	7	$ 6,000
Arkansas	1%–5%	5	25,000
Kentucky	5%–7%	2	25,000
Mississippi	2%–6%	5	25,000
North Dakota	3%–6%	4	15,000
Wisconsin	2%–7%	7	6,000

Columbia and produces about $1 billion annually for the states. This represents about 6.6 per cent of state tax collections and less than 4 per cent of combined state and local tax collections. It is equivalent to about two-thirds of the revenues the states derive from individual income taxes.

Most (31) of the state corporate income taxes predate World War II; nearly half of them (15) came into existence during the depressed 1930's; only 2 states (Delaware and New Jersey) joined the ranks during the present decade, both in 1958. Recent years have witnessed, however, extensive legislative activity in states with established corporate income taxes to increase revenues, frequently through rate increases.

The rate structure of the states' corporate taxes are summarized in Table 5 above. Most states (28) and the District of Columbia employ flat rates; six impose graduated rates. The flat-rate state taxes range from 1.75 per cent in New Jersey and 2 per cent in Iowa, Missouri, and New Mexico, to 8 per cent in Idaho. Five per cent rates are most frequent. Of the six graduated rate structures, Kentucky uses only two brackets and differentiates, as the federal government, at $25,000 of net income. Arkansas and Mississippi employ five brackets in their rate structure, the maximum rate applying to the excess over $25,000. Arizona and Wisconsin employ seven brackets and North Dakota four (Table 5).

In relation to the federal tax, the weight of the overlapping state taxes is moderate. In the 32 states which taxed corporate income during the six years, 1953–58, state revenues averaged about 6.9 per cent of federal corporate income tax collections and in the aggregate now equal about 2 1/2 percentage points of the federal tax rate. The net cost of state taxes to corporations, allowing for the deductibility of state taxes for federal tax purposes, was of the general magnitude of about 1 1/2 percentage points of the federal tax rate. This is one measure of the extent to which state corporate income taxes overlap the federal tax (Table 6).

On the basis of federal tax returns filed in 1955–56, the states with corporate income taxes accounted for 66 per cent of all corporations filing federal income tax returns, for 61 per cent of these corporations' reported net income and for 60 per cent of their federal income tax liability. The two new state taxes enacted in 1958 raise these respective percentages by about five points. About 28 per cent of corporations with net income, accounting for one-third of all corporate net income and federal tax liability, have their main offices in one of the fourteen states without a corporate net income tax. Some of these corporations, however, pay income taxes in one or more additional states since they derive income from them.

The obstacles to replacing the 34 state corporation income taxes with a share of the federal government's collections from this source are akin to those discussed above with reference to the individual income tax, but are here found in a more exaggerated form. They

TABLE 6

Federal and State Corporation Income Tax
Collections, Fiscal Years 1953–58
(in millions)

| | | STATE AND LOCAL | |
YEAR	FEDERAL	*Amount*	*Percentage of Federal*
1953	$21,238	$817	3.85
1954	21,101	778	3.69
1955	17,861	744	4.17
1956	20,880	890	4.26
1957	21,167	984	4.65
1958	20,074	981	4.89

SOURCE: Bureau of the Census, *Summary of Government Finances*. The 1956–58 totals exclude local collections which averaged $7 million in the earlier years.

stem from the uneven use the states make of this tax. Fourteen do not tax corporate net income. The other 34 states have relatively similar tax structures and employ tax rates of the same general magnitude (largely concentrated within the 4 per cent to 6 per cent rate range) but the revenue produced varies widely both in relation to the states' total tax revenues and more particularly in relation to federal revenues. In 1958 the corporate income tax supplied 17.2 per cent of New York's but only 1.3 per cent of Iowa's tax collections.

The evaluation of the relative weight of the states' corporate income taxes in terms of the federal tax presents even more difficulties than in the individual income tax area (Tables 7 and 8). The tabulation of federal collections by states is based on federal returns filed and taxes collected. Corporations typically file a single federal tax return at their headquarters or principal place of business, although a substantial number of them derive income in more than one state. Because their main offices are generally in urban industrial areas,

TABLE 7

Corporation Income Tax: State Collections as a Percentage of Federal
Collections, Fiscal Years 1953–58

STATE	FISCAL YEARS						
	1953	*1954*	*1955*	*1956*	*1957*	*1958*	*1953–58*
Alabamaa	5.5	5.3	6.0	7.9	8.3	7.8	6.9
Arizonaa	6.6	7.6	7.9	10.1	9.0	6.5	7.9
Arkansas	22.5	23.7	22.8	24.5	31.4	31.6	25.8
California	10.3	10.4	12.4	12.6	13.1	14.6	12.2
Colorado	4.2	4.7	5.3	4.8	3.4	8.9	5.2
Connecticut	5.2	6.0	7.5	8.6	8.9	9.3	7.5
Georgia	7.5	7.2	7.2	10.7	11.5	10.5	9.2
Idaho	14.0	14.2	11.1	16.2	20.4	18.6	15.5
Iowa	1.6	1.9	1.8	2.3	2.9	2.4	2.2
Kansas	2.1	2.7	3.0	3.4	3.8	5.2	3.3
Kentucky	6.3	5.5	7.9	7.7	10.5	11.4	8.2
Louisianaa	4.6	4.2	4.8	5.6	5.9	5.8	5.2
Marylandb	8.5	7.2	8.9	11.5	10.3	11.8	9.6
Massachusettsc	4.5	5.1	5.3	5.4	5.8	6.2	5.4
Minnesota	5.4	4.7	5.8	6.5	6.6	8.3	6.2
Mississippi	33.9	45.4	49.2	41.1	46.5	48.0	43.8
Missouria	1.9	2.0	2.3	2.7	2.8	3.1	2.5
Montana	6.9	8.6	7.1	12.8	10.2	10.3	9.4
New Mexicoa	3.6	3.9	4.3	4.8	4.8	4.9	4.4
New York	4.4	4.0	4.5	4.2	4.6	4.9	4.4
North Carolina	14.3	14.8	16.1	16.3	16.1	16.8	15.8
North Dakota	11.6	12.3	12.3	15.2	14.7	13.1	13.2
Oklahoma	4.6	4.7	5.2	5.4	5.6	6.1	5.3
Oregon	18.7	19.0	19.2	17.0	22.8	35.3	21.5
Pennsylvania	9.4	7.7	8.4	9.3	11.5	10.1	9.4
Rhode Island	8.7	9.0	9.8	11.3	10.7	11.7	10.1
South Carolina	18.5	19.3	17.8	24.2	24.5	23.1	21.2
Tennessee	12.4	13.6	13.6	11.2	14.3	14.9	13.3
Utah	8.3	11.4	7.0	9.2	19.9	13.8	11.8
Vermont	11.2	9.2	11.0	14.7	15.9	18.1	12.7
Virginia	9.2	11.5	12.4	13.0	11.7	11.5	11.5
Wisconsin	10.4	11.8	12.7	12.9	13.2	13.5	12.3
Total 32 States	6.3	6.0	6.7	7.1	7.6	7.9	6.9
Total (U.S.)	3.9	3.8	4.2	4.4	4.9	5.1	4.4

Caution: These data are subject to important limitations and the reader is urged to consider the qualifications noted in the accompanying text in interpreting them.

SOURCE: Federal collections from Annual *Report*(s) *of the Commissioner of Internal Revenue*. State collections from Bureau of the Census, *State Tax Collections*.

a Since the state income tax collections include both the individual and the corporate tax, the computation is based on combined federal and state collections from both taxes.

b Includes District of Columbia.

c State collections do not include corporation excise taxes and surtaxes measured in part by net income and in part by corporate excess, which are classified as licenses.

TABLE 8

Corporation Income Tax: State Collections as a Percentage of
Federal Collections, Fiscal Years, 1953–58

FREQUENCY DISTRIBUTION							
Under 5 Per Cent		*5 Per Cent to 10 Per Cent*		*10 Per Cent to 15 Per Cent*		*15 Per Cent and Over*	
Iowa	2.2	Alabama[a]	6.9	California	12.2	Arkansas	25.8
Kansas	3.3	Arizona[a]	7.9	North Dakota	13.2	Idaho	15.5
Missouri[a]	2.5	Colorado	5.2	Rhode Island	10.1	Mississippi	43.8
New Mexico[a]	4.4	Connecticut	7.5	Tennessee	13.3	North Carolina	15.8
New York	4.4	Georgia	9.2	Utah	11.8	Oregon	21.5
		Kentucky	8.2	Vermont	12.7	South Carolina	21.2
		Louisiana[a]	5.2	Virginia	11.5		
		Maryland[c]	9.6	Wisconsin	12.3		
		Massachusetts[b]	5.4				
		Minnesota	6.2				
		Montana	9.4				
		Oklahoma	5.3				
		Pennsylvania	9.4				
Number of states	5		13		8		6

Caution: These data are subject to important limitations and the reader is urged to consider the qualifications noted in the accompanying text in interpreting them.

SOURCE: Federal collections from Annual *Report*(s) *of the Commissioner of Internal Revenue.* State collections from Bureau of the Census, *State Tax Collections.*

[a] Since state income tax collections include both the individual and the corporate tax, the computation is based on federal and state collections from both taxes.

[b] State collections do not include corporation excise taxes and surtaxes measured in part by net income and in part by corporate excess, which are classified as licenses.

[c] Includes District of Columbia.

federal tax collection statistics understate the contribution of the nonindustrial and noncommercial states.

Since the states invariably tax all income derived within their borders, the less industrialized jurisdictions generally derive a large share of their corporate tax revenue from nonresident corporations which pay their federal taxes in another state. In consequence, the ratio of state to federal collections generally exaggerates the relative weight of state taxes in rural sections, and undervalues it in industrialized states. As Table 7 indicates, the ratio of state to federal collections (1958) is highest in Mississippi (48 per cent) where the corporate tax structure is not materially different from that of the other states. It will be noted that its ratio of state to federal collections has been consistently high over the years. This suggests that a large share of Mississippi's tax revenue is attributable to corporations which file their federal returns outside the state. This explanation may apply also to Arkansas. In Oregon, on the other hand, the high percentage (35.3 per cent) may in part be explained by high rates.

156

While the ratio of state to federal corporation income tax collections is not a meaningful measure of the absolute weight of a state's tax, it is indicative of the relative weight of the tax in comparable states. The existence of wide interstate variations is compelling with regard to the proposal that the states exchange their taxes for a share of federal corporate income tax revenues. During 1953–58, it would have required about 40 per cent of federal collections in Mississippi to compensate that state for giving up its own corporate tax. A sharing on this scale with all of the states would have produced large windfalls for all other states and entailed a vast cost to the federal treasury.

A noteworthy feature of federal-state corporate tax relations is the growing reliance of the states on the tax base computed for federal income tax purposes. Significantly, all three state taxes enacted since World War II (Rhode Island in 1947, Delaware and New Jersey in 1958) base their own tax on income computed for federal tax purposes. This is the practice in seven other states as well. The adjustments made in the federal tax base are relatively few. Each of the states requires that state income taxes excluded from the federal base be added back and that interest on federal obligations included for federal purposes be subtracted. Only two of the ten states (Iowa and Kentucky) which employ the federal tax base allow the federal income tax as a deduction. In fifteen of the remaining twenty-four states the deductibility of the federal income tax reduces the base of the state corporate income tax by nearly half. The states' reliance on federal definitions of taxable income, coupled with some standardization of rules for allocating multistate income among the participating states, has appreciably eased the compliance burdens of corporate taxpayers.[17]

D. ESTATE AND INHERITANCE TAXES[18]

A major performer on the stage of intergovernmental tax relations is the tax on the transfer of property at death. The taxation of such property transfers either to the estate or to the heirs of the decedent has a long history, as do the efforts to bring order into federal-state relationships in this tax area.

---

[17] Recent developments in the allocation of multistate income among the states merit more than passing reference but fall outside the scope of a paper concerned with federal-state relations.

[18] The gift tax, an integral part of the federal property transfer tax system, is not treated here. Twelve states now have gift taxes which collectively produced less than $7 million in 1958.

Inheritance and estate taxes are typically state, as distinguished from local levies, although a number of states share some of these revenues with local governments. Over the years, largely as a result of rising property values, the annual yield of this state tax source has risen. Collections aggregated $344 million in 1958 and $340 million in 1957, compared with $168 million in 1950 and $244 million in 1955. These totals include state imposed taxes retained by local jurisdictions in ten states (about $10 million in 1957).

In most of the states the institution of a tax on transfers of property at death was well established when, in 1916, the Congress enacted what proved to be a permanent estate tax. Similar impositions (1798 to 1802; 1861 to 1870; 1898 to 1902) associated with earlier national crises were retained only temporarily.

Objections to the entry of the federal government into a tax area pre-empted by the states and a simultaneous concern for the survival of state taxes in the face of overt interstate tax competition for wealthy residents stimulated the invention in 1924 of the credit against the federal estate tax for inheritance and estate taxes paid to the states. At first the credit was limited to 25 per cent of federal tax liability but in 1926 was raised to 80 per cent. This enabled the states, through appropriate legislation, to have in effect death taxes as high as 80 per cent of federal tax liability without adding to the net tax burden of their taxpayers. Within this limit state taxes merely pre-empted revenues which otherwise would be payable to the federal government. The credit provision was interpreted by many as congressional consent to share with the states the revenue yield of death taxes approximately in the ratio of 20 per cent federal and 80 per cent state.

Subsequent federal tax developments altered this relationship. In successive efforts to increase federal revenues the estate tax exemption was reduced (1932, 1935, 1942) and tax rates increased (1932, 1934, 1935, 1941), while the amount of credit remained geared to liabilities under the 1926 Act. This reduced the ratio of the state credit to federal tax liability in proportion to the increase in the latter.[19] Today the relative importance of the credit is least in the brackets where the post-1926 increases in tax liability were greatest; it is relatively largest where the increase in federal tax has been relatively

---

[19] The adoption by the federal government of the marital deduction in 1948 left the relationship of the maximum credit to federal tax liability unchanged, but reduced its dollar value by reducing the size of the taxable estate which determines the size of the credit.

TABLE 9

Credit for State Death Taxes as a Percentage of Federal Estate Tax
Liability, Returns Filed During 1957
(amounts and size classes in thousands)

Net Estate before Specific Exemption Classes	Credit for State Taxes	Federal Estate Tax Liability before State Credit[a]	Credit as Percentage of Federal Liability
Taxable Returns:			
60–80	–	4,296	–
80–100	–	16,890	–
100–150	439	68,406	0.6
150–200	2,428	71,393	3.4
200–300	5,815	120,570	4.8
300–400	5,891	88,452	6.7
400–500	5,633	72,617	7.8
500–600	5,056	58,906	8.6
600–700	4,543	49,514	9.2
700–800	3,596	36,815	9.8
800–900	4,002	38,902	10.3
900–1,000	3,115	28,621	10.9
1,000–2,000	25,377	200,395	12.7
2,000–3,000	13,521	94,233	14.3
3,000–4,000	7,758	50,809	15.3
4,000–5,000	7,542	49,147	15.3
5,000–7,000	10,325	62,196	16.6
7,000–10,000	7,153	37,620	19.0
10,000–20,000	11,932	62,811	19.0
20,000 or more	22,643	110,824	20.4
Total taxable returns	146,769	1,323,417	11.1

SOURCE: Internal Revenue Service, *Statistics of Income, 1956.*
a Before state but after other tax credits.

smallest. The state credit varies from zero on net estates below $100,000 and from less than 1 per cent of gross federal tax liability on net estates between $100,000 and $150,000, to 20 per cent on net estates above $20 million (Table 9).

In fiscal year 1957, the credit allowed for death taxes paid to states aggregated about $147 million, or approximately 11 per cent of federal estate tax liability (before the state credits). An approximately 10 per cent relationship between the credit for state taxes and federal tax liability has prevailed for more than a dozen years, a period of stability in federal estate tax rates. For several years preceding 1932, the credit approximated 75 per cent of federal tax liability (Table 10).

As a result of the dissatisfaction of the states with their reduced share of this revenue, the terms of federal-state relations in the death

TABLE 10

Federal Estate Tax Liability and State Credit, for Returns
Filed During 1929–57
(dollar amounts in thousands)

| | | STATE DEATH TAX CREDIT | |
YEAR	FEDERAL ESTATE TAX LIABILITY BEFORE STATE DEATH TAX CREDIT[a]	*Amount*	*Percentage of Federal Tax Liability before Credit*
1929	$165,414	$122,110	73.8
1930	152,391	113,388	74.4
1931	182,202	137,663	75.6
1932	84,006	61,642	73.4
1933	87,725	28,295	32.3
1934	129,053	33,769	26.2
1935	197,664	43,864	22.2
1936	239,486	44,218	18.5
1937	364,018	58,252	16.0
1938	374,230	59,842	16.0
1939	329,202	53,111	16.1
1940	295,654	45,337	15.3
1941	345,342	53,636	15.5
1942	353,933	45,626	12.9
1943	398,120	35,966	9.0
1944	450,888	46,285	10.3
1945	595,562	64,517	10.8
1946	n.a.	n.a.	n.a.
1947	691,817	69,850	10.1
1948	797,432	82,725	10.4
1949	633,250	65,831	10.4
1950	532,459	48,940	9.2
1951	641,935	64,535	10.1
1952	n.a.	n.a.	n.a.
1953	n.a.	n.a.	n.a.
1954	864,346	85,842	9.9
1955	864,591	86,249	10.0
1956	n.a.	n.a.	n.a.
1957	1,323,479	146,769	11.1

SOURCE: Internal Revenue Service, *Statistics of Income.*
[a] After other credits.
n.a. = not available.

tax area have been reviewed with much frequency, if not regularity. Resc utions on the subject have become a standard feature of gath ings of state officials. The inheritance-estate taxes have become a symɔol of the need for federal-state tax coordination entirely out of proportion to the contribution—less than 2 per cent—they make to the revenues of all governments in the United States.

In fiscal year 1957 about 40 per cent of the $340 million collected by state and local governments from inheritance and estate taxes was offset as a credit against federal tax; the remaining 60 per cent did not qualify for the credit. These are national averages and submerge wide interstate differences. In the five states where the state tax is limited to and determined by the maximum credit allowed under present federal law, about 100 per cent of the state tax qualifies by definition for the credit. In the remaining states this percentage falls below 100 per cent, depending upon the degree to which the state-imposed tax exceeds the allowable credit. In some states, only about a fourth (possibly even less) of the state tax appears to be offset by a credit against the federal tax. In these cases state-imposed taxes are, on the average, about four times as large as the maximum credit allowed under federal law.

To increase their revenues from this source, states have lowered exemptions, imposed taxes on small estates exempt from federal tax or ineligible for a credit, and raised their tax rates in excess of the maximum credit. The resulting structure is characterized by much diversity. Several types of death taxes are in use. The simplest of these are the five estate taxes (Alabama, Arizona, Arkansas, Florida, and Georgia) which correspond precisely to 80 per cent of tax liability under the 1926 federal law. Two other states (Mississippi and New York) also have estate taxes which are patterned on the 1926 federal law but depart from it in significant detail. Mississippi retains tax rates corresponding to 80 per cent of the 1926 federal rates, but uses a $60,000 (in lieu of a $100,000) exemption. It imposes also a temporary surtax equal to 14 per cent of liability under its permanent tax. New York's rates are 25 per cent in excess of the allowable credit. Its exemption varies with the relationship of the heirs to the decedent and is deductible from the first taxable bracket. Five other states (North Dakota, Oklahoma, Oregon, Rhode Island, and Utah) also have estate taxes but their rate and exemption structures bear no resemblance to federal law (Table 11).

Three-fourths of the states (37) employ inheritance taxes with diverse rates and exemptions, but all except two of these (Oregon and West Virginia) also have "pick-up" estate taxes which absorb any part of the allowable credit left unused by the inheritance tax. Oregon supplements its inheritance tax with an independent estate

TABLE 11
Types of State Death Taxes

State	Inheritance Tax	Estate Tax Based on Federal Levy (1926)	Independent Estate Tax	Differential Estate Tax
Alabama		X		
Arizona		X		X
Arkansas		X		
California	X			X
Colorado	X			X
Connecticut	X			X
Delaware	X			X
Dist. of Col.	X			X
Florida		X		
Georgia		X		
Idaho	X			X
Illinois	X			X
Indiana	X			X
Iowa	X			X
Kansas	X			X
Kentucky	X			X
Louisiana	X			X
Maine	X			X
Maryland	X			X
Massachusetts	X			X
Michigan	X			X
Minnesota	X			X
Mississippi		X		
Missouri	X			X
Montana	X			X
Nebraska	X			X
Nevada	–	–	–	–
New Hampshire	X			X
New Jersey	X			X
New Mexico	X			X
New York		X		X
North Carolina	X			X
North Dakota			X	
Ohio	X			X
Oklahoma			X	X
Oregon	X		X	
Pennsylvania	X			X
Rhode Island	X		X	X
South Carolina	X			X
South Dakota	X			
Tennessee	X			X
Texas	X			X
Utah			X	
Vermont	X			X
Virginia	X			X
Washington	X			X
West Virginia	X			
Wisconsin	X			X
Wyoming	X			X
Total	38	7	5	38

tax and West Virginia's inheritance tax rates are so high that tax liability in almost all situations exceeds the maximum credit. There are important interstate variations also in the structural features of state death taxes, especially in deductions allowed in determining the net estate. A fourth of the states (13) for example, allow a marital deduction for property passing to the surviving spouse, and half allow the federal estate tax to be deducted in determining the amount of the taxable estate for state tax purposes.

Since the inheritance and estate tax affects relatively few tax-payers, it is a tax area which arouses relatively little public interest. Proposals for coordination and more particularly for increasing the states' share of revenues have emanated largely from state officials, scholars and tax practitioners. Some are concerned primarily with increasing the states' revenues; others with tax simplification for the benefit of taxpayers and tax administrators.

Coordination Proposals

The most frequent proposal for increasing the states' share of death tax revenues is to raise the credit allowed against federal tax liability for taxes paid to states. It is commonly supported by the argument that the Congress is obligated to honor the 1926 principle which earmarked approximately 80 per cent of this revenue for the states.

It is not generally understood that an increase in the credit would not automatically increase the revenues of the great majority of the states; that for many states it would be difficult to benefit from the higher credit and the net result would be federal tax reduction.

As noted above, state imposed death taxes generally exceed the maximum credit allowed against federal tax. In the five recent years for which data are available, the credit claimed on federal estate tax returns represented 34 per cent of state inheritance and estate tax collections. In other words, the average estate could claim only $1 of credit against federal tax for every $3 it paid in state taxes. This relationship, however, varies widely among the states (Table 12) reflecting interstate variations in tax burdens. It varies also between different size estates within any one state. It follows that an increase in the credit would, in the first instance, enable the estate to take a credit against federal tax for a larger share of taxes paid to the states than hitherto (even though the state tax remained unchanged). Net federal tax liability and federal revenues would be reduced but

TABLE 12

Credit for Inheritance and Estate Taxes Claimed on Federal Estate Tax
Returns as a Percentage of State Estate and Inheritance Tax Collections
for Five Fiscal Years, 1949–51 and 1954–55[a]

FREQUENCY DISTRIBUTION							
Under 25 Per Cent		*25 Per Cent to 50 Per Cent*		*50 Per Cent to 75 Per Cent*		*Over 75 Per Cent*	
Colorado	16.3	California	32.1	Alabama	64.4	Arkansas	80.4
Idaho	16.1	Connecticut	37.8	Arizona	70.7	Florida	86.9
Indiana	17.1	Delaware	31.6	Georgia	73.4	Nebraska	159.3
Iowa	7.0	Illinois	45.6	New York	56.4	South Carolina	81.8
Kansas	24.9	Louisiana	33.8	Ohio	69.8		
Kentucky	15.9	Maryland	30.3	Texas	58.4		
Maine	14.6	Massachusetts	27.0				
Minnesota	20.6	Michigan	29.1				
Montana	9.4	Mississippi	40.9				
New Hampshire	21.4	Missouri	36.2				
North Dakota	18.5	New Jersey	27.1				
Oklahoma	21.0	New Mexico	26.9				
Oregon	17.1	North Carolina	25.4				
Pennsylvania	22.1	Rhode Island	44.3				
South Dakota	13.8	Virginia	49.9				
Tennessee	20.7	Wyoming	30.3				
Utah	7.7						
Vermont	23.6						
Washington	10.7						
West Virginia	12.6						
Wisconsin	17.8						
21		16		6		4	

SOURCE: Credits claimed from Internal Revenue Service, *Statistics of Income*; State collections from Bureau of the Census, *State Tax Collections*.

[a] These percentages provide only an approximate indication of the share of state taxes claimed as credit on federal returns because they are based on unaudited federal returns. Audited returns would show a larger federal tax liability with a corresponding increase in the maximum limitation on the credit. On the other hand, however, these computations are based on state tax collections only (excluding local) and in ten states (notably in Nebraska, Ohio, Illinois, and North Dakota) a part of state taxes is retained by local jurisdictions and is not included in state revenues.

would not be offset by increased state liability. State tax liabilities and revenues would be increased only to the extent that the increased credit was accompanied by state tax increases. This poses difficulties except in the very few states whose present taxes are limited to the credit and include "pick-up" provisions which would operate automatically if the credit limitation were raised.

An increase in the federal credit for taxes paid to states could take several forms, depending upon the objective sought. It is possible, for example, to leave the credit tied to the 1926 federal rate and exemption structure and raise the 80 per cent limitation to 100 per cent or more of the federal tax liability calculated under that structure.

This could be accomplished by appropriate adjustment in the credit schedule which the Congress in 1954 converted into equivalents of the current federal estate tax rates (Section 2011). An increase in the credit limitation to 100 per cent of 1926 liabilities would, in each case, raise the credit by 25 per cent; an increase to 200 per cent of those liabilities would raise it by 150 per cent, etc. Such proportionate increases in the credit would perpetuate all current variations in the relationship of the credit to federal tax liability among estates of different size. In other words, it would continue to deny any credit to net estates under $100,000, and, in all other cases, would increase the credit in the same ratio. As a result, the relative importance of the credit to federal tax liability would continue to increase as the size of the estate increases. The handful of states whose present taxes are determined by and limited to the maximum credit, would automatically raise their own taxes to pick up the exact increase in the credit. All other states, whose taxes exceed the present credit, would be free to choose between passing all of the increased credit to the benefit of their taxpayers or adjusting their rate structure (possibly through a "pick-up" tax) with a view to retaining it for the benefit of state revenues. Because the details of state tax structures typically vary substantially from the structure of the federal estate tax, that objective could at best only be approximated, and would necessarily entail net tax reductions for some taxpayers and net tax increases for others.[20]

Another possibility is to leave the present credit unchanged and to supplement it with a second credit based on net federal tax liability under current law. The credit would in each instance be increased in proportion to federal tax liabilities. This not only would perpetuate the complexity inherent in the 1926 rate structure, but also would aggravate it by superimposing an additional, albeit relatively simple, credit computation. Since the difference between tax liabilities under the 1926 and the current federal tax structure is relatively largest at the lower end of the rate schedule, this would increase the credit for small estates relatively more than for large estates. States could appropriate the increased credit for the benefit of their tax collections by enacting an additional pick-up tax measured by an appropriate

[20] The credit is a function of federal tax liability and bears no uniform relationship to state tax liability. For this reason, it is not possible to adjust state tax rates so as to increase the tax liability of each estate by an amount exactly equal to the increase in the federal credit, unless each state enacted an additional pick-up tax measured (for each estate) by the excess of the new credit over the old.

percentage of net federal tax liabilities, with attendant further complexities.

A third alternative is to scrap the present credit entirely and replace it with one based on current federal tax liabilities. It would require a credit equal to 20 per cent of gross federal tax liability to double the revenue significance of the present credit. The relative increase in credit would be greatest for small estates and would decline gradually as the size of the estate increased. Since, however, federal tax liability varies both in relation to the 1926 credit and state tax burdens, some states would experience great difficulty in matching the increased federal credit with an increase in state liabilities. None could achieve it completely; only approach it approximately. This arrangement, however, would ease taxpayers' compliance and tax administration problems by displacing the present credit calculations which vary bracket by bracket, with one consisting of a constant percentage of federal tax liability.

Technically, it is possible also to vary a credit based on federal tax liability with the size of the taxable estate, or bracket by bracket. A proposal advanced years ago would have allowed a 100 per cent credit up to $100,000 of taxable estate and 20 per cent on the balance. Such variations would add to the complexity of the credit computation and, depending upon the extent of the differentiation, would affect the relative importance of the credit for different size estates.

A favorite proposal of some state officials is that the federal government surrender the estate tax field for the exclusive use of the states. They support it on the grounds that the transfer of property at death is a privilege controlled by state law, that states provide for the administration of estates and were first to develop estate taxes, and that they have a relatively greater need for revenue than the federal government. The opponents point out that private wealth is derived, for the most part, through interstate commerce fostered by national programs and policies, that a transfer tax limited to the state of domicile of the decedent or the situs of the property would discriminate against other states which contributed to the creation of wealth, and that State taxation alone would enable the wealthy industrial states to monopolize an unduly large share of the revenue. It is feared also that if the tax were reserved for the states, their revenue take would only be temporary because competitive tax reductions would soon be revived.

Advocates of tax simplification suggest the reverse of the above proposal: that the states surrender this tax area to the federal government in return for an appropriate share of federal collections. They point to the multistate origin of family fortunes. This suggestion, however, elicits little sympathy from those who regard this to be historically a state tax.

Since the states currently obtain about $350 million of revenue from death taxes and desire to increase it substantially, they could be expected to be willing to give them up only on terms entailing a sizable net revenue cost to the federal treasury. Present state death tax revenues correspond to about 25 per cent of federal estate tax liabilities before credits for state taxes. In other words, they exceed the credits allowed by about $200 million a year. However, substantially more than 25 per cent of federal liabilities would be required to compensate the states for the revenue they would forego by abandoning their own levies, if distributions among the states were based on state of origin of federal collections.

States typically obtain a large part of their revenue from small estates which are either entirely exempt from federal tax or are subject to relatively low rates. While theoretically the federal tax take from this group of estates could be increased to replace state taxes, practical administrative considerations would militate against such a course. Moreover, since federal taxes are necessarily uniform in all 48 states, the substitution of a federal tax for the several state taxes would significantly alter the tax burdens on small estates. In those states which now limit their death tax to the credit allowed under federal law, any increase in federal tax would represent an increased tax burden; in the states with relatively very heavy state taxes, the substitution of an increased federal tax would not prevent some tax reductions.

A significant change in burdens would be an inescapable consequence of substituting a uniform federal tax for diverse state taxes, irrespective of whether an effort were made to recoup part of the federal cost by increasing federal tax rates. This would prevail even if federal revenues were distributed among the states in proportion to the states' own collections, rather than shared on the basis of the origin of federal collections.

Still another possibility is to divide the death tax area among the states and the federal government, giving the states exclusive tax jurisdiction over small and medium sized estates and the federal government over large estates. What is a "large estate" would presumably be determined by the amount of the revenue it is desired to leave with the federal government. If, for example, the federal government exempted from estate taxation all net estates below $500,000 (but retained the present specific exemption for those above this level), net federal estate tax liabilities would be reduced by about $315 million (at 1955 estate tax levels). If, in return, the federal government were relieved of the need to grant credits for taxes paid to states on returns subject to federal tax (above $500,000, exempted from state taxes) net federal tax liabilities on those estates would be increased by $70 million, resulting in a net revenue loss of approximately $250 million. This is a measure of the initial cost to the federal treasury of a division at the $500,000 level (at 1955 estate tax levels); not necessarily the ultimate cost.[21]

Since present state taxes on large estates frequently exceed the maximum credit allowed under present law, the exemption of these estates from state taxes would result in a corresponding reduction in the tax burden borne by them. An upward adjustment in federal rates to offset such reductions would reduce the federal cost below the $250 million level. This, however, would involve a tax increase for estates in those few states where the state tax above the $500,000 net estate level does not exceed the present federal credit.

Under this kind of federal-state division, the states would be left with complete tax autonomy with respect to smaller estates, while the federal government would be left with exclusive jurisdiction over the taxation of large estates, which presumably are likely to have multistate origins and in that respect provide a more appropriate basis for federal than for state taxation. To the extent inheritance and estate tax considerations are of relatively secondary importance in the case of small estates, the states would be free to shape their tax policies without fear of interstate tax competition for wealthy residents.

Under this division, the number of taxable federal estate tax returns would be reduced by more than 90 per cent (from 30,000 to about 2,000 at 1956 estate tax levels). The administrative task of the states might be increased, since they would be deprived of such assistance as they now obtain from access to valuations and related data available in the Internal Revenue Service. In other respects, however,

---

[21] Since the number and size of large estates can vary widely from year to year, a similar calculation based on another year's returns would probably show a different result.

the states' administrative task would be eased. They would be freed of the specialized problems typically associated with large estates, such as the valuation of contingent interests, especially complex under inheritance taxes since it is not certain at the time the tax is determined to how many beneficiaries and to what class of beneficiaries these interests will pass. Taxpayers' and practitioners' burdens would be eased by the division of this tax area on the basis of the size of the estate, since each estate would be subject to either federal or state taxes, not to both.[22]

E. EXCISE TAXES

Since World War II, a widespread point of view has developed with respect to the handling of sales and excise taxes in the rearrangement of federal-state tax relations: that the federal government relinquish those suitable for state or local administration for exclusive use by these governments. State and local governments are agreed that the federal government should relinquish them. Local governments add the qualification that the states, too, should relinquish them; that excises so relinquished be reserved for exclusive local use. In two or three recent instances, the federal government has moved in the direction urged by the states but this has contributed little, if at all, to the solution of their problems.

The federal taxes most frequently selected for transfer to state/local governments are these:

TABLE 13

Federal Excises Proposed for Transfer to the States

Federal Excise Tax	Collections, f.y. 1958 (in millions)
Gasoline	$1,637
Cigarettes	1,668
Admissions	54
Local telephone service	371
Sales of electrical energy	a
Club dues and initiation fees	60
Coin operated devices	18
Bowling alleys, pool tables	3
Safety deposit box rentals	6
Total	3,817

SOURCE: *The Budget of the U.S. for Fiscal Year 1960,* Special Analysis B, pp. 933–9.
a Repealed in 1951 when it yielded about $100 million.

[22] *The Second Report* of the Joint Federal-State Action Committee, December 1958, pp. 32–44, contains estimates of the effect of alternative increases in the credit for state death taxes on federal revenues and the state-by-state distribution of credits.

It is argued in support of the transfer of excises to the states that the federal government can dispense with them because its needs can be met from income taxation, while state-local governments, precluded from intensive use of income taxes, necessarily rely heavily on consumer taxes. Local governments see in some excise taxes an opportunity to supplement local property taxes without encountering intercommunity competition. In motor fuel taxation, the states base their claim on historical priority in the field and on their responsibility for building and maintaining streets and highways.

Spokesmen for the federal government have on at least one occasion (1949) accepted this objective conditionally "when budgetary conditions permit." Since federal budgetary conditions have rarely been propitious, such federal taxes as have been relinquished were picked without specific relationship to the objective of increasing the taxing resources of state and local governments. The proposal to transfer federal revenue sources to the states has recently been infused with fresh blood by the recommendation of the Joint Federal-State Action Committee to trade the states' tax sources for federal grant-in-aid programs.

Motor Fuel

The outstanding example of a federal excise coveted by the states is the gasoline tax. During the immediate postwar years, proposals for repeal of the federal gasoline tax had been frequent. Originally introduced in 1932 as a depression emergency revenue measure, this tax had remained in continuous use at rates of one to two cents per gallon for 25 years.

Repeal of the federal tax has had strong support from the states, the petroleum industry, highway organizations, and some members of Congress. While the imposition of the tax coincided with a substantial federal highway aid program, federal administrations regularly went to great lengths to explain that the two were unrelated; that gasoline was taxed for general revenue purposes and the size of the highway program was determined by need and not the yield of this tax. In 1953, advocates of repeal combined that proposal with the recommendation to discontinue federal grants for highways except to those states which would lose by it. Three years later, in the context of a concerted Administration effort to greatly improve and enlarge the nation's highway network, jurisdictional claims to the gasoline tax were removed from the arena of debate. The federal government relinquished use of the gasoline tax for general fund purposes and reserved it for the highway trust fund, to be expended through the states' highway departments. The Federal-Aid Highway Act of 1956 increased the tax rate from two cents to three cents per gallon, and together with the yield of some other automotive taxes, earmarked its proceeds for the Highway Trust Fund, reserved for financing an expanded, long-range highway program.[23] This assured the states collectively that the proceeds of a three cent tax were theirs to spend for highway construction, over and above the proceeds of their own taxes. Had the federal tax been repealed, its revenue equivalent would have been available for highway construction only to the extent that each state legislature made a corresponding increase in its own tax rate.

By relinquishing the gasoline tax (together with the new tax on tread rubber and the weight tax on trucks and buses, the revenue from an increased tax on tires, and half of the revenue from the increased tax on trucks and buses) from its general fund, the federal government has provided financing for 90 per cent of the cost of the enlarged interstate highway system. The states' highway financing problems have been relieved, but not solved. Several, particularly those with extensive mileage and relatively low-traffic loads, are finding it difficult to match (in the ratio of 1 : 9) their allocations from the highway trust fund, and to finance their other highway needs as well. During the past three years, ten states have raised their own tax rates which now range from three cents per gallon in one state to seven cents in ten, and other states are considering increases. The average state rate is now six cents, not including local gasoline taxes in seven states, typically at a one cent rate, but in a few cases as high as three cents per gallon.

Electrical Energy

Another federal excise long desired by local governments was that on the sale of electrical energy, originally imposed in 1932 at a 3 per cent rate and increased to 3 1/3 per cent in 1940. Sales of electrical energy, as other utility services, have long been taxed by state and local governments. In the years following World War II the Congress was urged to repeal the federal tax because it was particularly suitable for local collection. In 1951 the tax was repealed, not in response to

[23] In his January 1959 Budget Message the President recommended an increase in the gasoline tax rate from three cents to four and one-half cents.

local governments' pleas, but to remove the discrimination against private enterprise created by the tax exemption of electrical energy sold by publicly owned plants. Since its repeal at the federal level, state and local governments have shown little disposition to make increased use of the tax—at least not on a scale comparable to what the federal tax had been.

In 1956, the Municipal Finance Officers Association tallied some 215 separate municipal taxes on electrical utility gross receipts.[24] However, it did not segregate their revenue yield from the revenue produced by all utilities, which aggregated $98 million for gross receipts taxes on all public utilities in 341 cities. Inspection of the detailed data suggests that the cities may have collected as much as $30 million from the gross receipts of electric utilities, as compared with about $100 million produced by the federal tax on electrical energy sales of privately owned power plants six years earlier, at the time the tax was repealed.

Admissions

A timely illustration of local governments' failure to enter tax areas vacated by the federal government is the admissions tax. This tax area has long been sought by spokesmen for municipal governments, who have been seconded by those speaking for the states and the professional associations.

In the years following the war, the federal admissions tax provided nearly $400 million a year. The estimated yield is $30 million for the fiscal year 1960. During the interval, the rate of the tax was cut from 20 to 10 per cent and the larger part of the tax base was eliminated by increases in exemptions. Municipal taxation of amusements has been unaffected by these developments. In 1955 approximately 200 cities raised about $22 million from admissions taxes. The Municipal Finance Officers Association reported that "the tax has been confined to the same states in which it has been used in the past and has not spread to other states despite a decline in federal admissions tax rates from 20 per cent to 10 per cent that occurred in 1954. This is contrary to expectations of advocates of this type of tax for municipalities. It had been anticipated that the tax would be utilized more extensively by municipalities if federal taxes were reduced or eliminated."[25]

---

[24] Municipal Finance Officers Association, *Municipal Nonproperty Taxes*, 1956 Supplement to "Where Cities Get Their Money," p. 29.
[25] *Ibid.*, p. 20.

Anticipating that cities would have difficulty in imposing admissions taxes, the American Municipal Association suggested in 1952 that, in lieu of repeal, the federal government allow a credit for locally imposed admissions taxes. This suggestion received little consideration from a Congress interested in relieving a depressed industry; that objective would not have been served by a credit for local taxes.

Cigarettes

The cigarette tax now produces about $1.7 billion of federal revenue, approximately $200 million for each one cent of tax. Cigarettes are taxed also by state and local governments. In 1958, state revenues from tobacco products (mostly cigarettes), aggregated about $600 million; local revenues, an additional $50 million.

Cigarettes are taxed by 43 states. In six of these, some local taxes are added. In two others, the states' collections are distributed among local governments; Wyoming earmarks its tax for this purpose and Florida allows a credit for locally imposed cigarette taxes against the state tax. Currently only five states do not have cigarette taxes. In two, Colorado and Virginia, there are some local levies. Oregon, California, and North Carolina have neither state nor local taxes. In the latter two, the general sales tax applies to the sale of cigarettes.

These variations in state taxation reflect differences in attitudes toward consumer taxes in general and taxes on smoking in particular. In Oregon, where consumer taxes are given no quarter, the electorate has twice rejected a cigarette tax. North Carolina and Virginia are large tobacco producers and apparently labor under the misapprehension that a cigarette tax would adversely affect local tobacco growers, even though their produce is destined very largely for out of state consumers.

Given this heterogeneous attitude toward cigarette taxation, what basis is there for presuming that a reduction of the federal tax would be followed by a corresponding increase in state cigarette taxes? Some state rate increases would no doubt follow, but not on a scale which would add to state revenues an amount even approaching the federal loss. If some states failed to pick up all of the federal tax, interstate shipments to avoid tax could again become an important consideration. This problem, it will be recalled, arose in the past and created a need for the Jenkins Act which requires persons, who sell cigarettes in interstate commerce and ship them to other than a licensed distributor in a state imposing a cigarette tax, to forward to the tobacco tax administrator of that state monthly information on cigarette shipments.[26]

The federal government could place its revenue at the disposal of the states by utilizing the credit device—at least for a period of years until the state tax was well established. This would be state taxation by congressional compulsion, more akin to the credit in the unemployment insurance program than in the estate-inheritance tax areas, where it was invented to halt interstate competition. A tax forced on the states by the tax credit route varies from a grant-in-aid only in degree. Indeed, the grant has the virtues of economical administration since the federal tax is collected from a relatively few manufacturers, whereas state taxes have to be collected from a very large number of wholesalers and retailers. Moreover, its distribution among the states can be designed to favor jurisdictions with relatively greater revenue needs, whereas, under the crediting arrangement, benefits vary in proportion to cigarette consumption which tends to be correlated with income levels.

Local Telephone Service

The tax on local telephone service figures prominently in current tax coordination discussions as a result of the proposal of the Joint Federal-State Action Committee to transfer to the states four-tenths of the 10 per cent federal tax, in compensation for the termination of federal vocational education and waste treatment construction grants.[27]

The original proposal contemplated a credit against the federal tax for a 4 per cent state tax imposed over and above existing state rates. The proposal was subsequently modified to meet the objections of those states which would have lost through the exchange because the yield of a 4 per cent tax would have fallen short of their share in these grants. In a later version the credit was limited to a 3 per cent tax but the revenue equivalent of another 1 per cent is to be distributed among the states so as to produce for each a surplus in excess of the amount it now receives from these grants. However, repeal of this tax as of 1960 by the Rate Extension Act of 1959 has effectively shelved this proposal.

The proposal illustrates the technical difficulties encountered in

[26] P.L. 363, 81st Cong. 1st sess.
[27] *Progress Report No. 2*, December 1958.

compensating states for the termination of grants by transferring tax resources to them. Grants tend to reflect need (at least in part) and need generally varies inversely with the distribution of tax bases.

F. COORDINATED TAX ADMINISTRATION

This discussion should appropriately take note also of the potentials of coordinate federal and state tax administration although its contribution to state and local revenues, the object of this inquiry, can have only secondary importance. Where it has been adopted, administrative cooperation has improved state-local revenues by improving tax enforcement. In some instances, this has been at little or no cost, but if carried far, the terms of cooperation are likely to entail an increased investment in enforcement somewhere along the line.

As the foregoing discussion makes clear, the rearrangement of federal and state tax structures into neat packets which would leave each level of government with revenue resources in strict correspondence to revenue requirements, without overlapping, is not realizable. Interstate diversities in economic resources, perverse relationships between revenue resources and needs, fondness for independent tax structures, and lack of machinery for crystallizing a unanimous state viewpoint illustrate the objections.

In these circumstances administrative coordination can afford some relief and the dedication of tax administrators at all levels of government to tax enforcement objectives should contribute to it. As Professor William Anderson observed ten years ago:

"Within each group handling a function of government there develops a fellow-feeling, an *esprit de corps*, a concern for good results in performing the functions, that cut across geographical boundaries. . . . The function, not the unit of government, becomes the concern, and in the handling of the function, the various staff members even develop some resistance to interference by the units of government of which they are a part . . . the intrafunctional group loyalty tends to gain the ascendancy over the loyalty to a particular entire unit of government, such as the state, county, or city."[28]

Administrative coordination by two governments can range from very loose, almost casual relations to comprehensive integration of

[28] "Some Trends in Federalism and Intergovernmental Relations," American Political Science Association, December 30, 1948, Chicago.

enforcement activities. Two tax administrators with a high degree of mutual purpose and freedom could conceivably allocate their separate resources among the several phases of tax enforcement, so as to achieve essentially the results of a singly administered tax. Indeed, acting in concert they could develop a more efficient procedure than acting separately, improving the products of both.

Congressional recognition of the case for administrative cooperation dates from 1935 when disclosure of information from federal income tax returns to the states was authorized. It required the Internal Revenue Service, in response to the request of a governor, to open federal income tax returns for inspection by state officials for the purpose of facilitating the administration of state tax laws. The current version of that provision [Section 6103(b) of the 1954 Code] is the authority under which the Internal Revenue Service has developed its exchange information program with the states.

Before 1950, the program consisted largely of a transcript service to provide copies of federal tax returns to requesting state governors. It engendered little enthusiasm in the federal Revenue Service because it encroached on its already limited facilities. While the states reimbursed the Service for clerical expenses, their payments accrued to the credit of the general fund and not to the Revenue Service.[29]

In 1949, representatives of federal, state and local governments, meeting under treasury auspices, agreed to develop the potentials of administrative coordination, specifically through the exchange of audit information. Soon thereafter, arrangements were made for the exchange of audit information with Wisconsin and North Carolina (1950), with Kentucky and Montana (1951), and with Colorado (1952). While these pilot projects served the essential purpose of breaking ground in a field that previously had had only scattered attention, they did not prove to be a great success. Although all participating states derived some benefit, the federal Revenue Service found it to be a one-way street in all but one of the states. The information furnished by the other four states was poor in both quality and quantity and yielded little additional federal revenue.

In response to the recommendation of the President's Commission

---

[29] Some states have apparently found the program very productive from the viewpoint of additional revenue collected. See Federation of Tax Administrators, "State programs for photostating Federal income tax returns," RM-350, May 1958. Effective January 1, 1959, the charge for preparing abstracts of federal income tax returns and documents for state governments has been increased from $1.50 to $2.50 per hour. (IRB 1943–58, p. 47.)

on Intergovernmental Relations that income tax administrative cooperation be expanded, the Revenue Service redesigned the program to improve its value and attain a better balance between the benefits it receives and the costs it incurs. With these objectives in view, an exchange program has been concluded with Minnesota (1957) and the agreement with Wisconsin has been renegotiated (1958).

These two new agreements have given the program a new lease on life. The Revenue Service, plagued perennially with inadequate budgets, understandably has little enthusiasm for a program which drains its resources and contributes little in return at a time when an additional dollar invested in tax enforcement can produce several dollars of additional collections. To improve the prospects of federal-state audit exchange, the agreements have been expanded to include other aspects of income tax administration such as detecting delinquencies and unreported refunds, and embrace exchange of information on other types of taxes. The agreements also move in the direction of trying to encourage joint planning, joint action, and limited sharing of work.

Even assuming encouraging results from the broadened exchange effort, the bulk of duplicate costs in both compliance and administration would remain: dual receipt and processing of returns, dual accounting and collection, separate space, machine facilities and management. In the individual income tax field the federal government has moved predominantly to a refund basis with the mass of taxpayers, while many states continue on a tax-due basis. This means that the same taxpayer may be receiving a refund check from the federal government and almost simultaneously making payment to his state, instead of having the two transactions handled on a net basis. Interest in avoiding dual and parallel transactions with separate governments has produced a few straws in the wind. One recent example was the legislative proposal (reportedly introduced at the instance of some states anxious to protect their strict refund procedures), that the states process both federal and state gasoline tax refunds with lump sum federal reimbursement of the several states.

While the expanded audit exchange program affords a new attack on overlapping problems, the rate of progress does not promise large budgetary relief for the near future. Those probing for larger dividends from administrative coordination, whether in the form of additional revenue or economy in operation, are faced with numerous and substantial barriers. Some of these are primarily technical and could be removed with the adoption of strong policy positions fostering concerted action. As things stand, however, tax administrators have much concern and little precedent for their authority to join forces. General authority to exchange information is fairly well established by statute at both federal and state levels, but specific steps, whether aimed at enlarging revenues or saving costs, face questions of interpretation. Two procedural problems that have not been surmounted are the use by one jurisdiction of evidence (audit) provided by the other level of government, and authority for use of appropriated funds to do the work of another level of government. Of minor but more immediate irritation is the priority of liens for collection which now seems to be accorded to the federal government.[30]

A more imposing barrier to larger strides towards closer cooperation is the unequal quality of tax enforcement in the several states. Another, especially relevant in this instance at the federal level, is the compulsion every tax administrator feels to demonstrate the highest possible revenue return per dollar appropriated for his activity. Still another is to be found in the general framework in which coordination efforts are conducted. There is no organized channel for continuous dealing with intergovernmental tax relations on a comprehensive basis, only *ad hoc* commissions, committees, and forums. Such progress as has been made by interstate groups engaged in promoting state community of interests has found no focal point in the federal hierarchy where planning, legislation and execution of policies can be responsive. The recently created Office of the Deputy Assistant to the President for Intergovernmental Relations could remedy this situation.

The survival of administrative duplication can in part be explained by a lack of pressure. The era of expanding revenue bases since World War II has submerged the duplication problem. But the effect of full employment in filling revenue coffers has also been reflected in increased cost of tax administration and the difficulty of competent staffing. The search for administrative economies at both federal and state levels may bear fruit in bringing about more cooperative use of resources on enforcement work. The adoption of high-powered mechanization is also likely to highlight obvious duplication and suggest more joint planning at the management level. Moreover,

[30] National Association of Tax Administrators, "Federal Tax Liens and the Administration of State and Local Taxes," B-460, September 3, 1957.

different levels of government may come to appreciate that they are not competitive in the sense of business units competing for a share of the market, but can profitably pool their knowhow, training facilities and programming work. Here no preponderance of progress exists on one side, since there is strong evidence that both state and federal levels of government have lagged behind the business community in streamlining their operations.

With the rapid pace inherent in technological applications today those who would benefit therefrom must move fast. Internal Revenue is well along toward area-processing in three major centers servicing sixty-four district offices. Heretofore the district offices provided units of operation coinciding with state boundaries in most instances. Unless mechanization of state processing operations takes into account the changed federal setup, opportunities for coordination may continue to go by the board.

The testing now under way can provide a valuable feedback. Through more intimate association with each other's problems, state and federal administrators can bring up to the legislative and executive levels the kind of action necessary to clear the way to greater mutual benefits. But halfway coordination without support from topside can consume much effort while leaving benefits mostly unrealized.

3. Debt Financing

Since state and local governments are finding it necessary to cover a significant portion of their expenditures by borrowing—a condition expected to continue—and since many, particularly among local governments, cannot always borrow as cheaply as they may wish, this examination of ways and means to facilitate local government financing through intergovernmental action should logically embrace this problem as well. Time limitation precludes our doing here little more than assemble a partial inventory of suggested approaches to the problem.

State and local borrowing has averaged more than $7 billion during the last several years, raising the volume of outstanding debt from $30 billion in 1952 to about $57 billion by the middle of 1958. These totals compare with about $16 billion at the end of World War II. In 1957, the only recent year for which data are available, the combined state and local net long-term debt ranged from $42.69 per $1,000 of personal income in South Dakota to $219.25 in Washington.

TABLE 14

State and Local Tax Revenues and Interest Payments on General Debt,
Each per $1,000 of Personal Income, 1957

	FREQUENCY DISTRIBUTION						
TAX REVENUES PER $1,000 OF PERSONAL INCOME	Number of States with Interest Payments per $1,000 of Personal Income of:						ALL STATES
	$0.72–$1.57	$1.66–$2.39	$2.40–$2.77	$2.85–$3.18	$3.23–$3.76	$3.80–$5.93	
$48.96–$73.29	–	2	1	1	2	2	8
73.83– 79.95	1	–	1	3	1	2	8
81.88– 89.22	–	–	2	3	3	–	8
89.31– 93.98	–	4	1	–	1	2	8
93.99– 97.04	4	–	2	1	1	–	8
97.06–116.38	3	2	1	–	–	2	8
All States	8	8	8	8	8	8	

SOURCE: Bureau of the Census, *State and Local Government Finances in 1957.*

Interest charges on the general debt of state and local governments for that year ranged from 72 cents per $1,000 of personal income in South Dakota to $5.39 in Louisiana.[31] Since 1952, annual interest costs of all state and local governments have increased from about $725 million to nearly $1.5 billion, and annual debt redemption from about $1.8 billion to about $3.2 billion. Debt service on the general debt alone is now equivalent to about one-seventh of tax collections. Compared with earlier years these are striking magnitudes. They support the contention that variations in the cost of borrowing may appreciably affect state-local capacity to finance capital improvements.[32]

Some interpret the rapid postwar rise in state-local debt as evidence that these governments are finding it easy enough to borrow; that perhaps borrowing ought to be made more difficult to encourage more capital outlay financing out of current income, i.e., taxes. Others, on the other hand, are preoccupied with the problems of those jurisdictions which have been unable to borrow despite pressing needs for capital improvements substantially in excess of capacity to finance out of current income. They are concerned also with jurisdictions obliged to pay relatively high interest rates, whose borrowing potential would be enhanced by a rate reduction. As

[31] Bureau of the Census, *State and Local Government Finances in 1957.*

[32] For example, the savings in financing charges resulting from a reduction in interest rates from 3.5 per cent to 3 per cent on one year's $7 billion issue of serial bonds maturing over 25 years, would finance $392.5 million of additional borrowing.

180

Table 14 indicates, the debt burdens assumed by state and local governments appear to bear an inverse relationship to the tax efforts they are making. The states exerting the highest tax efforts—generally the low income states—report relatively small interest payments, even in relation to their low personal incomes. Since these states generally provide a relatively low level of government service (despite their high tax effort), the data can be interpreted as support for the view that a reduction in interest rates would facilitate capital improvements in the states where the need is greatest.

A. FEDERAL TAX SUBSIDIES

Exemption from federal income taxes has been a factor in the demand for state and local obligations since 1913. During most of this period, municipals shared this favorable position with federal securities, some wholly and some only partially exempt from federal income tax. After 1941, when the issuance of tax-exempt federal securities ceased, the relative tax position of municipals improved as federal obligations outstanding in 1941 gradually matured and were retired.[33]

The high level of federal tax rates which has prevailed for nearly two decades and the growing number of investors in the higher income brackets combined to enhance the value of the privileged tax position of state and local obligations. However, forces tending in the opposite direction have also been at work. State and local governments have poured an unprecedented supply of tax-exempt obligations into the market, a supply substantially in excess of the growth in savings seeking this type of investment.[34] An increasing proportion of savings has been channeled through institutional organizations to whom the tax exemption is of little or no value. Thus, exemption from income taxation is, and has been, of little immediate moment to mutual or cooperative financial institutions and qualified pension funds, and has had relatively little value to life insurance companies that have been subject to special low rates. It is of no interest also to regulated investment companies, precluded from passing the exemption privilege on to their members.

[33] Two small tax-exempt issues are still outstanding: $1,485 million in partially tax-exempt 2 3/4 per cent Treasury Bonds (1960–65) and $50 million in wholly tax-exempt 3 per cent Panama Canal Bonds (1961).

[34] Roland Robinson, *Postwar Market for State and Local Government Securities*, Princeton University Press for the National Bureau of Economic Research, 1960.

181

With a view to broadening the market for state and local obligations, the President has recommended legislation to permit special regulated investment companies with assets in state and local securities to pass on to their stockholders the tax-exempt status of the income they receive from these securities. This recommendation envisages a special class of regulated investment companies which invest substantially all of their assets in municipals and have both the facilities and the incentive to seek out the obligations of small jurisdictions unknown to most investors. This would channel into municipal obligations the savings of investors in mutual funds, a class of investor who presently does not purchase municipals.[35]

Those in quest of devices to broaden the demand for municipal obligations, mindful that some investment institutions' lack of interest in tax-exempt municipals at this time is explained by the preferential tax treatment they enjoy irrespective of the composition of their income, view with interest proposals to restrict the favorable tax treatment of these institutions.

It has been suggested that state and local governments could preserve a larger share of the value of the exemption of their securities from federal income tax if they exchanged this exemption for a federal interest subsidy commensurate with the government's present revenue loss.[36] If, for example (and these numbers are illustrative only), the annual federal revenue loss from tax exemption is equivalent to 1 per cent of state-local debt and the savings to state and local governments due to the exemption amount to only 0.5 per cent, state and local governments would find it profitable to forego their exemptions for a federal subsidy equal to more than 0.5 per cent of their future debt offerings. This would divert to state-local governments a corresponding part of the surplus which now accrues to high bracket taxpayers at the expense of federal revenues. It would involve state and local governments voluntarily foregoing their tax exemption privilege. In the process, an income tax problem would be eliminated, but only after the lapse of a number of years. During the interval, the supply of tax exempts already outstanding and held by investors to whom tax exemption is of relatively little value would gradually drift to high rate taxpayers (for a gradually increasing price).

[35] H. R. 1222, H. R. 4380, and H. R. 8811 introduced during the Eighty-fifth Congress incorporate the President's recommendation.

[36] *Federal, State and Local Government Fiscal Relations*, Senate Doc. No. 69, 78th Cong., 1st sess., 1943, p. 28.

B. SUBSIDIES FOR FINANCIAL STUDIES
AND IMPROVED REPORTING

Part of the borrowing problems of state and local governments stem from their operating methods—more correctly, from the fact that some of them operate without methods. Many local governments typically function without benefit of professional staffs knowledgeable in the financial markets of which none is more complex than that for municipals. Moreover, their governing bodies are generally composed of lay citizens also unversed in the technicalities of complex money markets. They lack the specialized skills required to manage a community's borrowing operations with a view to the most favorable credit terms; they lack the know-how of debt management. Their inability to promote investor understanding of the quality of their obligations by informative reporting contributes to the alleged inaccessibility to money markets experienced by some, particularly small, borrowers. The situation has been partially relieved in some states by machinery developed for assisting political subdivisions in debt management problems, including the marketing of offerings. Our host state, Virginia, for example, has a State Commission on Local Debt which assists cities and counties in this way.[37] Some states provide facilities for pooling the separate small offerings of a number of borrowers into a single offering more likely to interest the market. Some states use their sinking, trust, and investment funds to bolster the demand for local issues. Many obtain technical advice on the timing and handling of their borrowings from their bankers.

Part of the blame for inadequate investor interest in municipals is related to poor and disorganized financial reporting by borrowing jurisdictions. Potential investors find it difficult to ascertain the credit condition of a particular security offering and of necessity make their bids on the basis of the least favorable assumptions. The need for improved and more standardized financial reporting on the part of borrowing governments, and for channeling of such information to potential investors is recognized by all concerned with reducing borrowing costs. To facilitate this end, it has been suggested that the federal government support and encourage efforts to improve the quality of municipal financial reporting through the dissemination of guides to good reporting and possibly by sharing in its costs.

---

[37] The Commission is authorized to advise political subdivisions on the planning, preparation and marketing of bonds and to assist in the sale of such bonds. (*Code of Virginia* 15-590.2 and .3.)

In some states, obstacles to borrowing encountered by local jurisdictions stem from constitutional or statutory limitations which have grown out of improvident borrowing practices in former epochs. Necessity has fathered various devices to circumvent these prohibitions. Limitations expressed as a percentage of assessed valuation, for example, have been side-stepped by raising the ratio of assessed to market value of property. The public "authority" has been invented, adding to the complexity of the governmental structure. In still other places, "public spirited citizens" have organized nonprofit corporations to act on behalf of their local governments. They have undertaken to construct the required facility, lease it to the community, and finance its construction by debt secured with a long-term lease. School buildings, utility enterprises, and athletic facilities have been financed in this way.

These are half-way measures lacking in forthrightness. Direct solutions are preferred by most students of the problem: the revision of statutory and constitutional provisions to accord with present day needs.[38] With this in mind, suggestions have been made for federal financial aid to assist and encourage the states to finance studies looking to the updating of constitutional and statutory provisions, the development of more meaningful norms for debt limitation purposes, and to ensure widespread distribution of their findings to facilitate the public understanding prerequisite to bring about these changes. The grants for urban planning provided small communities under Section 701 of the Housing Act of 1954 illustrate this kind of federal assistance to enable local governments to help themselves.[39]

C. INSURANCE PROGRAMS

Proposals have been advanced also to insure state and local obligations. The excellent risk performance of these obligations suggests that this would entail a very low premium charge. Since a mandatory program is not compatible with the conventions of a federal-state relationship, such a program would presumably be offered on an optional basis. This, however, would tend to limit insurance coverage to the poorer quality obligations, and such adverse risk selection would markedly increase premium costs. Mandatory

[38] *Report* of the President's Commission on Intergovernmental Relations, June 1955, p. 98.

[39] Section 320 of the Housing Act of 1959, S. 7, 86th Cong., 1st sess., as passed by the Senate, would broaden eligibility for these grants.

coverage presents no problem for individual states with respect to their own political subdivisions. It is not known, however, whether any of the states has actively considered operating such an insurance program, or whether it would be practicable to provide facilities for sharing such state risks through a national reinsurance agency. Federal statutes contain a variety of insurance programs which are summarized annually in a special analysis of federal credit programs included as a regular feature of the President's Budget and need not be detailed here.[40]

D. FEDERAL GUARANTEES

With a view to reducing the cost of borrowing for various public objectives, such as housing and school construction, proposals have been considered on various occasions in the past that the federal government guarantee the particular obligations. In recent years this form of assistance has been urged to facilitate the construction of public school and college facilities. Such a guarantee applied to a municipal obligation would create a super security which possessed the safety of a federal obligation and the tax exemption privilege of a state or local obligation. The local public housing authority bonds backed by a government commitment to cover debt service costs in excess of the income from the property have been criticized for this reason. To avoid this result, the Administration's program to encourage the construction of college facilities makes the proposed guaranty of the principal of and interest on the bonds of educational institutions conditional upon the income from such bonds being subject to federal taxation.[41]

E. FEDERAL PURCHASE OF MUNICIPALS

To complete this inventory, mention should be made also of the suggestion that either through the treasury or through a specially created corporation the federal government stand ready to purchase municipal obligations when financing terms available in the market are unsatisfactory. These obligations would then either be resold under appropriate market conditions or held to maturity. A national credit agency could conceivably finance the purchase of state and local obligations by public offerings of its own obligations secured by its portfolio of municipals. Depending upon the terms of purchase,

[40] See, for example, *The Budget for Fiscal Year 1960*, Special Analysis E, pp. 957–69.
[41] Section 2(a) of S. 1017, 86th Cong., 1st sess.

this could assist some borrowing jurisdictions and incidentally curtail the flow of tax-exempt obligations to private investors.

In lieu of purchasing local obligations, the federal and state governments could jointly undertake to meet the debt service cost on obligations issued by needy jurisdictions under conditions that the community maintain a reasonable tax effort, and so long as it is unable to meet this obligation. This is a feature of the Administration's school construction assistance program under which the federal government would advance half of the cost of debt service on school construction bonds issued by needy jurisdictions, if the state undertakes to advance the other half.[42]

The problem of marketing municipal obligations is generally believed to be due in part to the absence of an adequate secondary market for municipal obligations, which tends to restrict the purchase of these obligations to investors prepared to hold them until maturity.[43] This suggests that an inventory of possible aids to state and local borrowing should include also possibilities for developing a more adequate secondary market. Conceivably this would then take any one of several forms, such as a national organization on the pattern of the Federal National Mortgage Association or regional organizations akin to the federal land banks.

Some of the devices here catalogued, employed singly or in combination, could probably facilitate state and local borrowing. Analysis is required to determine which, if any, would on balance serve the national interest. It is essential to keep in view, however, that the limitations on the borrowing capacity of a jurisdiction stem more from the limitations of its economic capacity to support debt than from technicalities of the money market or the jurisdiction's lack of skill to exploit it. This is not to deny that money market conditions affect credit operations, both public and private. If, for example, national credit policies pursued in the interest of economic stability increase borrowing costs, it is no more possible and desirable to insulate state and local governments than the federal government from such increases. Moreover, the effectiveness of national policies in achieving stable economic growth may, in the long run, have a more significant impact on the capacity of state and local governments to provide public services than factors within their own control.

[42] S. 1016, 86th Cong., 1st sess.
[43] Robinson, *op. cit.*

4. Financial Aids to State and
Local Government

In terms of net federal budgetary expenditures federal aid to state and local governments in cash and in kind equalled early in the 1950's about 9 per cent of total state-local general revenues. Recently, federal aid (including grants from the new highway trust fund) has declined to about 7 per cent, as direct revenues have increased more rapidly. Early in the decade, too, these payments equaled some 3 to 4 per cent of total federal cash payments to the public; currently they are running at 5 or 6 per cent, and the budget estimates for 1959 and 1960 indicate federal aid equaling 7 and 8 per cent of federal payments to the public.

Measured on the basis of the state-local accounts, the cash grants-in-aid and all other intergovernmental payments received from the federal government were just over one-tenth of all state-local general revenues for the five years 1953–57, inclusive. They financed 9.5 per cent of direct general expenditures of the state and local governments during the 5 years.

The importance of these aids in state-local finance varies greatly among the states and among particular programs. For federal finance, likewise, the differences between programs are substantial. Each type of variation will be reviewed.

First it should be noted, however, that we are dealing here with relationships that are only partly measurable in pecuniary terms—and for which, even in the measurable area, different figures are reported depending on the point at which data are compiled.

Some aid received from the federal government is not reflected in the financial accounts of state and local governments. This contributes to an understatement of the magnitude of state-local operations and perhaps to some understatement of the fiscal support they receive from the federal government.

Already noted is the indirect aid afforded by the deductibility of state and local income, property, and other taxes from personal and corporate incomes in computing federal income tax liability, and by the federal tax exemption of interest-income from municipal bonds. Also, the development of a direct federal program may provide indirect aid by relieving state and local units of related needs for expenditure; this is illustrated by the federal old-age, survivors, and disability insurance system in relation to federal-state-local public

TABLE 15

Federal Aid to State and Local Governments,
as Shown in the Federal Budget: 1951–60
(millions of dollars)

Fiscal Year	Total, Net Budget Expenditures[a]	Grants-in-Aid[b]	Shared Revenues	Loans and Repayable Advances, Net[c]
1951	2,434	2,256	31	147
1952	2,604	2,393	38	173
1953	2,857	2,781	51	25
1954	2,657	2,986	66	−395[d]
1955	3,124	3,126	78	−80[d]
1956	3,753	3,642	82	29
1957	4,111	3,943	96	72
1958	5,072	4,831	101	140
1959 estimated	6,695	6,266	106	323
1960 estimated	7,148	6,851	119	178

SOURCE: *Budget of the United States,* fiscal years 1953–60, special analyses.

a Includes grants paid from highway trust fund and loans from unemployment trust fund, fiscal years 1957–60.

b Includes grants paid from the highway trust fund, as follows:

1957	$ 953
1958	1,493
1959 estimated	2,425
1960 estimated	3,015

c Includes loans from the unemployment trust fund, as follows:

1958	$ 3
1959 estimated	116

d Repayments received exceeded new loans by the amount of negative expenditures shown here.

assistance. Similarly, federally sponsored fellowships and traineeships in public service fields of special concern to state and local governments—particularly health, education, and science—may promote the productivity and efficiency of state and local program operations. Indeed, federally sponsored research and development sometimes affects profoundly the content and objectives of public programs at all levels.

Even among direct federal aids, those involving cooperative administration, exchanges of personnel and services, and grants-in-kind usually leave no financial tracks in the state and local accounts. The various grants-in-kind are, however, included in the federal budget analyses of expenditures for aids to state and local governments. Of greater significance in the totals is the fact that the federal data include loans on a net basis. That is, in the federal government accounts, the amounts lent to state and local governments (whether through purchases of their securities or through other types of advances) are considered expenditures and any repayments received are deducted from expenditures. In recent years, repayments received have largely offset the loans made. In fact, in 1954 and 1955 the repayments exceeded the new loans, producing "negative expenditures" in this category of federal aid.

A ten-year summary of the federal budgetary totals is given in Table 15.

A. GEOGRAPHIC COMPARISONS RELATING
FEDERAL AID TO PERSONAL INCOMES

This section gives particular attention to interstate or interregional differences in the relative importance of federal aids because, as was noted early in this paper, the uneven geographic distribution of resources is the genesis of most problems in federal-state fiscal relations. These geographic variations have greatly complicated the task of the Joint Federal-State Action Committee which was set up in 1957 to develop practical proposals for increasing the fiscal resources available to state-local governments while reducing the volume of federal grants-in-aid. The Committee, after surveying intensively the broad problem of equalization, has suggested the possible necessity of "block" grants—i.e., grants for an unassigned general purpose in place of grants for specific purposes.[44] Some aspects of the Joint Committee's work, as well as the earlier report of the Commission on Intergovernmental Relations, are noted below.

A definite tendency for the existing federal grants to help equalize fiscal means relative to personal incomes and to state-local general revenues is evident in gross geographical comparisons for recent years. The summary data will be given for the fiscal year 1957.

In the broad groupings of Table 16, per capita federal grants in the aggregate and for each of several problem categories are highest in the group of low-income states and lowest in the high-income group. The inverse relationship exhibited in these broad groupings of states and of programs is sufficiently pronounced that if judgment were based on these data alone the pattern might seem creditable to design

[44] Cf. *Second Report of the Joint Federal-State Action Committee to the President of the United States and to the Chairman of the Governors' Conference*, Progress Report No. 2, December 1958, pp. 8, 47.

TABLE 16

Federal Grants to State and Local Governments
in Amounts Per Capita, by Function, as Related to Personal Income
Levels in Three Groups of States: Fiscal Year 1957

Program or Other Category	Continental U.S.[a]	16 Highest- Income States[b]	17 Middle- Income States	16 Lowest- Income States
Per capita federal grants, 1957:				
Total	$23.11	$18.76	$26.43	$30.54
Public assistance	9.23	7.29	10.07	13.38
Employment security[c]	1.89	2.22	1.47	1.41
Health services	.93	.60	1.06	1.58
Other welfare services	1.18	1.04	1.17	1.58
Education	1.18	1.01	1.46	1.31
Highway construction[d]	5.73	4.33	8.18	6.46
All other	2.97	2.27	3.02	4.82
Per capita personal income— annual average during calendar years 1954–56:				
Median State	$1,851[e]	$2,178	$1,670	$1,308
Range:				
Highest in group	2,630	2,630	1,827	1,546
Lowest in group	926	1,874	1,560	926

SOURCE: Adapted from Sophie R. Dales, "Federal Grants to State and Local Governments, 1956–57," *Social Security Bulletin*, June 1958, pp. 13–18, Tables 2 and 3, with additions as noted.

[a] Omits Alaska and Hawaii; includes District of Columbia.

[b] Includes District of Columbia.

[c] Includes distribution of certain federal tax collections to state accounts in unemployment trust fund.

[d] Included with "all other" in *Social Security Bulletin*. To make this separation, highway grants per capita were calculated approximately for each of the three groups of states and for the continental total, and deducted from the corresponding per capita amount of "all other" grants as shown in the *Bulletin*. The highway grants, by state totals, are from Secretary of the Treasury, *Annual Report on the State of the Finances*, 1957, p. 578, col. 13; population for the per capita averages, from Table 2 in the *Social Security Bulletin*.

[e] Per capita average for Continental U.S.

and intention. In fact, of course, the pattern is only in part a product of design; moreover, the broad groupings cancel out many internal deviations, and closer inspection of underlying data emphasizes that the progression is not regular or fully balanced. But the general picture is coherent enough to warrant further description.

The use of per capita averages and ratios to personal incomes for some of these comparisons is not meant to suggest that the need for or the level of particular services is best measured in this way. In some fields, such as highway construction or forest fire prevention, a simple population count (or a comparison of income levels) may be almost irrelevant to program objectives.

Yet there is logic in the use of such measurements for assessing the broad impact of federal aid. In our society, at any given time, the over-all magnitude of the needs of a state for public services is more directly affected by the size and affluence of the population than by most of its other attributes, and the fiscal capability of the state and local units is clearly dependent on the relative affluence of their constituencies. Apart from the stimulation of particular programs, the primary general purpose of assistance from the federal government is to assure support everywhere for some minimum standards in selected public services; and the need for the federal aid arises from variations in the fiscal capabilities of the states and their subdivisions. Almost certainly, the best general, comprehensive measurement of differences in the need for such aid is to be found in population and personal income differences. Moreover, the averages and ratios do afford a rough-and-ready basis for comparison—a point of departure for more thorough analysis.

Federal grant-in-aid objectives, it has often been observed, are not directed explicitly toward interstate equalization of per capita personal incomes.[45] A federal-aid system intended to redistribute income would be quite different from the heterogeneous, multi-purpose arsenal of many-sized aids presently included in the federal budget. Nevertheless if a by-product of these programs is some interstate redistribution of means, that tendency may be significant for an examination of interlevel fiscal problems, whatever the justifications that were advanced for establishing the individual programs.

Data for the fiscal year 1952, as analyzed by Selma Mushkin, support a conclusion that in that year at least, although federal government expenditures taken as a whole "appear to result in

---

[45] As Miss Mushkin has cautioned:

"Equalization of state (per capita) income and equalization of minimum program levels, paralleled by more uniform state and local taxing effort, are two different things. Moreover, they have different purposes. The design of federal grants to achieve a national minimum program level, without requiring disproportionate state and local tax burdens, needs to be considered without being confused with equalization of state income."

Selma Mushkin, "Federal Grants and Federal Expenditures," in *National Tax Journal*, September 1957, p. 197. Cf. Howard G. Schaller (whom Miss Mushkin quotes), "Federal Grants-in-Aid and Differentials in State Per-Capita Incomes, 1929, 1939, and 1949," in *ibid.*, September 1955, pp. 287–99.

redistribution of income additional to that effected by federal taxes," the federal grants as a group had "negligible equalizing effects."[46] Howard Schaller found that "all grants-in-aid combined reduced the relative difference in state per capita incomes by 2 per cent in 1949 and 1 per cent in 1939," whereas they had "negligible" effects in 1929. His measurements indicated that grants under the Social Security Act alone "significantly affected the relative differences, reducing them by 1 per cent in both 1949 and 1939."[47]

It may be that federal grants now exhibit somewhat greater equalizing tendencies relative to personal incomes than they did a few years ago.[48] This could well reflect both the narrowing of the range of interstate differences in per capita incomes and some increase in the ratio of aggregate federal aid to personal incomes. In 1929 and 1939, the highest state average of personal income per capita was more than four times the lowest, and in 1952 the ratio was 2.8 to 1; by 1957 the difference again had widened slightly, to a ratio of 3 to 1.[49] Aggregate federal-aid payments in 1929 equaled about one-eighth of 1 per cent of personal incomes; in 1952, just under 1 per cent; and in 1957, 1.2 per cent.[50]

Over the last 30 to 50 years, the rise in the relative magnitude of federal aid has certainly substituted federal taxes (with emphasis on the taxation of personal incomes at progressive rates) for the more

[46] Mushkin, *loc. cit.*, pp. 205, 208.

[47] Schaller, *loc. cit.*, p. 298.

[48] We have not equated our data directly with the series compiled by Miss Mushkin and Mr. Schaller in their articles.

Likewise we have not attempted to ascertain whether our observation as to present tendencies toward equalization relative to personal incomes indicates a change in the situation described by V. O. Key, Jr., in 1942, when he found that "the dominant form of grant compels the states and localities to bear a share of the cost of the aided programs that as between states becomes more burdensome from state to state as resources decline." (*The Matching Requirement in Federal Grant Legislation in Relation to Variations in State Fiscal Capacity*, preliminary draft; Federal Security Agency, Social Security Board, Bureau of Research and Statistics, Bureau Memorandum No. 46, February 1942, p. 57.) Key's analysis was based on interstate comparisons of the burdens involved in matching federal grants. Our analysis is based on the aggregate amounts of federal aid actually paid.

Also pertinent for its discussion of issues and objectives in equalization is Byron L. Johnson, *The Principle of Equalization Applied to the Allocation of Grants in Aid*, *ibid.*, Bureau Memorandum No. 66, September 1947.

[49] Cf. Department of Commerce, Office of Business Economics, *Personal Income by States since 1929, A Supplement to the Survey of Current Business*, by Charles F. Schwartz and Robert E. Graham, Jr., 1956, Table 2, pp. 142–3; and *Survey of Current Business*, August 1958, p. 13.

[50] Personal income totals from *ibid.*; federal aid totals from Census compilations and federal *Budget*.

diversified state and local tax systems as the means of financing a substantial volume of expenditures.

As a central objective of policy or as a qualifying consideration, the promotion of interstate equalization in personal incomes is several degrees less remote for federal aid programs than for the geographic incidence of federal taxes and the benefit or incidence distribution of aggregate federal expenditures, to which Miss Mushkin referred. Indeed, it seems evident that the federal-aid system, especially the grants-in-aid and the loans, grew up as one type of practical accommodation to problems that confront a multilevel political structure in which the subdivisions exhibit diverse economic, as well as political and social, characteristics.

Over the years, per capita personal income averages by states have been specified as factors in an increasing number of the statutory formulas for grant apportionment and grant matching. The language of hearings and debates suggests that the purpose—at least the expressed purpose—has usually been to improve upon simple head counts as a measure of relative need for a particular public service and relative capacity to finance it from state and local resources.

Not even in the consideration and approval of the successive statutory increases in the large public assistance grant program has interstate redistribution of incomes been identified as a purpose of the program. The case has been made almost wholly in terms of the fiscal inability of state and local governments to meet the particular, apparently irreducible, need. Still, the pressures for larger grants and for less state-and-local matching have been so persistent and so repeatedly successful as to warrant an inference that they derive some of their persuasive force from considerations outside the public assistance program itself.

The case is reminiscent of the origins of large state-aid funds for public schools in various states, where the stated interest of many proponents was to transfer the support of a major item of expenditure from local property taxpayers to state taxpayers. Public education was a program with wide popular support and of state-wide concern; a large measure of property-tax relief could be accomplished with state aid covering only a fraction of the cost.

It would be difficult to demonstrate that an analogous purpose has influenced congressional legislation for public assistance grants. The tendency to increasing reliance on financing by federal taxation is, however, evident in the results.

193

The commission on Intergovernmental Relations, in its report in 1955, said it did not believe that "the 'equalization' of the general fiscal capacities of the states is by itself a proper objective of National policy."[51] The Commission flatly rejected, without dissent, proposals for federal grants "to reduce fiscal disparities" among the states and the alternative of "a comprehensive subsidy program for general governmental purposes."[52]

More recently the Joint Federal-State Action Committee has raised anew the question whether it would be practicable to make interstate equalization a specific objective of policy. The Committee has therefore undertaken to study:

(1) the *feasibility* of replacing grants for *specific* purposes by an unassigned general purpose (*block*) grant as an alternative approach to revenue source adjustment; and (2) the practicability of revising grant formulas to relate grants to per capita incomes.[53]

Against this background of policy discussion, a description of existing relationships is of some interest. The geographic comparisons are summarized first in terms of aggregates and then by program categories.

In the aggregate. Taking all the federal grants together (but omitting other types of federal aid), the national per capita average in fiscal 1957 was $23.11. (Table 16.)[54] The over-all averages for three

---

[51] Commission on Intergovernmental Relations, *A Report to the President for Transmittal to the Congress*, June 1955, p. 135.

[52] *Ibid.*, pp. 110–15.

[53] Joint Federal-State Action Committee, *2d Report*, December 1958, p. 8 and appendix vi. (Italics in original.) Informal discussions suggest that the Commission's interest subsequently shifted from unassigned general purpose grants to functional block grants, e.g., a single grant for public health.

[54] This average and the statistics immediately below are from the *Social Security Bulletin*, June 1958, pp. 15 and 16, Tables 2 and 3, with some modifications. The payments represent grants only, and the total of $3,933 million shown for fiscal 1957 is very close to the $3,943 million reported in the federal Budget as actual grant-in-aid expenditures (see Table 15).

A per capita average of $22.57 is reported in the Census of Governments for 1957 for all intergovernmental payments from the federal government. Comparable detailed amounts for functional or program categories are not available from the Census.

All state and local government data in this section, unless attributed to another source, are from publications of the Department of Commerce, Bureau of the Census, Governments Division. Data for 1957 are from 1957 Census of Governments Advance Releases, No. 8, *State and Local Government Finances in 1957* (issued February 1959). Data for the period 1953–57, inclusive, are from the annual *Summary of Governmental Finances* for these years.

groups of states (including the District of Columbia but omitting Alaska and Hawaii) are as follows:

1. In the sixteen states with the lowest per capita personal incomes, the federal grants averaged $30.54 per capita—32 per cent *above* the national average. The median state in this group was 29 per cent *below* the national average for personal incomes.

2. In the sixteen states (including the District of Columbia) with highest per capita personal incomes, the federal grants per capita averaged $18.76—19 per cent *below* the national average. The median state in this group was 18 per cent *above* the national average for personal incomes.

3. In the seventeen middle-income states, average federal grants at $26.43 per capita were 14 per cent *above* the national average. The median state was 11 per cent *below* the national average for personal incomes.

Irregularities in the progression come to light in Tables 17 and 18, where 48 states (excluding the District of Columbia, Hawaii, and Alaska) are divided on the basis of per capita personal incomes into eight groups of six states each.[55] Table 17 reports for each six-state group the average annual personal income per capita during the four years 1954–57 and the share of each group in the 48-state total for 1957 of personal incomes, population, state-local general revenues (including revenue from the federal government), and state-local general expenditures. In Table 18 these revenue and expenditure data are converted to index numbers or relatives, with the 48-state average for each series taken as the base, or 100.

Thus, if state-local general revenues from the federal government were distributed among the eight groups of states in the same proportions as personal incomes, the index number for the series would be 100 for each six-state group. Instead, the range shown is from 70 in the next-to-highest income group (group 2) to 214 in the sixth group (comprising states that ranked 31st to 36th in per capita incomes—namely, Utah, Maine, Vermont, Idaho, Oklahoma, and New Mexico). State-local general revenues from their own sources and general expenditures for all purposes (including the federally financed expenditures) cluster much more narrowly about the average relationship to personal incomes than does the federal aid.

[55] These Tables are derived from data in the 1957 Census of Governments.

TABLE 17

Personal Incomes, Revenues, and Expenditures, by Groups of States: 1957

Groups of 6 States Each (Based on Rank-Order of Per Capita Personal Incomes, Annual Average for 1954-57 Inclusive) Group	Personal Income Per Capita, Annual Average for 1954-57		Personal Incomes, Aggregate Average 1954-57	Population (1954-57)	State-Local General Revenues, 1957 Total, All Sources	From Federal Government	From State-Local Sources	State-Local General Expenditures, 1957 Total, All Purposes	For Selected Functions Education	Highways	Public Welfare	Health, Hospitals
	Amount Relative[a]		*Percentage of Forty-eight-State Total*									
1 (highest incomes)	$2,393	126	28.5	22.6	28.6	21.8	29.4	28.6	27.1	22.9	25.6	32.4
2	2,157	113	24.8	21.9	21.9	17.3	22.4	22.8	22.4	23.5	20.9	24.1
3	1,924	101	13.7	13.6	11.9	11.6	12.0	11.7	12.3	10.9	11.7	11.0
4	1,783	94	6.7	7.2	7.7	8.1	7.7	7.8	7.9	9.6	8.5	7.5
5	1,669	88	11.4	13.0	12.2	13.6	12.0	12.0	12.7	14.1	10.3	9.8
6	1,560	82	2.8	3.5	3.6	6.0	3.3	3.5	3.7	4.1	5.1	2.5
7	1,364	72	5.8	8.1	7.0	10.0	6.7	6.8	6.8	7.1	9.6	6.5
8 (lowest incomes)	1,189	62	6.3	10.1	7.0	11.6	6.5	6.8	7.1	7.7	8.3	6.2
48-State Total	1,906[b]	100[b]	100.0	100.0	100.0	100.0	100.0	100.0	100.0	100.0	100.0	100.0

Sources: Personal incomes and population based on data in *Survey of Current Business*, August 1958, p. 13. State-local general revenues and general expenditures based on 1957 Census of Government advance releases, No. 8, *State and Local Government Finances in 1957*, February 1959.
[a] 48-state average equals 100.
[b] Average.

TABLE 18

Relationship of General Revenues and Expenditures to Personal Incomes, by Groups of States: 1957
(Average relationship for the 48 States = 100 for each column)

GROUPS OF 6 STATES EACH (BASED ON RANK-ORDER OF PER CAPITA PERSONAL INCOMES, ANNUAL AVERAGE FOR 1954-57, INCLUSIVE)	STATE-LOCAL GENERAL REVENUE, 1957			STATE-LOCAL GENERAL EXPENDITURES, 1957					
	Total, All Sources	From Federal Government	From State-Local Sources	Total, All Purposes	FOR SELECTED FUNCTIONS				
					Education	Highways	Public Welfare	Health, Hospitals
Group 1 (highest incomes)	100	76	103	100	95	80	90	114
2	88	70	90	92	90	95	84	97
3	87	85	88	85	90	80	85	80
4	114	121	114	116	118	143	127	112
5	107	119	92	105	111	124	90	86
6	129	214	118	125	132	146	182	89
7	121	172	116	117	117	122	166	112
8 (lowest incomes)	111	184	103	108	113	122	132	98
48-State Average	100	100	100	100	100	100	100	100

Based on Table 17, with the percentage for each column of revenues or expenditures divided by the corresponding percentage for aggregate personal incomes and the product multiplied by 100.

For general expenditures and for nonfederal revenues, as for federal aid, the highest ratio to personal incomes is in the sixth group of states.[56]

Revenues received from the federal government in 1957 tended not only to be highest per capita in the states with lowest personal incomes; they also tended, on the whole, to be greatest in states that drew most heavily on their own taxable resources.[57] To illustrate:

1. Of the twelve states with the highest ratios of nonfederal state-local general revenues to personal incomes, ten were among the top twelve in the ratio of revenues from the federal government to personal incomes. In this group of states, state-local general revenue from nonfederal sources ranged from a maximum of 15.9 per cent of personal income in North Dakota to 11.8 per cent in Oklahoma. The federal payments ranged from 4.2 per cent of personal income in Wyoming to 1.3 per cent in Minnesota. In North Dakota, the federal payments equaled 2.2 per cent of personal income.

2. Of the twelve states with the lowest ratios of nonfederal state-local general revenues to personal incomes, eight were among the lowest twelve for the ratio of revenues from the federal government to personal incomes. In this group of states, state-local general revenue from nonfederal sources ranged from a minimum of 6.8 per cent of personal income in Delaware to 9.4 per cent in Nebraska. The federal payments ranged from 0.4 to 1 per cent of personal

[56] The Census statistics on which these tabulations are based combine all types of revenue received from the federal government. An analysis confined to grants-in-aid alone (as are the preceding comparisons for three broad groups of states, based on the *Social Security Bulletin* Tables) might show a stronger tendency for federal assistance, insofar as it takes the form of grants, to be associated inversely with the level of personal incomes. However, emphasis upon public lands, total land area, and road mileage as factors in the distribution of the large federal grants for highway construction is a qualifying factor.

The high index number of 214 for the relationship between federal aid and personal incomes in the sixth group of states (in Table 18) is considerably affected by the highway grants. In this six-state group, highway construction grants received in 1957 averaged about $12.67 per capita, compared with a 48-state average of $5.74.

Shared revenues are more important in certain other groups of states. This is illustrated by data for the third group, which includes Wyoming—16th among the 48 states in personal income per capita. Wyoming derived under the Mineral Leasing Act between one-third and one-half of all state-local general revenues received from the federal government in 1957, whereas this category accounted for less than 1 per cent of all federal aid payments to all state-local governments. Federal payments to Wyoming state-local general revenues for all purposes in 1957 averaged $84.88 per capita.

[57] The frequency groupings that underlie this paragraph are derived from the 1957 Census of Governments.

income in New Jersey—the lowest among the 48 states—to 1.6 per cent in Missouri. For Nebraska, the federal payments equaled 1.3 per cent of personal income.

3. Among the middle twelve states in terms of the ratio of non-federal state-local general revenue to personal incomes, only five were among the middle twelve in the ratio of revenues from the federal government to personal incomes. In this median group, the range of state-local general revenue from their own sources was narrow—from 11.1 per cent of personal income in Florida to 10.0 per cent in Michigan. The range of federal government payments in the twelve states was not so narrow; it varied from 2.5 per cent in Arkansas to 0.6 per cent in New York. For Florida, the federal payments were 1.2 per cent of personal income—approximately at the nation-wide average; and for Michigan, 0.9 per cent.

Regional tendencies also are pronounced, as Table 19 indicates. Relative to personal incomes, state-local revenue from the federal government is lowest in the New England, Mideast, and Great Lakes states. With the exception of Vermont and Maine, the sixteen states in these three regions all rank from 34th to 48th in the ratio of federal revenue to personal income. It is highest in the Far West, Rocky Mountain, and Southwest states, where nine of the thirteen states are in the top one-third. In the Plains and the Southwest, the relationship is less evident.[58]

By program categories[59]—Taking the grants by separate functional or program categories shown in Table 16, the 1957 arithmetic means for three broad groups of states (including the District of Columbia but omitting Alaska) were as follows:

1. For public assistance, the average per capita federal grant in the sixteen lowest-income states was 45 per cent *above* the national average; in the sixteen highest-income states, it was 21 per cent *below* the national average.

2. For health services, the grant average in the lowest-income states was 70 per cent *above* the national average, and in the highest income states, 35 per cent *below*. Grants for all health programs were one-tenth as much as for public assistance.

3. For "other" welfare services, the per capita grant average in

[58] The data underlying this paragraph are from the 1957 Census of Government.
[59] Based on details in *Social Security Bulletin, loc. cit.*

TABLE 19

State and Local Government General Revenue from the Federal Government—
Total and Per Capita Amounts and Relationship to Personal Incomes and Total State-Local Revenues, by States and Regions: 1957

GEOGRAPHIC REGION AND STATE	STATE-LOCAL GENERAL REVENUE FROM FEDERAL GOVERNMENT, 1957				RANK ORDER FOR REVENUE FROM FEDERAL GOVERNMENT	
	Total Amount (millions)	Per Capita Amount	Per $1,000 of Personal Incomes	As Percentage of all State-Local General Revenue	Per Capita Amount	Per $1,000 of Personal Incomes
48-State total	$3,808.1	$22.47	$11.10	10.0%		
New England:	$182.1	$18.45	8.03	7.8	(6)	(6)
Maine	22.1	23.49	14.07	11.7	29	26
New Hampshire	10.5	18.24	9.81	9.3	37	36
Vermont	11.0	29.72	17.57	13.0	18	18
Massachusetts	87.9	18.21	7.74	7.2	38	40
Rhode Island	20.2	23.52	11.75	12.2	26	34
Connecticut	30.4	13.38	4.78	5.4	45	47
Mideast:	510.0	13.89	5.80	5.9	(8)	(8)
New York	254.2	15.74	6.21	5.6	43	43
New Jersey	56.0	9.97	3.97	4.7	48	48
Pennsylvania	139.9	12.70	6.00	6.4	46	46
Delaware	8.1	18.78	6.79	9.1	35	42
Maryland	51.8	17.90	8.30	8.6	39	39
Great Lakes:	555.4	15.85	7.16	7.4	(7)	(7)
Michigan	142.9	18.55	8.56	7.9	36	37
Ohio	147.2	15.99	7.10	8.0	42	41
Indiana	56.5	12.54	6.21	6.8	47	44
Illinois	146.1	15.06	6.20	6.9	44	45
Wisconsin	62.7	16.24	8.46	7.0	41	38
Plains:	$409.3	$26.74	$14.66	12.3	(4)	(4)
Minnesota	79.2	23.88	12.90	9.8	25	29
Iowa	62.0	22.27	12.26	9.7	30	31
Missouri	128.2	30.24	15.52	16.7	16	23
North Dakota	20.6	31.96	22.31	12.3	14	12
South Dakota	27.5	39.73	25.61	16.4	7	5
Nebraska	33.8	23.50	12.79	12.0	27	30
	58.0	27.63	15.20	11.7	20	24

Southeast:	930.6	25.02	17.53	14.1	(5)	(3)
Virginia	66.2	17.29	10.50	9.6	40	35
West Virginia	37.6	19.13	12.23	12.7	34	32
Kentucky	66.5	21.87	15.95	14.5	31	22
Tennessee	80.9	23.50	16.88	14.2	28	20
North Carolina	117.4	26.25	19.81	16.1	22	15
South Carolina	46.8	19.76	16.74	13.2	33	21
Georgia	97.1	25.75	17.96	14.3	23	17
Florida	89.4	21.25	11.89	9.7	32	33
Alabama	101.7	32.16	24.38	19.9	13	10
Mississippi	59.1	27.28	28.23	17.0	21	3
Louisiana	117.4	38.28	24.43	14.7	9	9
Arkansas	50.5	28.38	24.83	18.8	19	8
Southwest:	413.6	30.91	17.65	14.5	(3)	(2)
Oklahoma	92.0	40.75	24.94	17.5	5	7
Texas	233.7	25.47	14.28	12.8	24	25
New Mexico	54.2	66.68	38.75	22.5	2	2
Arizona	33.7	31.25	16.95	12.8	15	19
Rocky Mountain:	$177.6	$42.84	$22.97	16.4	(1)	(1)
Montana	32.8	48.84	25.95	17.7	4	4
Idaho	23.4	36.27	22.43	16.0	10	11
Wyoming	26.9	84.88	41.78	24.8	1	1
Colorado	66.6	40.02	19.93	14.8	6	13
Utah	27.9	33.25	19.37	14.5	12	16
Far West:	629.5	33.70	14.00	11.1	(2)	(5)
Washington	81.0	29.73	13.99	11.2	17	27
Oregon	67.1	38.53	19.84	13.9	8	14
Nevada	16.3	62.36	25.25	17.4	3	6
California	465.1	33.51	13.24	10.7	11	28

SOURCES: Bureau of the Census, Governments Division, 1957 Census of Governments advance releases, No. 8, *State and Local Government Finances in 1957*, February 1959, Tables 3–6, with 48-state and regional amounts per capita and per $1,000 of personal income supplied by using regional totals in *Survey of Current Business*, August 1958, p. 13. Regional percentages computed from Table 3 of the Governments Division compilation.

the lowest-income group was 34 per cent *above* the national average, and in the highest-income group, 12 per cent *below*.

4. For highway construction, per capita grants tended to be highest in the middle-income states. In the seventeen middle states, the average grant was 43 per cent *above* the national average. In the sixteen lowest-income states the grant average was 13 per cent *above* the national average. In the sixteen highest-income states, it was 24 per cent *below* the national average. The greatly increased grants for the 41,000-mile interstate network began in fiscal 1957.

5. Employment-security also reveals a special pattern. These grants are primarily for the full administrative expenses of the state unemployment compensation system and employment services. Their expense runs highest, relative to total population, in the more industrialized states—and these are the states with the highest per capita incomes. Thus, the federal grants for employment-security in the sixteen lowest-income states averaged 25 per cent *below* the national per capita average, and the average for the middle-income group was almost as low. In the sixteen highest-income states, the grants averaged 17 per cent *above* the national average.

6. In grants for education, the largest amount of federal aid in recent years has been for school districts especially affected by federal government activities, such as military installations. Education grants in the aggregate in the sixteen lowest-income states averaged 11 per cent *above* the national per capita average but they were still higher in the middle-income group—24 per cent *above* the national average. For the sixteen highest-income states, grants for education fell *below* the national average by 14 per cent.

7. All other grants, for a variety of programs taken as a group, exhibited some general tendency toward equalization relative to personal incomes. In the sixteen lowest-income states, the average per capita was 62 per cent *above* the national average, and in the sixteen highest-income states it was 24 per cent *below*. The middle-group average was close to the national average.

B. FUNCTIONAL OR PROGRAM DIFFERENCES

The foregoing comparisons relate federal aid in the fiscal year 1957 to per capita personal incomes. The pattern of federal aid may also be usefully described in terms of geographical or other variations in the direct, quantitative importance of federal support for the several functions of state and local governments. The following general and somewhat tentative account is drawn from a combination of data already published in Census reports and those available from other sources. It is based on summations for the five years, 1953 through 1957.

The importance of federal financial aid in particular program categories may be assessed from the separate points of view of the state-local and the national governments. The relationship to the state-local programs is described first.

FEDERAL AID RELATED TO STATE-LOCAL EXPENDITURES BY PROGRAM CATEGORIES. The concentration of federal aid upon two or three program categories is evident both in Table 16, giving per capita amounts, and in Table 20, giving aggregates over a longer period. Of

TABLE 20
Federal Financing of State and Local Functions in the
Five-Year Period, 1953–57, Inclusive
(millions of dollars)

Category	Total	From Federal Government	From State and Local Sources[a]	Federal as Percentage of Total
General revenue, total	$160,369	$16,140[b]	$144,229	10.1
Direct general expenditures:				
Total	169,484	16,158	153,326	9.5
By functions:				
Public welfare	15,692	7,215	8,477	46.0
Health and hospitals	13,131	481	12,650	3.7
Employment security administration	1,050	1,050	0	100.0
Education	59,575	2,644	56,931	4.4
Highways	31,681	3,305	28,376	10.4
Natural resources	4,168	438	3,730	10.5
Other and unallocable	44,187	1,025	43,162	2.3

SOURCE: Compiled from Bureau of the Census, Governments Division, annual *Summary of Governmental Finances*, 1955–56, and 1957, Tables 1 and 8.

a By subtraction.

b This tabulation reflects the Census classification of all intergovernmental expenditures by the federal government as general revenue to the state and local governments. Thus, the reported general revenue receipts of the states from the federal government in 1957 omit $30 million credited to unemployment trust fund revenues of the states; there was no corresponding item in the preceding years.

the $16 billion paid to state and local governments during the five years that ended with 1957, more than $13 billion, or five-sixths, was for public welfare, highways, and education.

The federal government financed nearly half—46 per cent—of all state and local expenditures for public welfare (and 49.8 per cent of that major segment of public welfare known as "public assistance").

Federal grants financed substantially all state administrative expenses for the employment security system (unemployment insurance and employment services).

Federal payments for highways, though substantial in amount, covered only 10.4 per cent of the $32 billion that state and local governments spent for highway purposes. The same percentage of natural resource expenditures was financed by federal aid; the dollar-amount of this aid, however, was much smaller.

Federal assistance for education has been dominated by the geographically spotty distribution to selected school districts. The aggregate federal payments covered but 4.4 per cent of the near-$60-billion total of state-local direct expenditures over the five-year period.

Health and hospital expenditures in the aggregate amounted to $13 billion in the five years—barely more than a fifth of the amount for education. Federal payments financed 3.7 per cent of state-local expenditures for health and hospitals.

For nearly all other functional categories of state and local service, federal grants were relatively small in aggregate amount and small in comparative importance. Important for particular programs were federal grants for airport construction, slum clearance, urban renewal, low-rent housing, disaster relief, soldiers' homes, and perhaps a few others, but all these programs summed together were a small part of state-local expenditures. Among state and local services entirely without federal assistance, probably the largest financially are police and fire protection. Several writers have pointed out that federal aid has been used to help finance the service programs rather than the regulatory activities of government.[60]

PUBLIC ASSISTANCE. In the public assistance program, the federal grants finance—by a complicated and frequently liberalized formula —the major portion of assistance provided by public agencies to four categories of needy people: the aged, the blind, the permanently and totally disabled, and dependent children. All other needy persons who may be given relief by public agencies are classified as receiving "general assistance," a category that is not federally aided.

[60] Cf. V. O. Key, Jr., *The Administration of Federal Grants to States*, Chicago, 1937, p. 381; Paul Studenski and E. J. Baikie, "Federal Grants-in-Aid," *National Tax Journal*, September 1949, p. 197; Commission on Intergovernmental Relations, *Report* (1955), p. 125.

Until the recent rise in highway construction grants, public assistance was for years the largest single avenue of federal financial aid to state and local governments. The needs for public assistance tend to be proportionately greatest in the less affluent states. Also the formulas for federal matching of state-local expenditures have given greatest weight to the lower average relief payments in those states. Consequently, the public assistance grants have long exhibited an inverse association with average personal incomes in the several states. Extensive amendments enacted in 1958 are strengthening somewhat further this equalizing effect, although their full influence will become apparent only gradually.

The past equalizing tendency, relative to personal incomes, is evident in Table 21, in which the federal grants are shown to have financed during the period 1953–57 about two-fifths of public assistance expenditures in the twelve states with the highest per capita incomes and about two-thirds in the twelve states with the lowest per capita incomes. The progression is not regular, however. Among the six-state groups, the percentages for groups 3 and 6 deviate most noticeably. The high over-all federal percentage of 51.3 for group 3 reflects especially a ratio of 64 per cent federal financing in Missouri. The comparatively low over-all ratio of 54.9 per cent in group 6 is substantially determined by Oklahoma, which accounted for more public assistance expenditures than the other five states combined.

FEDERAL AID RELATED TO FEDERAL EXPENDITURES BY PROGRAM CATEGORIES. As is evident in Table 22, the federal functional categories in which federal-aid payments were most significant during the five fiscal years, 1953–57, were (1) labor and welfare—83 per cent, and (2) commerce and housing—38 per cent.

Labor and welfare as a budget category includes public assistance, a program in which the grant payments accounted for all but one-tenth of 1 per cent of the federal expenditures. It includes also labor and manpower, in which the grants (predominantly for employment security) represented 75 per cent of the federal outlay; and education, in which they were 74 per cent. In the field of public health, including hospital construction grants, federal aid represented less than half—45 per cent—of all federal expenditures for the five years. Of the hospital grants, about half were for private, nonprofit institutions. There was no federal aid for correctional and penal institutions, although there were payments for the use of local jails. There would

205

TABLE 21

Public Assistance Financing, by Groups of States:
Five-Year Totals, 1953–57, Inclusive

GROUP OF 6 STATES (GROUPED IN ORDER OF AVERAGE PERSONAL INCOMES PER CAPITA, 4 YEARS 1954–57)	EXPENDITURES FOR PUBLIC ASSISTANCE,[a] 5 YEARS 1953–57			
	Total	*Federal*	*State*	*Local*
AMOUNT (MILLIONS)				
Group 1 (highest incomes)	$3,766	$1,543	$1,346	$877
2	3,282	1,341	1,525	416
3	1,660	852	710	98
4	1,297	542	443	312
5	1,485	940	467	78
6	798	438	340	20
7	1,440	927	460	53
8 (lowest incomes)	1,167	838	280	50
48-State total	14,895	7,419	5,571	1,905
PERCENTAGE OF TOTAL FOR THE GROUP				
Group 1 (highest incomes)	100.0	41.0	35.7	23.3
2	100.0	40.8	46.5	12.7
3	100.0	51.3	42.8	5.9
4	100.0	41.8	34.2	24.0
5	100.0	63.3	31.4	5.3
6	100.0	54.9	42.6	2.5
7	100.0	64.4	31.9	3.7
8 (lowest incomes)	100.0	71.7	24.0	4.3
48-State total	100.0	49.8	37.4	12.8
PERCENTAGE OF 48-STATE TOTAL				
Group 1 (highest incomes)	25.3	20.8	24.2	46.0
2	22.0	18.1	27.4	21.9
3	11.1	11.5	12.7	5.1
4	8.7	7.3	7.9	16.4
5	10.0	12.6	8.4	4.1
6	5.4	5.9	6.1	1.1
7	9.7	12.5	8.3	2.8
8 (lowest incomes)	7.8	11.3	5.0	2.6
48-State total	100.0	100.0	100.0	100.0

SOURCE: Basic data from *Social Security Bulletin*, Annual Statistical Supplements for 1953–57 inclusive.

[a] Comprises the four federally aided categories, general assistance, and administrative expenses.

TABLE 22

Federal Aid to State and Local Governments as an Element in Federal
Finance, in the Five Fiscal Years, 1953–57, Inclusive

MAJOR FUNCTION OR SUBFUNCTION IN FEDERAL BUDGET	AMOUNT (IN MILLIONS)		FEDERAL AID EXPENDITURES AS PERCENTAGE	
	Total Federal Expenditures[a]	Federal Aid Expenditures[a]	of this Category	of all Federal Aid
Federal Government, Total	$343,555	$16,502	4.8	100.0
Major national security	228,030	–	0	0
International affairs and finance	3,727	–	0	0
Veterans services and benefits	22,560	36	0.1	0.2
Labor and Welfare:				
Public assistance	7,214	7,205	99.9	43.7
Labor and manpower	1,761	1,318	74.8	8.0
Promotion of public health (includes hospitals)	1,703	764	44.9	4.6
Education	1,456	1,084	74.4	6.6
Science, research, libraries, museums	247	1	0.4	b
Correctional and penal institutions	144	–	0	0
Other welfare and administration	679	570	83.9	3.4
Total, Labor and Welfare	$13,204	$10,942	82.9	66.3
Commerce and housing:				
Provision of highways	3,593	3,293	91.6	20.0
Promotion of aviation	1,313	90	6.8	0.5
Promotion of water transportation	1,959	1	0.1	b
Housing, community development and facilities	295c	85	28.8	0.5
Civil defense	272	52	19.1	0.3
Other commerce[d]	1,833c	49	2.7	0.3
Total, commerce and housing	$9,265	$3,570	38.5	21.6
Agriculture and agricultural resources	19,399	1,332	6.9	8.1
Natural resources	6,393	419	6.6	2.5
General government	7,332	204	2.8	1.2
Interest	33,645	–	0	0

SOURCE: Compiled from "actual" fiscal year expenditures shown in the federal *Budget* documents for the fiscal years 1955–59, inclusive. Federal aid is the sum of grants, shared revenues, and net loans reported in Special Analysis G or H of the several *Budget* volumes.

[a] "Expenditures" here represent federal "net budget expenditures" plus highway trust fund expenditures for 1957, which was the first year of the trust fund.

[b] Less than one-twentieth of 1 per cent.

[c] After deducting receipts that were credited against expenditures.

[d] Comprises postal service deficits; aids to business; regulation of commerce and finance; and disaster insurance, loans, and relief. For "aids to business," there were $869 million of net receipts (negative expenditures) in the five years.

207

have been no federal aid for libraries, museums, science, and general-purpose research but for the introduction of demonstration grants for rural libraries in fiscal 1957.

In the commerce and housing category, the outstanding subject of aid is highway construction. For the five-year period, federal grants for state and local highway building took 92 per cent of all the federal expenditures for "provision of highways" (including in 1957 the highway trust fund expenditures). Airport construction grants represented under 7 per cent of federal expenditures to promote aviation. In the promotion of water transportation, only the federal grants to state marine schools are considered intergovernmental aids; these were $1 million in a five-year total of nearly $2 billion of expenditures. The large expenditures for river and harbor development and other navigation improvements are considered direct federal programs, not financial aids to states and their subdivisions.

In the case of housing, slum clearance, and urban redevelopment programs—also part of the commerce and housing category—measurement of the relative importance of federal aids is complicated by the accounting system. In these programs, a large part of the aids takes the form of loans rather than grants; as already noted, the loan disbursements are considered expenditures and any repayments received are considered "negative expenditures." For some parts of the program in some years—and indeed for the public housing programs as a group for the whole five years—the federal expenditures are negative; i.e., receipts exceed expenditures. Thus, neither the $295 million of total federal expenditures nor the $85 million of federal aids shown for housing and community development and facilities is an actual measure of federal financial operations in this field during 1953–57. A different handling of the transactions could easily change the ratio of federal aid to total federal expenditures in this category from the 28.8 per cent shown in Table 22 to some other magnitude. In fact, the same can be said for the over-all percentage of 38.5 for commerce and housing, since the stated amount of federal expenditures (budgetary plus the highway trust fund) is affected not only by the repayments on public housing, slum clearance, and urban redevelopment loans, but also by the deduction of other receipts credited against expenditures. Dependable measurement of the importance of federal aid as a component of this category of the federal budget would require special interpretations of the data.

The purported 6.9 per cent of expenditures classified as federal aid in agriculture and agricultural resource programs must be similarly qualified because the aggregate federal expenditures are a similar composite comprising not only the net amount of loan transactions, but also the net result of commodity purchases and sales. However, the 6.9 per cent certainly gives a correct general impression—that is, that federal aid to state and local governments is relatively a small part of the federal government programs for agriculture. The aids in this category are largely commodity distributions to the school lunch program and other state-local agencies. (Cash grants to the school lunch program are included in "other welfare services" and help explain the high proportion of federal aid in that subfunction of labor and welfare.) Also important are payments for cooperative agricultural extension work and agricultural experiment stations.

The similar magnitude for natural resources—6.6 per cent devoted to aid to state and local governments—is a reasonably clear figure. Direct federal programs dominate this functional category, also. Much of the aid is in shared revenues from mineral leasing, timber sales in the national forests, and TVA operations (the latter distributed as payments "in lieu of taxes"); the rest is largely in grants for wildlife restoration and forestry cooperation.

The reported federal aid for purposes of "general government"— measured at 2.8 per cent of all federal expenditures for general government—can be misleading, since the payments during 1953–57 were exclusively to the District of Columbia and various territories and possessions. None of these expenditures was for assistance to any state or its subdivisions.

Budget expenditures for interest on the public debt were slightly more than twice the total for federal aid in the period 1953–57.

C. SOME FEDERAL PROGRAM DEVELOPMENTS AFFECTING STATE-LOCAL FISCAL NEEDS

In some fields, such as public assistance, major highway construction, slum clearance, and urban redevelopment, the pressures for expanded federal financial assistance to state and local governments have operated inexorably. In others, such as education and resource conservation, pressures have been persistent and strong but the resistance has been stronger. An interpretation of the differences might be enlightening, but it would require more intensive analysis than can be undertaken in this paper, as well as subjective evaluations outside its intended scope. On the other hand, a sketch of some related developments seems necessary to a consideration of factors shaping the next decade.

FEDERAL PROGRAM OPERATIONS THAT RELIEVE STATE AND LOCAL GOVERNMENTS. When the federal government in 1928–30 took direct responsibility for completing the improvement of the Illinois Waterway and for its subsequent operation, it relieved the state of Illinois from the necessity of proceeding with a project on which the state had already expended $16 million. The federal government in the ensuing thirty years invested twice that amount in new work, besides $28 million for operation and maintenance. The Corps of Engineers has reported that in 1957 the original project was 96 per cent completed, but the revised project, which now includes related works even more costly than the original Waterway, was only 18 per cent completed. The revised cost estimate in 1957 was $160 million for project construction, with annual maintenance costs on the completed work averaging $1.8 million a year and expenditures for operation and care running even higher.[61] The state government finances no part of the waterway construction, maintenance, or operation.

Such a dramatic transfer of a specific responsibility, though not unique, is a comparatively rare event. Usually the shift is more generalized. When the program for the federal interstate highway network was enacted, with its provision of federal grants for 90 per cent of the construction costs of toll-free superhighways, one almost immediate result was a cooling off of enthusiasm for additional toll-charging turnpikes under state or special-authority auspices.[62] The toll roads, of course, have been financed by revenue bonds and operated as commercial-type enterprises, but in the Census Bureau statistics they are included in "direct general government." Initiation of the federal program had a strong impact on state and local activities in this field—though it is too soon to say whether the immediate response will prove to have been an acceleration or, as seems more likely, some lessening of the rate of increase in construction outlays from the state and local governments' own sources of revenue. The high standards of construction on the interstate network may permit some postponement of maintenance costs and retention of lower standards on some local roads.

Whatever the first reaction, it seems plausible in the case of the

---

[61] U.S. Department of the Army, Corps of Engineers, 1957 Annual Report, *Chief of Engineers, Civil Works Activities* (1958), Vol. 2, pp. 1274–5.
[62] Cf. *Business Week*, October 18, 1958, pp. 58–64.

highway program to expect that after a few years state and local financing for maintenance and operation of the road system will have to increase above recent levels—unless, of course, federal aid is broadened to cover these needs. Will future state-local outlays for construction, maintenance, and operation in the aggregate be greater or less than if there had been no special federal program?

In another field, urban renewal and slum clearance projects prosecuted with federal financial assistance may arrest the deterioration of central city areas, ultimately salvaging a significant part of the local tax base and strengthening city finances.

PUBLIC ASSISTANCE AND OASDI. Less direct and obvious, though equally real, is the relationship between the federally operated system of old-age, survivors, and disability insurance and the federal-state local system of public assistance.

As noted earlier, the pressure for increase in federal grants for this program has been practically irresistible. Since 1950 specific provision has been made to finance with federal grants a substantial part of the payments made to vendors of medical care for persons on public assistance. The matching formulas have been liberalized repeatedly. A further increase in the federal share, accompanied by adjustments in the formulas, was enacted in 1958; the effects will not be fully reflected in assistance payments and financing for another year or two.

At the same time, the gradual maturing of OASDI since its inception in 1935–39, coupled with its broad expansion in the decade of the 1950's, has greatly lessened otherwise mounting pressures for public assistance expenditures. So marked has been the effect that even in this era of rapidly growing population, with its especially rapid growth of the proportions who are in the dependent groups of the very old and very young, the number of recipients of public assistance now is somewhat lower than in 1950. In the face of rising personal incomes, living standards, and consumer prices, the aggregate of payments (excluding administrative expense) advanced 28 per cent from 1950 to 1957—an interval in which consumer prices alone advanced 17 per cent.[63]

[63] This is the increase in the average consumer price index for the calendar years. Medical care prices within the consumer price index advanced 36 per cent in the calendar year averages. Medical care is an especially important segment of public assistance expenditures, accounting in 1957 for $224 million of money payments directly to vendors of medical services in the four federally aided categories, to which should be added any direct expenditures by assistance recipients and the medical care expenditures made for recipients of general assistance.

The OASDI program has affected all the categories of public assistance but most significantly the major category, old-age assistance. In fact, the numbers drawing aid to dependent children and the blind rose nearly one-eighth from 1950 to late 1958. The number of the permanently and totally disabled receiving assistance rose also, but in 1950 this category was newly separated from general assistance and was identified in only a few states. The over-all total on public assistance rolls declined because of a 12 per cent decrease in the number of recipients of old-age assistance. Also, despite the recession of 1957–58, the number of persons drawing general assistance was less in late 1958 than in the post-recovery month of December 1950.[64]

For old-age assistance, federal, state, and local expenditures for assistance payments in calendar 1957 were $1,773 million, with 56 per cent of the total provided by the federal government.[65] On an average for the whole country, about one-sixth of the population of age sixty-five and over received old-age assistance payments—168 in each 1,000 in June 1957, and 162 in each 1,000 a year later. In the 1940's the average was 212 in each 1,000.[66] Suppose that proportion had persisted. In that event, the difference in numbers alone would have meant old-age assistance benefit payments in 1957 more than one-fourth greater, some $465 million more, than the actual total of $1,773 million. Moreover, an increasing percentage of the old-age assistance recipients—by June 1957, 571,000 persons, or close to one-fourth— were being given relatively small amounts of public assistance to supplement inadequate OASDI benefits. In the 1940's, relatively few persons drew both old-age assistance and OASDI benefits at the same time. The average assistance payment in 1957 necessarily would have been substantially higher in the absence of OASDI. The difference is not easily estimated, but each $1 additional in the over-all monthly average of old-age assistance payments for the year 1957 would have required $30 million more of federal-state-local expenditure for the 2.5 million persons then on the rolls.

Without OASDI, then, the larger number who would have been drawing old-age assistance and the higher amount of the average individual payment might easily have required some $750 to $850

[64] Data on numbers receiving assistance are from *Social Security Bulletin*, Annual Statistical Supplement, 1957, principally p. 74; and *Social Security Bulletin*, January 1959, p. 27.

[65] These aggregates include the District of Columbia, Alaska, Hawaii, Puerto Rico, and the Virgin Islands. *Ibid.*, Annual Statistical Supplement, 1957, pp. 74 and 84, Tables 105 and 108.

[66] Bureau of Public Assistance, *op.cit.*, p. 56.

million more of assistance payments. With federal grants at the 1957 proportion of 56 per cent—a proportion considerably higher than in the 1940's—an additional total outlay of this magnitude would have called for $330 to $375 million more from state-local sources.[67]

The maturing and expansion of the federal OASDI system has been almost certainly the major change taking pressure off old-age assistance—surely a stronger factor, even, than rising prosperity. This shift to primary reliance on a contributory insurance system was, indeed, an original advantage asserted for the social security law.

Public assistance, then, is an area in which a federal program has relieved the state and local governments of a growing share of a large responsibility. Even without further liberalization of the OASDI system, its effects should be still more pronounced a decade hence. At that time, less than 10 per cent of the aged population will lack eligibility for the insurance benefits.

When the Commission on Intergovernmental Relations examined the public assistance grants several years ago, it recommended that general assistance should continue to be financed and administered by the states and their subdivisions, and that, as total national-state expenditures for old-age assistance decrease, the contribution of the national government to this program be decreased by approximately the same amount. Also, it proposed revision of the formula governing federal financial participation in old-age assistance so that greater equalization of the burden will be achieved.[68]

The 1958 amendments moved in the direction of greater equalization relative to personal incomes. They provided, however, for an increased federal share in financing of the public assistance program as a whole and at the same time raised the insurance benefits.

What additional lessening of potential state-local responsibilities may follow this important legislation? How far can public assistance shrink in relative importance on the basis of the continuing expansion of federally administered social insurance? What other factors will operate in this general area?

Legislation has often been proposed and is currently being urged that would create a new federal-aid category for general assistance or,

---

[67] If the comparisons were based on averages for December rather than June, the additional outlay to care for the larger number of recipients would be $558 million, rather than $465 million. The wholesale calculation, with its rough allowance for the level of assistance payments, probably understates the aggregate reduction in old-age assistance even though it omits qualifications for the possible impact of the OASDI system on private pensions and savings, as well as refinements for interstate differences.

[68] In the Commission's Report, cited *supra*, cf. pp. 270–1.

in some versions, would wipe out all the categorical distinctions. An advisory council appointed by the Secretary of Health, Education, and Welfare is examining the whole question of public assistance, including its future relation to old-age, survivors, and disability insurance, and the desirable division of financial responsiblity between the federal and the state and local governments.

During the recession of 1957–58, not only were bills introduced in congress to bring the general assistance category under the umbrella of federal aid, but there was strong support for related proposals to pay from general federal revenues unemployment benefits for two groups of unemployed persons: those whose entitlement to insurance benefits under state laws was exhausted and those who had no insurance entitlement. The temporary extended unemployment compensation law that was enacted in 1958 provided for those whose rights were exhausted but not for the uninsured. Moreover, it calls for ultimate repayment of the federal expenditures made in the seventeen states that joined the program.

FEDERAL PROGRAM OPERATIONS THAT GIVE RISE TO SPECIAL NEEDS. Except in periods of war, there appear to be few instances of widespread need for state and local services created by program operations of the federal government. Perhaps the peacetime need for civil defense organization and preparations is one such instance, but it serves also in local and regional civil disasters. Another instance is the provision of schools and other local services for children living on federally owned land or for the children of persons who work in tax-free federal establishments.

Customarily, special federal aids have been provided in such circumstances. Thus there are grants-in-aid for civil defense and for the construction and operation of schools in communities especially affected by federal government activities; there are special schools for some Indian children who are wards of the federal government and special aids to local school systems that accommodate other children living on Indian reservations; there are special services for communities created for the atomic energy program and reclamation projects, and arrangements to help finance state and local governments in the area of the Tennessee Valley Authority.

Whatever may be the complexities or shortcomings of any or all of these special programs, the pertinent fact for the present inquiry is that we have here no policy vacuum. The policy issues that arise, rather, are those relating to consistency and equality that inevitably accumulate in a series of piecemeal provisions for interrelated problems.

OTHER ILLUSTRATIVE CASES. The significance of some federal programs for state-local finance may be real, yet indeterminate in fiscal direction.

A federal reclamation project, making possible the settlement and exploitation of a comparatively arid tract of land, may mean more services from and revenues for the county government or other local units. Whether the added revenues outweigh the added expenses depends on local circumstances.

The federal government has undertaken major research and demonstrations directed toward the production of useable water from saline and brackish sources. These efforts, if successful, may make available lower-cost water supplies for communities where the present or threatened scarcity of an adequate supply of potable water is a subject of concern and expense. Success may also mean more population—and more local government services—in areas that now are settled sparsely or not at all. Similar consequences could flow from weather-modification studies that have been authorized.

In fact, the general environmental situation in which all state and local governments will be operating ten or twenty years hence may be profoundly affected by the findings and the application of federally sponsored or federally stimulated research.

A striking current instance is the transformation of care for the mentally ill—a field worth reviewing in some detail as a case illustrating how a limited program of intergovernmental aid sometimes meets with a substantial response.

About half of the hospital patients in the United States are in mental institutions—most of them in state hospitals. For a century, these hospitals were little more than places of custody and detention —overcrowded asylums offering little hope to the hundreds of thousands of people who were brought within their walls.

In 1854, Congress yielded to the entreaties of that "angel of mercy," Dorothea Lynde Dix, by voting to donate federal lands to aid the states in the care and support of the mentally ill. President Pierce vetoed the bill. He held that this was an improper intrusion of the federal government into a field of local responsibility. There was no federal aid for care of the mentally ill until 1946, when the National Mental Health Act was adopted. That legislation established a National Institute of Mental Health, a research agency, in the Public

Health Service. It provided grants to research workers in state and private institutions; it provided help to medical schools to encourage them to train more professional personnel; and it inaugurated small grants to the states for community mental health services. The grant payments to all the states under the Act were $1.6 million in the first fiscal year, 1948; they are estimated at $4 million annually in the fiscal years 1959 and 1960.

Soon after the National Mental Health Act was adopted, a few of the states began to examine their mental health programs more closely. The major impetus for this reawakening, it has been said, was the federal legislation:[69]

"After the passage of the Act of 1946 the states bestirred themselves. They started to build buildings. They hired more doctors, nurses, and attendants and raised their salaries. They matched federal grants. They reorganized their mental health departments. They established preventive programs—community clinics, child-guidance clinics, out-patient clinics. By 1953 the states were spending three times what they had spent on their state hospitals nine years before—half a billion dollars a year. Some states had multiplied their expenditures fantastically during that same period—Kansas by 610 per cent. Capital outlays became enormous—New York alone spent $350 million building hospitals. New research and training centers were set up. Salaries were increased until in some states mental health officials were earning more than governors. State spending far outran federal."[70]

For the current operating costs of mental institutions, the states alone reported expenditures of $189 million in 1946. By 1953, the total had risen to $498 million and by 1957 to $686 million, with capital outlays approaching $200 million a year. The budget of New York State currently includes a larger amount for mental hospitals than was expended in 1946 by all the 48 states together.[71]

[69] John Bartlow Martin, "A Better Break for the Mentally Ill," in *Harpers*, February 1959, pp. 58–64, tells the story of these developments.

[70] *Ibid.*, p. 59. See, also, the same writer's book-length report, *The Pane of Glass* (Harpers, 1959), from which the magazine article is taken.

[71] Annual totals for state hospital operating expenses are reported on p. 44 in Council of State Governments, *The Mental Health Programs of the 48 States, a Report to the Governors' Conference* (Chicago, June 1950; 377 pages), prepared in response to a resolution of the Governors' Conference of June 1949. Data for 1953 and 1957 are from Bureau of the Census, Governments Division, *Compendium of State Finances*, 1953, p. 35, and 1957, p. 31. The New York State budget as proposed for 1959–60 included $203 million for mental hospital operations and $39 million for construction (*The New York Times*, February 3, 1959).

It may be assumed that the federal legislation, with its effect of prodding the states, was itself an outcome of the same rising medical, economic, and humanitarian concern that was pushing inevitably toward concerted action at all levels of government. The interest of individual states led to discussions in the Governors' Conference, a state-sponsored study of the subject, and the formation of an Interstate Clearinghouse on Mental Health for the exchange of information and ideas.[72]

The application of various new drugs, beginning on a large scale in 1953, has had much influence. This, however, is not directly an outgrowth of federal research and leadership.

Whatever the prime cause, it is clear that federal legislation and action contributed significantly to the mental health revolution of the last dozen years. The nationwide ferment led to further federal action in the form of a law enacted by Congress, the Mental Health Study Act of 1955, giving official sanction to a three-year study by a Joint Commission on Mental Illness and Health—a joint, nonprofit project of the American Psychiatric Association, the Council on Mental Health of the American Medical Association, and a score of national professional and lay organizations. Congress appropriated $1,250,000 for the Joint Commission, and the states and private sources have supplemented this financing. The Commission's interim reports have already influenced public attitudes toward the state programs for preventing and treating mental illness and promoting mental health.

Already the overcrowded mental hospitals have experienced some actual reduction of population—from 558,000 at the end of 1955 to 547,000 two years later.[73] What is more significant in terms of human welfare is that there has been some shortening of the average patient's stay. Between 1945 and 1957, admissions to state and local public mental hospitals increased from 115 to 150 for each 100,000 of

[72] Cf. the Council of State Governments report cited in the preceding footnote; also, by the Council's Interstate Clearinghouse on Mental Health, *State Action in Mental Health: A Summary of Financial, Legal and Administrative Developments in State Mental Health Programs*, 1956–57 (mimeo., 95 pages; April 1958).

[73] Department of Health, Education, and Welfare, Office of the Secretary—Office of Program Analysis, *Health, Education, and Welfare Trends*, 1959 ed., p. 36. Of a total of 623,938 resident mental patients in all United States hospitals at the end of 1957, 547,495 were in state, county, and city hospitals; 60,935 in Veterans Administration hospitals; 1,965 in United States Public Health Service hospitals; and 13,543 in private hospitals. For resident patients in state-local hospitals, the rate per 100,000 of the civilian population reached a peak of 441.0 in 1954 and declined during the next three years to 417.1 at the end of 1957.

civilian population. At the same time, releases rose from 154 a year to 175 a year for each 1,000 resident patients.[74]

Some researchers think schizophrenia and certain other mental illnesses may be linked significantly to the bodily chemistry of the patient; this avenue of research is one of the most hopeful in the whole field of mental health. The expense for each patient-day of residence will clearly be greater if the care is to be more intensive, more professional, and more efficacious. The possibilities in the realm of patient-costs may be suggested by some quick comparisons. The estimated average cost of maintaining a patient in a public nonfederal mental hospital in 1957 was $3.64 a day. This was 38 cents—12 per cent—more than the daily average only one year earlier.[75] It was more than twice the median cost for 1949.[76] The patient-day costs for neuropsychiatric patients in the federal government hospitals for veterans for many years have run far ahead of average patient-day costs in state mental hospitals—and the average length of the patient's stay in the veterans' hospitals has been decidedly shorter. Last year the operation and maintenance costs in the veterans' hospitals averaged $4.01 a patient-day; estimates for fiscal 1960 indicate a rise to $4.37.[77] An average increase from $3.64 to $4.37 for all the patients in state-local mental hospitals in 1957 would have meant something like $146 million a year of additional expenditures.

Suppose the state and local governments undertake to improve care. Will the greater expense for each patient-day mean, in the aggregate, greater or less expense over the hospital stay of each admitted patient? What will be the net effect on state and local finances (let alone the net effect on the national income) of the rehabilitation and renewed productivity of millions of helpless persons who, under present arrangements, are consumers only?[78]

D. SOME EVALUATIONS OF FEDERAL AID

This review has indicated that federal aid is an important source of revenue for state and local governments—a major source for

[74] *Ibid.*, p. 37.
[75] National Institute of Mental Health, *Facts on Mental Health and Mental Illness* (revised May 1958), p. 7.
[76] Derived from median annual cost in Council of State Governments, *Mental Health Programs of the 48 States*, p. 262.
[77] Calculated from operating costs and average daily patient loads shown in federal *Budget* for fiscal year 1960, pp. 217–8.
[78] For a prognostication based on the foreseeable effects of tranquilizers and energizers alone, cf. Rudolph Kieve, "The Chemical Revolution in Psychiatry: Its Effects on

financing certain of their functions, such as public assistance and highways, and a relatively negligible source for others, such as education, natural resources, and agriculture. As a channel for expenditures, federal aid is a sizable but not a major item in the federal budget. In the labor and welfare field, however, it is a dominant channel of expenditure.

Geographic variations in the distribution of federal aid tend to be associated with differences in personal incomes. In the aggregate and for several program categories, per capita federal grants have been highest in the group of low-income states and lowest in the high-income group. The services exhibiting this association are public assistance—the largest grant category and the program for which income-differences may be considered most meaningful; the health services, "other" welfare services, and a catch-all category of other programs taken as a group. In the highway construction, employment security, and education grants there has been no clear tendency for the highest proportionate grants to go to the states with the lowest incomes; each of these categories is a special case.

Over the last two decades, proposals have been advanced from time to time that the fiscal structure of interlevel relations might be simplified, and the independence and strength of the states enhanced by a simultaneous reduction in federal grants and selected federal taxes yielding an equal amount. The Commission on Intergovernmental Relations concluded that it could not support this proposition. It commented as follows:

"This approach would be inadequate in the current situation, since grants serve an essential purpose by assisting in the support of specific functional programs. Moreover, any general or selective reduction or repeal of federal grants coupled with an equivalent reduction in federal taxes would intensify the fiscal problems of the lower-income states, which would lose far more in grants than they would gain in taxes. On the other hand, a tax cut of sufficient magnitude to

---

the Care of the Mentally Ill," *State Government*, Spring 1959, pp. 104–8. Dr. Kieve predicts "that, not too far in the future, public mental institutions will not only have little claim for expansion—replacement of indispensable equipment aside—but that many will have to prepare for contraction," and that "it will not be possible much longer to shift so much responsibility—financial, legal, and moral—for the mentally ill from the municipality and county level to the state level," pp. 106–7. He suggests that the productive years of the mentally ill will be greatly increased and the costs of public care may be substantially reduced or recouped.

indemnify fully every state would result in a total loss of federal revenue that would far exceed the grant reductions."[79]

The Joint Federal-State Action Committee has examined various specific approaches to interrelated tax and grant reduction. It has documented one by one the practical difficulties involved in trying to work out such a program, and, as indicated in Section 2 above, has recommended a transfer of part of the federal telephone tax to the states in exchange for withdrawal of federal grants for vocational education and for construction of waste treatment plants, with state assumption of full responsibility for these programs. The tax reduction and distribution were estimated for 1958 at $147.5 million, and the grant reduction at $86.5 million. The President endorsed this proposal,[80] but neither in Congress nor in the states does favorable action appear to be imminent.

The Committee's program, it has been aptly said, makes clear that the practical choices are quite limited. They embrace (1) a choice between a carrot for state-local expenditure programs and a carrot for state-local tax programs, and (2) a choice between equalizing federal program grants and some type of equalizing fiscal grant.[81]

A general evaluation offered by the House Committee on Government Operations may provide a convenient summary for this review. After conducting extensive regional hearings in all parts of the country, after examining hundreds of replies to a comprehensive questionnaire and analyzing detailed statistical data supplied by federal agencies as well as by state and local governments, a subcommittee reported as follows—and the full Committee concurred unanimously:

"With relatively few exceptions, the subcommittee has found a favorable acceptance throughout the nation of the use of grants and of most existing grant purposes. Although a number of witnesses and questionnaire respondents signified that as a general principle their state or local governments would be willing to assume

[79] Commission on Intergovernmental Relations, *Report*, pp. 115–6. Four members of the 25-member Commission dissented, arguing that the tax and grant reductions, "with the reduced grants being more heavily equalized," would be a move in the right direction. They observed that "no nice balance is to be expected; tax and grant reductions should not even be respectively earmarked." (*Ibid.*, footnote.)

[80] Federal *Budget* for fiscal year 1960, p. M65.

[81] Selma J. Mushkin, "Fiscal Capacity of the States," address before the National Tax Conference, Philadelphia, October 29, 1958, published by the National Tax Association in the 1958, *Conference Proceedings* (1959), p. 304.

independent responsibility for aided functions if adequate tax sources were available, comparatively few specific grants were recommended for termination.

"In general, the subcommittee finds the grant a useful device for harnessing cooperative governmental effort in the accomplishment of a national legislative purpose. The opportunity for cooperation between the levels of government for the attainment of common objectives should be recognized as a resource of our federal system. In some circumstances the use of a grant may be the more practical and desirable method of administering an activity than confining complete responsibility to any one level of government."[82]

There is abundant reason, then, to conclude that federal aid in the form of grants, loans, and revenue-sharing—like many other practical expedients devised to meet specific needs—has become an institution firmly established as part of our federal system. As yet, a more efficient acceptable device for interlevel cooperation in the program side has not appeared.

On the other hand, federal aid is not appropriate to all types of interlevel problems. Clearly, each measure of fiscal accommodation must be applied selectively and with specific safeguards, limitations, and objectives.

In such a setting, as Harold Groves said a good many years ago, the pragmatic approach of "nibbling" promises most in the way of progress in what must be a complicated cooperative venture. Hopes for a grand solution of the fiscal coordination problem, or for a single comprehensive plan for immediate adoption, are doomed to disappointment.[83]

COMMENTS

Harold M. Groves, University of Wisconsin

Authors Ecker-Racz and Labovitz have presented a comprehensive exhibit of the fundamental research upon which the quest for practical

[82] U.S. Congress, House Committee on Government Operations, Federal-State-Local Relations: *Federal Grants-in-Aid—30th Report by the Committee*, 85th Cong., 2d sess., House Report no. 2533, August 8, 1958, pp. 26–7. The subcommittee report was adopted and submitted by the full committee.

[83] U.S. Treasury Department, Committee on Intergovernmental Fiscal Relations, *Federal, State, and Local Government Fiscal Relations: A report submitted to the Secretary of the Treasury*, 78th Cong., 1st sess., Senate doc. 69; 1943, p. 2. Harold M. Groves was chairman of the special committee that made the study; the other members were Luther Gulick and Mabel Newcomer.

solutions in intergovernmental fiscal relations must be based. They have also analyzed some of the practical difficulties involved in alternative suggestions for improvement. This is a first rate accomplishment and a valuable contribution. They have not devoted very much space to an attempt to define the problem. Perhaps this cannot be done without a good deal of "subjective evaluation" which the authors sought to avoid. Perhaps "Defining the Problem" is another paper which might have been on this agenda. Anyway, the discussant finds it difficult to say much about the practical solutions without considerable inquiry or speculation as to what they aim—or might or should aim—to accomplish in the first place. We don't need any practical solutions unless we have a problem.

Mr. Ecker-Racz suggests that the problem or major problem might be overlapping taxes. But it isn't at all clear to me that there is anything very objectionable about overlapping taxes. One tax utilized by two layers of government involves two administrations where one might suffice; but it probably involves less total administration than two different taxes, one designated for the top layer of government and one used by the lower units.

Perhaps the major difficulty is found in the fact that the states are now in considerable financial difficulty, caught in a squeeze between rising responsibilities (especially for education) and disappointing revenues. Mr. Netzer's paper offered some prognostications concerning the long-range aspects of this problem. It can be said on the reassuring side, as Ecker-Racz indicates, that very few if any states have exhausted their tax potential. Less than half the states have both income and sales taxes and very few if any of these, even within rate limits applied in other states, have exhausted these sources. As to recessions, it is true, of course, that the federal government could help the states immeasurably if it could somehow manage the economy to achieve stable prices, rapid growth, and low interest rates. But this surely is another paper. It is also true, of course, that the states' problem would be easier if the federal government did not pre-empt so much of so many taxes. The person who is in a position to do something "grand" about this is not the Secretary of Treasury but the Secretary of State.

Perhaps the problem is interstate and intercommunity competition—legislators caught in the frustration that, while they would like to raise state or local taxes to meet current demands for services, they are constrained lest the tax base or the richest part of it will move out or shun them. After all, if the states need more revenue, they have the same taxpayers in their jurisdiction that the federal government has in its. And the states enjoy all the important legal powers to tax. I expect that the competition factor is at the bottom of a considerable part of the demand—and need—for federal help. Ecker-Racz mentions it, observing that there is no creditable evidence that state taxes have affected industrial development. Whether his observation is valid, and I have no reason to question it, there is a lot of fear that it might not apply in specific cases. The fear cramps the style of the states and municipalities even if it has no valid foundation.

Perhaps the nub of our problem is increasing general property taxes. This raises a host of problems some of which carry us straight into subjective evaluation: How bad is the general property tax anyhow? Does it have any natural or other limits beyond those imposed by the constraints of intercommunity competition? On the sanguine side, we could cite the fact that while the general property tax is a heavy burden on housing, new homes are being built in large numbers. Moreover, it is not clear that property taxes have increased very much in relation to income and wealth. In Wisconsin, average state rates have been rising since 1953, but the rise has amounted to only about 10 per cent and is still less than half of a postwar drop.

Perhaps the federal government has grown too much and too fast, usurping through its aid system functions that had better be left with the states. But as Mr. Labovitz has documented, the Joint Federal State Action Committee working hard on this theme finally developed only the concrete suggestion that a part of the local telephone tax be surrendered by the federal government in exchange for assumption of full responsibility for vocational education by the states. It was a very modest program but it invoked little enthusiasm in Congress. Apparently the federal aid program is firmly established and popular.

Perhaps there is legitimate ground for the concern lest the growing importance of state and local taxes along with the erosion of the federal tax base enfeeble the progressiveness of the over-all tax system. Available data seem to indicate that the role of the tax system as equalizer is not very impressive nor is it becoming more so. However, the egalitarian debate into which this leads can hardly escape a large element of subjective evaluation.

Now, still in search for a cause of complaint or alarm, let us consider briefly some of the several major coordination institutions which our authors have passed in review.

Take for instance deductibility of state and local nonbusiness taxes against the federal income tax base. It is an old institution inaugurated apparently on the ground that income free of personal taxes is the appropriate measure of taxable capacity. The point was compromised however when a few years later federal income taxes were disallowed as a deduction. Currently, deductibility is most often defended as a coordination device. It is open to considerable objection on the grounds that it provides an uneven concession for taxpayers at different levels; it encourages the states to venture into excessive progression, largely at the expense of the federal treasury and it (as to property tax allowance) discriminates between landlords and tenants. This is a fairly impressive bill of indictment. On the other hand, deductibility affords the states some protection at the critical point of interstate competition; it is nominally neutral among state choices in their tax systems; and it has not as a matter of fact been abused. There are considerable difficulties and objections associated with alternatives that might be proposed. It is my personal view that an income tax credit could do the job now assigned to deductibility and do it better, but our authors, apparently, regarded this alternative as so inaccessible that they didn't even give it honorable mention.

Then we have the death tax credit. The person who does not have a large estate but who does favor reform wherever necessary could not examine the death tax and the credit associated with it without concluding that something should be done in this area.

Here again the first step should be an analysis of the purposes the credit is supposed to serve. It was established in the now fairly ancient past as a compromise between federal abandonment of the death tax and federal exploitation of the field with no regard for the states' preestablished interests in it. The credit was also inaugurated to mitigate the tendency of large taxpayers to migrate in contemplation of death. It was observed that it might provide the states some assistance in an area of administration where they were weak. Finally, it is apparent that a credit serves the purpose of directing the pattern of state death-tax institutions.

Suppose, for the exercise, that the last-named factor were given predominant weight in the remodeling program. Suppose the federal government, in conference with state officials, were to accept some model or modal schedule of effective state rates on estates, let us say on those with assets upwards of $20,000, presumably featuring the ideas that the states will exploit the small estates intensively and apply moderate graduation to the remainder of the scale. Suppose the federal government were then to extend the coverage of its tax to include all of these estates. Suppose the federal credit were tied to this model state-scale instead of the 1926 federal scale, and suppose that a high percentage credit—say 80 per cent—were applied to it to constitute the federal assistance to the states in this field. States could go beyond this at their own risk. The suggestion is probably utopian but it would at least have the advantage of a rationale more plausible than historical accident.

Let us turn finally to our federal aid program and inquire whether it meets the criterion of rationality which is one test of the adequacy of our coordination institutions. I find this an extremely elusive subject and I am grateful for the help of Labovitz's data and Musgrave's profound analysis. Aids can be viewed as a manifestation of federal interest in programs which are also of state interest. They can thus be viewed as federal expenditures *per se* and only incidentally a federal-state coordination device. They also may be viewed as a means for territorial equalization and of local tax relief. As presently constituted, they serve these latter purposes incidentally and not very effectively. A block grant on the Australian or British model might serve these latter objectives more advantageously. The block grant would also make more sense than our present program, if it be concluded that differential degrees of federal interest in local activities is indeterminable.

The rationale supporting present federal practice is one case where the benefits-received doctrine is still in vogue. The idea of reciprocation, of taxes justified if not measured by benefits, is the basis of the judicial doctrine that one jurisdiction cannot tax what lies outside its borders. It is only a logical extension of this idea to conclude that an over-all unit of government should not tax one district to relieve the budget of another. This is not to say, however, that a minimum standard for certain public services may not be a matter of general interest.

A community's interest in other communities' amenities has a distance preference somewhat similar to the time preference of individuals in classical theory. This is one reason why we have not only our lowest layers of government but also intermediate ones (counties and states) as well.

This philosophy assumes that it is possible to select amenities of government that are strictly of local interest, varying not only as to the amount of such interest but also as to the area over which it applies. It is a large order but perhaps not more difficult than other similar judgments which underlie the budget of any government in any democratic state. To add a value judgment, I am of the opinion that these distinctions are not so impossible as to warrant abandoning the attempt to make them.

Mr. Labovitz does neglect to cover what seems to me to be a fairly important (potentially) aspect of aids and that is their use to bring the states into the economic stabilization program. For instance, if federal participation in welfare is to be extended to include general relief, this could be done on a basis similar to that used in New York State where the aid is set to vary according to the percentage of population on relief. Replacement of tax-exempt securities by a public works aid tied to an employment index could hardly fail to score for the public interest.

One further desultory comment should be added. I disagree with the inference in one of the papers under review that state apportionment of tax bases and the immunities from state taxation associated with interstate commerce are not federal problems. It is my view, often enough propounded, that Congress should take the ball from the Supreme Court in these areas and that Congress itself should not act without full consultation with the interested parties in the states.

In conclusion, I fear that these remarks are more of a speech of my own than the careful commentary that two excellent papers deserve. The excuse is that I found these papers highly provocative.

C. LOWELL HARRISS, Columbia University

Apportionment for tax purposes of income of businesses engaged in interstate commerce seems to me, as to Professor Groves, to be more of a national problem than Dr. Ecker-Racz indicates. Compliance costs now put business to some sheer waste. The economy suffers from the use of skilled manpower in meeting diverse and intricate compliance requirements of different states. The variety of these requirements serves no useful purpose for the public as a whole. Waste results and seems likely to grow as many more firms will be affected. In terms of national accounts, the wastes cannot be large —but they are avoidable. Congressional action specifying uniform apportionment would yield real savings to the economy. Moreover, the prescription of a formula which conforms to economic reality as well as we can reasonably define it would help the economy a little by encouraging more efficient resource allocation. Formulas like those now in use create at least a slight inducement to distort affairs to save tax. The result is more expense, or a slightly smaller gross income, than if the tax law did not attach more importance to some details than their economic significance warrants.

Metropolitan Finance Problems: Territories, Functions, and Growth

JULIUS MARGOLIS
UNIVERSITY OF CALIFORNIA

1.

STUDIES of local public finance are typically replete with such alarming terms as crisis, problems, and emergency. The spirit of urgency permeates them. The dismal prophecies, if drastic remedial steps are not taken, are of slum-ridden cities, inadequately educated future generations, traffic clogged and abandoned central business districts, water-thirsty cities, mass flights to less encumbered areas, and patronizing and unpopular intervention of the federal government. Despite the fact that most of the nation's wealth is located in the metropolitan areas, a great part of the difficulties of local governments is attributed to their fiscal condition. Why, when the city[1] is the focus of economic activity, its residents have a more than proportionate share of the national income, its property is far more valuable than the nonurban sectors, it is the market place where most transactions occur, its fiscal base is far greater than other parts of the nation, must its governments operate under crisis conditions? What are the sources of these crises? Are they becoming more critical? These are the questions of this paper.

There is a tendency to view the fiscal problems of metropolitan areas as a function of the very heavy burdens imposed upon the taxpayers because of the expanded public facilities necessary to serve the booming urban population. However, not only has the growth in urban wealth kept pace with the growth in urban population, but the fraction of the nation's income which is locally taxed has fallen. Table 1 shows the trend in local real public expenditures as a percentage of real gross national product over the past 25 years. In recent years there has been a slight increase in local expenditures, but

Note: This paper was written with the assistance of the Real Estate Research Program, University of California, Berkeley.

[1] The following convention on terms will be followed. "City" refers to the urbanized area. "Municipality" refers to a part of the city incorporated under one government. Suburbs, satellites, and central cities are municipalities. The metropolitan area or region is the standard metropolitan area of the census.

TABLE 1

Real Local Revenues and Expenditures
as a Percentage of Real Gross National Product

Year	Revenue from Local Sources	Direct Expenditures
1932	10.42%	12.34%
1938	7.43	9.09
1940	6.41	8.51
1946	4.17	5.11
1948	4.16	5.75
1950	4.38	6.40
1954	4.54	6.50
1956	4.51	6.50
1957	4.69	6.71

SOURCES: Local revenues and expenditures: U.S. Bureau of the Census, Census of Governments Advance Release, *Governmental Finances in the United States 1902 to 1957*, March 1959. Table 6 for current data; p. 2 for price deflators.

Real gross national product: Council of Economic Advisers, *Economic Report to the President*, January 1959, p. 143.

the level is far below that of the prewar years. The fiscal crisis of local governments takes the conventional form—the search for tax sources; but more basic is the question of why public support has fallen behind previous levels. Perhaps part of the reason is a resistance to all taxes because of the large growth in the federal budget. In this paper I intend to explore some of the causes of the crises as they emerge from the structure of the city and its government.

The city is a densely settled area which is economically dependent upon other areas. It is always dependent on other areas for food, since its density precludes agricultural production, and it is frequently dependent for raw materials for production and markets for its products. The city as an aggregate is part of the division of labor in the economy, but more important for our problems is the differentiation of functions which occur within the city. The economic units which comprise the city—the households and firms—are functionally and spatially differentiated. The organization of functionally differentiated economic units into an economy which satisfies the needs of the people has been the central topic of economic analysis. Spatial differentiation has been neglected, but herein lies the core of the metropolitan finance problems.

Differentiation and specialization in economic functions make increasing efficiency possible, but at the same time they give rise to costs of organization. In the economy, the possible chaos which might arise because of functional differentiation is overcome by the

230

organization of markets. The pull of the market leads to shifts of units so as to result in a tolerably efficient production and distribution pattern. Even where the market is nonexistent, as within the administrative structure of firms, pecuniary evaluations of inputs and outputs which are derived from the market greatly facilitate the efficient organization of the firm.

Spatial differentiation, like functional differentiation, leads to the need for organization, but the role of the market as a spatial organizing force is quite different. Spatial differentiation refers to the fact that every activity must occupy a unique site within the city. Each site is unique since each bears a different distance and thereby time and cost relationship to any other site within the city. How shall the functionally differentiated economic units be distributed among the sites—or to put it in more conventional terms, how shall the sites be distributed among the different users? A market organization is one technique. Economic units bid for the site and in a way similar to that of labor or coal, land will be allocated to the higher bidders. But this form of an organization, though it is important, is minor compared to the other institutions which have developed to enable the city to function.

Governments perform the vital organizing role within the city. Though the activities of governments go far beyond those necessary to provide a structure to organize the spatially differentiated activities, many of the governments' activities arise because of the high social costs of using a market organization. At the minimum we could say that the inefficiency of the market is sufficiently great that even in an economy as ours, where the ideology of the market is so all-pervasive, there have been no serious proposals to replace government by a market organization. On the contrary, the role of the market has been steadily declining.

Space is an input which supports productive activities including the amenities of consumption, but at the same time it is an obstacle which must be overcome in order to communicate or transport. Though the same is true of every other input—e.g., labor is an input but it must be supervised; machines are inputs but they must be maintained—space has the peculiar feature that the use of the land input by one economic unit affects its costs as space to all other economic units. Furthermore, the input value of any site is partially determined by its accessibility, which in turn is affected by the space uses of all other units. The most obvious illustration of this problem is that of entry and egress. One site completely surrounded by other sites has little value unless the interior site-user has rights of passage over other sites. A very elaborate body of common law has developed around the rights and duties of adjacent land owners, and there exists market transactions which deal with influencing the uses of sites other than your own, but the dominant agency which is used to organize accessibility (and thereby the usefulness of sites) is the government.

Streets are probably the most significant factor in urban organization. Though one can imagine a private company providing street services where they would at a price link up each site with a common pattern of streets, comparable to the services provided by a telephone company, the cumbersomeness and inefficiency of this market organization would rule it out as a possible solution. Even telephone, water, and sanitation, when privately organized, have to be endowed with special government powers to establish their rights of way over property, in order to connect sites. Public streets are the most impressive instance of government organization of a spatially differentiated area. With low density and extensive land use, a private market might arrange for accessibility. With high density and intensive land use, the government arranges the facilities.

Similar to streets, we have the development of other public services to permit this high density development to survive—fire protection, sanitation, water development, police protection, etc. Though the government has established the basic functions which permit the city to develop, there is an active private market in the allocation of the sites which have been created and arranged by the government. Then, the market allocates the sites according to the profit productivities for firms and their living amenities for households.

The individual units as economic entities adapt themselves to government patterns, but the individual units also function as political entities. The public organization provides a necessary framework for an urban development and the residents as citizens influence the framework. As part of the political process, the individuals establish governments, manage functions, support expenditure, control programs, and assess taxes on themselves. As individuals they play both roles, political and economic, to realize their goals, selfish or altruistic. The fiscal problems of metropolitan areas are political as well as economic since they are concerned with the political and economic behavior of the individuals. Can the government effectively establish a framework for economic and social activity within the city? Do the economic incentives of the individuals i.e., a comparison of the benefits they receive and the costs they incur, inhibit or facilitate the development of a government organization of the city? Does the structure of government—its limited territorial jurisdiction, functional specialization, restricted fiscal tools—inhibit it as an efficient organization?

2.

Though the city at any given moment of time is composed of sites with unique locational characteristics, the sites are highly substitutible. The patterns of substitution are prominent features of the metropolitan fiscal problem. The degree of substitution among sites has not been analyzed but there are several hypotheses which seem reasonable in the light of the many specific land-use studies. It is rare that an unchangeable topographic feature dictates a specific land use. The most obvious case would be docking facilities along a river or bay. Even these, in most cases, could have been located at many other points along the water front. Once the port facilities are established, the possibilities of substitution among sites are far more restricted. The street pattern has become adjusted to the present location; rail freight facilities have been constructed; the multitude of necessary service industries have located themselves in view of the current port location. A shipping company which seeks a site outside of this complex for a docking facility would find itself denied all of these linkages which are necessary for its operation. In the short run, since complementary facilities are not mobile, high substitutibility among sites is restricted to neighborhoods. The same restrictions to neighborhoods exist for almost all other land uses in the city. Industrial usages are in industrial parks or areas; the department stores and office buildings are downtown. Within any given neighborhood the short-term substitutibility of sites is great and there exist very imperfect substitutions among neighborhoods. In the long run (for city structures the long run is extremely long) almost all sites are good substitutes. Long-run adjustments are hindered by the long life of public and private structures and the adjustments are facilitated by rapid growth. But neighborhoods exist whether they are in short-run or long-run equilibrium. This neighborhood pattern has serious implications for the fiscal problems of metropolitan areas. In fact, most analysts attribute the major source of the fiscal difficulties of the municipal governments contained within the metropolitan area to the partitioning of the metropolitan area into municipal governments which rule over different neighborhoods of the metropolitan area.

A neighborhood within a city is not a simple homogeneous area, though frequently the structures are similar. The locational advantages of an area for one activity will frequently hold for many similar activities so that branches of industry, transport, retailing, and types of residences will cluster together. Not only do these uses share common locational interests, but also there are strong forces to retain their concentration: they share many economies in efficient contact with suppliers and servicing firms which can reach efficient size if they are located near a large group of similar firms. Similarly, the firms' marketing role is enhanced if prospective purchasers can easily visit several firms. Many small firms, when located nearby, can economize on inventories if they can borrow from each other; they can reduce excess capacity if they can easily subcontract rush or large orders; they can reduce labor costs if the neighborhood attracts a standby supply of temporary workers. The same neighborhood effects extend to residences. The amenities of household residences such as parks, schools, neighbors, reduced traffic, and handy shopping are more efficiently supplied for clusters of residences rather than for a scatter, interspersed among many other uses. For households, neighborhood effects take on the additional attribute that the resident derives utility not only from his house but also from the character of his neighbors' structures and even their behavior—the play patterns of the children, the sociability of the wives, etc. Clusters of similar uses in a city create neighborhoods and within a neighborhood, sites are highly substitutible. And in the long run, neighborhoods themselves could have been located at many points within the city. With the growth of the metropolitan area, shifts in current neighborhood location patterns will arise.

A major determinant of the distribution of the neighborhoods of the city is the accessibility pattern. Those units which assign the greatest value to accessibility, the retailers, competitively bid up the price of sites in the center. The units which find the value of accessibility less crucial cannot outbid the retailers and therefore settle at points more distant than the center. The factor of general accessibility sets the pattern of rates in the center, but retail trade does not account for the majority of the central land uses. There are no authoritative studies of the central business district, but the study of Cincinnati which shows that retailing and business services have about the same total floor area is typical.[2] The business services includes usages such as: employment agencies, financial and insurance firms, legal and accounting firms, etc. Together, retailing and business services accounted for slightly less than half of the floor space.

Though all sites in the central business district are prepared to pay the high costs of rent in this area this is not because of its great general accessibility. Many business services require special accessibility to those units which require general accessibility. But whatever the motives of entry into the central business district, the many individual sites are highly substitutible for use by retail trade and central offices which enter the CBD and pay high prices for space there because of its general accessibility. The high prices in turn must be paid by those who do not value the general accessibility.

The differences in accessibility needs are in turn related to different demands placed upon the public organization of the city. The retailer requires rapid transit channels for shoppers and truckers and other amenities for shoppers such as close parking and pleasant walks, while the business services may require alleys for messengers, restaurants for conferences, and all-day parking for workers. The stores have large inventories to be protected, large shopping crowds to be moved; the business services have large all-day working forces relative to space. Public services capacity-requirements for these two types of users are quite different. Of course, the central business district at any given moment is far more complex. The point of peak accessibility and peak land values is constantly shifting. In its wake it leaves an area of declining land values and converted buildings. In its path there usually lies an area of better hotels, speciality shops, etc.[3] All that I want to establish here is the different facilities needed by the occupants of the neighborhood.

The conflicts over public policy by residents with different needs and incomes is significant for the fiscal status of the city. Consider the ever-recurring conflict over residential densities and zoning. There is a constant effort to maintain the amenities of uncrowded living by government sponsored rules to limit occupancy rates per acre. The usual standards deal with establishing minimum size lots, number of floors in an apartment house, or minimum open space on a

[2] *The Cincinnati Central Business District Space Use Study, A Summary*, Cincinnati City Planning Commission, 1956, pp. 1–2, 18.

[3] See an analysis of nine central business districts contained in R. E. Murphy, J. E. Vance, Jr., and B. J. Epstein, *Central Business District Studies*, Worcester, Clark University, 1955.

TABLE 2
Hypothetical Relationship Between Housing Expenditures,
Income and Density for a One-Block Area

Income Class	Number of Families	Ratio of Housing Expenditures to Income	Average Family Housing Expenditures	Total Housing Expenditures	Total Income
5,000	100	.20	1,000	$100,000	$500,000
10,000	50	.18	1,800	90,000	500,000
20,000	25	.16	3,200	80,000	500,000
25,000	20	.14	3,500	70,000	500,000
50,000	10	.10	5,000	50,000	500,000

building lot. In any case, the policy advocated for the government is to restrict density. This policy, though often adopted in a planning code is constantly frustrated in practice. The frustration of the policy arises because of the pressure of the market. The efforts to maintain the policy have implications for local finance.

Land which has greater accessibility is more valuable. This is true for residential sites as well as commercial and industrial. Their greater value arises because of the greater demand; individuals in order to avoid the costs of the lack of accessibility are willing to pay heavier for housing. The value of accessibility is significantly related to income. The lower incomes have fewer cars and can afford fewer trips with their cars. They also must be located closer to a variety of job possibilities since their jobs are less certain. When we plot the distribution of personal incomes on a gradient from the city center, ignoring the very wealthy apartment houses located at the center, we find that income rises with distance from the center. The poor are more centrally located. One of the reasons is that they can displace the rich. As income rises, the ratio of housing expenditure to income falls. As illustrated in Table 2, the lower incomes, because they are prepared to pay a higher per cent of their incomes in housing expenditures and live in more dense conditions, can outbid the upper incomes for sites. If the rich originally lived in the area analyzed in Table 2, it is to be expected that they would sell out. This process is familiar—the conversion of the town mansion to flats and finally rooms. The rich sell and move farther out where the accessibility costs are higher and where the lower incomes are discouraged from following. Though higher accessibility costs provide some protection to the rich, it is not sufficient. There is a dispersion of industrial plants throughout the city and an appreciable part of the lower incomes with job security and without the need of other job possibilities, might be tempted to follow the rich in search of cheaper land. To protect themselves against the inadequate barrier of high accessibility costs, the rich must impose zoning regulations in which they jointly deny themselves the possibilities of capital gains in the sale of their properties to the poor. Is this ordinance which restrains their freedom of action efficient from their perspective?

Some form of public controls are necessary if they are to maintain their properties. Men, when they buy homes, associate the amenities of the neighborhood with the home itself. Dense occupancy in adjoining blocks by lower income groups reduces the enjoyment of their homes. Of course they can sell out, realize a handsome capital gain, and relocate. Therefore, there has to be a personal advantage for them to accept willingly the self-denying zoning ordinance. One explanation may lie in the discontinuities which exist in available sites. Frequently, if one neighborhood is to be abandoned and another established, a lengthy leap to a new site may be necessary. There are no readily available areas which are only slightly less accessible. The move may be one of many miles with subsequent disruption of old neighborhood ties—church memberships, tennis clubs, school associations, etc. As the constant conversion from higher to lower income housing demonstrates, the differences in capital gains and the inability to maintain neighborhood solidarity has forced the rich to more and more distant points. Today, in the largest of the cities where the growth of population and its sprawl has become so great that a large per cent of the population lives outside the limits of the central municipality, the suburban city incomes are greater than those of the central city.

Municipalities or neighborhoods on the periphery of the metropolitan area are far from being solely refuges of the rich from the competitive, high-density bidding of the poor. Industry is fairly widely dispersed in the city and there are neighborhoods of workers in the periphery who constantly threaten the cheaper lands of the rich neighborhoods. The threat of higher density creates conflicting demands on public policy. The accessibility needs of the two neighborhoods as well as their attitudes towards density and industrial location are quite different. The richer tend to commute to the central core of the city while the lower incomes work much closer to home.[4]

[4] See R. F. Whiting, "Home-to-Work Relationship of Workers Living in Public Housing Projects in Chicago," *Land Economics*, August 1952, p. 287; and *Report on the Detroit Metropolitan Area Traffic Study*, Part I, J. D. Carroll, Jr., July 1955, pp. 95–7.

237

The problem of intra- and inter-neighborhood conflicts can be posed in its simplest form as an imbalanced distribution of taxes and the benefits of public services. Consider the property tax which is the mainstay of the local tax system. An extension of a public service will usually mean an increase in property tax rates. If the public services provide benefits equal in value to the taxes to be paid, the value of the property will remain unaffected. Fixed annual payments by the property owners will be increased by the tax and they will receive a set of services which in the aggregate are equal in value to the tax costs. However, this is too simple a story. The taxes do not support services which generate an equal set of benefits for each resident. Far from it. The benefits of the public services might be freely available to all land users in the area, but not all land users might be equally inclined to use the public services. For those who are disinclined, the services represent a fixed annual cost not compensated by an equal benefit. Benefits from services and the costs in the form of taxes may balance so as to leave the aggregate of property values unaffected, but there may be a redistribution effect which might prevent agreements about public services.

A similar analysis can be applied to the central business district. Transportation and parking and shopping amenities are critical for its expansion and growth. These improvements in accessibility if made will enhance the value of property, not only of the department store and central office buildings, but of adjoining land which contains substitute sites. Therefore, taxes need not lead to declines in values, possibly they may lead to an increase. Annual costs of holding property have gone up and so will rents. Business service units which require only linkages to the other units in the CBD need not directly benefit from the increase in accessibility. If they do not, then they are paying for an undesired service. Clearly, many of the business services are not so benefited.

The mechanics of unequal distribution of benefits and gains from some form of economic change, as described above, are widespread throughout a competitive economy. In the normal operations of a competitive private market economy, the redistribution of incomes does not lead to a frustration of economic change. If the department stores initiated credit departments they would hire more clerks to operate them. Their increased demand for clerks would force an increase in wages of clerks and a resultant increase in clerical costs for all other firms in the same labor market area, the central business district. This is the working of the competitive process. In the case of an increase in public inputs to enhance accessibility there is one major difference. The unbenefited firm has a right to vote whether any unit should have increased benefits and costs. It is as though the non-department stores, recognizing that the introduction of credit facilities in department stores would lead to an increase in clerical costs, had a vote in determining whether department stores could introduce credit offices. A vote by all land users in an area, or members of an industry, on the pecuniary external diseconomies associated with the growth of one of the land users or members would result in a vetoing of the expansion plans. This procedure is occasionally followed in some industries; it is the general practice in cities. The inhibitions on policy exercised by the veto power of those who suffer pecuniary external diseconomies is true for all governments. Taxes are not assessed in proportion to benefits received, but the frustrations of government reach an acute form in the metropolitan area where governments are smaller; their actions more visible; where specific public services are more directly related to tax payments; and where a multiplicity of governments compounds the difficulties of agreement.

In the above context, the principal fiscal problem of the metropolitan area is the difficulty of public decision-making. The resources of the metropolitan area are great. The needs have not become unsupportable. However, the ability to organize the public framework has become weakened because of an increasingly ineffective governmental structure of which financial problems are only symptomatic.

3.

The conflict between the beneficiaries and the taxpayers illustrated in the above pages is similar to that stressed by several writers on the normative theory of public expenditures who have discussed the difficulty, if not the impossibility, of determining an optimum pattern of public expenditures. These writings were normative—in contrast, the purpose of this paper is positivistic.

The normative analysis is directed toward two questions: When should the government displace private production? What are the conditions for an optimal level of public services? These are not our questions which are concerned with explaining actual expenditures. However, the normative analysis does suggest interesting hypotheses for the study of behavior.

It is argued that one of the cases where the government should intervene is where the product cannot be packaged so as to exclude certain users and therefore if it is produced it must be made equally available to all. In this case, a consumer will not voluntarily purchase the commodity but instead will allow others to purchase and then enjoy the product without payment. Therefore, no one will make the necessary payment since everyone will wait for his neighbor to act. The public is assumed astute enough to recognize this dilemma and therefore individually they are willing to allow the government to force all of them to make "fair" payments in order to produce this commodity. It is further argued that the level of services will not be optimal since the consumers will never reveal their true preferences for the commodity, as judged by the amount of funds they would sacrifice for the public service. The only way that they could reveal their true preferences is if the electoral system would allow them to cast as ballots not only ayes and nays but ballots which list the amounts they would be willing to subscribe for the services. This would result in the same situation which frustrates the private sector in providing the services. Individuals would offer less than their true estimate of the service, hoping that others would subscribe sufficient to provide the service which would be freely available for all. Therefore, the government must rely on a compulsory tax structure in which tax payments are not necessarily related to the values placed by the consumers on the services.

An extension of the logic of the argument of the public expenditure theorists is that if an optimal set of expenditures is not presented to the voters, then there will be some who will oppose the bill. Despite the opposition the bill will be carried if at least half of those voting prefer the situation with the bill to the situation without the measure. The political criterion of accepting a measure is therefore quite different from the criterion adopted by the welfare economists. Any situation A might be politically acceptable compared to a situation B though the welfare economist might not be able to compare these two situations since it might involve redistributions of income. On the surface it would seem simple to find politically acceptable solutions where at least one-half of the population is improved. These agreements are more numerous than the solution of the welfare economist who insists that there is an improvement only if all of the population is at least indifferent or better off. But there are forces which militate against and facilitate the development of a politically acceptable solution. Recent trends in the metropolitan area are making politically acceptable solutions more difficult.

One factor which sharply reduces the area of possible agreement is the issue of equity. For the welfare economic theorist, every public service is to be welcomed if someone is better off, and no one is worse off with the introduction or expansion of the public service. This allows possible situations where some persons are made very well off while others only slightly or not at all. To accept the welfare economists' criterion, some persons, and for many of the solutions possibly most of the persons, would have to agree to a reduction in their relative income status. Therefore, many persons who might favor a public service would refuse to support it if they felt that it would benefit others "inordinately." This would lead to a severe reduction in the range of politically acceptable solutions. In fact, the introduction of comparative judgment rather than simply judging a situation in terms of one's own income without considering the income of one's neighbors, if done without the introduction of majority rule, might lead to situations where there are no acceptable solutions. It is not inconceivable that the residents of suburbs and all the neighborhoods of the central city might each individually demand of a proposed improvement in public services that each of their relative statuses should improve. If the improved relative status is not forthcoming, each of the groups might prefer the status quo. Therefore, envying-equity considerations would sharply reduce the set of acceptable solutions, since individuals are concerned with both the absolute and relative levels of their incomes. It would be reasonable to argue that the more equitable the distribution of income and wealth, the more easy will it be to agree on efficient solutions since considerations of equity and status will be less significant. This factor is not trivial when we consider the marked divergency in income and social class among the suburbs and central cities of a metropolitan area.

Equity considerations of relative status narrow the range of acceptable solutions. Majority rule expands the range far beyond the optimal set. We will now observe how joint products, uncertainty, and moral sentiments greatly expand the set of acceptable choices.

The normal pattern of public choice is one of choosing a package rather than a single product. It is reasonable to hypothesize that the greater the number of products offered in the package to the voter the greater the likelihood of adoption. Even if the voting scheme were balloting with subscriptions, the strategy of many projects rather than one is more likely to be carried. It is clearly a better strategy for the government when the balloting is by yes or no and a majority or specific percentage of votes is required for adoption. The success of the multipurpose package is based upon the existence of consumers' surpluses of enough voters for specific projects so that they are willing to endorse the entire package rather than lose the specific project.

The bulk of decisions in regard to public services are not made by referenda, but instead are made through legislative processes. In this case the same sort of phenomena holds. The public exerts their influence on the formation of specific legislative acts either through direct action, as in the case of pressure groups, or, more generally, indirectly, through the election of legislators. In this case the elected official represents a very complex package. It is in the official's interest to create enough surpluses within his voting constituency to assure himself a majority of the vote.

Uncertainty is another significant factor in accounting for the acceptability of public services. There are many dimensions to uncertainty, but the element I want to stress is ignorance. Many governments are very complex, and the more complex the government the easier will it be for it to expand public services. The complexity of government, in addition to providing more variables for the political leader to juggle in order to shape a package acceptable to voters, provides a protective smokescreen for the public administrators through which the citizens cannot penetrate.

Another determinant of the range of acceptable public services even more seriously affects the strategy of political choice. Factors such as uncertainty and multiple products make individual computations and valuations of the elements of a public policy extremely difficult. Generally, voters, rather than acting as hard-headed shoppers, adopt ideological positions toward the whole program. The strategy of the voter may take the form of accepting the leadership of a political party, of a community group, of the primacy of principles, etc. The substitution of ideologies for self-interest as the basis of the support of a program is similar to the adoption by consumers of such strategies as brand preference, trusting a storekeeper, etc. In the case of the private sphere, advertising and habit replace calculation. In the case of the public sphere, political persuasion replaces rational self-interest. The restraint on government which might develop because of rational self-interest is thereby reduced.

The reliance upon ideology, in effect, substitutes a sense of public responsibility for self-interest. This is too narrow a concept of the morality of individuals acting as citizens. It may be true that individuals are prepared to sacrifice self-interest when faced by moral questions posed by public actions. This is not questioned. All that I wish to establish is that even if individuals were totally self-interested, their lack of knowledge would lead them to evaluate public actions on the basis of ideologies rather than calculations. Whichever motivation for this type of evaluation dominates, the introduction of ideologies greatly increases the freedom of the government in acting. The set of public policies acceptable to the voting public is increased.

The consequence of the forces which expand the set of acceptable programs is to permit the government of the city greater freedom in seeking out compromises. It is easier for the government to assess taxes and it is easier for the government to expand services than if only rational self-interest ruled. Ignorance and the acceptance of majority rule permit the resolution of conflicts by the political processes of persuasion and negotiation, while knowledge of consequences and their implications for one's own self-interest would lead to a frustration of policy by focusing on possibly irreconcilable conflicts.

Though ideological and utopian thinking become important in political decision-making, this does not mean an abandonment of self-interest. It is just that both enter into the public support of a program. The conflict between the social and private evaluations is reflected in the answers to a recent survey of Detroit-area residents on their attitudes toward government activities. They were asked whether the government is doing too much, too little, or the right amount in areas such as unemployment, education, and housing. Only 7 per cent thought that the government was doing too much while 40 per cent thought that the government was not doing enough. When the respondents were asked to compare the worth of government services to the contribution that the public must make for them, the support of the government dropped. Twenty-nine per cent thought that the government asks for more than it provides for the public, while only 13 per cent thought that the public gets more from the government than it pays. The support of the government dropped even further when the question became even more pointed and asked whether they should pay more or less taxes considering what they get from the government. Forty-one per cent thought that taxes were too high, while only 2 per cent thought taxes were too low.[5] These respondents were prepared to give overwhelming support to an extension of government so long as they were not subjected to the pressures of pecuniary evaluation of costs. Consistent with the above finding, we find the popular demands for the expansion of individual services associated with the sense of frustration about the inability to restrain the total.

The first section of the paper indicated some of the dimensions of conflict which existed among the individuals who use the sites of a city and the difficulties of resolution by a tax-supported government. The second section of the paper discussed some of the attributes of the government decision-making pattern which enables the government to establish an organization for the city despite individual conflicts. In the next sections we will analyze the structure of government of the city and try to assess its ability to resolve the conflicts of site users.

4.

The lack of consensus which creates obstacles for governments is partially overcome by the special nature of political decision-making described in the previous section. The political process counteracts the voters' constraint on government which arises because of self-interest. The structure of governments in the metropolitan area rather than helping to overcome the voters' constraints, aggravates the problems posed by conflicting interests. It is reasonable to expect that local governments would have more severe fiscal difficulties than central governments simply because knowledge and thereby self-interest can play a more significant role in local governments. The degree to which self-interest leads to the frustration of political action is increased by the functional and territorial balkanization of the metropolitan area.

Whereas the design of a policy containing many issues permits the development of a stable majority to support it, in local financing there are many single-function governments, e.g., education which precludes the possibility of adding voting strength by promising more voters more benefits. Similarly, territorial restrictions have the same effects.

[5] M. Janowitz, D. Wright, and W. Delaney, *Public Administration and the Public, Perspectives Toward Government in a Metropolitan Community*, University of Michigan Government Studies, No. 36, 1958, p. 36.

TABLE 3

Partitioning of a Five-Man City and Stable Voting Majorities

	INDIVIDUALS	PREFERENCE RANKINGS OF ALTERNATIVES				
		1st	*2nd*	*3rd*	*4th*	*5th*
Part I	A	X_1	X_2	X_3	X_4	X_5
	B	X_2	X_3	X_4	X_5	X_1
	C	X_3	X_4	X_5	X_1	X_2
	D	X_4	X_5	X_1	X_2	X_3
	E	X_5	X_1	X_2	X_3	X_4
Part II	A	X_5	X_2	X_3	X_4	X_1
	B	X_2	X_5	X_4	X_3	X_1
	C	X_3	X_4	X_5	X_1	X_2
	D	X_4	X_2	X_1	X_5	X_3
	E	X_4	X_1	X_2	X_3	X_5
Part III	A	X_5	X_2	X_3	X_4	X_1
	B + D + E	X_4	X_2	X_1	X_5	X_3
	C	X_3	X_4	X_5	X_1	X_2

The Arrow[6] voting paradox is the classic demonstration of the inability of getting a majority to decide on what is best, if the preferences of the voters are inconsistent. Arrow demonstrated that under certain conditions a group might cast a majority of votes for choice A when compared to B, and another majority might favor choice B when compared to C, and that it is possible that a majority of votes from the same group would be cast for C when compared to A. In this case, which is based upon a ranking of preferences for alternatives by individuals which are completely at variance, no single issue could receive a stable majority support. Policy would be frustrated. There are many reasons in actual practice why stable majorities would arise. One of the most important is that there does exist a great deal of agreement among many persons about the rankings of many issues. But unless there is complete agreement about preferences among all individuals in the city, it is usually possible to assign individuals to groups, give each group one vote, and then return to the original condition of not having a stable majority. Table 3 demonstrates this possibility.

The first part of Table 3 lists the preferences of a five-individual city, A, B, C, D, E, where each resident ranks his preferences among X_i in the order given. In this case, there is no possibility of a majority preference. If any X_i is put to a vote there will always be three people

[6] K. J. Arrow, *Social Choice and Individual Values*, Wiley, 1951.

who would prefer some other X_i. This is true for every X_i so that a stable majority is impossible. If three people should by chance vote for some X_i, then someone could propose another X_i for which three persons would also vote. This instability arises because of the diametrically opposed preference orderings of the individuals, which we would not expect to find in nature. The orderings illustrated in Part II of the table are more likely to be found.

In Part II there is a stable majority for X_4. No matter what alternative is posed in opposition to X_4, a majority would vote for X_4. In fact all the choices would be stable, or, to use the more technical language, transitive, i.e., X_4 is preferred to X_2, X_2 is preferred to X_5, X_5 is preferred to X_3, and X_3 is preferred to X_1. Any single alternative if preferred to another is also preferred to all alternatives which are not preferred to that other. It is likely that this may be the more typical situation. Of course, not every one is happy with this final order of preferences of the group. Individual A, who places X_4 low in his order of preferences, will be an active minority opposition. But he has no hopes of upsetting the majority votes. A decision can be taken by our five-man city, and this decision will be stable so long as they agree to accept the results of majority voting. This stability is lost, once the city becomes partitioned into certain combinations of separate governments.

Part III of the table illustrates the return of the voting dilemma after the partitioning of the five-man city into one combination of separate governments. Individuals B, D, and E are now joined in one government with one vote, while A and C represent two independent governments. If votes are now assigned, one to each government, there will be no stable majority among the governments, though the underlying preference orderings of the individual voters would have allowed for a stable majority. In the case of voting by governments, X_4 which is the stable majority of the individuals, would lose in a vote against X_3. This would hold despite the poor showing of X_3 in the voting choices of individuals. When all individuals voted as citizens of one city, X_3 would have been defeated by all alternatives except X_1.

The problem of achieving a stable majority translates itself into an important metropolitan area problem: The metropolitan area is divided into a great many governmental units. A multitude of governments, *per se*, is not a problem. After all there are many thousands of groceries, drug stores, etc., in any given metropolitan area. In the case of governments, the territorial and functional divisions create difficulties. The organization of a city is a public function which requires consistent planning for the entire area. There is a strong tendency for neighborhoods of a metropolitan area to become municipalities. If all of the municipalities were identical, then the possibilities of an agreement about common organizational problems would not be endangered by territorial partitioning. Instead, municipalities have widely diverging socioeconomic characteristics so that the interests of any given municipality may diverge greatly from the interests of many of the others. The possibilities of a successful exploitation of the rich fiscal resources available in the city are reduced by the difficulties of agreement among the municipalities.

In the 178 standard metropolitan areas, there are 15,658 governments. This is an average of 90 governments per standard metropolitan area, 18.3 governments per 100,000 persons. Though this seems to be a large number, it is small compared to the area outside the SMA. In the rural areas, there are 133 governments per 100,000 persons. Within the SMA's there are large stretches of rural territory, since the boundaries of the SMA are the county lines, no matter how far the county limits are from the urban area. The central counties of the SMA would approximate most closely an urban area. The central counties average 56 governments or 14 governments per 100,000 persons. As the SMA grows in population, the governments do not increase proportionally. The five most populous urban areas are on the average 71 times larger than the average area of 50–100,000 inhabitants, but they only average 16 times as many governments. Governments per capita in the largest areas are slightly less than 1/5 of the figure for the smallest SMA's. Some type of economies of scale are present though it is not obvious whether they are based upon politics, the technology of supply of public services, or the economic advantages of a larger service area for a unit.

Though the very large number of governments are accounted for by the many school and special districts which abound in local governments, municipal governments themselves are still numerous. There are 3,422 municipalities in the 178 standard metropolitan areas. School districts were almost twice as numerous as the municipalities and special districts appeared almost as frequently.[7] Though the number of municipal governments is quite large, the bulk

---

[7] The statistics on the frequency of governments in the standard metropolitan areas are taken from U.S. Bureau of the Census, U.S. Census of Governments: 1957, Vol. I, No. 2, *Local Government in Standard Metropolitan Areas*, 1957.

TABLE 4

Number of Municipalities and Their Population
in the Standard Metropolitan Areas in 1957

Population Size of Municipalities	Number of Municipalities	Percentage of Population of Municipally Governed Area of Standard Metropolitan Areas
50,000 or more	234	79
25,000–49,999	104	6
10,000–24,999	289	7
5,000– 9,999	386	4
2,500– 4,999	419	2
1,000– 2,499	753	2
Under 1,000	1,237	1

SOURCE: U.S. Bureau of Census, *Local Government in Standard Metropolitan Areas, 1957*, p. 6.

of them govern small areas and account for a small percentage of the urban population as can be seen in Table 4.

Though the bulk of the metropolitan population resides in the few large municipalities, the metropolitan area problem is not simply a big-city problem. First, the population of noncentral cities is growing relative to the central cities. Second, for many areas the central cities have a minor part of the population of the standard metropolitan areas.

As can be expected, the municipalities are highly diverse, with far greater differences existing among the satellites than among the central cities. Table 5 gives one dimension of the great diversity which exists—suburban cities tend either to be highly residential, or, interestingly enough, almost as frequently highly industrial. All cities of over 10,000 population in the SMA's of over 500,000 were classified by central or noncentral, and by the ratio of jobs in manufacturing and trade to the number of residents employed in those industries. The lower the ratio the more likely that the residents of the city in those industries have to go elsewhere to work. For the bulk of cities it is likely that this ratio can be used to classify the municipality as an employment or residential center. A high ratio would indicate an industrial city and a low ratio would mean a dormitory city.

The differences in the municipality economic characteristic most relevant to fiscal problems—the employment-residence ratio—is striking. Though most of the population of central cities are located in municipalities which are moderately a greater source of employment in manufacturing and trade than their supply of residents for those industries, there are appreciably large numbers of central cities

248

which export labor for those industries and others which import large numbers. The central cities show a marked bunching around a moderate job surplus status. The suburbs show an altogether different pattern. Rather than a balanced employment-residence structure being dominant, more than half of the population of suburbs reside in suburbs which can be characterized as highly specialized as dormitories or employment centers. The importance of suburbs as industrial satellites has been overlooked in the general tendency to view suburbs as the homing place of the central city workers. One out of five suburban residents of cities over 10,000 live in cities where local manufacturing and retail jobs are almost 50 per cent greater (and usually a higher percentage) than the number of residents who work in these industries.

The extreme diversity of suburbs has two aspects of interest. It is apparent that no simple generalizations can be made about the differences between central cities and suburbs. It is true that if a person lives in a residential city he most likely lives in a suburb, but it is also true that if he lives in a highly industrialized municipality he also most likely lives in a suburb. The too-easy generalization about the suburbs as dormitories and central cities as production centers is incorrect. The suburbs can be considered a collection of the many types of neighborhoods which exist in the urban area, with each neighborhood usually having its own government, although many suburban municipalities have more than one neighborhood. The one neighborhood which will not be found as a suburban municipality is the central office district, the major shopping centers, the entertainment and restaurant district. The suburban municipalities are not only distinguished by job-resident ratios, but also by income levels, rental levels, birth rates, educational levels, proximity to central city limits, occupational characteristics, and so forth.

The existence of neighborhoods as cities has the consequence of gathering into one government unit the individuals who have relatively similar preference orderings and who, as a group, tend to have orderings which are distinct from other groups. This has the effect of reducing the possibilities of agreement on public programs in a metropolitan area. Within any neighborhood there may be sufficient similarity for a stable majority to develop (and it is possible that a stable majority could be developed for the entire urban area), but partitioning the metropolitan area into cohesive sectors where each municipality has one vote reduces the possibilities of agreements.

TABLE 5

Percentage of Population in Cities with Different Employment-Resident Ratios, by Size of Standard Metropolitan Area and Type of City, 1954

RATIO OF JOBS AVAILABLE TO RESIDENTS EMPLOYED IN MANUFACTURING AND TRADE	SUBURBAN CITIES OVER 10,000 IN STANDARD METROPOLITAN AREAS OF				CENTRAL CITIES IN STANDARD METROPOLITAN AREAS OF				PERCENTAGE OF POPULATION OF RATIO GROUP IN	
	100,000 to 500,000	500,000 to 1,000,000	1,000,000 and Over	All Suburbs	100,000 to 500,000	500,000 to 1,000,000	1,000,000 and Over	All Central Cities	Suburbs	Central Cities
145 and over	18.8	3.7	23.7	20.5	11.5	8.4	0	4.9	55.4	44.6
130–144	18.4	5.4	3.1	5.5	15.5	20.5	8.4	12.8	11.3	88.7
115–129	13.9	2.8	8.6	8.6	27.2	34.0	19.4	24.5	9.4	90.6
100–114	8.5	8.3	14.6	12.9	24.5	29.6	63.2	45.8	7.7	92.3
85–99	12.4	25.7	10.0	12.3	16.0	7.4	8.4	10.3	26.0	74.0
70–84	4.9	18.9	8.0	8.9	4.3	0	.6	1.5	63.7	36.3
50–69	17.8	15.4	12.4	13.5	.9	0	0	.3	93.9	6.1
Under 50	5.3	20.0	19.7	17.7	0	0	0	0	100.0	0

SOURCE: Work sheets of Victor Jones and Andrew Collver, "Economic Classification of Cities and Metropolitan Areas," to appear in the forthcoming annual *Municipal Yearbook, 1959,* International City Managers' Association.

TABLE 6

Rate of Increase in Population,
by Metropolitan Status, 1940–50

METROPOLITAN STATUS	INTERDECADE RATES OF POPULATION INCREASE				
	1940–50	*1930–40*	*1920–30*	*1910–20*	*1900–10*
Total United States	14.5	7.2	16.1	14.9	21.0
Nonmetropolitan	6.1	8.5	6.0	6.7	13.6
Metropolitan	22.0	8.4	27.5	25.9	32.5
Central Cities	13.8	5.5	24.2	27.9	37.1
Rings	34.2	13.4	33.2	22.4	25.6
Urban	26.0	8.0	42.6	35.9	49.2
Rural	45.2	21.3	22.0	9.4	8.4
Incorporated	34.1	13.2	28.6	24.1	45.0
Unincorporated	46.5	22.3	21.2	7.8	5.6

Source: Leo F. Schnore, "Metropolitan Growth and Decentralization," *American Journal of Sociology*, September 1957, p. 172.

This reduction weakens the opportunities for the residents of the metropolitan area to use their superior fiscal capacity to carry out the necessary organization of the metropolitan area.

Is this differentiation increasing? Are the prospects for agreements worsening? The evidence is not clear. The most noticeable signs point to increasing differentiation. Suburbs are growing relative to central cities, central cities are becoming more dissimilar from the suburbs, and suburbs are increasing their distinctiveness.

Table 6 shows the changing trends in location of population growth in the metropolitan area. Metropolitan areas have consistently grown relative to the rest of the United States. Within the urban area, the suburbs, highly differentiated, have over time absorbed an increasingly larger percentage of the urban growth. In the years since the last census, this higher rate of growth by the suburbs has been maintained if not accelerated. Table 7 shows the distributions of building permits for 1954 to 1957 between central cities and the rest of the metropolitan area by type of construction. The shift of the population to the suburbs is indicated by the 70.6 per cent of the value of new dwelling units which are being located outside of central cities. The dominance of the noncentral areas in other types of construction is not as great, but they all indicate the relative growth of the noncentral. Industrial buildings permits are divided almost the same as residential. Only in construction for the clearly central-city functions, i.e., office building, institutional buildings, and commercial garages, are the central cities growing more rapidly than the noncentral. Although industrial

251

TABLE 7

Value of Building Permits Issued in Metropolitan Areas, 1954–57

| | DISTRIBUTION OF TYPE OF CONSTRUCTION BY PLACE, PER CENT | | IMPORTANCE OF TYPE OF CONSTRUCTION IN AREA, PER CENT | | |
TYPE OF CONSTRUCTION	Central Cities	Metropolitan Areas Outside Central Cities	Standard Metropolitan Areas	Central Cities	Metropolitan Areas Outside Central Cities
All building construction	38.7	61.3	100.0	100.0	100.0
New dwelling units	29.4	70.6	57.2	43.4	65.9
New nonresidential bldg.	48.7	51.3	32.6	41.0	27.3
Commerce building	56.9	43.1	10.9	16.1	7.7
Amusement	52.6	47.3	.6	.8	.5
Commercial garages	75.9	24.1	.4	.7	.1
Gas & serv. stations	43.6	56.4	.7	.7	.6
Office buildings	72.8	27.2	4.5	8.5	2.0
Stores	43.0	57.0	5.2	5.7	4.8
Community building	49.8	50.2	11.0	14.1	9.0
Education building	45.2	54.8	6.8	7.9	6.1
Institution building	67.4	32.6	2.1	3.6	1.1
Religious building	48.2	51.8	2.1	2.6	1.8
Garages	33.6	66.4	1.5	.9	1.8
Industrial	32.5	67.5	5.5	4.6	6.0
Public utility	54.0	46.0	1.6	2.2	1.2
All other non-residential	43.8	56.2	2.2	2.4	2.0
Additions, alterations, and repairs	59.1	40.9	9.5	14.7	6.2

SOURCE: Various May issues of *The Construction Review*, U.S. Department of Commerce and Labor.

buildings are divided almost in the same proportion as residential building and stores and other mercantile buildings are more than half in noncentral areas, this does not mean that the suburban growth is necessarily balanced. As indicated earlier, suburbs are highly differentiated, and it is pertinent to ask whether the growth of suburbs, which is balanced in the aggregate, results in an increase or decrease in the degree of differentiation.

Table 8 details the increase in population between 1948 and 1954 in different types of suburban cities over 10,000 in SMA's over 500,000. The table indicates that the suburban cities are retaining their pattern of differentiation and possibly accentuating it. Were there an equalizing movement, the balanced cities should have grown relatively more rapidly than other types of cities. Instead, the balanced cities, as defined by either 1948 or 1954 indices, grew the slowest. By far the lowest growth was experienced by balanced cities which remained balanced. The cities which retained their same

TABLE 8
Percentage Increase in Population of Suburban Cities from 1948 to 1954[a]

| | 1954 RATIO CLASSIFICATION | | | |
1948 RATIO CLASSIFICATION	*Employing Cities Ratio over 115*	*Balanced Cities 85–115*	*Dormitory Cities Below 85*	*Total*
Employing cities	16.2	31.7	26.7	19.7
Balanced cities	18.5	1.1	28.9	9.4
Dormitory cities	76.8	15.6	23.7	24.1
Total	18.7	9.0	24.4	18.7

SOURCE: Work sheets of Jones and Collver, *op.cit.*
[a] By 1954 and 1948 ratios of jobs in trade and manufacturing in city to residents employed in same industries. Suburban cities over 10,000 in standard metropolitan areas of over 500,000.

TABLE 9
Distribution of Population of Suburban Cities in 1948 and 1954[a]

| A. PERCENTAGE OF 1954 SUBURBAN POPULATION | | | | |
| 1948 Ratio Classification | 1954 Ratio Classification | | | |
	Employing	*Balanced*	*Dormitory*	*Total*
Employing	20.5	5.9	1.5	27.9
Balanced	4.4	15.5	6.1	26.1
Dormitory	1.4	3.5	41.1	46.0
Total	26.3	24.9	48.8	100.0
B. PERCENTAGE OF 1948 SUBURBAN POPULATION				
1948 Ratio Classification	1954 Ratio Classification			
	Employing	*Balanced*	*Dormitory*	*Total*
Employing	20.9	5.3	1.4	27.6
Balanced	4.4	18.2	5.7	28.3
Dormitory	.9	3.6	39.4	44.0
Total	26.3	27.1	46.5	100.0

SOURCE: Work sheets of Jones and Collver, *op.cit.*
[a] By 1954 and 1948 ratios of jobs in trade and manufacturing in city to residents employed in same industries. Suburban cities over 10,000 in standard metropolitan areas of over 500,000.

classification in both years grew the least. This is to be expected, since a large increase in population will have a temporary unbalancing effect, so that the economic character of the municipality will change. The population of cities with constant classification grew by 16.5 per cent, while the population of those cities which changed classification grew by 27.1 per cent. The greatest rates of population growth were registered in the dormitory cities whether classified by 1948 or 1954 indices. The continued pattern of differentiation is reinforced by Table 9 which shows the distribution of the 1954 and 1948 suburban population by type of city.

253

TABLE 10

Distribution of Area and Area Growth
by Size of Cities for Cities of over 100,000 Population in 1930

Size of City by Population (thousands)	Percentage of Total Area Growth during the Period 1900–1950 Attributed to Population Size-Class of City at Time of Growth	Percentage of 1950 Total Area by Population Size of City in 1950
49 and under	8.5	
50–74	8.1	
75–99	10.3	
100–249	26.1	24.3
250–499	33.6	28.3
500–749	7.5	13.3
750–999	3.9	7.8
1,000 and over	1.9	26.3
Total	100.0	100.0

SOURCE: U.S. Census, *Land Area and Population of Incorporated Places of 2,500 or More*, April 1950; *City Finances, 1942*, Vol. 3, pp. 200–9; R. D. McKenzie, *The Metropolitan Community*, McGraw-Hill, 1933, pp. 336–9.

The growth of the noncentral part of the metropolitan area relative to the central has been the repeated theme of hundreds of reports and conferences on metropolitan fiscal problems. Frequently this shift in population distribution is identified with mass movements of people who, once they have automobiles, feel free to abandon their crowded urban quarters to live expansively in the wide-open areas of a green suburbia. This decentralization is not an accurate depiction of the facts. There has not been an evacuation of the central areas for the periphery. The typical evidence dealing with decentralization is similar to Table 6 which shows the increasing rates of growth of the suburbs with declining rates of growth of the central city. There is nothing in this sort of evidence which is inconsistent with the hypothesis that population is normally distributed over an area and that each successive stage in a growth trend is also normally distributed.

Part of the phenomenon of decentralization is based upon the change in the pattern of area growth of cities. Table 10 summarizes some of the data on the area growth of the cities which had a population of 100,000 or over in 1930. From 1900 to 1950, the population of these 91 cities increased by 153 per cent and their areas increased by 83 per cent. As we can expect, the densities of these larger cities have grown. Over time, the population growth has tended to have the same general shape as the area growth with a somewhat greater concentration of area growth in the early decades of the century.

Undoubtedly, this unequal development of area and population has contributed to the identification of the year 1920 as the turning point in the growth of decentralization, though as we have seen the concept of decentralization is poorly defined.

Table 10 shows the area growth between 1900 and 1950 of the cities which had a population of over 100,000 in 1930. The first column analyzes the area growth of these cities according to their population size when they acquired additional acreage. The figures entered in the column are the percentages of the total area growth of the 91 cities distributed among the cities according to their population size when the annexations took place. The first item, 8.5, means that 8.5 per cent of the total area growth between 1900 and 1950 of all 91 cities was incurred when these cities had a population of under 50,000. The column understates the area growth of cities under 50,000 during this period since the percentages only refer to the growth of cities which reached 100,000 in 1930. Some cities under 50,000 in this period grew and reached 100,000 after 1930 but they would not be included in the table. The important point about the table is that though in each decade the areas of the large cities have been growing, lagging behind population but growing, there is little area growth of cities beyond the 500,000 population size. The 17 cities which had populations of over 500,000 in 1950 were only 19 per cent of the 91 cities analyzed, but they contained 47 per cent of both the area and population of this group of cities. It is this very important group of cities for which we can expect very little in the way of area growth. They are hemmed in by already incorporated areas which will zealously retain their identity. In the future, we can expect in these major urban areas a very rapid increase in noncentral populations relative to the increase in population in the central cities. Given the pattern of distribution of population increase among the suburban cities of the large metropolitan areas which was analyzed in the preceding tables, the difficulties of agreements about the mobilization of fiscal resources will most likely increase in the future.

The municipalities of the metropolitan area are becoming more diverse. Industry and residences and shopping centers are not distributed randomly among the municipalities. Cries of inequity, conflicting competition for fiscal resources, appeals to higher government, creations of new governments become common. The next sections will discuss some of the problems in more detail and the fiscal reactions of local governments.

5.

Discussion of the problems created by the increasing partitioning of the metropolitan area into ever-larger and more numerous municipality-neighborhoods is too frequently restricted to one issue— equity. Equity is important. Municipalities are less prone to cooperate in a sensible organization of the metropolitan problem if they feel that other municipalities are liable to reap most of the benefits, even if they should benefit somewhat. Solutions to metropolitan problems must consider equity, but they must also consider how best to find agreements when there are real conflicts of interest. Furthermore, even if conflicts were nonexistent, the structure of suburban governments handicaps the possibility of political action to expand public services.

The major arguments about equity are concerned with the central city *vs.* suburbs. The central cities argue that the suburbanite crowds their streets, demands police and fire protection while he shops and works, and then retreats outside the municipal boundaries into his valuable residential property, which the central cities believe should be taxed to pay for these public services. The suburban governments argue that they must educate the boom baby crop of the commuter; they must protect his family and his property, but the lucrative tax base which should support these services—the factories and office buildings—are located in the central city. Both sectors of the metropolitan area deplore their partial access to the taxable property of the metropolitan area, and both feel a sense of deprivation which they hope can be rectified by changes where each can achieve an improvement in their relative standings.

The only substantial evidence to support the claim of suburban exploitation of the central city has been the study of Amos Hawley.[8] He showed that the per capita public expenditures of central cities increase as the percentage of the population of the standard metropolitan area which lives in the central city declines. The central cities which comprise the smallest part of their metropolitan areas have the highest per capita public expenditures. This finding, which was based upon municipal expenditures and which could be challenged since it ignores the many differences in the use of special district governments among cities, is confirmed when we use the data on government payrolls of all local governments overlying central cities. Table 11 presents the data for the 36 largest standard metropolitan

[8] A. H. Hawley, "Metropolitan Population and Municipal Government Expenditures in Central Cities," *Journal of Social Issues*, VIII, 1951.

TABLE 11

Indexes of Local Government Costs and Fiscal Capacity
in the 36 Largest Standard Metropolitan Areas

CENTRAL CITIES POPULATION AS PERCENTAGE OF TOTAL URBANIZED AREA, 1950	PER CAPITA APRIL 1957 PAYROLLS		RATIO OF CENTRAL CITY PUBLIC PAYROLLS PER CAPITA TO TOTAL SMA GOVERNMENTS, APRIL, 1957	RATIO OF CENTRAL CITY PER CAPITA RETAIL SALES TO TOTAL SMA, 1954	RATIO OF CENTRAL CITY PER CAPITA EMPLOYMENT IN MANUFACTURING AND TRADE TO TOTAL SMA, 1954
	of Central City Municipal and Overlying Local Governments[a]	Total Standard Metropolitan Area			
35.9–65.4	$11.89	$9.05	1.31	1.35	1.31
66.1–73.6	11.11	8.67	1.28	1.08	1.13
74.9–81.7	10.19	9.04	1.12	1.56	1.56
83.3–97.5	7.76	7.31	1.06	1.07	1.03
Total	10.69	8.68	1.23	1.19	1.21

[a] County payrolls were allocated to the area overlying central city on basis of percentage of county population contained in central city. This most likely leads to some overstatement of central city payrolls. All of the special and school district payrolls were assigned to the central city even if these governments served a larger area.

SOURCES: Population: Work sheets of Jones and Collver, *op.cit.* Payrolls: U.S. Bureau of Census, *Census of Governments 1957*, Vol. II, No. 3, *Local Government Employment in Standard Metropolitan Areas.* Employment and Retail Sales: U.S. Bureau of Census, *County and City Data Book,* 1954. Ratio of Central to Urban Population: D. Bogue, *Population Growth in Standard Metropolitan Areas, 1900–1950,* USHHFA, 1953, pp. 73–4.

areas. The first column gives the per capita payrolls by groups of central cities with different ratios of central city to total urban area populations. The differences among the groups are not striking but it is clear that the greater the outside population relative to the residents of the central city, the greater will be the central cities' local public expenditures. The per capita public payrolls of the standard metropolitan areas do not bear the same relationship as do those of their central cities, which lends credence to the inference that the central city public expenditures relationship is a function of its outside population, and not some special characteristics of the area or region. This "inequity" is of special interest since the future booming growth of urban areas will result in central cities having still smaller shares of the metropolitan population and therefore incurring still larger public expenditures relative to the suburbs.

The last three columns of Table 11 evaluate the significance of the payroll differentials. The first shows the ratios of central city public payrolls to those of the entire SMA. The expected relationship holds—the ratio of per capita central city public payrolls to those of the total SMA increases as the percentage of the total urban population which resides in the central city falls. Differences in expenditures show that public costs per resident are greater as the population outside the central city grows, and therefore they indicate that the central city services a population much larger than its residents. Clearly, as the central city becomes a smaller part of the metropolitan area it is likely that it will contain a relatively larger share of the employment of the SMA and with this increased daytime population its local public costs would rise. This expectation is confirmed by the data of Table 12 which shows that the employment-resident ratio of the central city rises as its share of the population of the urbanized area falls. However, the large daytime population of the central city and the consequent higher public expenditures does not necessarily mean a higher tax burden on the residents. Associated with an increase in daytime economic activities of the central cities there may be larger fiscal capacities to support additional public services. The remaining two columns of Table 11 are partial indices of the fiscal capacities of the central cities of the 36 standard metropolitan areas. In only one of the four groups do the fiscal capacities fall appreciably below the expenditures indices. The evidence is too partial to allow for any clear conclusions about who exploits whom. But the fact that central cities contain a larger per capita tax base casts doubt on the validity

TABLE 12

Distribution of Urbanized Areas
by Degrees of Central Cities Jobs-Residents and Inside-Outside Population Ratios

RATIO OF JOBS IN MFG. AND TRADE TO RESIDENTS EMPLOYED IN MFG. AND TRADE 1954	RATIOS OF POPULATION TOTAL URBANIZED TO POPULATION OF CENTRAL CITIES, 1950					
	Below .60	*.60–.69*	*.70–.79*	*.80–.89*	*.90–1.00*	*Total No.*
130 and above	12	13	9	8	2	44
115–129	5	4	9	14	7	39
100–114	4	1	7	16	8	36
Below 100	0	3	3	6	12	24
Total No.	21	21	28	44	29	143

SOURCES: Work sheets of Jones and Collver, *op.cit.*; D. Bogue, *op.cit.*

of any inference drawn from their higher expenditure ratios. Retail sales and employment are important indices of fiscal capacity but they are far from complete. Family incomes are higher outside the central city than inside, for the larger metropolitan areas. It is likely that value of residence per family is also higher. But the higher valued residences are often offset by the greater per capita industrial and commercial property.

The argument that central cities are exploited by the noncentral cities is not well established. If anything, central cities may be relatively better off. Other alleged inequities within the metropolitan area may have a better basis in fact, and these may prove the obstacle to efficient fiscal arrangements.

A typical set of suburbs may include an industrial satellite with a low-income, densely settled residential district with an old shopping district; an upper-income suburb where zoning might exclude all commerce and industry and set a minimum-sized building lot of one or more acres; a middle-income city with shopping districts, minimum-sized lots of modest dimensions, and constantly on the lookout for clean industry; a lower-income city with aggressive plans to attract industry. The upper incomes commute to the central city. The lower incomes work in the industrial satellites or in plants on the periphery of the central city closest to the suburb. The middle-income group is mixed, containing central business district commuters and managers of peripherally located businesses. The demands for public services by these suburbs, and their fiscal capacities, are quite different. Fiscal inequities exist, but more important are the supposed

TABLE 13

Some Fiscal Indices of Cities in the San Francisco Bay Area

Type of City	Average Household Income	Real Property Value per Capita	Average Annual per Capita Municipal Expenditures	Average Annual Municipal Expenditure per Dollar of Household Income
	1950	1954–55	1952–55	
Central	$3,709	$4,802	$69.00	$.0188
Business suburbs	3,890	4,688	53.60	.0138
Higher income	4,495	5,156	53.35	.0119
Lower income	3,647	4,502	53.70	.0147
Dormitory suburbs	4,864	5,598	43.66	.0090
Higher income	5,809	6,692	49.19	.0085
Lower income	3,930	4,517	38.19	.0097

SOURCE: See J. Margolis, "Municipal Fiscal Structure in a Metropolitan Region," *Journal of Political Economy*, June 1957, pp. 231–2 for methodology. Some of the numbers in the above table do not agree with the numbers in the article. Not all of the cities in the Bay Area could be used for the above table since income could not be estimated for some.

or real inequities of any proposed changes in the development of the metropolitan area which attempts to treat all persons and municipalities in a uniform manner. For instance, a mass transportation plan with an orientation toward the central business district may provide great benefits to those suburbs containing the commuters— the upper- and middle-income suburbs—but they provide few benefits to the low-income suburbanite who does not work in the central business district. Frequently, the operations of these proposed programs require a subsidy by a property tax which might involve agreements by many municipalities. The unbenefited, but taxed, are not likely to agree.

In addition to conflicts among the governments, there is the further complicating factor that many of the municipalities might be too small and simple in structure to allow for the political flexibility necessary to extend public services. Table 13 shows some fiscal data for the cities of one metropolitan area, the San Francisco Bay Area, which casts some light on problems of equity and fiscal adaptability in the suburban areas. The business suburbs are those which have a substantial residential population and have local employment at least close to that of their resident labor force. They do not include the heavily industrialized satellites which are factory towns with very little residential development. The dormitories have few local jobs relative to the resident labor force. The differences in fiscal behavior among the suburbs is very marked. The dormitories have higher household incomes and higher per capita real property than the business dormitories, but their municipal expenditures per capita are appreciably less. Income differences in the case of dormitories lead to substantial differences in the levels of their municipal expenditures. The lower-income dormitories make a greater effort in terms of their incomes, but they still fall far behind the level of the higher-income dormitories. Both groups make a distinctly lower effort than the central cities or business suburbs. The latter group spends the same amount per capita independent of the level of income or value of property in their city. The low-income business suburbs make a much greater effort than the higher-income business suburbs to achieve the same magnitude of expenditures. The full explanation of the magnitudes of expenditures is beyond the scope of this paper, but the inability or the unwillingness of the dormitory suburbs to make the same efforts as the business suburbs is, I feel, explainable. My argument in the earlier sections of this paper stressed that the more complex the government the easier it is for the political leadership to expand its level of services. This is applicable here. The lower-income business suburbs achieve the same standards of services as the higher-income business suburbs though it means a much greater effort for them. The lower-income dormitory suburbs do not achieve the same expenditure levels as the upper-income suburb though they make a slightly greater effort. They do not approximate the efforts of the lower-income business suburbs though their per capita incomes are greater and their per capita real property values are the same. The inference seems clear that the more complex governments find it easier to muster the public support necessary to extend the level of public services despite the greater sacrifice required. The continuing dominance of the dormitory suburb among the noncentral municipalities prophesies a perennial shortage of funds for the new and rapidly expanding municipalities of suburbia.

6.

The creation of many municipal neighborhoods is only one dimension in the balkanization of the metropolitan area. Another has been the development of special-purpose governments. Historically, municipal governments expanded the scope of their functions to displace bodies which administered single functions. Today, there is a possibility that we may be returning to the earlier pattern. One solution offered to overcome the frustration of policy because of the too many small municipalities is to develop special governments which would have authority over an area large enough to handle the problems posed by the great interdependencies which exist within a metropolitan area. This has been especially true for such functions as water, sanitation, bridges, port development, and recreation. It is true that the larger jurisdictional area of these governments will enable them to better serve a planning role, but their specialized character which insulates them from some of the normal political processes of the metropolitan area may prove a handicap.

In previous sections, I stressed that governments with many functions may find it easier to raise funds by taxation. The voters' constraints could be eased by the development of a program with many services which could provide surpluses for a majority of the voters, and the uncertainty surrounding a complex program might enervate the opposition. If this is so, the single-purpose special districts may not find themselves with sufficient fiscal strength to fulfill their goals. One test of the reasonableness of this suspicion is the status of the largest group of single-purpose governments in the country—the school districts.

The school district, as a government, performs one function, education. Its territorial jurisdiction is usually small. These attributes permit the voters to have some knowledge of the scope and nature of its activities. It is not too difficult to become familiar with its activities, and it is easy for many individuals to relate what they believe is their self-interest to the functioning of the school. Support of schools is not restricted to those who have children in the schools. On the contrary, there is some evidence that the level of education of the voters is a better determinant of how they vote on school fiscal issues than the number of children of school age. Whatever the basis of individual support of an educational budget, the voters can readily develop a negative or positive attitude toward the extension of the school budget. Under these conditions, it is not surprising that schools are the major fiscal problems of local governments despite the nation's best organized public pressure groups—the parents and teachers associations.

Education services are supplied both by independent governments such as school districts, and multipurpose governments, such as counties, municipalities, and townships. There are 52,913 public school systems in the United States. The bulk of them, 50,887 are independent school districts while the others are fiscally dependent upon other governments. The nonindependent school departments are few in number, but they are significant in size—they have 22 per cent of the school enrollment. Over time, the independent school districts have been declining in number, because of increasing consolidation of districts.

Two aspects of school finance are of special interest to this paper. The school districts represent the pure form of a single function government, with local control and relatively widely known operations. Their difficulties are an accentuation of the difficulties confronting other local governments. The first question that I want to raise is whether fiscally independent school districts fare better than fiscally dependent school departments in raising funds. The second question deals with the solution by the school districts of the problem of their inability to overcome the constraints imposed by a lack of consensus on the part of the voters.

A comparison between fiscally independent school districts and fiscally dependent school departments is of interest since it indicates whether the public will spend more for a public service when it is presented as a single unit or as part of a package for which the specific benefit of the marginal tax dollar is uncertain. The evidence is far from weighty but it indicates that fiscally dependent departments spend more per pupil than fiscally independent school districts. "Woodward made an analysis of expenditures in 85 cities between 100,000 and 1,000,000 population over the period 1929–30 to 1943–44. During this period the mean per pupil expenditure was highest in the fiscally dependent cities. They spent about 4 per cent more than the independent districts in 1929–30 and nearly 12 per cent more in 1943–44."[9]

Ten of the 41 largest cities have municipal school departments. They spent in 1952–53, $346.11 per pupil in average daily attendance against $293.40 spent in the other 31 largest cities with independent school districts.[10]

Most states have independent school districts throughout the state. Where municipal departments are permitted, they are frequently

[9] Henry B. Woodward, *The Effects of Fiscal Control on Current School Expenditures*, Ph.D. thesis, Columbia, 1948. Cited in Paul R. Mort and Walter C. Reusser, *Public School Finance*, McGraw-Hill, 1941, p. 60.
[10] U.S. Office of Education, Biennial Survey of Education, 1953–54, *Statistics of City School Systems*, pp. 36–45.

associated with larger cities. New Jersey is a case where there are independent and dependent systems at all size classes. The six cities of over 100,000 had municipal school departments. They spent $383 per ADA. In the remaining cities, the municipal school departments spent $343 per ADA, while the independent school districts spent $293 per ADA.[11]

The evidence is not conclusive, but it does indicate that when a government function is broken out of the complex matrix of the multifunctioned government and becomes institutionalized in a separate government it finds greater difficulties in maintaining levels of services because of the fiscal constraints imposed by the necessity of developing a consensus among knowledgeable voters.[12]

Further evidence supporting the hypothesis that simple government structures are subject to more severe constraints is given by the decline in the fiscal independence of the school districts. In 1920, 14 per cent of the public elementary and secondary school revenues were derived from state taxes and appropriations. This increased to 39 per cent in 1950, and for the last year for which we have complete information, 1953–54, it stood at 35.5 per cent.[13] The secular shift of public support of education to the state government which is less subject to widespread knowledge and popular control is more clearly demonstrated when we consider the pattern of state support among the different states.

Table 14 shows that the poorer states, as measured by per capita personal income, make a greater effort to support education. The poorer states spend 3.23 per cent of their personal income on education against 2.60 per cent for the higher-income states. More interesting is the division of fiscal responsibility among the local governments and the distant state legislatures. In the high-income states, local governments raised 62.0 per cent of their school revenues while the poorer states raised only 38.7 per cent of their revenues from local sources. The greater effort made by the poorer states to support education is attributable to a shift of fiscal support from the local to the more complex state government.

[11] *Ibid.* Classification of fiscal dependence or independence made upon the basis of the state school directory.

[12] The above findings only refer to expenditures. They do not directly show that nonindependent school departments provide better education. It is possible that the political infiltration associated with the school department becoming part of a general budget may result in poorer education. My only point is that the school alliance with the professional politician eases their budget constraint.

[13] U.S. Office of Education, *Biennial Survey of Education in U.S., 1953–1954*, p. 26.

TABLE 14

State and Local Expenditures on Education by State Income Levels

	Personal Income Per Capita 1953–54	School Systems' Revenue Receipts as Percentage of Personal Income 1953–54	Local Revenue as Percentage of Total School Revenue 1953–54	Local Revenues as Percentage of Personal Income 1953–54
Higher Income				
States[1]	$1,225	2.60%	62.0%	1.61
High effort[2]	1,094	3.12	52.8	1.65
Low effort	1,313	2.30	68.9	1.59
Lower Income				
States	645	3.23	38.7	1.25
High effort[2]	567	3.74	33.6	1.25
Low effort	690	3.00	41.8	1.25

SOURCES: Personal Income: *Survey of Current Business*, September 1955, pp. 16–17. School Revenues: U.S. Office of Education, *Biennial Survey of Education, 1952–1954*, Ch. 2, pp. 70–1.

[1] The twenty-four states with higher per capita personal incomes.

[2] The twelve states in this group with higher percentages of school revenues receipts to personal income.

It would be hazardous to extend without modification this piece of school finance analysis to the proposed special districts and authorities which many municipalities are seeking. First, most of these special governments are not heavily dependent upon any special taxes and therefore they are less subject to voters' constraints. They frequently make use of user charges such as metered water, bridge tolls, and leases at airports. Controlling as they do commodities with inelastic demand, and assessing prices according to average cost principles, they find little difficulty remaining solvent and encounter little political opposition. But what if these governments were to extend their activities to include functions which necessitated reliance on a tax, usually the property tax? Would they find severe fiscal restraints? There is no easy empirical answer, since these groups have not been studied closely and the reported statistics lump under the single heading of special districts a most heterogeneous group— dominated by fire, and irrigation, and soil conservation districts. Some indications that they might then be severely subjected to voters' constraints can be inferred by their resistance to proposals to extend their scales of operations. For example, the New York Port

265

Authority is opposed to moving into the areas of mass transportation where financing methods other than average-cost pricing might become necessary.

To summarize: The single-function governments which are fiscally important in local finance (in 1957, the special and school districts spent almost as much as the municipalities) are very limited in their ability to mobilize their fiscal resources. They lack the freedom to jockey for support of a composite program. Their escape from this position is to depend upon support from more complex governments, the state, and to rely on pricing mechanisms which avoid the problem of nonaccord between the distribution of the benefits from the public services, and the costs of financing them.

7.

One reaction of governments to the voters' constraints is the substitution of pricing mechanisms for taxes. Prices have the great virtue that they provide a means by which to measure the residents' desires for the service, they are a flexible device to ration efficiently the supply of public facilities and service, and if they are the basis of financing a project they reduce voters' opposition since the unbenefited voters are not being asked to pay. Prices may not be efficient for all public services. However, there are several services for which they would have all three of the above virtues. A research study on the use of pricing mechanisms by governments would be a great boon to municipalities. Too frequently, simple average-cost prices are established which do not efficiently ration the supply, or generate information about desires for the service. Sometimes, the average-cost price does not free the government from seeking supplemental support from tax-raised funds, in which case they are returned to the old problem of voters' constraints, albeit modified.

Accompanying the growth of pricing mechanisms, is the shift in local debt from bonds backed by the tax base of the local governments to bonds backed only by earnings of specific activities or facilities or special assessment. In 1940, the nonguaranteed debt was 6 per cent of the total long-term debt of local governments. This percentage increased to 29 by 1957. A large part of the increase in local debt was incurred by school districts which could only issue bonds backed by the full faith and credit of governments. If we consider the debt of all local governments, excluding school districts, the nonguaranteed percentage increased from 6 to 43 between 1940

TABLE 15

Municipal Nonguaranteed Debt and Services Charges
by Size of City, 1957

Size of City (by population in thousands)	Revenues from Charges and Miscellaneous as Percentage of All General Revenues	Nonguaranteed Debt as a Percentage of All Long-Term Debt
All Cities	17.3	31.7
1,000 and more	13.3	21.7
500–1,000	13.3	15.2
250–500	23.7	39.5
100–250	17.0	36.3
50–100	18.6	35.6
25–50	19.9	40.5
Under 25	22.1	48.3

SOURCE: U.S. Bureau of Census, *Summary of City Government Finances in 1957*, July 1958, pp. 11 and 15.

and 1957. Most of this increase was accounted for by municipal and special district governments.[14]

Of special interest for this paper is the reliance on prices and nonguaranteed debt by size of city, a shown in Table 15. My argument would lead to the expectation that the smaller and more simple cities would feel a stronger voter constraint, and thereby would be forced to rely more on pricing mechanisms and on nonguaranteed debt. This expectation is confirmed. The smaller cities, those under 50,000, make a far greater use of nontax financing of local services and facilities than the larger cities—those over 500,000. This despite the fact that the larger cities had per capita municipal expenditures twice that of the smaller cities. If the smaller cities tried to approach the expenditure level of the larger cities, their reliance on nontax financing would have to be still greater.

8.

Another adaptation pattern of the neighborhood-municipalities to voters' constraints is the surrender of their fiscal independence. The school district is the classic case of a transfer of fiscal support to a more distant government, the state. There are persistent efforts to construct a single unified metropolitan government with sufficient fiscal strength and authority to plan and carry out plans for the

[14] Debt figures for recent years can be gotten from the U.S. Bureau of Census annual reports on *Summaries of Government Finance*. In earlier years they are available in their annual reports on *Government Debt*.

267

TABLE 16

Increases in Education and in All Other Grants
Between 1942 and 1957
(millions of dollars)

	Education Grants	*All Other Grants*
State to local	$3,304	$2,226
Federal to state	290	2,408

SOURCES: Census Bureau publications: *Historical Statistics of State and Local Government Finances, 1902–1953,* Table 2; *State Government Finance in 1957,* Tables 1, 15.

interdependent metropolitan area. So far these efforts have borne little fruit. Metropolitan government is still only on the banner of the professional administrators. It has not found a place on the political agenda. Although a metropolitan government remains nonexistent, there is a transfer of fiscal functions to higher level and more complex governments. The increasing role of the federal government in local affairs is apparent. Similarly, the state government has grown relative to the municipal governments in the last few decades, despite the growth or urbanism.

The major shift from local to state support has been in the form of the direct growth of state activities. Again, this can be related to the difficulties of the local governments to muster the political support to expand their services. The growth of the state relative to the local has been in the direct provision of services rather than through grants-in-aid. Table 16 shows that from 1942 to 1957 state payments to local governments increased by $5.5 billions and federal grants to states increased by $2.7 billions. Separating the grants between those for education and all others, it is apparent that except for education the state government has merely been a transfer agent between the federal government and the local government. The increase in federal grants to states for noneducational purposes has been only slightly greater than the increase in grants by the states to locals for noneducational purposes. Therefore, the increase in noneducational grants by the states does not represent a transfer of fiscal responsibility from the locals to the states. Educational grants do represent a growth in the fiscal importance of the state relative to local governments. The educational grants result in an increase in the proportion of state and local taxes raised by the state government.

Other than education, the transfer of fiscal responsibility to the states has taken the form of expanded services by the state government. Transfers have more commonly occurred, as would be expected,

268

TABLE 17

State and Local Payrolls and State Grants to Local Governments
as Percentages of Personal Income, 1957

	STATE AND LOCAL			STATE GRANTS	
	Total Payrolls	*Noneducation Payrolls*	*Local Non-educational*	*Educational*	*All Non-educational*
Higher Income					
States	4.61	2.66	1.61	1.08	1.03
Higher effort	5.24	3.01	1.80	1.34	1.33
Lower effort	3.91	2.27	1.40	0.80	0.72
Lower Income					
States	4.91	2.69	1.20	1.53	0.68
Higher effort	5.48	2.99	0.94	1.71	0.95
Lower effort	4.58	2.52	1.35	1.43	0.52

SOURCES: Payrolls: U.S. Bureau of Census, *U.S. Census of Government: 1957*, Vol. II, No. 1, *Summary of Public Employment*, 1958, Table 16. State Grants: U.S. Bureau of Census, *Compendium of State Government Finances in 1957*, 1958, p. 25. Personal Income: *Survey of Current Business*, August 1958, p. 13.

where political resistance to local services is the greatest. This is demonstrated in Table 17. Note that the aggregate noneducational payrolls of state and local governments for both high- and low-income states are a constant percentage of personal income. The local noneducational payrolls alone do not show the same pattern. In the states with lower incomes, the local noneducational payrolls are a smaller percentage of personal income than in higher-income states. The differences in local support of noneducational services as revealed by these figures is almost identical with the differences in local support of educational services as shown in Table 14. Clearly, low incomes discourage local public support for public services. The local resistance does not effectively restrain the state government. Though local efforts remain the same for educational and noneducational services, the reactions of the states are quite different. For noneducational purposes, the state payrolls as a percentage of personal income are distinctly greater for low-income states than for higher-income states. The states spend more relative to the local governments where local resistance to public services because of low income is greatest. The relatively greater effort of poor state governments results in the same amount of state and local payrolls per dollar of personal income for both poor and rich states.

269

It is interesting that, although local efforts for the support of education and noneducation services are the same, the total state and local efforts by lower-income states relative to the higher-income states, is much greater for education than noneducation. Does this mean that it is easier to overcome the fiscal resistance of local voters by means of a grant-in-aid program which retains a modicum of local control, than by means of a direct transference of functions to a higher government? This would seem to be a reasonable hypothesis. Possibly it reflects the power of the educational bureaucracy to exact support from the state while retaining its own independence. In any case, the political dimension is necessary to understand the fiscal problems of local governments.

COMMENTS

LYLE C. FITCH, Division of Administration, City of New York

In a general way, I concur in most of the conclusions reached by Margolis in his interesting and ingenious paper. But I am uneasy about some of the propositions which have led him to the conclusions.

I will comment, first, on the discussion of the structure of the urban community, and second, on problems presented by deficiencies of urban governmental machinery.

1.

Margolis' schematic pattern of the city is the conventional one of a core, which is the population center, surrounded by rings in which land-use intensity and population density decrease, and per capita income increases, with distance from the center.

I think this schema hides about as much as it reveals about today's rapidly changing metropolitan areas, certainly about New York. First, there is great diversity in the size and configuration of metropolitan areas. Second, most metropolitan areas are rapidly changing shape.

Raymond Vernon points out in his recent CED pamphlet, *The Changing Role of the Central City*, that many of the centrifugal forces which tied industrial, commercial, and white collar employment to the city's center are weakening. The concept of accessibility, on which the Margolis scheme so heavily relies, must be redefined.

Some types of employment are leaving central business districts because new transportation forms make suburban locations more accessible for their purposes than the central city with its characteristic traffic jam. For many firms, accessibility which once depended upon central concentrations is now provided in part by far-ranging trucks and automobiles.

Along with this changing role of the central city goes a great heterogeneity of developments in the older, built-up sections. As the evolutionary process continues, buildings are progressively demoted to less valuable uses; this trend in itself is a powerful developmental force, comparable in some ways to the gradual exhaustion of agricultural land. Building and land values tend to decline as obsolescence progresses. We find the phenomenon in many older central cities of vast stretches of so-called gray areas, characterized by obsolescent buildings which are not removed simply because of the difficulty and high cost of assembling land and preparing it for new uses. Cost of clearance in Manhattan, for instance, may run to $200,000 or $300,000 an acre, whereas land can be had in the rings, with more adequate accessibility for industrial purposes, for a small fraction of this clearance cost.

Some central land, it is true, is being reclaimed for high-priced office buildings and luxury apartment houses. Other land is being rescued from advancing blight by urban redevelopment programs, with the high cost of acquisition and clearance paid for in part by the federal and local governments. But in most cities of my knowledge, these countermovements have been quite inadequate—gray areas are extending faster than they are being removed.

The gray area is typically a central city problem; it is one which can be attacked only with great expense and effort; and it is one of the main manifestations of governmental inadequacy in urban areas today.

2.

In Margolis' system of things, the high-income groups are driven out of the city by economic pressure of low-income groups, who are willing to bid more per square foot for space. This abstraction also hides about as much as it reveals. The concentration in the center of low-income groups is due in part to the existence there of large amounts of inferior housing, which they can command and for which they have little competition from higher-income groups.

But it is due also to a great complex of other factors, including political and sociological factors.

3.

Margolis' main questions are concerned with the role of government in the modern urban area.

Can present local governments effectively establish a framework for economic and social activity within the City?

Answer: No.

Does existing governmental structure—limited as to territorial jurisdiction, functional specialization and restricted fiscal tools—reduce the organizational efficiency of government?

Answer: Yes.

Great stress is put on fragmentation of governmental responsibility in urban areas, among many governmental units. Individuals with relatively similar preference-orderings find it possible to cluster together. This weakens possibilities of agreement on public programs in a metropolitan area, and weakens opportunities for residents to use their superior fiscal capacity to carry out the necessary organization of the area.

Here is an implicit value judgment, basic to Margolis' thesis as I understand it, on the point of whether values of the individualist society are served by allowing possibilities of choice as to levels of government service by clusters of individuals of like tastes. Margolis thinks not. But Charles Tiebout finds positive values in the ability of like-thinking people to express their preferences by choosing compatible local jurisdictions. (Two basic difficulties, of course, lie in spillover effects which may benefit communities who do not pay therefore, and in large disparities of fiscal capacity relative to "basic" or "minimal" local needs, however defined.)

Another point concerns the size of the package of governmental services which are voted upon. The larger the package, within reason, the more services which may be supplied, relative to the situation where consumers vote on each service individually. To quote: "The success of the multipurpose package is based on the existence of consumers' surplus of enough voters for specific projects so that they are willing to endorse an entire package rather than lose the specific project."

But cannot this argument, based on a theory of log-rolling, be turned around? Can we not equally well say that the failure of the multipurpose package is due to the existence of the consumer's deficits of enough voters against specific projects so that they are willing to lose the entire package rather than take specific projects which they do not desire to pay for, or to which they may violently object? Logs may be rolled backward as well as forward, and frequently are.

To illustrate my point, New Jersey, a large governmental unit and one of the wealthiest states, is one of the most niggardly in support of governmental services. New York State, next door, is one of the most generous.

New Jersey, I submit, is a case of backward log-rolling, where the forces predisposed, or not indisposed, toward low state taxes find more in common than the forces favoring more governmental services.

I therefore would not want to gamble on a principle of organization based on the thesis that larger jurisdictions and more complex jurisdictions make it easier to extend the scope and quantity of governmental services.

4.

Despite my questions about Margolis' specific points, I of course agree that existing urban government is not adequate for modern urban problems. New forms of organization are needed for certain functions which can be handled efficiently only by jurisdictions encompassing entire urban areas. Some services and benefits can be provided most economically on a large scale, some are efficient only when they are integrated, and some can be handled only by having a central authority to resolve intra-area conflicts.

The New York City area, for instance, needs a unified program for water supply, waste disposal, pollution of air and water, recreation, and a unified comprehensive transportation policy and structure. Some or all of the same items are predominant needs of most metro communities.

One great need to be served by area-wide governmental machinery is that of efficient tax administration. Though the largest central cities are big enough to avoid typical difficulties of local taxation which arise from small-scale administrative organization, smaller jurisdictions generally are not. (The jurisdiction should be large enough and isolated enough to prevent avoidance by persons and firms moving over boundary lines or shopping outside the jurisdiction. And it should be large enough to afford the specialists and machinery necessary for efficient tax administration.)

Another major problem concerns the disparities of fiscal capacities among fractionated governments.

5.

I continue with a specific example of local governmental inadequacy whose causes are considerably more varied and complex than those discussed by Margolis. The Washington metropolitan area is just winding up a three-year study of its transportation requirements which indicates a need for constructing about $1.8 billion worth of highways and a $500 million rail transit system in the next twenty years. The rail transit system, it is agreed, cannot be entirely self-supporting; part of the costs of construction will have to be met by revenue sources other than fares. Unless the federal government is willing to finance the entire system, the region itself will have to put up a substantial amount to get the highways and rail transit system built.

The bulk of construction costs will be for construction in the District, while the bulk of the benefits will accrue to residents of Maryland and Virginia using the system for the journey-to-work. Increments to property values resulting from regional development (made possible in part by transportation facilities) will be concentrated largely outside the District. Hence there is no neat formula by which present local governments, acting by themselves, can match costs and benefits. A region-wide tax or combination of taxes, related as closely as possible to benefits, is indicated.

In addition to taxing powers, other powers would be required for an efficient transportation system. These include the power to control the flow of traffic on arterial roadways, the entry of vehicles into congested areas, and, of course, regulatory controls over private transit companies. Vesting such controls in a region-wide agency impinges on the jealously guarded power of existing local governments, and of state regulatory bodies. The transportation agency would also require the power to condemn land, another jealously guarded prerogative.

An organization capable of financing and operating the system, in a region comprising parts of two states and the District of Columbia, will have to be created.

The most adequate device would be a regional transportation agency, with the powers mentioned above, created by an interstate compact of the two states and the District of Columbia. But interstate compacts are always difficult to negotiate, and the greater their proposed scope, the more difficult it is to set them up. No compact agency to serve local areas has ever been endowed with taxing powers, or with other powers as broad as those listed above. Add to other obstacles, the low regard of the Virginia state government for the interests of urban northeastern Virginia, the proprietary interests of the federal government in the District, and matters relating to income levels and racial composition of various sectors, and it looks as if the cause of transportation improvement in the Washington region may be stalled for a long time to come if it has to wait on an interstate compact agency.

The only alternative to an interstate compact organization is a federal corporation, with the same territorial jurisdiction and the same powers (except taxing power, which cannot be exercised by a federal corporation). Such an agency could be created by an act of only one legislature, the federal Congress. But here again, are formidable obstacles. The corporation would need not only unusual powers, but also generous grants of federal funds, since it could not impose taxes. The very idea of having to live and share power with a federal corporation ·is anathema to many local politicians and government officials. Some observers therefore see little more chance in the foreseeable future for a federal corporation than for an interstate compact agency.

6.

In conclusion, the inadequacy of local government for the requirements of the urban age has many and varied roots. It is only one example of the general tendency of development of social institutions to lag behind technological and other developments, including population growth. But the prospects for improvement are not entirely dark. There are encouraging notes in the widespread interest in metropolitan problems, and moves in many metropolitan communities, amounting at least to getting a toe in the water, for dealing with them.

WILLIAM F. HELLMUTH, Oberlin College and the University of Wisconsin

Congratulations to Julius Margolis for a stimulating and, on several points, a pioneering paper. The theoretical statement of the relation of functional and spatial differentiation within metropolitan areas to fiscal needs and resources is excellent. Comparison of the criteria of welfare economics with those of political choice offers an interesting and useful insight. Introduction of the concept of "envy-equity" and broadening the horizons beyond the equity issue are commendable.

The assignment in these comments, as I have interpreted it, is to discuss the Margolis paper in light of the data and analysis developed from the studies of the Cleveland metropolitan area.[1] The Cleveland metropolitan area is a large but relatively uncomplicated area, entirely within a single state and with 95 per cent of the 1950 population in a single county.

The Cleveland METRO study offers mountains of data to verify many of Margolis' points. The great diversity of municipalities within a metropolitan area, for example, can be vividly documented. Hunting Valley—the most exclusive residential village with dividend and interest income averaging $7,000 per capita, residential assessed valuation of $37,000 per residence on a 40 per cent assessment ratio, and police service which includes delivery of the morning paper— and Cuyahoga Heights—the epitome of the industrial enclave with two huge steel plants to support 785 residents with per capita municipal expenditures of $527 on a municipal tax rate of about 1/4 of 1 per cent on true value—represent the diverse but richest suburbs. Oakwood with a per capita assessed valuation only one-one-hundredth that of Cuyahoga Heights, and Woodmere which is both small and poor requiring about a 1.5 per cent tax on true value of property just to maintain a full-time police force, exemplify the poorer communities.

The Cleveland study gives results which conflict with two of Margolis' points. First, Margolis contends that single-purpose

---

[1] Cleveland Metropolitan Services Commission, a private, nonprofit research organization, has published a series of studies on many aspects of the metropolitan problem. For those relating especially to government finance in the metropolitan area, see Sacks, Egand, and Hellmuth, *The Cleveland Metropolitan Area: A Fiscal Profile* (1958) and Sacks and Hellmuth, *Financing Governments in a Metropolitan Area: the Cleveland Area Experience* (Free Press, Glencoe, Illinois, 1960).

governments find it more difficult to gain local tax support for their programs. Independent school districts are cited as the prime example of this situation. All school districts in Ohio are separate and independent from other local governing bodies. School districts in the Cleveland area find it easier to muster political support than do the municipalities. Ohio has a limitation of ten mills on the property taxes which may be imposed without a referendum. One of the few advantages of this tax limitation is that it produces a scoreboard showing the popular support for expenditures for different functions.

In Cuyahoga County over the five-year period 1953–57, the municipalities put 126 operating levies on the ballot, of which 74 or 58.7 per cent passed, while school boards presented 95 levies to the voters of which 91 or 94.5 per cent passed, as shown in Table 1. Of the 95 municipal bond issues, 68.3 per cent passed, but of the 72 school bond issues, 90.3 per cent passed. The percentage required for passage is 50, 55, or 60 per cent of the votes cast, depending on the sponsoring government, the purpose of the issue, the duration of the tax rate, and the type of election. School issues polled more popular support in every classification by percentage required. County and municipal officials regard with envy the ease with which school issues are passed.

And voter support for schools is strong despite the high level of school tax rates relative to municipalities'. The school share is exactly half of the average property tax rates in Cuyahoga County, equal to the combined state, county, and average municipal rates. The tax rate in 30 of the 32 school districts exceeds the comparable municipal tax rates. And the school tax rates have increased more rapidly than rates for municipal and county purposes, with schools increasing their share of the property tax levy from 35 per cent to 50 per cent since 1940. State support for schools in Cuyahoga County has decreased on a relative basis, from 22.6 per cent of total revenue in 1940 to 16.5 per cent in 1956.

A check of the Census data which Margolis used at page 263 to show that payroll per pupil for April 1957 was less in independent than in dependent school districts, leads me to the opposite conclusion. My calculations indicate over $21 of payroll per pupil in all *independent* school districts against less than $17 per pupil for all *dependent* school districts, reversing the relationship shown in his text. The Margolis figures show payroll per pupil comparing *all* independent school districts with *only municipal* dependent school

TABLE 1
Number of Tax Levies and Bond Issues Succeeding and Failing by Vote in Cuyahoga County Municipalities and School Districts, 1953–57

PERCENTAGE OF VOTE RECEIVED	TAX LEVIES — Percentage Required for Passage						BOND ISSUES — Percentage Required for Passage		
	50% Municipal	50% Schools	55% Municipal	55% Schools	60% Municipal	60% Schools	55% Municipal	55% Schools	60% Schools
75 and over	2	10	–	–	9	2	13	12	8
70–74.9	2	12	7	–	9	3	8	11	4
65–69.9	2	18	2	3	7	2	25	11	5
60–64.9	–	20	6	5	9	4	27	7	4
55–59.9	6	5	10	4	7	–	22	3	1
50–54.9	3	3	5	–	11	1	22	1	–
45–49.9	6	2	6	1	6	–	6	2	–
40–44.9	1	–	1	–	2	–	8	–	1
Under 40	4	–	2	–	1	–	8	1	1
Number Passing	15	68	25	12	34	11	95	44	21
Number Failing	11	2	14	1	27	1	44	4	3

SOURCE: O. Waldby and A. Theuer, *Problems of Financial Management in Cuyahoga County*, Ch. 4, Cleveland Metropolitan Services Commission, 1959.

278

districts. Exclusion of the generally lower-cost dependent school districts operated by county and township governments accounts for the different results.

This evidence suggests that single-purpose governments with a popular function may attract more support than governments providing a complex of functions each with minority support.

A logical case can be made that state support for public schools has increased in order to escape the disadvantages of the property tax. Except for one or two states, the property tax is the sole local revenue source available to independent school districts. When the education function is included in the budget of municipalities or counties, other revenue sources besides the property tax are usually available. Thus, when a county or municipal budget includes the education function, other local revenue sources are available to supplement the property tax.

With inflation, the postwar bulge in school enrollments, and a more widespread desire to equalize educational opportunities and standards in public schools throughout the state, most states have increased their aid to education in preference both to heavier local dependence on the property tax and to providing other local revenue sources to the independent school districts. State grants shift the burden from the local property tax to sales, excise, and income taxes. These taxes have advantages over the property tax in that they can be administered more effectively and economically at the state level, are more responsive automatically to increases in income and prices, and avoid the sometimes harmful competition among jurisdictions within the state to keep rates low. The effect of an intrastate educational equalization program shows clearly in Cuyahoga County. The Ohio School Foundation Program, which provides minimum aid to every school district and additional aid to the poorer districts provided 34 per cent of the funds to support public schools in the state in 1957. But the Cleveland area school districts—richest in the state in terms of local tax capacity measured by assessed property value per pupil—received an average of only 17 per cent of their revenues from the state.

The hypothesis that financing or functional responsibility is shifted to higher levels of government to gain political support seems to neglect the greater taxing capacity of the higher-level governments. The Cleveland METRO staff report, for example, is recommending that when substantial additional amounts of revenue are needed, a county-wide income tax would be preferable to new taxes in the 58 municipalities and 32 school districts in the county. This new tax would be available both to finance increased needs and to correct the existing imbalance in revenue needs and capacities between different jurisdictions.

The hypothesis that complexity of government organization facilitates political support, though not borne out by schools, is substantiated by comparing the tax support received by 36 villages with that of the 21 cities excluding Cleveland. Villages generally provide fewer and lower-quality services than cities in part due to lower tax rates. The average millage levied by villages in 1956 was 5.3 mills compared with 10.0 mills in the cities.

Second, evidence from the Cleveland study suggests that the fiscal position of the central city government relative to the suburbs is more difficult than Margolis indicates. The Cleveland area conforms to the quantitative data, presented in Table 11 of the original paper, showing the greater per capita expenditures in the central city and allegedly the even greater per capita revenue capacity. But taxable real and tangible property, on which Margolis' data is less conclusive, is the major local source of revenue. The county is the assessing jurisdiction in Ohio. In Cuyahoga County, Cleveland has 58.6 per cent of the population and 67.8 per cent of the municipal current operating expenditures (58.9 per cent including schools), but only 56.6 per cent of the assessed valuation. Despite the heavy concentration of commercial, industrial, and utility property in the central city, the assessed valuation per capita is only $2,964 in Cleveland against $3,066 in the entire county. County, state, and Census sources indicate that assessment ratios in Cuyahoga County are higher for commercial and industrial properties than for residences. As residences constitute a higher proportion of the tax base in the suburbs than in the central city, adjusting assessed values to full values would show an even greater differential in favor of the suburbs over Cleveland. Per capita and per family income are also lower in the central city than in the entire county, as shown in Table 2. Thus the central city has a greater absolute need and a lower absolute capacity in the Cleveland area. Margolis' data in Table 13 shows for the San Francisco area also that average household income is lower in the central city than in the suburbs.

Margolis' analysis explains the lower expenditures per capita in the suburbs compared to the central city in terms of the simpler

TABLE 2

Fiscal Indices of Central City and Suburbs
in Cleveland Metropolitan Area, 1956

	Cleveland	Suburbs
Population	926,052	654,501
Average income per capita	$2,089	$2,590
Assessed value per capita	$2,964	$3,210
Municipal expenditures per capita[a]		
Current operating	$59.30	$39.80
Capital	18.00	18.20
Total	80.60	60.20
Municipal total expenditures to income	3.86%	2.32%
Municipal tax rate (mills)	16.80	7.53
School expenditures per capita[a]		
Current operating	$42.20	$60.30
Capital	3.00	23.50
Total	45.20	86.90
School total expenditures to income	2.16%	3.35%
School tax rate (mills)	12.80	17.58
School ADM[b] to population	12.9%	16.6%
Municipal plus school expenditures, per capita[a]		
Current operating	$101.50	$100.10
Capital	21.00	41.70
Total expenditures	125.80	147.10
Combined total expenditures to income	6.02%	5.68%
Combined tax rate (mills)	29.60	25.11

[a] Interest expenses are not shown separately. Expenditures for transit, water, and electricity are excluded.
[b] Average daily membership.

nature of government operations, making a coalition in support of different functions less likely. This analysis neglects the different needs and preferences for government services of the diverse neighborhoods and jurisdictions. Higher total expenditures per capita in the central city and industrial enclaves, represent a different product-mix of services from that of the dormitory communities. The mix differs both in range and emphasis. The central city spends more for welfare, urban renewal, slum clearance, police, and fire due to greater traffic, different type of property, and the composition of its population by employment stability, income level, and density. The industrial enclaves had very high expenditures per capita for general government, police, fire, streets, and total expenditures but little or no spending for most other municipal functions. The municipal expenditures of the business suburbs, other than the industrial enclaves, are not distinguishable from the dormitory communities in the Cleveland area.

281

The parts of the Margolis study comparing the central city and the different classes of suburbs seems to cover *only municipal* expenditures, and *not school* expenditures. The Cleveland area shows a pattern of school expenditures almost diametrically opposed to the pattern of municipal expenditures. Although municipal expenditures are higher per capita and in terms of effort in the central city, school expenditures are higher per capita and in terms of effort in the rest of the county. Capital outlays, especially for schools, are sharply higher outside the central city—$23.50 per capita in the suburbs versus $3.00 in Cleveland. As school expenditures are larger now than municipal spending, the current operating expenditures per capita for municipal and school purposes combined are now about equal in the central city and the suburbs. (See Table 2.) If capital outlays are included, the suburban expenditures per capita are $147.10 against $128.80 for the central city. The tax effort of the central city is greater, however, due to its low capacity and less borrowing.

Another point deserving comment is the question whether municipalities in metropolitan areas are becoming more diverse. The evidence is not conclusive either in Margolis' paper or in the Cleveland area. A number of factors and developments point toward greater diversity:

1. Population growth is most rapid in the 36 villages, 21 of which have areas of less than 5 square miles and another 10 of which are between 5 and 10 square miles. The smaller the area, the more likely only one or two neighborhoods and a narrow range of interests will be included.

2. Almost no land area is left to enlarge existing municipalities. Less than 15 square miles of area in Cuyahoga County is currently outside municipalities. With municipal home rule protecting existing municipalities no matter how small or how poor, the prospect of reducing the number of municipalities is very dim.

3. The racial composition of the central city is steadily growing more different from the suburbs. The nonwhite population in Cleveland is now estimated at about 25 per cent of the total, compared with 9.7 per cent in 1940 and 16.3 per cent in 1950. No more than 4 of the 57 suburban municipalities have over 5 per cent nonwhite population. However, the future increase in the nonwhite population due to in-migration is expected to slow down.

4. Much of the future population and economic growth in the

Cleveland Metropolitan Area will take place outside of Cuyahoga County. Lake County to the east, already included in the metropolitan area by the Census definition, had less than 6 per cent of the metropolitan population in 1950. Future growth will occur in several counties to the south and west as well, complicating the problem across county boundaries and involving adjacent metropolitan areas, such as Akron.

On the other side, several factors suggest less diversity in the future:

1. Population growth and spread have converted Cuyahoga County into an urbanized county. The greatest diversity of interests exists between urban neighborhoods and rural villages and townships. But the rural areas have almost disappeared. Only 0.02 of 1 per cent of assessed real estate valuation is agricultural. Only 2 villages out of the 58 municipalities have more than 10 per cent of their real estate assessed values in agricultural uses. Growth has created greater similarity of services from local governments in the metropolitan area. This greater uniformity is also reflected in the narrowing of the range of local property tax rates between different jurisdictions in Cuyahoga County since 1940. Especially the very low rates of the former rural areas have moved much closer to the mean tax rates for cities and villages. The coefficients of dispersion for the 58 different municipal tax rates around the city and village means have declined almost half since 1940.

2. The county has recently taken over responsibility for several functions formerly performed by municipalities. Welfare administration, Cleveland City Hospital, and schools for delinquent boys and girls have been transferred to the county, with popular vote supporting the additional county property taxes to finance these functions.

3. In November 1958, the people of Cuyahoga County voted to establish a county charter commission. This commission is now at work on a charter which will be presented for approval or rejection at the November 1959 election. To pass, the proposed charter must be supported by a majority of voters in the central city— Cleveland—and by a majority of voters in the rest of the county. An amendment to the Ohio Constitution in 1957 removed the former requirement that the voters in a majority of municipalities in the county had to approve the charter. The importance of each neighborhood under this procedure depends more on its voting strength than on its existence as a separate political entity. A county charter

thus offers real possibilities for more integrated government in the Cleveland area.[2]

The popular vote on transfer of functions to the county and on establishing a county charter commission indicates Margolis' "envy-equity" principle. Generally the vote in the lowest- and highest-income neighborhoods favored the changes. The voters in lower-middle income areas—who do not clearly see gains for themselves, who perhaps see their relative position threatened, and who are not motivated by *noblesse oblige*—have generally opposed the changes.

My parting comment is directed to Margolis' first table, which he introduces to show that local support of local government is below *prewar* years. Use of the depression year of 1932 as the first year in the series, probably dictated by the availability of continuing series for GNP and implicit price deflators, causes the decline in local revenues and expenditures to appear larger than if any other year of a local government census were chosen. My admittedly crude estimates for 1922 and 1927 still show a decline but a much smaller one than if 1932 is the starting point. (My calculations indicate revenue from local sources of 5.9 per cent in 1922 and 7.6 per cent in 1927, with direct expenditures of local governments 7.1 per cent in 1922 and 8.4 per cent in 1927, each expressed as a percentage of real gross national product to fit with Margolis' data in Table 1.)

A methodological question arises also about a real measure of local government revenue as used in Table 1. Which is the best price index to use to deflate government revenue? The implicit price deflator for the appropriate government sector measures the real purchasing power to the receiving government. The consumer price index, however, would measure better the loss in real buying power to the individual taxpayer. Some might prefer the implicit price deflator for total GNP. In the Cleveland study the decision was to deflate local government expenditures with the implicit price deflator for state and local government purchases and to adjust local revenues with the consumer price index. This procedure creates a new gap between revenues and expenditures due to the two types of "constant" dollars. We would be glad to get your reaction to this method.

---

[2] Since this paper was presented, the proposed charter for Cuyahoga County was defeated at the 1959 election, failing to receive a majority either in Cleveland or in the county outside of Cleveland.

WERNER Z. HIRSCH, Washington University and Resources for the Future

Julius Margolis has courageously plunged into the difficult undertaking of seeking an answer to the questions "What are the sources of the fiscal crises of metropolitan areas?" and "Is the crisis likely to become more acute?" If I understand him correctly, his main thesis can be summarized as follows: Spatial differentiation of economic activity in metropolitan areas causes conflicts of interest among individuals, particularly as taxes are not assessed in proportion to benefits received. The smaller the local governments, the more visible their actions, the more directly related to tax payments specific public services, and the more government units in a metropolitan area—the greater the frustration of local government, and the greater the fiscal crisis. On the other hand, "multipurpose package" voting and ignorance of the people permit the resolution of conflicts by the political process of persuasion and negotiation and, thus, the alleviation of the fiscal crisis. To quote Margolis on this latter point, "Ignorance and the acceptance of the rules of the game implicit in majority rules permit the resolution of conflicts by the political processes of persuasion and negotiation, while knowledge of consequences and their implications for one's own self-interest would lead to frustration of policy by focusing on possibly irreconcilable conflicts."

My comments will attempt to examine the basis of two major tenets of Margolis' thesis and their implications, and then consider some issues connected with the framework for analyzing metropolitan finance problems.

Package vs. Single Product

In analyzing the "normal" pattern of public choice between "multipurpose package" and "single product," it appears useful to distinguish between policy and legislation. Except for a few "omnibus" bills of Congress, legislation, particularly on the local level, is usually specific. On the other hand, there is available evidence which indicates that people in voting for a party or candidate tend to vote for the policy for which they think the party or candidate stands. This too, however, is less true on the local than on the national level. To me, it appears not so evident why "it is reasonable to hypothesize that the greater the number of products offered in the package to the voter the greater the likelihood of adoption." Likewise, more careful analysis is needed before we can be sure that "voters . . . are willing to endorse the entire package rather than lose the specific project (close to their heart)." A very large number of people called upon to vote on local fiscal matters appear satisfied with the status quo. Often no specific project is close to their heart. Furthermore, a careful study remains to be made as to whether the following hypothesis does not offer a better explanation: combining many projects into one package affords strong political or special interest groups an opportunity to seize on one issue, possibly a minor one, dramatize it and defeat the entire package.

To back up his contention, Margolis states that the schools are the major fiscal problem of local governments. As reason he cites that the single purpose district permits voters to "readily develop a negative or positive attitude toward the extension of the school budget." In this very characteristic, to my mind, can lie not only the weakness but also the strength of the single purpose district. Again more work appears in order before generalizations are possible. No doubt there are other, perhaps more important sources of schools' fiscal problems. Much of the difficulty of schools arises from the fact that their budgetary needs are so great compared to other public services. In suburbia often more than two-thirds of all current local government expenditures are for schools. For example, in St. Louis County, Missouri, school districts spent during 1951–55 an average of 66 per cent of the total outlay by local units, compared to 17 per cent expended by its 96 municipalities and 15 per cent by the county government.

Furthermore, in accordance with widespread state practices, property tax limitations are applied to local governments. For example, the permissible tax rate in Missouri for urban school districts, other than St. Louis, is 1 per cent of assessed valuation; the limit for St. Louis is 0.89 per cent, and for other school districts in Missouri it is 0.65 per cent. School districts may increase their rates to three times the specified limit, but only by annual popular vote. All school bond issues in Missouri must be submitted to a popular vote and must be passed by a two-thirds majority, while the total amount of indebtedness represented by general obligation bonds cannot exceed 10 per cent of the assessed valuation of taxable tangible property. It seems fair to say that restrictive tax and bonding limits written into state constitutions are the results of package and not single-product votes.

As further evidence designed to support the hypothesis that simple government structures are subject to more severe constraints, Margolis presents mean per-pupil expenditure data for fiscally dependent school departments and fiscally independent school districts. While the first are somewhat higher than the second, I would suggest that a simple comparison could be dangerous. States differ in their school subsidy program. Our study of factors affecting expenditures for public education appears to point to a host of factors which can significantly bear on per pupil expenditures.[1] How treacherous simple comparisons can be is illustrated in the St. Louis County experience with fire protection. In 1952 and 1955, the fourteen fiscally dependent fire departments spent on the average more per person than the eighteen fiscally independent fire districts. And yet from 1952 to 1955, the latter's per capita expenditure increased more (10 per cent) than that of the former (4 per cent). Our empirical analysis suggests that the wealth of residents, service levels, extent of commerce and industry, etc., greatly affect per capita expenditures for fire protection.

Margolis cites the heavy reliance of school districts on state subsidy as further support for his thesis. If the relatively large state subsidy for primary and secondary public education could be attributed to the fact that this service is rendered to a large extent by fiscally independent school districts (with single product votes), would we not expect special single purpose districts (other than school districts) to receive similarly important subsidies? But Census figures indicate just the opposite. Thus, in 1957 intergovernmental revenue payments for primary and secondary education, which was rendered only in part by fiscally independent school districts, amounted to 42 per cent of total school expenditures, while those to special districts not engaged in education were merely 8 per cent of their expenditures.[2]

Ignorance vs. Knowledge

Little, if any, evidence is offered to support the thesis that the ignorant voter helps solve local fiscal problems more than his knowledgeable brother. The same holds for the claim that political persuasion replaces rational self-interest. Is it really true that

[1] Werner Z. Hirsch, "Projecting Local Government Expenditures in Metropolitan Areas," *Proceedings of the Business Economics Section of the American Statistical Association* (1959).

[2] U.S. Bureau of the Census, *Summary of Governmental Finances in 1957*, August 1958, p. 22.

self-interest must be subdued and that it cannot be made to work toward the solution of metropolitan area problems?

Ends vs. Means—Question of a Framework

Margolis defines the fiscal crisis of local governments as a frantic search for tax sources, with public support possibly falling off. Yet, it is not clear that, if allowance is made for intergovernmental revenues for schools, highways, etc., real revenue from local sources as a percentage of real gross national product actually declined between 1932 and 1957. Even without such adjustments, the percentage has been steadily increasing ever since the end of World War II.

Such an approach, however, tends to look at metropolitan finance as an end in itself, when for many purposes the opposite is much more appropriate. I submit that in many respects metropolitan finance is better understood and its problems can be more successfully analyzed and attacked by looking at the dynamics of metropolitan areas in general. Metropolitan finance then becomes one of a number of different means toward a variety of ends. From the viewpoint of the area, public services and taxes provide residents with a more or less desirable place to live and work, and business and industry with an environment for more or less profitable business operations.

Within such a broader framework one of the great metropolitan area problems is to decide on the area's future image and the scope and quality of public services compatible with it. Other significant problems are developing means to improve fiscal capacity and finding revenue to finance these services, and establishing an environment which assures that they are provided efficiently.

How can imaginative and intelligent decisions be made as to what the area should look like ten, twenty, or more years hence and therefore what the appropriate fiscal needs of the area are? In planning the future of the area, it is important that the officials and the electorate have a reasonably clear picture of the main dimensions of the area's health and well-being. Among them are economic growth, increases in welfare, i.e., in per capita income, employment stability, amenities of life, etc. Alternative plans can then be judged in the light of the contributions they can be expected to make in specific terms.

In this connection, it is important to quantify the impact of specific local fiscal steps on the area's health and well-being and attempt to find a rough balance between benefits and costs. Such an impact analysis is rather complex. First the impact of a given fiscal policy on private decision-makers must be assessed. How will their decisions with regard to the area be affected? Second, the impact of these induced private decisions on the region's health and well-being must be traced and estimated.

An area's health and well-being is not only affected by its local public and private activities. Exogenous forces beyond its control, too, have a far-reaching impact. They can upset local plans and create a variety of financial exigencies. For example, legislation in connection with the Federal Housing Administration has made possible the purchase of new homes with very small down-payments and monthly payments not much larger than monthly rent. As a result, many young families have been induced to become home owners in suburbia, stretching themselves to their financial limit. Not only is this legislation an important force contributing to urban sprawl, but also it transplants large numbers of families to suburbia at a time when their need for public services is at a maximum, while their ability to pay for them is at a virtual minimum. This FHA legislation, regardless of its other salutary effects, is no doubt responsible for some of the financial difficulties of public schools.

Municipal governments would be wise to charge much larger building permit fees designed to cover more of the capital expenditures for schools, highways, fire houses, etc. However, it is fair to assume that many governments will be reluctant to take such a step for fear that other municipalities will be more accommodating and, thus, grow more rapidly. Perhaps a better procedure would be to put at the disposal of the FHA a revolving fund from which suburban governments could borrow to help finance urban public capital expenditures needed by those who were induced by it to buy new homes in suburbia.

Another source of difficulty, though much less important, is that many areas compete with one another for new industry by keeping taxes to industry low or by even offering tax concessions to new-comers. There exists also much confusion about the financial blessings of industry. All too often merely the tax payments of the plant are compared with the costs of providing it with public services. A proper analysis would attempt to estimate direct and indirect changes in local economic activity brought about by the new plant. Once this was done, receipts and expenditures of the various govern-ments associated with these activities would be estimated, added, and compared. This final figure alone can indicate whether the new industry is a fiscal asset or liability.

Within this framework, what are possible vistas to the solution of metropolitan finance problems and what are their chances for success? I admit that philosophically my position stems from inherent, though somewhat moderated, optimism, and from a deep conviction that people and governments are fundamentally eager to make rational decisions. During the next decade or two, the perfection of a well-conceived and powerful general framework for making intelligent decisions on metropolitan area problems should be in our reach. Appropriate data should become available to implement important parts of it. With such help imaginative and rational solutions to metropolitan problems in general and fiscal problems in particular must and can be found. It should become increasingly possible to show the electorate that the individual's welfare is closely tied to that of the entire area. Once we can assess the indirect effects of local fiscal and other action, and cost and benefits of specific projects can be estimated and more adequately shared, I would hope that conflict-reconciling policies can be advanced. When we can show how much one section or industry of the area depends upon others and how apparently convenient short term temporary solutions can produce serious long term disadvantages and losses, appropriate action will, I trust, be forthcoming.

For instance, the St. Louis study made two empirical stabs at this issue. To illustrate the economic interdependence of the area, regardless of geographical location, it estimated the number of persons directly and indirectly employed by a large brewery and determined their place of residence. Located in the heart of the core city, it employed 6,000 employees (about 4,800 of whom lived in the core city itself). Directly and indirectly it provided employment for about 6,800 core-city residents, about 2,600 residents of St. Louis County and about 900 residents of the Illinois counties in the metropolitan area.

Another attack relied on the regional input-output table to show, on an industry-by-industry basis, the direct and indirect employment and income impacts of alternative industrial development policies.

Both types of information can help convince the voters that the entire area's welfare and growth is their concern. For example, public measures hurting the brewery enough so as to force it to move part or all its operations out of the area would have serious repercussions for many residents of other municipalities in the area. But even without such a detailed study, it is not too difficult to show that low service-levels in some of the area's police departments can threaten much of the area with blossoming crime and high theft insurance rates.

No doubt there will be occasions when personal and public interests will seem irreconcilable. In such cases, higher levels of government will have to be called upon to establish an environment which can facilitate a creative resolution. Before this can be done, we must attain a better understanding of the exogenous effects of state and federal activities upon metropolitan areas. This is necessary also for another reason. As time goes on, the political power of metropolitan America will grow and the national government will become more and more responsive to the problems of metropolitan areas. At the same time, it will become increasingly important that the relationship between local public and private policies and the balanced growth of the national economy be more closely watched.

While state and federal government should play an important coordinating role, local governments should be encouraged to be increasingly active in fields to which they are suited. Let us not forget that, fundamentally, local governments offer the closest and potentially best link between people and government. In a democracy this link deserves continuous strengthening. Very large local governments often prove unresponsive to the needs and desires of the people.[3] Then the people tend to lose interest and their attitude to local officials and their tax needs can become negative. Efficiency considerations may not call for very large governments. The St. Louis study has shown that there are hardly any significant economies of scale in local government services. Exceptions are for water supply and sewage disposal.

There is, of course, a strong tradition of local self-government in the United States, which will make difficult, for instance, any attempted shift of land-use planning from a local to a higher level of government. But because of great differences of wealth and the conviction that every citizen should benefit from at least a minimum service level, the tax base of metropolitan areas or whole states should be pooled to underwrite a floor below which local public

[3] Lennox L. Moak, "Some Practical Obstacles in Modifying Governmental Structure to Meet Metropolitan Problems," *University of Pennsylvania Law Review*, February 1957, p. 611.

services cannot fall. Then it will be up to the specific community to poll its electorate and decide on service levels for schools, fire protection, refuse collection, etc., above the prevailing floor, and tax themselves accordingly.

However, some functions, such as traffic and transit and industrial development and planning, are area wide, and they must be handled on an area-wide basis. Other services, such as water supply and sewage disposal appear to benefit from economies of scale and can be most efficiently provided on an area-wide basis. In these cases, multipurpose districts and other arrangements can help meet these challenges and provide for the necessary financing.

The hope to the solution of metropolitan finance problems, to my mind, lies in more knowledge, which should enable us to weigh intelligently the local government services we desire against our ability to afford them. Then we can more judiciously establish priorities and plan for needed sources of additional revenue, in ways likely to be acceptable to an informed electorate.

MORRIS BECK, Rutgers University

The Margolis paper is a solid contribution to the literature on local public finance. However, his choice of 1932 as a standard for comparing the relationship between local public expenditures and GNP is unfortunate, for a longer view tells a somewhat different story. Direct expenditures of local government rose from 5 per cent of GNP in 1913 to 7 per cent in 1927. The relatively high ratios of the thirties are attributable to the depressed level of total output. Since World War II, the local-expenditure component of GNP has again exhibited an upward trend with the ratio approaching seven per cent. Data for years prior to 1932 are shown below:

	1913	*1922*	*1927*
Gross national product, bil. of $	40.0	69.9	90.9
Direct expenditures of local governments,			
bil. of $	2.0	4.6	6.4
as % of GNP	5.0	6.6	7.0
Local government revenues from own sources,			
bil. of $	1.7	3.8	5.7
as % of GNP	4.3	5.4	6.3

SOURCES: Gross national product: J. F. Dewhurst and associates, *America's Needs and Resources: A New Survey*, New York: Twentieth Century Fund, 1955, Appendix Table 4-2. Based on unpublished data from Simon Kuznets.

Local revenues and expenditures: U.S. Bureau of Census, *Historical Statistics on State and Local Government Finances, 1902–1953*, Table 3.

Decision-Making in Taxation and Expenditures

CHARLES E. LINDBLOM
YALE UNIVERSITY

Introduction

THE planners of this conference believed that it might be possible eventually to formulate more workable standards for government tax and expenditure decisions by interweaving a search for clarification of actual decision processes with a search for workable norms. In undertaking such a project as they proposed, I am accordingly pursuing a refinement of normative economics in a roundabout way. Most of what I have to say will be positive, not normative and, for that matter, will be more derived from political science than from traditional economics. The facts to be alluded to are on the whole familiar. The norms sought are of two kinds: for taxers and spenders and for designers of decision-making machinery. Given the purposes of such Universities-National Bureau conferences as this one, I take it that in the interpretation of facts, hypotheses will often be welcome. If at critical points in the argument I fall back on the plea for additional research, I assume I am within my scholarly rights.

1. Contemporary Practices and Norms

Beginning then with facts, let us take note of some characteristics of government expenditure and taxation decisions in the United States, especially in the federal government, that are significant to economists.[1]

1. Legislative decisions that authorize expenditures are typically made without benefit of any formal machinery that brings budgetary considerations to bear on them. The authorization committees of the Congress on one hand, and the appropriations committees, on the other, are relatively independent of each other and not locked in close cooperation.

2. The costs and benefits of authorized programs are not typically

---

[1] Most of the characteristics of decision making to be listed are familiar. All can be documented in Arthur Smithies, *The Budgetary Process in the United States*, McGraw-Hill, 1955.

weighted against each other, systematically and explicitly, when legislative decisions are made.

3. Policy-making is not systematically and explicitly viewed as a problem in the choice among alternative means for the achievement of desired ends. Even in decisions in which the necessity of allocating scarce funds might appear to make the means-ends problem especially acute, decision-making is not typically marked by explicit comparison and deliberate choice among means. The military's penchant for the "best" of everything—the best planes, the best mess kits, the best gloves—is coming to be the classic example of reluctance to evaluate means in the light of ends. Points 2 and 3 are, of course, merely two aspects of the common failure of government decision-makers to employ an adequate concept of cost.

4. Some major expenditure or taxation policies are set or altered as an accident or by-product of other decisions. That is to say, a policy is not always a decision; it is often simply upon us without deliberate and explicit choice. A "decision" to run a surplus or deficit is, for example, often not a decision at all but simply an outcome.

5. More generally, many of the financial and other implications of a decision are ignored when a decision is made. The decision-maker, whether administrator or legislator, permits pressure of work and limits on his own concerns to confine his attention to less than all of the important relevant variables.

In the budgetary process, most of us see a partly realized, partly potential, technique for making expenditure and taxation decisions more rational. This brief list of characteristics of financial decisions can be extended to note certain aspects of budgeting.

6. Many major explicitly financial decisions are outside the budgetary process. Tax decisions are, of course, wholly outside; so also deficiency appropriations. And in wartime, as might be expected, appropriations to the military are so generous that availability of physical supplies, not budgetary considerations, set expenditure rates.

7. As many economists have noted, there is in the federal budgetary machinery no explicit provision for coordinating revenues and expenditures.

8. Formal congressional review of the budget is concentrated in appropriations subcommittees whose interests are focused on segments of the budget considered largely in isolation from other segments.

9. Neither the appropriations committee as a whole nor the Congress as a whole gives extended formal consideration to the budget as a whole, nor does the appropriations committee as a whole play a strong coordinating role for the subcommittees.

10. Moreover, even in considering segments of the budget, the subcommittee members are repeatedly drawn into scrutiny of details rather than of the major expenditure alternatives, although this phenomenon varies from one subcommittee to another.

11. Being torn between two possibilities—using budgetary scrutiny for detailed administrative control or using it for planning broad public policy—legislators are drawn toward the first to a degree that reduces significantly their explicit attention to the latter.

12. Congress does not enact the budget as a whole at the termination of budget review but instead enacts a series of appropriations bills.

13. Budgeting is marked by conflict between President and Congress, between the two houses of Congress, and among subcommittees.

Familiar as these provisions are, they are essential to what follows.

The accepted contemporary norms for the budgetary process reflect widespread dissatisfaction with the characteristics of the budgetary process just summarized. I would expect widespread agreement on such a list of norms as the following, taken from Smithies (page references are to Smithies) though altered somewhat in emphasis and presentation. Some are norms for taxers and spenders; some are norms for designers of decision-making machinery. Some are general norms, and some are norms pertaining to coordination, which is a special aspect of decision making.

1. Governmental objectives should be as clearly and explicitly defined as possible (25ff.).

2. Alternative policies should be explicitly regarded as alternative means toward the achievement of objectives (28).

3. Specifically, expenditure decisions should be made explicitly and deliberately in the light of all of the objectives they are intended to achieve (16).

4. In the interests of a rational comparison of alternatives, final expenditures decisions should not be made until all claims on the budget can be considered (16).

5. Revenue and expenditure decisions should be deliberately coordinated (192).

6. For each expediture, some systematic and deliberate appraisal of benefits and costs should be made (12ff.).

7. Policy-making, including budgetary policy making, should achieve a unified policy (23).

8. A comprehensive overview of policy-making on expenditures and revenues should be attempted (16, 25).

9. All taxation and expenditure decisions should be somehow embraced in the budgetary process (175ff.).

10. Specifically, the legislature should undertake a comprehensive, unified, rather than segmented, review of the budget (164, 169, 193).

11. Decisions should be made on the basis of a cooperative division of function between the legislature and the executive (45).

For present purposes, it does not matter that some of these norms overlap others and that some are more specific statements of others. It is important, however, to observe that a few central principles run through this and similar lists to be found elsewhere in the literature. In such lists economists reveal themselves as esteeming, not surprisingly, such conventional principles as:

1. A comprehensive overview of factors relevant to a decision
2. Clarity of definition of social objectives
3. A means-end approach to policy
4. Deliberate and explicit choice among policies
5. A calculation and minimization of cost
6. Reason and cooperation rather than arbitrariness, coercion and conflict
7. A unified decision-making process for decisions that are highly interdependent.

Most, perhaps all, of the listed norms are applications in varying degrees of specificity of these more fundamental principles.

2. Discrepancy Between Practices and Norms

For all the immediate appeal of both norms and underlying principles, an objection to them is that they do not emerge from a skeptical analysis of the actual decision-making process, good and bad, in government but appear instead to be derived from a paradigm of a rational decision process. They stem from criticisms of government decision-making that take the form of observations that the process is not what one would suppose a rational process to be.

Reconsider now in this light the characterizations of decision-making with which this paper opened. They are invariably read as shortcomings of decision-making, although I did not present them as such. They are thought to be shortcomings, I suggest, not on a demonstration of their effects but by implicit or explicit appeal to obvious standards of rationality. Or look again in this light at the seven underlying principles on which the norms rest. Why are they as persuasive as they are? Because, again, they represent almost universally accepted ideas on how to be rational in any kind of problem-solving.

It is possible that we are all betrayed by these obvious standards for rational problem-solving. Perhaps they are more limited in their applicability than we have thought. Although one's ideas of what is rational suffice to predict that using a milk bottle to drive spikes into 4 × 4's will ordinarily be inferior to using a hammer, one cannot be confident for such a complex process as governmental decision-making that such principles of rationality as comprehensiveness of overview, explicitness of choice, means-ends calculations, and clarity of definition of objectives are appropriate. These are standards drawn largely from our own intimate experiences with small scale, relatively more simple, problem-solving.

That conventional norms do indeed follow paradigms of rational processes rather than reflect independent diagnosis of decision-making and that they may lead us astray can be illustrated. It is a commonplace norm that revenue and expenditure decisions should be coordinated through some formal congressional machinery now lacking. Why? Because fiscal policy is a powerful device for economic stabilization, from which it seems "logically" to follow that Congress should have formal machinery for taking account of the fiscal consequences of a prospective surplus or deficit. But is it in fact true that Congress is without methods for coordinating revenue and expenditure decisions? No, it is only without *formally prescribed* procedures, and we should know by now that informal operating procedures are often superior to formal. And is Congress typically unaware of a deficit when it occurs? No, except to the degree that fact-collecting cannot keep up to date in any organization. Do such deficits and surpluses as do occur (other than those justified by stability considerations) appear at random? No, they are probably the result of a combination of congressional attitudes toward fiscal policy and pressures upon Congress. Do then "economically unwise" surpluses and deficits demonstrate a need for formal coordination? No, not unless formal coordination can be shown to be an intermediate step to the achievement of changed congressional attitudes and to the restructuring of pressures on congressmen.

What is it about government decision-making that might make "obvious" principles of rational choice inappropriate? A first answer is that complex decision-making is molded by limitations on human problem-solving capacities not taken account of in the conventional picture of rational choice.

Consider man's limited capacity to undertake usefully a comprehensive overview of the variables relevant to a complex decision. If sufficiently ambitious, all attempts at a comprehensive overview run into two major limits: first, man's limited intellectual ability, that is, his limited ability to grasp, calculate, and remember; and, second, limited information. Some problems lie so far beyond these two limits that it would be irrational for man to attempt an informed and reasoned solution to them; better he flip a coin, adopt a rule of thumb, or decide by any of several "arbitrary" means.

Commonplace though not trivial decisions as to whether to marry, what occupation to choose, or how many children to produce are not so much comprehensively calculated as resolved through a limited evaluation; or they are drifted into, unthinkingly decided, taken as by-products of other decisions, or settled by rule of thumb. While the role of what might be called "reason" in such decisions might well be increased for some people in some circumstances, I see no evidence that these decisions would always be more rational (unless "rational" is defined as "reasoned") if approached through an inevitably only partly successful comprehensive overview of the relevant variables. I would not be so foolish as to make the attempt myself and did in fact satisfy myself with a very limited view of the variables.

If these relatively simple personal decisions call for intellectual capacities and knowledge beyond our reach, all the more so do complex governmental decisions. The federal budget document runs to 2,000 pages, and prints of committee hearings on it cover many thousands more. It is not at all obvious, and indeed doubtful, that any man or committee can achieve a sufficiently intimate understanding of the budget as to make the thousands of comparisons and evaluations required in a genuinely comprehensive overview, even if these printed materials were all one were required to master. In fact, of course, one cannot understand the variables relevant to budgetary decisions without knowing, grasping, remembering, and relating to the decisions a prodigious amount of information about government, the economy, and the wishes of the citizenry.

These difficulties do not mean that men think and express conspicuously irrational thoughts when faced with the budget, or that they flee in panic, or that the budgetary process comes to a grinding stop. They do mean, however, that most budgetary decisions are in fact made in ways economists are accustomed to call arbitrary, that thousands of important comparisons are never in fact made, that many major issues never come to the attention of decision-makers, and that such agreement as various decision-makers reach is less owed to the exhaustiveness of their scrutiny of the budget than to common ideology, prejudice, or even common ignorance when they all miss the same relevant issues that might have divided them.

If this is true, as can easily be documented and as I should like to see documented by research, then it does not at all follow that even more ambitious attempts at comprehensiveness of overview, as is conventionally recommended, will increase the elements of rationality in government taxation and expenditure decisions. It is quite possible that overtaxing man's limited capacities still further will make the situation worse.

An objection to this line of argument springs to mind. It is that limits of man's capacities have been pushed back by dividing up the decision-making process, that is, by factoring out subdivisions of the decision tasks. It is true, everyone agrees, that limits on man's problem-solving capacity can indeed be pushed back by factoring out parts of problems and enlisting the cooperation of a number of individuals or groups, each of whom attacks its own assigned part of the problem. If it were not for this possibility, even the small federal budgets of earlier decades would have been beyond our grasp. But pushing back the limits is not the same as eliminating them. Hence, even with subdivision of the decision-process in the administration and in Congress, a $70 billion budget presents a staggering decision-making problem. Is it not obvious that, even with subdivision, thousands of important comparisons are not made and many major issues are not brought to the attention of decision-makers?

We can see why subdivision only pushes back but does not remove limits by looking at subdivided decision-making processes. Observers report such familiar difficulties as the following:[2] (1) coordination

[2] See for example, Ely Devons, *Planning in Practice*, Cambridge University Press, 1950.

of subdivisions is a continuing task of top decision makers; (2) substantial interdependent elements that cannot be factored out remain the responsibility of top decision-makers; (3) appropriate lines of division are unstable, as changing conditions create new patterns of interdependency; (4) difficulties of communication, many of which are intended by subordinates, misrepresent to top decision-makers the facts required for their decisions; (5) motivational difficulties, illustrated by divergence between organizational goals as seen by top decision-makers and as seen by subdivisions, inevitably distort decisions. If this last point is not clear, it predicts, for example, that appropriations subcommittees take a segmental view of the budget not only because they lack a strong central coordinating committee, but also in large part because a subdivision or sub-committee inevitably takes on goals and attitudes of its own.

Now, again, these difficulties in subdividing the task of compre-hensive overview do not mean that decision making becomes chaotic when subdivided. They simply represent specifications of *limits* on man's capacities to carry off successfully a comprehensive overview of a complex problem. And to return to our main point, they buttress the allegation that government decision-making is molded by limits on man's capacities that are not taken account of in contemporary conventional norms and principles.

Another illustration of the failure of conventional norms and principles to take sufficient account of the facts is that government officials often cannot cast a policy problem into a means-ends framework, as the norms require.

An immediate and obvious difficulty on this score is that decision-makers, to say nothing of the electorate, do not in fact wholly agree on objectives or values.[3] To be sure, on many they agree roughly; but the scope of government decision-making is not limited to their areas of agreement. Nor do men generally aspire to universal agree-ment on objectives of social policy, prizing instead diversity and change. Still, it may be questioned, do we not agree that governments shall take as their working objectives those preferred by the majority? Do we not consequently enjoy a working agreement on objectives of governmental policy?

This is a question of fact, and for several reasons the answer is no. In the first place, it has been shown that majority rule is a process

---

[3] For present purposes, I shall use interchangeably such terms as "values," "objec-tives" (including "constraints"), "goals," and "ends."

through which it is not usually possible for citizens to indicate preferences on specific policies.[4] If a winning candidate differed from his defeated opponent on, say, an issue in foreign policy (among other issues that divided them), it does not follow that those who voted for him favored his stand on the foreign policy issue. Hence, neither the winning candidate nor anyone else can say what policy objective is to be taken, by majority rule, as the government's objective.

Second, most policy choices open to government, including almost all budgetary choices, are never even raised during election campaigns as campaign issues. Again, therefore, a public official is without a clearly defined governmental objective. Third, even in abstract principle we do not in fact agree on majority rule as a basis of working agreement. For in a large number of decision-making situations, citizens differ as to how far the equality principle implicit in majority rule ought to be compromised to take account of differences in intensity of preference among citizens and differences in their circumstances. We have even gone so far in the United States as to subject some policy decisions to a vote in which only farmers in particular categories participate. And, of course, the United States Constitution makes numerous systematic provisions for inequality, as in its basis for representation of senators and the bicameral legislature. On all these counts, it is clear that government decision-makers are often without clear instructions from the electrorate on policy objectives.

At one extreme, the impossibility of a means-end approach to policy is clear when one decision-maker's mean is another's end. To one decision-maker or citizen, for example, tax reduction comes to play such a role in his thinking that we can only call it an end or objective for him. To another, tax reduction is considered simply as one of several means to an objective like full employment. A government such as ours survives because it takes advantage of agreement among two such individuals where it finds it; to require them to agree with each other on which is end and which is means and then ask for their agreement on both ends and means is not only to pose insuperable problems of calculation to them but also to endanger political stability. The political scientists tell us democracies cannot be fussy about the terms on which their citizens reach agreement.

[4] R. A. Dahl, *A Preface to Democratic Theory*, University of Chicago Press, 1956, pp. 124 ff.

I should like these specific failures of the conventional principles to take account of the character of government decision-making to be taken as illustrative of two more general failures that will become clearer as we move through succeeding stages of the analysis. The failure to account for man's limited capacities and for the frequent impossibility of casting a problem into a means-end framework is sufficient to reveal the possibility that conventional norms and principles have not taken sufficient account of either (1) the sheer complexity of government decision-making or of (2) the special problems of handling values or objectives. Almost any other specific aspect of decision-making we might have looked into will reveal the same two underlying problems: complexity and special difficulties in evaluation.

It was suggested above that our ideas of what is rational in problem-solving are derived in large part from introspective observation of our own problem-solving processes from which many of the complexities of collectivities, including certain value problems, are absent. In addition, recent new insights into decision-making carry a powerful bias. With few exceptions, the formal theory of decision-making has not faced up to the possibility that complexity can outstrip limited intellectual capacity.[5] And the success of conventional principles in such sophisticated application as operations research have perhaps tempted us to forget the limited competence of these applications and the possibility that extremely complex rational decisions have to be approached quite differently. Aware of this, Charles Hitch writes:

"I would make the empirical generalization from my experience at RAND and elsewhere that operations research is the art of suboptimizing, i.e., of solving some lower-level problems, and that difficulties increase and our special competence diminishes by an order of magnitude with every level of decision-making we attempt to ascend. The sort of simple explicit model which operations researchers are so proficient in using can certainly reflect most of the significant factors influencing traffic control on the George Washington Bridge, but the proportion of relevant reality which we

[5] See the survey: Ward Edwards, "The Theory of Decision-Making," *Psychological Bulletin*, July 1954, pp. 380–417. The older theory has, of course, been extended, through statistical and mathematical theory, to deal more adequately with limitations on information.

can represent by any such model or models in studying, say, a major foreign-policy decision, appears to be almost trivial."[6]

3. Incremental Decision-Making

We need now to pause to make clear and rather exact the significance of the fact that conventional principles do not face up to either the complexity of decision-making or its special value problems. A common but too quickly despairing inference is that we have no alternative but to press on as far as possible toward comprehensive overviews of our collective problems, toward clarification of objectives, toward structuring each decision as a means-end problem, toward deliberateness and explicitness of choice, and the like. Those who make this inference will grant that man's capacity to employ these methods successfully is indeed limited, that government expenditure and taxation policies, therefore, will at best be none too good; but they may somewhat paradoxically take heart from the discrepancy between practice and norm by believing that the only continuously serviceable norms are those impossible to reach.

But *if* for rational decision-making there is any alternative to comprehensiveness, the means-end approach, deliberateness and explicitness, and the like, the more sensible inference would be to employ these methods only when their limits permit and to employ an alternative when available. A big "if," it will be replied. Let us see. A fundamental characteristic of the literature on expenditure and taxation decisions is that it has not explored the possibility of alternatives, as I now propose to do.

There are a number of ways in which a decision-maker, within government or out, can approach a rational decision that departs considerably from the practice of the conventional principles outlined above.[7] Herbert Simon, for example, has constructed a model of "satisficing" rather than maximizing. It takes account of limits on man's cognitive capacities, by simplifying both the welfare or pay-off function and the process of search for a satisfactory solution.[8] Its implications for government decision-making procedures remain to be explored but are not, I should think, trivial.

[6] Charles Hitch, "Operations Research and National Planning—A Dissent," *Operations Research*, October 1957, p. 718.

[7] It is apparent by now that I am not going to define rationality. The reader is invited to supply his own definition, for I think what I have to say about rationality is as true for one concept of it as for another among the common definitions.

[8] Herbert Simon, "A Behavioral Model of Rational Choice," *Quarterly Journal of Economics*, February 1955, pp. 99–118.

Problems of resource allocation in wartime led E. A. G. Robinson to the hypothesis: "The golden rule of all planning is that it must be done in terms of the scarcest of the resources."[9] This, the "bottleneck principle," is hardly more than a hint at still another model of rational decision-making; but it may be the germ of a principle for drastically simplifying a complex problem so that it can be as rationally decided, for all the makeshift appearance of the decision, as through an inevitably futile attempt to comprehend all the complexities of the problem.

Still other ways of simplifying decision-making tasks to avoid irrationalities might be mentioned. Among them is one I have elsewhere described in some detail under the label of the incremental method.[10] I suggest that it is actually the most common method through which public policy decisions, including decisions on taxes and expenditures, are approached. That it is a method commonly practiced has led us to take it for granted rather than formalize it in terms like those that formalize incremental consumer choice, to which it is obviously related.

The incremental method is characterized by its practitioner's preoccupation with: (1) only that limited set of policy alternatives that are politically relevant, these typically being policies only incrementally different from existing policies; (2) analysis of only those aspects of policies with respect to which the alternatives differ; (3) a view of the policy choice as one in a succession of choices; (4) the *marginal* values of various social objectives and constraints; (5) an intermixture of evaluation and empirical analysis rather than an empirical analysis of the consequences of policies for objectives independently determined; and (6) only a small number out of all the important relevant values.

Of these six characteristics, the first three are recognizable characteristics of political decision-making, as practiced by both officials and most policy-minded academic analysts. I shall not linger over them except to point out that anyone whose approach meets the first three conditions has enormously simplified his policy problems compared to what they would be if he literally and strictly followed the conventional prescription to attempt a comprehensive overview. The fourth and fifth strike at the value problem in

---

[9] D. N. Chester, ed., *Lessons of the British War Economy*, Cambridge University Press, 1951, p. 57.
[10] Lindblom, "Policy Analysis," *American Economic Review*, June 1958, pp. 298–312.

policy-making; and the sixth strikes at the general complexity of policy analysis, although in what appears to be a shocking way.

Let us first consider problems of handling values. In the incremental method, political decision-makers handle values through marginal comparisons in the same way that consumers do. Although economists describe rational consumer behavior by reference to utility surfaces, indifference curves, demand schedules, and the like, a rational consumer need know nothing about them. He need not first determine his indifference curve for oranges and apples and subsequently decide his purchase policies accordingly. Nor need he first try to comprehend all possible product mixes (or even a few alternative product mixes), then decide which one he prefers, and only then make those purchases necessary to attain the preferred mix. The rational consumer proceeds directly to marginal comparison of alternative specific purchases. The way in which we economists can, for our own professional purposes, conceptualize consumer choice obscures the great difference between what the consumer can be conceived of as having done but does not actually do—ascertain a function, then choose so as to maximize it—and what he actually does—simply compare policies at the margin and choose directly the preferred policy.

Like the consumer, the incremental decision-maker in governmental affairs does not make use of a utility function, in his case a social welfare function. He does not think in terms of "all the variables that might be considered as affecting welfare: the amounts of each and every kind of good consumed by and service performed by each and every household, the amount of each and every kind of capital investment undertaken, and so on."[11] He can hardly be said to know even a point or two on such a function because he does not think in terms of alternative social states; and, if he can be said to value one social state higher than another, this fact is more to be inferred from his choices than said to control them. He makes specific choices, as does the consumer, at the margin.

Similarly, incremental decision-makers closely intermix empirical and value elements in choice as do consumers. We may describe a consumer who buys a car as having decided upon such a purchase policy in order to attain such objectives or values as speed of movement, ready accessibility of transportation, improved status, and

---

[11] Abram Bergson, "Socialist Economics," in H. S. Ellis, ed., *A Survey of Contemporary Economics*, Blakiston, 1947, p. 417.

conformity, as well as the pleasures of novelty, display, color and form, and acquisition itself. To decide whether to buy a car and, if so, which car, requires then that he both choose among combinations of such values as these and empirically investigate the consequences of alternative purchase policies for the attainment of each of these values. Thus he must make two kinds of choices: (1) the preferred value-mix and (b) the purchase best suited to the attainment of the preferred value-mix. In actual fact, however, he makes these two choices simultaneously when he decides upon his purchase; he does not in one choice determine the preferred value-mix and then make his purchase in its light.

Moreover, he would find it difficult to describe, even to himself, his preferences among the objectives except by pointing to the purchase made and those rejected. Furthermore, he would confess that many of the objectives or values served by his purchase appeared to him as relevant only after alternative purchase policies began to compete in his mind. He did not, for example, first consider buying a car in order to satisfy his esthetic senses, but esthetic values quickly became relevant once he contemplated buying a car.

Although it is customary to analyze values as a first step in policy making, it is a characteristic of the incremental method that such an analysis is cursory, short-lived, and only a prefatory clarification of a few of the many goal-values that will be affected by policies to be considered. Sometimes such an analysis is omitted entirely. Either at once or very quickly in incremental decision-making, the analysis turns directly to alternative policies. *Predicting* consequences of alternative policies and *evaluating* the consequences then become intertwined to the degree that, as in consumer choice, only in the final choice among policies is the final choice among objectives or values itself made.

For example, many policy analysts find it extremely difficult to decide how much inflation they are willing to tolerate in order to achieve some specified reduction in unemployment except in contemplation of some particular set of policy alternatives offering marginally different prospective amounts of inflation and un-employment. Or, again, none of us do very well in describing to others—or even to ourselves—the relative value of economic security and rapid economic growth. But we make the choice when confronted with alternative policies offering different increments of the two values. Again, we do not determine our welfare function, then choose, but instead choose directly and, in so doing, simultaneously both indirectly define a part of a welfare function and maximize it.

It is also a characteristic of the incremental method that the decision-maker is much more tentative about his objectives or values than he is considered to be in conventional models. He counts on policy choices to lead him to fresh perceptions about values, he expects to learn about his values from his experiences with pursuing and enjoying them, and he is inclined to think that in the long run policy choices have as great an influence on objectives as objectives have on policy choices.[12]

If incrementalism is a method through which a single decision-maker can rationally evaluate alternative policies, it also offers a solution to the problem of disagreement among decision-makers on values. Incrementalism sidesteps problems posed by disagreement on values because decision-makers deal directly with policies, as has just been explained; no virtue attaches, as it does in the conventional method, to prior discussion of and agreement on objectives or values.

This characteristic of incrementalism makes agreement possible in at least three distinguishable ways. First, ideological and other differences in values that loom large when considered abstractly do not necessarily stand in the way of agreed marginal values. Second, the practice of evaluating only in actual choice situations often leads decision-makers to reconsider values in the light of practical constraints, and reconsideration often moves them toward agreement. Third—and much more important—individuals can often agree on policies even if they hold conflicting values. A group of decision-makers can agree, for example, on the desirability of a sales tax without agreeing on objectives; they may have quite different values and reasons in mind. It will be shown in a later section that incrementalism makes still another attack on the problem of disagreement: sometimes incremental policy-makers are coordinated by methods that do not require them to agree with one another on either values or policies.

---

[12] How then distinguish, it might be asked, a rational and irrational decision? The conventional model defines a rationally chosen policy by its relation to a set of objectives. A rational policy, for example, is one that attains its objectives, or maximizes the probability of doing so, or is, by warranted beliefs, best suited to attainment of its objectives. But since for complex public policy decisions, the decision-makers' objectives are defined by the policy choice he makes, the principal characteristic of the rational decision—perhaps the defining characteristic—turns on the accuracy of the decision-maker's predictions about the outcome of his policies. We shall, however, say more about this below.

As for the general problem of complexity in policy-making, the most drastic simplification of complex problems achieved in incremental decision-making is, as already indicated, through outright neglect of important consequences of policies. Neglect of important variables is so widely preached against that it may be worthwhile to make the point that all policy analysts practice such neglect and intend to go on doing so. In academic policy analysis, we economists routinely leave a mound of unfinished business for the political scientist, sociologist, or psychologist to attend to; and we only sometimes remember to qualify our results accordingly. We leave to the psychologist, for example, the appraisal of malingering when we analyze the desirability of liberalizing benefits under unemployment compensation. Less obvious but no less common is every policy analyst's neglect of imponderables, even when they are considered to be important. Beyond these omissions are many others, some of which appear at least superficially to be arbitrary or random, others of which are traceable to our ignorance. Examples are extremely long-run consequences for family solidarity of increasing urbanization achieved as a result of agricultural expenditures (or restrictions of expenditures) that induce farmers to leave the land; short-term consequences for corporate concentration of military procurement decisions; and consequences for the development of socialized medicine of liberal expenditures on veterans' medical care.

If important consequences are neglected, can the method still be described as one suitable for rational decision-making? Or is omission of important consequences a proof of irrationality? Whatever one's concept of rationality, I suggest that the answer in principle is clear. If the consequences are not neglected in the processes by which policies are determined, then that they are neglected by any given decision-maker is not evidence of irrationality in decision-making. Less cryptically, if values neglected by some decision-makers are the concern of other decision-makers, public policies taken together can be rational. We often permit the fallacy of composition to obscure this insight. Or, to put it another way, we often miss this point because we have applied to politics a confusion of partial and general equilibrium analysis.

Consider a hypothetical example. The President and some of his advisers agree on a greatly expanded program of highway expenditures. Their objectives are national defense, reduction of highway congestion for civilians, and economic development. Consequences of the program for the parity of the 50 states as recipients of federal funds are ignored, as are possible consequences for auto fatalities, design of automobiles, profits of existing toll roads, destruction of homes and recreational areas, sales of automobiles, sales of home furnishings, character of home life, participation in organized religion, and so on.

When the program is presented to Congress, if not before, some of the neglected values will be spoken for by, say, representatives of the states or of toll-road authorities. These interests may come to terms immediately with the original proponents of the program, not necessarily by each representative's taking into account each other's values but by agreement directly on modifications of the program. Other interests will wait until congressional consideration of the program is underway, and still other interests will be brought to bear on the administrative officials eventually responsible for implementing the program. And years later, when it becomes apparent to churchmen that too many people are out driving on Sunday rather than attending religious services, they will stir themselves to find ways of combating the tendency. When they do so, they will not necessarily associate the tendency with the earlier highway program, and it is not at all necessary that they do so in order to deal with their problem.

I intend the example to do no more than show the possibility that decisions can be rational even if each decision-maker ignores important values, if only the values neglected at one point are attended to at another. It is not necessary to show that all values are given equal consideration; they are not in the conventional method. Nor is it necessary to show that their inequalities are systematic or are understandable in terms of some formula; they are not in the conventional method. Nor is it necessary to show that all important values are brought somehow to bear on each decision, even if not on each decision-maker. For sometimes a neglected value will move no one to action until a decade later when it becomes clear that it is being endangered.

The example I chose was not after all very hypothetical; the processes illustrated are familiar. Let us, therefore, explore further the possibility that interconnections among decision-makers in actual fact accomplish rational decision-making despite the apparent irrationalities of each decision taken by itself. We turn thus to an aspect of decision-making that can be posed explicitly as the problem of coordination.

4. *Coordination Through Partisan Mutual Adjustment*

Coordination is worth exploring for several reasons. First, we have been lead into it by an exploration of ways in which decision-makers simplify their problems and hence achieve a rationality that would be denied them if they tried to comprehend their problems fully. The possibilities that decision-makers are achieving some notable degree of rationality through the practice of what we have called the incremental method depend in large part on how the decisions are related to each other. Second, quite aside from incrementalism, coordination is an aspect of decision-making with its own special difficulties usually not sufficiently distinguished from decision-making in general. Third, in the study of expenditure decisions, budgeting usually emerges as the dominant coordinating process, and we shall want later to reconsider budgeting in the light of alternative coordinating mechanisms actually in use or potentially useful.

One group of possible coordinating devices includes, of course, the very same procedures that have already been described for decision-making generally: the conventional method with its attempt at comprehensiveness of overview; and the alternative methods for simplifying decision-making, i.e., bottleneck planning, satisficing, and incrementalism. These are all similar in that, if they are used for coordinating decisions, the principal coordinating mechanism is a centrally located mind or centrally located, closely cooperating group of minds. Consideration of their prospects for achieving rational coordinating decisions raises the same questions as we have already raised about them, and I shall consequently pass them by with only two comments.

With respect to the conventional method, because limitations on rationality are posed both by value conflicts and by the complexity of problems, these limitations would appear to be even more serious in the case of coordinating decisions than for decisions generally. With respect to the incremental approach to decisions, it is indeed a possible coordinating method; but, because one of our claims for it is that individual decision-making irrationalities are compensated for by characteristics of a coordinating mechanism appropriate to it (and yet to be explored), to defend incrementalism itself as an approach to coordinating decisions is, though not impossible, difficult.

To what extent the coordination of, say, total federal revenues and expenditures—they are coordinated, even if not ideally—is accomplished through this first group of coordinating methods is not clear. As we have seen, the absence of formal machinery for a centrally comprehended coordinating decision does not prove the absence of central coordination. Assuming some degree of central coordination, achieved perhaps through informal consultation, we do not know what mixture of such approaches as the conventional and the incremental is employed. In any case, inspection of such a problem in coordination as this one would quickly lead us to believe that a second type of coordination, not marked by central comprehension, is also exploited.

The second type, so far as I know, has been best elaborated, though with some troublesome ambiguities in presentation, by Michael Polanyi in a little known essay in which he attempts to generalize from market coordination processes.[13] This is a method in which each of a number of decision-making centers desiring a solution to a commonly recognized problem that cannot be centrally solved independently makes an adjustment to the positions taken at each other decision-making center. A long succession of such independent adjustments eventually achieves a solution to the problem when no center needs make a further adjustment. Polanyi draws an explicit analogy with certain forms of mathematic problem-solving.

His assumption, on which he perhaps wavers, that participants in such a process recognize a common problem and deliberately cooperate is an assumption explicitly to be denied in describing still a third kind of coordination: the mutual adjustment of partisan decision-makers. In this kind of coordination, adjustments to each other are made by decision-makers who do not share common criteria, differ in the values they think important, do not necessarily cooperate with each other or recognize any common problem. It is an especially significant kind of coordination for incremental decision-makers because, to the extent that they simplify their problems by concentrating on some values to the exclusion of others, they become the very kind of partisan we have just described. It is in this third kind of coordination that we shall find the mechanisms

[13] Michael Polanyi, "Manageability of Social Tasks," *The Logic of Liberty*, University of Chicago Press, 1951.

through which incremental decisions are often made parts of a larger rational policy-making process.

Partisan mutual adjustment is commonplace for coordination of any two or more of such individuals and groups as the President, Director of the Budget Bureau, individual legislators, congressional committees and subcommittees, administrators at various levels, and countless private groups. At least three major types of partisan mutual adjustment can be distinguished although any one individual or group is often simultaneously engaged in all three.[14]

A. ATOMISTIC. This first type is suggested by atomistic mutual adjustment in the hypothetical purely competitive market. Each decision-making group simply ignores the repercussions of its decisions on other groups in deciding upon its own policies. The decision-maker may or may not know that his decisions have repercussions for other groups; in either case he ignores them. It follows that he does not attempt to manipulate other groups. In the example above, protagonists of a highway program can simply ignore the consequences of their policies for church groups, for taxpayer associations, or for wildlife conservationists. Typically, a group acts atomistically with respect to some but not all other groups. The atomistic method is, I think, the equivalent of Polanyi's method except for what I believe to be his assumptions of a common recognition of a problem and of deliberate cooperation.

In the atomistic method, each partisan group will find itself constantly adjusting its policies as it finds that other groups have created the need for an alteration in its course of action. A continuing process of mutual adjustment could conceivably work through successive approximations to an equilibrium in which no further moves are necessary; but, equilibrium tendencies or not, it interlocks the various groups whose policies are consequential for each other.

B. DEFERENTIAL. In this adjustment process, each decision-maker avoids any policy that would constrain or adversely affect another group. In our own private affairs, each of us is accustomed to leaving unchallenged to each of our associates certain areas of personal choice. Similarly, there develops in the political arena a set of mutual

---

[14] It will be apparent to many that in exploring these processes I am following the tradition of the pluralists in political theory. But my professional interests in the application of the results of these inquiries to problems of collective expenditure and other economic decisions turns my interest toward the calculation aspects of these processes rather than the control aspects. More concretely, where a political scientist asks whether these processes safeguard us against an overconcentration of power, I ask whether they can aid us in rational choice.

concessions of jurisdiction or authority among decision-makers, individual or group. In addition, private citizen and public policy-maker alike defer in order to avoid adverse counter moves. In such a process as this, decision-makers seek a way to attain their objectives in the areas of free movement left open by the activities of other decision-makers. Some congressmen will not pursue their policy objectives if they turn out to challenge the President's program; and similarly in some areas of choice formally open to the President, he will defer, say, to a congressional coalition. Again, decisions are closely interlocked by this process of mutual adjustment.

C. STRATEGIC. In this method, decision-makers manipulate each other in a variety of ways. They may do so by partisan discussion, in which they try to win other decision-makers over to their preferred decisions by whatever purely verbal appeals they think might be effective. This kind of discussion differs from discussion that proceeds in the light of agreed objectives or end values, and its possibilities for achieving coordination throw, I suggest, a new light on the loose but stimulating older concept of democracy as government by discussion. It is the kind of discussion in which an advocate of tax reduction in the Senate might appeal to his high-expenditure colleague not through values shared but by calling the colleague's attention to facts favorable to tax reduction or by reference to his colleague's values or objectives.

Second, decision-makers may manipulate each other by the exchange of effective threats and promises. The Pick-Sloan plan for the Missouri River is an example of the product of an exchange of promises, in this case between the Army Engineers and the Reclamation Bureau. An exchange of threats and promises is a common outgrowth of partisan discussion, but I mean to define partisan discussion to exclude it, so that it can be seen as distinct. Such an exchange I shall refer to as bargaining, following, in so doing, one common usage. Partisan discussion and bargaining, as I have defined the latter, are typically intermixed.

Third, they may manipulate each other by a variety of pressures on each other beyond partisan discussion and bargaining, that is, by injuring, forestalling, or crippling each other directly. For this no intercommunication is required, as in partisan discussion and bargaining; and the frustrated group or decision-maker may not even know the source of the frustration. Here, as also in bargaining, one of the principal strategies is to form an alliance or coalition.

Among several advantages gained through alliance, one is that, where one group is without a direct method of influence on a third, it may use a second as an instrument, as when the President is induced by one group to dismiss the head of an agency that stands in the way of the first group. The National Wildlife Association and the American Forestry Association are examples of a pair of conflicting decision-making groups both powerless to make legislation and administrative decisions alone, hence both engaged in building alliances with legislators, other interest groups, and individual voters.

How often these methods for partisan mutual adjustment achieve a rational coordination of decisions is not realized. That they interlock decisions made at various points in the body politic is clear enough; that they are methods for interlocking a multiplicity of incrementally approached decisions is also clear. In addition, whatever its defects, partisan mutual adjustment achieves whatever coordination it does achieve without making coordination a staggering intellectual task. To the extent achieved, coordination is a by-product of decision-making, as in market processes. Nor does coordination, so achieved, make staggering demands for information, because the facts needed to achieve an intellectual coordination are required by no one. Finally, coordination so achieved does not depend upon agreed objectives or values. In short, partisan mutual adjustment strikes at both the complexity problem and the values problem.

But what if the interlocking of decisions is without any perceivable desirable pattern? It has to be shown that coordination so achieved is rational in some sense going beyond what we have already said. I suggest the following hypotheses:

1. *Partisan mutual adjustment is a process through which any value held to be important by any group of people can be made influential on policy-making.* The common objection that not all important interests are participant in each decision is, for reasons discussed above, not valid; it is sufficient for the truth of this hypothesis that each interest be somewhere influential.

2. *It often achieves a satisfactory weighting of conflicting values or interests in policy-making.* Because, as argued above, there is no agreed formula for weighting of conflicting values in our society, any one of a large range of possible systems of weights is no less satisfactory by any agreed standard than another. And since any system of weight used in conventional methods of coordination is

to a degree arbitrary, it need only be shown that the system of weights used in mutual adjustment is sometimes better.

While accidents of strategic position and other factors will produce a wide variety of weight from one policy area to another, a supporting hypothesis is that policy will respond relatively more to widely shared and/or intensely held values than to less widely shared and/or less intensely held values and that, consequently, values will in effect often be weighted in a satisfactory way. This supporting hypothesis is all the more probable because of the practice of groups to form alliances around common or adjacent interests. It does not imply that all individuals express their values and the intensity of their values by the degree to which they participate in the mutual adjustment of groups in the political arena. On the contrary, a satisfactory system of weights could evolve from the mutual adjustment of groups representing a small minority of citizens if the distribution of values and intensities among the participating minority corresponded roughly to its distribution in a larger population consisting of citizens not indifferent to policies even if not participating. Again, the system of weights does not have to meet any very restrictive conditions in order for it to be satisfactory in the light of alternative methods of coordination.

3. *In particular, the weighting of interests in mutual adjustment meets the requirements of consent.* Put down roughly, for brevity's sake, the hypothesis takes account of the alleged precondition of democratic government: that citizens must agree on certain fundamental values and procedures, despite their disagreements on others. Societies can be thought of as purchasing this agreement, or consent to continuation of democratic government, by conceding to each interest group whatever it requires as a price for its consent. (If too many groups demand too high a price, their demands cannot be met, and democratic government is impossible.) Mutual adjustment is a process in which, when the intensity of frustration of group interests threatens democratic consent, the fact is plain; and the option is open to other groups to pay the necessary price. This is an aspect of mutual adjustment much to be prized, I suggest, even if it is sometimes converted into blackmail, as perhaps it has been in the fight against desegregation.

These three hypotheses deal directly with the suspicion almost all of us entertain that mutual adjustment is an arbitrary coordinating mechanism. I suggest that they are sufficient both to call into question the widespread view that central coordination is generally superior and to argue the desirability of comparative study of the two methods, with the hope of discovering just when the one is superior to the other.

Three additional hypotheses throw further, though indirect, light on the value of mutual adjustment as a coordinating process.

4. *Partisan mutual adjustment clarifies citizens' perception of their own preferences and leadership's knowledge of citizens' preferences.* I can only allude briefly to competition among potential group leaders for followers as having the effect of stimulating each leader to outdo his rivals in articulating for the group its preferences and its best avenues toward their gratification.

5. *It also often dissipates conflict stemming from narrow or hastily considered views of group interests by group members.* The search for allies in multilateral bargaining, for example, puts enormous pressure on group leaders to find a way of defining a group's interest so that it can be harmonized with the interests of potential allies. Mutual adjustment will often achieve not merely a compromise of interests but what Mary Parker Follett has called an integration of interests.[15]

6. *Whether mutual adjustment is or is not more coercive than centrally achieved coordination depends upon the rules of the game by which the mutually adjusting groups play.* In view of some tendencies to stress the coercive aspects of mutual adjustment, it is relevant to emphasize its contribution to winning consent, to point up the inevitability of coercion in central coordination, and finally to point out that, while mutual adjustment could and does under some rules lead to violence, as between nations, in other circumstances it can be and is played by rules that respect traditional constraints on the use of coercion.

5. Implications for Norms and Principles

We now turn to the implications of all the foregoing for norms and principles for decision-makers and designers of decision-making machinery in the field of taxation and expenditure decisions. To the extent that incrementalism together with partisan mutual adjustment is a set of processes for rational decision-making, its first implications for norms and principles in decision-making are already

---

[15] H. C. Metcalf and L. Urwick, eds., *Dynamic Administration: The Collected Papers of Mary Parker Follett*, Harper, 1942, pp. 31 ff.

obvious from the foregoing discussion. Although these first implications are destructive more than constructive, to go very far beyond them requires research and reflection that has hardly yet been attempted and which has in fact been inhibited by the common preoccupation with conventionally conceived decision-making.

The first and obvious implication is that, to the extent that incrementalism and mutual adjustment are defensible, every single one of the conventional norms explicitly listed in the early pages of this paper is invalidated. Some of them are reduced to norms appropriate to particular circumstances in which central comprehension is possible; others are entirely inappropriate.

It would be tedious to discuss each in turn; inspection of them in the light of the foregoing argument should be sufficient. But it may be helpful to recapitulate some principal points of the foregoing argument as explicit comment on each of the seven listed principles on which the more numerous prescriptions rest. Each of the seven is in some substantial way invalidated.

A. COMPREHENSIVE OVERVIEW. It follows from all the foregoing that deliberate omission of important relevant values from the analysis of a decision is desirable for sufficiently complex decisions, or for decisions in which decision-makers cannot agree on values; and the circumstances in which each omission is satisfactory increase with the adequacy of partisan mutual adjustment for the coordination of the decisions so made.

B. DEFINED SOCIAL OBJECTIVES. For collective decisions, they cannot be defined if they cannot be agreed upon, as is typically the case for large-scale social choice. Often social objectives can be defined only through actual marginal policy choices by individuals or by groups within which values are agreed upon. It is then sufficient that such individuals and groups agree on policy, even if they do not agree on objectives; and atomistic and deferential mutual adjustment achieve policy-making even without agreement on policy. Hence the principle is often inappropriate in that it defines a quite unnecessary requirement for rational collective choice.

C. MEANS-END APPROACH. Where values cannot be agreed upon, it is not desirable that participant decision-makers look upon their problem as a collective means-end problem; it is sufficient that they simply find a basis for agreement without regard to which variables are means and which are ends. Or it is sufficient in some types of mutual adjustment, such as atomistic and deferential, that they see the policy problem only as a problem of adaptation of means to their own private partisan ends. Moreover, since ends and means are simultaneously finally chosen in incremental policy-making, it is not desirable that policies be chosen as means to previously clarified ends. Finally, it is desirable that ends be considered as quite tentative and that they be reformulated with each policy choice in such close interconnection that it can be said that ends follow choice of means as much as means follow choice of ends.

D. DELIBERATE AND EXPLICIT CHOICE. It is desirable that some policies be set as a by-product of partisan mutual adjustment rather than deliberately and explicitly. Just as we do not have in a price system a deliberate and explicit choice among resource allocations but permit allocation to be determined as a by-product of a multiplicity of market decisions, so policy on, say, income distribution in the United States may be an example of a policy best achieved as a by-product of more particular decisions on factors affecting income distribution. Or, for another example, it may be desirable to let the aggregate size of the military budget emerge as a by-product of decisions on specific expenditure programs and not raise the aggregate as an explicit problem at any time. On values and objectives, it follows from comments on the means-end approach that values or objectives should quite commonly not be made the object of explicit and deliberate choice but should be chosen implicitly at the margin through an actual policy choice and should not be articulated as an unnecessary obstruction to agreement on policy.

E. UNIFIED DECISION PROCESS. This normative principle, specifying the general appropriateness of hierarchical forms of organization to knit decision-makers together, simply leaves no room for co-ordination through partisan mutual adjustment.

F. REASON AND COOPERATION. The whole point of the argument of this paper might be reduced to the proposition that reason runs out, cannot bear the burdens imposed on it, therefore has to be employed in the light of its limitations. A general prescription to employ reason in decision-making, however persuasive, is less wise than a prescription to use reason in establishing such decision-making machinery as reduces the demands made on reason and achieves a coordination of only partly reasoned decisions through processes of adjustment other than those that go on in the human mind.

Because partisanship is an asset (because it simplifies), conflict becomes not a problem but a method of coordination. Conflict is as useful, therefore, as cooperation. Conflict between the President and Congress, for example, or between two administrative agencies is, within limits still to be explored, to be prized as an essential element in partisan mutual adjustment.

G. CALCULATION AND MINIMIZATION OF COST. This principle requires more extended comment than given to the others, although the principal grounds for qualifying the principle are inferrable from the above comments on the means-end approach.

Let us take the example of expenditures for inspection of income tax returns, an allegedly clear case in which a larger expenditure than at present would easily recoup its costs in increased tax receipts. Assume that those making the decision are divided among those who want the increased receipts and are willing to expand the necessary funds to accomplish their objective, those who welcome an opportunity to weaken income taxation, and those who, while favorably disposed to income taxation, are not happy about the extent to which its enforcement requires detailed investigation of personal affairs by revenue officials. Each can calculate costs as he sees them, both monetary and intangible. Typically, at some stage a policy will in fact emerge; but, given the assumption that their values differ, they will not have aggregated their values into a pay-off or welfare function (assuming, of course, they do not have an overriding agreed value in the form of such a function). Hence the policy finally arrived at by agreement or by other mutual adjustment is just that—a policy, not their response to an agreed compromise or aggregation of their conflicting values.

Given this solution to their problem, it cannot be asked and answered whether the costs of achieving a social objective were minimized or not, except by the arbitrary injection of the personal values of the observer who asks the question. In this case, a prescription that costs be calculated and minimized could be appropriate only for the partisan problem-solving of the participant decision-makers, which is not the way in which such a prescription is ordinarily intended. As a prescription intended for some collectivity like the House of Representatives, it is not operational, for the House as a whole cannot agree on what is value received and what is cost.

To go further, it would not even always be desirable, even if possible, for the House to agree on an aggregating rule for conflicting values so that, in the light of such an aggregation, choices could be made that did maximize values received or minimize costs. For presumably such a rule would itself be a product of partisan mutual adjustment. To minimize costs under such circumstances would therefore be simply to make policies consistent with prior partisan adjustment of conflicting values. It is not at all clear that this is to be preferred to the direct partisan mutual adjustment of policy conflicts without prior resolution of value differences. The arbitrary element is only more apparent in the one method than in the other.

The same line of argument holds for choice among expenditures on, say, heavy bombers, medium bombers, and missiles of various kinds. It is easy to advocate the policy of providing the biggest bang for a buck; but, in the absence of agreement among bargainers for various branches of the military or among congressmen on just what weapon has the biggest bang, the prescription reduces to the advice to the partisan interests to minimize costs or maximize objectives as they narrowly see them, or else the prescription is again nonoperational.

One appropriate alternative prescription in cases such as these is that expenditures should be undertaken that participant decision-makers can voluntarily agree on, assuming only that each participant has, in his own limited view, acted economically. Another appropriate prescription is simply that each decision-maker act economically and that their independently decided courses of action be coordinated (policy achieved as a by-product) through atomistic, deferential, or some type of strategic adjustment not even requiring their agreement, assuming only that the process of adjustment meets certain conditions.

Still further, let us assume no disagreement whatever on values but a problem so complex as to go beyond the successful comprehension of any individual or committee. Under these circumstances, breaking the problem down into its aspects and throwing decisions into the hands of partisan groups linked through mutual adjustment may still be desirable. If so, the appropriate prescription is, again, not that costs be calculated but that the policy be that on which the participants can agree or be that policy achieved as a by-product of mutual adjustment without agreement. Here the impossibility of achieving a value aggregation in the light of which costs can be minimized stems not from conflict but from complexity.

I want now to depart from summary comment on the listed conventional principles to identify several further illustrative implications of the foregoing argument for norms for expenditures and tax decisions. One of these is interwoven with the last principle discussed. We have just said that under certain assumptions policymakers should take their own voluntary agreement as a criterion for policy. No doubt this will strike many as curious advice for policymaking, since one might think that a norm ought to be useful in distinguishing between agreement on foolish policy and agreement on wise. The norm of agreement is not, however, so inadequate as it might seem because it specifies voluntary agreement as sufficient only when each partisan has in his own limited view calculated his costs.

Similarly when we said that in some cases a sufficient condition of a "good" policy is that it be arrived at through partisan mutual adjustment, this was saved from being a foolish prescription because we also required that the adjustment processes themselves meet certain conditions. For lack of research, we cannot now say when the adjustment processes are and are not satisfactory, but the distinction is valid, just as is the distinction between workable and unworkable competition or competition and monopoly despite our inability to define and agree on what kinds of real world market structures are workably competitive.

The important point in both prescriptions is that in many circumstances we need no test of a correct or wise policy other than that it has been achieved through one set of processes rather than another. To pursue the market analogy further, in many circumstances we need no test of the superiority of one pattern of resource allocation to another other than that one pattern is achieved through one set of practices rather than another, the one set being characterized by open opportunities for comparison, substitution, and choice, and the other by restrictions. If we can clarify different structures or circumstances in which mutual adjustment proceeds badly or well, we should be able to define rational expenditure and tax policy in many cases without regard to outcome.

In any case, it is not a reasonable objection to mutual adjustment that I cannot show directly that its outcomes are superior to other outcomes. As with the most social processes, we argue the superiority of the outcome from the process, not of the process from the outcome. The constancy of the economist's objection to this conclusion when applied to governmental rather than market decisions simply often reflects the fact that, while some economists are not disturbed that consumer preferences lead to allocation policies other than best respond to their own personal tastes, when political preferences lead to government policies not consistent with his informed and considered preferences, they are tempted to attribute irrationality to government. When my professional colleagues and I complain that research and education are starved for public funds, we have by no means necessarily seen in this fact evidence of irrationality; it may be evidence only of the discrepancy between our and others' tastes.

A further implication is that consistency in government decisions is not an appropriate norm. As has been explained, atomistic mutual adjustment and some forms of strategic adjustment take place through conflicts among programs of government agencies. In-consistency in government programs is thus inevitable and part of the mechanism of partisan mutual adjustment. A quite different reason for inconsistency is that there is no set of "social" preferences about which the question can be asked: Is their ordering transitive? (If A is preferred to B and B to C, is A then preferred to C?) Still further, if we look at observable policies as evidence of an ordering of preferences, we must not forget that incrementally approached policies proceed through a continuing succession of adjustments to ever-changing ends as policies and objectives interact. Hence we should not even wish to find in the record of actual policy choices an evidence of transitively ordered preferences.

The next implication suggests a revision of traditional notions of the appropriate organizational structure for government decision-making. It is commonly assumed that factoring out or subdividing decision-making problems is best achieved when interdependent problems and decisions are grouped together in the same subdivision and when, correspondingly, problems and decisions of low or simple interdependency are separated into different subdivisions. It follows, however, from what was said about mutual adjustment that problems or decisions with a high degree of interdependency should sometimes be assigned to separate subdivisions so that their interdependencies can be taken account of not by internal coordination within any one agency but through partisan mutual adjustment among the agencies.

Another implication is that gross disparities in group influence on decisions, disparities going beyond what by any ordinary estimate would be called a defensible weighting of conflicting interests, are not to be dismissed as evidence of irrationality if they turn out to be simply the evidence of the price that some groups pay to others as a condition of the latters' consent to playing the rules of the game of constitutional democracy. We may regret the price paid; but we would do well to be clear on just what aspect of the decision-making process we are complaining about. Our norms should not simply proscribe these disparities.

Let us now look at some of these implications taken together in application first to the allocation in the large of federal expenditures and then to the budgetary process. Consider such a choice as that between social welfare and defense expenditures. How to choose?

We must first distinguish sharply, as conventional approaches to this problem do not, between the problem of the individual decision-maker and the problem of coordinating individual decisions, which may or may not be a decision-making problem itself. It follows from all the foregoing that, for the individual decision-maker, whether Director of the Bureau of the Budget, the President, a cabinet member, or congressman, it is a possibility much to be considered that he cannot make a reasoned decision between defense and welfare when they are both aggregated. It is true he can think he is thinking; but whether there is anything for the mind to seize upon when faced with a choice of some marginal increase in the defense budget as against a 10 per cent increase in welfare expenditures is problematical. Faced with aggregates which it must compare and among which it must choose, it is possible that the mind does not so much calculate as default—in some quite capricious or arbitrary way turning up a choice, or leaving the mouth or the hand to make its own decision. And if the mind tries to break the aggregates down and calculate the value of their components, it seems clear that it cannot encompass and interrelate more than a fraction of components at the level of specificity to which it must descend.

Conceding a considerable looseness in my description of mental processes, I nevertheless want to make the point that to sit in a chair and try to think about defense and welfare is not to guarantee that the mind will do anything with the problem that could properly be described as systematic calculations. It is quite likely that more rational decisions can be reached by an individual who tries to compare some fairly specific, concrete—and newly proposed— military expenditure with some similarly specified innovation in welfare expenditure, making his choice on specifics and letting the aggregates be determined almost wholly as a by-product or residual decision.

Gross determinations of military or welfare expenditures the decision-maker can make, I believe, by calculating in aggregates. But gross determinations are not the repeated business of government decision-makers; each year presents them instead with choices among relatively small variations.

There are, however, so many small choices to be made that the legislature cannot possibly attend to them. As a result the making of expenditure policy has to pass in large part to civilian and military administrators, who can attend to the specific kind of comparisons in which the mind can successfully engage. But these administrators can at best make rational comparisons of specifics within their own agency's field, not between them. Hence, without substantial administrative reform, it would appear that a congressman would do well to become a specialist in interdepartmental and interagency program comparisons. Since even this assignment is too large, ideally a congressman ought to ask each major subdivision of government to identify a small variety of marginal expenditure programs, permitting the congressman then to approach expenditure allocations as a specialist in marginal comparisons among the lowest valued increments to programs of various major subdivisions.

Although I have not qualified this prescription adequately, it serves to emphasize the probable desirability of specific rather than aggregate marginal comparisons in Congress and of a highly selective policy with respect to the specific comparisons to be made. Some of Congress' much deplored refusal to deal with the larger issues in expenditure policy and its preoccupation with haphazardly selected detail is, I think, a laudable even if fumbling attempt to proceed by such a prescription.

As for the coordination of decisions reached by individual administrators, politicians, and others, it is only necessary to state again that debate on the objectives of the military and the objectives of welfare programs will ordinarily accomplish relatively little. Similarly, debate on policy alternatives conceived of in large aggregates of expenditures will help relatively little. If agreement can be reached through debate on specific comparisons and marginal choices, agreement is sufficient, assuming that the individual comparisons of specific alternatives have been well done. Agreement failing, all we should ask is that the processes through which mutual adjustment will produce policy as a by-product meet certain conditions yet to be defined by research.

What then is the appropriate role of the budgetary process in expenditure and tax decisions? I think the answer requires an investigation of the budgetary process from a point of view that has not been taken by previous writers. The literature on the budget, I think it fair to say, has not given extended consideration to the implications of incrementalism and partisan mutual adjustment; were it to give such extended consideration, many firmly held beliefs would turn out to be either erroneous or undemonstrated. My view of the conventional norms for the budgetary process is, therefore, that of an agnostic, except for my explicit rejection of certain budgetary norms listed in the first pages of this paper.

To indicate what might follow from verification of the hypothesis that incrementalism and mutual adjustment are major avenues to rational decision-making, let me speculate as follows, limiting, however, my examination of the budget process to its expenditure programing functions.

It appears possible that the formulation of a comprehensive federal budget as a strong recommendation to Congress for its expenditure decisions should be abolished. As a proposal for expenditure programs, the budget document is not very helpful to the kind of rational decision-making we have been describing; and, as a recommendation from the President and Budget Bureau that the expenditures-mix for the coming year should be as presented rather than slightly different, it is not very convincing. The circumstances of its formulation do not generate much confidence in it as an incremental program proposal, even if its formulation in some ways is well suited in congressional eyes to congressional control over the administrative branch.

In any case, a formal, comprehensive congressional overview of the budget should not be attempted, for it would only drive congressmen into the kind of abstract comparison of aggregates that we have argued is less satisfactory than highly selective comparison of specific programs. I might even suggest that the submission of the budget to Congress as a program for appropriations is made more defensible the less Congress is induced by its presentation to attempt to comprehend it in the large.

A comprehensive budget is best used, it may follow, as a background document to which any decision-maker can refer for reference and such guidance as he can take from it, playing a role in decision-making much like the role, as I understand it, of the Indian Five-Year Plan. A frequently revised budget, embodying both a report on prospective expenditures already authorized and recommendations of the Budget Bureau and President for programs not yet authorized might well always be available to but never thrust upon Congress.

Accordingly, congressional appropriations practices would be altered to permit Congress to make many successive appropriations for relatively limited numbers of functions or agencies, without a concentration of budgetary decisions at any one time of the year and, it might be hoped, to provide for automatic renewal of a very large number of expenditures so as to permit Congress to revise its programs in these fields only when it wished.

One of the standard complaints about present practice is the separation in time and attention between the authorizing legislation and the appropriations legislation. A major barrier to bringing the two together may be the conventional insistence on the inclusion of all appropriations decisions in the budgetary process. The effect of my proposals is to get appropriations out of the present budgetary process so that in a feasible way appropriations can be linked very tightly to basic legislation.

For income and employment stabilization, the aggregate of expenditures and revenues must, of course, be systematically adjusted. But there are many ways in which the need for adjustment comes to the attention of congressmen and many ways in which they can meet the need for systematic adjustment. Above I have expressed skepticism on the need for new formal machinery, for it appears that this is a kind of coordination best handled, in view of conflicting values, through mutual adjustment. If, however, formal machinery is needed, the budgetary machinery is excessively complex for the purpose.

Granted that this line of prescription for the budgetary process flies in the face of a sustained movement toward increasing dependence on the budget as a major coordinating instrument, no one has yet made a convincing case that the budgetary process is today an effective and rational coordinator; it has largely been assumed to be so. It is quite possible that the present line of budgetary reform, which goes back at least as far as the Taft administration, was suited to the much smaller government programs of earlier years.

But when the Department of Defense alone uses roughly a tenth of the national product, when it spends more than the national product of some nations, when it purchases forty times as many products as marketed by Sears Roebuck,[16] it is no longer safe to assume that the budgetary problem is still basically the same old problem.

Without raising any questions about budgeting within agencies, I suggest in short that comprehensive budgeting for the American government may be a prerevolutionary method of programing the expenditures of a government that has indeed gone through a revolution in its size, complexity, and involvement with citizens' values.

COMMENTS

ABRAM BERGSON, Harvard University

In his very interesting and provocative paper, Professor Lindblom analyzes governmental decision-making within a democratic framework. He also explores implications regarding budgetary policies and practice. I shall focus my remarks on the more general topic.

Professor Lindblom's main theme, as I understand it, concerns the nature of rational government decision-making. Economists tend to misunderstand this. Whereas they assume that certain "conventional principles" are generally applicable, in fact rationality very often calls for the employment of an alternative and analytically distinct approach, the "incremental method." The presuppositions of economists regarding government rationality, I am sure, are sometimes open to question, but I must confess some doubts as to the fruitfulness of Professor Lindblom's attempt to distinguish on this basis between "conventional principles" and the "incremental method."

As seen by Professor Lindblom, economists misconceive rationality in various ways. Among these, not the least is in the view taken of the alternatives open and, in association with this, the degree of delineation of values that is entailed. According to "conventional principles," the government official ordinarily must choose between a wide range of alternative social states. Accordingly, one ideally

[16] From calculations made in the Procurement Task Force of the Second Hoover Commission, summarized in a letter of March 17, 1959, from Jay Westcott to C.E.L.

takes as a point of departure, a "social welfare function" defining the values to be attached these alternatives. As seen by Lindblom, the choice in fact is very often quite restricted by political considerations. Not only is the set of alternatives limited but also, typically, these differ from each other only in rather marginal ways. It follows that rational action calls for the valuation of only these limited aspects. This, I believe, is a cardinal feature of the "incremental method."

In elaborating the presuppositions of economists, Professor Lindblom takes as a point of departure Professor Smithies' study of the budgetary process, but on a theoretical plane he evidently refers throughout to the conception found in welfare economics. I think we must concede that this discipline is, from a political standpoint, notably abstract. Among other things, the variety of social states considered is generally not restricted to those that might be politically relevant. Moreover, Professor Lindblom might, with no less justice, have added that the analysis is not especially easy to apply where political constraints are introduced. The principles to be observed in selecting the "second best" are not necessarily the same and indeed may often be rather different from those applying where the concern is with the "first best."

But granting all this, I wonder if Professor Lindblom has sufficiently considered what is involved even in the appraisal of limited alternatives to which he refers. After all, even the most restricted actions of government are apt to have pervasive effects. Without some fairly extensive commitments regarding the shape of the "social welfare function," it is open to question whether one would be able even to begin to appraise the alternatives rationally. Moreover, the commitment ordinarily will be hardly any less restrictive than that usually made in welfare economics.

More specifically, a principal effect of government action ordinarily is in respect to the volume of goods and services produced and marketed privately. How is one to value the diverse goods and services affected? At their market prices? If not, how otherwise? If different households are affected differently, how is this aspect viewed? The import of the questions is evident. Even to begin to think systematically about such alternatives one cannot very well dispense with the principle of "consumers' sovereignty" or some variant thereof. Moreover, if one adds to this some general standpoint on income distribution one has already gone as far as the welfare economist ordinarily does in defining on a theoretical plane the "social welfare function."

I have been referring to the question of the alternatives open and the degree of delineation of values. Logically, prior to the latter aspect is the question of the general nature of the valuation process itself. As seen by Professor Lindblom, there may be dubious preconceptions here also. Among other things, reference is made ordinarily to a value scale that is both explicit and relatively static. These notions, too, have become embodied in "conventional principles." In fact, however, the situation may often be quite different. "In the incremental method, political decision-makers handle values through marginal comparisons in the same way that consumers do." If the official "can be said to value one social state higher than another, this fact is more to be inferred from his choices than to control them . . . . We do not determine our welfare function, then choose, but instead choose directly and, in so doing, simultaneously both indirectly define a part of the welfare function and maximize it." Moreover, the "decision-maker is much more tentative about his objectives or values than he is considered to be in conventional models. He counts on policy to lead him to fresh perceptions about values."

It is true that the presuppositions of welfare economics as to the nature of rational decision-making may often be overly formal and correspondingly too restrictive. On the other hand, one might easily err also in stressing unduly the aspects Professor Lindblom describes. No doubt both the consumer and the public official may often behave rationally without consciously applying any previously determined value scale, but at least for the official the choices, as we have seen, are highly complex. Without reference to some guiding principles, it is permissible to doubt that any high degree of rationality could be achieved. This still is not to say the official must carry in his mind some textbook "social welfare function." No doubt the principles applied might often be of a more commonsense sort. Most importantly, the official might as a matter of course take the money values of marketable goods sacrificed or added as measures of social costs and returns. On the other hand, even such an approach necessarily is treacherous. What, for example, if the prices at which goods and services are valued are generated in a ration system rather than through an open market? One might easily go astray at this point. Tentativeness might also be carried

331

too far. Presumably, however novel they may be, choice situations always are in some degree repetitive. Indeed, one wonders whether the question of whether the individual is rational can fruitfully be discussed in any other context. At the same time, so far as there are repetitive elements, are we not compelled to suppose some limitations, given rationality, on the variability of values?

Professor Lindblom properly assumes that in welfare economics rational decision-making is ordinarily seen as proceeding within a "means-end framework." Although he is not entirely explicit, one gathers that this is not necessarily so in the case of the "incremental method." The view that must be taken here of this aspect I believe is already sufficiently evident and needs no further elaboration.

Professor Lindblom is certainly right in contending that disagreement on values poses a difficulty for rational governmental decision-making of a sort that welfare economists usually envisage. He feels, however, that the difficulty consists in the fact that "government decision-makers are often without clearly defined policy objectives." I wonder whether it might not be somewhat more accurate to say rather that in implementing his own values the official is subject to complex political constraints posed by other people's. In any case, it is not easy to see how the difficulty is disposed of, as is contended, by use of the "incremental method." As Professor Lindblom is aware, disagreements persist even within the politically relevant range. As he contends, individuals can often agree on policies when they disagree on principles, but as I have explained, a fairly extensive commitment to principles hardly can be avoided. Possibly he is, nevertheless, right in assuming as he apparently does that economics textbooks stress insufficiently the implicit and tentative nature of valuations. Possibly, too, as he seems to assume also, this has tended to exacerbate disagreements among decision-makers, but I believe this is a problem that is more properly considered under the sociology of politics than in an inquiry into the conditions for rational decision-making.

Professor Lindblom feels that as envisaged by the incremental decision-maker, the problem of governmental decision-making is much simplified in comparison with the usual conception. This arises partly from the concentration on a limited range of alternatives that are relevant. I believe it also arises partly from the different conception of the valuation process. I have also said all that I have to say on these two aspects. On the other hand, the simplification seemingly also is achieved because of the conscious decision to focus on only "a small number out of all of the important relevant values." This feature has not been commented on previously, and I think I should at least record briefly some mixed feelings on this score. Professor Lindblom's main concern at this point, I believe, is simply to underline the familiar fact that consequences neglected by one decision-maker may be considered by another. Hence the whole decision-making process may be rational even though individual decisions are not. I agree that in a fully realistic formulation of rationality one must consider the costs of acquiring and utilizing information on alternatives. One wonders, however, whether the official who neglects important aspects on the ground that they would be properly weighed in the decision-making process as a whole might not often be disappointed.

At the outset of his essay, Professor Lindblom informs us that "most of what I have to say will be positive not normative." In my opinion, the analysis of rationality on the part of public officials is apt to be more fruitful in a normative than in a positive context, but I do not undertake to consider here the question that is posed as to the extent to which government decision-making in practice can be understood as rational. On the other hand, in commenting so far I have sought to do so without violating Professor Lindblom's declared aim. It may be in order at this point, therefore, to consider to what extent one's view of the problem he discusses might be affected if one adopts a normative rather than positive standpoint. A review from this standpoint is the more in order since the "conventional principles" he describes were elaborated primarily in a normative rather than positive context. Moreover, despite his initial declaration of purpose, Professor Lindblom himself is clearly much concerned with normative aspects.

Taking a normative standpoint, then, what is to be said of the usual presuppositions regarding the nature of rational decision-making and of the "incremental method" as an alternative? I believe essentially all that has been said already still applies. On the other hand, given a normative standpoint, the concern on a theoretical plane presumably is to formulate general precepts that might guide public officials. For this purpose, it seems all the more difficult to see the merit in the avoidance of prior and explicit commitment to values which Professor Lindblom stresses. In ways that cannot be explored here I believe the problem posed by dis-agreements in values is also somewhat altered when the analysis proceeds in a normative context.

GERHARD COLM, National Planning Association

Lindblom has made a very significant contribution to a realistic analysis of the decision-making process in public policy determination. I would like to comment on one aspect of his "Coordination Through Partisan Mutual Adjustment." I would be concerned if the various means of coordination were to be understood as (1) *exhaustive* and (2) *normative*. Perhaps he did not mean it that way. However, it appears to me that a very important aspect has been left out of his discussion. What I am concerned with is the concept which may be called the general interest or the general welfare to use terms of the "conventional norm." I suggest that this concept has and should still have a crucial place in the analysis of the decision-making process of public policy.

I emphasize the role of the general interest also because it has no adequate place in the theoretical framework suggested by Musgrave and Tiebout. The welfare approach looks at the benefit derived from public services as in principle analogous to the benefits derived from private goods. In this respect the welfare economists and the partisan strategists are similar. Only Lindblom does not refer exclusively to the welfare of individuals but also to individuals as members of a partisan group.

It can of course always be said that the interest of the individual or the interest of a partisan group includes the satisfaction they expect to derive from seeing the general interest pursued by policies of the government. This argument of the old hedonists is of course not logically wrong but it omits the distinctions which are essential if a theory of public finance is designed to analyze the peculiarities and interactions of the public and the private sectors of the economy.

Also the spillover effect in its geographic or interpersonal meaning cannot substitute for the concept of the general interest without again stretching the meaning of that term. I wonder particularly how the individuals of generations still unborn can express their preferences with respect to programs which will have a spillover effect on them.

It is useful to distinguish between the market process and the budget process. In the first, individuals or corporations pursue their self-interest within certain limits and the general interest presumably is taken care of as a result of the interplay of all the individuals and corporations pursuing their self-interest. It is a basic problem of the theory of public finance to explain why under certain conditions and with respect to certain activities this coordination through the market does not work or does not reach the desired results. This, then, forms the basis for a rationale of government action.

I do not deny, of course, that the individual voter or the partisan group are pursuing their self-interest also in their political activities. With respect to some government activities (for instance, building a sewer in a certain street) the individual interest is decisive and arguments that this activity is in the general interest would not be of major importance. In some cases it may be possible that, as Lindblom suggests, one partisan group may appeal to the partisan interest of another group in order to form an alliance. For other government activities, particularly those at the national level, but also many of those at the state and local level, the "strategic coordination" requires that those in favor of government action argue for the proposed measure in terms of the general interest. In a pluralistic society this might often be the only way to find support of individuals and groups which have different or indifferent personal interests with regard to a specific issue. Important as particular interests are in the determination of public policies, they do not provide a workable criterion for the appraisal of many programs. For purposes of policy appraisals the general interest must be translated into tangible national objectives, such as economic growth, national security, stability, resource development, opportunities, and so on.

If I buy a refrigerator, I do not argue with the dealer that lowering his price or giving me a better quality product not only serves me better, but also is in the interest of economic growth, economic stability, national defense, or other objectives which may reflect my concept of the general interest. On the other hand, if I am in favor of an increase in defense expenditures it would not be very effective if I argued that I am for this increase in expenditures because it adds to my business (if I happen to be in the defense business); or because I happen to live in an exposed part of the country; nor would it be very effective if I argue for a reduction in the top-bracket rate of the income tax only with the reason that I happen to be in that bracket and prefer to pay less taxes. Thereby I hardly would find the support of the people in the lower brackets without whose consent such tax reform could not be adopted. In the market mechanism, everyone pursues his self-interest and the general interest is taken care of as a result of these interactions. In contrast, the process of democratic policy determination also requires that the individual or the partisan group reconcile in their own thinking their particular interests with the general interest.

Some people will be inclined to dismiss such reconciliation as mere ideological "rationalization." I think it is one of the tasks of a science of public finance to either "debunk" or to confirm the claims made by advocates of various government measures.

I do not underestimate the difficulties involved in the concept of the general interest or the general welfare. Every individual's and every partisan group's concept of the general interest is influenced by their position in society and their special interests among other factors. What is adjusted in the process of "partisan coordination" is to a large extent not merely differences in various personal wants but differences in the concepts of the general interest or, we may also say, differences in the image of good government.

The economist analyzing various policy proposals in terms of the general interest will have to recognize not only the common ground but also the differences in the hierarchy of values reflected in different articulations of the general interest. The fact that a concept poses difficulties which result from the pluralistic character of our society is no reason for dropping such a concept, as long as it is essential. You would not leave the role of Hamlet out of a performance of *Hamlet* because there are several competing interpretations of his character.

In the theoretical discussion, reference was made to the "rational" decision based on self-interest and the emotional and ideological motivations which appear to spoil this neat process of decision-making. (Or rather: a neat but purely formal expression of decision-making.) If I vote for an issue of a school bond but have no children in school and no direct interest in schools, this theory will make me appear as irrational. I wonder whether it is really true that a person who votes in line with his concept of the general interest to the best of his lights, is really as "queer" as this theoretical approach makes him out to be. Or might it be that this theoretical approach is too narrow for grasping all aspects of decision-making in government policy and for serving as a general theoretical frame of reference for a theory of public finance? I am inclined to think that the latter is the case.

Evaluating Alternative Expenditure Programs

ROLAND N. McKEAN
THE RAND CORPORATION

ONE problem of choice that falls, at least partly, into the domain of public finance is the allocation of government resources among broad activities and the determination, therefore, of the scale of its various activities. In order for us to get the most out of the nation's resources, we should devote fewer millions to an activity if some of its output is worth less than the cost—and spend still more millions on it if extra output would yield greater value than the other things the money could buy. This way of looking at the problem is not universally accepted. Some persons apparently believe that the scale of activities should be determined in the light of cost alone. They name some figure and say: "That's all we'll pay, and that's that." Others apparently believe that activities should be planned on the basis of need alone. In determining the scale of defense outlays, for example, defense leaders are often asked to reveal what they "really need." Some simply say that the task of determining budget size has to be done one way or the other:

"In general, there are two ways in which the problem of balancing defense needs against fiscal requirements can be approached. One way is to ascertain essential defense needs and then see if the funds can be made available to meet them. The other is to predetermine, as a matter of fiscal policy, a dollar limit for defense expenditures; and thereupon refuse to satisfy any defense needs that cannot be compressed within that limit."[1]

The truth is, however, that one cannot properly plan expenditures

Note: Parts of this paper are also presented, though in somewhat different form, in Chapter 4 of a book entitled *The Economics of Defense in the Nuclear Age,* by Charles Hitch and Roland McKean, published in 1960 by Harvard University Press.

In various parts of the paper, I am indebted to David Novick of The RAND Corporation, especially for access to unpublished materials.

For other discussions of some of these points and of related topics, see Arthur Smithies, *The Budgetary Process in the United States,* McGraw-Hill, 1955, especially pp. 229–77, and Jesse Burkhead, *Government Budgeting,* Wiley, 1956, pp. 110–81.

[1] *Airpower*, Report of the Subcommittee on the Air Force of the Committee on Armed Services, U.S. Senate, 84th Congress, U.S. Government Printing Office, 1957, p. 9.

337

on the basis of either cost alone or needs alone. There is no budget size or cost that is correct regardless of the payoff, and there is no need that should be met regardless of cost. One has to make judgments about *both* costs and gains. What we should like, therefore, in evaluating alternative expenditures, are estimates of both costs and gains. Or, where estimates cannot be in terms of a common denominator, we should like at least relevant clues to both costs and gains so that more informed judgments about them can be made.

1. How Much for Programs vs. How Much for Objects?

In order to derive meaningful clues to the gains as well as the costs of broad governmental activities, we probably have to think in terms of "programs"—that is, combinations of activities that produce distinguishable products. A program is the counterpart of an "industry" in the private sector of the economy—and is just as ambiguous, as hard to define, and probably as useful a concept—as an industry.

There is one important difference, however. In the private sector of the economy, markets reveal prices for industry outputs, even if they are intermediate products. In the governmental sector, there are no markets for most outputs, and the significance of the products, especially intermediate outputs, becomes especially hard to judge. To facilitate judgments about their value, therefore, programs should be aggregations of activities yielding outputs that can be at least subjectively appraised. In general, we should move toward thinking in terms of programs that perform tasks and yield end-products (speaking rather loosely) rather than actions that yield objects or intermediate products.[2]

For example, consider the attempt to derive clues to the gains and costs of defense programs. (Since defense accounts for a large proportion of government expenditures, I shall use defense activities to illustrate many points.) We can think in terms of activities that perform tasks or missions, or we can think in terms of objects. Certain activities of the Air Force, Army, and Navy produce retaliatory striking power or deterrence and might be grouped together as a *program*. In providing deterrence, the Services use *objects* such as missiles, manpower, food, and transportation.

---

[2] I use this terminology largely because *The Budget of the United States Government* distinguishes between "programs" and "objects."

338

Several points about programs and objects should be noted. First, decisions about the size of programs and those about the things to be bought are interdependent. One would not make one of these decisions in complete ignorance of the other. If the desired striking power is increased, different types of equipment may become the most efficient means, and if some new type of equipment appears (e.g., more accurate ballistic missiles), a different level of striking power may become the proper choice. But to some extent these choices have to be made separately—by different people or at different times. In making one choice we must try to make reasonable assumptions about the other.

Second, as suggested previously, just what one means by a "program" is not unambiguous. The line of demarcation between programs and objects is not clearcut. Is the Military Air Transport Service (MATS) a program or simply an activity supporting, say, the Tactical Air program? Or is the latter merely something to be purchased for a program that might be called "deterrence and fighting of limited wars"? Even such tasks as providing deterrent striking power and forces for limited war have interrelationships. Neither is solely a supporting activity of the other, yet each can influence the credibility and effectiveness of the other. It may seem that one is driven to regard every defense item and activity as an object purchased for and contributing to *one* program—national security. Such an aggregation, however, would be too broad; we have no conception of units of "national security" that are being purchased.

Despite these complexities, officials do find it helpful to think in terms of programs, and there is hope of developing still more useful categories. Complications and difficulties abound, and yet for some such programs we can make judgments about (or even develop quantitative clues to) their value as well as their cost. To be sure, attention should also be given to the detailed objects of expenditure. The way government agencies use materials and manpower deserves hard scrutiny—even at the highest levels. If Congress can, through the review of expenditures, perceive better ways to combine objects or discover wasteful purchases that can be eliminated, it should certainly insist upon the increased efficiency. But objects of expenditure do get a goodly share of attention at the Congressional level. The annual hearings on appropriations are to a considerable extent about such matters as maintenance costs, the utilization of surplus butter and cheese by the Services, travel costs, and the location of flag officers' quarters. Here, however, I wish to stress that the broader problem, the selection of the scale of programs, also deserves careful attention. At whatever degree of efficiency can be achieved, the question remains: Should the nation buy larger or smaller programs? Are the last increments to existing programs worth their cost? Would further increments to particular programs be worth more than their cost?

To these questions, we cannot provide definitive quantitative answers, of course. No analysis can yield solutions to the problem of choosing program sizes that would necessarily be valid for all congressmen and voters. There is no use, as I see it, in trying to find optimal solutions to *this* problem by means of elaborate linear programing models and sophisticated computational techniques. Each person's answer depends upon how much value he attaches to the outputs of various governmental programs. It depends upon his attitude toward risks and uncertainty—that is, upon whether he is inclined to gamble or to hedge. It depends upon his valuation of "spillover effects" on other programs and impacts that cannot be made commensurable (in any *generally* valid way) with the main effects of the programs. Nonetheless, we can devise budgetary exhibits and analyses that facilitate weighing the gains and costs of alternative program sizes.

In the following sections, I turn first to exhibits of costs and then to the possibilities of appraising gains. Most of the time, I shall use the defense budget and defense activities to illustrate these possibilities. It might be noted too that I am regarding certain changes, such as more extensive crossing of departmental lines, as being politically feasible. Such reforms could be achieved either by organizational changes or by the preparation of special exhibits separate from the main budget documents.

2. Breakdowns of Cost in Recent Budgets

Since 1949, budgetary presentations have been improved. Proposed obligational authority and expenditures[3] have been collected into

---

[3] In the United States budget, "obligational authority" is total authority to make commitments during the designated fiscal year, whether the cash is to be expended in that year or later on; and "expenditures" are the estimated disbursements during the fiscal year, whether the obligations were incurred in that year or previously. I shall refer mostly to obligational authority here, believing that it approximates future costs more closely than would the scheduled disbursements.

one document and put into somewhat more meaningful categories than had previously been used. These recent presentations probably make possible more informed judgments about expenditure levels than could be made in earlier years. Nonetheless, the current document falls far short of being an effective program budget. Perhaps the best way to bring this out is to discuss briefly a few sample exhibits from a recent budget.

A. THE BROAD FUNCTIONAL BUDGET

There is, first, the functional budget in which activities are put into extremely broad programs like labor and welfare, commerce and housing, and international affairs and finance.[4] (Defense outlays are collected into one huge program called "major national security.") To appreciate the cost and significance of such programs is almost impossible. Few persons have any subjective "feel" for the worth of the outputs from these categories. And there is little hope of ever devising quantitative measures that would shed much light on the worth of such conglomerations. To try to sort out less inclusive programs would seem to be a more promising approach.

B. THE CURRENT "PERFORMANCE" BUDGETS

The present budget does classify expenditures into less inclusive categories that have often been called programs.[5] There are fairly detailed exhibits in terms of both programs and objects. In the Defense Department Section, however, the classification of expenditures by program turns out to be a classification by organization unit (Army, Navy and Air Force) and account title,[6] though the exhibit for each account title is accompanied by a few paragraphs purporting to describe "program and performance." Consider the summary presentation of the Air Force budget that appeared (until the Budget for 1960) at the front of the section. (In order to conserve space, Table 1 omits proposed expenditures and shows only proposed new authorizations.)

Note the nature of these "programs." Few of the items on this

[4] *Budget of the United States Government for the Fiscal Year Ending June 30, 1958,* Table 2, "Summary of Net Budget Expenditures by Function and Agency," U.S. Government Printing Office, 1957, p. A5.

[5] In the Budget for fiscal-year 1960, these categories are labeled "appropriation groups," and the amounts for the Army, Navy, and Air Force are combined into totals for the Defense Department instead of being shown separately. The points presented here, however, still apply.

[6] The "account titles" are the major "programs" listed in Table 1.

TABLE 1

Budget Authorizations and Expenditures (Air Force)
by Organization Unit and Account Title

DEPARTMENT OF THE AIR FORCE	NEW AUTHORIZATIONS (millions of dollars)		
	1956 Actual	*1957* Estimate	*1958* Estimate
Aircraft and related procurement	$6,287	$6,849	$6,200
Procurement other than aircraft	350	1,140	1,225
Research and development	593	712	661
Operation and maintenance	3,597	3,743	4,225
Military personnel	3,709	3,690	3,840
Reserve personnel	44	59	57
Air National Guard	192	259	263
Military construction	739	1,228	–
Miscellaneous:			
Contingencies	–	–	–
Preparation for sale or salvage of military property (indefinite, special account)	6	10	10
Total, Department of the Air Force	$15,517	$17,690	$16,481

SOURCE: *The Budget of the United States Government for the Fiscal Year Ending June 30, 1958*, p. 488.

list are even remotely like end-product missions, and the dollar amounts are not the costs of achieving capabilities in such missions. Instead, the items are collections of objects used in a variety of Air Force missions; and the dollar figures are the sums of selected costs from all of them. For instance, "military personnel" covers officers and men for the Strategic Air Command, tactical air capability, and all other activities. How does one choose the amount that should be spent on categories like across-the-board procurement or military personnel?

As might be expected, the further breakdown of these items helps little in appraising program levels. Consider, for instance, the breakdown of expenditures for military personnel into activity-categories—shown in Table 2. These so-called "activities"—e.g., pay and allowances, clothing, subsistence in kind, and travel—are really species of objects, and are just as remote from tasks or functions as is "military personnel."

It was mentioned at the outset that current budgetary exhibits include breakdowns of expenditure both by programs (so-called) and by objects. In order to make clear what these objects are and why they do not convey useful information about end-product

TABLE 2
Obligations for Air Force Military Personnel,
by Activities

	OBLIGATIONS (millions of dollars)		
	1956 Actual	1957 Estimate	1958 Estimate
Program by Activities:			
1. Pay and allowances	3,284	3,250	3,332
2. Individual clothing	75	74	70
3. Subsistence in kind	150	159	161
4. Movements, permanent change of station	204	210	227
5. Other costs	5	5	51
Total obligations	$3,718	$3,698	$3,840[a]
Financing:			
Comparative transfers from (−) other accounts	−9	−8	−
Appropriation	3,709	3,690	3,840

SOURCE: *The Budget of the United States Government for the Fiscal Year Ending June 30, 1958*, p. 548.
[a] Totals may not add because of rounding.

TABLE 3
Obligations for Air Force Military Personnel,
by Objects

	OBLIGATIONS (millions of dollars)		
	1956 Actual	1957 Estimate	1958 Estimate
1 Personnel services: military	$3,372	$3,337	$3,410
2 Travel	106	111	120
3 Transportation of things	66	66	72
5 Rents and utility services	−	a	6
7 Other contractual services	19	19	21
8 Supplies and materials	150	159	161
10 Lands and structures	−	−	a
11 Grants, subsidies, and contributions	a	a	a
12 Pensions, annuities, and insurance claims	4	5	4
14 Interest	1	1	a
15 Taxes and assessments	−	−	46
Total obligations	$3,718	$3,698	$3,840
Comparative transfers from (−) other accounts	−9	−8	−
Appropriation	$3,709	$3,690	$3,840

SOURCE: *The Budget of the United States Government for the Fiscal Year Ending June 30, 1958*, p. 549.
[a] Less than $500,000.

programs, Table 3 presents a sample breakdown of authorizations by objects—the one for Air Force military personnel.

The amounts proposed for these object classes (e.g., personnel services, transportation of things, supplies and materials) may aid officials in locating inefficiencies; though systematic analysis would be necessary before anyone could be reasonably sure where inefficiency existed. Such a list of amounts can scarcely assist anyone, however, in weighing alternative program levels.

3. Improving the Breakdown of Costs

The first step toward getting more useful exhibits is to put budget figures into categories that more nearly correspond to end-product functions. Officials can make more perceptive judgments about the importance to the nation of these functions than they can make about the worth of categories like those listed above. Moreover, as will be indicated later, there is hope of devising useful quantitative clues to the importance of end-product missions. Thus, for these programs, there would be both rough estimates of the costs and a chance of gauging the gains.

Let us follow through the Defense Department illustration, keeping in mind that the aim would be, for any part of government, to think in terms of more meaningful programs. In the Defense Department, activities that contribute to an end-product program are seldom confined to one branch of the service. Naval operations and the Army's role in active defense contribute to strategic deterrence. All three departments—Navy, Army, and Air Force—contribute to limited-war capability. Hence, a budget designed to show the approximate cost of "end-product programs"[7] would have to cross departmental lines.

In Exhibit 1, there are essentially three broad programs—(1) deterrence or fighting of all-out war, (2) deterrence or fighting of limited war, and (3) research and development. Each of these would be divided into component missions. Many of the latter would be interdependent to a considerable degree (the broad programs to a lesser degree), and the incremental costs of one would depend in part upon the sizes of the others. Some parts, such as a submarine force or a transport fleet, would contribute to both the nuclear

---

[7] As stressed previously, I use the term loosely. At best, no aggregation of defense activities yields an output that is unambiguously an independent end-product, and *some* "programs" will inevitably comprise left-overs or aggregations for which no clear-cut end-product can be defined, let alone measured.

EXHIBIT 1

Pro Forma National Security Budget

Programs and Subprograms	Proposed Force Composition (No. Military Units, Where Applicable)				Expenditures Implied by Proposed Programs			
	'60	'61 ...	'64	'65	'60	'61 ...	'64	'65
	—	—	—	—	—	—	—	—
Deterrence or Fighting of All-Out War								
Nuclear striking force (AF, Navy)								
B-47								
B-52								
Atlas								
Polaris								
etc.								
Active defense (Army, Navy, AF)								
Early warning								
Interceptors								
F-102								
etc.								
Local defense								
Nike								
Bomarc								
etc.								
Passive defense (OCDM, FCDA)								
Dispersal								
Shelters, evacuation								
Recuperation planning								
Deterrence or Fighting of								
Limited Wars								
Ground forces (Army, Marine)								
Sea power (Navy)								
Tactical air (AF, Navy)								
Transport (AF, Navy)								
Air								
Sea								
Military aid to other countries (mutual security)								
Reserves for mobilization								
Military units (AF, Army, Navy)								
Defense production (OCDM)								
Research and development (AEC, AF, Army, Navy, etc.)								
Exploratory								
Weapon systems								
General Administration								
Miscellaneous								

deterrent capability and the limited-war mission. For this reason (as well as others), the costing of programs would necessarily be approximate.

In principle, one always wishes to know the incremental cost of whatever policy or program he is considering. In the budgetary exhibits suggested here, the costs of programs and program-increments would be rough approximations. Joint costs might be allocated among programs according to crude rules of thumb, or sometimes assigned to one program with recognition that others were being aided (or hindered, as the case might be). Some items used jointly, such as top administration, could be considered as separate aggregates (called, for the sake of convenience, "programs").

The particular aggregations in Exhibit 1 simply represent one set of possibilities. There may be other aggregations that would be equally or more useful. Additional meaningful programs might be formulated from the activities in the "all other" or "miscellaneous" category. I believe that Exhibit 1 does indicate, however, the direction in which our budgetary exhibits should be evolving.[8]

4. Indicators of Performance in Recent Budgets

Budgetary presentations today do attempt to describe the product that is being purchased. Since 1949, when the Services were instructed to submit "performance budgets," they have classified proposed outlays into programs or appropriation-categories such as those previously discussed, and they have tried to indicate the output or performance that would be purchased. The indicators are not very revealing, however, chiefly because the categories into which outlays are grouped are remote from end-product programs. As an example, consider the paragraphs on the performance of the "military personnel" category—the one that also served in Tables 2 and 3 to illustrate other points:[9]

[8] The use of the exhibits just suggested would call for, or be aided by, a number of changes in current estimation procedures—for example, increased emphasis on the use of statistical cost factors and a shortened budget cycle, increased attention to costs *during* the formulation of proposed programs (i.e., prior to their translation into budgets), and an improved system of accrual accounting and costing of programs. Some of these reforms are discussed in Smithies, *op.cit.*, pp. 237–65, and in David Novick's *Weapon-System Cost Methodology*, Report R-287, The RAND Corporation, February 1, 1956.

[9] This passage, including the title at the beginning and the numbers at the end, is an excerpt from *The Budget of the United States Government for the Fiscal Year Ending June 30, 1958*, pp. 548–49.

Program and Performance

1. *Pay and allowances.* Provision is made for pay, separation travel, and other allowances of military personnel, including aviation cadets and cadets at the United States Air Force Academy. Also included are personnel of the Reserve components while on active duty for purposes other than undergoing training such as duty under section 265 or 8033 of title 10, United States Code. The 1958 estimate includes the cost of enacted legislation for increased pay and allowances for doctors and dentists.

Provision is made for amounts otherwise available as quarters allowances to be paid (1) to the revolving fund for "Acquisition, rehabilitation, and rental of Wherry Act housing," in cases where such housing is assigned as public quarters, and (2) as mortgage payments on Capehart housing.

The revised 1957 estimate provides for an end strength of 15,300 below the number previously approved and a reduction of 5,957 man-years.

2. *Individual clothing.* Provision is made for the payment of authorized monetary clothing allowances, including initial uniform allowance, maintenance allowance and special supplemental allowances, to enlisted personnel and aviation cadets for individual clothing requirements.

3. *Subsistence in kind.* Provision is made for the procurement of subsistence supplies for issue as rations to enlisted personnel, including emergency and operational rations.

4. *Movements, permanent change of station.* Provision is made for permanent change of station movements of individuals and groups of military personnel and their dependents, including dislocation allowance, storage of household goods in commercial facilities, movements to and from overseas by Military Sea Transportation Service, and for transportation of household effects and personal automobiles. . . .

The number of military personnel provided for by type is shown in the tables on page 348.

The only parts of the above passage that convey much are the numbers at the end; and they, since personnel are ingredients rather than end-products, are not very informative. Sometimes descriptions of performance are a good deal worse, constituting merely colorful

Average Number

Type:	1956 Actual	1957 Estimate	1958 Estimate
Officers	142,127	142,273	142,655
Enlisted personnel	792,275	769,296	775,599
Aviation cadets	3,502	2,776	2,381
Air Force Academy cadets	270	518	776
Total	938,174	914,863	921,411

Fiscal Year End Number

Type:	1956 Actual	1957 Estimate	1958 Estimate
Officers	142,093	142,500	143,500
Enlisted personnel	764,609	774,890	778,265
Aviation cadets	2,993	2,800	2,475
Air Force Academy cadets	263	510	760
Total	909,958	920,700	925,000

pleas for a program. It is not surprising that some officials prefer a budget in terms of objects to be purchased. With the latter one can at least try to say something about the internal efficiency of programs. The advantages of a program budget are considerably reduced if the indicators of performance are uninformative.

5. *Improving the Indicators of Performance*

If activities are grouped into more appropriate aggregates, however, it seems likely that better subjective appraisals of output can be made and also that better indicators of performance can be provided.

A. PROGRAMS FOR WHICH DOLLAR GAINS CAN BE ESTIMATED

There are a number of government activities for which gains in terms of dollars can be estimated.[10] Wherever reasonable estimates of this type are feasible, gains and costs of increments to programs

[10] Results of surveying the Federal Budget for possible programs of this sort are summarized in the writer's *Efficiency in Government Through Systems Analysis, with Emphasis on Water Resource Development*, Wiley, 1958, pp. 279–309.

can be directly compared. There will still be serious difficulties in reaching decisions because of such things as interdependencies among programs, uncertainties and variability of outcomes, and "spillover effects" that are not commensurable with the other costs and gains. But estimates of predicted outcomes (plus perhaps some clues to variability, interdependencies, and spillovers) can lighten the burden of weighing these various considerations and lead to better-informed decision-making.

The possibilities of estimating dollar gains from increments to certain governmental tasks have been illustrated in several studies.[11] William A. Vogely has tried some promising techniques and lines of reasoning for measuring the gains from the land, minerals, and grazing programs in the Bureau of Land Management.[12] The estimates strongly suggested, for example, that increments to the grazing program at the present time would have an extremely low rate of return.[13]

B. PROGRAMS FOR WHICH GAINS IN MEANINGFUL PHYSICAL TERMS CAN BE ESTIMATED

In most government programs, however, the dollar gains cannot be measured. Once again consider defense activities as an example. It is obviously impossible to put a generally valid price tag on the output. The gains from program increments cannot therefore be expressed in the same units as the costs, and the two cannot be compared in terms of a common denominator. But there is hope of describing the product meaningfully, and some ways of describing it are more meaningful than others. Similarly, no researcher can measure the ultimate worth of a new car to a particular consumer. But there is hope of describing this product, and what the car will do is a more meaningful description to the consumer than the car's chemical composition.

Changes in Force Structure

As a first approximation, force structures for each category in Exhibit 1—numbers of B-52 wings, Atlas squadrons, army and naval

---

[11] For example, *ibid.*, pp. 253–78, where an attempt was made to estimate the prospective gains from increments (positive or negative) to forest-service activities, and William A. Vogely, *A Case Study in the Measurement of Government Output*, Report RM-1934-RC, The RAND Corporation, July 9, 1957.

[12] *Ibid.*, pp. 29–49, 63–84, 98–114.

[13] *Ibid.*, pp. 108–109.

units of various types—are closer to end-products than numbers of personnel. To some extent, the quantity of wings and divisions in each category suggests what is being purchased. This information is constantly used at present by officials in the Services and in the Defense Department, and by our legislators in various Congressional hearings. Numbers of wings and divisions, however, do not reveal enough about capabilities. For one thing, force structure *per se* does not tell anything about the enemy's position or about his probable reaction to changes in our force structure. Yet what our forces buy for us is clearly relative to the enemy's capability and his reaction to our decision. Can he easily counter our move? What deterrent capability (or ability to fight local wars) will we end up with? Will our action yield a better basis for finding mutually advantageous weapon limitations?

For another thing, force structure *per se* may not tell much about the kind of capability that it provides. An augmentation of our forces may increase our capability to strike first, but not our ability to strike second. If so, it may produce negative deterrence. Or, additional divisions may increase our ability to fight World War III but not our strength in more likely kinds of conflicts. If so, they may produce small gains.

Changes in Designated Capabilities

Fortunately, it is often possible to indicate more meaningfully what program increments will buy. Quantitative analyses can be made comparing alternative ways of carrying out broad missions such as the strategic deterrence mission. Such analyses usually seek to answer questions like: What combination of means yields the greatest deterrent capability for a given budget? Capability might be measured by the destruction that could be inflicted on potential enemies in selected contingencies, even if we received the first strike. Similar analyses can be devised to answer a different type of question: What capabilities are yielded by different program levels? What changes in capability result from program increments or decrements? The analyses would by no means point to the preferred program levels—but they would give highly relevant indicators of performance.[14] Analysis can also provide revealing indicators of another gain from portions of the strategic deterrence mission—namely,

[14] The quantitative nature of these problems is indicated by Albert Wohlstetter in "The Delicate Balance of Terror," *Foreign Affairs*, January 1959, especially pp. 213–7.

the contribution of retaliatory capability, active defenses, passive defenses, and recuperation planning to the chance of survival in the event of enemy attack. Analysis can give a rough yet informative picture of, say, people and stocks that would survive a plausible enemy attack.

In addition, analysis of this sort might be able to reveal what different program-levels could accomplish in the limited-war mission (another of the broad programs listed in Exhibit 1). Calculations might give clues to the scale and kinds of local aggressions that could be "handled" with alternative programs for limited-war capability. The results would constitute quantitative clues to what we could do in various plausible contingencies. Obviously the outcomes of such conflicts could not be projected with precision. Nonetheless, such clues to our capability would probably be more revealing than numbers of divisions, tactical air units, and so on.

These indicators of gain would not embrace all possible effects of program changes. There would be "spillover effects" on other programs. For instance, a change in strategic deterrence capability would have some influence on our prospects regarding limited conflicts. There would also be other impacts not reflected in the suggested indicators of performance—impacts on our relations with neutral or friendly nations, on the basis for trying to reach mutually advantageous agreements with enemy nations, and so on. Nonetheless, such indicators of gain would help sort out the *major* implications of alternative program-levels, facilitating the task of weighing the costs and gains of program increments or decrements.

As for the research-and-development program, there is probably no good way of indicating the performance that would be purchased with alternative program-levels. Estimating the results of research is even more uncertain than measuring the consequences of, say, future programs for limited war. We can try to estimate the potential gains *if* certain break-throughs or developments can be accomplished, and such estimates are valuable clues in shaping research and development programs. Even though estimates of potential payoff are helpful, however, tremendous uncertainties must be recognized. Hence, while the output of research and development is of great significance to future capabilities, that output is highly uncertain in both form and magnitude, and there is no way to show what a particular year's program will bring.

It is partly for this reason that it seems to be appropriate to break out research and development as a separate program. In a sense it is a supporting activity. But we do not know to what extent it will turn out to support strategic deterrence and to what extent it will support other missions. Moreover, because the program's objective is to explore rather than to carry out a well-defined task, research and development should be managed differently from operational missions. It is best, therefore, to regard research and development as a separate program—but no over-all indicator of performance in these activities (or in Administration and Miscellaneous!) can be provided.

Where meaningful indicators were feasible, they would have to be separate exhibits, not just a few numbers in another column of Table 4. But they would be introduced *along with* the breakdown of costs by broad missions. In the case of defense programs, the breakdown of costs, the indicators of performance, and the underlying analyses might all have to bear a military classification. These tools, nonetheless, could be valuable to military planners, to officials in the Defense Department and the Budget Bureau, and to congressional leaders.

For many other governmental activities, too, meaningful measures of gain from program-increments can probably be devised. As an illustration, I have talked mainly about defense, gains from which are typically regarded as being particularly difficult to assess. What I hope this discussion suggests is that, in many governmental operations, there is hope of measuring more meaningfully what we are buying. We can often do better than to measure the number of manhours used, the number of post offices built, or the number of trees planted. We can often devise measurements that get at least somewhat closer to what we really *want* to buy—and get close sometimes to the *value* of what we want to buy.

COMMENT

JESSE BURKHEAD, Syracuse University

The combative discussant always looks forward to reading the paper prepared for comment. There is the search for errors of analysis or interpretation with which to confound the author. A careful reading may disclose a passage that suggests an inadequate historical perspective. A phrase may be lifted out of context and employed for purposes of harassment. We might call this the Art of Discussantmanship.

Unhappily, Mr. McKean's paper is a disappointment in this regard. The traditional devices of the combative discussant are not available; the search for error has been unavailing; the major conclusions and most of the subpoints are unassailable. McKean is surely right in pointing out that a further analysis of costs and gains is desirable for government expenditure programs, that the national defense budget is particularly inadequate in its cost/gain aspects, that the first step in improvement is a better definition of programs within the Department of Defense, that there will always be difficulty in measuring dollar gains for defense, but that at least the major implications of program levels can be quantified, and that there are some expenditure areas, such as research and development, that are particularly difficult.

These conclusions suggest comments that will be directed here to three points. The first will consist of a rapid review of the whole range of efforts in the last ten years to improve the quality of budgetary decisions in governments in the United States. The second, an examination of some specific measurement problems, to indicate answers to the question: Where do we go from here? And the third, a brief restatement of the goals of traditional budget-making.

1. Recent Progress in Budget Measurement

The last ten years have brought a rather large number of developments in the practice and more recently in the theory of budgeting. The first of these, in point of time, is the introduction of performance budgeting by a rather large number of cities, and a few states and other units of government. In some cases, as in Richmond, Virginia and the state of Maryland, the performance units selected for measurement are simply broad programs, resting on existing organizational structure. In other cases, as in Los Angeles, there has been a serious effort to provide a firm cost-accounting support for budget justifications, with careful and detailed measurement of work units and activities. And in dozens of other jurisdictions there has been a thorough reclassification of expenditures, conducted in the name of performance or program budgeting. Unfortunately, no one has surveyed and analyzed all or even a major portion of these efforts.

353

Two significant developments have taken place in the national government. The first can also be described as the performance or program approach. The Department of Defense has taken the lead here but in that Department the heightened tempo of organizational change, changes in definitions of programs, projects and sub-projects, and the reassignment of budgetary responsibilities make it impossible for the outsider to appraise the results. The insiders are apparently too busy accommodating to change to be able to analyze the state of improvement, if any.

The development of performance budgeting in the national government has produced the cost-type budget statement whose applications are being continuously extended. This classification, utilized by both the military and other agencies, is a careful analysis of program costs. It does not attempt to measure gains in dollar terms other than those revealed by savings in costs for a government output level as authorized.

The second development at the national government level is the expanded use of an old technique developed by the Navy—the stock and industrial fund, or the "public enterprise fund," as it is commonly called. This has been useful from an administrative standpoint in segregating some kinds of activities that are notoriously difficult to budget.

Apart from reforms within government agencies, a significant development in budgetary theory and practice has come by way of the work of the RAND Corporation. The major effort has been directed to the military, with efforts to measure costs, objectives, alternative production possibilities for achieving these objectives, and performance. The major conceptual advance has been on the gain side of the cost/gain ratio. McKean's paper is an outgrowth of this, and shares, with the other work of RAND, a concern for both the conceptual apparatus and the arduous task of measurement.

The public finances of water resources have also been subject to particular examination, as a part of the theory of public expenditures. Major theoretical and measurement contributions have been made in the work of Krutilla and Eckstein on multiple purpose river development, of Eckstein on benefits and costs, and of McKean on water resource project analysis. Finally, there is the more purely conceptual work of Samuelson and Musgrave which contribute substantially to a more sharpened analysis of the activities of the public sector.

354

All of this adds up to a considerable amount of effort devoted to thinking about government activity, to the measurement of government activity, to improvements in budgetary technique. It is sometimes instructive, when contemplating a major shift in professional and practitioner concern such as this represents, to ask, "How come?" Why is it that the theory and practice of public expenditures, so long neglected, suddenly comes to the center of attention? The answer may be obvious. It may be that the sheer growth in the public sector has caught the attention of economists with their traditional concern for resource allocation and efficiency. But I suspect there is a bit more to it. Efficiency and economy have been around a long time, as have government cost accounting and work measurement. It may be that this heightened concern with the analysis of government programs is a simple out-growth of strong pressures from the private sector to protect that sector from what are thought to be the threats of big and uncontrolled government. The professional concern with measurement may be a manifestation of the same concerns as the recent taxpayers' revolts in state capitals, and the current popular identification of inflation with any increase in government expenditure.

However, it should hastily be added that the practice of economy and efficiency must not be regarded as evil. Improvement in the effectiveness of government programs is a laudable objective even if its by-product is the protection of the affluent taxpayer. But surely there is a bit of irony in a situation where efficiency and economy in government will contribute to the expenditure of tax-released dollars on prestige symbols such as larger automobiles, that will in turn force larger public outlays for such programs as highways and parking facilities. I am inclined to agree with Galbraith that we need additional resources in the public sector. We might do better to worry more about how to increase the dollars in this sector than to worry about the effective employment of the dollars already there. Efficiency in the interest of retrenchment is one thing; efficiency in the interest of an improved quantity and quality of government services quite another.

2. Where Do We Go From Here?

As we turn to more technical considerations, it may be appropriate to say a few words at the outset about the cost aspects of the cost/gain ratio. For a great many public programs the measurement of cost poses no particular problem. The attribution of government staff costs to programs or activities would appear to be as difficult but no more difficult than the attribution of overheads to product costs in industry. In most instances, this can probably be handled best by simply neglecting it, that is, by measuring program costs with an appropriate break-out of fixed and variable and by the treatment of departmental overheads as a separate program or activity whose end product is not subject to measurement.

Far more serious is the case of joint costs in government, as, for example, in water resource programs. A multiple purpose dam and reservoir produces a number of water derivatives such as flood control, hydro power, and water supply. In these circumstances in the private sector Alfred Marshall told us that price is a function of demand. But for a public project, demand cannot be measured directly and we must resort to a synthetic attribution of joint costs in terms of alternative costs for specific water programs. This is conceptually unsatisfactory, but it is not easy to see any way out.[1] Unfortunately, substantial elements of joint costs in government programs are a pervasive phenomenon, as in the public works departments of municipalities.

There is a further range of cost problems that may be mentioned but not elaborated. These arise in comparisons of government activities with private activities. Here an effort is made to answer the question, as with hydro power development: how do public sector costs compare with private sector costs for an identical project? Even an approximation to the answer requires careful analysis of interest costs, depreciation, allowance for risk and uncertainty, and taxes. These issues have been thoroughly explored in recent literature, but it could hardly be said that all controversy is settled.[2]

Nevertheless, and although the measurement of government program costs is not always easy, the problems are at least translucent. The gains side is more obscure but also more intriguing, because we are dealing here with a fine tangle of economic measurements, political processes, administrative procedures, and value judgments.

Starting at the definitional level, our concern is with the allocation

---

[1] Eckstein has recently stressed the arbitrary nature of joint cost allocation for resource projects but points out that there is no resulting distortion in public investment patterns as long as the cost allocation does not affect project justification. See Otto Eckstein, *Water-Resource Development*, Harvard University Press, 1958, pp. 259–72.

[2] See Eckstein, pp. 81–109; John V. Krutilla and Otto Eckstein, *Multiple Purpose River Development*, Baltimore, 1958, pp. 78–130; Roland N. McKean, *Efficiency in Government Through Systems Analysis*, Wiley, 1958, pp. 103–82.

branch, to follow the Musgrave terminology.[3] Considerations affecting stabilization and distribution may be laid to one side, although the latter must be reintroduced later, together with the distinction between gains from the satisfaction of social wants and gains from the satisfaction of merit wants. Gains may be described as falling in three general categories, in accordance with the language of cost-benefit analysis. Direct or primary benefit is the immediate value of the output of government goods and services to the program beneficiaries. Indirect or secondary benefits are those "stemming from or induced by" the program, such as profits from additional economic activity that would not otherwise have been undertaken. This category is imprecise since it is never very clear as to how many rounds of activity should be embraced as indirect. Intangibles are all noneconomic or nonefficiency values, including the political, cultural, and social. Third party or spillover gains or benefits may arise in either the secondary or intangibles category but are separate from primary benefits.

With these categories as reference points, let us now attempt to divide measurement problems into three broad classes. The first are the cases where not even primary gains can be measured with precision, let alone indirect and intangible gains. The second class embraces cases where primary gains can be measured with some accuracy, but where secondary and intangible gains, not susceptible to measurement, may be more significant than the measurable gains. The third class consists of the cases where nonprimary gains do not predominate and where some rather precise measurements of gains and costs are possible on an incremental basis.

The first group, where there are the greatest difficulties in the measurement of even primary gains, includes two of the largest government programs—national defense and public education. As McKean says of defense, "It is obviously impossible to put a generally valid price tag on the output." Hoffman, of the RAND staff, in his AEA paper last December, concluded that the most that could be done was further exploration of alternative ways of achieving stated objectives.[4] But the objectives, as Hoffman said, must be established by higher criteria, that is, by nonefficiency considerations. It may be laboring the obvious to emphasize that

---

[3] Richard A. Musgrave, *The Theory of Public Finance*, McGraw-Hill, 1959, pp. 6–17.
[4] Fred S. Hoffman, *The Economic Analysis of Defense: Choice without Markets*, RAND, Santa Monica, 1958.

concepts of consumer well-being, or alternative private cost have no applicability in this area.

Now it may well be, as some have suggested, that the value of national defense is infinite, and if so, we have no cause for concern; all resources except those for subsistence living must be channeled into defense. But even at a less philosophically absurd position it is most evident that we cannot even measure whether we are better defended this year than last. If the objectives themselves cannot be quantified, nor progress in achieving objectives, the contributions of the economic analyst will not be very significant. It can only be hoped that the political process will come to our rescue.

The measurement of gains from public education is almost as formidable as the measurement of national defense. But here, at least, we can describe the categories of gains. Education brings substantial primary, tangible benefits in terms of the increased earnings of those educated. But we cannot estimate the value of these either for particular individuals or for a whole society. If decisions about educational expenditure were made solely by households, it seems likely that the total volume of education would fall short of its potential social contribution. Neither is it possible to attach monetary values to the components of an educational system—to the life adjustment courses and the math courses. Then, of course, there are the third-party, tangible but nonmeasurable benefits, such as accrue to the employers of graduates of a vocational high school, and the intangibles, such as the value of an informed and cultured citizenry. Since the primary benefits cannot be measured, there is no way of knowing whether they are more important than the tangible and intangible third-party benefits.

Government programs of this first class—where all significant gains cannot be measured—are not likely to be undervalued because of this fact. Legislators and administrators are not waiting for measurements of gains from national defense and education. Decisions about the totals of such programs are not likely to be improved by additional measurements. The preferences of strong interest groups are well revealed in these areas and will continue to dominate public decision-making.

The second class of problems covers a rather large group of government programs for which some measurements are possible, but where the task is that of making sure that that which is measured is meaningful. Consider the case of an urban renewal program that includes slum clearance, the construction of new housing units, widened streets, and the provision of public parks. Many of the gains from such a program can be added up in dollar terms— increases in property values, and in economic activity in and adjacent to the area. But such intangibles as the reduction of crime and disease rates and the improvement in urban esthetics cannot be put into the summation.

When this kind of problem is encountered in cost-benefit analysis for water resource projects it is customary to measure that which can be measured and describe that which cannot as a part of project justification. No doubt this is the best that can be done, but, in consequence, projects tend to be justified in terms of the measurable and the project values that are nonmeasurable are relatively neglected. This is the case with recreation, whose benefits are now valued in federal water-resource project-justification at an arbitrary $1.60 per visitor day. This figure reflects average daily expenditures of public park visitors for admission and parking fees, outlays for food and beverages, and other concessions within the park area. Even if this were an adequate measure of average vistior benefits, which it is not because the admission fee is a subsidized price, the $1.60 figure would omit such tangible but nonmeasurable gains as the long-run improvement in the health and productivity of a society with adequate recreation facilities. In consequence of this valuation technique, reservoir-based recreation facilities are not now highly developed and at the moment we have an Army-Interior land-acquisition policy that is not only restrictive in it present scope, but also destructive of recreation values that might be developed in the future.

Another kind of measurement difficulty, again from the field of water resources, arises with hydro power values. The next several decades will undoubtedly bring multipurpose projects to a number of eastern river valleys. Hydroelectric power will be one of the project purposes. Prevailing practice requires that this power be valued, for purposes of project justification, at its most efficient use. This means hydro for peaking purposes, and if these values are to be realized in project operation, the power must be sold to large, integrated private companies with substantial peaking requirements. The preference customers—public bodies and cooperatives—are seldom in a position to utilize substantial amounts of peaking power; their needs are for base power. As a result, a *prima facie* case can be made in terms of economic efficiency for modifying existing preference policy,

359

shunting the public bodies and cooperatives to one side and selling the power to private distributors. But the efficient solution is, in this case, a single-faceted kind of efficiency that neglects the values of a long-range power-marketing arrangement embracing both private and public distributors, an arrangement that can be sustained only by the continued application of the preference clause. It can be demonstrated, I am convinced, that our mixed system of public and private power gives rise to a kind of competition that checks monopoly, supplements traditional rate regulation, and produces significant long-run gains in terms of lower retail rates and wider markets for electric power. To preserve these long-run efficiencies it will be necessary to continue to provide governmental support that will have the unfortunate appearance of a subsidy to the inefficient.

These examples—urban renewal, recreation, public hydro power—illustrate that in some areas decisions about alternative government expenditures cannot be based solely on the things that can be measured. Very often the nonmeasurables have a societal significance that exceeds the significance of the measurable values. In other cases the efficiency values that can be measured reflect short-range expediencies. There are "higher criteria" in areas of public expenditures other than national defense. The general point is that not all values in our society center on the private market and on the preferences of the sovereign consumer.

The third class of government programs is made up of those where measurable gains are significant indicators of performance and where additional quantification is likely to be productive of results useful for decision-making. Vogely of the RAND Corporation has provided an excellent case study of this type in his examination of the Bureau of Land Management of the Interior Department.[5] McKean has suggested additional cost/gain measurements, on an incremental basis, for the Forest Service and for other resource management programs.[6] Techniques of this type are now rather widely applied to decisions about highway expenditures at the state and even the local level.

Unfortunately, the dollar volume of all programs of this type is not large. For the national government, defense outlays, veterans' benefits, welfare expenditures and agricultural price supports, to

[5] William A. Vogely, *A Case Study in the Measurement of Government Output*, RAND, Santa Monica, 1958.
[6] *Op.cit.*, pp. 247–309.

name major areas only, must be excluded. For state and local governments it would be necessary to exclude welfare, education, and police protection, although the costs and gains of many aspects of institutional care and public works construction and operation could be measured with reasonable accuracy. There is work to be done here by both economists outside government and by the budget practitioner.

There is a final point affecting all types of measurement problems in government expenditures. This can best be elaborated in terms of the Musgrave framework that conceptualizes a separation between the allocations branch for public goods, and the distribution branch where considerations affecting income by size class must be dealt with.

Musgrave has recognized that in the real world these branches are not, in fact, separated, and that decision-making about government programs must necessarily embrace both branches simultaneously. Let us look at some aspects of this interrelationship by examining budget-making as a political process.

There are a great many public goods that are demanded not by individuals, acting in their capacities as consuming householders, but by individuals acting in their capacities as representative of producer groups. Government programs for almost all aspects of resource development—navigation, flood control, and reclamation, and programs for farmers, and for highways and airports fall in this category. The public goods that are demanded here are not for the satisfaction of the nonrevealed preference of consumers, but for the satisfaction of the strongly-revealed preferences of producer groups.[7] What is it these producer groups want? Their demands are in fact for a larger share of the national income. The employees and stockholders of an electronics firm are very likely to have a greater preference for national defense expenditures than the employees and stockholders of a diaper manufacturing concern. A steel company that operates a fleet of ore boats will have a greater preference for navigation improvement than will a railroad. The demands of producer groups for government goods are, of course, distributional demands, but not of the kind that can be taken care of by an income tax directed at the distribution of income by size class. Economic power considerations are at stake here.

---

[7] A similar point has been made by Julius Margolis, "A Comment on the Pure Theory of Public Expenditures," *Review of Economics and Statistics*, November 1955, pp. 347–9.

It would be possible to conceptualize a model to deal with these cases. For example, intermediate goods to be provided by government, such as a resource development program, could be isolated and maximizing equations elaborated. Principles could be devised for the compensation of the losers by the producer groups that gain. And as Musgrave has proposed, goods to satisfy social wants could be distinguished from goods to satisfy merit wants, with a dividing line between the two described in terms of the exclusion principle.[8] But models drawn along these lines would have no relation to reality. Once an activity is within the public sector, decisions about expenditures combine program and distributional considerations.

This is the reality of interest group pressures with which the administrator and legislator must deal continuously. The economist who attempts to measure program gains in terms of consumer preference is not talking about the same world as the administrator or legislator who must look continuously to the relative distribution of economic power among producer groups. The public decision-maker does not proceed on the assumption that social goods are consumed equally by all. His assumption is quite the opposite—namely, that all government programs have distributional consequences; the political process is an assessment and balancing of the relatives of economic power.

3. The Traditional Role of Budget-Making

In government budgeting our zeal for quantification and the emphasis that we attach to it may well cut us off from communication with the political decision-maker, particularly if we insist that efficiency and economy, as measured by market techniques, is the primary consideration.

An expanded role for the economist in the measurement of alternative government expenditures must be found within the existing framework of budgetary processes and procedures. I would submit that the traditional budgetary process, as practiced in governments in this country with strong executive leadership patterns, where implemented by competent central budget staff and where legislative

[8] If the exclusion principle means simply that the enjoyment of government goods by A does not limit B's enjoyment, there is little difficulty with the concept. But if it means that government goods must be provided equally for all or consumed in equal amounts by all, the principle is an uncertain basis for classifying government activities. It is hard to find a government program, even national defense, that does not discriminate among beneficiaries in accordance with income, occupation, geographical location, or personal tastes and habits. See Musgrave, *op.cit.*, pp. 9–17, 37–41, 133–5.

review procedures are reasonably adequate does, in fact, contribute a great deal to the maximization of gains over costs. Further, it provides a mechanism for equating, insofar as possible, efficiency values with political values, and tangibles with intangibles. McKean says that procedure is no substitute for analysis. True, but traditional budgetary procedure in government embraces a good deal more analysis than is revealed in budget documents. Cost/gain considerations are very often examined with great care, often explicitly, and always implicitly.

In well-staffed and well-organized central budget offices, efficiency considerations are the continuous responsibility of the budget examiner. In most budget procedures proposed increases in appropriations are examined with particular care. New programs are subject to special scrutiny and changes above last year's appropriation to special justification. This, of course, is incremental budgeting as an assessment of marginal costs. Marginal gains, unfortunately, are not always examined with the same circumspection, but very often this is not the fault of the budget examiner, revealing a lack of understanding of effective resource allocation. Rather, the general dimensions of the program under review and the area or groups to be benefited have been specified in basic legislative enactment, and the examiner is not in a position to propose a revision in the authorizing legislation. This kind of incremental budgeting is practiced very widely. In fact, it may so dominate the work of a central budget office that total justification, that is, the re-examination of the whole program of an agency, may be neglected.

Traditional budget procedure also imposes a kind of efficiency by way of ceiling requirements. It is common practice in many governments for the chief executive or the budget officer to initiate the budget cycle with an announced ceiling within which agencies and departments must submit their requests. This technique forces on the agencies a re-examination of inputs and outcomes and serves as a kind of disciplinary ingredient that secures more effective resource allocation.

Finally, traditional budget examination is based very heavily on ordinary, run-of-the-mill measurements and comparisons. The Veterans Administration engages continuously, aided and abetted by the Bureau of the Budget, in the comparison of costs among field offices and among hospitals. Strong state budget offices, as in New York State, undertake comparative cost studies of institutional care as a basis for budget decisions about operating expenses, and as a basis for selecting hospitals that shall remain open or be closed.

The budget examiner can achieve certain kinds of efficiencies. In addition, a well-articulated budget procedure will unite considerations affecting the kinds of efficiencies that may be subject to economic measurement with considerations based on other kinds of values to be maximized.

A central budget office does not necessarily conduct a better budget examination than a departmental budget office, but it conducts a different kind of examination. The department budget officer is close to program operation and program needs. The central budget office, if it is competent, has a perspective on many programs, on their interrelations, on the total program of the chief executive, and on the probable reception to the program by the legislature.

Similarly, legislative review is a different kind of budget examination than review by administration officials. The Congress, for example, is very much interested in costs and gains. But, as noted, it is also interested in the relative welfare of interest groups, the welfare of states and congressional districts, and the welfare of Democrats and Republicans. This is both the accommodation of conflict and the building of consent. All of this makes budgetary decision-making imprecise, which is simply another way of saying that budget-making is a political process well adapted to a pluralistic society.

Budget procedures and organization in the Commonwealth countries and in governments in the United States are a product of Anglo-Saxon patterns of executive leadership in administration. The executive budget system in the United States government is an outgrowth of the evolution of the Presidency since the turn of the century. In his institutional capacity the President is the general manager of administrative agencies and departments, the head of a state, and the leader of a political party. The Office of the Presidency thus becomes our most significant national political institution in the broadest sense of the word political. The budget of the United States government is a major instrumentality both expressing and contributing to the strength of the Presidential office.

The measurement of the economic costs and economic gains of government programs can be a significant part of budgetary decision-making. But it cannot and will not be the predominant concern. Budgeting is far more than a device for the allocation of public resources.

Defense Planning and Organization

ALAIN ENTHOVEN and HENRY ROWEN
THE RAND CORPORATION

Preface

SINCE this paper was written expressly for an audience of professional economists, we felt free to use the technical language of formal economic theory. Those readers who are not economists are warned that some of the words used in the paper, such as "efficiency," are used in a definite technical sense and not in their more general meanings.

This is an exploratory essay on the organization of the Department of Defense. We use the word "organization" in a broad sense, to include not merely the assignment of roles and missions, but rather the whole set of mechanisms through which the business of defense is conducted. In this essay we attempt to do three things. First, we explain what we think are some of the shortcomings of the present organization. Next, we consider the general question of intelligibility of defense allocation problems. Finally, we develop some of the implications of the principles we have discussed, and we put forward a few practical suggestions.

Defense organization is a controversial subject. Being aware of this, we ask the reader to keep in mind three disclaimers. First, we believe that the problems of choice in defense are intrinsically difficult. The uncertainties in political, strategic, and technological factors are usually great, and the pace of technological change is especially rapid. Our views on defense organization are influenced a good deal by a realization of our own fallibility in dealing with these problems. Second, we believe that the failings in our defense organization are to be attributed mostly to the difficulty of the problems and to the system, not to the people involved. The people directing our defense establishment are honest, patriotic, of above average intelligence, and they work extremely hard for limited rewards. Finally, our conclusions are still tentative. We regard this paper as a vehicle for discussion and as a progress report on our thinking on the matter, not as a definitive statement of our point of view. In fact, since the writing of this paper, we have come to feel that we understated the harmful effects of interservice rivalry.

We have benefited, in the preparation of this paper, from discussion with and criticisms and suggestions from Gene Fisher, C. B. McGuire, Charles Hitch, Malcolm Hoag, Burton Klein, Roland McKean, Charles Lindblom, William Niskanen, Thomas Schelling, William Taylor, Albert Wohlstetter, and Charles Wolf. We would like to acknowledge gratefully their assistance.

1. Introduction

Since the end of World War II, there has been a widespread and growing belief that the organization of our military establishment has not been satisfactory. This has not been changed by the various reorganizations which have taken place during the past decade. It is possible to identify two points of view or schools of thought on the shortcomings of defense organization and what ought to be done about it. One school includes among its members President Eisenhower, Secretary of Defense McElroy, Henry Kissinger, and the authors of the Rockefeller Report. At the risk of some over-simplification, their point of view might be summarized roughly as follows: The roles and missions of the separate Services are defined in terms of modes of transportation rather than by missions or purposes which are relevant to the strategic problems of the day. This situation has prevented the development of unified strategic planning to accomplish broad military objectives, it has encouraged "wasteful" and "harmful" interservice rivalry, rivalry which has also diverted attention away from the important problems, and it has led to an undesirable amount of "duplication and overlap," particularly in research and development. Although complete unification of the Services would not be politically feasible because of the power of vested interests, both in the Services and in Congress, an end to interservice rivalry brought about by unification would be desirable and we should move as far in that direction as political realities will permit.

In April 1958, President Eisenhower made a series of proposals for defense reorganization, and a bill providing for them was introduced into the Congress. The President's message suggested very strongly that the cause of the difficulties in the defense organization was to be found in the rivalry and in the "duplication and overlap" between the separate Services.[1]

[1] The following paragraphs are illustrative.

"The products of modern technology are not, in many cases, readily adaptable to traditional service patterns or existing provisions of law. Thus there has tended to be

Writing in *Foreign Affairs* a year earlier, Henry Kissinger also put the blame for the failings of defense organization on interservice rivalry: "In the absence of doctrinal agreement, interservice disputes can be resolved only by compromises which may define merely the least unacceptable strategy or by adding to the number of missions and weapons systems."[2] The Rockefeller Report on the problems of defense took a similar view. It listed the following as the three defects in defense organization:

"The roles and missions assigned to the individual military services have become competitive rather than complementary because they are out of accord with both weapons technology and the principal threats to our national safety; the present organization and responsibilities of the Joints Chiefs of Staff preclude the development of a comprehensive and coherent strategic doctrine for the United States; the Secretary of Defense is so burdened with the negative tasks of trying to arbitrate and control interservice disputes that he cannot play his full part in the initiation and development of high military policy."[3]

If the blame can be placed on interservice rivalry, then the corollary must be that unification is desirable. What can be said for disunity? Must not the opponents of unification be partisans of special interests? This seems quite clearly to be the view of Kissinger:

"It would still be the wisest course to move in the direction of a single service initially by amalgamating the Army and the Air Force.

[2] Henry Kissinger, "Strategy and Organization," *Foreign Affairs*, April 1957, p. 385.
[3] *International Security—The Military Aspect*, Special Studies Report II of the Rockefeller Brothers Fund, New York, 1958, p. 27.

confusion and controversy over the introduction of new weapons into our armed forces and confusion and controversy over the current applicability of long-established service roles and missions.
". . . Confronted by such urgent needs, we cannot allow differing service viewpoints to determine the character of our defenses—either as to operational planning and control, or as to the development, production, and use of newer weapons. To sanction administrative confusion and interservice debate, is, in these times, to court disaster. I cannot overemphasize my conviction that our country's security requirements must not be subordinated to outmoded or single-service concepts of war.
". . . While at times human failure and misdirected zeal have been responsible for duplications, inefficiencies and publicized disputes, the truth is that most of the service rivalries that have troubled us in recent years have been made inevitable by the laws that govern our defense organization."

See "The President's Reorganization Plan," *Air Force*, May 1958, pp. 103–8.

The strategic problems of the Navy may remain sufficiently distinct not to require integration and in any case resistance to complete unification in the Navy would be so bitter as to obviate its advantages.[4]

There is an alternative point of view that we consider deserving of at least equal attention. Briefly stated, it is that the fundamental defects in defense organization are to be found largely in the inadequacies of the mechanism of choice among alternatives in research and development, in procurement and operation, and in the allocation of the defense budget in general. While some of these inadequacies stem from the existing lines of division of the Services and from interservice rivalries, most would remain and some perhaps even worsen if there were complete unification. Thus, unification is neither necessary nor sufficient for improvement, nor is it necessarily desirable. Indeed, interservice rivalry has some real benefits. What may be needed is an improvement and strengthening of the system that will channel interservice rivalry into more productive outlets. Although we do not profess to know exactly how it should be constructed, a mixed system which includes both strengthened unified commands, defined in terms of purposes, along with the traditional Services, has the possibility of capturing the advantages of competition among the Services and the advantages of organizations defined in terms of missions which correspond to current strategic requirements.

This is not to suggest that interservice rivalry has no harmful effects. The separation of responsibility for missions that depend for their execution on the closely knit interaction of forces from two or more Services has made efficient planning extremely difficult. The problems of continental air defense or of limited war operations, for example, are very complex and would be taxing even if there were no service rivalries to contend with. One result of these rivalries is that much of the staff of each of the Services is busy, in effect, developing debating points to be used against the others. Moreover, interservice rivalry strengthens a tendency toward underestimating the costs and overestimating the performance of both old and new weapon systems, and encourages each Service to compete with the others, in the public press, in making exaggerated claims in its own behalf—claims that cannot easily be controverted because of the limitations imposed by the requirements of secrecy. These effects are

[4] Kissinger, *op.cit.*, p. 390.

serious. They have been recognized and some improvements have been made by the Administration and the Reorganization Act of 1958 through the strengthening of command channels and the authority of the Secretary of Defense.

However, it is important to recognize that a single command structure of the kind that is needed for fighting a war is not necessarily the best structure in peacetime for developing a flexible capability to meet a wide range of contingencies over the long term. As the House Armed Services Committee observed in its Report on the Defense Reorganization Act of 1958, such a command structure is efficient in time of war because it suppresses alternatives and reaches decisions quickly.[5] But in peacetime, as technology and international conditions change in ways difficult to predict, it is important that alternatives be developed and that old choices be continually reconsidered. One of the most important things any defense allocation mechanism should do is to help prevent gaps from appearing in our capability. We need a broad spectrum of capabilities because the enemy, free to apply pressure at the weakest point, can choose the form in which he will challenge us. If anything, we should err in the direction of duplication. But rather than charge one group with responsibility to think of all important contingencies, it seems to us safer to have an organization in which competing groups have an incentive to think of gaps that need filling along with a central staff able to choose among the alternatives offered. Thus, it is valuable to have the separate Services "looking for business," trying to expand and take on new jobs. The solution to difficult problems of choice cannot be found by changing the system so that it will not develop alternatives. Human limitations being what they are, there is good reason to believe that a decentralized competitive system, in which people have incentives to propose alternatives, will usually meet this test more effectively than a highly centralized system.

The values to be found in interservice rivalry, then, are the values of competition. We need diversity, experiment, discussion, and criticism (the motives for the criticism are not the important thing). Competitive incentives can act as a powerful stimulus to change and improvement, a stimulus which helps to offset the inertia of bureaucracy. But, one may ask, doesn't competition with the Soviet Union provide enough stimulus? The answer is that the Soviet

[5] *Department of Defense Reorganization Act of 1958, Report,* Committee on Armed Services, House of Representatives, Report No. 1767, May 22, 1958, pp. 27–8.

challenge often seems too distant and hypothetical and uncertain, whereas the possibility of losing part of the budget to a sister Service is a clear and present danger.

Even some of the apparently unpleasant facets of the rivalry serve very important purposes. In the absence of periodic wars, critical discussion must play an important role in exposing error and inefficiency. The competing Services have not only the incentives but also the military expertise to be each other's critics. The famous B-36 hearings are a good example. This episode was valuable in raising questions and stimulating discussion about the missions and performance of the Navy's supercarriers and the Air Force's B-36's. Whether the motives of the Services are purely patriotic or tinged with self-interest is less important than that the discussion take place. Moreover, criticism inspired by self-interest has the advantage of being persistent. In the absence of the separate Services, our defense programs would not have the benefit of as much expert military criticism.

It is interesting to note that the House Committee on Armed Services was particularly aware of these points. The introduction to the Committee Report emphasizes that

"Our defense organization must be flexible; it must be responsive to rapidly changing technologies; it must be dynamic and versatile; it must have our national survival as its one and only objective. But the organization of our defense system must also recognize certain fundamental concepts that do not change. It must at all costs be capable of correct decisions. Those decisions must represent the divergent views of several military experts, not the doctrine of one individual . . . . It must at all costs retain the capability to meet any type of aggression, not merely one type of aggression."[6]

The existence of the separate Services with their own traditional interests provides a stability in military policy that can often be very valuable. Mankind is often the victim of fashion. For example, the view that nuclear weapons provided a solution to our principal military problems, to limited as well as general war, has been widely held. It received its initial impetus from our atomic monopoly and, later, from the "more bang for a buck" principle adopted by the Administration. Accordingly, there has been a premium on all-out

[6] *Department of Defense Reorganization Act of 1958, Report, op.cit.,* p. 2.

war capability and our limited-war forces have been cut back. Those branches of the Services with limited-war forces resisted the cuts in part by trying to show that they too had atomic delivery capabilities and should therefore be counted as all-out war forces. Though this has left the United States weak in conventional, limited-war forces, the situation might well have been worse if there had not been some organizations vitally interested in conventional warfare whose members believed that they had an important and unique contribution to make to that mission. Because the aggressor can, to a large extent, choose his weapons, it is better to be too slow than too fast about discarding apparently obsolete missions. This is a useful aspect of vested interests.

It is curious that, although interservice competition has probably stimulated development of better weapon systems than would otherwise have been produced, as well as the development of new tactics and doctrine, (e.g., the remarkable development of the Sidewinder air-to-air missile in competition with the Falcon; the development by the Marines before World War II of amphibious techniques later adopted by the Army), competition in the field of research and development seems almost universally agreed to be the most undesirable feature of interservice rivalry. For example, in his address, the President emphasized that "The Secretary must have full authority to prevent unwise competition in this critical area. He needs authority to centralize, to the extent he deems necessary, selected research and development projects under his direct control. . . ."[7] In this, the President was following one of the recommendations of the Rockefeller Report.[8]

In commenting on the effects of the Reorganization Act of 1958, Secretary McElroy provided his hearers with an insight into the way he views the problems of research and development management.

"However, I believe that there will be savings and I think they can be quite substantial, principally in the direction of a more orderly development of new weapons through better over-all supervision and direction of the research and engineering program which should be supplied by the newly authorized Director of Defense Research and Engineering. There has been some coordination in this area in the past, but *our real problem is to avoid getting started on research*

[7] "The President's Reorganization Plan," *op.cit.*, p. 107.
[8] See *International Security—The Military Aspect, op.cit.*, p. 33.

programs that are duplicative, overlapping, or of marginal usefulness. Once a thing gets moving down the road, it is very hard to stop it. . . . Then you get contractors involved, vested interests, and all kinds of other considerations which you understand. *The thing that is important in order to avoid getting into duplication and waste is to think it through right at the very beginning.*" (Italics added.)[9]

As we pointed out earlier, the solution to difficult problems of choice cannot be found in simply not developing alternatives, as Secretary McElroy would seem to suggest. Again, the problem lies largely in the method for making choices and enforcing decisions, and the solution must be found here, in strengthening and improving it. Rather than preventing duplication of research projects, research and development policy should aim at preventing the creation of a few, large-scale programs, which large and powerful interests will want to preserve, before the major uncertainties have been resolved and before sound choices can be made. As Admiral Rickover put it "There ought to be a 'chopper-off'er' in every research and development organization who chops off complete developments or parts of them."[10]

In research and development, we should want competition, duplication, and overlap because research and development deal with matters that are uncertain and unpredictable, and duplication and overlap is the price we pay for the reduction of uncertainty. It simply is not possible "to think it through right at the very beginning." If it were, it would not be research. As Burton Klein has argued, "research and development is being crippled by the official refusal to recognize that technological progress is highly unpredictable, by the delusion that we can advance rapidly and economically by planning the future in detail."[11] In an uncertain and rapidly changing world, what we cannot afford is to be without alternative means of doing important jobs. The single way without alternatives is the expensive way; the costs are the undiscovered cheaper ways of doing the job.

[9] Department of Defense Appropriations for 1960, Hearings before the Subcommittee of the Committee on Appropriations, House of Representatives, 1959, pp. 194–5.
[10] See *Inquiry Into Satellite and Missile Programs*, Hearings Before the Preparedness Investigating Subcommittee of the Committee on Armed Services, United States Senate, Part 2, 1958, p. 1435.
[11] See Burton Klein, "A Radical Proposal for R. and D." *Fortune Magazine*, May 1958, p. 112.

2. The Defense Economy

The defense economy is more like the economy of a college student being supported by his father, than like the economy of a household trying to allocate its expenditure efficiently within a fixed set of income possibilities. The college boy may receive a set allowance to cover minimal living or operating expenses, but beyond that he must persuade his father of the value of particular projects for which he wants financial support. One day he may want a set of new law books, another day a new automobile. How much he gets will depend on how much he asks for, how he plans to spend it, and also on how he has spent his money in the past. The important characteristic of his economy is that he does not attempt to allocate optimally within a fixed budget constraint. Because the typical father considers himself to be the moral guardian of his son, budget level and allocation are inseparably tied together, and it would not be rational for the son to ignore this.

The independent household, by way of contrast, generally has a fixed set of income possibilities, and it must attempt to allocate efficiently within them. Within rather broad limits, the employer, unlike the father, is not concerned with the allocation of the employee's income. This is not the case in the Department of Defense. The military departments estimate their needs or "requirements" and then send them on to be joined with the requests of other departments. These requests are not determined on the basis of a pre-existing budget constraint which is assumed to be binding and unchangeable. The military departments, like the college boy, know full well that how much they get depends very much on what and how much they ask for. During the allocation process, various agencies, such as the Service staffs, the Defense Comptroller and Assistant Secretaries, the Bureau of the Budget, and then the Congress, try to "weed out" requests for things which they deem to be unnecessary, while the military departments defend their requests as being in accord with their "needs if they are to be able to defend the United States." The question of efficient choice among alternatives is rarely raised, even when appropriate. Rather, both budget allocation and level are determined by a never-ending process of bargaining; that is, a series of exchanges of offers and counteroffers, sometimes explicit and sometimes implicit, pertaining to budget level, allocation, and effectiveness. What the participants in this process say and do must be judged by the effect of their actions on the over-all results, and not simply on the assumption that each alone is making the decisions.

A. SOME VIEWS ON DEFENSE ALLOCATION

A regrettably widespread view of the nature of efficient choice in defense allocation, and one which should be disposed of quickly, is that it is primarily one of efficiency in the small or avoidance of "obvious waste," for example, one service selling as surplus and at a low price supplies which another service is buying new, or people sitting about with nothing to do, or duplication and overlap in research and development. Congressional hearings on military appropriations provide ample evidence that problems of this sort consume a great deal of energy at the expense of more important issues. By efficient choice, we mean allocation of the budget and other scarce resources in such a way as to maximize the relevant output. Efficient choice is concerned primarily with decisions as to whether or not to adopt alternative programs, secondarily with how well the programs are run. Genuine efficiency, in our sense, may generate apparent waste. For example, the cost of improving the coordination of all of the military departments and organizations in their buying and selling may exceed the extra savings which can be obtained thereby, in which case it would be better to tolerate the apparent waste than to try to correct it. (Unfortunately, the potential savings are likely to be more easily identifiable than are the costs.) Or again, apparently wasteful duplication and competition in research and development are popularly regarded as evidence of inefficiency. The problem of allocating defense expenditure wisely is far more subtle and difficult than mere identification of apparent waste.

One major school of thought which seems to have more adherents in the military than elsewhere follows what might be called the "requirements approach." During the Symington Committee Hearings of 1956, Senator Goldwater illustrated its view very neatly.

"If I have any criticism of the Air Force since the second war, it has been their seeming timidity to put down on paper what they want and then let those of us who believe in them fight for that amount, and let the money take care of itself.

"I have felt for a number of years that we were not approaching the total Air Force properly and that goes probably over ten years, that we ought to say we need X number of air planes and X number of men to do the job.

"I am convinced that if we can come up with a figure like that the American public will back it and we can provide it.

"I do not necessarily mean that we need 10,000 air planes or a thousand air planes.

"Certainly these professionals know what the figure is, and if we can convince the top commanders in the services to come up with it, we can get a balanced, over-all program."[12]

The essence of the requirements approach is that there are certain absolute needs, stated in terms of military hardware and manpower which must be met regardless of cost, if the security of the United States is to be guaranteed in some absolute sense. Taken seriously as a set of principles for the determination of the level and allocation of the defense budget, this approach has major shortcomings. It is based upon a failure to recognize that both we and our opponents have a wide range of alternatives from which to choose to accomplish any objective, and a failure to recognize the existence of the uncertainty, both strategic and technological, intrinsic to military planning. It contains the implicit assumption that the world is deterministic. The concepts used are drawn more from engineering ("technical requirements") than from economics ("efficient choice") and the theory of games ("alternative strategies"). It assumes that intelligence makes estimates of the enemy "threat" for various future dates, and that these are point estimates, not interval estimates. The possibility that the enemy may choose to do something different—perhaps influenced by our own choices—is ignored. The estimates are handed to the military planners who calculate the forces "required" to overcome this fixed enemy, and the results become our military requirements. The uncertainty in our estimates and the uncertainty in the performance of our future weapon systems is ignored.

The requirements approach is not the same thing as the specification of a set of objectives and the determination of the minimum cost method of achieving them. The two differ in several ways. First, in the requirements approach, costs are considered irrelevant except for purposes of a rough check of fiscal feasibility. Second, there is little if any systematic consideration of alternatives. Third,

[12] See *Study of Airpower*, Hearings Before the Subcommittee on the Air Force of the Committee on Armed Services, United States Senate, 1956, pp. 230–1.

the requirements are stated in terms of military hardware and man-power rather than in terms of purposes or objectives. They are thus stated in a way which predetermines the means and precludes consideration of alternatives. There is little need to dwell on the fact that here is a series of misconceptions. There is nothing absolute about national security. We attempt to reduce our insecurity by spending money on national defense. The real issue is, considering the other demands on our resources, how far and by what means can and should we reduce it. There is no possibility of eliminating it altogether.

As a position in the bargaining process, the requirements approach is a convenient way of presenting and defending requests for resources. By proceeding from the hypothesis that what has been requested "is necessary if the job is to be done," the bargainer can portray any cut in his program as a threat to national security. Programs are presented as entities with strong internal interdependencies, whose contents are all of equally high value, and whose value will be impaired seriously if tampered with. An implicit denial of the existence of alternatives makes possible the avoidance of the notion of marginal items. By avoiding discussion of marginal items, it is possible to direct attention away from the relationship between costs and benefits at the margin, where it would be possible to discuss intelligently changes in the scale of the program, and to focus it on the much less relevant total value of each program. If the issue is total acceptance or rejection, in the case of many military programs the security of the United States *will* be at stake.

Another popular conceptual framework for dealing with problems of allocation in defense is a variant of the requirements approach—the use of the priority list. The priority list seems to be favored by Congress because it is a way of attempting to force the exposure of marginal items and of getting some insight into what is really of greater and lesser value in the program under discussion. Of course, the demand for a priority list, if it is for this purpose, is vulnerable to a fairly obvious counter. The relative priorities can be adjusted so that the items at the bottom of the list are either of obvious and substantial military value or known to be favored by an influential congressman. In other cases, the priority list is an instrument used by the Services to increase the budget level. The organization using the priority list insists on its number one priority item until it gets it, and then points to all the complementary things that are needed to make it work properly.

As an instrument for allocation, the idea underlying the priority list is that all projects or expenditures can be ranked in order of their priority, so that when the budget level is determined the projects to be funded will be revealed automatically. This overlooks two important possibilities. First, at a higher budget level it may be better to spend the extra money on modifications of, or increments to, items included in the program at a lower budget level rather than on the next items on the list. Second, given a larger budget, it may be rational to drop out some items included in the smaller budget, replacing them with better ways of accomplishing the same purpose. In fact, with larger budgets we may find it desirable to change some programs in very fundamental ways.[13]

In their bargaining for larger budgets, the Services find themselves opposed by a group of people whose attention is riveted almost exclusively upon costs and the budget. We may describe the views of this school as "budget first." It is possible to distinguish at least two variants of this view. One group holds that national security is best served by a healthy economy, and that the health of the economy would be seriously impaired by further increases in government spending.[14] They would argue that if the defense budget were increased substantially the inevitable consequence would be inflation and bankruptcy. Now there is no possibility of bankruptcy of the federal government in the literal sense. But the danger of inflation is a real one. However, at least within the range under consideration, there is no question but that the extra inflationary pressures of increased defense spending could be offset by tax increases. There is no basis in fact for the argument that we cannot afford more defense spending. We can afford more. The real issue is one of balancing extra sacrifices against extra gains.

The other budget first group, whose members are to be found, for example, in the Bureau of the Budget and in the office of the Comptroller of the Department of Defense, conceives its job to be entirely a matter of holding the line on the defense budget. In the bargaining process they are the custodians of the budget, just as the Services are the custodians of military effectiveness. The essentially limitless

---

[13] For one example of the misconception of what a priority list can do, see the discussion in *Military Construction Appropriations for 1958*, Hearings before the Subcommittee of the Committee on Appropriations, House of Representatives, 1957, pp. 416–27.

[14] For a good example of this position, see the Interim Report of the Cabinet Committee on Price Stability for Economic Growth, *The New York Times*, June 29, 1959, p. 16.

DEFENSE PLANNING AND ORGANIZATION

demands of the Services and the inevitable limitations on total expenditure place the Comptroller and the Bureau of the Budget in a strategic position. Someone has to reconcile the competing demands with the limited resources available, and the Services are unwilling to do it because this would mean tacit acceptance of the existing budget level. ("If they can live within the budget they have, then they don't need more.") And, in a sense, this reconciliation *is* the formulation of defense policy, since this is the place at which choices must be made, and to make choices is to determine policy. However, both the Comptroller and the Bureau of the Budget are handicapped in the performance of this reconciliation in two ways. First, neither in principle nor in fact do they have the military expertise of the Services. This means that they are without adequate criteria of military effectiveness for determining where programs should be cut. As a consequence, political resistance often seems to be the criterion employed. If the defender of a program shows any uncertainty or lack of determination, he is likely to find his program cut, and this perhaps quite independently of its merits. Second, the focus of attention is inevitably on the current budget since it is within the current budget that choices must be made. Next year's budget is always a year away, and both sides feel, quite correctly, that anything can happen between now and then. The budgeteers are neither in a position to bargain over questions of current allocation insofar as they affect future budgets, nor do they seem to us to be particularly interested in doing so. As a result, present expenditures which will bring about future net savings tend to be neglected.

If the requirements approach and budget-first views are unbalanced, what is a balanced view? Only a brief sketch can be given here. Broadly speaking, our defense objectives derive from higher goals of national policy. We wish to defend the United States and its allies from attack and to provide for a secure and just peace in the world. These goals can be furthered, though not achieved absolutely, by our defense establishment. The defense establishment pursues lower level objectives, such as defense of the United States against bomber attack, which promote the achievement of national security goals. Generally speaking, our defense objectives cannot be achieved absolutely either. It is always a question of more or less. Our society, on the other hand, has limited resources, whence it cannot do everything that would otherwise be desirable. Part of these resources, measured by the budget limitation and other constraints, are turned over by society to the defense establishment for the purpose of achieving the various national defense objectives. It should be the task of the defense establishment to allocate these limited resources in such a way as to achieve as much as possible of that combination of defense objectives which brings us closest to the achievement of the goals of our national policy.

For any combination of defense objectives, an allocation of the budget can be described as *efficient* if there is no alternative allocation which does at least as well with respect to all objectives and better with respect to some. Efficiency is a standard by which we can evaluate how well the budget is used. As a practical matter, we cannot hope to reach perfect efficiency, or even anything very close to it. The problems are too difficult for that: our objectives are not that clear, and the technology with which we achieve them is changing too rapidly. But we can hope to avoid gross inefficiency in the sense of avoiding choices which are inferior, unambiguously and by a large margin, to other alternatives open to us. And we can hope to make improvements, in the sense of reallocations within the same budget and other constraints which leave us in a better military position. Above all, we can hope to avoid the worst kind of inefficiency, the situation which leaves us with completely open gaps in our capabilities which are exploitable by an enemy. The concept of efficiency relates the achievement of our objectives to cost and to the budget. Whatever the interests of the contending parties in budget level and defense effectiveness might be, they should have a common interest in efficient allocation, that is in spending whatever budget is agreed upon in such a way as to maximize military effectiveness, or, what amounts to the same thing, in achieving whatever level of the objectives has been agreed upon at minimum cost.

B. CONFLICT OVER BUDGET LEVEL AND
THE EFFICIENCY OF ALLOCATION

We have examined briefly the language of defense allocation and found it lacking. One school emphasizes effectiveness and does not give adequate attention to cost, particularly the cost of alternatives. Another emphasizes cost and the budget at the expense of military effectiveness. However, we do not want to place ourselves in the position of criticizing the defense allocation process on the grounds that nobody is trying to do the right thing, much less on the grounds that what people say does not suggest that they are doing the right thing. It is altogether possible that even though no individual appears to be taking a balanced view and attempting to allocate the budget efficiently, the process may be producing satisfactory results. Charles E. Lindblom has made the point that ". . . the notion that to accomplish a social objective someone must try to accomplish it degenerates into a proposition that most of us would reject at once—that only do-gooders do good."[15] Moreover, if the process does produce satisfactory results, it might well be positively undesirable that any of the participants in the process individually take a larger view. If the Bureau of the Budget were to forget its preoccupation with the budget and worry about military effectiveness, we might soon find ourselves with an undesirably large defense budget; or if the Services were to stop bargaining for more money, we might find ourselves with an undesirably small defense program. Moreover, if they were to offer balanced programs at alternative budget levels to Congress, thus exposing their marginal items, the Services might expose themselves to large cuts, and the rest of us to undesirable military risks. Given the structure of the present system, it is therefore not obvious that any party should abandon its current bargaining positions and try to act consciously but naively in the public interest.

It is worth emphasizing that the results of the defense allocation process could be worse, indeed much worse, than they actually are, and that it would be undesirable to upset the existing balances of bargaining power without some expectation that the new set of relationships would produce better results. But unfortunately, the system as it now exists does contain biases which work against efficient allocation and which are not corrected by countervailing forces. As a result, the bargaining between the Services and the Office of the Secretary of Defense and between the Department of Defense and the Bureau of the Budget and Congress produces allocations which in many cases are quite inefficient. Part of the problem can be illuminated by drawing a contrast between the defense economy and the classical model of the competitive private market economy. In the competitive economy, the motive of private profit gives the businessman an incentive to minimize his costs of production and to reduce prices and expand output until marginal costs are equal to the corresponding competitive market prices.

[15] Charles E. Lindblom, *Bargaining: The Hidden Hand in Government*, The RAND Corporation, RM-1434-RC, February 22, 1955, pp. 6–7.

Given the admittedly unrealistic assumptions of the model, this produces an efficient allocation of resources in production, whence, at least from the point of view of the efficiency of allocation, private interests are consistent with the public good.

By way of contrast, in the private economy as it exists and still more in defense, the legitimate interests of at least some of the individuals and organizations involved are not entirely consistent with the public interest, and the latter seems remote and unclear. For example, the military services are concerned with the performance of our defense establishment, that is, with effectiveness, and not with cost as such. In the pursuit of greater defense effectiveness, for the Services improved efficiency and larger budgets are often alternatives. Moreover, seeking a larger budget may be easier than improving efficiency. Improved efficiency requires hard choices and generates conflict within the organization; the opposition to a higher budget is external, and it is easier for the organization to unite against the outside world. Furthermore, because the case for a higher budget is based upon need, improved efficiency may make it harder for a service to get future budget increases. In this sense the two are conflicting alternatives. In any given year with a given budget, effectiveness will be greater, the greater the efficiency. But in the long run, when budget levels are variable and subject to negotiation, it is not at all clear that the efficient route maximizes output.

We do not mean to suggest that this is a conscious choice or that anyone is intentionally wasting money. The point is simply that the Services are concerned primarily with the defense of the United States and not with saving the taxpayers' money.

The tendency to fight for higher budgets is strengthened by the difficulty of making an objective estimate of how well defense activities perform. Fortunately from most points of view, the actual wartime performance of most military systems must remain hypothetical. But this does mean that the importance of an activity, and therefore of the people directing it, tends to be judged by the amount of resources it uses, or by the size of its budget and the number of people it employs. This is still another reason to fight for a larger budget. The incentives now at work cut against improvements in efficiency and in favor of expensive programs, for the rational response at a higher level to improvements in efficiency at a lower level is usually to realize some of the potential savings by cutting the improved activity's budget. Improved efficiency thus appears to be penalized, and the system of incentives is perverse. Only at a very low level are there rewards for improvements in efficiency.

This emphasis on getting more budget stems in large part from the fact that the budgetary process does not provide *ex ante* budget constraints, either for the Services or for major combat commands, within which they are free to allocate. This is not to say that there are no prior guidelines sent down through the Bureau of the Budget and the Office of the Secretary of Defense. But the guidelines appear to the Services as moves in a bargaining process and not as binding constraints.[16] Furthermore, they are not generally presented in such a way that they appear as constraints within which the Services will be free to buy alternative programs on an equal budget basis. Rather, they are "one-sided" constraints. The limitation side is emphasized. The promise that would be implicit in a genuine budget constraint— that the organization constrained can trade weapons on a dollar-for-dollar basis—is not given. If the Services give up a project, they are not assured of getting the money for another project of higher value. In defense, a dollar saved is not a dollar earned. New projects must be considered anew "on their own merits." As a consequence, the Services are reluctant to give up approved systems because they represent a budget category. This leads to hoarding of large and expensive programs of relatively low marginal value.[17] The other side of the constraint does not work either. When fighting for approval of new projects, the Services do not typically feel called upon to offer compensating cost reductions of an equal amount elsewhere. If they were to offer such reductions they would have good reason to fear that the proposed cuts would be accepted without the increase being granted, at least in the next budget cycle, because such proposals are taken to be a sign that the programs to be cut back are "not really necessary." As a result, every question of allocation is a potential battle between the Services and the budgeteers over budget level.

The struggle over budget level fosters the use of what might be called "foot-in-door tactics" for getting larger budgets. One variant of this is the use of the priority list in the manner we have described.

---

[16] For an explanation of an example of this, see the testimony of Assistant Secretary of Defense W. J. McNeil in *Department of Defense Appropriations for 1960*, Hearings Before the Subcommittee of the Committee on Appropriations, House of Representatives, 1959, Part 2, pp. 2–3.

[17] This is a point made by Kissinger, *op.cit.*, p. 384. "Because to relinquish a weapon system may mean to relinquish the appropriations that go with it, every service has a powerful incentive to hold on to every weapon even after it has outlived its usefulness."

The organization using the priority list insists on its first priority item until it gets it, and then points to all the complementary things that are needed to make that item have any military value.[18] In its extreme form, this tactic can be characterized as the "critical weakness" strategy. A military department will buy only part of a system and then later point to the obvious gaps that need closing if the system is to be useful. This technique exploits the strong complementarities between the components of a weapon system, and it exploits the continuing character of the bargaining process. The same device can also be used to forestall budget cuts as well as to press for increases. Budget cuts are represented as affecting the most vital areas. The trouble with this from the point of view of the allocation of the defense budget is that it leads to unbalanced programs and incomplete weapon systems, and sometimes leaves large gaps in our defense capability over substantial periods of time.

The general character of the situation fosters a downward bias in the estimation of the cost of new weapons and of new ways of using existing ones. From the time the cost of new weapons is first presented, at a point when the weapons are still a gleam in the eye of the designers, until they are actually produced and in the field, often their estimated cost increases many times over. This happens mainly because there is little incentive on the part of anyone to take a realistic view. The contractor wants to sell the weapon, the using command wants to have it (and does not have to pay for it), and the Service wants to get a commitment to the weapon and hence whatever money is needed for it. This introduces an uneven bias into the choice among new weapon systems, and it causes distortions in their design. Moreover, the cost underestimation leads to an important bias in the choice between existing systems and future systems. It often prevents us from doing things that we should do now because of the belief that something very cheap and effective will soon be here. Then, when it proves that the new system is not so cheap and not so effective, we are left with a gap in capability.

The structure of the bargaining situation also poses a temptation to the Services to exploit the effect Secretary McElroy alluded to when he testified "once a thing gets moving down the road, it is very hard to stop it . . . . Then you get contractors involved, vested interests, and all kinds of other considerations. . . ."[19] By making large

---

[18] For an illustration, see *A Study of Airpower, op.cit.*, pp. 96, 231–2.
[19] *Department of Defense Appropriations for 1960, op.cit.*, pp. 194–5.

commitments of money to research and development programs very early, before the technical uncertainties are resolved and before large commitments are really necessary to the rapid progress of the program, it is possible to prejudice the choice which must be made when the uncertainties have been resolved. Not only does this interfere with rational choice but also it leads to conducting some development programs on a wasteful scale.

We have mentioned already the position of the Defense Comptroller and the Bureau of the Budget. As custodians of the budget they inevitably play a part in the reconciliation of the limitless demands of the Services and the limitation of the current budget. But as we noted earlier, given the nature of the situation, they cannot do much bargaining over future plans. They must focus attention on the current budget because that is where their power lies. This leads to a very high implicit discount rate applied to prospective future savings, and thus to a neglect of current expenditures which will yield larger future savings. Ideally, if the allocation of the current budget is to be efficient, it should be based on a projection of future budget levels. Despite the bargaining, large changes in budget level *ex post*, that is changes large enough to have an appreciable effect on allocation, generally occur only in response to large and unforeseen changes in the international situation. Therefore, the best working assumption is probably that this year's budget level will be in force indefinitely (adjusted for price level changes, and perhaps growth in income).[20]

The problem of expenditures now for savings later was posed for the Bureau of the Budget and the Administration by the Cordiner Committee proposals in the Spring and Summer of 1957. The Cordiner Committee was appointed to study the problems of military pay. In the Spring of 1957, it published a report which contained an explanation of the serious problem of keeping skilled manpower in the Services, a proposal for a set of pay increases designed to ameliorate the problem, and estimates of the cost of the increased salaries and of the savings which would result.[21] Since the savings

---

[20] Of course, part of the peacetime job of the military services is to be ready to expand rapidly in time of emergency; i.e., to be able to exploit sudden and large increases in the budget. But this capability should be identified as a kind of output and should not be confused with attempts to allocate in such a way as to bring about an increase in the peacetime budget.

[21] See *A Modern Concept of Manpower Management and Compensation for Personnel of the Uniformed Services*, Volume I, Military Personnel, Defense Advisory Committee on Professional and Technical Compensation, May 1957, which we refer to as "The Cordiner Report."

would be the result of improved retention, they would not be realized until the program had been in effect for a year or two, whereas the extra costs would be felt right away. In the first full year of operation, the net increased cost of the program was estimated to be about $300 millions. By the fifth year of operation of the plan the projected extra costs (gross) were about $660 millions whereas the projected (gross) savings were about $660 millions in material and maintenance, $430 millions in personnel savings, mainly in training costs, and about $4 billions in measurable increases in combat effectiveness.[22]

The evidence that military salaries were too low, just from the point of view of retention, was quite clear cut.[23] It is also clear that large gains in military effectiveness and substantial cost reductions in training and accidents could be obtained with even modest improvements in personnel retention. One could reasonably dispute the estimated savings projected in the Cordiner Report, and it might have been open to question whether the proposed salary scales were really just the right ones.[24] But the evidence suggested very strongly that the Cordiner proposals were a step in the right direction. It is difficult to believe that the Bureau of the Budget and the Administration really were opposed to the idea. Nevertheless, they did oppose the recommendations.[25] A reasonable hypothesis to explain this may be that the Department of Defense offered no offsetting budgetary savings in the first years of operation of the plan and as a result the Bureau of the Budget felt called upon to resist the pay increases probably because it had no way of enforcing the realization of the savings in the form of budget reductions in later years. On this hypothesis, the alternatives to the Bureau were improved efficiency and a higher budget or rejection of the plan and a maintenance of the same budget.[26]

As well as biasing the resulting allocation in the direction of inefficiency, the bargaining process by which a "coordinated"

[22] *Ibid.*, pp. 25–42.
[23] As well as the Cordiner Report, see the testimony of the personnel officers before the Symington Committee, *A Study of Airpower, op.cit.*, and Alain C. Enthoven, "Supply and Demand and Military Pay," The RAND Corporation, Paper P-1186, September 30, 1957, or "An Economist's View of the Cordiner Recommendations," *Air Force*, Vol. 41, No. 1, January 1958, pp. 38–41.
[24] In fact, Secretary Wilson did just this. See *The New York Times*, July 7, 1957.
[25] See *The New York Times*, April 27 and July 7, 1957.
[26] Interestingly enough, the early returns suggest some improvement in re-enlistment rates since the enactment of the pay increases, and this despite a decrease in civilian unemployment. See *Department of Defense Appropriations for 1960, op.cit.*, pp. 105, 354, and 382.

position is arrived at imposes costs of its own. A policy-making organization can make two types of error: it can decide to do something which should not be done, or, what is likely to be more serious, it can fail to do something which should be done. Unfortunately, the former often seems to be more identifiable than the latter. Perhaps partly as a consequence of this, the typical coordination process in the Department of Defense is biased against getting things done, particularly against getting them done quickly. The effects of this are particularly pernicious in research and development where changes must be made and failures must occur if there is to be any progress at all.[27] In the structure of checks and balances, there are too many layers of authority with veto powers.[28] Authority without responsibility can cause undesirable and unnecessary delay because it conveys a veto power which can be used without sufficient cost to the user. It costs one nothing to delay a project if one is not responsible for the results. The costs and incentives are unbalanced unless those who can cause delay have a corresponding interest in avoiding it.

All this is not to suggest that bargaining is necessarily a bad thing or that, even if it could, it should be replaced by a well-defined hierarchy in which decisions are made unilaterally. Rather, we wish to suggest only that in the defense establishment the conflict over budgets and the failure to separate questions of allocation from questions of budget level, insofar as the two are separable, does produce inefficient allocations. This should not be taken to imply

[27] For a discussion of this point, see Burton Klein, "A Radical Proposal for R. and D.," *op.cit.*

[28] The testimony of Admiral Rickover on this point is illuminating. In discussing the purchase of nuclear cores for naval ships before a Senate Committee, Rickover related the following episode.

"Next time the purchase of nuclear cores came up there was a six-months' delay. Even though the Chairman and the General Manager of the Atomic Energy Commission were for it, it wound up with the necessity for an official request from the Navy to the Atomic Energy Commission via the Secretary of Defense. The matter was handled by General Loper, the Chairman of the Military Liaison Committee. I went over to see General Loper with the draft of the letter which he agreed to and which he initialed. After that it took the initials of fifteen or twenty officials in the Pentagon and a month's delay before the letter got out of the Pentagon.

"So it took six months just because one staff person with no responsibility but with authority had on his own decided that the policy was wrong. This is the sort of thing we face. So therefore I get back to the point that if you want these research and development jobs done expeditiously you had better see to it that somehow or other you do not separate responsibility from authority."

See *Inquiry Into Satellite and Missile Programs, op.cit.*, Part 2, p. 1,394.

that a system in which budget level and allocation would be determined without any bargaining would necessarily be better than the present one, or that the existing bargaining process could not be changed in such a way that it would produce better results. Some of the defects in the present system which we have described should be remediable; some may be inescapable costs of an otherwise advantageous system; some may be intrinsic in all large administrative structures. We are not now prepared to say to which category each belongs. Neither are we prepared to advance an entirely different method for allocating resources in defense which we would consider to be unambiguously superior. Further study is required.

Obviously some method is needed for determining budget level as well as allocation and, the problems of information in a context of rapidly changing technology being what they are, the choice of budget level is bound to be a collective decision in which the agencies affected have some voice. This almost inevitably opens up the possibility that agencies which believe (perhaps quite justifiably) that more resources should be devoted to their activity will use whatever leverage they have to increase their budgets. However, it is all too easy for the participants in the budget struggle to lose perspective, to feel that they must resort to extreme bargaining tactics, and to over-value the effectiveness of the tactics. The stability of the total budget over the past several years does suggest that the budget level forces are fairly evenly balanced. (This is not a prediction that there will not be a large increase in the defense budget in the next few years.) The changes that are made in allocation turn out in retrospect to be roughly one-for-one dollar trades. Over-all allocation would be improved if both sides in the contest over budget level could recognize this stability, separate questions of budget level from budget allocation, and redirect some of their energies from the struggle over budget level to the problem of improving allocation.

C. BUDGET STRUCTURE

The budgetary process does not provide *ex ante* budget constraints by classes of military output in a form that can be a guide for military planning. There are guidelines or expenditure totals for each service sent down by the Administration early in the budgetary process. But as we pointed out earlier, these are partly bargaining counters and only partly constraints and, moreover, they have little effect on military planning except in the single year for which the budget is being prepared. In general, the following observation by Arthur Smithies holds good:

"Planning and programing precede budgeting, and programs provide the basis on which budgets are prepared. Programs, however, are prepared in terms of military concepts and not in terms of dollars. When a program is completed the cost in dollars is not known."[29]

The defense budget is subdivided into input rather than output categories, and Congress and the Services consider allocation in terms of these subbudgets. The appropriation titles are military personnel, operation and maintenance, procurement, research and development, and military construction, rather than, say, strategic offense, continental air defense, antisubmarine warfare, and the like.

The subdivision of the budget along input rather than output lines is both a symptom and a cause of one of the principal weaknesses in the structure of the defense economy. The concept of military output as something which exists and can be measured independently of inputs is neglected. The issue of criteria is rarely raised. It is all too easy to measure the strength of our fleet in the Pacific by the number of its ships rather than by its ability to accomplish some objective. As a result, there is not enough explicit consideration given to raising military output by trading among inputs within a subbudget. The existing budget classifications make this situation worse because they do not present decision-makers with very manageable allocation problems. They do not enable the decision-makers to factor out reasonably independent "suboptimization" problems because there is no common set of criteria spanning the items considered in such a subbudget. Consider the aircraft procurement category. This subbudget covers procurement of bombers, tankers, transports, fighters, and other aircraft. In order to allocate this budget efficiently, the allocator would have to know, among many other things, the marginal product of another bomber in SAC, and then the marginal product of more SAC in our over-all strategic offensive position, and, in turn, the marginal product of more strategic offense for national security. Then he would have to know the marginal product of another interceptor in our air defense system, the marginal product of more air defense in our over-all national security, and so forth. These decisions, in turn, should

[29] Arthur Smithies, *The Budgetary Process in the United States*, New York, 1955, p. 241.

depend on what is being done in personnel, installations, and else-where. And at the same time, another committee is allocating the installations budget in comparable circumstances.

There are important interactions between air defense and air offense, for example, but these are much less strong and much more manageable than they are between the personnel, equipment, and installations that go into a bomber system. Members of a board charged with responsibility for the allocation of the aircraft pro-curement subbudget could not possibly master simultaneously the range of questions they would have to understand in order to make the decisions efficiently. Not only are the criteria governing the different types of aircraft different in detail, they are also different in kind. For example, the marginal product of another fighter in the air defense system is a relatively easily analyzed quantity by comparison with the marginal product of more strategic offensive power in our over-all national security position.

In practice, of course, there is informal communication between the different committees and boards making the various decisions, and some communication is assured by overlapping memberships. This communication does help to minimize the gross and obvious errors. But there is no reason to believe that the results are efficient. Quite the contrary. The impossibility of constructing criteria which span an input budget means that it is not possible to compare alternative allocations of a subbudget in terms of a definable military output. Moreover, this budget structure leaves the division of total service budgets between alternative activities to be decided largely by a number of independent committees.

The operating commands are organized broadly along output lines. They are organized to accomplish certain missions. However, within the operating commands there is, in general, no possibility for trading between budget categories. For example, there is no such thing as a budget for the Strategic Air Command or Continental Air Defense in the *ex ante* sense. There is no point in trying to persuade an operational command that it should give up, say, some personnel in order to get more aircraft, or give up some aircraft to get more installations, since by the nature of the budgetary process these trades do not appear to be open to it.

Since resources are not as a rule charged to the using command, there is little incentive to economize on their use. Personnel, for example, are either free or unobtainable. Similarly, supporting services (airlift or depot maintenance or trained men) are free if they are available. If demand exceeds supply, the inputs in short supply have to be rationed and, as a result, are often simply not available when needed. In any case, their costs do not enter into the calculation of the organizations that use them, or if they do enter, it is as an absolute constraint (e.g., a method of operation might be rejected because there is no prospect of getting the necessary crews from the training activity).

The subbudgets treated separately by decision-makers in the Department of Defense are also treated separately by Congress. This congressional method may be partly accounted for by the notion that the military departments are going to Congress for *means* (i.e., inputs) to accomplish hard-to-understand objectives on which they are expert, and by the tendency of congressmen to concern themselves more with how and where the money will be spent than with military objectives and ways of attaining these objectives. Nowhere in the budgetary process from the bottom to the top is there an explicit analysis of the possibilities for trade-offs between installations and personnel and equipment. (Fortunately, some new weapon systems are being treated more as a system than as an independent collection of inputs. Unfortunately, however, there is no evidence that this modest but very promising reform is about to be extended to the whole of the military establishment.)

The treatment of military construction presents an especially important obstacle to efficient planning. Construction is handled separately from procurement of weapons and personnel. The Congress examines construction proposals in considerable detail and makes specific appropriations to individual projects. This rigidity in the treatment of construction, which leads to underbuilding and to a neglect of passive defenses (shelter and dispersal) has been especially dangerous in a period in which the performance of entire weapon systems and even our ability to deter general war can depend critically on the speed with which construction plans can be initiated and carried out. There is little consolation in having more than enough money for bombers and missiles if there is no money for bases and for shelters which are essential if the bombers and missiles are to be able to deter war or to fight effectively if war comes.

The Congress is not inflexible in its budgetary procedures. There have been important changes in the past ten years in the direction of allowing greater flexibility to the Services. For example, in the late

1940's, there were about 110 rigid budget categories in which money was appropriated for the Army; today there are about 10.[30] However, the treatment given to construction and to some other categories remains extremely detailed. Each construction project, and many are quite small, must be approved individually by Congress. There is little possibility of transfer within this category, and, of course, none between it and other categories.

In view of the budgetary procedure of the Department of Defense, it is hardly surprising that our military services do not operate with a concept of scarce resources. They think in terms of needs and feasible solutions to meet the needs. Any characterization of "military thought" is likely to be inaccurate, but it does seem to be the case that the explicit consideration of alternatives as such is less interesting to the military than it is, say, to private industry. Choice between alternative means as such rarely enters in nor, given the institutional framework we have described, should we expect it to.

D. ORGANIZATION STRUCTURE AND DECENTRALIZATION

Paralleling the lack of correspondence between budgets and objectives is a lack of correspondence between organizations and objectives. It is now a commonplace that the military services are organized along the traditional lines of ground, air, and sea combat that no longer reflect military objectives. This is in conflict with the establishment of an orderly system of decentralization of decision making. It would be impossible to construct a set of criteria for evaluation of the performance of, say, the Army, which spans all of the activities of the Army. The "output" or product of the defense establishment is too remote for the Services to consider the relative merits of many alternative allocations. Like the budgetary breakdown, the organization of the Services along lines that do not correspond to military missions tends to divert attention from output and ways of improving it.

In order to focus attention more on output and to facilitate the development of performance criteria, it is particularly desirable that each organization have a reasonably homogeneous set of purposes. Herein lies the particular merit of the proposal of the President to organize the military forces into unified commands. These organizations can concentrate their attention on efficient ways of carrying out their missions. It is undesirable to have missions and organizations

[30] *Reorganization of the Department of Defense, op.cit.*, p. 6,577.

separated when they interact strongly. Two good illustrations of this are the separation of close air support for infantry from the Army and the separation of local defenses for SAC bases from the Air Force. In both cases, not only should the supported or defended force be able to buy its own support or defense in the amounts desired, but also it should be required to pay for it.

On the other hand, there are advantages to having more than one organization to carry out any particular mission. Diversity fosters desirable variation; the existence of different organizations for the same mission encourages competition. Thus, merging the Army and Marines or the strategic offensive forces of the Navy and the Strategic Air Command into single combat commands would appear to offer limited prospect for increased efficiency and a clear reduction in desirable competition which fosters large gains in effectiveness.

The case for reallocating roles and missions should therefore be tempered by the value of preserving competition in the attaining of given ends by keeping easily distinguishable and largely independent activities separate, and it should be based on evidence that gross inefficiencies exist as a consequence of separate planning and control of highly interdependent activities. When there are different organizations serving the same general purpose, however, the organizational structure should provide for another body at a higher level whose job it is to allocate budgets and parts of the general mission between them.

Some decentralization of decision-making is both unavoidable and desirable in a large organization such as the Department of Defense. In allocating a budget of $40 billion a year, there must be subbudgets in order to permit specialization in particular problems of allocation. However, it is one thing to decide which subproblems can be factored out and another to determine at which level in the organization different classes of decision should be made. The problem is complicated in defense by rapidly changing technology. This makes it difficult to specify in advance which decisions will be routine and unimportant and which will be of very great importance. Nevertheless, it should be possible for the character of decentralization in the Department of Defense to be improved. The Department has in fact become very highly centralized, with many decisions of a relatively unimportant character being made in the office of the Secretary of Defense. The Secretary of Defense and his staff, however, are too remote to be able to manage efficiently and in detail all of these questions. Moreover, the Joint Chiefs of Staff provide a battlefield for the contending services, but not, in practice, an instrument for effective planning. As a consequence, in spite of the apparent high degree of centralization of control, many critical decisions of great national importance are actually made at remarkably low levels of authority. This stems largely from the fact that higher officials are absorbed with a great mass of relatively unimportant detail. They simply do not have time left over to reflect on and decide all of the major issues that they should. Rather than focusing attention on how to carry out missions and achieve objectives which have been assigned to them, subordinate commands actually determine much of our national policy. As long as high officials and congressmen continue to concern themselves with such questions as the need for extra fuel hydrants on Base X, much more important questions will continue to be decided by default at lower levels.

E. THE LACK OF PERMANENT STAFF

Underlying the whole problem of defense organization, the issue of roles and missions, the adequacy of our strategic planning and our command channels, and our budgetary process, is the adequacy of the staffs of the office of the Secretary of Defense, the Joint Chiefs of Staff and in the service headquarters. At the present time, the staffs of the three Services are composed of officers who have a three-year tour of duty which, under special conditions, can be extended to four. This is a statutory limitation. There are many reasons advanced why officers should not spend more than three or four years in staff positions. The arguments have to do with the generalized experience the officers require and with fears on the part of some congressmen that a professional military staff would be a danger to our democracy. If these arguments are persuasive, the alleged benefits are not without cost. Moreover, many civilians at high levels, including political appointees in particular, often remain in their jobs for even a shorter time than do military staff officers. This rapid turnover of personnel would damage seriously the efficiency of any organization, and in defense, the damage is worsened by the extraordinary changes in weapons technology taking place all the time.[31] The important problems are objectively difficult and uncertain and many are highly technical. Nevertheless, staff officers, most of

[31] See, for example, the comments of Admiral Rickover on this problem in *Inquiry Into Satellite and Missile Programs, op.cit.*, p. 1,391.

whom do not have the appropriate technical background, are expected within a short time to master these problems and to make critical decisions. This impermanence of personnel means not only that much time is lost in educating new arrivals, but also that it proves difficult for more than a very few officials to acquire over time the deeper wisdom on defense matters that should be possessed by a sizable core of permanently assigned officials.

There are several ways of increasing the quality of the professional management of the Department of Defense. No single measure is likely to be sufficient. Undoubtedly a relaxation of the rule restricting military officers to short tours of duty would be beneficial. It might be useful to expand the number of civil servants employed as full-time experts, at the expense of a reduction in the large number of part-time experts serving on committees, and to offer better career opportunities through promotion within the Defense Department. Finally, there should be higher pay at top levels. The number and, if possible, the salaries of higher grade civil service posts should be increased. While it is commonplace in government that relatively poorly paid civil servants are responsible for decisions concerning billions of dollars, and the obstacles to pay increases are well known, in the case of the defense establishment more than our money is at stake, and we should be prepared to pay handsomely for the services of the people who run it.

3. Some Theoretical Aspects of Defense Organization

The shortcomings in the workings of the defense allocation process which we have discussed testify to the fact that the problems are difficult. The Defense Department is large, and it has grown rapidly. Its very objectives are subject to constant revision, and the technology which it must use to carry out its objectives is changing at a fearsome rate. In these circumstances, can the problems of defense policy be made intelligible? The rapidity of change in military technology and the very nature of the problem, which make the accumulation of relevant experience and experimentation particularly difficult, combine to make a theoretical understanding of the problem especially important. As in all sciences, there is a "trade off" between theory and experience; the scarcity of the latter increases the extent to which we must rely on the former. It is therefore interesting to inquire whether the economic theory of rational choice can be useful in the construction of a theoretical framework which can illuminate the problem of defense budget structure and organization.

The answer to these questions is "Yes," although there is good reason for modesty. The problems are not easy. Current economic theory cannot guide us to a total solution, except in a very formal and empty sense. However, it often can be a useful guide to finding improvements. Indeed, this is the basis for fruitful analysis. Because of the difficulty of the problems of weapons choice and operation, it is always likely to be the case that major improvements will be possible whereas total over-all optimum solutions will continue to elude us.

Ideally, it would be desirable to organize much of the problem of allocating the defense budget into a set of independent subproblems, each divided into further independent subproblems, and each capable of being decided in terms of a relevant criterion or set of criteria.[32] Corresponding to a hierarchy of subproblems of allocation of increasing scope, it would be desirable to have a hierarchy of criteria increasing in generality and measuring the achievement of more and more general objectives. Such a structure would have numerous advantages. Factoring out independent subproblems would make possible a high degree of decentralization and specialization. Separate organizations could be charged with the responsibility of allocating their budgets in such a way as independently to maximize definable criteria. The required information flow within the whole organization would be small, being composed mostly of budgets, marginal costs, and marginal products. The allocator of each subbudget would need to know only his budget and criterion and the costs of alternative ways of accomplishing his assigned objectives. The resulting specialization would be particularly valuable because, in so many areas, it requires a specialist to keep up with the pace of technological change. However, as one attempts to construct such a hierarchy and to extend it to cover broad objectives, some formidable difficulties appear.

A. WHICH CRITERIA? WHOSE CRITERIA?

The first problem is the selection of criteria for making allocation decisions. Of course it is possible to discuss the efficiency of allocation

---

[32] A structure of this kind would be reminiscent of Robert Strotz' "utility tree." See "The Empirical Implications of a Utility Tree," *Econometrica*, April 1957, pp. 269–80.

only in terms of a specified criterion. But what criterion? Whose criteria should be used? How are good criteria to be identified? These questions are at the heart of the whole problem of defense policy. The criterion problem is an extremely difficult one on which we have no satisfactory general statement and no clear cut position. We can only suggest some principles which seem to us to be relevant.

Good criteria can be found only by working with the problems. We do not believe that it is possible to develop a set of criteria for defense policy *a priori* independently of cost and technology.[33] Ends and means interact. Particular objectives are often themselves means to higher objectives. Therefore, the desirability of attempting to accomplish an objective cannot be decided independently of the possibility and cost of achieving it and of achieving alternatives. For example, the United States has adopted the broad policy of strategic deterrence as the primary means of protecting itself from Soviet attack. This decision could be made only in the context of the costs and technological possibilities of alternatives such as active air defense. For these reasons one cannot deduce intermediate criteria "from the top down" nor construct them "from the bottom up." One must break into the problem somewhere in the middle, work up and down and out, attempting to carve out reasonable partial orderings of alternative possibilities. Also for these reasons criterion problems must be dealt with by people who understand the relevant aspects of the technology and the economic possibilities. But this does not tell us what or whose criteria.[34]

There are many areas in which there is widespread agreement among informed people on at least the broad outlines of criteria. For example, there now appears to be widespread agreement that an important criterion for the performance of our strategic offensive forces is their ability to survive a surprise attack designed to destroy them, and then to be able to carry out their missions. Also there are many areas in which intermediate criteria can be deduced from

[33] The contrary view seems to be suggested by Henry Kissinger in *Nuclear Weapons and Foreign Policy*, New York, 1957, Ch. 12.

[34] Beyond the identification of reasonable goals, there is a problem of choosing the form in which they are to be stated for purposes of analysis and decision. Here there are some rules for selection though they are primarily negative rules. For example, as a general matter, it is important to avoid using the ratio of an output to an input as a criterion for allocation. For the literature on this subject, see e.g., Roland N. McKean, *Efficiency In Government Through Systems Analysis*, New York, 1958, Part 2; Charles J. Hitch, "Suboptimization in Operations Problems," *Operations Research*, Vol. 1, May 1953, pp. 87–99.

agreed upon policies. This is generally the case with decisions in the small. Moreover, many disagreements over criteria are of the kind which can be resolved by analysis, agreement on the relevant facts, and appeal to agreed upon higher level criteria. Our analysis is directed primarily to problems in these areas. It is possible to find inefficient allocation even where objectives are understood and agreed upon.

There are, however, important areas in which there is no general agreement among informed people on objectives and criteria. There are strong differences of opinion, for example, on whether our tactical forces based overseas should be designed primarily as atomic striking forces with conventional capability only as a by-product, or designed primarily as conventional forces with atomic capability as a by-product. Issues of this kind cannot be settled directly by the democratic process because the subject matter of defense policy is esoteric. The relevant information is largely technical and abstruse and there is an inevitable requirement for secrecy. As a result, it is not possible to get an informed public opinion on most issues. Moreover, most of the people who are informed have access to information because of their institutional commitments. For this reason, also, the fact of general agreement may not be an entirely reliable guide to the merits of a policy.

It is important that there be open agreement within the defense establishment on criteria (on the reasons for policies) and not just on the policies themselves. Moreover, as much as possible, decisions should be defended in terms of explicit criteria. There are several reasons for this. First, it helps to limit the extent to which purely private interests govern. Second, though imperfect, open discussion is the best method for determining, refining and improving criteria that we know. Third, technology and circumstances are changing rapidly. A policy that is decided upon in terms of good criteria made explicit is more likely to change in the right direction as circumstances change than a policy which owes its existence solely to the fact of agreement. Where there is no agreement on criteria, we have nothing of general significance to say about the efficiency of allocation decisions.

B. THE MULTIPLICITY OF CRITERIA

Consider, for example, the problem of designing forces for fighting all-out war. It seems natural to structure the problem into strategic offense and continental air defense, and then to divide air defense into warning systems, area defense and local defense systems, and passive defenses, and to divide strategic offense into the different weapon systems designed for the purpose. Indeed, as Roland McKean has suggested, such a breakdown has a great deal of merit both for budgetary and for organizational purposes.[35] But what should we use as a criterion for evaluating alternative allocations among these categories? And what should the criteria be for evaluating alternative offensive and defensive systems?

The problem is not a shortage of criteria, but rather an over-abundance. We have a number of general war objectives, and corresponding to them, a number of criteria for the design of our forces. Our primary objective in maintaining all-out war forces is deterrence. That is, we attempt to maintain forces which will be able to inflict damage on our potential enemies that is sufficiently severe that they will not find it to their advantage to attack us or to commit other aggression warranting retaliation. In effect, in pursuing the deterrence objective, we attempt to adjust the payoffs to alternative courses of action open to potential enemies so that they will not choose, as the result of a rational calculation, a course of action severely disadvantageous to ourselves.

But deterrence may fail, and we may find ourselves involved in an all-out war because of miscalculation or an inadequate deterrent. In such circumstances, we have other objectives which we would like our forces to accomplish for us. For example, we would like to limit the damage we suffer. This can be done by defensive forces shooting down attacking vehicles, and it can be done by offensive forces striking at the bases of the enemy's offensive striking power, that is by "counterforce" attacks. But a good counterforce capability may weaken our deterrent by reducing the value, to the enemy, of not attacking us because it may make him think that we are more likely to go first. Thus deterrence and limiting-damage partially conflict.[36]

Beyond these two objectives, one can think of others. We would like our all-out war forces to give us the power to win the war, or at least to terminate it on satisfactory terms, if war does occur. This may call for a force which differs in some respects from a pure

[35] See Roland N. McKean, *Evaluating Alternative Expenditure Programs*, The RAND Corporation, Paper P-1602, January 27, 1959, p. 14.
[36] For a discussion of this and related problems, see T. C. Schelling, *Surprise Attack and Disarmament*, The RAND Corporation, Paper P-1574, December 10, 1958.

deterrent. And we have, of course, many other military and foreign policy objectives which interact with and are furthered by our ability to wage all-out war successfully.

How does one deal with multiple objectives in making choices? Formally, the problem could be solved by defining a single criterion for ordering alternative combinations of levels of satisfying the multiple objectives. But as a practical matter it is very difficult to do this explicitly, even though it is done implicitly by decision-makers every day. The formal possibility offers little comfort to the analyst who is interested in helping his country to survive.

First, we can seek unambiguous improvements, that is changes in allocation which leave performance as good as or better than before with respect to all important criteria. At the end of this road would be efficient postures, that is postures which do not admit of unambiguous improvements. But as a practical matter, perfect efficiency in this sense is simply not attainable, and to seek it in one area would require forgoing the opportunity to seek large improvements elsewhere. Instead, although we may be unable to resolve our multiple objectives into one, we can seek to design systems which are at least tolerable in all circumstances with respect to the important criteria. That is, we can solve higher level criterion problems when they are easy; when they are not easy it *may* be because they are not important.

Usually, it is not necessary to pay a high price in terms of one objective in order to improve performance with respect to another if the system is designed to maximize achievement of the first objective to begin with. This is a reflection of the ubiquity of diminishing marginal returns and of the fact that related objectives are not generally directly opposed. If we care about several objectives, and a design performs extremely well with respect to one of them but extremely badly with respect to the others, we are likely to be willing to yield some in performance with respect to the one if by doing so we can improve performance with respect to the others. At what point do we stop trading? If we are uncertain about the answer, it may mean that performance is in a range in which we do not feel strongly about minor differences. This is another way of saying that the problem is no longer important.[37]

---

[37] A similar point can be made with respect to uncertainty. If a system performs satisfactorily and we are uncertain about the net effect of marginal variations in design, then uncertainty may exist because the effect is not important.

C. INTERACTIONS

Another obstacle to the factoring of the whole defense allocation problem into a hierarchy of independent subproblems is the existence of direct interactions between apparently separate elements of the defense organization.[38] The natural separation between strategic offense and continental air defense, for example, is much more apparent than real. Air defense can contribute a great deal to the value of the offensive systems by providing them with warning of attack and by providing them direct protection.[39] Thus there are both area and local defenses protecting SAC bases. Our offensive systems, in turn, help the defenses limit the damage we suffer by disrupting or destroying the enemy's striking power on the ground in his own territory. Even more distant parts of our defense establishment interact in important ways. We attempt to deter potential enemies from launching an all-out attack on us by the threat of all-out retaliation. But we can attempt to deter peripheral challenges by combining the threat of all-out attack with the use of conventional ground and air forces. By increasing the range of challenges that we meet with the threat of an all-out response, we increase the probability of general war, and thereby increase the burden on our damage-limiting active and civil defenses.[40] To ignore such interactions is to run the risk of making serious errors in defense planning.

In order to understand the theoretical significance of direct interactions, consider a very simple allocation problem in which we wish to maximize an index (in one dimension) of performance which itself depends upon the performance of two systems (each measured in one dimension), subject to an over-all budget constraint, by appropriate choice of the combination of the two systems and by appropriate design of the systems themselves. Let the performance of the two systems be measured by the variables "x" and "y" respectively, and suppose that groups or individuals designated as "managers" are responsible for designing each of the systems, and that a "coordinator" is responsible for combining the two systems in

---

[38] This is analogous to the phenomenon of direct non-market interaction in a market economy which leads to problems for Welfare Economics similar to the ones which we discuss for the defense economy. For a lucid discussion of the problem for Welfare Economics, see Francis M. Bator, "The Anatomy of Market Failure," *Quarterly Journal of Economics*, August 1958, pp. 351–79.

[39] Indeed it is not at all clear that the warning function should "belong" more to the defense than to the offense; if anything, quite the contrary.

[40] For a discussion of this point, see Malcolm W. Hoag, "Is 'Dual' Preparedness More Expensive?" *Bulletin of the Atomic Scientists*, February 1957, pp. 48–51.

such a way as to maximize the over-all performance index. It would be desirable to factor the whole problem into three independent problems so that decision-making can be decentralized in such a way as to minimize the amount of information that the managers and the coordinator need to have about the rest of the problem in order to do their jobs, both to permit specialization and in order to minimize the costs of communication.

If the performance of each of the systems is independent of the performance and design of the other, i.e., if there are no direct interactions between the systems, the decentralization problem is easy. Each manager needs to know only the technology of his own system, his budget, and the prices of the inputs he buys. If, given this information, each manager maximizes the performance of his own system, an over-all maximum can be achieved by the coordinator by dividing the total budget between the two systems appropriately. To do this, the coordinator needs to know only the marginal costs of x and y and their marginal products in terms of the over-all performance index.[41]

Suppose, however, that the output of one system, say x, depends on y, the output of the other. This may be described as an interaction between outputs. Such an interaction increases the amount of knowledge that each participant must have about the rest of the system if he is to make his decisions correctly. Beyond what he needed to know when there were no interactions, the manager of system x must now know the aggregate performance of system y, since his allocation will depend on it. The coordinator must know how y affects x, i.e., the marginal product of y in x, and this, in turn, may mean that he must be acquainted in some detail with the design of system x since the marginal product of y in x is likely to depend on the character of system x.

However, in the case of a simple interaction between outputs, an over-all maximum can still be attained if each manager maximizes the performance of his own system, subject to his budget constraint, and if the coordinator divides the total budget correctly. The interactions will play a part in determining the optimal division of the total budget into subbudgets—the marginal product of the air defense system in limiting damage to cities will have an indirect

[41] This assumes constant or diminishing marginal returns everywhere. If there are increasing returns, the coordinator will need to know more about costs and the relationship of x and y to the over-all performance index. But the important point for present purposes remains: the information requirements are aggregative and simple.

component by way of protecting SAC—but the allocators of sub-budgets can act independently. If the interactions are positive, that is if improvements in the performance of each system increase the effectiveness of the other system(s), there will be no possibilities for cooperation between managers in the sense of increasing total effectiveness at the higher level by doing anything other than maximizing independently within the budgets which are given to them and which they take as fixed. If there are some negative interactions, that is if improvements in one system directly reduce the effectiveness of another, there may be possibilities for cooperation. If improvements in system y reduce the effectiveness of system x, the designer of system y may be able to increase over-all effectiveness at the higher level by not using up his whole budget. This will be so if the reduction in over-all effectiveness caused by a reduction in the effectiveness of y is more than offset by the consequent improvement in x. In this case, however, it would pay the coordinator to reduce the budget for y and spend it on x. Although cooperation may be possible if there are negative interactions, it is not necessary for reaching the over-all maximum if the budget division between the two has been correctly arrived at (i.e., if someone else at a higher level does their cooperating for them).

But the output of system x may depend not on the aggregate performance of system y but rather directly on the *design* of system y, or, in other words, on the combination of inputs chosen to produce y. This may be described as an interaction involving inputs. The retaliatory power of SAC is a function of the amount and reliability of warning, irrespective of how that warning is produced. This is an interaction between outputs. However, the cost of any specified amount of warning depends not only upon the ability of the radar system to detect and count aircraft and missiles but also upon the deployment of SAC. Decisions on how SAC is based affect the minimum number of aircraft the enemy must send in an attack to accomplish a given amount of destruction, and therefore the ability of the warning system to detect attack. In this type of interaction, the particular inputs of one system affect the output of another.

Weapon systems which have multiple purposes lead to interactions of this kind. The aircraft carrier, which carries both tactical aircraft for conventional, limited-war operations and longer range aircraft with nuclear weapons for purposes of strategic retaliation, is alleged to be an example of this. Suppose one organization employs a multiple-purpose weapon system which has a value to another organization. Then there is an interaction between the two organizations because the product of the second depends on the extent to which the first uses the system, and therefore on its weapons mix.[42]

When there are interactions involving inputs, the problem of decentralization becomes more complicated. A simple scheme in which the two system managers maximize the performance of their respective systems independently, taking all relevant features of the other system as parameters, and in which the coordinator controls only the division of the total budget, cannot be expected to lead to optimal results. There is an analogy to game theory here. By acting independently, the designers of the two separate systems overlook any possibilities for over-all improvement through cooperation. Perhaps by modifying his design in such a way as to reduce the performance of his system only slightly, the designer of one system might make it possible for the performance of the other system to be improved more than enough to offset the effect of the reduction in the performance of his system in terms of the higher level criterion. For example, perhaps at the cost of a very modest reduction in its ability to defend cities, the air defense system might, by shifting resources to the protection of SAC bases, be able to bring about a large increase in the power of our deterrent and thereby greatly reduce the expected damage to cities.

If the interactions take place in one direction only, that is, if x depends on the composition of system y but not vice versa, a division of the whole problem into two parts could be brought about if the coordinator were to join with the manager of system y and design that system in such a way as to maximize over-all performance rather than to maximize y. In such an organizational scheme the manager of system x could be left independent and instructed to

---

[42] In his writings on Welfare Economics, Professor Samuelson has introduced the concept of *public goods*, goods which contribute to the utility of many, but which cannot be rationed by the private competitive market mechanism. At the heart of this concept is the nonallocability of the services produced by these goods. We all benefit from national defense, and the extent to which I derive utility from it does not affect the extent to which others derive utility from it, at least to a first approximation. See P. A. Samuelson, "The Pure Theory of Public Expenditure," *Review of Economics and Statistics*, November 1954, pp. 387-9. There are counterparts in the defense establishment. As we pointed out earlier, both the offensive and the defensive weapon systems benefit by improvements in the amount and reliability of warning. The extent to which one system benefits does not affect the extent to which the other benefits, at least to a first approximation. "Public goods" of this kind can lead to interactions of both kinds.

maximize x. However, he would have to know all the relevant aspects of system y since, by our definition of the problem, his performance and therefore, in general, his allocation depend on them. The coordinator and the manager of system y together would have to know x's technology since their decisions would depend in part on the effects of the design of system y on x (and this depends on the design of system x), and, of course, y's technology also. That is, in effect, the coordinator would have to know everything. Alternatively, the coordinator could leave both managers independent and tax and subsidize system y's use of the various inputs as well as setting budgets for both x and y in order to bring about an over-all optimum. But again the coordinator would have to know enough to solve the whole problem himself. When there are interactions involving inputs, then, unless the circumstances are particularly favorable in the sense that few inputs are involved and the effects of the interactions are not extensive, decentralization of information is no longer compatible with over-all maximization. Whether decentralization for purposes of computation is desirable depends on the circumstances.[43]

[43] Mathematically, all this could be stated as follows. Let the coordinator's task be to maximize $F(x, y)$ subject to an over-all budget constraint and a list (vector) of prices, p. Let $x = f(v^1)$, $y = g(v^2)$ where v^1 and v^2 are vectors of inputs used by the respective systems and controlled by their managers. In this case, there are no interactions. An over-all maximum can be reached if the coordinator knows only $F(x, y)$ and the marginal costs of x and y, and if each system manager knows his production function, f or g, and his budget and the prices of inputs. Each manager maximizes his performance index and the coordinator divides the budget. This is the standard case in Welfare Economics. Now suppose $y = g(v^2, x)$. This is an interaction between outputs. Then, assuming F, f, and g are concave and differentiable, the over-all maximum will be defined by conditions of the form

$$\frac{\partial F}{\partial y} \frac{\partial g(v^2, x)}{\partial v^2} - \lambda p \leqq 0 \quad \text{and} \quad \left[\frac{\partial F}{\partial x} + \frac{\partial F}{\partial y} \frac{\partial g(v^2, x)}{\partial x}\right] \frac{\partial f}{\partial v^1} - \lambda p \leqq 0.$$

The y manager who controls v^2 can satisfy the first set of conditions if he maximizes independently and knows x. The x manager does not need to know y, but the coordinator must know $\dfrac{\partial g(v^2, x)}{\partial x}$ and, therefore, in general (though not always), v^2 and g, in order to determine the optimum budget division. Finally, suppose $y = g(v^1, v^2)$. This is an interaction involving inputs. Now, under the same assumptions, the over-all optimum will be defined by conditions of the form

$$\frac{\partial F}{\partial y} \frac{\partial g(v^1, v^2)}{\partial v^2} - \lambda p \leqq 0 \quad \text{and} \quad \frac{\partial F}{\partial x} \frac{\partial f(v^1)}{\partial v^1} + \frac{\partial F}{\partial y} \frac{\partial g(v^1, v^2)}{\partial v^1} - \lambda p \leqq 0.$$

The y manager can proceed to maximize y independently, though he must know v^1 to do so, and this will be consistent with an over-all optimum. But the x manager must take into consideration the effects of v^1 on y if his allocation is to be consistent with an over-all optimum. To do this, he must know $F(x, y)$, $g(v^1, v^2)$, v^2, and of course $f(v^1)$, i.e., he must know all the elements of the problem.

We discuss decentralization in terms of setting budgets instead of prices for output

Moreover, the above illustrations are rather simple cases. It is not difficult to imagine or to find cases which combine both kinds of interaction and which are complicated further by multiple criteria of performance.

What can be done to offset or to remove complicating interactions? It is important to remember that their existence and strength is a function of the way in which the larger problem is factored into subproblems. For example, the trouble with factoring the budget for central war into subbudgets for equipment, personnel, and installations is that the interactions between these categories are particularly strong and involve inputs. The advantage of factoring the problem into offense and defense, and then into the different offensive weapon systems, area defense and local defense, and warning, is that the resulting interactions are weaker and are more between outputs, though interactions involving inputs remain. In general, an important objective in the decomposition of large allocation problems should be to minimize the remaining interactions and to restrict them wherever possible, to those between outputs.

D. THE SIGNIFICANCE OF GAME ASPECTS

As well as the multiplicity of criteria and the problem of finding subdivisions sufficiently free of direct interactions, the strategic or game aspects of most defense problems complicate the task of constructing a set of orderings and subproblems. Game aspects enter at every level. The balance which we select between offense and defense should depend on the balance which our opponent selects, and the kind of offensive and defensive forces which we choose must depend upon his. Our allocation between ballistic missiles and bombers depends on the level of, and balance between, his active and passive defenses. The design of our bomber systems should be influenced by the offensive and defensive choices of our opponent. We can trade, in the design of our bomber systems, between vulnerability in the air to his defenses and vulnerability on the ground to his offense. The extent to which we should shelter and disperse our bombers depends on the characteristics of his

---

because, as a general matter, defense outputs are only ordinally measurable. Cardinal numbers are used, of course, but their significance is generally largely ordinal.

In principle, the coordinator could find the optimum, with independent maximization of x and y, without knowing f and g, by an infinite number of experiments at setting subbudgets and taxes and subsidies on input use and evaluating the resulting value of F. But such a possibility has little practical significance.

offensive vehicles. Even at the level of design of the electronic system for the bomber, an important game is involved. In fact, the electronic countermeasure and counter-countermeasure game bears a striking resemblance to the two-person, constant-sum game.

The reason that game aspects complicate the task of structuring defense allocation into a hierarchy of criteria and independent subproblems is not that *we* have a broad range of alternatives available for countering his strategy, for we would have this even if he were fixed in his choices, but rather that *he* has a list of possible alternative strategies which includes the possibility of countering our moves in very indirect ways. This gives rise to a kind of interaction which would not occur if he were fixed in his choices. If we should improve our air defense radars to the point where he is unable to blind them with electronic countermeasures, he may look for such broader alternatives as using decoys or other penetration aids, or equipping his bombers with air-to-surface missiles; or he may try to increase the numbers of bombers which he can deliver by reducing their vulnerability on their own bases, by sheltering and dispersing them; or he may choose to increase his missile force at the expense of bombers; or he may attempt to reduce the need for strategic bombing capacity by improving his ability to respond to challenges in other ways. A conceivable response to a reverse in the electronic counter-measure game is an improved civil defense program. And the significant point is that each of these responses to our improved radars reduce our capability in some other, possibly remote, area.

E. THE POWER AND LIMITS OF ANALYSIS

But these difficulties should not be allowed to obscure the fact that there are many important cases in which it is useful to optimize with respect to one criterion, in which the criterion is definable with some vital interactions and game aspects embodied in it and others consequently able to be ignored, so that it is possible to use the standard economic model of efficient allocation, or, to use an expression of C. J. Hitch, to "suboptimize."[44] Often it is possible to factor a larger problem so that a subproblem naturally meets these conditions. In some cases in which there are multiple criteria, one

[44] See C. J. Hitch, "Suboptimization in Operations Problems," *Journal of the Operations Research Society of America*, May 1953, pp. 87–99; also "An Appreciation of Systems Analysis," *Operations Research*, November 1955, pp. 466–81. By the standard economic model of efficient allocation we of course mean maximization of a quasi-concave ordinal function of variables constrained to lie within a convex region.

criterion may dominate, in the sense that what is optimal from one point of view is optimal from other points of view also, or one criterion may be sufficiently important relative to the others that it is useful to optimize system design on the basis of that criterion and then to make marginal adjustments to allow for the others. We would judge the latter often to be the case with strategic offensive systems, for example. There, the deterrent mission is sufficiently important that an optimum design from the point of view of deterrence is likely to serve as a good first approximation to an over-all optimum. And sometimes it is also possible to neglect interactions and game aspects in arriving at a good first approximation to an over-all optimum.

Some problems which otherwise meet the requirements for sub-optimization are complicated by increasing returns. However, this is generally not an important qualification, affecting as it does only the computational procedures. Moreover, the increasing returns can often be turned into decreasing returns by applying a higher level criterion.[45] For example, the usual models of bomber penetration of enemy defenses which are based in large part on saturation phenomena indicate that there are increasing returns to scale in penetration. Physical target damage displays strong diminishing returns, however, so that the over-all relationship between bombers attempting to penetrate defenses and the damage they achieve is likely to exhibit diminishing marginal returns.[46]

We wish to emphasize the importance of a constructive approach as opposed to an analytical approach. What is at once the most fruitful and the most difficult part of the study of defense policy is the factoring out of meaningful subproblems, the construction of partial orderings in terms of relevant criteria, and the design of alternative solutions. Next comes the analytical part, the problem of relating alternative means of achievement as measured by the criteria. When this is done, the remaining computation is often trivial, or at least the easiest part of the problem. Most of the current literature on military operations research quite incorrectly gives the opposite impression.

[45] See Malcolm W. Hoag, "Some Complexities in Military Planning," The RAND Corporation, Paper P-1531, *World Politics*, July 1959, pp. 553–76.

[46] This example is used by Hoag, *ibid.* For a still higher level criterion increasing returns may reappear. For example, over a considerable range the increasing marginal disutility to the enemy of having his remaining cities and military installations destroyed may increase our deterrent power at an increasing rate.

What are the limits to this approach? Can we structure the whole defense establishment in terms of a hierarchy of criteria and semi-independent subproblems? While this would be desirable, it is not essential if we are looking for improvements instead of for that elusive grand optimum. Because of the rapidity of change and the inherent difficulty of the problems, it will be possible to make improvements as long as we can factor out and define meaningful sub-problems. As we work toward greater levels of generality, the criteria become less definable and more uncertain. Political and sociological effects become more important and their relevance becomes harder to escape.[47] What is the optimum balance between threats of strategic bombing and a readiness to commit conventional ground and air forces in deterring a communist invasion in Southeast Asia? A host of intangibles and uncertainties enter into the problem. As we work toward greater levels of generality, the range of alternatives increases, and the number of different possible choices which we can make is multiplied by the number of strategies which the opponent can pursue. Even at the highest levels, however, analysis can be fruitful in providing insight and in narrowing the range of un-certainty. Moreover, as the level of generality increases, the importance of the problems increases and with it the potential gains from analysis. With or without criteria or analysis, high-level decisions are made every day. This fact should help to offset the modesty that must be inspired by the difficulty of the problems.

4. Some Suggestions for Improving Defense Organization

If anything should be clear in the complicated and ever-changing business of defense, it is that there is no panacea. Unification of the Services and elimination of interservice rivalry will not solve the problem of poor allocation. Nor will it be solved by the establishment of unified commands, by the institution of an improved budgetary process, or by reduction in the rate of turnover of managerial personnel, although these measures would help a great deal. It is unfortunate that so much of the discussion of defense organization has been in the language of total solutions, as this has, to some extent, diverted attention from the more important quest for improvements. Unified commands, output oriented budgets and many other proposals can lead to a better defense system; the standard by which

[47] See, for example, C. J. Hitch, "Operations Research and National Planning—A Dissent," *Operations Research*, October 1957, pp. 718–23.

408

they should be evaluated should be the ability to ameliorate rather than to solve the problems.

A. BUDGETING FOR MISSIONS AND WEAPON SYSTEMS

For much of the defense organization, the right kind of question is "how to allocate a given part of the budget in order to maximize an appropriate set of outputs." What are the general implications of this for the defense organization and budget structure? There are several. First, one basic conceptual framework brought to bear on the problem should be centered around the notion of a constrained maximum. Alternative defense budgets might be possible in the future, but at any point in time a given set of resources has been allocated. The problem should be to use those resources so as to maximize a relevant set of measures of output or military worth. This sounds so obvious that it appears to be trite. But as we have pointed out earlier, this basic idea is not a part of the approach brought to defense policy by many people.

Perhaps the most important step that must be taken in order to bring about this needed change in concepts is to identify outputs independently of inputs. Military objectives at all levels should be made explicit and, to the extent that it is possible, relevant standards of performance which relate weapons to objectives should be developed. Then different weapon systems can be considered for the various missions. For example, discussions of the operation of our existing bomber force or of plans to buy more bombers should be focused on precisely what job these bombers are intended to accomplish. The justification for buying more bombers should not be merely that it gives us more bombers, or that more bombers are needed for the defense of the United States, but rather that more bombers will contribute in a measurable way to the objectives for which we maintain strategic offensive forces, and that they will contribute more to our attainment of those objectives than, say, the extra missiles that could be bought and operated for a comparable amount of money. We discussed earlier the question of criteria for strategic offensive forces, and we observed that, among other things, we maintain strategic offensive forces in order to deter attack on ourselves and our allies, to limit damage to ourselves should war occur, and to enable us to terminate all-out war on acceptable terms. Strategic offense may be a relatively favorable case from this point of view, but these objectives do admit of some useful quantification and of sensible discussion with people who are not military experts. In general, the criteria upon which the allocation of the defense budget is based should be discussed, distinguished from other criteria that might appear to be sensible, and the choice defended. The general problem of criteria for defense allocation certainly cannot be solved by methodology or by procedure alone, but we are convinced that explicit discussion of this problem would help a great deal.

Along with the identifying of outputs or kinds of defense effectiveness, a major contribution to the decision-making process would be made if programing and budgeting were to be made to correspond to output categories. In fact, most of the defense budget, except for research and development and overheads, should be identified with combat commands which are organized around purposes or missions. There should be budgets for general-war and limited-war forces; within the former, for example, there should be strategic offense and continental air defense. Within output subcategories, the basic input units should be weapon systems rather than the traditional equipment, personnel, installations, etc.[48] (Weapon-system budgets, of course, can be broken down into the traditional categories.) In any case, weapon-system cost accounting has proven to be essential.[49] In the absence of information about all the major costs of weapon systems such as the costs of maintenance and operation as well as the procurement cost, an intelligent decision as to whether to procure another aircraft carrier, for example, can only be made as the result of blind luck. While the existence of multiple-purpose weapon systems will provide some inevitable exceptions, it should be possible to fit into this scheme almost all of our military forces. This means a primary budget division by purposes and weapon systems rather than, for example, a budget for the Army which is then broken down into procurement of equipment, installations, and personnel categories, because these are not spanned by any reasonable set of identifiable criteria which correspond to identifiable outputs. The equipment, personnel, installations breakdown should be regarded as secondary in importance. Along with it, congressional consideration of military appropriations which is now only on the

---

[48] See Roland N. McKean, "Evaluating Alternative Expenditure Programs," *op.cit.*
[49] See David Novick, *Efficiency and Economy in Government Through New Budgeting and Accounting Procedures*, The RAND Corporation, Report R-254, February 1, 1954. Also, "Weapon System Cost Analysis," The RAND Corporation, Paper P-794, February 24, 1956.

personnel, equipment, and installation lines should be replaced by consideration of choices between different kinds of military objectives, by broad classes of capabilities to achieve these objectives, and by different levels of alternative weapons systems.

In the absence of such output oriented programs and budgets, it is difficult for defense officials or congressmen to know how much we are spending for example, on all limited war capabilities; within this category, on tactical air power, at the next lower level on tactical missile systems, etc. These basic quantities should be well known to anyone with an over-all responsibility for defense matters.[50]

This change, which is intended to produce a closer correspondence between missions and budget categories, should work in both directions; that is, there should be a purpose or related set of purposes for each subbudget and a subbudget for each related set of purposes. If each subbudget corresponds to a set of objectives, relevant criteria can be constructed which will span a wider range of competing alternatives. For example, the Navy's ship-building budget now includes funds for minesweepers and for submarines designed to carry Polaris; the Air Force's major aircraft procurement budget includes funds for bombers and fighters. It would be better if the Navy were to have, for example, a subbudget for the Polaris *weapon system*, including not only the submarines but also the missiles, manpower, tenders, special port facilities, etc. The number of Polaris submarines should not be considered as an alternative to more minesweepers and carriers; Polaris should compete directly in the same budget with the ICBM, the land-based IRBM, and manned bombers.

Independently of these changes in budget procedure, the possibilities for improved allocations could be increased considerably if alternative allocations, in the large, of the same total budget, were constructed and tested. Also it would be desirable if budget preparation were closer in time to budget execution. The time required to prepare one budget is now very long, being of the order of two and a half years. This is largely attributable to the vast detail included in the budget, detail which can only serve to create a false impression of accuracy. The Defense Department should follow Professor

---

[50] Even with present budget procedures it would be possible to do cost accounting by output category. There are, of course, many uses for such a cost breakdown apart from the budgetary process.

Smithies' suggestion and adopt planning factors (statistical average cost estimates) for preparation of the whole budget, rather than the detailed accounting procedures now used.[51] This would occasion no loss of significant information and it would shorten and simplify the budgetary process, thus freeing resources which might be used more profitably elsewhere.

With the budget structured in the manner suggested, it should be easier for "high-level" decisions to be made at "high levels" and "low-level" decisions to be made at "low levels." The desirability of this should be fairly obvious. At a high level, decision-makers can take into account a broader range of alternatives, and they can test the performance of alternative combinations of the systems under their purview against more general criteria.

Finally, somehow, a partial separation between the questions of budget level and allocation must be found, so that the extent to which this year's allocation can be used as an instrument to increase next year's budget can be reduced, and so that the problem of efficient allocation within a given budget will be faced directly. This will not be easy, and we do not wish to suggest that we think we have found a solution. For one thing, budget level and allocation are related intimately; the best budget level for any activity does depend upon the efficiency of allocation within that budget, and the allocation depends on the budget level. Moreover, budget levels must be decided upon somehow, and it is only natural that any agency should be represented in the process by which its budget is determined, since it knows best how the money would be used and what it would accomplish. But if an agency can bargain for more budget, it cannot be expected to act on the assumption that what it does has nothing to do with how much it receives. Doubtless, whatever is done to improve upon the existing situation will be imperfect. However, an interesting possibility, and one which illustrates the kind of idea which deserves some consideration, would be to require the commands and Services to prepare plans and budgets and to present each year, as a part of their budget submission, a five-year program based on a projection of the current budget, showing proposed expenditure year by year for the period. Such a budget would reveal the implications of current decisions for future expenditure. It would show, for example, the operating costs that will be incurred in the future if a new weapon system is procured this year. It would not be necessary

[51] Arthur Smithies, *op. cit.*, Ch. XI.

that the budget for each of the five years be equal to the budget this year. For example, an agency might quite sensibly propose a large investment in the first year or two which would lead to savings later on. The point of the procedure would be to force into the open the implicit assumptions made about future expenditure and thus make them the objects of bargaining and control. Guidelines might be used which specify five-year totals and amounts of substitution permissible between years. The preparation of budgets of this nature would not be much of an extra burden if statistical cost factors (e.g., the average annual cost of operating a destroyer) were used instead of very detailed estimates. Moreover, the Services and commands already do have programs extending several years into the future. Furthermore, budgets are prepared in terms of new obligational authority required for the coming fiscal year, and not planned expenditures, and these requests involve projections over several future years anyway.

B. DECENTRALIZATION THROUGH THE USE
OF BUDGETS AND PRICES

In order to reduce the volume of detailed decisions which are made centrally in the Department of Defense, consideration should be given to the idea of decentralizing much of the decision making by the granting of some spending authority to subordinate commands. We do *not* mean that these commands should be given complete authority over the spending of their budgets. As we pointed out earlier, the choices made with respect to one activity often affect strongly the level of performance of other activities. And many decisions with respect to the combat commands so directly affect the security of the country that they should not be delegated. However, it does appear that extensive spending authority should be given to the operating commands for the *current operation* of their forces and, in fact, this authority might be delegated within the commands to units as small as an air wing or a naval squadron or to still smaller units. For the most part, our military forces in peacetime engage in training activities and have outputs which are fairly specific and quantifiable. Moreover, the operation of many single units is a large one by standards of industry, often involving tens of millions of dollars annually.

In order for this spending authority to have any useful effect, it would be necessary to eliminate or modify many of the programs sent down from higher headquarters that deal not with questions of *what* performance is expected of subordinate units but precisely *how*, in detail, the activities of subordinate units shall be carried on in order to attain these objectives. We believe, in general, that it is possible to set up measurable standards of performance for the current operation of subordinate units. Given these standards, unit commanders should have considerable freedom in deciding how to allocate their resources to meet the standards their superiors have set. For example, in the case of a bomber wing, the measurement of performance might include the combat readiness of bombers, the alertness of crews, and navigation and bombing skills as shown in bombing competitions, and the wing's safety record. Since such measures of performance of subordinate units must be assessed by higher commanders in any case, this would impose no additional burdens upon them, while higher staff levels would be partly relieved of the task of directing in voluminous detail such a vast organization.

In addition to having spending authority over operating budgets, limited authority over capital expenditures should be granted to operating commands. Perhaps a quite small percentage (say 5 per cent) of their capital budgets might be left to the discretion of these commands, for example, for the procurement of auxiliary equipment, for additional construction, or for additional research and development. The major part of the capital budget of combat commands should remain under the authority of those agencies which must take account of higher level criteria, including the important interactions we have discussed.

Out of their operating budgets, the combat commands should have to pay (in the sense of giving up something to get them, or getting something else for giving them up) for a broad class of supporting services. The principal source of funds for such activities as supply, depot maintenance, procurement, training, transportation, and medical services should come from the commands that use these services. No longer should most of these services be either free or of infinite cost (i.e., not available at all). Moreover, the using commands should have to pay not only for the direct cost of the supporting services consumed in peacetime but probably also for the capital cost of any excess capacity held in readiness for an emergency.[52]

[52] The problem of charging using commands for capacity is somewhat complicated by the fact that extra capacity may be used by different commands in different sorts of emergency. Airlift capacity might be claimed more by ground forces in one situation and by tactical air in another.

C. THE DEFENSE REORGANIZATION OF 1958

The main objectives of the President's proposal and the modified Department of Defense Reorganization Act of 1958 passed by the Congress were to facilitate the establishment of a system of unified commands and to promote more unified strategic planning, and to eliminate "harmful" interservice rivalry, especially in research and development, by strengthening the authority of the Secretary of Defense. We have commented on the second objective. What about the first one? The unified command idea has a great deal of merit. Unified commands (e.g., Strategic Air Command, North American Air Defense Command) are organized around missions. The choices that must be made in designing a force for a unified command are the kind that can be governed by a related set of criteria. These are the output oriented organizations we are seeking. They can concentrate attention on finding efficient ways of doing a relatively well-defined job. A well-designed unified command structure may, for example, be able to coordinate better the planning between the ground forces and tactical air forces meant to support them, and between the ground forces and their air-lift. The unified commands have another advantage also. It has been observed frequently enough that changes in technology have outmoded the traditional lines of separation between the Services. As circumstances and technology change, it is reasonable to expect that the present unified command structure will also become outmoded. Other missions and groups of missions will replace them. In these circumstances, the unified command system is much more flexible than the roles and missions of the separate Services. Unified commands are the creatures of the Secretary of Defense. They can be changed at his discretion without new legislation.

We have argued both for the retention of the separate Services as organizations with a good deal of autonomy able to pursue, within broad limits, improvements in their capability that will further both service and national interests in the long run, and for the unified commands which cut across service lines. In fact, we have argued that the power of the unified commands should be increased by giving them some budget authority. In effect, we believe in a mixed system which has both. In some respects, the 1958 Reorganization Act has moved the defense organization in this direction. It leaves the Department of Defense divided into an output or demand side and an input or supply side. The Joint Chiefs of Staff and the unified commands represent the output side, the military missions. The separate Services supply the forces and weapon systems used by the commands. We believe that this kind of division has a great deal of merit, and that a mixed system which contains both unified commands and the traditional Services should be able to capture the advantages both of output oriented organizations seeking to accomplish definable missions and of competing separate services looking for ways of expanding their usefulness.

Of course, it is not surprising that this may create some problems. For example, the personal loyalties of officers to their separate services may conflict with joint planning at the unified command level. The competitive attitude which is appropriate in research and development is likely to be quite inappropriate for officers in unified commands whose job is to select a combination of weapon systems generally from more than one service. The purpose of the unified commands will be defeated if their planning staffs become interservice battle grounds. This problem is intensified by the fact that an officer's career is still in his own Service. The two ideas put forward by the President to ameliorate this—the ability of officers to transfer between Services and the making of promotion beyond the level of major general dependent on the Secretary of Defense— should help, but they are likely to leave a good deal of room for improvement.

The reorganization leaves budgeting and appropriations by Services rather than by commands, and this has the disadvantage that it leaves the commands without budget constraints within which they must do their planning. In fact, the change may have widened still further the gulf between planning and budgeting (or effectiveness and cost). "The unified commander submits his forces and his requirements to the Joint Chiefs of Staff,"[53] but there is no provision

[53] The budgetary procedure was described by General Twining in testimony before the House Armed Services Committee as follows:

Mr. Blanford. All right. Tell me who will submit the budgets for the forces assigned to unified commands?

General Twining. The Services actually put in their own budgets to supply their forces and whatever they need to carry out the unified commander's plan. The unified commander assembles his components. The unified commander submits his forces and his requirements to the Joint Chiefs of Staff.

If that is approved, then each Service gets the money to carry out its own part of the mission, just like it does now.

The Chairman. Let the committee understand whether the Service, as they do today,

so that he can and must trade forces on an equal budget basis. Nor is there provision that the separate Services, which will continue to present their own budgets, will support adequately the over-all mission-orientation of the commands.

There are several ways in which budgets could be introduced for the unified commands. For example, the Department of Defense could begin the budgetary process with guidelines sent to the Services for them to budget for those of their activities which are not in unified commands. In such a process, the forces requested of the Services by the unified commands would have to fit into the command budgets. Appropriations might be to a mixture of Services and commands, or entirely to the Services. There is especial value in appropriating funds to the separate Services for research and development so that they can develop new weapons, doctrine, and tactics and do long-run planning. The commands are too busy with recurring day-to-day crises to give adequate consideration to the future beyond the procurement of weapon systems already developed. In any case, Congress doubtless will want to see the breakdown of the defense budget by Services and it will want to be able to appropriate in such a way that the existence of the Services is preserved. Clearly, the best balance between the Services and the commands will be difficult to ascertain. There is no particular reason why the balance needs to be the same for each combat mission and for each service supporting function. However, with ingenuity, it ought to be possible to construct a mixed system which can reconcile these conflicting aims in such a way as to be a distinct improvement over the existing arrangement.

---

makes the request for the money, or the Joint Chiefs of Staff takes into consideration their unified commands?

General Twining. The Services will do all the budgeting, but their over-all plan is approved by the Chiefs of Staff. I am talking about the magnitude of them. But the Services do it.

Mr. Blanford. Then it is clear that it is the intent of this proposal that the budget requests for unified commands will go through the military Secretaries, that they in turn will support that budget request before the Appropriations Committees of the Congress?

General Twining. That is correct. That is my understanding.

Reorganization of the Department of Defense, Hearings Before the Committee on Armed Services, House of Representatives, 1958, p. 6,261.

COMMENT

ARTHUR SMITHIES, Harvard University

This paper is a clear demonstration of the fact that the economist has an essential role to play in deciding questions of administration and organization. Readers of the paper, including economists, may feel utterly bewildered by the complexity of the problems involved. But no one can deny that the questions raised by the authors are of central relevance, or that any discipline other than economics can provide the answers. Yet economists do not customarily find themselves members of committees to reorganize the Defense Department. Part of the reason is that, until recently, the economics profession has considered such matters beyond or beneath the range of their interests. Another point is that noneconomists fail to realize that an essential part of administration is to make rational choices among alternatives, subject to budget constraints.

I am afraid, however, that our authors have not provided us with a blueprint for the organization of the Department of Defense. Rather, they have produced an essay on the principles of decision-making that every defense official should read and consider. Perhaps that is the most important thing. Although they assert that the problem is one of organization rather than personnel, the quality of decision-making might be greatly improved if everyone, from the Secretary down, could take a graduate course at The RAND Corporation. As it is, reorganization plans seem to assume that Secretaries spring fully armed from the head of Jupiter. Since they do not, they should at least be provided with civilian and military staffs who are well-educated in the process of decision-making.

I should now like to turn to some practical difficulties that still leave me very perplexed.

1. The paper properly criticizes present procedures for concentrating on military inputs: personnel, procurement, maintenance, and operations; and proposes that the emphasis should be placed on outputs such as missions and weapons systems. But this is easier said than done.

The forces required to perform a mission are extremely hard to determine with precision. Perhaps the easiest problem is strategic deterrence of general war. The various components of a deterrent system are well known and the objective is clearly defined. But even here the problem defies quantification. Many of the differences of opinion concerning the adequacy of the strategic force relate not to technical factors but to differences of opinion concerning the attitude of the enemy. What damage to his own territory would he regard as an acceptable price to pay for his objective? And what degree of certainty does he require that his losses will be held to the acceptable level?

When one considers limited war missions, difficulties increase. What is our mission in Southeast Asia; and what forces, in the hands of ourselves or our allies, are required to perform it with some reasonable likelihood of success? What are our requirements for mobile support forces when war can break out at any one of a number of places, or a number of them at once? Is economic aid in any sense a substitute for military aid? To what extent does our strategic deterrent deter limited attack? I have recently had occasion to consider our military problem in Asia, and have found that rational processes do not seem to yield conclusive answers. But this does not mean that the traditional emphasis on inputs is the way out of the difficulty. I am merely suggesting that whatever budgetary system is employed, there will be ample scope for the exercise of judgment and intuition.

2. The new reorganization of the Defense Department emphasizes outputs through the unified commands and inputs through the existing services, which now become supply organizations. Budgeting, however, is left with the services. This may tend to perpetuate the existing system of decision-making—despite the reorganization. On the other hand, to transfer budgeting to the unified commands would probably mean that consideration of feasibility would be unduly neglected. Interestingly enough, the problem thus posed does not seem to have received any consideration when the new arrangements were made.

Perhaps the correct answer is that budgeting must be a highly centralized operation conducted by a staff, in the office of the Secretary, which will take due account of mission requirements and supply considerations. The Defense Comptroller would be an adjunct of such a staff, rather than a high authority on strategic matters.

3. The paper does not tell us how to deal with the question of allocation between the present and the future. How much of our current resources do we put into immediate strength and how much

to strength in the next decade? How much do we spend on weapons systems that we know will be obsolete in a few years? Should we take increased risks at the present time in order to allocate more resources for research and development? How should the research and development program itself be devised with due regard for the great uncertainties of the future? I cannot think of any answer except to say that decision-making should rest in the hands of officials who are prepared to pose and answer the right questions—even though the answers must rest heavily on their own judgment.

4. Finally, the paper is confined to decision-making within a given budgetary constraint. It does not deal with how the constraint itself is determined. It correctly deplores the notions of obsolete requirements on the one hand or budget ceilings on the other, but does not present an alternative. How is the President or the Congress to decide whether the defense budget should be $30 billion, $40 billion, or $50 billion? Is there any practical alternative to the adversary procedure in which the Secretary of the Treasury says that the economy cannot stand more than x billions, while the military authorities assert that the country cannot be defended for less than y billions? Can the President feasibly present anything other than a single-figure recommendation to the Congress?

One obvious answer is that budgets should be submitted in the form of alternatives. The President should have an opportunity to consider the implications of $30, $40, and $50 billion budgets and to achieve his own balancing between security risks and domestic costs. But this suggestion ignores the fact that within the Defense Department the budget results from competition among unified commands or services and that outside it defense has to compete with agriculture, public works, veterans and the taxpayer. Since the future of the country is not to be ordained by an all-wise rational being, the budgetary process must contain a strong bargaining element. But this does not mean that processes of rational choice must be discarded.

I come back to an earlier point. I believe the kind of work Enthoven and Rowen are doing is invaluable. It may lead to significant changes in organization and formal procedures. But its main contribution may be in the education of the people who have to make something like the present system work.

User Prices *vs.* Taxes

O. H. BROWNLEE

UNIVERSITY OF MINNESOTA

I INTERPRET my assignment to be to indicate very generally the role of rationing governmental services by the price mechanism and of financing the provision of such goods and services at least partially from "sales receipts" rather than rationing these services according to criteria other than price and financing their provision from general revenue sources.

In cases in which the price mechanism can be employed, it is possible to assure that no one pays for services that he does not consider to be worth the price *and* that anyone can obtain service providing that he is willing to pay the cost. At least some of the ambiguity in statements about our "needs" for public services can be eliminated.

Although I favor using price as a rationing device wherever a reasonable opportunity exists, I believe that the appropriate area for application of market pricing to the determination of how much of various goods and services government should produce is a relatively small one. Opportunities undoubtedly exist for financing such items as fire and police protection partially on the basis of service actually rendered. Nevertheless, such cases would be relatively insignificant in terms of the over-all pattern of public expenditure. I see few *major* services that ought to be financed exclusively from sales revenue that are not already being financed in this way. However, the criteria currently used for establishing prices and for determining how much to produce are not necessarily the best ones. Furthermore, charges at less than cost might well be established for some services that are now provided free.

My criteria for evaluating whether a service is being rationed appropriately and whether the amount produced is optimal do not include the effects upon the distribution of income. If agreement could be reached with respect to how various income distributions should be ordered, the best one could be achieved independently of the production pattern of government services.

1.

A virtue of rationing services by the price mechanism is that such a procedure permits obtaining information regarding how users value these services relative to other things that they might obtain. Together with appropriate cost information, such demand data would permit one to determine whether too little or too much of a service was being produced. For services which have no external economies or diseconomies in consumption or production, i.e., the consumption level of one person does not enter directly as a variable in the utility functions of other persons and the production level does not affect the physical productivities of resources in other uses, setting the price equal to marginal production cost and noting whether there is excess demand or excess supply can, under certain conditions, tell one whether too little or too much is being produced—provided, of course, that the optimal level of output is not zero. If there are external economies or diseconomies in production or consumption, services still might be allocated by the price mechanism, but the optimal amount to produce would not be that at which price is equal to marginal cost.

The validity of these assertions and the conditions which must prevail in order for them to be used as the basis for good rules to guide resource allocation are well known. I will not reproduce the "proofs" here. Instead let me try to indicate their applicability to determining which services should be "priced" and how the resulting pattern might compare with the existing one.

2.

Among the goods and services that should not be priced are those currently labeled by economists as "public" or "community" goods, i.e., those which can be consumed by one person without a reduction in the quantities available to others.[1] "Voluntary" contributions for the support of such activities will not necessarily be sufficient to obtain the best amounts of them, since there seems to be no reasonable way of inducing persons to reveal their true preferences

[1] Paul A. Samuelson, "The Pure Theory of Public Expenditures," *The Review of Economics and Statistics*, November 1954, pp. 387–9; Stephen Enke, "More on the Misuse of Mathematics in Economics: Rejoinder," *ibid.*, May 1955, pp. 131–3; Julius Margolis, "A Comment on the Pure Theory of Public Expenditure," *ibid.*, November 1955, pp. 347–9; Samuelson, "Diagramatic Exposition of a Theory of Public Expenditure," *ibid.*, November 1955, pp. 350–6; Samuelson, "Aspects of Public Expenditure Theories," *ibid.*, November 1958, pp. 332–8.

for such goods relative to others. Although there is no unanimity with respect to which services fall in this class, expenditures for defense and associated activities fit this classification and bulk large in the over-all expenditure pattern.

At the other pole is the class of services produced under conditions of constant or increasing marginal production cost and of a character such that there are neither external economies nor diseconomies of production or consumption associated with them. These should be rationed by price (or a mechanism comparable to the price mechanism), and the output at which the market clears when price is equal to marginal cost is the appropriate one to produce. For the most part, such services are not produced by government except in cases where the cost of collecting from users in accordance with quantities used is high relative to production costs. However, there is no inherent reason why government should not produce such goods providing that it attaches appropriate values to the resources that are used in production, allows for the restrictions that it imposes upon private producers in determining costs *and* does not cover losses from general tax revenues. That one or more of these conditions would be violated is not unlikely.

In between these two extremes are those services which have external economies in consumption and/or decreasing marginal production costs leading inherently to monopoly. Those with pronounced external economies in consumption generally have been produced by government; those with obvious increasing returns generally have been subject to regulation.

3.

A detailed description of governmental services which can be classified accurately according to the three categories suggested— "public goods," services with pronounced external economies in consumption and/or production, and services which should be priced at marginal cost—is not readily available. However, a cursory examination of aggregate data suggests the following somewhat crude allocation of some of the major service categories: (Table 1, on following page.)

The above classification is somewhat arbitrary and does not reveal the things that are of interest in determining whether services are being produced in appropriate quantities. Although it is a picture for only one short period of time, this picture is not an atypical one.

TABLE 1

Categories of Government Service[a]

	Expenditure	"Sales Receipts"
	(billions of dollars)	
A. "Public goods"		
1. Federal government		
a. General government	1.7	
b. National defense, including atomic energy, USIS, mutual security, State Department, and research and development	48.6	
c. Health, hospitals and medical (largely veterans)	2.4	
2. State and local governments		
a. General control	1.7	
b. Public safety[b]		
(I) Police	1.5	
(II) Fire	0.8	
c. Health, hospitals and welfare		
(I) Welfare	3.4	
(II) Hospitals[b]	3.2	
B. Services with pronounced external economies		
1. State and local governments		
a. Elementary and secondary Education	11.9	
b. Sanitation		
(I) Sewage	0.9	
(II) Other sanitation	0.5	
C. Saleable services		
1. Federal government		
a. Postal service	4.1	4.0
b. General aids to business	0.2	
c. Higher education	0.45[c]	
d. Highways		1.0
2. State and local governments		
a. Higher education	1.5	0.4
b. Highways	7.8[d]	4.0[e]
c. Public utilities	3.5	2.9
d. Liquor stores	0.9	1.1

[a] Data for the federal government are for 1960, and are from Executive Office of the President, *The Federal Budget in Brief*, Fiscal year 1960. Those for state and local governments are for 1957 and are from *State and Local Government Finance in 1957*, Bureau of the Census, February, 1957.

[b] Police and fire protection as well as hospitals contain a component that is clearly not in the category of "public goods." However, I prefer to err on the side of making the category of saleable goods too small rather than too large.

[c] Included in state and local expenditure and should not be counted separately.

[d] Includes some capital expenditures that should not be charged exclusively to current services.

[e] Estimated. 1955 fuels taxes and auto, truck, and bus registration fees were $3.65 billion.

Of particular interest is that (1) there are no "sales receipts" from services that benefit both the users and other parties (i.e., have pronounced external economies in consumption)—although some such receipts probably should be attributed to sanitation—and (2) there is a substantial amount of support from general tax funds for a service that I have classified as one that should be sold at marginal cost—higher education. Included in the expenditures for this service are those for research, so that all of the difference between expenditures and receipts should not be attributed to higher education. Nevertheless, I believe that nearly everyone agrees that tuition receipts at publicly supported institutions of higher education are less than the costs that reasonably could be allocated to the teaching function.

Even though expenditures and receipts are approximately equal for the postal service and may be approximately equal for highway services—if capital expenditures were accurately estimated—it does not follow that these services were produced in the optimal amounts since their prices were somewhat arbitrarily determined and the cost computations probably omitted imputed property taxes and underestimated capital costs.

4.

As I asserted earlier, the fact that a service has external economies associated with its consumption does not imply that it should not be priced. Consider some of the implications of pricing the services of elementary and secondary schools.

Elementary education is a commodity that is believed to have such important effects upon persons other than those who obtain it that it has been made not only free but compulsory. To make persons pay for something which they may not wish to consume generally would not be considered desirable. However, there may be decided advantages to widening the choice of what might be consumed; and there are potential gains from inducing suppliers to minimize the cost of producing whatever they produce. Combining payments to persons conditional upon these payments being spent upon elementary education with institutional arrangements whereby any entrepreneur who meets certain minimum production requirements is qualified as a seller could further both of these objectives.[2]

[2] See Milton Friedman, "The Role of Government in Education," included in Robert A. Solo, ed., *Economics and the Public Interest*, Rutgers University Press, 1956.

Adoption of such a proposal would not answer the question, "Are we spending the correct amount upon education?" but it would provide a more satisfactory answer to the question of whether that which was being made available was being provided at minimum cost.

Services that benefit persons other than the immediate users could be offered to users at a price below marginal cost or a subsidy could be provided to users, as was suggested above in the case of elementary education. The latter procedure appears to me to be preferred in that it permits a greater element of competition among suppliers. Thus rather than directly providing innoculations, medical examinations, etc., the government might give each person a minimum grant conditional upon its being used for such purposes and let the person select his own supplier.

5.

Let me now turn to the potentialities of the pricing mechanism for determining the appropriate production levels for highway services and higher education. The former service is one that many persons contend ought to be priced; the case for pricing the latter is less generally accepted.

In this discussion I shall not consider the problems of city streets. The metropolitan transportation problem is one of congestion together with pronounced external diseconomies in consumption to some urban residents. The purely mechanical problems of charging tolls for the use of the street system along with the space-saving features of mass transport suggest subsidization of bus and subway transportation on a large scale. My concern, however, is with the so-called trunk highways and rural roads.

The benefits from investment in such highways have properties such that a highway investment can be evaluated in the same manner as can any investment designed to produce goods and services that are to be sold. To speak of highway services as if they constituted a single homogeneous commodity is to err in the same way as to speak of food as a single good. I will avoid discussion of how such services should be defined except to assert that some of our difficulties in analyzing highway problems arise from inappropriate definitions of highway service. Traveling a particular distance, at a given speed and with given comfort and safety may be as different—in the mind of the highway user—from traveling this same distance at another speed and with other degrees of comfort and safety as a pound of sirloin steak is from a pound of potatoes. Truck travel differs from auto travel, etc.

Although there are many different kinds of highway services, nearly all of them benefit the highway user—in the case of services provided by passenger car travel—or the benefits are passed on to other persons from whom a collection can be made—through commodity prices, in the case of truck services—in the same way as are the benefits from technological improvement or additional capital used in a farm or factory. In general, highway services are like food in that one person has no interest in another's consumption pattern (except for its effect on prices).[3] The case for distributing highway services and for determining their appropriate levels of output by a price-cost mechanism is as strong as that for any other commodity group.

The statement that the distribution and production of highway services should be guided by price-cost criteria does not mean that we should set up toll stations at every street corner and every cross-road. Because of collection costs and inconveniences that may be more distasteful than congestion, toll roads can play a very limited role in the highway system. However, in principle, one could establish an over-all fee schedule of motor fuel taxes, weight-distance taxes, license fees, and other charges which would yield a rational allocation of whatever road and street facilities were available. And, we could account for costs and revenues so that we could get about the right amount of highway investment and distribute it fairly well geographically. In fact, the structure of charges to highway users already may be fairly reasonable and actually improving, although we are without some of the information required to construct a good fee catalog. The provision of facilities probably is less rational, relatively speaking, than is the fee schedule, although we can only make rough guesses about this from existing data.

Except on toll roads, the basic charge for the passenger auto is

[3] That different degrees of highway congestion are not all equally satisfactory to a highway user might appear to nullify the assertion that one man's consumption is of no concern to other men, and vice versa. However, if we consider travel at one speed, safety, etc., as a different commodity from travel at another speed, safety, etc., there is no contradiction in the formal statement. More congestion is analogous to the higher price for steak that would result from an increase in its demand. The highway user would be indifferent to some higher fee with lower congestion and the low fee with more congestion.

the motor fuels tax.[4] Fuel consumption is an index of distance traveled for any vehicle, although distance traveled and amount of service are not uniquely related as long as highways and speed of travel differ. However, to account for highway quality differences by differences in fuel taxes probably is not feasible. Since passage for the passenger auto is the least costly to provide, the fuel tax can be used as a kind of toll. Special fees for passenger cars may be warranted in large cities where congestion is a problem, such fees being in accordance with the higher costs of providing a given level of service in areas where land values are high. Similarly, special assessments or special license fees for residents of very sparsely settled areas may be advisable. In this case, such fees are in accordance with the high value of the service rendered by the highway.

For trucks and busses, fuel taxes are supplemented by license fees in recognition of the differences in costs imposed by passage of vehicles of different characteristics. However, license fees cannot be varied sufficiently to tax equitably the many different classes of weight and distance combinations. Weight-distance taxes are preferable and could permit different fees for different routes. In fact, weight-distance taxes might be administered in a manner similar to that used in collecting the personal income tax from self-employed persons. Estimates of tax liabilities to be incurred during a year might be filed, and taxes paid on this basis. Differences between actual and estimated liabilities could be settled at the end of the year.

Some of the implications of using price-cost comparisons to a greater extent in making highway decisions are of interest.

1. If prices and costs are appropriately determined, not only the highway system as a whole, but each separate entity should "pay for itself" in an accounting sense when the system is optimal.[5] Otherwise sectors of the system that are "making a profit" and ought to be expanded may be supporting sectors that ought to be contracted. This possibility cannot be detected when only the revenues and costs of the system as a whole are examined.

[4] Data relative to the demand for highway services as well as to the costs of providing them are not adequate for determining what prices to establish. Engineers are undecided as to whether a highway designed to carry heavy axle loads can carry passenger cars at zero marginal maintenance and construction cost. Economists generally would argue that a highway having such characteristics is "overdesigned," i.e., the capital investment is excessive. However, if such a relative cost relationship actually exists and congestion costs are zero, passenger car operators should pay only for the privilege of using the highway—i.e., license fees.

[5] Because of indivisibilities, equality between imputed revenues and imputed costs may not be achievable.

That highway users should pay for the highways has much, though not universal, support. However, that each clearly distinguishable sector should pay for itself is less widely supported—except possibly for toll roads. In particular, it is my belief that generally there has been relative overconstruction of rural nontrunk highways, although this belief can neither be adequately supported nor refuted with existing data.

2. The prices that have to be paid for resources are taken as reliable estimates of the value of the product that has to be sacrificed in order to expand production of one good. Government pays the same prices for labor and materials as do other users. However, it borrows money at more favorable terms (at a lower rate of interest) than does the typical private borrower. This lower interest rate reflects primarily the confidence of the lender in government's ability to repay—not in the relative merits of the projects. Government can tax (or print money, if it is the federal government) to repay loans. Private borrowers must repay out of earnings. If government borrows at, say, 3 per cent, whereas private producers borrow at, say, 6 per cent, and both government and private producers use amounts of capital such that rates of return are equal to borrowing costs, government will be using too much and private producers too little. Shifting capital from the government to the private sector would expand total product. Government also should not invest in projects unless they would yield, say, 6 per cent, if capital is to be allocated in the best manner. Thus, decisions to build highways *and to* make other governmental investments should not be based on the rate at which government can borrow but on the rate of return on capital in other uses.[6]

3. Tax differentials, as well as differentials in costs of borrowing affect the relative prices of governmentally produced goods in comparison with privately produced goods. In the transportation field are special excise taxes affecting some kinds of transport (but not others) that encourage use of the highway system rather than alternative forms of transportation. These taxes ought to be abolished. However, there are also property taxes applying to nearly all private property. I do not consider a complete evaluation of the property tax to be appropriate for this discussion. However, to obtain

[6] See Arnold C. Harberger, "The Interest Rate in Cost-Benefit Analysis," included in *Federal Expenditure Policy for Economic Growth and Stability*, Joint Economic Committee, 85th Cong. 1st sess., 1957, pp. 239–41.

a better distribution of resources among various kinds of transportation, imputed property taxes on highways ought to be considered in arriving at highway costs, just as a "shadow" interest rate equal to the marginal rate of return on capital in private investment rather than the cost of borrowing ought to be employed.

To try to make my last two points clearer, imagine that there are two services—call them "rail transport" and "highway transport"—both of which could be produced at the same constant unit costs, if resource prices were the same to both industries. Assume also that the amount of either service demanded varies inversely with its price and directly with the price of the competing service. With the same interest charges and no taxes, the prices would be identical and certain amounts of each service would be produced. However, if one industry were charged more for capital than was the other and also had to pay taxes proportionate to the volume of service produced, its service would be priced higher than that of the other industry. Less of it and more of the other would be used than would be economic, i.e., than would be the case if "true" costs determined prices.

It should be noted that if the highways were to "pay for themselves" in the sense of yielding revenues equal to costs, including the imputed ones, there would be diversion of highway revenues to the general governmental fund. This diversion would be equal to imputed property taxes plus, say, 2 or 3 per cent of capital outlays—this 2 or 3 per cent being a rough estimate of the differences in borrowing costs to government and private borrowers.

4. Although it is not economically feasible to collect tolls except on a very small percentage of the highway system, tolls can be equitable rationing devices and can permit accurate accounting of the revenues attributable to a particular sector of the highway system. For these reasons, rather than minimizing the number of toll roads, I would employ them wherever feasible. However, certain practices in administering toll roads are not consistent with best use of the highway system. In particular:

a. requiring that toll roads pay for themselves out of tolls is uneconomic. Motor fuels tax receipts also should be credited the toll roads. To do otherwise will result in underutilization of such roads and overutilization of, or overinvestment in, freeways.

b. tolls should be much more flexible than toll authorities have been inclined to make them in the past. Varying tolls with the demand would smooth the traffic flow and could make it approximate more closely that for which the road was designed. Ideally, tolls might fluctuate as do the odds at parimutuel betting booths or stock market quotations. In areas such as Manhattan where access is by tunnel or bridge, tolls to the island certainly should exceed those away from the island during the morning rush hours, and vice versa during the evening hours.

Fluctuations in tolls not only would aid in controlling traffic flows, but also would permit improved estimates of the demand for highway services. Such data are required for determining how much investment to make in highway facilities, and very few of them are available.

The service, higher education, is obtained by consumers because of its impact upon earnings—in which case it can be treated as an investment good—or because the knowledge is desired for its own sake—in which event it can be treated as a consumption good. In either event, I believe that investing in such education is like investing in any other capital asset and that the consumption of higher education by one person does not enter other persons' utility functions.

The statement that one person's consumption of higher education does not enter the utility functions of other persons is an assertion without either adequate proof or disproof. Some persons state flatly that they prefer to live among persons that have attended colleges or universities and that they are willing to pay to increase the number of such persons. Others believe that college trained people make "better citizens" and hence that support from general funds is warranted. This latter contention could be tested by analysis of such items as memberships on civic committees, attitudes on certain public issues where basic value premises are identical, etc. I believe that such analyses would show that, after standardization for such factors as native intelligence and incomes, there are no significant differences between persons with and persons without higher education. However, this belief may be contradictory to fact.

If my belief is correct, state colleges and universities should receive support from general tax sources only for research, tuition should be raised to cover instruction costs, and the terms under which people can borrow to invest in education should be the same as those under which they can borrow to make other kinds of investments. I am not the sole protagonist of this general proposal and it has by now been widely enough voiced so that I need not develop it further.[7]

We have little information about the demand for educational services so that I can not make a good guess about what the pattern would be if such a proposal were put into effect. However, one would expect the distribution of education to be altered somewhat. Persons now attending college but not willing to pay the full costs would not attend; and persons willing to pay the costs but not now able to obtain funds would attend college. Also one would expect the costs of providing a given level of service to be reduced. Most important of all, the question of whether we need more facilities for higher education could be answered more satisfactorily than it can be at the present time.

6.

Allocating government services by pricing them has limited applicability. To me, an appeal of the price mechanism is that it provides information that would permit us to settle some debates about whether an expenditure is too large or too small. The use of prices in guiding how to produce a given level of service is an area that has not been discussed here. It also offers possibilities for improving resource allocation.

COMMENTS

E. CARY BROWN, Massachusetts Institute of Technology

In general, I agree with Mr. Brownlee's view that pricing is of limited applicability in the governmental sector. Practically, what prices should be charged even in the limited areas where they seem feasible is, however, a baffling question.

1. It is difficult to go beyond the general but empty principle that the best use of resources requires that marginal social benefit be equated with or exceed marginal social cost. Discussions of how this principle should be implemented run into trouble. The usual beginning is the view that the pricing system can perform admirably when there are no externalities in production or consumption nor increasing returns to scale in the particular industry in question.

[7] See Milton Friedman, *op.cit.*, for example.

From there on, depending on value judgments about governmental activity, we find assertions about the demand and cost conditions of various commodities that I find unconvincing.

Consider the following statements of Mr. Brownlee:

"In general, highway services are like food in that one person has no interest in another's consumption pattern . . ." (p. 427).

"In either event, I believe . . . that the consumption of higher education by one person does not enter other persons' utility function" (p. 431).

While these views may mirror Mr. Brownlee's tastes, they are unlikely to mirror everyone's. I would be interested in knowing how he reached such a general conclusion.

One piece of evidence I can offer is that other people's consumption of these two commodities does affect *my* utility. The satisfaction I derive from a social system is a function of its quality. In a tightly knit society such as ours, the quality of that society will depend on the education of its members, directly through the kinds of laws it enacts, if in no other way. I have, therefore, a considerably greater interest in other people's consumption of public education, both higher and lower, than I have in their consumption of oats, peas, beans, and barley.

My second assertion is that there may be extraordinarily large external diseconomies from the consumption of highway services that sometimes fail to be reckoned in. Otherwise attractive landscapes have been hideously scarred by roads; ugly strips of gasoline stations, eating joints, and billboards have moved such men as De Voto to crusade against them; hikers, cyclists, and the like have been driven off our streets; our cities are crowded with cars, fumes, and smog, and cluttered with stoplights, parking meters, and road signs; macadam glades bedizen factory and shopping center. Indeed, will the American future be that of a land flattened completely by bulldozers and embedded in a few feet of concrete, thus permitting auto travel by optimal great circle routes? To treat the output of highway services and higher education in the same way as the output of lollypops seems to me remarkable.

2. Some of our sharpest debates in public finance have been over such excise taxes as those on tobacco, an industry that perhaps is characterized by relatively few externalities. What is the best output

for this industry, whether operated privately or publicly? There are an infinite number of excise taxes, both positive and negative, and consequent prices that could be charged to consumers in this situation. Surely, it is not obvious that price equal to marginal private cost would necessarily be best. That depends on the unresolved argument regarding consumer sovereignty. Much of our debate in this sphere is whether or not price is a proper measure of marginal benefit—whether smokers are not just harming themselves.

3. That leads to the next point—the removal from discussion by Mr. Brownlee of distributional considerations in the choice between user prices and taxes. Both from a pedagogic and theoretic point of view, there is much merit in separating distributional from efficiency considerations. Since, in theory, a system of lump-sum taxes and subsidies can distributionally bail out any price configuration, attention can be directed either toward the rationing function or the distributional function of prices. Much can be learned from this instructive exercise, provided the rules of the game are not confused with those of the real world. For here, there simply do not exist nondistorting taxes and transfers that can make appropriate distributional adjustment. Indeed, the feasible political alternatives may be very limited. It is necessary, therefore, to appraise both distributional and efficiency considerations in any realistic political situation. Unfortunately, we must be satisfied with second best. It may be a closer approach to an optimal situation to employ the price system to redistribute income, even though a divergence between marginal rates of transformation and marginal rates of substitution may result, than it would be to make price decisions on the assumption that somehow the proper distribution of income will be achieved by other social policies. We must, therefore, make interpersonal comparison of utilities.

4. Now, suppose we do wish to follow marginal-cost pricing. Mr. Brownlee would have cost computations based not on the interest cost of funds to the government, but instead on the rate of return on capital in alternative uses. He refers approvingly to Harberger's study in this connection. I find myself in general agreement with this view, but do not reach the same policy conclusion as he reaches. He considers, for example, the case in which the government interest cost is 3 per cent and the private rate is 6 per cent. As I understand it, he would charge the 6 per cent rate against government projects, rather than the 3 per cent rate. Yet if, as Brownlee

says, the differential interest cost of 3 per cent is attributable "primarily [to] the confidence of the lender in the government's ability to repay—not on the relative merits [or riskiness] of the projects," should not the 3 per cent rate be used in private projects rather than the other way round?

The government rate presumably reflects the greater pooling of risks, just as in the private sphere we find many different borrowing costs depending on size of firm and its ability to combine risks. In an ideal world would it not be desirable for all investment decisions to be made on the basis of a rate of interest from which was absent a premium for lender's risk? Is it obvious that we would move closer to an optimum by saddling all investment decisions with this premium, rather than taking steps to reduce or eliminate it? True enough, there may be underinvestment in the private sphere because marginal private cost exceeds marginal social cost. But is it clearly incorrect for the government to base its decisions on the pooling gains from scale that it achieves? One would find, I expect, that, if lender's risk were fully eliminated, the government interest cost might be raised somewhat higher than the 3 per cent rate. But I fail to see why it should move all the way to the private rate.

Even were private interest cost the proper rate to use, the empirical rate indicated by Brownlee and Harberger seems to me to be overstated for two reasons. One is the failure to distinguish between marginal and average rates. The other is the inclusion of yields on equity capital grossed up by the profits tax. If the interest cost of the government and of large business concerns were compared, not nearly as large a differential is found as the ones they use.

I also have the uneasy feeling that inclusion of the property tax in the computation results in imposition of the same distorting effects in the public sphere that we find in the private sphere. Such a movement does not necessarily lead us toward an optimum.

Granted that there has been much loose thinking about criteria for governmental investment decisions, Brownlee and others have performed a real service by emphasizing the relevant factors. But it may be a disservice to overcorrect the governmental decision. The application of frictions present in private investment decisions to governmental decisions may worsen things, not improve them.

5. Economists must ever be alert to the advantages of the price system. But we may not be adding to social output if we insist on its inevitable advantages when these depend only on particular value

judgments applied. In the area of user prices versus taxes, where the interpersonal comparison of utility is required, and where our choice must be between second best alternatives, an agnostic posture would seem to conform more closely to the present state of our knowledge.

C. HARRY KAHN, Rutgers University

As Mr. Brownlee suggests, the division between services with pronounced external economies (Category B) on the one hand, and saleable services (Category C), on the other, is apt to be somewhat arbitrary. I think this is not primarily because of any lack of "detailed description of governmental services" but rather in the nature of the classifications chosen. The arbitrariness is introduced because the services listed in Category B are apparently considered not saleable because of their pronounced externalities whereas Category C-services are presumed to have no externalities and to be produced under conditions of increasing or constant marginal production costs and therefore saleable.

Actually such a dividing line is well-nigh impossible to draw. Almost all the services under B and C can be sold and have externalities. Category C, as defined, is practically nonexistent as Brownlee himself notes (p. 425). Few services produced by government have no external economies or diseconomies or increasing returns to scale. On the contrary, one or the other is usually the reason for governmental performance. Can it be shown that externalities are greater for sewage than for the postal service and highways (not to speak of higher education)? And are higher education and highways "saleable" in the same sense as liquor?

In short, I suggest that the difference between B and C is one of degree rather than kind, and that a simpler and more useful procedure would be to list all of the services in Brownlee's B and C categories as "saleable services," ranked in descending order according to the degree of external economies associated with each service, and hence in ascending order according to the degree of saleability. Such rankings would still involve considerable judgment and arbitrariness, but at least an arbitrary conceptual division would be removed.

Can all government services then be subsumed under either the public goods or saleable category? I would find it useful and convenient to add a third, "redistributive expenditures." Practically all government expenditures have, of course, incidental redistributive effects, but for some the stated purpose is clearly redistributive. Among others, welfare expenditures and veterans services would fall into this category. Such services are, almost by definition, not saleable, and they can hardly be considered public goods if one defines them—as Brownlee does—as goods which can be consumed by one person without a reduction in the quantities available to others.

The merit in dividing government expenditures into public, saleable, and redistributive groups is thus that the dividing lines are sharp and meaningful.

A Survey of the Theory of Public Expenditure Criteria

OTTO ECKSTEIN

HARVARD UNIVERSITY

THE theory of expenditure criteria has received a lot of attention in recent years, stimulated by the practical needs of the world. In the United States, the evaluation of public works, particularly in the field of water resource development, has led to the evolution of techniques and criteria for project evaluation. This work was largely pioneered within the federal government. The need for devising development plans for underdeveloped countries has led to extensive theoretical study of investment criteria for that particular economic context.

This paper presents the elements of the theory. Rather than propose or defend specific criteria, I try to indicate the issues about which assumptions must be made. First, possible objective functions are discussed—What, if anything, is to be maximized? There follow sections on constraints, interest rates, repercussion effects, and the treatment of risk and uncertainty. Finally, with the taxonomy of the problem in hand, most of the more important decision-models that have been developed are surveyed and discussed.

Some limitations should also be mentioned. First, there is very little empirical work in this study, in particular, no real allocation-problems are presented or solved. In view of the scope of the problems to be covered at a theoretical level, intensive treatment of specific empirical situations was not attempted. Second, there is no treatment of the various technical maximization methods, such as Lagrangian techniques, linear and nonlinear programing, simulations,

NOTE: This research was sponsored by Resources for the Future, Incorporated, as part of their regular program in Water Resources. I am grateful to Dr. John V. Krutilla of that organization, who was most helpful in the design and execution of this study, and with whom I have collaborated over several years in this general area.

I have benefited from participation in the lively controversies of the Harvard University Seminar on Water Resource Planning. Professors Robert Dorfman, John Meyer, Arthur Maass, Peter Steiner, and Harold Thomas, Dean Fair, Messrs. Maynard Hufschmidt, Stephen Marglin, and Donald Farrar, and other some-time members of the Seminar have all left their imprint on this paper. Professors Bergson and Dorfman have read and commented on the paper and have improved it. Responsibility for anything said rests entirely with me, of course.

queuing theory, and game theory, since excellent treatments are now available. Third, the macro-economic decision models developed by Frisch, Tinbergen, and Theil are not discussed, even though they are closely related conceptually. Nor is the theory of public expenditures, advanced by Wicksell and others, and developed further by Samuelson and Musgrave, treated here. This theory concerns itself with those expenditures for which conventional value theory breaks down completely. My concern is largely confined to public works and development projects of a sort for which measures of value can be established empirically.

1. The Objective Function

A. INTRODUCTION

The most fundamental consideration in a decision model is the choice of an objective function. Should the model seek to maximize (or minimize) some operationally definable measures? And if so, what should the measure be?

Typically, in economics, the analysis presupposes that we seek to maximize economic welfare, however this may be defined. The notion of maximization is perhaps the central analytical concept of economics. Recently, Simon[1] has questioned this idea, and at least as a description of the real world has suggested that people and corporations merely seek to obtain a satisfactory state of affairs, rather than some optimum.

One could reconstruct prescriptive (or welfare) economics along Simon's lines, letting the analyst indicate what policies keep the state of affairs within the tolerance levels of the interest groups affected inside and outside government. The "putting out fires" approach to policy, which frequently characterizes American political leadership, certainly suggests that politicians are also "satisficers," in Simon's phrase. Nevertheless, the present study takes the view that economic analysis will play a more productive role if it seeks to maximize something. The extent to which policy makers decide to accept the economist's optimizing analyses will probably be decided by satisficing considerations.[2]

---

[1] Herbert Simon, *Models of Man*, 1957, Ch. 14, "A Behavioral Model of Rational Choice," reprinted from *Quarterly Journal of Economics*, February 1955, and *Administrative Behavior*, 2nd ed., 1957, Introduction and Chs. 4 and 5.

[2] For a different view, that politicians are maximizers of votes, see Anthony Downs, *An Economic Theory of Democracy*, Harper, 1957.

B. WHAT SHOULD BE MAXIMIZED? WELFARE ECONOMICS

Assuming a maximizing approach, a yardstick which will define the optimum must be specified. Economic welfare is the usual objective, but there are a number of alternative ways of defining this broad concept.

First, in Western economics, economic welfare is almost always related to individual welfare; it is postulated that there can be no welfare other than what accrues to individuals. This is a rejection of the organic theory of the state: the state as an entity enjoys no welfare, only the people that compose it.[3]

Following Bergson,[4] the function for social economic welfare at any point in time can be written formally:

$$W = W(W_1, \ldots, W_n),$$

where W_i is the economic welfare of individual i. A change in economic welfare can be written

(1.1) $$\Delta W = \Delta W(\Delta W_1, \ldots, \Delta W_n).$$

When can the change in social economic welfare caused by a policy be said to be positive? A definition of this positive change is needed for to strive to maximize welfare, all changes which serve to increase it must be undertaken. An optimum point is defined as a situation in which no further positive changes in social welfare can be accomplished.

Clearly, if all individuals are made better off ($\Delta W_i > 0$ for all i) economic welfare is improved according to any nonmalevolent standard. A somewhat weaker, although still very strong, requirement is this: Let no one be made worse off and let at least one person be better off. ($\Delta W_i \geq 0$ for all i, with at least one $\Delta W_i > 0$.)

There are few (or no) economic changes which could pass this test. Usually, some person is affected adversely, which is sufficient to preclude this criterion from ruling on the desirability of the change.

---

[3] For the view that economics only encompasses the case of individually based welfare, see Howard Ellis, "The Economic Way of Thinking," *American Economic Review*, March 1950, pp. 1–12. For a reply, see Bushrod W. Allin, "Is Group Choice a Part of Economics?" *Quarterly Journal of Economics*, August 1953, pp. 362–79, and "Replies," *ibid.*, November 1953, pp. 605–14.

[4] A. Bergson, "A Reformulation of Certain Aspects of Welfare Economics," *Quarterly Journal of Economics*, February 1938.

A test which promised to yield an answer in a wider range of situations was introduced by Kaldor[5] and Hicks.[6] They did not require that no one be made worse off, only that the gainers of any economic change be able to compensate the losers, though the compensations need not necessarily be carried out. In this way, it was hoped that the production features of economic policy could be separated from their distributional implications. Presumably, pure lump-sum transfers of income can achieve any distribution of output that is desired. If the total value of output minus the value of factor services is increased, presumably the gainers can compensate the losers, and economic welfare is increased. If the economic change is so small that prices are unaffected, this is a simple and unambiguous test. Where prices change, Hicks suggested use of the new prices, Kaldor of the old.[7]

An implicit assumption of this approach is that the economic welfare of any individual (or family) only depends on the goods and services consumed and supplied by him; his welfare is not affected by the welfare of his neighbors. For if there were such external effects of consumption, even an increase in total net value which made more goods and services available to everyone might reduce economic welfare—by causing envy, for example.[8] Of course, if all individuals were so noble as to derive only happiness from an increase in other people's consumption, this result would be ruled out.[9]

The Kaldor-Hicks compensation criteria were subjected to much criticism. Scitovsky showed that if the economic change is large enough to cause prices to change, the criterion may become inconsistent; the gainers could compensate the losers after the change, yet the potential losers might be able to compensate the potential gainers prior to the change.[10] He found that an unambiguous increase in welfare required that the value of net output must increase both at the new and the old prices. Samuelson deepened this line of criticism, contending that all the potential distributions of welfare

[5] N. Kaldor, "Welfare Propositions and Interpersonal Comparisons of Utility," *Economic Journal*, 1939, pp. 549–52.

[6] J. R. Hicks, "The Valuation of Social Income," *Economica*, 1940, pp. 105–24.

[7] This is the interpretation of J. de V. Graaff, *Welfare Economics*. For a different view, see I. M. D. Little, *A Critique of Welfare Economics*, 2nd ed., Ch. 6.

[8] This phenomenon is stressed by W. J. Baumol in *Welfare Economics and the Theory of the State*, Harvard University Press, 1952, pp. 88, 127. Also see J. de V. Graaff, *op.cit.*, pp. 43–5.

[9] See Stefan Valavanis, "Schadenfreude and Freudeschaden," to be published.

[10] T. Scitovsky, "A Note on Welfare Propositions in Economics," *Review of Economic Studies*, 1942, pp. 98–110.

of any given production situation be considered relevant. One situation would be ruled superior to another only if every potential distribution of welfare possible under it is superior for at least one individual, and is inferior for none. This statement, which would be extremely difficult to implement empirically, eliminates some cases which would be ranked even under the Scitovsky double criterion.

Another line of criticism questions the use of potential compensation.[11] Can one situation be considered to yield greater economic welfare if everyone could be made better off even though, in fact, the necessary compensation payments are not made? Hypothetical payments, according to most later writers, are not an adequate device to remove the distribution issue. On the other hand, actual compensation payments have not been accepted either, since they would attach particular desirability to the income distribution before the economic change. The most widely accepted modern view insists that the redistribution of income of any economic change be evaluated separately on the basis of specific ethical judgments. As formulated by Little,[12] an appropriate criterion for the desirability of an economic change would be the following:

1. the gainers must be able to overcompensate the losers and/or the losers must not be able to overcompensate the gainers, and

2. the redistribution of income must be good. This assumes that the option of making pure redistributions is excluded; otherwise different criteria apply.

The above criterion permits the comparison of any two situations on the basis of what is probably rather close to a minimum of restrictions that must be imposed on the economic welfare function.

As a theory of economic policy, this formulation leaves much to be desired, however. First, as Graaff has argued persuasively, the prevalence of external effects in consumption contradicts a necessary assumption of the theory. Second, analysis of real-world situations is usually ill-suited to be couched in terms of choices among two alternatives. Third, since most policies involve a loss of welfare to someone, a formal basis for interpersonal comparisons is needed,

---

[11] W. J. Baumol, *Welfare Economics*, . . . , p. 123; I. M. D. Little, *A Critique of Welfare Economics*, Ch. 6; C. F. Kennedy, "The Economic Welfare Function and Dr. Little's Criterion," *Review of Economic Studies*, No. 52, 1952–53; R. Baldwin, "A Comparison of Welfare Criteria," *ibid.*, No. 55, 1953–54, p. 154.

[12] I. M. D. Little, *A Critique of Welfare Economics, op.cit.*, p. 105.

and since the economist has no particular right to attach social weights to individual welfare in the social welfare function, this is sufficient ground to rule out rigid prescriptions. Of course the economist can stop short of this judgment, leaving the evaluation of distributive effects to the politician. But even under this view the economist will find it very difficult to sidestep the distribution issue altogether. After all, he cannot conduct his analyses in terms of the names of the millions of people in his country, and grouping of population into categories—by income class or geography or anything else—already prejudges the distributive issue.[13]

The complexity of the criteria, their inability to resolve most practical issues, and the inherently ethical problem of judging the distribution of income has brought many of the leading students of welfare economics to very pessimistic conclusions. Baumol, in his "Epilogue: The Wreck of Welfare Economics?" stresses the prevalence of interdependence effects which invalidate the use of market prices and rejects the standard marginal optimum conditions. Historically, the main use of welfare economics has been the derivation of these conditions and the proof that laissez-faire is the best economic system;[14] thus, Baumol's stress on interdependence strikes at the heart of the theory. Other than as a means of exploding fallacious arguments, he writes, the fact that categories like "external economies" and "external diseconomies" remain largely empty economic boxes prevents any further applications of welfare theory as it now stands.

"Is there any hope of further progress based on empirical investigation and analysis of the problem of the interdependence of activities of economic units? I cannot pretend to offer even tentative answers. It seems to me, however, that if the subject is to achieve primary importance for practical men, this question must be faced and answered."[15]

Graaff's[16] pessimism rests on two grounds. First, he does not believe that there will be agreement on the ends of policy. He is concerned not only with the distribution of income, but also with

---

[13] For other difficulties of the concept of distribution of welfare, see K. J. Arrow, "Little's Critique of Welfare Economics," *American Economic Review*, December 1951, pp. 923–34, esp. 931–2.

[14] K. E. Boulding, "Welfare Economics" in *A Survey of Contemporary Economics*, Vol. 2, B. Haley, ed., p. 24.

[15] Baumol, *Welfare Economics* . . . , *op.cit.*, p. 167.

[16] Graaff, *Theoretical Welfare Economics*, pp. 170–1.

the attitude toward uncertainty, the time horizon, and the rate of progress. The external effects in consumption which he stresses also hopelessly complicate the problem. He concludes that economists had best devote themselves to factual studies of the functioning of the economic system, perhaps predicting the effects of policy on some index numbers, but attaching no prescriptive value.

C. A MORE MODEST ROLE FOR WELFARE ECONOMICS:
THE OBJECTIVE FUNCTION

Its critics underestimate the usefulness of welfare economics. It is true that it has failed in the tasks which had been set for it: it has not (1) proved the superiority of laissez faire; (2) provided simple criteria for judging economic changes or economic optima, or (3) provided a method of isolating the economic aspects of policy from ethical considerations. But the failure to accomplish these objectives is due to their grandiose nature. There are more modest objectives of analysis for which welfare economics must play a crucial role.

What I propose is this. First, the rather casually dispensed advice of the critics of welfare economics should be taken seriously. I follow Baumol and seek to establish what interdependence effects should be measured, and to indicate the methods that may be appropriate. I follow Graaff by emphasizing measurement rather than absolutist advice. But this should be no senseless retreat into hypothesis-testing unrelated to potential action, nor the collection of random sets of facts; rather it should be the establishment of decision-models which will reveal explicitly what actions will maximize the achievement of specified objectives.

I do not insist that the economist be given the objectives in polished, formal manner. Rather, the economist must interpret the desires of the policy people whom he is serving and express them in an analytical form as an objective function. He then seeks to maximize this function, given the empirical relations in the economy and the institutional constraints that may be appropriate to the analysis. In this manner, the economist can play the role of technician, of bringing his technical equipment to bear on policy problems, with maximum effectiveness.

The specification of the objective function thus is not primarily meant to let the economist play omnipotent being; rather, it is a device for bridging the gap between the positive quantitative research which is the main stock-in-trade of the economist, and the normative conclusions which policy requires.[17]

D. SINGLE *vs.* MULTIPLE INDICATORS

Individual and "Social" Welfare—The Problem of Income Distribution

In formulating the objective function so as to express our notion of economic welfare, there is a question about the number of variables to be employed. From a theoretical point of view, the ideal function would define at least one variable for each individual measuring his welfare, and probably more than one, say, a measure of expected gain in real income plus a measure of the probable dispersion. Thus the objective function might take the form

$$(1.1) \qquad W = W(\bar{y}_1, \sigma_{y_1}, \bar{y}_2, \sigma_{y_2}, \ldots, \bar{y}_n, \sigma_{y_n})$$

where $\bar{y}_i$ is expected gain in real income of individual y $(i = 1, \ldots, n)$ and σ_i is the standard deviation of that gain. Were we given individual preferences about risk, so that we could write $u_i = (\bar{y}_i, \sigma_{y_1})$, and perhaps of higher moments, (1.1) could be rewritten

$$(1.2) \qquad W = W(u_1, u_2, \ldots, u_n).$$

But functions of this form are a counsel of perfection. Policy problems rarely present themselves in a form suitable for such ideal evaluation. Thus, W must be given some other form.

A particularly simple version weights a dollar of expected gain (or loss) of different individuals equally and ignores risk. Thus

$$(1.3) \qquad W = (\bar{y}_1 + \bar{y}_2 + \ldots + \bar{y}_n),$$

this is the form of the function which stresses economic efficiency to the exclusion of all else. The welfare theorists of the Kaldor-Hicks school sought to give strong normative significance to (1.3) through the compensation tests. In more recent literature, (1.3) plus an independent ethical judgment on the distribution of the

---

[17] This is not to say that an objective function must always be specified when economics is used for policy purposes. Perhaps in most cases, particularly where the analysis involves few steps, such as the mere marshalling of figures, it would be excess theoretical baggage. But once the analysis takes on some complexity, an explicit objective function becomes more important if normative recommendations are to be derived. At the least, the function is a means of forcing the technician to state his normative assumptions; at its best, it is a powerful analytical aid, eliminating uninteresting areas of exploration, and permitting the ranking of alternatives.

incomes $\bar{y}_i$ has found considerable favor and has been applied. This can be written as

$$(1.4) \qquad W = W(\Sigma_i \bar{y}_i, \bar{y}_1, \ldots, \bar{y}_n),$$

where the detailed list of individual incomes permits judgment about the income distribution, a judgment to be rendered by the policy-maker. This information cannot, in fact, be specified for individuals since it would be an impossible statistical task. It can be presented for income classes however, either by size class or functional type of income, or the data can be developed by regions.[18] This specializes (1.4) to

$$(1.5) \qquad W = W(\Sigma_m \bar{y}_i, \Sigma_{r_1} \bar{y}_i, \ldots, \Sigma_{r_k} y_i)$$

where i in m includes all individuals in the nation (or world), i in r includes all individuals in region (or income class) i, and so on.

When the policy-maker uses the objective function, he can attach any weights he wishes to the national and regional groupings of income. The economist *qua* economist has no right to attach these social utilities to the incomes of individuals. But he usually cannot escape the task of defining the groupings for which income distribution data are to be constructed. The efficiency minded economist will stress the national (world?) grouping and no other. The regionally oriented economist may stress the regional breakdown, and so on. Certain objective functions could be identified as bad economics if labeled as serving the public interest, e.g., the case where weight is only attached to the income of a specific pressure group.

While (1.4) and (1.5) have found most common application, they do not exhaust the possibilities of dealing with the distributional question. The policy-maker may specify more detailed rules. He may impose distributional side conditions, insisting that any policy produce a certain pattern of gain, or alternatively, that a certain minimum accrue to some group, or perhaps that no group suffer a net loss.

The economist can also feel free to perform experiments in policy evaluation using specific objective functions, treating the results as free of absolute normative significance. For example, he can assume a certain shape for the marginal utility of income functions. He may assume some elasticity to this curve, or he may choose to use a form

[18] For an example, see J. V. Krutilla and O. Eckstein, *Multiple Purpose River Development*, 1958, Chs. 7 and 8.

of the function that has been implicitly produced by the political process. The effective marginal rates of the personal income tax at different income levels can be interpreted as implying a marginal utility of income curve. If the government is assumed to act on the principle of equimarginal sacrifice, then marginal effective tax rates can be the basis for deriving a measure of the government's notion of marginal utilities of income.

The kind of question that could be posed when such a function is applied to the analysis of a policy is of the following form: assuming the values placed by the government on marginal income of different income classes in its personal tax legislation, will a policy raise total national economic welfare?[19]

Single vs. Multiple Objectives

Economic welfare can be viewed as a one-dimensional quantity for each individual or group, related presumably to the goods expected to be enjoyed, plus perhaps some allowance for the associated risk. The tools of economic analysis are not always designed to yield this type of answer; in practical work, the objective function has to be tailored to the analysis. For example, a public works program may produce certain outputs over a long period of time, generate a certain amount of economic growth, have a counter-cyclical potential, alleviate a pocket of local poverty, reduce some natural risks, create a potential for a future recreation facility, dot the landscape with beautiful monuments that have symbolic signifi-cance at home and abroad, and so on. Insistence on one-dimensional welfare indicators would either produce a meaningless hodge-podge, or a slighting of all objectives other than expected tangible output. In principle, the many outputs may be considered reducible to common units for each individual, assuming a scalar utility function to exist; in practice the many effects must be grouped into meaningful categories of objectives. These categories can be related to such factors as: (1) economic circumstance; for example, full employment benefits, which may be measurable from market data, can be considered a separate objective from depression benefits, which are more critically related to timing and to the employment and purchasing power generated; (2) the tangibility of the effect—is it measurable in some objective manner, or is it a rather arbitrary valuation? (3) reliability

---

[19] When the technique is applied to actual policies on an *ex post* basis, it yields a kind of consistency test of government attitudes.

of the estimates—with outputs meeting clear demands treated separately from more conditional benefits which may depend on various repercussion effects; and (4) the date of the benefits—with the usually more uncertain remote benefits treated as a different kind of benefit.

Policy people rarely view their problem as one-dimensional. A multiple objective function corresponds more closely to their view of the world. In particular, it leaves to them the all-important weighting of the various objectives, giving them the results of the technical analysis in the most useable form. The extent of elaboration of objectives is an issue that must be resolved between the policy-maker and the technician. But in no event should the technician arrogate the weighting of objectives to himself by presenting a one-dimensional answer after burying the weighting process in a welter of technical details.[20]

E. WHAT ARE THE BENEFITS?

Since the objective function must be suited to the problem and must often be multiple in nature, the definition of benefits is also a relative matter. On some assumptions, benefits are defined in a particularly simple way. For example, under full employment conditions, with the marginal utility of income the same for all individuals, and with perfect markets and no external economies or diseconomies in production and consumption, prices are perfect measures of benefit. If a project is so large as to affect the prices of its outputs, a simple result is obtainable if the marginal utility of income is assumed not only the same for all individuals, but also constant over the range of variation. The area under the output's demand curve then constitutes a measure of benefits, and if the curves are assumed linear, an arithmetic average of old and new prices multiplied by the number of units will measure benefit. Another interesting case is the following: if the underlying individual indifference curves are assumed hyperbolic, Fischer's "ideal" index number constitutes an indicator of benefit.[21]

In other cases, benefit cannot be defined so simply. While in principle it is always possible to measure the change in utility of individuals (assuming some cardinal concept that can be identified

[20] Examples of this practice abound in the evaluation practices in the water resource field. See my *Water Resource Development*, Harvard University Press, Cambridge, 1958, Ch. 7.

[21] This special case is discussed in R. L. Marris, "Professor Hicks' Index Number Theorem," *Review of Economic Studies*, October 1957, pp. 25–40.

with willingness to pay), in practice this is an enormous task and short cuts must be devised. Often there is the question of what chains of repercussion should be pursued in benefit estimation; this issue is treated in Section 4, below. And where public services are genuine collective goods, benefit estimation often becomes impossible.

F. A SPECIAL CASE: COST MINIMIZATION TO ACHIEVE FIXED OBJECTIVES

A case which has been found to have very wide applicability, particularly in the general field of operations research, is the case where the objectives are strictly fixed and the remaining economic problem is to minimize the real cost of accomplishing them. This is only an interesting economic problem where there are several alternative and quite different ways of achieving the objectives. The problem can be approached through the neoclassical theory of the firm, from which the theorem about marginal productivities can be drawn, through linear programing, through simulation, or through the other maximizing procedures. While, this paper does not elaborate on these techniques, the importance of the case for public expenditure analysis must be stressed, since it provides at least some role for economics even where the nature of the collective goods precludes benefit estimation.

2. The Constraints

A. INTRODUCTION

Economic policy is rarely concerned with the attainment of the best of all possible worlds. Rather, it seeks to improve economic welfare in the face of constraints. The economist, in devising a policy model, must decide how many of the constraints he will build into his analysis. Just as in the case of the objective function, there comes a point where the assumptions are so specific that they produce "bad" economics. Constraints can be assumed to rule out all solutions except one, which automatically is then justified. This procedure can be viewed as excluding the application of economics to the problem. On the other hand, to prohibit the use of constraints altogether is to confine economics to a very narrow—and usually utopian—range of problems.

B. SOME TYPES OF CONSTRAINTS

There are many different sorts of constraints, originating in various institutional or physical limitations. In a sense, they mold the analysis, giving shape to the problem under study and determining the general nature of the solution.

For the kinds of public expenditures to which our analysis is meant to apply, several types of constraints can be distinguished. First, there are *physical* constraints. The most general of these is the production function, which relates physical inputs to outputs. There may also be absolute limits to the size of structures, or else such sharp discontinuities to the cost curves that any point beyond them can be considered beyond the domain of analysis.

Legal constraints also may need to be incorporated into the model. A program or project must be in accordance with laws, whether it be water laws, property laws, treaties, or whatever. In admitting legal constraints, care must be exercised not to assume laws as fixed which could be affected by the analysis. This is one of the areas where the economist is in peril of accepting so many constraints that he will exclude the interesting solutions.

Administrative constraints may be imposed by the capability of the agency. Limits on the rate of expansion of a program, caused by the need to expand personnel and to diffuse administrative know-how, is one example. Excessive complexity of the planning process, requiring consideration of too many variables, or perhaps requiring excessive centralization of decision-making, is another.

We have already considered *distributional constraints*, which may impose a fixed pattern on the distribution of benefits and costs, or which may impose side conditions of minimum benefits for different groups.

There can be constraints of many other forms. *Uncertainty* can be introduced via constraints; for example, the condition may be imposed that the net gain of a project be positive at some specified probability level. Political constraints can also be imposed, though the line between realism and bad economics is particularly hard to draw on this point.

The final type is *financial* or *budget* constraints. In general, they specify that the amount of money available from some source is limited. In deriving expenditure criteria, this is a critical matter because it is the limited kind of money which must be allocated optimally, and it is to the constrained kind of funds that expenditure criteria address themselves. Elsewhere,[22] I have explored the effect of alternative financial constraints on the form of expenditure criteria.

[22] *Water Resource Development, op.cit.*, pp. 47–80.

If there is only one constrained financial resource and one category of benefits, the criterion requires that the rate of net benefit per dollar of the constrained funds be maximized. This maximization is accomplished by computing ratios of benefit to constrained funds for each project (or smaller unit of choice where possible), ranking projects by these ratios and going down the ranked list to the point where the scarce funds are exhausted. Although the ranking is by ratios, it is not the maximization of the ratio which is the objective but rather the total net gain that is possible, given the constraint. Examples of the use of various constraints will be found in the discussion of various models in Section 6 below.

C. CONSTRAINTS AND THE THEORY OF BUDGETING

Constraints are rarely an accurate description of an institutional reality. Budgets are not rigidly fixed except over very short periods— and even then there can be supplemental appropriations. Financial requirements, e.g., that an operation be self-liquidating, are rarely followed if circumstances change. Particularly if a constraint severely interferes with the achievement of economic welfare, the constraint is likely to give way.

Nevertheless, the use of budget constraints is a powerful analytical device. It freezes one (or more) financial resource(s) and then permits an answer to the question: What is the best use of this scarce resource? The analysis then allocates the scarce kind of money in the optimal way. This is a meaningful procedure where, in fact, it is possible to identify the resource which serves to limit the over-all size of the program.[23] A government agency allocating a budget that has been determined at a higher level, or a planning commission in an under-developed country drawing up an investment plan subject to limited domestic capital and foreign exchange, can view its problem in these terms. Thus, in a fundamental sense, the theory of constraints is at the heart of the theory of budgeting.

D. CONSTRAINTS AND OPPORTUNITY COSTS

The acceptance of a budget constraint removes the possibility of reaching the *optimum optimorum* solution. In particular, it prohibits solution of the problem of determining the optimal level of

[23] If there were a high degree of substitutability among financial resources, no resource would serve as a limit, and it would make no sense to use a constraint. Thus the constraint approach presupposes that the unconstrained financial resources cannot be a perfect substitute for the constrained resource.

expenditure of the constrained financial resource. Thus, an analysis using a constraint is restricted to optimum allocation of a fixed "second-best" budget level, but it cannot determine the level itself.[24]

The latter problem requires some notion of the cost of budget money. What are the opportunity costs in other sectors of the economy and in fields of the budget outside the particular one under analysis? The extent to which these costs can be measured is still an open question, though some types of opportunity costs can definitely be estimated.

But whatever the difficulties of measurement, it is important to distinguish between two different problems. Where an undertaking must be assumed to be financed out of extra funds made possible by the political process, it is incorrect to compare it to projects within some budget constraint. The relevant comparison is between the project and the opportunity cost of the resources in the sector out of which the resources are drawn, whether by taxation, borrowing, or inflation. On the other hand, if a budget is accepted as fixed, the comparison must be made within that budget.

Wherever possible, constraints should not be accepted blindly. Even if there is an upper limit to expenditures in a particular budget, not only should the scarce funds be allocated in an optimal way, but also, a further test, which assures that the marginal expenditures yield a benefit as great as they would if spent outside the budget, must be performed.

3. Interest Rates

A particularly difficult problem in specifying an objective function is the choice of an interest rate. With outputs accruing at different points in time, it is necessary to place relative values on them, depending on the date at which they occur. Similarly, the dates at which costs are incurred may affect the value they represent. In this chapter, some of the possible approaches to specifying interest rates are examined.

A. THE INTEREST RATE AS A MEASURE OF VALUE OF OUTPUTS AT DIFFERENT POINTS IN TIME: PLANNERS' TIME PREFERENCE

There are several bases on which the interest rate for valuing outputs can be chosen. Acceptance of consumer sovereignty is, in

[24] For a general discussion of the theory of "second-best" see R. G. Lipsey and R. K. Lancaster, "The General Theory of Second-Best," *Review of Economic Studies*, Vol. 24 (1), No. 63, pp. 11–32.

one sense, most consistent with individualist welfare economics. It requires that the interest rate used by households in their saving-spending decisions be applied. Clearly the use of this particular rate (or rather rates) makes sense only if the consumers' decision about the amount of saving and investment is also accepted; with the time profile of future output dependent both on the interest rate used for planning and on the amount of investment, rejection of consumer sovereignty with regard to one of the two variables requires modification of the other, even if consumer sovereignty is given full weight. Thus consumer sovereignty must be judged with respect to both variables simultaneously.

There is a long literature of criticism of consumer sovereignty for intertemporal choices.[25] Pigou, Ramsey, Dobb, Baumol and others reject the rationality of time preferences which prefer consumption earlier rather than later simply by reason of the date. Strotz[26] has recently shown that a series of decisions made under pure time preference for the present lead to a total history of individual experience which contains less total satisfaction than would be possible in the absence of such "myopia." As the period of comparison lengthens, there is also the problem of comparing the welfare of future generations. And what assurance can there be that present consumers will make adequate provision for unborn generations?

An alternative approach has the public decision-maker, whether congressman, budgeteer, or central planner, exercise his own time preference. In a democratic society, the preferences on which he acts presumably bear some relation to the population's desires, though in practice, judging by the interest rates used in planning in most countries, there is also a good deal of concern with remote payoffs.

A theoretical foundation can be provided for planners' optimal time preferences, based on the notion of the diminishing marginal utility of individual income. If we assume that this marginal utility falls, then the value of marginal output falls as per capita income rises. Since the interest rate is designed to reflect the relative value of marginal output at different points in time, this rate should be lower the smaller the expected increase in per capita output, and where a decline in per capita income is in prospect, possibly due to excessive

[25] For a summary see F. D. Holzman, "Consumer Sovereignty and the Rate of Economic Development," *Economia Internazionale*, 1958, pp. 3–20.
[26] R. Strotz, "Myopia and Inconsistency in Dynamic Utility Maximization," *Review of Economic Studies*, 1955–56, pp. 165–80.

TABLE 1

Interest Rates Based on Diminishing Marginal Utility
of Per Capita Consumption and Growth Rate of
Per Capita Consumption[a]

ELASTICITY OF MARGINAL UTILITY OF INCOME FUNCTION	PER CAPITA GROWTH RATE OF CONSUMPTION			
	-2%	0	$+2\%$	$+4\%$
2.0	−4.0	0	4.0	8.0
1.5	−3.0	0	3.0	6.0
1.0	−2.0	0	2.0	4.0
0.7	−1.4	0	1.4	2.8
0.5	−1.0	0	1.0	2.0

[a] The underlying model is the following:

Let $W = W(y_1, \ldots, y_t, \ldots)$, where y_t is per capita consumption in year t.

Let $\dfrac{\partial W}{\partial y_t} = (y_t)^{-\epsilon}$, where ϵ is the elasticity of the marginal utility of consumption.
Then

$$\frac{\partial W}{\partial y_t} \Big/ \frac{\partial W}{\partial y_{t+1}} = \frac{y_t^{-\epsilon}}{y_{t+1}^{-\epsilon}} = \left(\frac{y_t}{y_{t+1}}\right)^{-\epsilon} = (1 + r)^{\epsilon},$$

where r is the growth rate of per capita consumption.

But $\dfrac{\partial W}{\partial y_t} \Big/ \dfrac{\partial W}{\partial y_{t+1}}$ is the ratio of marginal values of consumption, and thus equals the interest factor, $1 + i$. Therefore

$$1 + i = (1 + r)^{\epsilon}.$$

This is the formula used for the table. If we decompose the growth rate of per capita consumption into the growth rate of population, π, and of consumption, ρ, we get

$$1 + i = \frac{(1 + \rho)^{\epsilon}}{(1 + \pi)^{\epsilon}}.$$

Recently, Samuelson has examined a similar problem and pointed to the relation between population growth and the interest rate. P. A. Samuelson, "An Exact Consumption-Loan Model of Interest With or Without the Social Contrivance of Money," *Journal of Political Economy*, December 1958, pp. 467–82.

population growth, the interest rate can even be negative.[27] Given the kinds of empirical magnitudes that actually prevail in the world, the interest rates suggested by the model are relatively low, 4 per cent or less, even for fairly large elasticities of the marginal utility of income curves. Table 1, which is reproduced from an earlier study, summarizes these results.

One paradoxical result is suggested by the analysis: the lower the

[27] For a formal model reflecting these notions, see my "Investment Criteria . . . , *op.cit.*, pp. 76–8. An earlier model, which has some points of similarity, can be found in R. F. Harrod's *Toward a Dynamic Economics*, Macmillan, 1948, pp. 35–62. A model which derives the optimal rate of investment from utility functions is given in J. Tinbergen, "The Optimal Rate of Saving," *Economic Journal*, December 1956, pp. 603–10; but see the important comment by A. K. Sen, *ibid.*, December 1957, pp. 745–50.

rate of growth, the lower should be the interest rate. Since, typically, the lowest rates of growth of per capita income are found in the poorest countries, low interest rates should be used in these countries. Yet these are the places where the pressure for early consumption is greatest. The resolution of the paradox is simple: the interest rate relates not to the absolute level of consumption, but to the relative changes over time. Thus, high-growth countries, whatever the present levels, can afford the luxury of high valuation of present consumption versus future consumption, since they will have higher levels in the future. The association of high interest rates with low income levels is based on other phenomena, particularly the scarcity of capital and pure preference of present over future consumption. Pure time preference has often been believed to be greater at low levels of income.

Should the objective function of the planner allow for pure time preference? Or should it be above such "irrationality"? Even from the narrow point of view of economic efficiency, this question cannot be resolved without use of strong value judgments. Preference for experiences in the near future can be rational for individuals, given the uncertainty of the duration of life. A lifetime consumption plan which stresses early years is more certain of fulfillment than one which emphasizes later years, since the probability of survival to the expected consumption dates is greater. Even if rationality is defined to exclude aversion to risk there is room for pure time preference. The utility to be enjoyed at each future moment must be multiplied by the probability of being alive at the time, and since this probability falls with the remoteness of the period, a kind of pure discount factor emerges. This assumes individuals to be narrowly selfish, caring nothing about the wealth they leave behind when they die.

Numerical values for this discount factor can be computed from mortality statistics. For consumption one year after the present moment, the factor is equal to the probability of not surviving the next year; for longer intervals, it is a geometric average of annual rates.[28] Table 2 gives numerical values for the probability of surviving the next year at different ages. The figures, which are given for an advanced country, the United States, and an underdeveloped country, India, are based on mortality statistics compiled by the

---

[28] For the theory of deriving long-term interest rates from a structure of short-term rates, see F. A. Lutz, "The Structure of Interest Rates," *Quarterly Journal of Economics*, November 1950, pp. 36–63.

TABLE 2

"Rational Individual Time Preference," Based on Survival Probabilities,
United States and India Both Sexes

Age	United States (1950) (in per cent)	India (1941–50) (in per cent)
5–9	0.04	1.50
10–14	0.04	1.10
15–19	0.07	0.85
20–24	0.10	0.95
25–29	0.10	1.25
30–34	0.15	1.60
35–39	0.25	1.90
40–44	0.40	2.15
45–49	0.65	2.50
50–54	1.00	3.10
55–59	1.45	3.80
60–64	2.10	4.90
65–69	2.90	6.15
70–74	4.50	7.50
75–79	5.85	8.95
80–84	7.45	10.55
Life expectancy:	68	32

SOURCE: United Nations, Department of Social Affairs, Population Branch, Population Studies No. 22, *Age and Sex Patterns of Mortality, Model Life Tables for Underdeveloped Countries*, New York, 1955, ST/TOA/Series A/22, pp. 30–1.

[a] The figures are the average values for the five-year interval.

United Nations; similar tables could be computed for many other countries, for either sex, and for the mortality experience at different points in history.

The figures for the United States turn out to be amazingly low. Up to age fifty the probability of not surviving the next year is less than 1 per cent, and below age forty-five less than 0.5 per cent. Thus, the pure time preference of the rational individual as I have defined him, should be less than 1 per cent a year up to age fifty. Or to cite a long-run figure, a twenty-year-old person looking ahead to a date fifty years away should discount at an average annual rate of 0.9 per cent. In old age the rate rises, of course, as the probability of survival diminishes.

The figures for India are considerably higher. Pure time preference based on rational mortality expectations never gets much below 1 per cent, and ranges up to 5 per cent even for moderate ages. For example, a rational Indian at age twenty, evaluating utility to be enjoyed fifty years hence, would discount it at an annual rate of 2.8 per cent. Thus, in underdeveloped countries, where life expectancy

457

is short, even "rational individuals" are governed by substantial pure time preference.

Two factors must be kept in mind in interpreting these figures. First, these pure time preference factors measure only one component of interest rates reflecting the intertemporal values of individuals. The time profile of expected incomes interacting with the shape of the marginal utility of consumption curve at different ages also affects the "rational" interest rate. A person with a rising income stream will find the marginal utility of early consumption greater and will use a higher interest rate in his intertemporal choices. Conversely, an older person with a falling income stream will find it worth while to postpone marginal consumption outlays to a time when the marginal utility of consumption will be greater; his valuation of present versus future marginal consumption may involve an implicit negative rate of interest. The second factor, trends in the marginal utility of consumption with age, probably works in the same direction; the cost of rearing children makes consumption expenditures in the younger, more active, years of greater utility than later on, i.e., the marginal utility of consumption function drifts downward in the conventional diagram.

Besides considering the other factors that enter into the "rational" marginal valuation of consumption at different points in time, the desire to leave an estate may modify intertemporal valuations. Thus the high time preference rates of old-age that would be derived from mortality expectations may be overruled by a desire to transfer wealth to a wife or to future generations.

Despite the significance of these motivations, our computations have some suggestive implications. First, for all countries, the uncertainty of survival leads to a purely rational preference of present consumption over future. Thus, the condemnation of all time preference as "due to weakness of the imagination" (Ramsey) is based on the unrealistic view that individuals live forever. Second, in advanced countries, the pure time preference discount rate is very low over a wide range of ages. But in underdeveloped countries, this pure discount rate is considerably higher, though even in a country with as bad a mortality experience as India, the factor ranges only from below 1 to 5 per cent over a range of ages which encompasses most of the population.

Granting then the existence of perfectly rational preference of earlier consumption for individuals, the question remains whether a public planning body should take such preference into account. As has been pointed out in numerous places, the society goes on forever, and in the absence of thermonuclear war, there is almost certainty about the perpetual life of the population as an entity. If the social welfare function is a sum of utilities enjoyed by individuals, regardless of when they live, then mortality probabilities of specific individuals become irrelevant, and pure time preference is eliminated.

An interest rate can still be based on the diminishing marginal utility of income as per capita income rises, but rates based only on this mechanism are relatively low for plausible combinations of rates of increase of per capita income and elasticities of the utility curves.

A planner's welfare function which ignores individual time preference may well be in the long run interest of the society, but, strictly speaking, it is not a preference derived from individual desires, and hence falls into the category of dictatorial preference functions. Now a welfare function which adds up the utility of everybody, present and future, may be a defensible value judgment by which a policy-maker may choose to operate. Where government is democratic, the population may choose to operate by this value judgment through the political process; that is to say, its politicans may find decision-making according to low interest rates a successful component of their platform. But there is nothing in economic analysis *per se* which justifies this particular welfare function over all others.

What is more, there is growing and abundant evidence that the people of underdeveloped countries do place a considerable premium upon benefits in the early years of development projects. In India, for example, there has been some dissatisfaction with investment plans that yield little for quite a while, partly because of long periods of construction. Even in Russia there has been some revamping of investment plans, reducing the number of new projects being started for the sake of more rapid completion of the vast amount of work in progress;[29] there has also been some shift away from gigantic long-lived projects, such as huge hydroelectric dams, toward smaller, less durable and less capital-intensive projects, including steam plants.

The planner may feel that he is protecting the nation against its

[29] Reported in *The New York Times*, June 12, 1958, p. 14.

own shortsightedness by using low interest rates. But where this flies in the face of popular desire, he runs some risks that he may lose the chance of development on the Western model altogether. And even within the narrow perspective of economic analysis, early benefits may have morale effects which yield extra production and generally add momentum to the development effort.

Thus the choice of interest rates must remain a value judgment. I have discussed some of the elements that enter into the choice and have presented two models which derive elements of interest rates from empirical magnitudes, to show that there are some objective factors that can enter into the choice. But these must be combined with subjective judgments that cannot be value-free.

B. THE RATE OF RETURN *vs.* PRESENT
VALUE COMPUTATIONS

Since the selection of an interest rate requires subjective judgment, the ranking of projects by means of rate of return comparisons has been an attractive alternative. The interest rate issue could be side-stepped, since each project has an internal rate of return which can be computed. Given a limited amount of capital, projects could be ranked by their rates of return, and the projects with the highest rates could be undertaken. The rate of the marginal project, the cut-off rate, could then serve for technological choices in project design.

This procedure is meaningful only under a regime of perfect competition, in which the capital market contains no rationing and is equated by the interest rate serving as the price.

Hirshleifer has recently shown, that only in very peculiar cases other than perfectly competitive capital markets does the use of the rate of return criterion result in optimal results.[30] Once the marginal returns inside the budget being planned differ from returns elsewhere in the economy and from the rates being offered to suppliers of capital, the internal rate of return loses any normative significance. Hirshleifer's neat and exhaustive analysis, which shows the inexorable relevance of the subjective time preference of the planning agent, disposes, once and for all, I think, of the rate of return criterion.

Other attempts to escape the necessity of specifying an interest rate have been made, and some of them are discussed in Section 7

---

[30] J. Hirshleifer, "On the Theory of Optimal Investment Decision," *Journal of Political Economy*, August 1958, pp. 329–52. Also see my "Investment Criteria . . . ," p. 64, where the same point is made.

below.[31] It will be argued there that none of these attempts is satisfactory. Relative values on the outputs of different periods must be established, and only an interest rate can do this. Once interest rates are used, present values of benefits and costs can be computed and utilized in decision criteria.

One of these present-value criteria is closely related to rates of return, and has sometimes not been sufficiently distinguished from it. This is the SMP, or social marginal product of capital criterion,[32] proposed by Chenery.[33] The SMP of a project is the rate of present value of net benefit per dollar of capital cost. It applies where capital is a constraining factor on a budget, the case where the rate of return criterion might appear to apply. But while focusing on a rate on capital, it differs from the rate of return in the crucial respect that it requires an interest rate to be specified for the computation of the present value of net benefit. Thus the SMP is one of a family of present value criteria, while the rate of return is not.

Č. THE OPPORTUNITY COST OF CAPITAL
AND THE INTEREST RATE

Just as some form of social time preference is required for planning within the expenditure field, it is also needed for measuring opportunity costs. For efficient resource allocation, the capital in a specific use must yield as much satisfaction as in the opportunity which is foregone. But this cost must be expressed in terms comparable to the benefits. The foregone flow of satisfaction must be reduced to a present-value concept by means of a social rate of discount.

Elsewhere,[34] I have measured the opportunity cost of capital raised by federal taxation in the United States, and expressed it as an interest rate. This rate proved to be 5 to 6 per cent. It is no more than an empirical approximation to the desired magnitude, since it does not employ a social discount rate.[35] To convert this opportunity cost rate to a present value concept, the chosen rate of social discount must be used in the following manner: suppose the opportunity cost

[31] See the discussion of the model of Sen below.
[32] For example, in *Water Resource Development*, p. 61, I mislabel the SMP criterion a rate of return criterion.
[33] H. B. Chenery, "The Application of Investment Criteria," *Quarterly Journal of Economics*, February 1953, pp. 76–96.
[34] J. V. Krutilla and Otto Eckstein, *Multiple Purpose River Basin Development*, 1958, Ch. 4.
[35] Peter O. Steiner first saw this point. See his "Choosing Among Alternative Public Investments," *American Economic Review*, December 1959.

rate is 6 per cent; as measured in my empirical study, this is a perpetual stream of .06 cents per dollar of capital. Assume that the chosen rate of social discount is 3 per cent, i.e., that the benefits of a project are reduced to a present value by discounting at that rate. Then in order to compare the benefits of the project with the foregone benefits of the opportunities in the private economy, the perpetual stream of .06 cents per dollar must also be valued at 3 per cent. In the present example, the present value of a dollar invested in the private opportunity is $2, since a perpetual stream of .06 discounted at 3 per cent has a present value of 2.[36] As an expenditure criterion, assuming the above numbers, this implies that public projects should only be undertaken if the ratio of present value of net benefits to capital cost is 2.0.

The particular notion of opportunity cost which was measured, the cost of capital raised by a particular tax system, is only of relevance in models which link expenditures to taxes, rather than to reduced other expenditures, inflation, foreign borrowing, tighter monetary policies, or whatever other method the government may devise to raise the capital. Each method has its own opportunity cost which must be measured, and valued with a social rate of time discount.

Thus both opportunity cost and an interest rate must be specified for expenditure models. For example, in conventional benefit-cost analysis, a present value of benefits must be computed, using some interest rate. The rate at which costs result in present value of benefit, that is, the marginal benefit-cost ratio, must then be compared with the rate at which present value is foregone elsewhere, i.e., the opportunity cost. A correctly constructed criterion will pass a project only if the rate of present value of benefit per dollar exceeds the rate of present value per dollar of opportunity cost. Even if a low rate of interest is chosen, this does not mean that projects which yield low rates of return can be built or that scales of development can be pushed to a point where increments yield a low return. It only means that the present values, both on the benefit and the cost side, are computed using a low interest rate.[37]

[36] If the opportunity cost is not expressed as a perpetual stream, for example, if the time profile of returns of the private opportunities can be identified, a present value has to be computed explicitly.

[37] The procedure proposed in my book, *Water Resource Development*, corresponds to this logic. A low interest rate is coupled with marginal benefit-cost ratios sufficiently in excess of 1.0 to assure that the project exceeds its opportunity cost.

The procedure of the Hell's Canyon study (in Krutilla and Eckstein, *Multiple Purpose River Development*) takes the short-cut of comparing opportunity cost with a rate of

The necessity for measuring opportunity costs springs from the fact that there is no perfect market mechanism which measures the cost of resources from the private sector. In the perfectly functioning market economy, opportunity cost of resources is fully measured by the price of factors of production purchased for a project, and there is no need to worry about the concept separately. It is because there are imperfections in the private economy, particularly in the capital market, that opportunity cost must be measured and utilized as a criterion in determining public budgets, and must be valued at a social rate of interest.

4. Repercussion Effects

A. INTRODUCTION: PRICES *vs*. INTERDEPENDENCE RECOGNIZED

In devising an analytic framework for maximizing any given objective function, there is an important choice in the selection of the chain of effects which should be pursued, both on the benefit and on the cost sides. The proper circumscription of the analysis is one of the critical points in the economics of public expenditures. It is all too easy to find myriad favorable effects of a social nature, both tangible and intangible; it is equally easy to lapse into such rigid acceptance of the rationale of the perfect market mechanism that the broader public viewpoint is lost altogether.

So far in economic science, only one approach has been developed for defining the proper area of analysis. It uses the perfect competition scheme as a point of departure; as is well known, under perfect competition, with price ratios equal to marginal rates of transformation in production and marginal rates of substitution in consumption, prices are precise indicators of value, and there is no need to pursue any repercussion beyond the most immediate market;

---

return of alternative plans. None of the results would have been affected by going through the intermediate step of revaluing the alternatives and the opportunity costs at a social rate of interest and then comparing the present values.

An alternative interpretation of the latter study, the interpretation given in the theoretical derivation of the opportunity cost concept, is the following: the proper social rate of interest is stated to be the rate which the taxpayers who are forced to finance the project choose to be their marginal rate of time preference. That is, the time preference of individuals is accepted for the government. This model is certainly closer to the strict concept of economic efficiency based on individual tastes. The upshot of the present discussion is this, however: even if individual time preference is rejected for public decision-making, opportunity cost, including foregone consumption, is a critical parameter that must be in the model.

the market mechanism produces an efficient allocation of resources. Because the real world is not perfectly competitive, some repercussions ought to be pursued, but in this approach each instance is justified by showing how the specific situation fails to conform to the competitive ideal. As will be seen in what follows, the range of repercussion effects that can occur is very wide, and while the use of perfect competition as a point of departure may impart some conservative bias against measuring them, it is a small bias and a shrinking one, as economists concerned with the problems of underdeveloped countries discover more and more cases in which the repercussions count. Further, the need to justify inclusion of repercussions improves the quality of the analysis and provides a framework for empirical measurement; it gives specific meaning to the "social" effects within an individualist welfare economic point of view.

We shall assay no comprehensive treatment of repercussion effects, since they vary from case to case. But we shall list the major categories, and give some indication of the techniques which would measure them.

B. A LIST OF LOCAL EFFECTS

Local, including some regional, effects involve simpler considerations than over-all national repercussions; they are listed first, not necessarily in the order of their importance.

Physical Interdependence

If a project has off-the-site physical effects, a particularly common phenomenon in water resource projects, their economic implications clearly require inclusion in the analysis. Where off-the-site effects are small, it may be possible to make simple allowances for such benefits and costs. For example, when an upstream storage reservoir is added to a system, its incremental benefits to projects downstream can be computed directly. But as the number of projects increases above one and the interrelations become more complex, centralized planning must be applied to the river basin as a whole. The Harvard Seminar in Water Resource Planning is experimenting with various planning techniques, including elaborate simulations, programing, and marginal analysis; actual physical interdependence relations turn out to be very complex, involving mixtures of competitive and complementary relationships. From the researches of this

Seminar it is clear that the problem is soluble for the water resource case—which is perhaps the most complex—but that it tests the analytic and computing technology of modern engineering and economics.

Economic Interdependence: Investment Coordination

Where a project produces outputs that are producers' goods. the value depends on the existence of industrial markets. If the growth of industry in a region is rapid, additional outputs cannot be considered to be incremental, and must be evaluated as part of an overall investment plan.[38] In this field, too, planning techniques have not been perfected, but linear and nonlinear programing, utilizing input-output data, offer considerable hope of solution.[39]

Large Changes in Inputs and Outputs

If a project is so large that it changes the prices of its outputs and inputs, market prices cease to be unambiguous indicators of value. This is a matter we have touched upon in Section 1, where we saw that reasonable approximations, such as arithmetic or geometric means of old and new prices, are readily at hand. In some cases, such as large power projects, finer approximations are possible by analyzing separate segments of the demands.

Local Unemployment

Where part of the factors of production, including labor, are un- or underemployed, their market price overstates their opportunity costs. If their opportunity cost is zero, their real cost for purposes of project planning may also be zero. Should their employment generate other costs, however, such as large food consumption or urbanization costs, these need to be considered, of course.

Social Overhead

All productive enterprises require certain complementary investments in public facilities, such as police and fire protection, public

[38] For more detailed discussion of these matters, see R. Nurkse, *Problems of Capital Formation in Underdeveloped Countries*, pp. 1–24, where they are treated as part of the problem of balanced growth. Also see T. Scitovsky, "Two Concepts of External Economies," *Journal of Political Economy*, April 1954, pp. 143–51; and J. A. Stockfisch, "External Economies, Investment and Foresight," *ibid.*, October 1955, pp. 446–9.

[39] See the forthcoming book by Chenery, and H. B. Chenery and H. Uzawa, "Nonlinear Programing in Economic Development" in *Studies in Linear and Nonlinear Programing*, Arrow, *et al.*, eds., Stanford, 1958, pp. 203–29.

health services, schools, workers' housing, etc. These are all real costs, of course, whether the project is charged a price for them or not.

Local Monopoly and Monopsony

If the project deals with monopolists, either in selling its outputs or in purchasing its factors of production, market prices may not measure value; the project then generates monopoly profits, which after all, are also part of national income (though they might be given a weight of zero in some objective functions). For example, if the profits in the processing of output include a monopsony element, then the price is below the value of output. Measurement is very difficult in this case, since accounting profits include normal profits and the regular return on equity capital.

C. EFFECTS ON THE ECONOMY AS A WHOLE

Repercussion effects on the economy as a whole should properly be measured and included in the analysis to the extent that there are specific imperfections in the economic system. Unemployment, capital shortage, foreign exchange imbalance, and excessive population growth are some of the items that fall in this category. We treat a few of the more important.

Keynesian Unemployment

In a situation of general unemployment, the conventional multiplier measures the repercussion effects on national income which are caused by the increase in purchasing power. Recent empirical studies suggest that the total multiplier in the American economy is on the order of 1.4 or so,[40] when all the various leakages, including taxes and retained earnings, are taken into account.[41] Of course the multiplier differs from project to project, depending on the marginal propensities to consume of the income recipients; but the recent work of Strout, using input-output techniques, implies that the differences,

[40] J. S. Duesenberry, Otto Eckstein and Gary Fromm, "A Simulation of the U.S. Economy in Recession," paper presented at the December 1958 meetings of the Econometric Society (to be published).

[41] If it is assumed that government expenditures are limited by revenues, i.e., that the government has a marginal propensity to spend equal to 1.0, the multiplier becomes much larger. Also, if the impact on inventory fluctuations is included—an impact that has to come quickly because of the speed with which inventory fluctuations occur—the multiplier becomes larger.

at least as far as off-the-site purchases of goods and services are concerned, are extremely small.[42]

Whether multiplier effects should be incorporated in the analysis depends, in part, on administrative policy. Past experience with investment projects suggests that their time-table makes them rather ineffective in counteracting the swift disturbances that have characterized the postwar period in advanced economies. Some speed-up of work in progress does appear feasible in recession, but this does not require that original investment plans need reflect this possible repercussion; symmetry would also suggest that if multiplier effects in potential recessions be included in the analysis, similar effects in inflation also be measured. In underdeveloped economies, on the other hand, Keynesian lack of effective demand may not be the critical dimension of the unemployment problem.

Structural Unemployment and Underemployment

Where an underdeveloped economy simply has an inadequate number of jobs for its population, or where many people are in occupations in which their productivity is very low or zero, the expenditure decision model must take some cognizance of this state of affairs. From the point of view of maximizing national income, money-wages are not likely to be reasonable measures of opportunity costs, and so some "adjusted" wage, possibly equal to zero, may be needed. In addition, employment-creation may be an important part of the objective function; separate quantitative analysis may be needed to measure the performance of projects on this scale, including the employment generated in subsequent stages of production; input-output analysis appears the logical quantitative technique.

Capital and Foreign Exchange Scarcity

In many countries, the desired rate of economic development is limited by the scarcity of capital and of foreign exchange. This can be introduced into the expenditure model in at least two ways: first, the two sources of finance may be treated as budget constraints, determining the choice of criterion. Second, the repercussion effects of projects in this regard can be measured, including the indirect

---

[42] Alan Strout, "Primary Employment Effects of Alternative Spending Programs," *Review of Economics and Statistics*, November 1958, pp. 319–28. Strout analyzes employment multiplier effects, but since differences in marginal propensities to consume largely relate to differences between wage-earners and others, his conclusions carry over to income-multipliers.

effects caused in other industries and in the purchases of consumers. The generation of reinvestible capital out of the income payments of projects is a particular instance of these repercussion effects.

Population effects

If it can be shown that some expenditures change the environment of workers in such a manner as to reduce the rate of population growth, and if the objective function is expressed in terms of *per capita* income, expenditure analysis must include population repercussions. This factor is often cited as making investment in urban areas relatively more attractive.[43]

D. CONCLUDING COMMENT

These lists of possible repercussions that ought to be measured in certain cases are far from complete. Each situation has peculiarities of its own, which make different repercussions of relevance. The only analytically valid principle that has been advanced so far for determining their inclusion or exclusion is the technique of comparison of the actual case to the perfectly competitive model.

5. The Treatment of Risk and Uncertainty

A. INTRODUCTION

Expenditure criteria must take some cognizance of the risky and uncertain nature of the economic world. Unfortunately, welfare economics has no complete apparatus for dealing with risk, no applicable optimum conditions from which decision criteria can be derived.[44] Nevertheless, it can easily be shown that for many reasonable objective functions, some account must be taken of risk, and some approaches will be indicated.

In evaluating these various adjustments for risks and uncertainty, it must be borne in mind, however, that something is being given

---

[43] This factor, as well as the importance of generating reinvestible capital, was put into the center of discussion by Galenson and Leibenstein. They also stress the effect of projects on the skills of the workers. W. Galenson and H. Leibenstein, "Investment Criteria, Productivity and Economic Development," *Quarterly Journal of Economics*, August 1955, pp. 343–70.

[44] But see K. J. Arrow, "Le Rôle des Valeurs Boursières pour la Répartition la Meilleure des Risques," *International Colloquium on Econometrics*, 1952, pp. 41–47, Centre National de la Recherche Scientifique, Paris, 1953, reprinted as Cowles Commission Paper, N.S. 77, where an interesting model which seeks to incorporate risks, gambling, and insurance into the competitive model is presented. Also see, M. Allais, "L'Extension des Théories de l'Équilibre Économique Général et du Rendement Social au Cas du Risque," *Econometrica*, April 1953, pp. 269–90.

up in exchange for the greater security, and that from the point of view of the country in the long run, short-run adjustments may not prove to be optimal. For example, if there is an empirical foundation for the idea of a risk premium, i.e., that risky investments have to have a relatively higher expected gain, then the national income will rise more if risky investments are undertaken, even though more risk is being experienced. It is possible that a series of risky, high-return investments not only give the country a higher national income, but also will put it in a more secure position in the long run than safe, low-return investments. Thus, even though there is a strong case for various adjustments in the direction of secure actions, the sum of a lot of adjustments may have the opposite effect of what is desired.

B. SOME CRUDE ADJUSTMENTS

The traditional adjustment for risk is simply to be conservative. In expenditure analysis, this has often taken three forms: (1) contingency allowances, which arbitrarily raise certain categories of costs by a certain percentage or reduce benefits through price assumptions which are below expected prices; (2) a limit to economic life shorter than physical life but also shorter than expected economic life; and (3) a risk premium in the interest rate. The first of these adjustments, which in many instances is a part of standard engineering practice, may simply be an allowance for errors in forecasting which past experience suggests will recur. Contingency allowances for costs are particularly of this character, since some unexpected costs always occur in construction. Thus, in a sense, they simply improve the quality of forecasts by allowing for expected errors.

A limit on economic life, which is particularly significant for projects like dams which have no definite terminal date, partly serves to standardize analysis of different projects. It also is an adjustment for technological progress, since it implicitly assumes that the economic value of the project goes to zero at some future date; this is clearly a very crude adjustment. The risk premium in the interest rate accomplishes the same purpose more delicately, since it discounts remote benefits progressively more heavily. The risk premium can have a precise basis where the probability of failure is known and remains constant over time. For example, if the probability of failure, defined as an economic value of zero after some date, is equal to .04 per year, the risk premium should be approximately[45] 4 per cent. But this precise application is only possible in connection with credit risks on securities with which there is lots of experience; for physical projects, there is, so far, no empirical method for determining the premium.

These crude adjustments are intellectually not very satisfying, and one should try to derive better adjustments from explicit objective functions and from the specific probabilistic nature of benefits. But where the probability distributions are unknown or based on very little information, or where it is difficult to specify an objective function that can fully value the effects of risk or uncertainty, the crude adjustments are appropriate and important; at least there is some cognizance of the problem.

C. THE CASE OF PURE RISK: PUTTING RISK ATTITUDES
INTO THE OBJECTIVE FUNCTION

Following conventional terminology, we call "risk" the state of affairs in which a probability distribution can be specified without error. Strictly speaking, the evidence is never complete and the parameters of the probability distribution are given with some error. But when such error is small, good results can be obtained by treating the problem as one of pure risk. While events which can be characterized as risky are rarely encountered in the analysis of public expenditures, the water resource field is replete with them because of the dependence of projects on hydrology; flood control benefits depend on the probabilities of flood events; irrigation benefits depend on stream flow probabilities. Social insurance is another field subject to risk, actuarial risk in this case.

There are several different ways of handling risk in the analysis.[46] With probability distributions of outcomes known, means, variances, and possibly even higher moments can be put into the objective function.[47] In the most general form, the objective function can be written

$$(5.1) \qquad\qquad W = (\mu, \sigma, \dots).$$

[45] It is only an approximation because the proper risk premium is $\sum_t (1 - p)^t$, where p is the probability of loss in a period. This expression is only approximated by $\sum_t \dfrac{1}{(1 + p)^t}$, the expression in the text. I owe this point to Donald Farrar.

[46] The need to include risk attitudes in the objective function was impressed on me by Harold Thomas in the Harvard Water Resource Seminar. See his paper discussed below.

[47] For a survey of authors who have made this suggestion, see K. J. Arrow, "Alternative Approaches to the Theory of Choice in Risk-Taking Situations," *Econometrica*, October 1953, pp. 269–90.

If we confine ourselves to the first two moments, this can be represented by an indifference map with the mean on one axis and the standard deviation on the other.[48] If there is aversion to risk, the indifference curves will slope away from the origin, with an increase in expected gain offset by an increase in the standard deviation.

Maximization of Expected Utility

Following Bernoulli[49] a utility function can be specified for which the expected value is maximized. Unless that function is linear, implying a constant marginal utility, it will result in the utilization of the probability distribution of outcomes in the optimizing analysis. This maximization of expected utility has been argued widely to be the rational form of behavior under conditions of risk. As a descriptive hypothesis, it can be tested empirically,[50] and is certainly not a perfect description of human behavior. But in normative welfare economics, as a prescription of what the rational consumer ought to do, it may serve the same purpose as the conventional theory of the consumer under certainty.

A particular problem in applying the approach to public expenditures is the choice of the person(s) whose utility function is to apply. Is it the utility function of the planner or of the affected individuals? This is a problem analogous to the choice of interest rate. From a strictly individualist ethical point of view, the functions of the individuals should be used and weighted in some way. But in connection with the loss of utility due to risk, as with the loss of expected utility due to mortality risks, the group as a whole may suffer less than the individual. The variance of the total outcome may be relatively smaller than for each individual because of pooling.

An Example: Flood Control Design

This example is a highly simplified illustration of the effect of introducing utility functions on flood control design. It will be shown that for a broad class of utility functions, utility maximization leads to

---

[48] This is drawn, for example, in F. Lutz and V. Lutz, *The Theory of Investment of the Firm*, 1951, pp. 190.

[49] See Daniel Bernoulli, "Exposition of a New Theory on the Measurement of Risk," (1738) translated by Louise Sommer in *Econometrica*, January 1954, pp. 23–46 for the original statement. For a summary of the literature see K. J. Arrow, "Alternative Approaches to the Theory of Choice in Risk-Taking Situations," *Econometrica*, October 1951, pp. 404–37.

[50] Early tests provide some support, but at this time the evidence must still be considered mixed. See K. J. Arrow, *ibid.*, p. 12, for a survey and further references.

more flood control than income maximization. The latter is equivalent to minimizing the expected cost of damages plus the cost of control works.[51]

Suppose utility is related to income by

(5.2) $$U = F(y),$$

and let $F'(y)$ be strictly decreasing with increasing y. Let s be the height of floods in the absence of control, expressed in feet of flood stage, and let r be the number of feet by which flood stage is reduced through control works such as a dam. Let

(5.3) $$x = s - r$$

be the number of feet of flood stage after control works are installed (s is determined by rainfall and other hydrological factors). The probability of occurrence of any particular value of s is described by the probability distribution $p(s)$, where s takes on only integral values.

Income is affected by a flood of x by an amount $g(x)$, measured by damages. Thus

(5.4) $$\Delta U(x) = F(y_o + g(x)) - F(y_o) = h(x),$$

where y_o is the level of income without flood.

We wish to minimize the expected value of this loss of utility due to floods, where r is the policy variable. The loss comes from two sources, the flood damages and the cost of control works. Let $\delta(r)$ be the cost of r. Thus the function to be minimized is

(5.5) $$\rho(r) = \bar{h}(r) + F'(y_o) \cdot \delta(r),$$

where $\bar{h}(r)$ is the expected value of $h(r)$ if control works serve to cut flood stage by r, and where $F'(y_o) \cdot \delta(r)$ is the marginal utility of income multiplied by the cost of r.

We must set

$$\rho'(r) = 0,$$

i.e.,

(5.6) $$\bar{h}'(r) + F'(y_o) \cdot \delta'(r) = 0.$$

But

$$\bar{h}(r) = \sum_{s=r+1}^{\infty} p(s)h(s - r),$$

so that

(5.7) $$\bar{h}'(r) = - \sum_{s=r+1}^{\infty} p(s)h'(s - r).$$

---

[51] The following argument is due to E. C. Schlesinger of the Department of Mathematics, Wesleyan University.

Hence the condition which minimizes the loss of utility is

$$(5.8) \qquad \sum_{s=r+1}^{\infty} p(s)h'(s-r) = F'(y_o) \cdot \delta'(r),$$

which must be solved for r.

Next, suppose we seek to maximize income, i.e., minimize the loss of income caused by floods. We substitute $g(r)$ for $h(r)$. Then we must minimize

$$(5.9) \qquad \psi(r) = \bar{g}(r) + \delta(r),$$

the expected damages plus the cost of control. This requires

$$\bar{g}'(r) + \delta'(r) = 0,$$

or

$$(5.10) \qquad \sum_{s=r+1}^{\infty} p(s)g'(s-r) = \delta'(r),$$

which is to be solved for r.

We now contrast the two solutions (5.8) and (5.10). Suppose r_o satisfies (5.10), the minimum cost solution, and that (5.8) has only one solution. It will be shown that

$$\rho'(r_o) < 0,$$

from which we can conclude that the optimal value of r for (5.8) is larger than that for (5.10).

The proof is based on (5.4) and on the assumption of the decreasing nature of $F'(y)$. From (5.4) we obtain

$$h'(x) = F'(y_o + g(x)) \cdot g'(x),$$

and from the assumption about the utility function we obtain that

$$(5.11) \quad h'(x) > F'(y_o) \cdot g'(x), \quad \text{since} \quad g(x) < 0 \quad \text{for} \quad x > 0.$$

We substitute (5.11) in (5.8). This yields

$$-\rho'(r_o) = \sum_{s=r+1}^{\infty} p(s)h'(s-r_o) - F'(y_o) \delta'(r_o).$$

The right side is greater than

$$F'(y_o) \left\{ \sum_{s=r+1}^{\infty} p(s)g'(s-r_o) - \delta'(r_o) \right\},$$

which equals zero by our assumption that r_o satisfies (5.10). Hence $\rho'(r_o) < 0$, as asserted.

This shows that utility maximization leads to more flood control than income maximization. This is no more than an application of the theory of insurance. It is interesting that the procedures actually applied in the design of flood control works reject income maximization, requiring substantially more control. The extent to which a utility-maximizing solution exceeds the income-maximizing result depends on the distribution of flood probabilities and the elasticity of the marginal utility of income curve. The more frequent and routine the flood losses, the smaller will be the deviation between the two solutions. An optimal set of flood-control design principles can be derived from a model which maximizes expected utility.

Models Utilizing Means and Standard Deviations of Outcomes[52]

In the general case, the maximization of expected utilities requires knowledge not only of the utility functions, but also of the complete probability distribution of outcomes. Decision criteria which require less knowledge have long had practical appeal. Several theoretical bases have been found for criteria that employ only the mean and standard deviation of outcomes.[53] Cramer[54] derived such a criterion in connection with insurance companies from the idea that the probability that income would fall below a certain level be minimized. A similar idea was applied by Roy.[55] He writes the objective function $W = f\left(\dfrac{\bar{B} - D}{\sigma_B}\right)$, where $\bar{B}$ is expected gain and D is the disaster level of outcome, the occurrence of which is to be minimized. The specification of the disaster level, which is a critical parameter for the ranking criterion, is a problem which appears to be of the same order of difficulty as specifying the utility functions. And the use of the standard deviation to measure the probability of failure is appropriate only if the probability distribution is normal, if it is of some other form that can be fully characterized by mean and standard deviation, or if all the alternatives have the same form of probability distribution.

[52] This section has benefited from my reading Don Farrar's, "The Investment Decision under Uncertainty," Harvard Water Resource Seminar Paper, September 1958, which discusses the models by Roy and Thomas, as well as an interesting model by Steindl.

[53] The indifference curves which correspond to this criterion are a series of parallel lines on a plane which has mean on one axis, standard deviation on the other.

[54] H. Cramer, "On the Mathematical Theory of Risk," Forsakringsaktiebolaget Skandias Festskrift, Stockholm, 1930, pp. 7–84, cited in Arrow, "Alternative Theories . . . ," *op.cit.*, p. 423.

[55] A. D. Roy, "Safety First and the Holding of Assets," *Econometrica*, July 1952, pp. 431–49.

A model of the same general type has been advanced by Thomas[56] for ranking water-resource projects. He argues that a project should have a positive pay-off over its life at some prespecified probability level. He suggests that an insurance fund be set up of such size that it is capable of making up the losses in any specific year, and that it have a positive balance at the end of the undertaking. It turns out that if the outcomes are normally distributed, the size of this insurance fund depends on the mean and standard deviation of outcomes and the specified probability level that the fund be adequate. With the fund considered part of costs, the objective function takes the form $W = \bar{B} + a\sigma$, where a depends on the probability level at which the success of the insurance fund is to be guaranteed. Where Roy minimizes the probability of disaster, Thomas maximizes net gain, including an insurance charge against failure. As in the previous model, the determination of this probability level is a problem akin to the specification of utility functions.[57]

The models of this type have a greater ring of concreteness than the maximization of expected utility. Yet except for those rare cases where there is an institutional basis for specifying the disaster level of outcome or the even rarer cases where the acceptable probability level of failure can be empirically determined, they are arbitrary adjustments to risk, perhaps not as crude as the "crude adjustments" discussed earlier, yet considerably removed from modern optimizing criteria. They stand in the same relation to expected utility maximization as the classical theory of statistical inference stands to modern decision theory[58].

Further Comment on Utility Maximization

If we insist on the specification of utility functions, we must be prepared to give some empirical implementation to this idea. While this is not an easy problem, it is an unavoidable one, since even in the classical models the specification of disaster levels of income or of confidence levels of probability presumably would need to be derived

[56] H. A. Thomas, Jr., "A Method for Accounting for Benefit and Cost Uncertainties in Water Resource Project Design," Harvard Water Resources Seminar Paper. For an empirical application see J. S. King, "A Method for Consideration of Risk and Uncertainty in Water Resource Project Evaluation," Harvard Water Resource Seminar Paper.

[57] L. Telser has employed the same model as Thomas' in an analysis of hedging behavior. See his "Safety First and Hedging," *Review of Economic Studies*, 1955–56, pp. 1–17.

[58] See R. D. Luce and H. Raiffa, *Games and Decisions*, Wiley, 1957, pp. 318–24.

from implicit estimates of utility functions. Certain elements of these functions can be derived from objective data. For example, in irrigation and hydroelectric power the money losses of shortage of stream flow are a crucial variable, and similarly in navigation and low flow control. Thus the derivation of these loss functions is a necessary and empirically feasible first step toward deriving optimal criteria. In addition, the shapes of individual utility of income functions must be specified, admittedly a heroic task. But reasonable assumptions about their general shape can be made, which, if not derived from experimental data, may be in the nature of value judgments (see Section 2 above). To fail to specify them is not to solve the problem, but simply to leave its resolution to the random process of picking the function which is implicit in the selection of values of other, more "pragmatic" parameters.

D. THE CASE OF UNCERTAINTY[59]

By uncertainty we mean the case where information about the probability distributions of outcomes is incomplete, that is, that their parameters are not known precisely. Strictly speaking, this includes all empirically derived probability distributions; but in this section we are concerned with that range of cases in which it is not a reasonable assumption for policy purposes to treat the distributions as known.

Even for individual action there are few settled conclusions about what constitutes rationality under conditions of uncertainty. In a few cases, considerable theoretical progress has been made. The most important of these are games of strategy involving at least two players. Here the Von Neumann-Morgenstern theory and subsequent developments (including bargaining theories) provide principles of decision. Public expenditures for national defense clearly require this type of analysis, as may expenditures which are primarily part of domestic political games.

Leaving genuine games aside, there still remain stubborn problems where decisions must be made with imperfect information. For example, no empirical probabilistic description can be given to the problem of price projection or to the forecasting of floods so extreme that the historical record contains only one or even no instance. Several principles have been advanced that might be applied. From the theory of games, the minimax principle has been drawn, which

---

[59] A critical survey of the relevant literature can be found in Luce and Raiffa, *ibid.*

would require that course of action which would minimize the losses which would occur if the worst possible circumstance arose. Where no rational opponent is involved, this is too conservative a principle. In flood control or irrigation design, for example, it would make decisions depend exclusively on the worst possible event that human imagination could visualize for the project, regardless of how remote the possibility. A somewhat different principle is the "minimax regret" criterion,[60] suggested by Savage. In choosing between two alternatives, it minimizes the difference between what would happen in the better outcome and in the worse outcome. Choices among more alternatives would be made by a series of comparisons among pairs. It is doubtful that this concept of regret is a desirable principle of action in the areas with which we are concerned; this criterion also suffers from excessive influence of very unlikely extreme values and has the additional fault that the optimum choice can be altered by the introduction of irrelevant alternatives. Hurwicz has suggested a third criterion, a weighted average of the best and the worst possible outcomes, with the weights left to the inherent pessimism or optimism of the decision-maker. This criterion, while it has the advantage of introducing both good and bad possible outcomes into the decision, still suffers from excessive influence of the extreme values.[61]

I can only echo Arrow's conclusion "that we do not really have a universally valid criterion for rational behavior under uncertainty. Probably the best thing that can be said is that different criteria are valid under different circumstances." For the range of decisions that is our concern, expenditure decisions that are not strictly strategies in a game, there is one important property that the decision criterion ought to reflect: while the probability distributions are not known, there is some experience, some knowledge which ought to aid in the decision. Typically the uncertainties are cases of difficult forecasting of prices, of rare floods, of industrial location patterns in the case of transportation facilities, and of other events the underlying mechanism of which is not fully understood.

The use of a priori probabilities is one possibility, in which the

[60] Besides Luce and Raiffa, there are several other interesting surveys of these criteria. See K. J. Arrow, "Utilities, Attitudes, Choices: A Review Note," *Econometrica*, January 1958, pp. 1–23; Roy Radner and Jacob Marschak, "Note on Some Proposed Decision Criteria," *Decision Processes* (1954); R. M. Thrall *et al.*, eds., pp. 61–8; and John Milnor, "Games against Nature," *ibid.*, pp. 49–59.
[61] Luce and Raiffa criticize this criterion on other grounds.

qualified "expert" attaches subjective probabilities on the basis of the evidence and of his intuition. Given these probabilities, including the joint probability distributions of the various dimensions of output, the problem can then be treated like a problem in risk. Since the subjective probability mechanism is no more than a method of utilizing a combination of evidence and intuition, there is a question as to whether it is the best method. This is a matter of personal taste; some may find the mechanism natural to their thinking processes; others may find it an encumbrance.

Another possibility is to use some sort of contingency approach, in which the major hazards are identified to which the undertaking is subject and which have some minimum a priori probability of occurrence. Strategies can then be devised which will reduce the maximum possible loss caused by each contingency to some bearable level. Within these constraints, some maximization of expected values might then be carried out. Alternatively, striking a completely defensive posture, the probabilities of certain loss levels might be minimized, with the weights given to the prevention of different contingencies determined from some preference function. The similarity of contingency planning to the models of Thomas, Roy and others discussed above will be seen.[62] It also has some strong similarities to Simon's "satisficing" analysis.[63]

I am sure enough has been said to indicate that this particular problem is far from a solution. In the meantime, judgment methods must be used, whether verbal or formal, with the identification of the major contingencies and some provision being made against them constituting a minimum program for the design of reasonable decision procedures in the face of uncertainty.

6. *A Survey of Some Recent Models*

A. INTRODUCTION

Having set up a taxonomy of the problem of public expenditure criteria, I shall now use it to classify the various models that have been advanced in recent years. No attempt will be made to present

---

[62] For discussion of contingency planning, see H. Kahn and I. Mann, *Techniques of System Analysis*, The RAND Corporation, RM-1829-1, ASTIA Doc. No. AD133012, June 1957, pp. 85–113. For a similar view, applied to research and development decisions, and stressing the resultant need for preserving flexibility, see Burton Klein and William Meckling, "Application of Operations Research to Development Decisions," *Operation Research*, May–June 1958, pp. 352–63.

[63] See Section 1, above.

each model in full detail; in particular, the algorithms that have been advanced for the numerical solution of some of them will not be given. But the taxonomy should permit us to give the essence of each model, and to show the interrelations between them. The models designed for projects of water resource development are presented first, followed by a model for transportation, and concluding with more general models for economic development planning.

B. U.S. GOVERNMENT PRACTICE IN EVALUATION
OF WATER RESOURCE PROJECTS

The federal government evaluates water resource projects by means of benefit-cost analysis. There is no single model which is employed by all agencies;[64] one of the problems in evaluation practice has been the lack of uniform methods among agencies. But there are certain characteristics from which an "ideal" model of federal practice can be derived.[65]

The objective function of this model has two kinds of benefits; "direct" benefits which are largely net additions to individual incomes, and "indirect" benefits which are miscellaneous repercussion effects. At least in principle, the difference between benefits and costs is to be maximized in determining the scale of projects, while project ranking is to be based on the ratio of total benefits to total cost, the crude benefit-cost ratio. Except for the inconsistency between pursuing the scale of individual projects to a point where marginal benefit equals marginal cost while the benefit of marginal projects has to exceed costs at a rate equal to some benefit-cost ratio greater than one, this procedure corresponds to a model in which benefits minus costs are maximized subject to a constraint on cost. A dollar of benefit is given the same weight, no matter "to whom it may accrue," suggesting an objective function of the form (1.3) in Section 1.

The constraint is not applied to the same concept of cost by all agencies. *Proposed Practices* . . . suggests project costs as the proper denominator of the ratio, and hence implicitly as the proper constraint. These are all the costs incurred on the project itself and are contrasted with associated costs, the costs of associated enterprises.

---

[64] A detailed account of actual practices can be found in my *Water Resource Development*.

[65] The classical statement of the general approach of the government can be found in Federal Interagency River Basin Committee, Subcommittee on Benefits and Costs, *Proposed Practices of Economic Analysis of River Basin Projects*, May 1950.

The Corps of Engineers follows this concept. The Bureau of Reclamation uses federal cost, the cost borne by the federal government. The constraint is applied to costs occurring in all periods, present and future, discounted by the interest rate.

The interest rate needed to discount benefits and costs to derive present values[66] is specified independently and related to government borrowing costs. Since the funds for projects are rarely borrowed but rather raised by taxation, the government borrowing rate is irrelevant. Being rather low, it may be a reflection of social time preference however.

Repercussion effects are measured in the form of "indirect" benefits. These include profits created in processing and in sales to the project, in increased production and wage payments made possible by eliminating floods, and in several other ways. Most of these "indirect" benefits cannot be derived from any reasonable objective function unless a particularly heavy weight is attached to the income—and particularly to the profits—earned in the immediate proximity of the projects, and no weight at all is attached to the offsetting losses elsewhere in the economy.

There is relatively little adjustment for risk and uncertainty. Benefits that are particularly uncertain, usually only expected to begin to accrue in the future, are to be discounted at a higher rate of interest, injecting a slight risk premium. Also, there is general use of engineering contingency allowances in cost estimation. In flood control, some provision is made to stress control of rare "disaster" floods.

Without seeking to subject the federal techniques to systematic critique, five points should be made: (1) The objective function is consistent with the traditional individualist welfare economics and can fairly be interpreted as representing the national interest. (2) In the ranking procedure, there is recognition of the existence of a budget constraint, though the resultant implications for project design are not followed. Some ambiguity remains about the concept of cost to which the constraint is applied. (3) The opportunity cost of budget money is not brought into the analysis; no test is performed to assure that benefits on marginal outlays exceed these opportunity costs. (4) Measurement of repercussion effects largely seeks to measure irrelevant effects. Finally, (5) the model presented is an

---

[66] In actual practice annual equivalents are employed. These correspond to present value concepts, expressed as an annual average figure.

"ideal," with actual practice rarely utilizing the rankings by the benefit-cost ratio; the analysis is primarily used as a test by which projects with ratios less than 1.0 are rejected, with the scores above 1.0 having only a minor influence in project selection. Also, marginal principles are frequently not followed in project design, particularly in choice of scale.

C. A MODEL FOR BENEFIT-COST ANALYSIS

In my book, *Water Resource Development, the Economics of Project Evaluation,* I present a decision model which was designed to be appropriate to the budgeting problem of the federal water resource programs. This model maximizes the increase in real national income, assuming equal marginal utilities for individuals, subject to a constraint on federal cost. This constraint applies to both capital and operating and maintenance costs; in particular, it applies to the present value of these costs, measured with the interest rate of the analysis. This constraint was chosen over several others. A constraint only on capital was rejected because operating and maintenance costs represent a serious drain on the federal budget in several fields, particularly flood control and navigation; and in the others, e.g., irrigation, these costs are borne by local interests, and hence would automatically fall outside the constraint as far as appropriate. It was also chosen over separate constraints applicable to the funds used in different periods because there was no evidence to suggest drastic changes in the future pattern of availability of funds, and so a perennial constraint equal to present conditions was selected; this assumes that project opportunities are generated at the same rate as funds become available. Finally, while there is some exploration of constraints that include the funds generated by the reimbursable portions of a project, I reject this constraint, because, in actual federal practice, revenues of projects go into general treasury funds, and not into further expenditures for water resource programs.

The interest rate is to be chosen as an expression of social time preference. To bring the opportunity cost of budget money into the analysis, the marginal benefit-cost ratios which correspond to the opportunity costs of budget money raised by taxation are given. In the event that the benefit-cost ratio of marginal projects that can be undertaken within the budget constraint falls below this opportunity cost rate, the latter rate serves as a cutoff, and not all of the available budget money is to be spent.

Repercussion effects are limited in the model, because it is assumed to be applied in full employment conditions and in the mature market economy of the United States, where prices are on the whole, adequate indicators of value. Where there are genuine external economies, largely of a physical nature, these should be measured, of course. Also, in the case of decreasing cost transportation industries, marginal costs rather than actual freight rates measure value.

The treatment of risk and uncertainty is confined to "crude adjustments," particularly risk premiums in the interest rate. In connection with flood control, some recognition is taken of the effect of diminishing marginal utility of income, justifying departure from minimizing the expected total cost of floods in the direction of paying more attention to "disaster-type" floods, but no specific criteria are advanced.

D. MULTIPLE PURPOSE RIVER DEVELOPMENT

Some closely related models were used in a volume of empirical studies.[67] Four investigations were undertaken; (1) the opportunity cost of tax-raised budget money was estimated; (2) an economic analysis of alternative plans of development of the Hell's Canyon project was prepared, using the social cost of capital, as measured by opportunity cost; (3) the extent to which private development is likely to produce the potential nonmarketable outputs of multi-purpose projects was investigated through a case study of the Coosa River, Alabama, and (4), the income distribution effects of a project in the Pacific Northwest were measured under the alternative conditions of private and local, and federal development, with both costs and benefits allocated to regions and income classes. The fourth of these studies seeks to implement an objective function of the form (1.5) of Section 1, identifying distribution of gains and costs by region and of federal costs by income class. No effort is made to rank the alternatives, a task left to the political process; but the necessary data for judgment are presented. It turns out that federal development redistributes income toward the region, compared with other places. The distribution of federal costs by income class depends on the assumed tax changes, but under some likely assumptions falls heavily on the lower income groups. The third study determines the flood

[67] J. V. Krutilla and O. Eckstein, *Multiple Purpose River Development: Studies in Applied Economic Analysis*, Johns Hopkins, 1958. Also see G. L. Reuber and R. J. Wonnacott, "The Cost of Social Capital in Canada" (to be published), where the opportunity cost of funds raised by borrowing is estimated.

control and other nonmarketable benefits that could be produced by the project of the case study, compares them with the incremental costs, and then analyzes the private plan of development. It turns out that the private plan provides virtually none of the nonmarketable benefits.

The remaining two studies are interrelated. The opportunity cost of tax-raised funds is measured from what Musgrave calls the differential incidence of taxation; if the level of expenditures is changed, what tax changes would accompany it, assuming that stabilization policy requires some offset and that fiscal policy is the device chosen? Specific assumptions are made about these tax changes, based on judgment, the tax burden is traced to its ultimate incidence, and insofar as it falls on investment, the foregone rates of return are estimated. Foregone consumption is valued at the time preferences of the affected consumers, as revealed by their saving-borrowing behavior. The resultant average cost of marginal tax funds turns out to be on the order of 6 per cent. This rate is then applied to the Hell's Canyon case, and using it as a test, it turns out that a two-dam plan that costs less than the actual private three-dam plan of development but produces more output is the best choice. The incremental investment required for the one large dam, the public proposal, yields less than 4.5 per cent, assuming fully integrated operation. With opportunity costs at 6 per cent, this increment is rejected.

This model uses rate-of-return comparisons, though they are applied through a benefit-cost terminology. A strict efficiency point of view is taken, in which the interest rate of the analysis is based on individual time preference of the people who are taxed. Had a social time preference been used, perhaps including a lower interest rate, the results would have been the same. The opportunity cost would have had to be revalued into a present-worth concept at the preferred interest rate, and compared to the incremental benefit-cost ratios of the alternative plans. The empirical conclusions would have been identical, since the benefit-cost ratio of the foregone opportunities would have been on the order of 2.0, assuming an interest rate of 3 per cent, while the incremental investment of the large dam plan has a ratio of only 1.5; the two-dam plan would have continued preferable to the private plan, since it has lower costs and greater benefits.

This analysis assumes no budget constraints. This is justified because Hell's Canyon was not a question of choosing the best public projects, but rather to compare competing private and public plans. A victory for the public plan would have meant that the additional budget money would have been voted; in fact, such a victory would have resulted in a general expansion of public power programs, since it was a symbolic showdown between public and private power advocates. To have used a budget constraint might have condemned the public plan on the grounds that it prevented other good public undertakings, a line of reasoning which was contradictory to the institutional reality of the situation.

There was no concern with risk and uncertainty, and repercussion effects were limited to physical downstream power benefits. Much of the difference in benefits among the plans proved to be in these repercussions, which are nonmarketable for a private developer and which therefore are not considered in private decisions.

E. THE STUDY BY McKEAN

A recent book by McKean devotes a great deal of attention to the theory of expenditure criteria.[68] I cannot summarize the entire discussion, much of which is devoted to practical problems of implementation, to saving the innocent from fallacy, and to setting out the fundamental principles of selecting criteria—a discussion which to some extent parallels this paper, but from a rather different conceptual point of view. I present only the bare outline of McKean's argument with regard to the criteria he considers appropriate. McKean stresses the many objectives of policy, and the limited weight that is to be attached to criteria that reflect only economic efficiency. In the economics, he seeks to maximize the expected gain of real income, though he also stresses the need for consideration of intangibles and of adjusting to uncertainty.

McKean takes the maximization of the difference of the present values of benefits and costs as the ultimate objective (p. 76). The interest rate he would use to compute present values is the marginal internal rate of return. As McKean points out, this is tantamount to a strict rate of return criterion, though there is still an open question about the interest rate to be used in the design of supramarginal projects. McKean makes clear the assumptions that are required for this to be the correct criterion. Either of two sets of assumptions suffices: (1) funds are available without constraint at an interest rate equal to the marginal rate of return—an assumption which makes many criteria, including benefit-cost ratios, come to the same result.

[68] Roland N. McKean, *Efficiency in Government Through Systems Analysis, With Emphasis on Water Resource Development*, A RAND Corporation Research Study, Wiley, 1958, esp. pp. 25–150.

(2) There is a constraint on investment funds, public and private, and the net returns can be reinvested at the marginal rate of return when they accrue (p. 85). McKean makes the necessity of the re-investment assumption abundantly clear. He is concerned with the sensitivity of the results to the rate of return at which reinvestment occurs, and in view of the necessary arbitrariness on this matter, he proposes that supplementary data be submitted as part of the analysis which give some idea about the time profile of benefits and costs. By giving this profile, the need for any interest rate is eliminated, and the decision-maker, whether Congress or President, is forced to apply his own time preference. Recognizing the need for simple criteria, however, McKean ultimately does propose the internal rate of return as the best simple decision-rule.

McKean rejects benefit-cost ratios (pp. 113–8). He correctly seizes on the critical issue: What are the financial constraints which limit the program? McKean argues that the constraint only applies in the immediate future when the investment costs are incurred, that operating and maintenance costs are financed out of revenues generated by benefits—including the revenues recaptured through taxation. He also feels no need to distinguish between federal costs and other costs. Finally, he prefers to treat the benefits as being reinvested. In my own work, I have preferred other assumptions on these matters. First, I believe budget money will remain scarce for a long, long time, and operating costs a decade from now will prove as much a drain on a scarce financial resource as current investment outlays. Second, since it is the preparation of a federal program which is at stake, I prefer to treat only federal cost as the constrained financial resource. Third, I assume that there is no reinvestment, partly because the benefits of projects and the institutional arrange-ments in this particular field are such that there is very little direct revenue generated, and what there is does not return to the water resource field; as for benefits recaptured through taxation, in fields such as flood control and irrigation virtually no taxes are created, while in power and navigation it is not clear that the resultant taxes are more than the taxes that would have been paid by the alternative private investments that might have occurred.[69]

---

[69] This controversy repeats some of the issues of the Lutz-Hildreth exchange of the 1940's. Lutz rejected the internal rate of return in favor of a strict present-value concept, though he did not select the constraint issue as the critical one. Hildreth, in reply, used an illustration which had the reinvestment property which validates the internal rate of return. See F. A. Lutz, "The Criterion of Maximum Profits in the Theory of Investment,"

On analytical grounds, I believe there are no contradictions between the study of McKean and my own. Different assumptions are made, but these are matters on which reasonable men can disagree.

F. THE STEINER PREEMPTION MODEL

Steiner has extended models of this general type in an important way.[70] He employs the same general objective function as the models discussed above, maximizing the difference between present value of benefits and costs. He stresses the need for specifying an interest rate, not only to compute present values of benefits and costs of projects, but also to compute present values of opportunity costs. There is no treatment of risk and uncertainty. The novelty of his approach lies in a combination of constraints and of sectoral analysis which brings out some interesting features of public development in a predominantly private economy.

Steiner defines four sectors of the economy: (1) the public sector the budget of which is being allocated; (2) the private sector which would contain private alternative developments of the particular public projects being considered; (3) the broader public sector in which funds left over from the particular budget would be spent; and (4) the general private sector containing marginal opportunities into which private funds displaced by public projects are pushed.

The total outlay for projects in sector (1) is limited by a budget constraint. This outlay has certain direct benefits in sector (1) of course, but in addition, it leads to repercussions in the other sectors. Sector (3), the general public sector, may receive some funds from the budget of sector (1). This comes about in two ways: first, some funds may be diverted because the marginal returns in sector (1) fall below the opportunities in sector (3). Thus the introduction of public sector (3) assures that marginal projects yield benefits at a rate equal to the opportunities elsewhere in the public sector. Second, funds spill over into (3) because Steiner employs discrete projects and a fixed budget, and so a small amount of money is likely to be left over because the project costs do not exactly equal the constraint.

The other repercussion effect which emerges is the change in

[70] Peter O. Steiner, "Choosing Among Alternative Public Investments," *American Economic Review*, December 1959.

Quarterly Journal of Economics, November 1945, pp. 56–77 and C. G. Hildreth, "Note on Maximization Criteria," *ibid.*, November 1946, pp. 156–64. Also see the later and much extended discussion which resolves some of the issues in F. and V. Lutz, *The Theory of Investment of the Firm*, 1951, pp. 16–48.

benefits earned on private investments because an investment opportunity has been preempted by the government. This forces private funds from the preempted opportunity into a marginal investment, or in the terminology of Steiner, from sector (2) to sector (4). This creates a loss in the private economy.

Steiner also explores the case where there is no budget constraint, the case where funds are drawn from the private economy and where opportunity costs play a key role. He brings the preemption problem into this case as well.

To summarize his model, Steiner writes a general equation

$$y_{ij} = (G_{ij} - a_1 k_{ij}) - (G_j - a_2 l_j) - a_3 m_{ij},$$

where y_{ij} is the net gain from the ij^{th} project, G_{ij} is the present value of benefits minus costs of the project, a_1 is the opportunity cost in the general public sector (2), k_{ij} is the project's drain on the limited public budget, G_j is the present value of the preempted private opportunity, a_2 is the opportunity cost in marginal investments in the private sector (4), l_j is the capital cost of the pre-empted private project, a_3 is the opportunity cost of funds transferred from the private sector by taxation, borrowing, inflation, or whatever method is actually employed, and m_{ij} is the amount of such funds actually transferred for project ij. This equation can assimilate combinations of budget constraints and transfers of funds from private to public sectors, can assure full recognition of opportunity costs elsewhere in the public and private sectors as far as this proves appropriate, and can reflect the losses caused by preemption of private opportunities.

The empirical magnitudes necessary to implement the model, other than the usual benefit and cost data for each project, include the three constants a_1, a_2, and a_3 (the three opportunity costs) and a rate of interest. Steiner does not advocate any particular interest rate, nor does he propose any specific method of measurement of the opportunity costs. As an empirical matter, in the general public sector, where many outlays do not produce outputs that can be measured with prices, it is extremely difficult to place a value on alternatives which would be comparable to the values attached to the projects being analyzed. The private opportunity cost of marginal investments could presumably be valued; in fact, in a market economy, money costs should be such a measure and no explicit treatment needed. The opportunity cost of funds transferred from the private sector to augment the public budget is measured by computations of the sort discussed above in connection with the Hell's Canyon study, or by similar computations applied to funds raised by public borrowing, or perhaps even by inflation. Thus Steiner's emphasis on the opportunity costs in the general public sector, sector (3), is likely to remain a counsel of perfection, but the rest of the analysis could probably be implemented empirically.

G. TINBERGEN'S TRANSPORTATION MODEL

Tinbergen has devised a model designed to measure the change in national income due to projects which improve the transportation system of a country.[71] This model consists of a set of geographical points in which production and consumption are carried on. For each product, supply and demand equations are determined, as well as the transportation costs for each product among all points. Each supply function contains the price of the product and of the other products in the geographical point; the demand functions contain the product's delivered price, and hence reflect transportation costs. Given these functions, it is possible to determine what will be produced in each place, and hence what its total production and income will be.

A transportation project will change some of the transportation costs in the model. The equations can be solved again assuming the new, lower transportation costs, and the change in total production and income can be seen from the difference between the two solutions.

This model is a technique for estimating benefits of transportation projects. It allows for the repercussions on production caused by broadening the markets in which the output of a place can compete. This increase in production and of income leads to further increases in demand and production. The resultant estimate of the impact on national income is greater than the estimate produced by conventional benefit-cost analysis, where the impact on national income is limited to the savings in transportation cost. The extent of the difference depends particularly on the supply elasticities, high elasticities implying large increases in production.

To apply the model as an expenditure criterion, a symmetrical analysis must also be carried out for the cost side. Presumably,

[71] J. Tinbergen, "The Appraisal of Road Construction: Two Calculation Schemes," *Review of Economics and Statistics*, August 1957. Also see H. C. Bos and L. M. Koyck, "The Appraisal of Investments in Transportation Projects: a Practical Example" (to be published).

repercussion effects on production and income would also result from alternative uses of the resources. Some assumptions would also have to be made about interest rates and budget constraints.

H. CHENERY'S SMP MODEL

H. B. Chenery has advanced an expenditure model designed to aid in the planning of investment budgets for economic development.[72] The objective is to maximize the present value of benefits minus costs, i.e., to maximize the present value of the real national income. In the closed-economy model, a constraint is applied to capital funds, with the resultant criterion, the Social Marginal Product (SMP), consisting of incremental ratios of present values of benefits minus operating costs divided by the requisite increment of capital. This criterion can be applied to the design of projects, and to project selection, with individual projects treated as increments in the determination of a program. Thus the technique is similar to the use of incremental benefit-cost ratios, except that the denominator contains only capital costs.

The criterion requires an interest rate. Chenery avoided this issue by confining his criterion to projects within the same field and with very similar capital intensities, so that the rankings of projects would be unaffected.

Chenery also applied the model to an open economy where foreign exchange has a higher opportunity cost than the nominal exchange rate. The SMP in this case consists of two terms.

$$\text{SMP} = \frac{B - M}{K} + f\frac{E}{K},$$

where B is present value of benefits, M of operating costs, f is the premium on foreign exchange, E the total effect of the project on the balance of payments, and K is the capital cost. Chenery has a very sophisticated repercussion analysis to estimate the balance of payment effect, including direct foreign exchange needs of the project, import savings made possible, as well as the import demands generated by the increase in the national money income caused by the multiplier effects of the project. These models are applied to development planning in several countries.

[72] H. B. Chenery, "The Application of Investment Criteria," *Quarterly Journal of Economics*, February 1953, pp. 76–96. There is an earlier literature by N. S. Buchanan, A. E. Kahn, and J. J. Polak, which is discussed by Chenery. Kahn introduced the SMP criterion.

I. CHENERY'S PROGRAMING MODELS

More recently, Chenery, in collaboration with others, has used programing techniques to solve the same type of problem. The practical advantage of programing is the great potential of empirical implementation. While some simplifying assumptions must be made to make the problem fit the apparatus of linear (and nonlinear) programing, complete solutions of the investment allocation problem of rapidly changing economics are possible. The marginalist approach, based on Lagrangean multipliers, is fundamentally a partial equilibrium approach (though in principle it could of course be applied to centralized planning of an economy as well).[73] When applied to expenditure decisions, it usually requires, at the least, that prices be projected. In advanced economies, particularly where the programs being planned are a small part of the economy, such projections can be made and are likely to be more accurate than prices which emerge from a programing computation. But where an economy is being transformed by rapid development, the supply and demand relations are so strongly modified by the development program itself that prices cannot be assumed. Even prices for planning must emerge from the planning computations; the programing technique produces such prices, in addition to solving for the over-all quantities.

Without seeking to present the results of the programing approach, the key characteristics of these models will be presented, particularly the assumptions made about objective functions, constraints, interest rates and the other matters with which we have dealt above.

In a study of development planning for Southern Italy, Chenery and Kretschmer[74] employed the following model: the economy is divided into 14 sectors, each of which is an industry aggregate. The sectors are divided into subsectors which have the property that they have the same input-output structure except for differences in capital inputs. A set of targets is specified, a list of goods, which is derived from demand projections based on income elasticities. The objective of the program is to meet these targets at a minimum total investment, with the total availability of labor and of foreign exchange acting as constraints. The production relations of the economy consist of two

[73] At a high level of abstraction, linear programing and the quadratic programing problems used by Chenery are logically equivalent to a Lagrangean problem, following the Kuhn-Tucker Theorem. See Chs. 1, 3, 4 and 5 of *Studies on Linear and Nonlinear Programing*, K. J. Arrow, L. Hurwicz and H. Uzawa, eds.

[74] H. B. Chenery and K. S. Kretschmer, "Resource Allocation for Economic Development," *Econometrica*, October 1956, pp. 365–99.

parts: first there is the input-output matrix of the 14 sectors (applied also to the subsectors). This matrix, together with the capital co-efficients, defines one method of production for each subsector. Purchase from abroad, at a given import price, is an alternative method. The good of each subsector also has an export demand curve, relating the price the good can command abroad to the amount being sold. This foreign demand curve, assumed to be a declining straight line, introduces a nonlinearity into the model and makes it a case of quadratic programming.[75] When solved, the model reveals what demands should be met by production in domestic subsectors as well as their total outputs, what and how much should be imported, and how much of various goods should be exported. It also reveals the total amount of investment that is required and in what sub-sectors it has to be placed. In the event more capital is available than is needed, the targets can be raised, of course.[76]

Models of this type clearly have an enormous potential for expenditure analysis in many areas. In water resource planning, for example, the most efficient program of meeting specified needs could be derived. Similarly in planning regional development, the most economic means of raising, say, the average income of substandard regions could be approximated.

J. REINVESTMENT MODELS

Galenson and Leibenstein[77] proposed that several sets of reper-cussion effects which had not been considered previously in formal analysis ought to be given an important place in decision models. They stress three effects: first, education of the labor force on the job is considered a benefit of some projects; second, if per capita growth of income is in the objective function, differential effects of projects on population growth should be included in the criteria.

[75] In a subsequent paper, this is generalized to declining demand curves both at home and abroad. See H. B. Chenery and H. Uzawa, "Nonlinear Programing in Economic Development," in *Studies in Linear and Nonlinear Programing*, K. J. Arrow, L. Hurwicz, and H. Uzawa, eds., 1958, Ch. 15.

[76] In a paper to be published in the *Essays in Honor of E. S. Mason*, Chenery applies a similar model to illustrate several problems in development planning. He shows, with realistic empirical magnitudes, how much is gained (1) by using cost figures that reflect real costs rather than money costs, (2) by using a changing price structure suggested by the programing solution rather than constant prices, and (3) by including urbaniza-tion costs in the analysis. He also shows (4) how programing can be used to measure the value of generating reinvestible funds in a dynamic (three-period) program.

[77] W. Galenson and H. Leibenstein, "Investment Criteria, Productivity and Economic Development," *Quarterly Journal of Economics*, August 1955, pp. 343–70.

Finally, if a government finds it impossible to achieve an optimal level of investment, the capability of projects to generate further capital out of benefits should be considered, and a marginal reinvestment coefficient is advanced as a measure. All three of these repercussion effects, it is argued, would favor industrial projects in urban locations as opposed to agricultural or handicraft investments in the countryside. Galenson and Leibenstein do not propose a formal criterion;[78] they make their points by illustrative example.

In a subsequent model, I sought to incorporate the reinvestment factor in a formal decision model. The present value of benefits minus costs, or real national income, is maximized subject to a capital constraint. Each alternative has a reinvestment coefficient which states what fraction of its benefits is reinvested, either through private saving or through taxation. The resultant criterion has two components: an efficiency term indicating the present value of benefit minus operating cost per marginal dollar of investment, plus a term which places a premium on that portion of the output which is to be reinvested. This premium has to be derived from the productivity of the reinvestible capital. Because of the long perspective over time, the resultant criterion is very sensitive to the choice of interest rate, and it was in this connection that the analysis of planner's time preference in Section 3 above was worked out.

K. THE MODELS OF A. K. SEN[79]

A. K. Sen has advanced a series of theoretical models designed to illustrate the problem of development planning in an underdeveloped country. These models are not meant to be used in practical planning, but to provide the theoretical underpinning for rules-of-thumb that are empirically feasible.

Sen is particularly interested in exploring the right degree of capital intensity for development, particularly when viewed in relation to the level of reinvestment that might be generated and to balance-of-payments effects. He sets up a simple sectoral model for an underdeveloped country, and by means of it evaluates the alternative strategies of development.

There are two sectors, a backward sector containing lots of

[78] Subsequent criticism interprets the reinvestment coefficient as a decision criterion, and shows it to be wrong or incomplete. But I think this interprets their position too broadly.

[79] A. K. Sen, "Some Notes on the Choice of Capital-Intensity," *Quarterly Journal of Economics*, November 1957, pp. 561–84.

unemployment, which can supply labor in any amount without loss of output, and an advanced sector which contains two departments, one producing capital goods, the other "corn." Two techniques can be employed to add to the output of "corn," one requiring relatively little capital, with labor having relatively low productivity, the other being more capital intensive but having a higher productivity. Following Ricardo, all of wages are consumed, all of profits constitute a surplus and are reinvested. In order to maximize the rate of growth, the rate of reinvestment per dollar of original investment is to be maximized, and this requires that the technique be chosen which produces the greatest surplus. With labor productivity greater under the capital-intensive technique, the rate of surplus per unit of output will also be greater. But there will be less output per unit of investment. The empirical question, which can only be answered by getting magnitudes for the parameters of the model, then becomes this: is the extra surplus per worker made possible by the more capital-intensive technique sufficiently great to offset the loss of total surplus caused by the smaller output which results from sinking the capital into intensive uses?

In a second model, Sen adds foreign trade to this scheme. He assumes that the capital-intensive technique requires imports of foreign machinery, which can be purchased by means of the export of some of the corn being produced. The rate of surplus of corn still needs to be maximized, but in addition to the corn going into wages, the corn absorbed by exports must be subtracted from the total to derive the reinvestible surplus.

Maximization of the rate of growth of output is an odd objective function, and in realistic cases with alternative time profiles, it is ambiguous. However, in Sen's model, if the parameters are assumed to remain unchanged, the growth rate remains constant unless there is a switch in technique. And so, assuming the target date is chosen far enough in the future, the higher growth rate will always dominate short-run losses of output. Maximization of the rate of growth is considered by Sen to be a polar case in which only the economic situation at a remote point in time is considered.[80] Sen views simple turnover criteria, which only takes the first period into account, as the other polar case.

To bring time discount back into the analysis, Sen employs the concept of a "recovery" period. If it is true that the capital-intensive

---

[80] He identifies Galenson-Leibenstein with this particular case.

technique produces less output in the early years but more later on, the only case in which there is a real problem of choice, then there must be some number of years over which both techniques produce the same amount of output. It is up to the government to decide how many years of output it wishes to consider in its objective function, and by comparing the "recovery" period of the capital-intensive technique with the government's time horizon, a choice of technique can be made.

These models allow the analyst to bring certain important empirical features of underdeveloped countries into the analysis. Particularly where broad strategic choices are concerned, such as the concentration on urban industry or rural cottage industries, empirical evaluation of models of the type proposed by Sen may prove valuable. It is my feeling, however, that whatever can be done by means of these explicit sectoral models, which must simplify reality enormously in order to keep the mathematics from getting out of hand, can be done more easily and more completely by means of programing techniques.

In Sen's particular illustrative models there is a weakness, I think, in the choice of objective function. Maximizing the rate of growth will, among interesting choices, bury more detailed time preferences of the objective function; the decision-maker will not be applying sufficient judgment to the issue, and will essentially leave it to chance. Similarly, the "recovery" period, which is the same as the "pay-out" period of private investment criteria, is arbitrary, placing equal value on output at any time within the period, and a zero value on any output thereafter.

7. Concluding Comments

Since this paper is a commentary on the problem of expenditure criteria and models, little further remains to be said. I have tried to bring out the major issues on which the choice of economic criteria turn. A deliberately narrow economic point of view has been taken, not because noneconomic factors are unimportant, but rather because we ought to be clear about things about which we can be clear. I would also pass the judgment that there is no excessive preoccupation with the economic aspect in public expenditures decisions, and that improvement of the economics of government activities can be justified by higher criteria.

COMMENTS

JACK HIRSHLEIFER, University of Chicago

Professor Eckstein has given us the benefits of his thinking on a wide variety of topics covering the field of public expenditure decisions. His over-all conceptual organization of the subject I find unexceptionable, and about a great deal of his content all that I could do would be to record agreement. To avoid such a dull proceeding, I shall center my remarks about one general subject on which Eckstein does, I feel, stray somewhat from the true path—the question of what interest or discount rate to use in making decisions on adoption or rejection of public expenditure alternatives. This discussion will, therefore, concentrate on Eckstein's Section 3 ("Interest Rates"), though there are certain spillovers (to use our private jargon) to a number of other Sections—most especially to Section 5 ("The Treatment of Risk and Uncertainty").

The first topic I shall discuss under this heading is "The Interest Rate as a Measure of Value of Outputs at Different Points in Time." Eckstein's argument here may be summarized as follows, I believe. The acceptance of the market interest rate for public decisions involves the acceptance of consumers' saving-spending decisions. But these decisions based on personal time-preference rates have been criticized as representing "myopia" or intertemporal selfishness. Eckstein provides a theoretical foundation for planners' time-preference free of "myopia"—based on expected growth of income together with diminishing marginal utility of income. That is, given the growth rate and the schedule of diminishing marginal utility, the relative utility value of marginal units of income in different periods, and consequently the interest rate, can be inferred. If marginal utility of income declines 2 per cent for each per cent rise in income, and we expect a 4 per cent higher per capita income next year, a planners' interest rate of 8 per cent is implied (Table 1). Next, Eckstein shows (as did Rae and Fisher long before) that on the purely individual level, a certain amount of time-preference is "rational" because of the risk of dying, an eventuality known to impair enjoyment of deferred consumption. Using plausible numbers, Eckstein finds that both of these considerations under present world conditions indicate positive but low interest rates. His conclusion is that the planners'

THEORY OF PUBLIC EXPENDITURE

decision as to what "social" rate of discount to use remains necessarily a value judgment.

This approach to the question of what discount rate to use is defective, I believe, in overemphasizing one element of the problem, time preference. Following Fisher's analysis, we know that the interest rate ruling in the market represents the interaction of the factors of *time preference* and *time productivity* of savings, given the initial distribution of consumable income as between individuals and also over time. Eckstein is of course aware of the influence of these other elements of the problem, but his analysis brings them in only through a side door—for example, postulating a rate of growth of income in Table 1 may be regarded as representing either an initial distribution of income over time or alternatively the product of a quantum of savings and the average productivity thereof. It is clear, however, that this is not the correct form of analysis: the rate of discount adopted for investment decisions will affect the rate of growth of income, which cannot therefore be taken as a datum in determining a "social" rate of discount.

The important practical implication of this theoretical consideration is that the choice of a rate of discount for a particular public project, or for the public sphere in general, is not quite as unconstrained a value judgment as Eckstein indicates. Since the interest rate represents a marginal balance of time preference and productivity, a 4 per cent market rate implies not merely a 4 per cent rate of marginal time preference but also a marginal productivity of investment equal to 4 per cent, setting aside for the moment market imperfections. In such a case the use of a 2 per cent rate in public investment decisions will be inefficient—public investments yielding just over 2 per cent will displace private investments yielding 4 per cent. Now, of course, value judgments can still enter; for example, there may be a political preference for "socialist" versus "capitalist" projects. But it is not true that a planner can correctly reject the market 4 per cent rate and use his own value-judgment 2 per cent rate instead unless he is prepared to accept a loss of economic efficiency.

I cannot forbear from making two additional comments, though they are not centrally relevant here. There is much confusion between time preference as a particular rate and time preference as a *schedule*, akin to the elementary confusion between the demand schedule and a particular quantity demanded. A positive interest rate need not imply time preference "myopia" in the schedule sense: that is, the time-preference utility isoquant may be perfectly symmetrical when diagrammed on the axes of present income versus future income. On the other hand, the productive opportunity locus for current versus future incomes may be (and usually is) of such a shape as to indicate positive marginal time preference *at the optimal point.*

The second comment relates to Eckstein's "paradoxical" result that the lower the rate of growth, the lower should be the interest rate. (This is his planner's optimal time preference interest rate, based on diminishing marginal utility of income combined with a postulated rate of growth of income.) The paradox is that poor countries having low rates of growth should then use a low public discount rate, but in these countries there is pressure for early consumption (that is, high market interest rates). Eckstein explains the high interest rates there as being based on "pure time-preference" at low levels of income. A more satisfactory analysis of this phenomenon would separate different possible reasons for low growth of income in poor countries. First, the productivity of available investments may be low (Fisher's "hard-tack" illustration), in which case the real rate of interest will necessarily also be low, regardless of time preference. More frequently, perhaps, highly productive investments will be available and the market interest rate consequently high even in the absence of "pure" time preference (in the schedule sense), though this possibility need not be excluded. The low growth nevertheless observed of per capita income may be due largely to population expansion, or else may be low only in an absolute sense while still large relative to the initial level. Perhaps the most important explanation of all is that the observed high interest rates are probably not the real riskless rates we have been talking about, but are nominal monetary rates incorporating adjustment for the very high default and confiscation risks faced by potential investors in such countries as well as a very high inflation risk. I will turn again to this matter of risk and uncertainty later.

The next major topic I will discuss is Eckstein's attempt to reconcile his "social" discount rate with the opportunity cost of capital. His basic error, I believe, is in arbitrarily establishing the social rate independently of the time productivity of savings. If it is intertemporal selfishness that we are worried about, what we want to do is to increase current sacrifice for the benefit of the future. Once we do this, by a system of taxes and subsidies for example, the interest yield on projects will be driven down to lower real values over the economy in general. No separate "social rate of discount" is necessary, and if one is used in the public but not the private sphere inefficiency will result.

This error vitiates, I believe, Eckstein's analysis of the opportunity cost of capital, which is based upon measuring opportunity cost and converting it to a present-value dimension by dividing through by the social rate of discount. Thus, if opportunity cost is 6 per cent, and the social rate is 3 per cent (for investments yielding perpetual streams), present value of $2 is foregone elsewhere for each dollar invested. This leads to Eckstein's prescription, for this case, that project cost and benefits should be discounted at 3 per cent, but that a benefit-cost ratio of 2 to 1 should also be required. The purpose of this peculiar device is to incorporate into the criterion the social time preference rate (3 per cent) while still precluding adoption of projects inferior in yield to alternatives foregone. The first of these aims is misguided, I have maintained. The second will not in general be achieved, since Eckstein's rule is biased in favor of alternatives with higher futurity of yield. For example, his rule would prefer (discounting at 3 per cent) an investment yielding 12 per cent after a lapse of two years (cash-flow sequence: $-1, 0, 1.12$) to one yielding 6 per cent in one year (cash-flow sequence: $-1, 1.06, \epsilon$—the terminal ϵ is an infinitesimal added to give the projects the same life). But if the marginal opportunity rate remains 6 per cent compounding of the quicker-yielding investment will dominate the slower one—whatever the rate of discount used in the comparison.

Eckstein at times implies that the per cent yield of a project cannot in general even be measured except by first postulating a discount rate—e.g., "his social rate of discount." Of course, if the marginal yield on alternative projects cannot be unambiguously determined, we cannot speak of the opportunity cost of capital as an interest rate appropriate for discounting public projects and Eckstein's concentration on time preference as the source of the discount rate becomes understandable.

While Eckstein seems to have been influenced by an article of mine[1] he cites in this connection, that article did not prove or assert inability to measure project yields independently of interest rates. While showing the limitations, as an investment criterion, of project

[1] "On the Theory of Optimal Investment Decision," *Journal of Political Economy*, XVI (August 1958), 329–52.

"rate of return" as familiarly defined—that discount rate which equates the present value of the cost-revenue stream to zero—the article went on to attempt a reconstruction of the important concept of yield of a project. The basic idea of the reconstruction is that project yield for any investment *can* be defined independently of the interest rate, but only as a vector or sequence of two-period yields. This conception has been improved and generalized in a paper by Martin Bailey.[2] In sum, we can continue to speak of opportunity yield foregone as a per cent rate, and the market rate of interest—setting aside market imperfections—as equating marginal time preference *and* marginal productivity.

A possible counterargument to my position on opportunity cost of capital could be based upon imperfection of the capital market—for example, that marginal time preference is not equal to marginal time productivity. In such a case, it might be possible to justify low-yield projects if the funds for them were diverted from low interest-rate sectors of the imperfect market. All that can be here said is that the possibility may be worth empirical study.

Eckstein refers in this paper to his empirical work with Krutilla which estimated the opportunity cost of capital as in the neighborhood of 5 to 6 per cent. His own criticism here of this work, that it fails to incorporate a social rate of discount, I do not accept. It is vulnerable to criticism on another ground, however. While I cannot go into the details here, I believe that the procedure used was faulty in crudely averaging nominal interest rates rather than expected yields. In considering alternative uses of funds secured via personal taxes, for example, a weighted average was made of the earnings of funds in such items as government bonds (3 per cent), stocks (6 per cent?), and reduction of consumer debts (12 per cent). Obviously, these rates incorporate varying risk allowances, and in general the over-all 5 to 6 per cent arrived at is an average of nominal market rates representing some undetermined average riskiness, and thus exceeds the expected yields. My own belief is that the riskless money interest rate for any given term can be estimated by the corresponding rate on United States government obligations, now about 4 per cent for long terms. Yields on such obligations, while (nearly) free of default risk, still represent some allowance for price-level or inflation risk. I think that presently $3\frac{1}{2}$ per cent would be a closer approximation

[2] "Formal Criteria for Investment Decisions," *Journal of Political Economy*, LXVII, October 1959, pp. 476–88.

of the real rate of interest—the rate that a riskless purchasing-power bond would yield. On the other hand, incorporating a risk adjustment comparable to that implicit in the market evaluations of private utilities can be shown, I believe, to lead to the prescription to use rates in the neighborhood of 9 to 10 per cent for government investments—the assumption being that these are of comparable riskiness with those of private utilities.

This discussion has now brought us to the next main topic—risk and uncertainty. While my previous comments on the discount rate have been designed to correct what I believe to be errors in Eckstein's analysis, here my remarks will be mainly of a clarifying nature. First, it is important to distinguish between two logically separate types of "adjustment" for risk. The first or "expected-value adjustment" would correct a nominal or quoted interest rate to allow for the probability of partial or complete default. For example, a nominal 12 per cent rate on consumer debt is not inconsistent with an expected yield to creditors and expected interest cost to debtors of 6 per cent or even 3 per cent. The second or "risk-aversion adjustment" starts from the expected value of a risky (high standard deviation) interest yield and adjusts it downward to allow for risk aversion (or upward for risk preference) as compared with a security with equal expected value but smaller standard deviation of yield. The first adjustment, then, says that a 4 per cent bond of Fly-By-Night, Incorporated really has an expected yield of but 3 per cent, after allowing for default probability. The second says that a particular individual will evaluate Fly-By-Night stock yielding 8 per cent on an expectational basis, but with a high dispersion of outcomes, as no better than the stock of Safe-and-Sure, Incorporated, yielding an expectation of 7 per cent with small dispersion of outcomes. An interest rate correction designed to allow for the notorious cost underestimates of government agencies would be an expected-value adjustment. Incidentally, as Eckstein points out, it is neither necessary nor always convenient to allow for risk through a high discount rate in planning projects; however, this is a familiar way in which the capital market reflects risk.

In the earlier part of Section 5, where Eckstein quotes an example using a specific probability of failure, he is clearly speaking of an expected-value adjustment. Later on, however, and in particular for the discussions of the Roy and Thomas criteria, it is risk aversion which is under discussion, the question being how high an expected

value is required to compensate for higher dispersion of outcomes.

This distinction clarifies the familiar argument about the advantages
of "pooling" of risks—that government has a natural advantage in
undertaking risky projects because it can pool the risks of a great
many such together. Eckstein has some remarks on this subject,
whose point I did not grasp. The contention about the advantage of
pooling is correct insofar as the argument relates to private risk
aversion, assuming that risk aversion rather than risk preference
dominates in the private sphere (since the law of large numbers
reduces the dispersion of the average outcome). It is not correct
insofar as it relates to expected-value adjustment: projects will fail
for governments as well as for private investors, and this must be
allowed for. The 9 to 10 per cent figure mentioned above incorporated
only an expected-value adjustment, and is just as applicable for
pooled as for unpooled investment alternatives.

As a minor comment, I think that the main lesson to draw from
Eckstein's flood-control example in this Section is that risk aversion
follows from an assumption of diminishing marginal utility of
income. Of course, the same point was made by Marshall in "proving"
the irrationality of gambling.

In conclusion, let me say that Eckstein's abstract formulation of
the problem of social decision in this field is admirable, despite my
criticism of particular points, in its logical organization, its many
original touches, and its attempt to boldly measure parameters that
others have merely hypothesized about. I must admit to an uneasy
feeling, however, that all our logical improvement of the theory of
decision may be getting us no closer to stopping, for example, the
federal reclamation scandal. Perhaps the fruitful topic for research
in this field is "Imperfections of the Political Decision Process";
if we knew more about this, I would feel more confident of the usefulness of theories of optimal public expenditure criteria.

BENJAMIN TOREN, Bureau of the Budget, Ministry of Finance,
Jerusalem, Israel.

Both Mr. Eckstein and Mr. Hirshleifer[1] present a very strong case
in favor of the present value approach (or cost benefit analysis),
rather than the internal rate of return approach (or profitability

[1] Hirshleifer presents his case in a paper cited by Eckstein, "On the Theory of Optimal
Investment Decision," *Journal of Political Economy*, August 1958.

THEORY OF PUBLIC EXPENDITURE

analysis). This preference is based on a rather theoretical argument— as more limiting assumptions are needed in the case of the internal rate of return to lead to ideal allocation of resources than in the case of the present value approach.

We do not know how much more actual limitation is introduced into the analysis by the rate of return approach, and to what extent resources may be misallocated by following this efficiency criterion. The only thing we do know is that a highly elaborate and complicated procedure is recommended.

The rate of return analysis uses as its basic tool a detailed profit and loss estimate, with adjustments on income and expenditure sides. The data is on an annual basis, as in any financial report of any business. And it goes without saying that to the public whatever in government looks like business, looks sound.

The present value argument embraces 20–50–100 years in its analysis and can be understood only by the quite complex notion of present value for future money flows, computed by using a compound rate of discount.

There is no difference whatsoever in the two approaches, neither in the process of price adjustments, i.e., replacing market prices by "real" accounting prices, nor in the process of introducing indirect benefits or costs into the analysis.

There are further the enormous statistical problems inherent in all of these studies, which make one worry much less about the perfection of the model, than about the availability of reliable data. The internal rate of return approach makes it possible to do the analysis without specifying the rate of interest. It is precisely this problem of specifying the applicable price of capital which is the least clear and most disputed element in the whole benefit cost analysis, as the discussion of Eckstein, Hirshleifer, Vickerey, and Buchanan clearly indicates.

In arranging a list of investment projects according to priority, the rate of interest does not enter the picture. It does enter the picture only if instead of a list of priorities, a classification between "good" and "bad" projects, is necessary, because then a borderline of minimum efficiency has to be fixed. The rate of interest may also be a necessary consideration, when we compare projects with different pay-off intervals.

Public opinion in Congress, government, business or elsewhere is very much inclined to reject rational efficiency evaluations as the sole basis for decision making, as it narrows the sphere where "mutual partisan adjustment" rules.

Congress recently has had a very good opportunity to prove its fullest interest in the regional allocation of water programs, and its fullest disinterest in the application of a rational way to evaluate these programs. In hearings before the Committees of Interior and of Public Works, the Bureau of the Budget and its circular A-47 were sharply criticized. The benefit cost approach in this circular was denounced as a political device to fight against federal water resource development.[2]

Nothing would be easier to rationalize an opposition to efficiency evaluation of government programs, than the mere fact that nobody understands the tool used, or that experts cannot agree on the right prices involved.

We should be cautious not to trade too much clarity, public acceptance, and statistical needs for an elaborate model with conceptual perfection.

Reply by Mr. Eckstein

The fundamental issue between Professor Hirshleifer and myself is quite simple: the interest rate in the model underlying his discussion serves its classical function, of equating the marginal rates of substitution in production and consumption. The profusion of interest rates in the economy is considered to be due to differing risk premiums. My model assumes the capital market to be imperfect, to be rife with rationing, ignorance, differential tax treatments, reluctance to finance investment from external funds, slow adjustment processes, etc., which destroy the normative significance of actual rates found in the market. The enormous gaps between the investing and savings rates in the system, with savers typically receiving 3 per cent and investment decisions being made at 20 per cent and more (and yielding similar *ex post* returns), is strong evidence against the pure, classical view.

Once the interest rates in the markets are denied their normative role, the rate for public decision-making must be derived from other considerations. It can be derived from individual revealed preference, from a planner's preference model, or from a vision in a dream; it is a value judgment, pure and simple.

[2] Report No. 2686, Senate, 84th Cong., 2nd sess., on S. Res. 281.

To assure a correct allocation of funds, capital or otherwise, marginal yields must be equated—the yield being present value, measured at the social rate of discount. The productivity of capital enters into the analysis as the rate at which present value can be created in alternative employment.

I agree that the determination of the social discount rate cannot be divorced from the over-all investment plan, and have tried to show the interrelation elsewhere.[1] The notion of schedules of rates, related to growth rates of output per capita or elasticities of the marginal utility functions is part of the model, of course.

Finally, I want to echo Professor Hirshleifer's call for getting on with the job of applying the criteria to public expenditures. The potential of this type of economic analysis is large and it is important that our theoretical quarrels not interfere with our empirical performance in this area.

[1] "Investment Criteria . . . ," *op. cit.* pp. 78–82.

Author Index

506

Subject Index

Agriculture, 6, 9, 207, 209, 219

Air transport: federal expenditures for, 207–208; projection of federal expenses, 14, 52, 54, 57–59

Allocation: budget funds, *see* Decision-making process; Defense Department, budgetary allocations for resources, 306, 320, 323, 355; city sites, 133–135; effect of fiscal activity on location, 92–93, 120–129, 132–133 public goods, *see* Public goods, spatial aspect of; *see also* Welfare economics

Assessments, 28, 33–35, 64, 72, 76–77, 139, 143, 184, 280; *see also* Taxes, property

Asset holdings, 67–68, 136

Benefit-cost analysis, 461–463, 479–495, 498, 501

Benefit principle, 80–81, 87, 89, 115n.; interarea effects and equality, *see* Fiscal residue; marginal vs. total analysis of, *see* Fiscal residue; related to spillover, 95

Borrowing: state and local government, 135–136, 179–181; effect of inflation on, 64–65; federal-state relations, 181, 187; projection of, 57–64, 68, 74 debt redemption, 135–136; *see also* Interest payments

Budget classifications: breakdown of costs in, 340–346, 356; gains side of; 346–352, 354–362, 363; recent progress in, 353–355; *see also* Decision-making process, accepted norms; Defense department, budgetary classification of

Budget constraints, *see* Constraints

Canada, 141

Capital gains and loss, state laws concerning, 151

Capital intensity, 492–493

Central fisc: relation to individuals, 97–98, 116ff., 122ff., 132–133 relation to member states: equalization plans, 99–111, 113–116; incentive plans, 111–114 *see also* Incentive effect, central fisc; Redistribution, by central fisc

Cities: causes of fiscal problems, 230, 239, 288

envying-equity principle, 241, 256, 276, 284; functional differentiation, 244, 246–247, 261–265, 272, 276–277, 285–287; territorial differentiation, 244, 246–247, 249–261, 272–276, 280–285

spatial organization of, 230–239; suburban-urban population growth, 251–255; surrender of fiscal independence, 267ff., 277, 279, 283, 291; use of nonguaranteed bonds by, 266–267

Commission on Intergovernmental Relations, 137n., 176–177, 184n., 189, 194, 204n., 213, 219–220

Community development, *see* Urban development

Compensation criterion, *see* Redistribution, as problem in welfare economics

Competition among areas, 151, 170, 222–224, 289

Constraints: lack of in defense budget, 373, 380–387, 395, 400–402, 412; in recent models, 479ff.; theoretical importance of, 452–453; types of, 450–451, 467

Consumer surplus, 120n., 133; *see also* Benefit principle; Fiscal residue

Cordiner report, 384–385

Cost-type budget statement, 354; *see also* Budget classifications, breakdown of costs in

Death taxes, *see* Taxes, estate and inheritance

Decision-making process: bottleneck method, 305–306, 312; characteristics of, 295–296; city problems affected by, 239–247, 249; incremental method, 305–313, 318–319, 324–327, 329–334, 363; norms: accepted, 297–298; applicability of, 299–312; *see also* Budget classifications

partisan mutual adjustment, 312–318, 318ff., 334ff.; "satisficing" method, *see* "Satisficing" method; stable and unstable majorities, 245–246, 249

Deductibility: federal income tax, 147, 157, 224; nonbusiness taxes, 224; property tax, 139; state corporate tax, 153; state income tax, 151

Defense Department, budgetary allocations: biases against efficiency in,

507